JEWS IN AMERICAN POLITICS

JEWS IN AMERICAN POLITICS

General Editor
L. SANDY MAISEL
Colby College

Project Director and Editor
IRA N. FORMAN
The Solomon Project

Associate Editors
DONALD ALTSCHILLER
Boston University

CHARLES W. BASSETT
Colby College

A SOLOMON PROJECT BOOK

ROWMAN & LITTLEFIELD PUBLISHERS, INC.
Lanham • Boulder • New York • Oxford

ROWMAN & LITTLEFIELD PUBLISHERS, INC.

Published in the United States of America
by Rowman & Littlefield Publishers, Inc.
4720 Boston Way, Lanham, Maryland 20706
www.rowmanlittlefield.com

12 Hid's Copse Road
Cumnor Hill, Oxford OX2 9JJ, England

British Library Cataloging-in-Publication Information Available

Library of Congress Cataloging-in-Publication Data

Jews in American Politics / general editor, L. Sandy Maisel ; project director and editor, Ira N. Forman ; associate
editors, Donald Altschiller, Charles W. Bassett.
    p. cm.
    "A Solomon project book"
    Includes bibliographical references and index.
    ISBN 0-7425-0181-7 (alk. paper)
    1. Jews—United States—Politics and government. 2. Jews in public life—United States—Biography. 3. Jewish
judges—United States—Biography. I. Maisel, Louis Sandy, 1945– II. Forman, Ira N. III. Altschiller, Donald. IV.
Bassett, Charles Walker, 1932–

E184.36.P64 J49 2001
973'.04924—dc21   2001019219

Printed in the United States of America

∞™ The paper used in this publication meets the minimum requirements of American National Standard for
Information Sciences—Permanence of Paper for Printed Library Materials, ANSI/NISO Z39.48-1992.

To the generations who brought us to this great nation,
who taught us the meaning of democracy and the importance of participation
and to
S. Daniel Abraham, Dr. Edward L. Steinberg,
and
Bernard (B) Rapoport,
generous in support of democracy
and of this project that tells of the democratic aspirations and
achievements of our people,
role models for coming generations of Jewish political activists

CONTENTS

PREFACE

When Bella Abzug died in the spring of 1998, newspapers around the country reported that she had been the first Jewish woman elected to the House of Representatives. That was false. Florence Prag Kahn served in the House from 1925 to 1937, but few journalists knew that—and no obvious sources occurred to them to check their fact.

Ira Forman, research director of the Solomon Project, saw this example as just one of many in which basic information about the participation of Jews in American political life is largely unknown. To be sure, anecdotal evidence exists, and many books have been written on various aspects of Jewish political behavior, but to no one source could a scholar or journalist turn to find both analytical and factual information covering the range of American Jewish political experience.

Forman's inspiration led directly to this book—and he is particularly well placed and well suited to have directed its progress. Forman is an amateur political historian. He is a font of political information—some of it important, some trivial; some of it analytical, some anecdotal; all of it fascinating. He saw a gap in Jewish literature and was determined to fill it. The Solomon Project's mission is to educate American Jews about the history of Jewish civic involvement and to foster—particularly among younger Jews—opportunities for discussion, education, and involvement in the public policy arena. The goal of the Solomon Project is to invigorate that aspect of Jewish culture that calls for active involvement in improving the life of the communities in which Jews live. A book highlighting the contributions of two centuries of Jewish leaders to American political life fit as perfectly into the Solomon Project agenda as it did into Forman's own interests.

Ira Forman knew in general terms the kind of book he envisioned. To flesh out that vision, he called together a group of practitioners and scholars interested in Jews and politics. The Editorial Advisory Board—Douglas Bloomfield, Michael Levy, Ann Lewis, Geoff Garin, Mark Mellman, Ron Rapoport, Stuart Rothenberg, Mark Talisman, and

I—met throughout the late spring of 1999 to define the kind of book we felt should be produced. The decision was that the book should fulfill two purposes: to provide the kind of information lacking in one source and to put the American Jewish experience in an appropriate analytical framework.

The two parts of this book follow from that direction. The first section of the book includes fourteen analytical essays—by political scientists, historians, practitioners, journalists—that examine various specific aspects of Jewish participation in American political life and American government. Some examine Jewish participation in particular institutions—the executive branch, the Congress, the Supreme Court, political parties, interest groups, and the media—while others examine areas that cut across those institutions—patterns of leadership, voting behavior, contributions to conservative or radical political thought, the unique role of Jewish women, and the importance of American foreign policy for Jews involved in politics. Each of the authors (or coauthors) was chosen for expertise, not for point of view. The resulting essays provide a complete spectrum of Jewish participation.

While the authors were not asked to develop a particular theme, it is difficult to read these essays as a group without seeing a theme emerging. When one reads accounts of Jews in American politics at the turn of the last century, or even at the mid–twentieth century, the common theme is that Jews have achieved prominence in art, literature, academia, certain businesses, and entertainment, but not in politics or government. The Jewish politician, even the Jewish appointed official, was the exception, not the rule. Other immigrant groups—the Irish and the Italians, to be sure—used politics as a means for social advancement. The Jews, by and large, did not.

In the last third of the twentieth century, however, that pattern changed. By 2000, Jews had become as prominent in the political realm as they have been in the other aspects of American life. If analysts are worried that the best and the brightest of the nation's leaders are turning away from politics generally, the same cannot be said of the Jewish community. And perhaps more to the point, Jewish participation is accepted for the contributions that these activists make, not because of their Jewishness. Nothing could symbolize this trend more cogently than the nomination of Joseph Lieberman for vice president in 2000 and, as David Shribman discusses in his brief commentary that follows Senator Lieberman's introduction to this book, the national reaction to his candidacy. The essays in the first section of this book in one way or another all seem to explore this theme.

The second section of the book provides very brief biographical sketches for more than four hundred Jews who have played prominent roles in American political life. Who these individuals are and how they were chosen is described in detail in the separate Introduction to the Biographical Profiles. Suffice it to say at this point that those sketches and the rosters that follow provide much of the basic information that we felt was lacking in one place prior to this project.

ACKNOWLEDGMENTS

An enormous number of debts are incurred in undertaking a project of this scope. As editor, I first want to thank Ira Forman. I did not know Ira before I received a call out of the blue asking me to come to a meeting about this project. For the past year I have probably spoken with Ira more than any individual other than my wife. He has been my collaborator and colleague and has become my friend. And I should repeat what I said earlier: this book is a result of his vision and his enterprise. Similarly, the members of the Editorial Advisory Board contributed greatly to this project, not only at its inception but also during its development. Their feedback, fact checking, and judgment have been most valuable to me in all aspects of this work.

Donald Altschiller and Charles Bassett have served as associate editors for this book. Donald is responsible for the Annotated Sources and Suggested Readings, for the sidebars that appear through the essays, and for checking many of the facts that appear in this work. As has been the case with much of what I have written throughout my career, Charles is responsible for the clarity and fluidity of the prose. He has worked with each essay to ensure readability and consistency.

I also want to thank those who have written the essays for this book. Never in my career have I dealt with a group so dedicated to the overall success of a project and so willing to meet what were often difficult deadlines. The quality of this book is a tribute to their skills and professionalism. Twenty-five different individuals contributed biographical sketches. They are mentioned by name in the introduction to those sketches, and I am indebted to all of them for their efforts. Tracking down sometimes-obscure historical figures—and extracting information for sometimes-unresponsive contemporary ones—was often difficult. None failed to provide the information needed. I want to single out three of those who wrote these sketches—Jeanna Mastrodicasa of the University of Florida, Jocelyn Wilk of Columbia University, and most especially my own student,

Theresa Wagner—for efforts beyond what any editor could expect. When this project was nearing completion and the last sketches remained, they answered my plea—and I am most grateful.

I cannot express thanks enough to Senator Joseph Lieberman for writing the introduction to this book. He had agreed to write his piece before Vice President Gore asked him to join the national ticket. Typical of Senator Lieberman, even in the trying days of the Florida recount, there was never a doubt that he would fulfill his promise. His words—here and elsewhere—on the importance of public service inspire a coming generation of political activists.

Very special thanks goes to our Solomon Project research assistants, Dana Reichman and Jason Silberberg. Dana is an amazing researcher. Whenever Ira could not track down a fact, whenever Ira had a large amount of data to bring together in a useable format, whenever Ira needed to find a long out-of-print book, he turned to Dana. Whenever I needed to track down Ira and pin down some esoteric point he was making, I turned to Dana. She never let either of us down. Dana also oversaw other Solomon Project staff who worked on this book. As the project neared completion, Jason took on the difficult task of checking our lists and tracking down information others had been unable to find. The Solomon Project summer 2000 interns Joshua Samis, Risa Berkower, and Stephen Krupin were responsible for a number of research assignments, including much of the work of creating a database of Jewish elected officials and their partisan attachments. Julie Fishman, a fall 2000 intern, was of tremendous help in finishing this database and researching voting-behavior data from Jewish neighborhoods at the turn of the twentieth century.

At Colby College, Cathy Flemming, Kase Jubboori, Rebecca Ryan, David Sandak, Kim Victor, and Theresa Wagner all helped in researching lists of those Jews who have held particular posts. I hope that their research skills have benefited from this project as much as it has from their efforts.

Others who helped with particular aspects of the project included Richard Baker, Dan Gerstein, ambassador Robert Gelbard, J. J. Goldberg, Ira Rosenwaike, Jonathan Sarna, Lee Sigelman, and Fred Yang. I particularly want to acknowledge Tom Keefe and David Quintin, who, along with Ira, allowed us to photograph scores of historical items from their personal memorabilia collections for use as illustrations throughout the book. The Solomon Project also benefited from the legal advice of Sheldon Cohen and Tomer Inbar of the firm Morgan Lewis and Bockius LLP. Ken Gross of the firm Skadden, Arps, Slate, Meagher & Flom has been helpful with both legal advice and with his insights on the funding of modern American political campaigns.

David Steiner served as president of the Solomon Project during the time when this book was conceived and written. David was one of the driving forces behind this book. Without his personal commitment of time and energy this project would have never come to fruition. A small number of very generous individuals and foundations were largely responsible for providing the funds of this book. They include S. Daniel Abraham, the Hassel Foundation of Philadelphia, Walter Kaye, the Marjorie Kovler–Peter Kovler Fund, the Bernard and Audre Rapaport Foundation, and the David and Sylvia Steiner Charitable Trust. Major supporters of the Solomon Project over the course of this book project include the Ambassador Arthur and Joyce Schechter Foundation, the Abettor Foundation, the Jewish Community Fund of Metrowest, the Goldman Sonnenfeldt Foundation, Paul and Alice Baker, Daniel D. Cantor, Monte Friedkin, Cynthia Friedman, D. Jeffrey Hirschberg, Lewis Katz, Fredric Mack, Bernice Manocherian, the Pritzker Cousins Foundation, Henry and Sheila Rosenberg, the Clifford and Barbara Sobel Philanthropic Fund, the Samuel and Helen Soref Foundation, Saul I. Stern, and Donald Warren.

Individual authors would like to make the following acknowledgments:

- Connie L. McNeely and Susan J. Tolchin note that chapter 3 was prepared with the help of Kenneth E. Cox, a research associate with the School of Public Policy at George Mason University.
- Jerome A. Chanes acknowledges his appreciation to Martin J. Raffel, Albert D. Chernin, and Morris Amitay and to Arnold Aronson of blessed memory, a mentor. Chapter 6 benefited as well from the probing questions of Steven Bayme.
- Ira N. Forman would like to acknowledge that chapter 8 was prepared with the help of Lee Sigelman, professor of political science, George Washington University.
- Edward Shapiro would like to acknowledge that the writing of chapter 10 was facilitated by a grant from the Myer and Rosaline Feinstein Center for American Jewish History at Temple University.
- Joyce Antler wishes to note that some of the material in chapter 12 is adapted from Joyce Antler, "American Feminism," in *Jewish Women in America: An Historical Encyclopedia,* ed. Paula Hyman and Deborah Dash Moore (New York: Routledge, 1997), and Antler, *The Journey Home: How Jewish Women Shaped Modern America* (New York: Schocken, 1998).
- Steven L. Spiegel notes that the following volumes were consulted for specifics in chapter 13: Peter Grose, *Israel and the Mind of America* (New York: Knopf, 1983); Arthur Hertzberg, *The Jews in America* (New York: Simon & Schuster, 1989); Howard Sachar, *History of the Jews in America* (New York: Knopf, 1992); and Steven L. Spiegel, *The Other Arab-Israeli Conflict: Making America's Middle East Policy, From Truman to Reagan* (Chicago: University of Chicago Press, 1985).

Ira and I want to thank Delores Henderson of the Solomon Project staff, and I want to offer my special thanks to Sarah Ward, secretary of the Department of Government at Colby College. Their efforts in keeping track of this project and in preparing the final manuscript are more valuable than they will ever know. In each case they play a most important role in allowing us to do our work.

Jennifer Knerr, our editor at Rowman & Littlefield, is, simply put, the best editor I know. She had faith in this project from its inception and has had a most important role in each stage of its development. As in the past, I feel fortunate to work with her. I would also like to thank her assistant, Brigitte Scott, who has worked on this project throughout and has assumed the responsibility for choosing the photos that enhance these pages. Lynn Weber has been a most efficient manager of this project as it has gone through production; readers rarely know of the efforts put in by those involved in production of books, but authors and editors are keenly aware of the contributions of talented people like Lynn. I also want to thank our copyeditor, Laura Larson, and Nancy Rothschild, who has handled publicity for this book.

Finally, I want to thank my wife, Patrice Franko. She encouraged me to undertake this project when I was not certain it was a direction I should pursue. Her advice was simple and direct—"Your religion is important to you, but you have never done anything professional that deals with it. It's a great opportunity"—and it was right on the mark, as it has been since I have known her. As this project has neared completion, she has been most patient with me—when I have not been with anyone. This project reminded me once again how fortunate I am to have such a perfect life partner.

In thanking these individuals, Ira Forman and I want to assure them that we hold none of them responsible for any errors of fact or interpretation found in these pages. For those, we alone are to blame.

L. SANDY MAISEL
Rome, Maine
June 2001

CREDITS

INTRODUCTION
SENATOR JOSEPH I. LIEBERMAN

It has been over a year since I finished my book *In Praise of Public Life*, in which I argue that it is more important than ever for the best in our society to enter into public service and aspire to elected office. In the past year, I experienced a more intense exposure to the "challenges" of public service than I ever could have expected when I decided to write that book.

The experience I had during the 2000 presidential campaign has only deepened my feelings about public service. It reinforced my basic faith in the goodness and tolerance of the American people, my belief that there is an important role for idealism in public life, and my conviction that each individual can make a contribution to a better society. It has also convinced me as never before that American Jews have an important and special role to play in the civic life of this great country.

The editors and authors in this book summarize the long history of Jewish participation in the historic experiment that is American democracy. Just as I was inspired to enter politics by the examples of those who came before me—the Roosevelts, the Kennedys, and the Ribicoffs—I hope this volume will help inspire a new generation of American Jews (and for that matter non-Jews) to dedicate themselves to public life and public office.

As you will read in the following chapters, Jewish Americans have not always been as deeply involved in American politics as we are today. A hundred years ago, while some ethnic groups, such as the Irish, thrived in politics, Jewish Americans were not particularly involved in public life. This disengagement was strange because of Judaism's emphasis on the individual's responsibility to the community.

Although politics was not exactly a Jewish profession in the early days of the republic, individual Jews did throw themselves into the democratic process. Some were traditional politicians, such as Judah Benjamin, who represented Louisiana in the Senate before serving in the cabinet of Confederate President Jefferson Davis. Others entered politics as machine politicians. Many more, such as Emma Goldman and the radicals of the early twentieth century, were inspired by the ideal that they had a duty to repair the world—Tikkun Olam.

Some of these people took the route of elected or appointive office through the major political parties. Individuals such as Oscar Strauss, the first Jew to serve in a president's cabinet, were at the center of the reform tradition in American politics. Many others entered public life as outsiders. They fought for equal rights for the working class, for equal rights for their co-religionists abroad, for abolition of slavery, and for voting rights for women. But whether as establishment politicians or as radicals, these Jewish Americans seemed to have been influenced (consciously or unconsciously) by Scripture's mandate: "Justice, justice, justice shalt thou pursue."

Today, Jewish American are broadly represented in all aspects of American civic life. They have been elected to public office in historic numbers and serve in high appointive office, as members of the president's cabinet, as ambassadors, and as judges at all levels of the federal and state judiciaries. Jews have gained prominence as political journalists, political pundits, political theorists (of the right, the left, and the center), civil servants, community activists, campaign consultants, staff to elected officials, as well as sources of campaign contributions.

Many reasons account for this change from the early decades of the twentieth century. As my candidacy for vice president illustrated, the forces of antisemitism in America have been relegated to the extreme margins of society, if not eliminated. In the last half-century, the principle of meritocracy has increasingly opened the doors of opportunity to those ethnic and racial groups that had been relegated to second-class citizenship in past decades. A Jewish child in America today can dream of becoming not only president of the United States but CEO of Microsoft. Moreover, the idealism and purpose that were spawned by the movements for civil rights, equal rights for women, opposition to the war in Vietnam, environmentalism, and other causes drew many Jewish Americans into the political arena in the last half of the century.

But if young Jews have been drawn to public life in the last four decades, there is no guarantee that they will continue to do so in the coming decades. The corrosive cynicism toward politics that afflicts our society today and the coarsening of the public debate can infect Jewish Americans as it has infected so many others.

We cannot let that happen. Today more than ever, the difficult problems our society faces will not be solved unless we can attract the best and the brightest to public life. We all have a stake in the health of this unique, free, pluralistic country. And America needs the commitment to justice, spirituality, and communitarian ethic of Jewish tradition.

John Kennedy inspired a generation of Americans to politics when he said, "Ask not what your country can do for you. Ask what you can do for your country." American Jews are further admonished to help perfect the world by the ancient wisdom of Rabbi Tarfon, who tells us, "You are not required to complete the task, yet you are not free to withdraw from it." That is the spirit I hope readers—particularly young readers—will draw from this excellent book.

PROLOGUE

The Lieberman Candidacy

DAVID M. SHRIBMAN

He keeps kosher. He walks to *shul*. He doesn't campaign on Saturdays. He has a wife named Hadassah. He gabs in Yiddish. Mainstream historians will remember the 2000 campaign for its emptiness, its closeness, its flirtation with endlessness. But Jews will remember it for the Democratic vice-presidential nominee and for his Jewishness.

Senator Joseph I. Lieberman was a curiosity when he joined the Senate in 1989. He was a symbol when he joined the Democrats' national ticket a dozen years later. Shock, disbelief, *nacchus*—all that plus a smidgen of fear. For years America's Jewish mothers told their children they could be anything they wanted, except for being elected president or vice president. Suddenly that truth was shattered, along with one of the last great barriers in American life.

But along with the pride—and in truth there was an upswelling of pride for the ages, an emblem of arrival in the ultimate nation of arrival—there was fear. Fear that Lieberman might provoke a backlash of antisemitism. Fear that he might be blamed if the Gore–Lieberman ticket lost. Fear that *something might happen to Joe.*

Some of that was not unfounded. Only hours after the senator took his star turn on a Tennessee stage, the Reuters news service moved a story on the rants of antisemites that carried an extraordinary warning to editors: "contains offensive language throughout." It didn't take Internet message boards long to fill up with invective and vulgarity.

For a while there was a lot of talk of miracles and *chutzpah,* and everywhere he went Lieberman was talking of blessings and quoting Scripture. It was enough to make even the Anti-Defamation League scream, "Enough!" Abraham H. Foxman, the group's national director, wondered aloud whether Lieberman was "almost hawking" his Jewish beliefs.

Shortly after Barry Goldwater won the Republican presidential nomination in 1964, the humorist Harry Golden quipped that it was only natural that the first Jewish candidate for president would be an Episcopalian. When Goldwater delivered his famous uncompromising acceptance speech in the Cow Palace in San Francisco, one Republican leader said with astonishment that the GOP's nominee was "going to run as Barry Goldwater."

When Lieberman took to the stump, it was clear that the Connecticut senator was going to run as a Jew. And he did. He ran particularly hard in Florida, a state that, by all rights, Al Gore should not have found competitive. The governor of the state, after all, was the brother of George W. Bush, the Republican nominee. But Lieberman campaigned in Florida as if he were running for the state senate, visiting with the shrewd old bosses of the condo high-rises (a *mezuza* on every doorpost, or so it seemed) and talking the old-time religion, which is to say pride in country, integrity in Social Security, trust in Israel, and plenty of bagels and borscht afterward. He rallied the spirit, but most important he rallied the troops, and the result was clear on election day and on day after day after day as Florida's election went into triple overtime.

Overall, Lieberman's Jewishness wasn't a big deal, which itself was a very big deal. The percentage of Jews who supported the Democratic ticket in 2000 (79 percent) was nearly identical to the rate won by the Democrats in the previous two elections. A *Wall Street Journal*/NBC News survey, taken in mid-September 2000, showed how little Lieberman's religion mattered to Americans. Indeed, more than three Americans out of four said nothing about Lieberman's selection troubled them. The poll showed that among those who had reservations, no single reason emerged—a few worried that Lieberman didn't believe Jesus Christ is the Son of God, and a few worried that the senator was too close to Israel—but overall Americans had little to say about Lieberman's religion. More Americans said they were worried about the power of religious Christian groups than about Jewish organizations. And nobody blamed the Democratic ticket's loss on Lieberman.

"While my faith was the focus of much of the early media reaction to my candidacy, it was not even mentioned at the end of the campaign," Lieberman stated when he returned to the Senate chamber in mid-December 2000. He used his remarks to celebrate the "absence of bigotry," adding that the absence of any overt antisemitism "should, I think, encourage every parent in this country to dream the biggest dreams for each and every one of their children."

Even so, the selection of a Jew to join the ticket headed by a Southern Baptist was a remarkable act. But so was its timing. It came only ten days after Republicans openly begged a black man, retired General Colin L. Powell, to join the Bush ticket. Suddenly one of the nation's most enduring truths—that Jews could advance to the very top in American finance, journalism, and the arts but not in politics—had become yesterday's myth. And there was every reason to believe that it came at a moment in history where it was not unrealistic to believe that Americans of all flavors were less inclined to stress their differences than to celebrate the breakthroughs of another of the groups that provide the American stew with its richness and spice. That was the achievement, and the meaning, of the extraordinary selection of Joseph Isador Lieberman to join the Democratic ticket in what would prove to be an extraordinary political year.

PART I

THEMES, TRENDS, AND AMERICAN POLITICAL INSTITUTIONS

IDENTITY AND POLITICS

Dilemmas of Jewish Leadership in America

BENJAMIN GINSBERG

Jewish political life in America poses a basic dilemma. Can the Jews succeed where others have failed and lead America while still remaining separate from it? On the one hand, Jews have risen to positions of influence and leadership in America far out of proportion to their numbers. On the other, leaders of the American Jewish community have struggled to maintain Jewish identity and distinctiveness in a nation that "melts" its ethnic groups—at least its white ethnic groups—into a barely distinguishable mass.

The importance of Jews on the American political scene dates from Franklin Roosevelt's New Deal. Small numbers of Jews had achieved political prominence before FDR's administration; but, generally speaking, Jews began the 1930s handicapped by political isolation and social ostracism. During the ensuing years, however, Jews became politically powerful and won full access to social institutions, such as the elite universities that had systematically excluded them. Today individuals of Jewish origin serve on the Supreme Court, in the Senate and House, as cabinet secretaries, and in virtually every significant position in American government and political life. In 2000, of course, the Democratic Party nominated Connecticut senator, Joseph Lieberman, as its vice presidential candidate. Lieberman became the first Jew named to a major party's national political ticket. Jews have also achieved positions of prominence in industry, in the media and professions, and in the universities, including service as presidents of schools that had been among the most restrictive—Harvard, Columbia, Dartmouth, and Princeton.

To achieve the status and win the opportunities they currently enjoy, Jews made use of the political process. Beginning in the 1930s, they were able to forge alliances with prominent politicians and major political forces and to become an important element of the leadership of national and state governing coalitions organized by the Democratic Party. Their leadership positions within these alliances permitted Jews to use governmental power to combat threats to their religious freedom; to further their educational, employment, and housing opportunities; to protect themselves from attacks by antisemitic groups; and to influence U.S. foreign policy in order to bring about the creation of a Jewish state in Palestine.

As the reach and power of American national government expanded, first during the New Deal era and again with the Great Society programs of the 1960s, Jews used their positions of importance in the Democratic Party and the national government to break down barriers to their full involvement in American life. As they did so, Jews not only served their own interests but also helped create a more inclusive America in which all groups could hope to achieve a piece of the American dream.

WHERE THE JEWS LED AMERICA: EQUALITY AND OPPORTUNITY

The Jews' unique contribution to America has been to force the nation to make good on its promise of liberty and justice for all. In the areas of education and employment opportunity, for example, Jewish groups made substantial use of both the national and state governments to end discrimination and to provide Jews and others with access to opportunities from which they had long been excluded. In 1944, several major Jewish organizations, including the American Jewish Committee (AJC), the American Jewish Congress (AJCongress), and the Anti-Defamation League (ADL), joined with a number of smaller groups to form the National Jewish Community Relations Advisory Council (CRC) to combat discrimination against Jews in employment, education, and housing.

Employment

The CRC was instrumental in securing enactment of legislation prohibiting discrimination in employment in a large number of states during the late 1940s and early 1950s and in monitoring compliance with that legislation. Corporations like AT&T, Pacific Gas & Electric, and major New York law firms (long bastions of discrimination) were compelled to open their doors to all job applicants.

During the 1960s, the AJC enlisted the support of the federal government in its campaign against employment discrimination. A 1965 executive order issued by President Lyndon Johnson in response to AJC efforts prohibited firms holding federal contracts from engaging in employment discrimination on the basis of religion or race. This policy was later extended to banks handling federal funds and to insurance companies serving as Medicare carriers.

Education

The AJC and the ADL launched major efforts to combat religious and racial discrimination in college and professional school admissions as well. At the turn of the

IN 1776 BENJAMIN FRANKLIN, THOMAS JEFFERSON AND JOHN ADAMS RECOMMENDED FOR THE FIRST OFFICIAL SEAL OF THE NEWLY PROCLAIMED UNITED STATES A DESIGN WHOSE THEME WAS THE ESCAPE OF THE ISRAELITES FROM EGYPT. IT HAD PICTURED ON IT THE ISRAELITES CROSSING THE RED SEA WITH PHARAOH AND HIS LEGIONS PURSUING AND PERISHING IN THE BACKGROUND. AROUND THE EDGES OF THE PROPOSED SEAL RAN THE MOTTO: "REBELLION TO TYRANTS IS OBEDIENCE TO GOD," FROM THE BOOK OF MACCABEES."

—TINA LEVITAN

twentieth century, many major American colleges and universities imposed Jewish quotas, drastically limiting the percentage of Jews admitted to both undergraduate and professional programs, as a response to the growing number of children of recent Jewish immigrants seeking admission, especially to universities in the Northeast. Jewish enrollments declined sharply, particularly in the most prestigious colleges and in the top medical and law schools. For example, at the beginning of the century nearly half the students enrolled in Columbia University's College of Physicians and Surgeons were Jews. By the beginning of World War II, less than 7 percent of Columbia's medical students were Jews. The Jewish enrollment in Cornell's School of Medicine fell from 40 to 4 percent between the world wars; Harvard's, from 30 to 4 percent.

During the 1940s and 1950s, Jewish organizations used the threat of legal action to compel universities to end overt discrimination against both blacks and Jews in their admissions policies. In 1945, for example, Columbia University altered its restrictive admissions procedures when the AJCongress's Commission on Law and Social Action initiated a legal challenge to the university's tax-exempt status. Cohen and Orren show that other universities, including Yale, moved to preclude similar suits by modifying their procedures as well. Through these actions Jewish organizations allied themselves with blacks, although the number of African Americans seeking admission to elite universities in the 1940s was very small. By speaking on behalf of blacks as well as Jews, Jewish groups were able to position themselves as fighting for the quintessential American principles of fair play and equal justice, rather than the selfish interests of Jews alone. College admissions would not be the last instance in which Jewish organizations found that Jews and African Americans could help one another.

In New York, Jewish groups played a major role in persuading Governor Thomas Dewey to establish the commission whose work led to the creation of New York's state university system in 1948. At that time Jewish leaders despaired of ever completely ending discrimination against Jews in private college admissions. Moreover, New York City's Jewish residents had, for decades, sent their children to schools in the city's public college system. Indeed, many of the nation's most distinguished senior Jewish scientists, physicians, attorneys, and university professors earned their undergraduate degrees at the City College of New York because they were unable to break through the barriers barring most Jewish applicants to private universities. After World War II, however, large numbers of New York's Jewish families moved to the Long Island suburbs, thus losing access to the city college system. Consequently, Jews fought for the creation of a public university that would provide educational opportunities for Jewish students on a statewide basis.

At the national level, Jewish organizations induced President Truman to create a number of panels to investigate discrimination in employment and education. The President's Commission on Higher Education recommended that university applica-

tions eliminate all questions pertaining to race, religion, and national origin. Similarly, the President's Committee on Civil Rights attacked Jewish quotas in university admissions. As colleges and universities were increasingly beginning to rely more heavily on federal funding, especially to pay for the staff and equipment needed to remain competitive in the physical sciences, higher education could not afford to ignore such federal guidelines.

Housing and Civil Rights

Jewish organizations also lobbied vigorously for state legislation prohibiting discrimination in housing. In 1948, the AJCongress and AJC submitted friends-of-the-court briefs to the United States Supreme Court in the case of *Shelley v. Kramer*, urging that restrictive covenants in housing be declared unconstitutional. In these endeavors to end discrimination in housing and employment, as in their campaign against restrictions on access to higher education, Jews continued to join forces with African Americans on the theory that they could be important allies in the struggle against bigotry. Gains achieved on behalf of one would serve the interests of both.

. Throughout the 1960s, of course, Jews played a major role in the civil rights movement. Stanley Levinson, a Jewish attorney, was one of Martin Luther King's chief advisers. Kivie Kaplan, a retired Jewish businessman, was one of his prominent fundraisers and contributors. Marvin Rich and Alan Gartner were important advisers to

WHILE I WAS POLICE COMMISSIONER [1895], AN ANTI-
SEMITIC PREACHER FROM BERLIN, RECTOR AHLWARDT,
CAME OVER TO NEW YORK TO PREACH A CRUSADE AGAINST THE
JEWS. MANY OF THE NEW YORK JEWS WERE MUCH EXCITED AND
ASKED ME TO PREVENT HIM FROM SPEAKING AND NOT TO GIVE
HIM POLICE PROTECTION. THIS, I TOLD THEM, WAS IMPOSSIBLE;
AND IF POSSIBLE WOULD HAVE BEEN UNDESIRABLE BECAUSE IT
WOULD HAVE MADE HIM A MARTYR. THE PROPER THING TO DO
WAS TO MAKE HIM RIDICULOUS.

ACCORDINGLY, I DETAILED FOR HIS PROTECTION A JEW SER-
GEANT AND A SCORE OR TWO OF JEW POLICEMEN. HE MADE HIS
HARANGUE AGAINST THE JEWS UNDER THE ACTIVE PROTECTION
OF SOME FORTY POLICEMEN, EVERY ONE OF THEM A JEW. IT WAS
THE MOST EFFECTIVE POSSIBLE ANSWER.

—THEODORE ROOSEVELT

James Farmer, head of the Congress of Racial Equality. Attorney Jack Greenberg headed
the National Association for the Advancement of Colored People (NAACP) Legal Defense Fund. And thousands of Jews participated in demonstrations, sit-ins, and freedom
rides, including the "Freedom Summer" of 1964 when two young Jews, Michael Schwerner and Andrew Goodman, along with their black colleague James Chaney, were murdered by racist thugs in Mississippi.

Religious Freedom

Jews played a major role in the coalition that worked to end officially mandated school prayer and other forms of public (and almost always Christian) exercise of religion. The AJCongress, together with the AJC and the Anti-Defamation League, joined with the American Civil Liberties Union (ACLU) and a Protestant group—"Protestants and Other Americans United for Separation of Church and State"—to initiate a series of federal court suits opposing school prayer. Fearing an antisemitic backlash, the three Jewish organizations were very anxious to diminish the visibility of Jews as opponents of school prayer. The AJC, for example, insisted that the ACLU find both a non-Jewish plaintiff and non-Jewish attorney for its ultimately successful attack on a New York state law providing for released time from school for religious instruction.

The ACLU complied with the AJC's wishes. Ironically, the public generally assumed that plaintiff Tessim Zorach and attorney Kenneth Greenawalt—both Gentiles—in the 1952 case of *Zorach v. Clausen* were Jews. Similarly, according to Samuel Walker, in 1962, in *Engel v. Vitale*, challenging the constitutionality of New York's nondenominational school prayer, the New York Civil Liberties Union (NYCLU) assigned William Butler, the only non-Jew on the NYCLU lawyer's committee, to the case.

Other Areas of Policy Leadership

As early as the 1930s, Jewish defense organizations such as the ADL began to secure the cooperation of federal and state law enforcement agencies in collecting information on antisemitic groups and activities. In recent years, the ADL has often worked in cooperation with the Southern Poverty Law Center's Klanwatch program to maintain extensive surveillance of the Ku Klux Klan and other neo-Nazi or racist groups. Information collected has been shared with law enforcement agencies and also used as the basis for civil litigation designed to undermine racist and antisemitic groups by forcing them to pay large damage claims.

Beginning in 1948, American Jews were also able to use their access to federal officials to exercise a substantial measure of influence over American foreign policy. During World War II, American Jews had been reluctant to intercede with the Roosevelt administration even to attempt to save the European Jews. After the war, some American Jewish groups unsuccessfully sought a revision of America's restrictive immigration laws to permit European Jewish refugees to enter the United States. Both the Displaced Persons Act of 1948 and the McCarran–Walters Act of 1952 continued the policy in effect since the Immigration Act of 1924, a "national-origins" quota system that favored immigrants from northern and western Europe and effectively held Jewish immigration to a trickle.

This failure was more than offset, however, by the greatest triumph of American Jewish organizations during the postwar period: recognition of the state of Israel. Despite the opposition of large segments of the British government and the U.S. State and Defense departments, American Jewish groups succeeded in securing President Truman's support for the creation of a Jewish state to house Jewish refugees from Europe. Over the ensuing decades, American Jews successfully urged the U.S. government to provide Israel with billions of dollars in American military and economic assistance. In recent years, Jewish groups have fought not only for aid for Israel but for American humanitarian intervention in other regions of the world as well.

HOW THE JEWS ROSE TO POWER IN AMERICA
The New Deal

Before the New Deal, the American Jewish community was politically weak and its role in American society precarious. During the Roosevelt era, however, the government's needs and the capacity of Jews to serve them launched Jews on the path to political influence and social acceptance.

When he came to power in 1933, Roosevelt and the Democratic Party were opposed by much of the nation's established Protestant elite. As a result, Jewish attorneys, economists, statisticians, and other talented professionals became critical sources of leadership and expertise for the Roosevelt administration. Jewish labor leaders, most notably Sidney Hillman, president of the Amalgamated Clothing Workers, played an important role in Roosevelt's political campaigns. Geoffrey Ward claims that more than 15 percent of Roosevelt's top-level appointees were Jews—at a time when Jews constituted barely 3 percent of the nation's populace and were the objects of considerable popular antipathy. A majority of Jewish appointees were given positions in the new agencies created by the White House to administer New Deal programs. As these agencies came to prominence during the Depression, Jews came to constitute a large and highly visible group. The term *New Deal* itself was coined by one of Roosevelt's Jewish aides, Samuel Rosenman. For their part, Jews found the Roosevelt administration and New Deal programs to be a major route to power, status, and employment in a society that had subjected them to severe discrimination in virtually every occupational realm.

One Jew who achieved a position of considerable influence in the Roosevelt administration was Harvard law professor Felix Frankfurter. He was a key adviser who played a central role in formulating New Deal programs and in channeling large numbers of bright young Jewish lawyers, known as "Frankfurter's happy hot dogs," to Washington to work in the New Deal. In 1939, Roosevelt appointed Frankfurter to the Supreme Court.

Among the most important of Frankfurter's protégés was Benjamin Cohen. Cohen was instrumental in writing major pieces of New Deal legislation, including the Securities Act of 1933, the Securities and Exchange Act of 1934, the Public Utility Holding Act of 1935, the Federal Communications Act, the Tennessee Valley Authority Act, the Wagner Act, and the Minimum Wage Act. Other Jews prominent in the Roosevelt administration included Supreme Court Justice Louis Brandeis, who advised the administration on ways of securing Supreme Court approval for its legislative enactments; Treasury Secretary Henry Morgenthau Jr.; Abe Fortas, who joined the Security and Exchange Commission (SEC) and later served as undersecretary of the interior; Isador Lubin, who became head of the Bureau of Labor Statistics and was Roosevelt's chief economic adviser; Charles Wyzanski in the Department of Labor; White House special assistant David Niles; SEC Chairman Jerome Frank; TVA Chairman David Lilienthal; and Housing Administrator Nathan Straus.

> "THE JEWS HAVE 'DREI VELTN—DI VELT, YENE VELT, UN ROOSE-
> VELT'—THREE WORLDS—THIS WORLD, THE OTHER WORLD,
> AND ROOSEVELT."
> —JUDGE JONAH GOLDSTEIN, NEW YORK CITY MAGISTRATE

For Jewish professionals, lawyers in particular, New Deal agencies were a critically important source of employment and a vitally important route to professional status and successful careers. Jews faced significant discrimination in the private sector and previously had few career options in the public sector. Talented Jews were more than able to hold their own against the Protestant elite in college, graduate school, and professional school but found that academic success did not give them access to remunerative jobs and high-status careers. Major law firms and law school faculties refused to hire Jews except under the most extraordinary circumstances.

Service with the Roosevelt administration conferred status and ultimately power on the many bright Jewish professionals who had few other options. Roosevelt, for his part, was happy to take full advantage of this pool of underemployed talent to develop programs and to staff his agencies. Thus, the New Deal provided Jews with opportunities and advantages and, by the end of Roosevelt's first term in office, most Jews had given the president and his party their allegiance. To this day, Jews largely remain in the Democratic camp as voters, activists, and financial contributors.

Jews and the "New Politics"

Despite the opportunities made available during the New Deal, Jews did not fully enter the American political mainstream until the 1960s, when they assumed prominent roles in the so-called "New Politics" or public interest movement. From the New Deal to the

early 1960s, Jews served as advisers, political operatives, congressional staffers, "idea men," and powers behind the throne. In the late 1960s and early 1970s, Jews rose to political prominence in the civil rights and anti–Vietnam War movements. From the 1970s on, Jews led or were influential in most, though not all, of the political reform, feminist, consumer rights, gay rights, environmental, and other public interest groups and related foundations and think tanks that came to dominate the Democratic Party.

Today Jews play important roles in a diverse group of liberal political and public interest organizations as Environmental Action, the Center for Democratic Renewal, the Center for Policy Alternatives, the Women's Legal Defense Fund, the Center for Science in the Public Interest, Common Cause, People for the American Way, the Judge David L. Bazelon Center for Mental Health Law, the National Organization of Women, the U.S. Public Interest Research Group, the Center for Law and Social Policy, the Children's Defense Fund, Save Our Security, the National Coalition against the Misuse of Pesticides, Citizens against PACs, the Institute for Policy Studies, and hundreds of others.

The various political reforms enacted during the 1970s gave these organizations and issue-oriented liberal activists a greatly enhanced voice in the Democratic Party's presidential nominating process and in the nation's policymaking and administrative procedures. Jews had always been *the* most active of liberal activists—willing to invest incredible time, energy, and money in politics—and were thus particular beneficiaries of the Democratic Party reforms adopted in the 1970s.

In addition to the Democratic presidential nominating process, public interest groups and liberal activists became extremely important in the national congressional electoral arena. While American presidential races have become increasingly media contests, candidates in individual congressional districts continue to rely on volunteers and activists to register and mobilize voters. These individuals have a stake in the domestic expenditures and programs championed by the Democrats and have become the political army that leads the battle for Democratic causes and candidates.

These organizations and institutions, in alliance with congressional Democrats and the national media, form a kind of permanent government, providing the Democrats with a continuing ability to influence the nation's policies even when they do not control the White House. These same organizations, moreover, serve as the base from which liberal Democrats launch their congressional and presidential bids. For example, in 1992, many of the key staffers and policy advisers who organized Bill Clinton's presidential campaign had backgrounds associated with such public or quasi-public institutions. These include major universities and colleges (Robert Reich from Harvard, Stanley Greenberg from Yale), think tanks and public interest groups (Rob Shapiro from the Progressive Policy Institute), public programs (Mickey Kantor, a board member of the Legal Services Corporation), and liberal consulting firms (Ira Magaziner). These individuals, and a host of other Jewish advisers, became key Clinton staffers during the president's two terms in office.

Because of their political activism, their willingness to make major financial commitments to the Democrats, and the leadership role that they play in this complex of agencies and organizations and, in turn, in the Democratic Party, Jews have come to play a major role in electoral politics and policymaking in the United States. In this way, in little more than a half century, Jews were able to move from social ostracism and political isolation to established positions of considerable power in American government and politics.

Jewish Liberalism

This historic background and the continuing relationship between Jews and the national government help explain one of the most notable characteristics of Jews in American politics: their strong adherence to liberalism, and especially to the Democratic Party, as loyal voters, leading activists, and major financial contributors. Geoffrey Brahm Levey has ascribed Jewish liberalism to the inherently humanistic character of Jewish values and traditions. This explanation seems somewhat fanciful, however, since in some political settings Jews have managed to overcome their humanistic scruples enough to organize and operate rather ruthless agencies of coercion and terror such as the infamous Soviet-era NKVD.

Like the politics of the Catholic Church, often liberal where Catholics are in the minority but reactionary where Catholics are in the majority, the politics of Jews varies with objective conditions. Jews have, at various times and in various places been republicans, monarchists, communists, and fascists, as well as liberals. In the United States, Jews became liberal Democrats during the 1930s because in the face of social discrimination, Jews found protection and opportunity in a political coalition organized by the Democrats around a liberal social and economic agenda.

This coalition greatly expanded the American domestic state, providing Jews with opportunities not fully available to them in the private corporate sector. Over the subsequent decades, Jews gained access to and positions of prominence in the public or quasi-public economy of government agencies, helping professions, private foundations, think tanks, and universities much more fully and rapidly than they did in the private corporate economy. This discrimination reinforced Jews' stake in the liberal ideologies that justify the role played by these institutions and in the Democratic Party that serves as the public economy's political champion.

The liberal Democratic coalition also promoted and, to some extent, continues to promote principles of civil rights that serve the interests of Jews. Democratic civil rights policies have worked to Jews' advantage in a direct way by outlawing forms of discrimination that affected Jews as well as blacks. Equally important, these policies have served to expand the reach and power of the federal government (an institution in which Jews exercised a great deal of influence) relative to the private sector and sub-national jurisdictions (where Jews' influence was less).

Finally, membership in the liberal Democratic coalition has provided Jews with access to and favorable treatment from important social institutions that had excluded them. For instance, participation in the liberal Democratic coalition meant that Jews would now receive privileged treatment in the media. While it is clearly not true that Jews control the American news media, Jews and the liberal political coalition are closely tied to some of the nation's major organs of news and opinion. Beginning in the 1960s, these media declared antisemitic expression to be extremist and un-American and, at least for a time, banished it from mainstream political discourse. The benefits they have derived from membership in the liberal Democratic coalition explains why Jews continue to support liberalism and the Democrats even though, as has often been observed, Jews' financial success might seem to suggest that many should be Republicans.

To be sure, a number of prominent Jewish Republicans and Jewish donors are significant factors in GOP fund-raising endeavors. Most Jews, however, are Democrats. Membership in the Democratic coalition allows Jews to exercise considerable political influence and has provided them with access to important social institutions. Moreover, the Democratic Party defends the institutions that are part of or depend upon the public economy, such as universities, in which Jews have a major stake. Jews remain liberal Democrats despite their contemporary economic status and even though their affiliation may require them, at times, to support positions that run counter to their short-term class or communal interests.

JEWISH LEADERSHIP AND THE LEADERSHIP OF THE JEWS

For most American ethnic groups, success and assimilation have gone hand in hand. Though many Jews seem thoroughly Americanized and "marrying out" has become a major issue in recent years, some argue that Jews remain less assimilated than other American ethnic groups of European origin. The continuing identity and distinctiveness of the Jews is a tribute to communal leadership. Jews have helped lead America for a few decades, but this is but a brief moment in the extended history of Jewish leadership. For more than two long millennia, Jews have practiced and honed the leadership skills needed to maintain communal coherence in the Diaspora. Everywhere that a sizeable Jewish community has existed, Jews have also established a complex of religious, educational, and communal institutions that collectively serve as a Jewish government in exile, regulating the affairs of the Jewish community.

Often, these institutions were created or transplanted in response to antisemitism and discrimination. However, once established, as is true for any other government, this government in exile has a vested interest in maintaining itself by maintaining its constituency as a separate and distinct group. Whether or not Jews need Jewish institutions, these institutions certainly need Jews if they are to survive. The survival of Jewish institutions, moreover, depends on the continued existence of the Jews as a separate and distinct group. Hence, these institutions and their leaders have promulgated a doctrine of separatism beginning with a religion that emphasizes the uniqueness of Jews as God's "chosen people" and a version of history that emphasizes the danger posed by non-Jews.

The government-in-the-Diaspora is responsible for maintaining Jewish identity despite the temptation faced by Jews to defect. A complex of lay and religious leaders and institutions, making use of secular techniques of governance as well as religious rituals and laws, maintain the existence of a Jewish community. The Jewish philosopher, Ahad Ha-am, once observed, "More than the Jews kept the Sabbath; the Sabbath kept them." This observation could be expanded to assert that Jews do not create Jewish institutions so much as these institutions create Jews and work to ensure their continued existence. It is because of the continuing efforts of these institutions that there continue to be Jews in America.

Through the eighteenth century, European Jewish communities were governed by a communal authority, or *kehillah,* which regulated the community's religious, cultural, and political affairs on the basis of *halakhah*, the Jewish legal system based on the divine revelation of the Torah. The *kehillah* was never established in the United States. However, even without the *kehillah*, contemporary Jewish communities support a complex of institutions that seek to preserve the Jewish community as an entity apart. Virtually all Jewish groups and organizations, secular as well as religious, are united on the overriding importance of this goal, though they sometimes differ on means. Indeed, even what might seem to be theological disputes among the different branches of Judaism are at heart really debates about how best to preserve Jewish identity. Orthodox Jews, for example, maintain that strict adherence to Jewish law and religious precepts is essential for maintaining the integrity of the community. The leaders of the Reform community assert that Jewish practice must be made more consistent with the secular life led by Jews in order to persuade them to remain in the community.

The Jews are undoubtedly the most, if not the best, organized communal group in the United States. At the heart of every Jewish community is a synagogue, presided over by a rabbi who usually serves as both its spiritual and secular leader. Many synagogues operate elaborate educational, cultural, and social programs catering to various segments of the Jewish community. Most synagogues also sponsor "sisterhoods" as a basis for women's activities and "men's clubs" for their husbands. Synagogues typically also arrange for the burial of their members in a Jewish cemetery or reserved section of a general cemetery.

Beyond the synagogue is a network of often overlapping and affiliated organizations and agencies that undertake religious, educational, cultural, social, economic, and political tasks. The *American Jewish Yearbook* lists nearly five hundred national Jewish organizations that each year collectively raise and spend as much as $2 billion for communal purposes. In addition, the American Jewish community supports some

180 local welfare boards, federations, or community councils; approximately 184 daily, weekly, or monthly periodicals focusing on Jewish issues; some 80 political action committees that, together, contributed nearly $5 million to candidates for political office in the most recent presidential and congressional elections; and last, but not least, a complex of schools that enroll nearly half a million students (one hundred thousand of these in Jewish day schools).

The most important Jewish organizations include the AJC and AJCongress, both of which concentrate on protection of the civil and religious rights of Jews throughout the world; the Anti-Defamation League of B'nai B'rith, which focuses on combating antisemitism; the Conference of Presidents of Major American Jewish Organizations, which works to maintain American support for Israel; the National Jewish Community Relations Advisory Council, which coordinates the eleven national and more than one hundred local Jewish community relations agencies; and the Simon Wiesenthal Center, which seeks to preserve the memory of the Holocaust and sponsors research and education on the Holocaust. Dozens of others could be listed.

In addition, each of the major Jewish religious groups and their numerous affiliates sponsor a variety of organizations to promote appropriate religious practices and to provide religious education and training. For example, the Jewish Reconstructionist Foundation coordinates the Federation of Reconstructionist Congregations and Havurot, the Reconstructionist Rabbinical Association, and the Reconstructionist Rabbinical College. At the other end of the Jewish spectrum, the Merkos L'Inyonei Chinuch (the Central Organization for Jewish Education) is the educational arm of the Lubavicher movement; it seeks to stimulate interest in Jewish education and observance and maintains a network of offices, schools, camps, and Chabad-Lubavitch Houses. The Rabbinical Alliance of America is an organization of Orthodox rabbis. The United Synagogue of America is an organization of 850 Conservative congregations throughout the United States.

This enormous complex of organizations and agencies asserts that they exist to serve the needs of the Jewish people. And, of course, they do. They work to combat antisemitism, deliver social services, provide educational opportunities, ensure religious training, resettle immigrants, and protect Israel's interests. However, the major goal of most, if not all these organizations, agencies, and institutions is what Jonathan Woocher has called "sacred survival." That is, they work to ensure the continuity of the Jewish people as a distinctive group both by struggling against enemies seeking to destroy the Jews and, at the same time, struggling to prevent the assimilation of the Jews into the larger society.

Moreover, on the one hand, Jewish organizations are forever vigilant against any and all manifestations of antisemitism, believing that the ultimate aim of every antisemite is the annihilation of the Jewish people. On the other hand, as frightening as annihilation may be, Jewish organizations are equally worried about the danger that Jews will disappear as a result of assimilation. Major Jewish organizations have made the fight against assimilation a primary goal. Through their cultural and educational programs Jewish groups emphasize three major points. First, Jews today have a debt to their ancestors to pass on their Jewish heritage to their children. To fail in this duty is to betray the millions of Jewish martyrs who fought and died for their faith and their people over the past four thousand years. Second, Jews as a people have made an enormous contribution to civilization through the philosophical ideals and scientific principles they have introduced. Thus, Jews have an obligation to humanity to maintain their distinctive identities, "because we are struggling to teach men how to build a better world for all men," as Woocher has said. Finally, only as self-conscious members of the Jewish community, the Jewish leadership avers, can Jews lead meaningful lives.

Thus, the great key to Jewish survival over the centuries: a government in exile that has struggled to preserve the identity and integrity of its people; a government in exile, moreover, that has had centuries to perfect three instruments on which it relies in its fight to maintain a Jewish community. These are law and religious practice, education, and communal mobilization.

Law and Religious Practice

A central precept of Jewish law and religion is the distinctiveness or "chosenness" of the Jewish people. Jewish religious practice, moreover, serves to reinforce this distinctiveness by maintaining the unity of the community and separating it from the Gentile community. For example, Jews have their own rituals, their own holidays, their own dietary codes. All these are justified as the special duties of Jews stemming from their special relationship with God. The effect of these practices is to remind the Jewish practitioner—and the Gentile observer—that Jews are different and distinctive, in order to separate Jews from the influence of Gentile society.

The notion of the Jews as a people chosen by God begins with God's covenant with Abraham in Genesis: "I will maintain My covenant between Me and you, and your offspring to come, as an everlasting covenant throughout the ages, to be God to you and your offspring to come. I assign the land you sojourn in to you and your offspring to come, all the land of Canaan, as an everlasting holding, I will be their God." This covenant is renewed in Exodus, which suggests that the Jews, as God's chosen people have a special mission. "You have seen what I did to the Egyptians; how I bore you on eagle's wings and brought you to Me. Now then, if you will obey Me faithfully and keep My covenant, you shall be My treasured possession among all the peoples. Indeed, all the earth is Mine, but you shall be to Me a kingdom of priests and a holy nation."

Chosenness implies a special mission. And what is the mission of a "kingdom of priests and a holy nation"? Jews were chosen to bring all of the people of the world to an acknowledgment of the sovereignty of God and to accept the values revealed by God. Jews were chosen, according to Abba Hillel Silver, to work toward the establishment on

Earth of a universal brotherhood under God. The chosenness of the Jews and their special mission, in turn, can require them to remain apart from other nations. "To carry out successfully the task assigned to it," says Silver, "Israel found it necessary to live in the world but apart from it" (75). As Balaam puts it in the Book of Numbers, "There is a people that dwells apart, not reckoned among the nations." Similarly, the Prophet Jeremiah compares Israel to an olive tree in that other liquids readily mix with one another, while olive oil refuses to do so and keeps separate. From the beginnings of Jewish history, as Silver observes, Jews were admonished to separate themselves from the customs of the people around them and to follow their own moral precepts and way of life. As expressed in Leviticus, "You shall not copy the practices of the land of Egypt, where you dwelt, or the land of Canaan, to which I am taking you; nor shall you follow their laws."

The injunction to Jews to keep themselves separate from the people around them is an important component of Jewish law expressed in the Mishnah and later in the Talmud. The Mishnah, a six-part code of laws formulated under the authority of Judah the Patriarch, the head of the Jewish community of Palestine at the end of the second century A.D., lays out numerous provisions regulating and restricting the relations between Jews and Gentiles, warning Jews of the dangers inherent in associating with Gentiles. Similarly, according to Talmudic law, Jews were forbidden to eat food cooked by non-Jews, to engage in sexual relations with non-Jews, or to eat bread baked by non-Jews. Needless to say, Jews were forbidden to marry non-Jews unless the latter submitted to a process of religious conversion.

Of course, in the contemporary world, most of these prohibitions are ignored by all but the most strictly Orthodox Jews. Indeed, most Jews are probably unaware of many of the prohibitions governing their relationships with non-Jews and cheerfully eat bread that has been baked by Gentiles and drink wine that has been handled by Gentiles. However, even if they do not deliberately refrain from associating with Gentiles, many particular and parochial elements of Jewish observance can serve to isolate Jews from their Gentile neighbors. The Jewish Sabbath and Jewish religious holidays take place on different days from Gentile religious holidays. Jews celebrate their religious beliefs when the community around them is engaged in its normal affairs. As all Jewish children who absent themselves from public school on Rosh Hashanah and Yom Kippur know, this distinction has the effect of reminding Jews that they are different from their neighbors and of reminding those neighbors of the difference as well. As Hayim Halevy Donin puts it, "By staying out of school on these days, the child is taught to assign priority to his religious commitments and to assert his Jewish self-respect in an overwhelmingly non-Jewish society" (123).

Similarly, Jewish dietary laws, if observed, inhibit social relations between Jews and Gentiles. Observant Jews find it difficult to eat in their Gentile neighbors' homes, to attend business luncheons with Gentile colleagues, and to join Gentile friends or associates for dinner in restaurants, even if they have no personal desire to avoid Gentiles.

Some Jewish groups have sought for decades to eliminate public forms of religious expression precisely to diminish the discomfort and sense of difference that Jews feel when confronted with the Gentile community's religious observances. Ironically, their very success has reduced the overt sense of distinctiveness that Jews feel, and it has thus eroded the barriers to assimilation that many of these groups fear even more than antisemitism.

Education

Every year, hundreds of thousands of Jewish children attend Jewish educational institutions, ranging from Jewish day schools, through afternoon Hebrew schools, to morning Sunday schools. These schools offer a variety of different curricula. In the Hebrew day schools, a great deal of instruction is offered in the Hebrew language and in Jewish law and history. In the afternoon Hebrew schools, some of which meet only once a week, the curriculum is abbreviated. In the weekly Sunday schools, with typically shorter sessions still, the curriculum is very limited.

The differences among these schools are instructive. As instructional time is reduced and curricular content abbreviated, training in the Hebrew language is usually the first subject to be eliminated. Next to go is the study of Jewish law. Next is training in prayer and ritual. What is left, then, when everything else has been dropped from the curriculum? The irreducible minimum, conceived to be more important than law, religion, or language, is the inculcation of Jewish national identity and loyalty. In other words, even where children are taught hardly anything about the substance of Jewish belief and practice, an effort is made to teach them to identify themselves as Jews, to take pride in their difference from other people.

Jewish identification and distinctiveness are also the themes of the three holidays that form the pillars on which the education of Jewish children is presently built: Passover, Purim, and Hanukkah. As is often pointed out by religious purists, these three celebrations are not the most significant events in the Jewish religious calendar. Yom Kippur, Rosh Hashanah, and several other festivals are more important. Nevertheless, it is Passover, Purim, and Hanukkah that are chiefly emphasized

in the Jewish schools. Not only are these cheerful holidays, deemed likely to appeal to childish sensibilities, but these three holidays help teach three fundamental concepts to Jewish children. Passover teaches chosenness, Purim emphasizes the potential duplicity of Gentiles, and Hanukkah emphasizes the evil of assimilation.

A major impact of Jewish education is to stimulate a sense of communal identification among Jewish children. Obviously, a Jewish education does not guarantee that a child will forever identify with the Jewish community. However, in this as in so many other areas, Jews treated to several years of Jewish education can never fully escape its effects.

Communal Mobilization

The making of Jews does not end with religious practice and the education of Jewish children. Organizations and institutions comprising the Jewish government in exile employ a third mechanism for maintaining the identity and distinctiveness of their followers. This technique, which could be called *communal mobilization,* involves the use of campaigns, meetings, books, rallies, and outright propaganda to present Jews with issues and problems that will remind them of their Jewish heritage and induce them to take part in communal affairs—most important, by contributing time and money to the organizations charged with managing those affairs.

The two most important topics used for communal mobilization are Israel and the Holocaust. Indeed, these two matters have become the central features around which Jewish communal life, fund raising, political activity, and even, to some extent, religious observance have become organized. These are central to the efforts of Jewish institutions to create and maintain Jewish identity. In recent years, of course, both the state of Israel and the Holocaust have also become major topics in most Jewish schools and in Jewish religious observance as well.

Israel

Very few American Jews have ever been Zionists in the literal sense of the term; that is, few have ever seriously thought of emigrating to Israel. Indeed, few American Jews are fluent in Hebrew or know much about Israeli culture or politics. Hardly any subscribe to English-language newspapers, such as the *Jerusalem Post,* that provide day-to-day coverage of events in Israel. Nevertheless, most American Jews have a sense of kinship with Jews in Israel and a sense of commitment to Israel's well-being and survival. This support is based on tradition and identification and on Israel's martial prowess. For American Jews, Israel's military success is a refutation of the stereotype of the Jew as a coward and a draft dodger. American Jewish support for Israel is also, in part, based on something that Jews will admit to one another but seldom to non-Jews, a fear that, as has occurred so often in Jewish history, Jews just might some day find themselves compelled to leave America and seek refuge elsewhere. Israel, to many Jews, represents a form of insurance policy against a major upsurge of anti-semitism in the United States.

To American Jewish institutions, however, Israel has been more than a form of insurance. To the Jewish government in exile, Israel has been the key to survival in the present. In the period following World War II, American Jewish organizations supported the creation of a Jewish homeland to provide a place where Jewish refugees from Europe could be sent other than the United States. American immigration policy was too restrictive to permit the acceptance of more than a small number of homeless Jews, and American Jewish groups were not successful in liberalizing these policies. Moreover, American Jews were concerned that an influx of "unassimilated" Jewish refugees from Europe could heighten antisemitic sentiment in the United States.

Despite these reasons to support the creation of a Jewish state in Palestine, some American Jewish leaders and major organizations, such as the AJC, were less than enthusiastic about the enterprise. The existence of a Jewish state might raise questions in America about the loyalty of American Jews. Moreover, a Jewish state in Palestine might pose a threat to the primacy of the institutions forming the "Jewish state" in America. In a sense, the rebirth of a Jewish state in Israel represented as serious a threat to the leadership of the American Jewish community as the return of Christ represented to Dostoyevsky's Grand Inquisitor.

In the immediate aftermath of Israel's creation, a fierce struggle developed between the fledgling Israeli government and the American Jewish leadership over primacy in the Jewish world. David Ben-Gurion, Israel's first prime minister, in effect claimed leadership of the entire Jewish world by declaring that all Jews belonged in—and hence to—Israel. Abba Hillel Silver, leader of the American Zionist movement, asserted that Jews everywhere had a special relationship to Israel and therefore had the right to exert influence over the decisions of the Israeli government. Silver's position implied that American Jewish organizations had a right to intervene in Israeli policies and politics. Ben-Gurion's famous response was that no one "could sit in Cleveland and give directions to Tel Aviv." He invited Silver to move to Israel and exert as much influence as he could through the Israeli domestic political process.

In the early 1950s, an accommodation was reached between the Jewish state in Israel and the Jewish state in America. The Israeli government agreed to stop embarrassing American Jews and undermining the American Jewish leadership with declarations that Israel was the only true home for a Jew. The American Jewish leadership, for its part, agreed to provide financial and political support for Israel but to refrain from attempting to meddle in Israeli policies. In the aftermath of this accommodation, previously non-Zionist American Jewish organizations like the AJC became staunch supporters of Israel. The position developed by American Jewish organizations and given the blessing of Israeli leaders was that American Jews had a religious and moral commitment to support Israel but no obligation to come to Israel to live. Indeed, some prominent Jewish leaders in America argued that American Jews could best fulfill their moral obligation to Israel by remaining in America, where they could use their political influence and organizational strength to assure Israel of American financial and military support.

In this way, the threat posed by the state of Israel to the Jewish "state" in America was defused and transformed into an opportunity. American Jewish vacationers, participating in guided tours arranged by Jewish organizations in the United States, began to *visit* Israel in large numbers and to return to America with a strengthened sense of Jewish consciousness and solidarity. This made them more willing to participate in and contribute to Jewish affairs in New York City, Chicago, Cleveland, and Baltimore. Through participation and charitable contribution, one could be a good Jew and still live comfortably in the United States.

Beginning in the late 1950s after Israel's victory over Egypt in the Suez War, and heightened after Israel's spectacular victory over all the Arab nations in the 1967 Israeli-Arab War, Israel became the central focus of American Jewish life. Support for Israel became the major theme around which American Jewish institutions organized their communal, political, and fund-raising efforts. As Jews became less religious and more secular, Jewish institutions found that Israel, and especially pride in the military prowess and achievements of the Jewish state, was the most effective rallying point for their fund-raising and membership activities. Indeed, as Israelis often charged during the 1960s and 1970s, American Jewish organizations invoked Israel as a vehicle for fund-raising activities even though many of the funds raised were actually spent in the United States. Over the past several years, however, the centrality of Israel has begun to diminish and to be replaced by other mobilizing themes.

The Holocaust

After the Likud bloc came to power in Israel during the mid-1970s and especially after the 1982 Israeli invasion of Lebanon, Jewish organizations began to feel American Jewish support for Israel weaken. In addition, during the 1980s and 1990s, as evidence of Israeli military superiority and chances for peace grew, American Jews felt less anxious about Israel's very survival. Thus, the importance of Israel as a motivating issue weakened. The response of Jewish organizations was to reduce Israel's role in their fund-raising activities and turn to other rallying points. Support for Israel has never been abandoned. However, to avoid alienating Jews on the political left who sometimes oppose the policies of the Israeli administration, Jewish organizations have sought to develop other, less "controversial," mobilizing themes.

For example, through the 1960s and 1970s, the annual UJA spring fund-raising drive, conducted through direct solicitations and telethons in every Jewish community in the nation, had focused mainly on the need to help Israel. Solicitation letters and calls emphasized Israel's military needs, housing needs, desert reclamation, and children's programs. By the 1980s and 1990s, faced with some unease about Israel's right-wing political leadership and treatment of Arabs, the annual campaign moved toward a policy of reduced emphasis on Israel and greater emphasis on other issues such as the Holocaust and antisemitism in Eastern Europe. The fund-raising letter sent to Jews in Ithaca, New York, in the spring of 1982, is a typical example:

> It never seems to end. Threats to Jewish life are more ominous than ever. Periods of economic hardship . . . bring anti-Semitic tendencies out of the woodwork and focus them into overt acts of violence and hatred. . . . Witness the pitiful remnant of Poland's Jews accused . . . of responsibility for Poland's food shortages; even more incredible witness the denial of the Holocaust! . . . Throughout history Jews have acted on the premise that we all share a common destiny and a common fate. . . . That historical obligation has been voluntarily assumed by each generation in its turn and now falls upon us; it is an integral part of our consciousness as a people.

The letter goes on to describe the uses to which the funds raised will be put. Significantly, Israel is not mentioned, though there is a brief reference without explanation to "Project Renewal," which is a program for urban redevelopment in Israel.

As the emphasis in this letter suggests, over the past twenty-five years, the Holocaust has become one of the most important vehicles for rallying support and raising funds in the Jewish community. Three major Holocaust museums have been built in the United States in recent years, and Holocaust history has become an important curricular focus for all levels of Jewish education.

While this acknowledgment of the tragedy that took place is important, during the actual Holocaust, unfortunately, American Jewish organizations were mainly silent, more concerned with antisemitism at home than with the fate of millions of Jews in Europe. For example, Leon Wells relates that when Joseph Proskauer became president of the AJC in 1943, his acceptance speech, which dealt with the problems American Jews were likely to face in the postwar period, made no mention whatsoever of the ongoing slaughter of European Jews or of any possible rescue efforts. Similarly, in *Deafening Silence* Medoff states that the "Statement of Views" adopted by the AJC's 1943 annual meeting has no mention of the Germans' ongoing efforts to destroy the European Jews, something that was already known by American Jewish leaders at that time.

The silence of American Jews regarding Hitler's campaign of murder continued even in the years following the war. Jewish organizations for the most part were quiet about the Holocaust; the few survivors to reach America were typically made to understand that they should not speak about their experiences. Many American Jewish leaders were embarrassed about the cowardice these Jews had shown, eager to avoid charges of inaction, and never anxious to link themselves in any way to the Jews of Europe. One source of shame, of course, was the apparent absence of Jewish resistance to the Germans. American Jews often felt contempt for their European brethren who, the Americans thought, had "allowed" themselves to be killed. The Americans resented being associated with people who seemed not only to confirm but to give new meaning to the stereotype of Jewish timidity. Jews, it appeared, had been too spineless to fight even when being herded toward the gas chambers. (My own parents, both Holocaust survivors, were told by their relatives to "keep quiet" about their experiences when they arrived in the United States. See Wells, chap. 9.)

During the 1970s, however, a new generation of American Jewish leaders emerged, men and women who had no complicity in the events of the war years and who could use the inaction during the Holocaust to discredit and displace the established leaders. The story of the Holocaust, moreover, became a useful parable on the dangers of assimilation and the evil of which even the best Gentiles were capable. After all, had not the Jews lived in Germany for centuries? Did many German Jews not regard themselves as Germans first and Jews second? Did their German friends and neighbors not turn on the Jews in a murderous rage? During the 1970s, this version of the story of the Holocaust began to join or even to replace Bible stories as mechanisms through which to teach American Jews—especially American Jewish children—to be wary of identifying too closely with the world of Gentile America.

As Jewish organizations began to make the Holocaust an increasingly central focus of their activities, Holocaust survivors were honored rather than told to be quiet. Holocaust studies became a major focus of activity for the young. Holocaust memorials and museums and commemorations became central parts of the agenda of all Jewish institutions. The Holocaust even entered the Jewish liturgy as a special day of prayer and remembrance; Yom Hashoah was added to the religious calendar by Conservative and Reform Jews, though usually not by the most Orthodox synagogues.

Rare today is the fund-raising appeal from a Jewish organization that does not remind the potential donor of the Holocaust and of contemporary efforts by neo-Nazi "revisionists" to claim that the Holocaust never took place. Rather than feel shame over the lack of Jewish resistance to the Germans, American Jewish organizations now celebrate the Warsaw ghetto uprising, which is said to have held the Germans at bay longer than the entire Polish army had been able to do in 1939.

The prominence currently given to the story of the Warsaw ghetto tragedy is especially ironic given the lack of a response among American Jewish leaders to the uprising when it actually occurred. In April and May 1943, as the ghetto was being liquidated by the Germans, Jewish resistance fighters made a series of dramatic broadcasts and desperate calls for help over their clandestine radio station. On April 22, the station told the

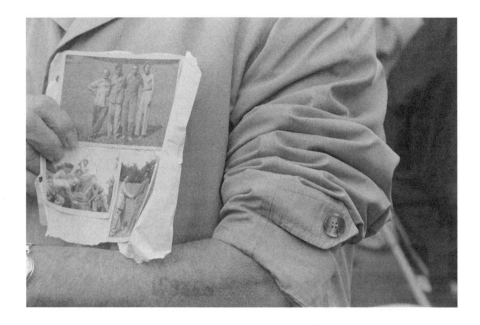

world that "Gun salvos are echoing in Warsaw's streets. Women and children are defending themselves with bare hands. Come to our aid!" On May 25, the BBC reported monitoring a broadcast telling of Jews being executed by firing squads and being burned alive. Yet many American Jewish organizations had other priorities and gave little attention to the grim news from Warsaw. Only years later, when it became an important vehicle for communal mobilization, did the story of the Warsaw ghetto become a prominent focus of American Jewish concern.

A similar story could be told about another contemporary focus of Jewish organizations' mobilizing efforts—the discovery of the plight of the Russian Jews. When Stalin was actually murdering hundreds of thousands of Jews, little interest in this tragedy was expressed in the West. In the United States, as Paul Appelbaum has observed, "The few calls for concerted action [to help the Soviet Jews] were, for the most part, gently put and generally ignored" (614). Indeed, many left-wing American Jewish organizations and leaders denied that Jews were actually persecuted in the Soviet Union. In later years, however, when the utility of Israel as a rallying point for fund-raising and organizational activities was compromised, American Jewish organizations made much of the importance of saving the Russian Jews.

Communal mobilization has thus been the third instrument through which leadership has preserved the Jewish community in America. Religious practice, education, and communal mobilization have prevented the Jews from completely disappearing into America. Because of the community's leadership, the Jews continue to maintain a measure of cohesion and identity in a nation whose other European ethnic groups are now largely indistinguishable.

THE ENDS OF LEADERSHIP

Jews have had a twofold political response to the American experience. On the one hand, Jews have risen to high positions of leadership in the United States. At the same time, though, the leaders of American Jews have struggled to maintain the coherence and identity of the American Jewish community. How long can America's Jews simultaneously lead the United States and resist assimilation by it? The answer is not clear. Total immersion into American politics exerts enormous pressure on Jews' capacity to retain their ethnic and religious identification. Ironically, when Jews were the victims of discrimination, there was no problem. According to Alan Dershowitz, America forced Jews to remain separate. But how can a group fail to immerse itself fully in a country in which some of its leading lights serve as senators, high court justices, and cabinet secretaries? The wonder is not that there is so much "marrying out" but that there is so little.

The other side of the coin, of course, is that if Jews insist on retaining their distinctiveness, their ability to retain a position of leadership in America is threatened. Would it really be appropriate for a future Jewish president to declare, "Next year in Jerusalem" at the conclusion of the Passover Seder? This is the dilemma Jews face in America. It is, of course, a dilemma born of freedom, opportunity, and success, but a dilemma nonetheless. Should Jews choose to lead in America, risking their identity as a people, or should they focus upon their communal identity at the risk of diminishing their position in America? Sooner or later, it becomes problematic to have it both ways.

2

AT THE SUMMIT

Presidents, Presidential Appointments, and Jews

DAVID G. DALIN

When Vice President Al Gore named Joseph Lieberman as his vice presidential nominee on the eve of the 2000 Democratic National Convention, Jews throughout the country swelled with pride. "Did you think you would live to see this day?" An observant Jew stood on the brink of holding our nation's second-highest office.

In truth the Lieberman nomination represents the next step—a large step, to be sure—in what has been an impressive history of Jews serving their country in the executive branch. The number of Jews serving in early administrations was extremely small, but they effectively represented Jewish interests. Historic strides were taken at the turn into the twentieth century, with the appointment of Oscar Straus as the first Jewish member of a president's cabinet. The progression since then has been steady and persistent until we reached the point, in the Clinton administration, at which no position was thought unusual for a Jewish public servant. The Lieberman nomination was historic—as all firsts are by definition—but the groundwork had been set by early in the twentieth century for Jews serving at the pleasure of presidents of the United States.

NINETEENTH-CENTURY PRESIDENTIAL APPOINTEES

The tradition of Jews receiving presidential appointments is almost as old as the nation itself. For much of the nation's first century, those Jews who received presidential appointments represented the United States in diplomatic posts. Presidents James Madison and James Monroe, for example, appointed Jews to several consular posts.

The best known of President Madison's Jewish appointments was political journalist Mordecai Noah who, in 1813, was appointed U.S. consul to Tunis. According to Jonathan Sarna and David Dalin, Noah had lobbied for the job as a Jew and won appointment, in part, "because it was hoped that he might establish beneficial ties with North Africa's powerful Jewish community" (89). The Muslim rulers of Tunis, however, later protested his appointment because they did not want to deal with a Jew. As a result, the State Department decided to recall Noah. "At the time of your appointment as Consul at Tunis," Secretary of State Monroe wrote him, "it was not known that the religion which you profess would form any obstacle to the exercise of your Consular functions. Recent information, however . . . proves that it would produce a very unfavourable effect" (90). Sarna has noted that the Madison administration had other compelling reasons for wanting to recall Noah, but President Madison explained his reason for rescinding Noah's appointment as being "the ascertained prejudice of the Turks against his Religion, and it having become public that he was a Jew" (28). Most Jews took President Madison at his word, believing that anti-Jewish prejudice lay behind Noah's recall. To this day, Madison's recall of Noah remains the only instance in American history in which overt antisemitism was a factor in the rescinding of a presidential appointment of a Jew.

These appointments from the small, rather isolated American Jewish community of the early eighteenth century were the exception, not the rule. The next major Jewish presidential appointment was made by Franklin Pierce, who named August Belmont, the influential financier and Democratic Party fundraiser, to the post of U.S. minister to The Hague. As the first Jew to hold this high rank in the American diplomatic service, Belmont represented the United States in the Netherlands from 1853 to 1857.

MADISON'S RECALL OF NOAH REMAINS THE ONLY INSTANCE IN AMERICAN HISTORY IN WHICH OVERT ANTISEMITISM WAS A FACTOR IN THE RESCINDING OF A PRESIDENTIAL APPOINTMENT OF A JEW.

In the fall of 1857, United States Senator Judah Benjamin turned down an offer from President James Buchanan to appoint him U.S. minister to Spain. Five years earlier Benjamin had also declined President Millard Fillmore's offer of a seat on the Supreme Court. When Louisiana seceded from the Union in February 1861, however, Benjamin, a passionate southerner, resigned his Senate seat. Soon thereafter, Confederate President Jefferson Davis appointed Benjamin attorney general of the Confederacy, making him the first Jew to hold a cabinet-level office in any American government. He subsequently served as the Confederacy's secretary of war and secretary of state.

Between the end of the Civil War and the turn of the nineteenth century, almost all Jews who received presidential appointments were nominated for diplomatic posts. Often their religion was important in the decision to appoint them to particular posts. In 1870, President Ulysses S. Grant appointed Benjamin Franklin Peixotto, a prominent San Francisco attorney and Jewish communal leader, U.S. consul to Bucharest, Romania. In sending Peixotto to Bucharest, which was then a hotbed of virulent antisemitism, Grant endorsed the new consul's intention to use the American consulate to promote Jewish rights and political emancipation in Romania. Max Kohler and Simon Wolf cite a letter that Peixotto carried with him from President Grant to Prince Charles of Romania: "The bearer of this letter, Mr. Benjamin Peixotto . . . has undertaken the duties of this present office more as a missionary work for the benefit of the people he represents who are laboring under severe oppression than for any benefits to accrue to himself. The United States, knowing no distinction of her own citizens on account of religion or nativity, naturally believes in a civilization the world over which will secure the same universal views" (382). Active in Republican presidential campaigns, Peixotto was later named U.S. consul to Lyons, France, where he served throughout the Garfield and Arthur administrations.

In 1887, President Grover Cleveland appointed Oscar S. Straus U.S. minister to Turkey, the second Jew to hold this rank in the American diplomatic service. With the financial help of his brothers Isidor and Nathan (who in 1888 became partners in, and later sole owners of, New York City's famed R. H. Macy's Department Store), Oscar Straus was able to devote his life to public service. In 1882, he entered politics as leader of a citizen's movement dedicated to municipal reform. Two years later, he played an active role in Cleveland's presidential campaign, speaking widely on his behalf.

When Straus's appointment to Turkey was announced, detractors pointed out that part of the U.S. minister's role in Constantinople was the protection of Christian missionaries and Christian colleges. Several Protestant clergy, however, actively supported the appointment of a Jew, including the enormously popular Brooklyn preacher Henry Ward Beecher, who wrote to President Cleveland, "The bitter prejudice against Jews, which obtains in many parts of Europe, ought not to receive any countenance in America. It is because he is a Jew that I would urge his appointment as a fit recognition of this remarkable people who . . . deserve and should receive from our government such recognition" (Dalin and Kolatch, 107).

Strauss was an immensely successful and popular minister to Turkey. His gift for diplomacy enabled him to win an invitation from the sultan to arbitrate a business dispute between the Turkish government and Baron Maurice de Hirsch, the Jewish financier and philanthropist who had built the first railroad connecting Constantinople to the cities of Europe.

In appointing Oscar Straus the first Jewish U.S. minister to Turkey, President Cleveland established a precedent that every president—Republican and Democrat alike—would follow during the next thirty years. Presidents Cleveland, Benjamin Harrison, William McKinley, Theodore Roosevelt, William Howard Taft, and Woodrow Wilson each appointed Jewish ministers (and, later, ambassadors) to Constantinople. American presidents recognized the symbolic importance of the Turkish embassy for American Jews, and especially for the growing number of Zionists within the American Jewish electorate, since the Jewish homeland of Palestine remained under the direct control of the Turkish government. During this era, the ambassadorship to Turkey came to be considered a quasi-Jewish domain.

Although Straus had resigned his ambassadorship following Cleveland's defeat for reelection in 1888, he remained a close friend and political confidant of the ex-president, helping renominate him at the Democratic National Convention of 1892. As a member of Cleveland's "kitchen cabinet" during his second term, Straus was a frequent guest at the White House, offering advice on monetary policy and immigration issues of Jewish concern.

However, as an advocate of "sound money" and of the gold standard that the Republican Party championed, Straus opposed the Democrats' nomination of William Jennings Bryan in 1896 and broke with his former party, actively campaigning for William McKinley. With McKinley's election, Straus again had easy access to the White House; he advised McKinley on a variety of issues relating to international diplomacy and foreign affairs. In 1898, McKinley asked Straus to resume his former post as minister to Turkey. In the aftermath of the 1897 Turkish massacre of Armenians, American relations with Turkey had deteriorated. The Turkish sultan refused American claims for property destroyed during the massacres, and American citizens in Turkey called for American warships to back up their claims. Dalin and Kolatch suggest that in asking Straus to return to Turkey, President McKinley told Straus that it was his duty to return as "the only man in the United States who could save the situation" (118). Straus returned as U.S. minister to Turkey for more than two years.

Throughout the nineteenth century, the few Jews who received presidential appointments were chosen because their personal connections to the presidents; they were asked to serve in posts deemed especially appropriate for Jews. While no Jews served in high-level administration posts, a number of Jewish leaders, including Joseph Seligman in the Grant administration, and both Oscar Straus and his older brother Isidor in the Cleveland administrations, were important presidential advisers. The movement of Jews from the periphery of executive branch power to the center awaited the turn of the century and the administration of Theodore Roosevelt.

A HISTORIC FIRST:
THE CABINET APPOINTMENT OF OSCAR S. STRAUS

In 1906, President Theodore Roosevelt appointed Oscar S. Straus as secretary of commerce and labor, the first Jew named to a president's cabinet. Roosevelt, who also appointed the first Catholic cabinet officer, Charles C. Bonaparte, his secretary of the navy (then a cabinet portfolio), introduced more religious diversity into presidential cabinet making than had any of his predecessors.

IN 1906, PRESIDENT THEODORE ROOSEVELT APPOINTED OSCAR S. STRAUS AS SECRETARY OF COMMERCE AND LABOR, THE FIRST JEW TO BE NAMED TO A PRESIDENT'S CABINET.

When Theodore Roosevelt assumed the presidency after the McKinley assassination, Straus, who had known Roosevelt for several years, soon became a close political adviser. In 1902, Roosevelt appointed Straus a member of the Permanent International Court of Arbitration at The Hague. A few months after Roosevelt's 1904 election, speculation that Roosevelt planned to name Straus to the post of commerce and labor was rampant in Washington. When Straus visited the White House in January 1906, the president confirmed the report. While Straus's ability and experience certainly were factors in Roosevelt's decision to appoint him to the cabinet, so too was his religion. Straus related the following comment made to him by the president: "I don't know whether you know it or not, but I want you to become a member of my Cabinet. I have a very high estimate of your character, your judgment, and your ability, and I want you for personal reasons. There is still a further reason: I want to show Russia and some other countries what we think of Jews in this country."

A number of ingredients are always involved in presidential cabinet appointments. The criteria of objective merit or ability often compete with the need for achieving both geographic and religious "representation" or balance in the selection process. In the case of Roosevelt's selection of Straus, analysts continue to debate whether the Jewish appointee was selected primarily on the basis of merit or, rather, because he was a Jew. Straus's biographer, Naomi W. Cohen, has noted that, in 1912, newspaper reports circulated that at a public dinner the previous year, at which both Roosevelt and Straus were speakers, the Jewish financier and philanthropist Jacob Schiff, one of the preeminent Jewish Republicans in America, had introduced Roosevelt, remarking that American Jews owed him a debt of gratitude because of his historic appointment of Straus. In his remarks, Roosevelt had stated that Straus had been appointed on the basis of merit and ability alone; the fact that he was Jewish had played no part in Roosevelt's decision to appoint him. A few minutes later, in introducing Straus, Schiff, who was a bit deaf and had evidently not heard Roosevelt's remarks, recounted how Roosevelt had sought his advice as to who would be the most suitable and eminent Jewish leader to appoint to his cabinet (Cohen, 1969, 147).

A FREE AND UNBOSSED CANDIDATE FOR GOVERNOR

COPYRIGHT 1912

Pirie MacDonald N. Y.

OSCAR S. STRAUS

WHAT PROMINENT MEN SAY.

"I desire to express to you my highest gratification upon your signal success, which has produced widespread satisfaction throughout the United States."—GROVER CLEVELAND, Former President of the United States.

"I judge that he would make a Governor superior to anyone likely to be nominated in opposition to him."—Dr. HENRY MITCHELL MACCRACKEN, Ex-Chancellor New York University.

"Providence inspired your nomination—may it continue to guide your every undertaking."—Father J. J. CURRAN, Wilkesbarre, Pa.

"Mr. Straus is a man of noble qualities appropriately blended in rare proportions; high ability, rock-bound integrity, warm energy, keen sagacity, and kindly humanity."—Rev. Dr. W. H. HUGHES.

Roosevelt's selection of Straus probably involved both the nominee's proven ability as a successful businessman, diplomat, and public servant *and* his religion and reputation as a respected Jewish communal leader. Clearly, Roosevelt wanted to make a Jewish appointment in 1906. He had appointed a Catholic to his cabinet the year before and sought an opportunity to appoint a Jew. As Naomi W. Cohen has concluded, while he upheld the Progressive ideal of appointments on the basis of merit and ability alone, he had an "equally strong . . . desire to show American Catholics and American Jews that they had the same opportunities as others" (148).

Theodore Roosevelt's appointment of Oscar Straus received wide and favorable coverage in the nation's press. As the first Jewish cabinet member, Straus's religion evoked more press comment that it had on the occasion of his other appointments. Cohen has noted that many newspapers used his appointment "as a point of departure to praise the contributions of the Jews in the United States, to express surprise that no Jew had filled a cabinet post heretofore, to laud T. R.'s liberalism, and to discuss the official posts filled by Jews in America and in foreign countries" (150).

In the twenty-eight years between Theodore Roosevelt's appointment of Oscar Straus and Franklin D. Roosevelt's appointment of Henry J. Morgenthau Jr. in 1934, no Jews served in any presidential cabinets. Jewish influence remained informal. For example, Woodrow Wilson relied on the advice of financier and philanthropist Bernard Baruch and consulted with Louis Brandeis, whom he would eventually name as the first Jew on the Supreme Court. President Hoover wanted to appoint his friend Julius Rosenwald, the president of Sears, Roebuck and Company and one of the preeminent Jewish philanthropists in America, as secretary of commerce, but his desire was thwarted by Rosenwald's wish to stay in his Chicago home because of his age and failing health.

INCREASED PRESENCE IN THE EXECUTIVE BRANCH:
FDR AND TRUMAN

During his twelve years in the White House, Franklin Roosevelt appointed more Jews to public office than had all previous presidents combined. Although he named only one Jew to his cabinet, according to Geoffrey Ward, more than 15 percent of Roosevelt's top-level appointees were Jews (254). Harvard law professor Felix Frankfurter, whom FDR appointed to the Supreme Court in 1939, was an important Roosevelt adviser and political confidant from the beginning of his administration. Not only did Frankfurter play a central role in drafting New Deal legislation and in formulating New Deal programs, but he also sent many of his brightest Jewish Harvard Law School students to Washington, where they found work in various New Deal agencies.

Benjamin Ginsberg claims that Jews were especially prominent in the Department of Interior (105). Upon the advice of Frankfurter, Nathan Margold was appointed Interior Department solicitor. Abe Fortas, who would be appointed to the Supreme Court by President Lyndon B. Johnson in 1965, began his public career in the 1930s as a young lawyer in the Interior Department, serving first as director of the department's Division of Manpower and later as undersecretary. Felix Cohen, a New York attorney, wrote the Interior Department's legislation concerning Native Americans.

Jewish attorneys were also appointed to influential positions in the Department of Labor, the Security and Exchange Commission, the Tennessee Valley Authority, and several other New Deal agencies. Among the several Jews who were appointed to ambassadorships by FDR, Jesse Isidor Straus, the nephew of Oscar Straus, was named ambassador to France, where he served from 1933 to 1936.

Franklin D. Roosevelt's closest Jewish friend and his one Jewish cabinet appointee was Henry Morgenthau Jr., who served as secretary of the treasury from 1934 to 1945. Morgenthau's father had served as finance chairman of the Democratic National

Committee during Woodrow Wilson's 1912 and 1916 campaigns and as ambassador to Turkey from 1913 to 1916. Independently wealthy and a Democratic Party activist, Morgenthau Jr. had become a gentleman farmer, growing apples and raising dairy cattle on a thousand-acre farm in Duchess County, New York, not far from the Roosevelt estate at Hyde Park. As neighbors, Henry and Elinor Morgenthau and Franklin and Eleanor Roosevelt became fast friends; the Morgenthaus were among the earliest supporters of FDR's candidacy for governor of New York in 1928. During the 1928 gubernatorial campaign, Morgenthau, who had become a prominent figure in New York state agricultural circles, advised Roosevelt on agricultural policy. After his election in 1928, Roosevelt appointed Morgenthau chairman of the newly created New York State Agricultural Advisory Commission, the first of several important positions that Morgenthau would hold under FDR as governor and president.

With Roosevelt's election to the presidency, Morgenthau had hoped for a cabinet appointment as secretary of agriculture, a position for which he was, by experience and ability, well qualified. However, FDR conformed with the long tradition of appointing an agriculture secretary from the heart of the nation's farmland, far west of Duchess County, New York. Morgenthau was sorely disappointed at being passed over for a cabinet post. According to George McJimsey, however, Roosevelt "soothed Morgenthau's hurt feelings at not being named Secretary of Agriculture by naming him to head the new Farm Credit Administration" (56), one of the three New Deal agencies established by Congress to provide credit to America's farmers.

In the first year of the Roosevelt presidency, FDR's first secretary of the treasury, William Woodin, became fatally ill; the undersecretary of the treasury, Dean Acheson, became the acting head of the Treasury Department but resigned within a few months over policy differences with FDR. The president turned to Morgenthau. After serving briefly as acting secretary, Morgenthau was appointed secretary of the treasury, the second Jew to serve in a president's cabinet. As FDR's secretary of the treasury from 1934 to 1945, Henry Morgenthau Jr. was the longest-serving treasury secretary and the longest-serving Jewish cabinet member in U.S. history.

Another of Roosevelt's closest political confidants and most trusted advisers was Samuel Rosenman. When Roosevelt was elected governor of New York in 1928, Rosenman, who had served for four years as a member of the New York State legislature, joined his staff in Albany as a speechwriter and special legal counsel. It was Rosenman who, in 1932, is credited with first bringing together the distinguished group of academic experts known as the "Brain Trust." He also is credited with coining the phrase *New Deal*. While serving as a New York State Supreme Court justice from 1934 to 1943, Rosenman continued to advise Roosevelt on an informal basis. In August 1941, Roosevelt asked Rosenman to draft a reorganization plan to prepare the government for wartime production. Rosenman's plan resulted in the creation of

I N SEPTEMBER 2000, JOSHUA ADLER BOETTIGER, THE GREAT-GRANDSON OF PRESIDENT FRANKLIN D. ROOSEVELT, BEGAN SEMINARY STUDIES AT THE RECONSTRUCTIONIST RABBINICAL COLLEGE IN PHILADELPHIA. HE IS THE FIRST AND ONLY KNOWN DESCENDANT OF AN AMERICAN PRESIDENT TO STUDY FOR THE RABBINATE.

THE GRANDSON OF ANNA (FDR'S DAUGHTER), BOETTIGER HAS A JEWISH MOTHER, JANET ADLER, WHO RAISED HER CHILDREN AS REFORM JEWS. GROWING UP IN WESTERN MASSACHUSETTS, JOSHUA ATTENDED SYNAGOGUE AND TOOK JEWISH STUDIES COURSES AT BARD COLLEGE. HE STUDIED HEBREW BIBLE AND MISHNAH AT THE PARDES INSTITUTE IN JERUSALEM BEFORE APPLYING TO RABBINICAL COLLEGE.

—DAVID G. DALIN AND ALFRED J. KOLATCH

the Supply, Priorities, and Allocations Board. Subsequently, Rosenman played a major role in creating the National Housing Authority, the War Manpower Commission, the Office of War Information, and the Office of Economic Stabilization. In September 1943, Rosenman resigned his judicial post to serve on the White House staff as special counsel to the president, a position in which he continued to serve President Truman for a year after FDR's death.

Another close Roosevelt adviser was David K. Niles, who joined the White House staff as assistant to the president in 1942. Sometimes referred to as Roosevelt's "House Jew," Niles was the president's unofficial liaison to the Jewish community. According to Michael Cohen, he advised the president "which Jewish leaders to receive and which might be rejected politely without causing too much political damage" (76). He was the first of a series of special assistants assigned to liaison between the president and the Jewish community. Like Rosenman, Niles stayed on with President Truman after FDR's death. As a special assistant to the president, he had a major influence on Truman's decision to recognize Israel.

A third important Jewish member of FDR's White House staff was Benjamin V. Cohen, one of the most talented of Felix Frankfurter's protégés. Serving on the White House staff as a speechwriter, Cohen was instrumental in writing several major pieces of New Deal legislation, including the Security and Exchange Act of 1934, the Federal Communications Act, and the Minimum Wage Act. More than occasionally, Cohen would leave the White House to lobby for New Deal programs on Capitol Hill in the days before the White House had an official Office of Congressional Liaison.

While President Truman used several Jewish advisers on his White House staff, he did not appoint any Jews to his cabinet, the only Democratic president after FDR not to have done so. One of Truman's latter appointments, Lewis L. Strauss, an influential investment banker and Jewish communal leader, and a Republican when he was appointed to the newly created Atomic Energy Commission (AEC), would become quite controversial in the Eisenhower years.

DECREASED PRESENCE IN THE EISENHOWER YEARS

No Jews played prominent roles in the Eisenhower administration. Few of his top-level appointees and only one prominent member of the White House staff, Maxwell Rabb, were Jewish. Rabb was assistant to the president in charge of civil rights, immigration, and labor problems; he helped shepherd the Refugee Relief Act of 1953 through Congress. Rabb also served as secretary to Eisenhower's cabinet from 1956 to 1958. He continued the tradition of having a Jewish member of the White House staff serve as liaison to the Jewish community.

But the Jewish appointment that was most controversial in the Eisenhower administration was one that was never confirmed. Eisenhower had elevated Lewis Strauss, the Truman appointee, to the chairmanship of the AEC in 1953. For the next five years Strauss was the most influential shaper of U.S. atomic energy policy. On October 24, 1958, President Eisenhower nominated Strauss as secretary of commerce, the only Jewish Cabinet designee of this administration. When the Strauss nomination was sent to Congress for confirmation in January 1959, however, it met the strong and unrelenting opposition of the Democratic-controlled Senate. The opposition was based on the public controversy, during Strauss's tenure as chairman of the AEC, over his prominent role in the revocation of the commission's security clearance to J. Robert Oppenheimer, father of the atomic bomb and one of the nation's most eminent physicists.

Oppenheimer had allegedly had past associations with communists; he was also suspect because of continued opposition to the development of the hydrogen bomb. At Strauss's urging, the AEC ruled that Oppenheimer was a security risk and denied him access to classified information on U.S. atomic energy policy. As chairman of the AEC, Strauss had also repeatedly failed to respond to the requests of the Joint Atomic Energy Committee for information. According to G. Calvin Mackenzie, Strauss had "so infuriated the Senate in this and his evasiveness at his confirmation hearing that it took the highly unusual step of refusing to confirm a nomination to the President's Cabinet" (143). In June of 1959, Strauss's nomination as secretary of commerce was defeated by a Senate vote of forty-nine to forty-six, the only Jewish cabinet nomination to be denied Senate confirmation.

THE KENNEDY AND JOHNSON YEARS:
JEWS AS PART OF THE WHITE HOUSE TEAM

President Kennedy was the first American President to name two Jews to his cabinet, Abraham Ribicoff and Arthur Goldberg. He and his successor Lyndon Johnson also used a large number of Jews in advisory capacities.

One of the most popular vote getters in Connecticut history, Ribicoff is the only American Jew to have served in both houses of Congress, as governor of his state, and as a member of a president's cabinet. Ribicoff and Kennedy first met after Ribicoff's election to Congress in 1948. During the four years when they were both young Democratic congressmen from neighboring New England states, Ribicoff and Kennedy became close friends and political allies. In 1954, when Ribicoff was running for the Democratic nomination for governor of Connecticut, Senator John F. Kennedy gave the keynote address at the Democratic state convention at which Ribicoff was nominated. At the Democratic National Convention in 1956, Ribicoff delivered the speech nominating Kennedy for vice president.

In 1960, Ribicoff played a pivotal role in Kennedy's campaign, serving as convention floor manager at the Democratic National Convention. After Kennedy's election, Ribicoff was offered his choice of cabinet positions; he selected secretary of health, education, and welfare (HEW). While secretary of HEW, Ribicoff drafted the original Medicare plan, which was defeated after intense lobbying by the American Medical Association. In 1962, after only sixteen months in the Kennedy cabinet, Ribicoff returned to Connecticut to run successfully for a seat in the United States Senate.

A native of Chicago and 1930 graduate of Northwestern University Law School, Arthur Goldberg had specialized in labor law and had earned a reputation as the preeminent labor lawyer in the United States. In 1948, Goldberg became general counsel for the Congress of Industrial Organizations (CIO) and helped draft the historic agreement merging the American Federation of Labor (AFL) and the CIO in 1955. For the next six years, before joining the Kennedy administration, Goldberg served as special counsel to the AFL-CIO. Kennedy had first met Goldberg during the Senate's consideration of labor legislation during the late 1950s and had been impressed. Indeed, as Arthur Schlesinger Jr. has recalled, Kennedy thought so highly of Goldberg, who was an early supporter of Kennedy's candidacy, that his appointment to the Labor post was almost inevitable. In 1962, when Felix Frankfurter

RIBICOFF IS THE ONLY AMERICAN JEW TO HAVE SERVED IN BOTH HOUSES OF CONGRESS, AS GOVERNOR OF HIS STATE, AND AS A MEMBER OF A PRESIDENT'S CABINET.

announced his retirement from
the Supreme Court, President
Kennedy appointed Goldberg to
fill the vacancy on the high court.

No one would deny the symbolic importance to Jews of Ribicoff's and Goldberg's simultaneous service in JFK's cabinet. But
perhaps more important, in terms
of the overall role of Jews in American politics, was the fact that the Jewish role and influence increased significantly on the White House staff and in subcabinet appointments
during the Kennedy and Johnson years.

Walt W. Rostow, who had been a distinguished professor of economics at MIT and
author of several influential books on economic history and international affairs, was appointed Deputy Special Assistant for National Security Affairs in 1961. When his boss,
McGeorge Bundy, left the White House in 1966, Rostow became President Johnson's
special assistant for national security affairs, the first Jew to hold the position of chief national security adviser.

Myer Feldman, a Washington lawyer who had handled Israeli and Jewish affairs
on JFK's Senate staff, was appointed a deputy special counsel when Kennedy became
president. In that capacity, he held the "Jewish portfolio" that David K. Niles had under
FDR and Truman. In 1961, Kennedy sent Feldman on a secret mission to Tel Aviv to
promise Israel protection by the U.S. Sixth Fleet and to arrange the sale of Hawk anti-
aircraft missiles that the Eisenhower administration had previously refused to sell to Israel. He had played a key role in reversing the Eisenhower administration's decision.
Shortly after Lyndon Johnson succeeded to the presidency, Feldman replaced Theodore
C. Sorenson as special counsel to President Johnson, a position that he would hold for
close to two years. As such, Feldman was one of seven Jews to hold that portfolio in the
last third of the twentieth century.

Richard N. Goodwin had joined John F. Kennedy's Senate staff as a speechwriter in
1959. During the Kennedy presidential campaign, Goodwin wrote speeches on Latin
America, coining the term "Alliance for Progress." Subsequently, he served on the White
House staff as a speechwriter before being appointed deputy assistant secretary of state
for inter-American affairs. He rejoined the White House staff during the Johnson administration as a speechwriter on Latin American and urban affairs and is credited with
having originated the term *the Great Society*.

Jerome B. Wiesner, a professor of electrical engineering at MIT, who had been a
member of President Eisenhower's Science Advisory Committee, was appointed special
assistant for science and technology by Kennedy in 1961. He also served as the director
of the Office of Science and Technology in the Kennedy and Johnson administrations.

Another high-level Jewish appointment was that of Sheldon Cohen as commissioner of the Internal Revenue Service in 1965. By the end of the Johnson administration, the presence of Jews in high positions in the executive branch was hardly noticed. While one Jewish assistant continued to hold the "Jewish portfolio," others played leadership and advisory roles on the entire spectrum of issues that defines American politics.

NIXON AND THE JEWS: A STUDY IN PARADOXES

The relationship between President Richard Nixon's personal view of Jews, on the one hand, and his appointment of several Jews to important positions in his administration, on the other, remains paradoxical. The more than four hundred hours of Nixon White House tapes, made public in the summer of 1999, reveal a level of antisemitic prejudice unique among American presidents. And yet, despite Nixon's uncomplimentary comments about Jews, his personal dealings with individual Jews were highly cordial, and he reached out to several Jewish appointees to serve in his administration.

His most influential Jewish assistant was Henry Kissinger. Kissinger, the foreign policy adviser on whom Richard Nixon relied more than any other, was appointed President Nixon's special assistant for national security affairs in January 1969. Kissinger's achievements in that role were many. In July 1971, he became the first American government official to visit China since 1949 and was instrumental in establishing diplomatic ties between the United States and the People's Republic, paving the way for President Nixon's historic visit to China the following February. Kissinger also had a principal role in negotiating the SALT I Agreement with the Soviet Union in May 1972. One of Kissinger's most notable achievements while serving President Nixon was negotiating a cease-fire with the North Vietnamese in January 1973, for which Kissinger received the Nobel Peace Prize.

In August 1973, Kissinger replaced William P. Rogers as secretary of state, becoming the first Jew to serve in that cabinet position. While secretary of state, he retained the title of special assistant to the president for national security affairs, the only secretary of state to do so. No Jew did as much to shape and determine U.S. foreign policy as Kissinger, who was unquestionably the most powerful and influential Jewish cabinet member or White House adviser in American history.

But Kissinger was far from the only Jew to serve in a prominent role under Nixon. Arthur Burns, a respected Columbia University economics professor who had served as President Eisenhower's chairman of the Council of Economic Advisers, was appointed chairman of the Federal Reserve Board; Walter Annenberg was named ambassador to England, the first Jew to be appointed to that most prestigious diplomatic post. Jews were among his closest White House advisers. Herbert Stein chaired Nixon's Council of Economic Advisors; William Safire served as one of the

> BEFORE WE COULD DISCUSS THIS ANY FURTHER, STEVE BULL CAME IN TO SAY THAT RABBI BARUCH KORFF WAS WAITING FOR HIS APPOINTMENT. I HAD ASKED ZIEGLER TO TELL HIM THAT I HAD DECIDED TO RESIGN AND THAT HE SHOULD NOT TRY TO CHANGE MY MIND. RABBI KORFF SUMMONED HIS USUAL ELOQUENCE AND SAID THAT ALTHOUGH HE WOULD ACCEPT WHATEVER I DECIDED, HE FELT OBLIGATED TO SAY WHAT HE THOUGHT. "YOU WILL BE SINNING AGAINST HISTORY IF YOU ALLOW THE PARTISAN CABAL IN CONGRESS AND THE JACKALS IN THE MEDIA TO FORCE YOU FROM OFFICE," HE SAID. HE SPOKE WITH THE FIRE OF AN OLD TESTAMENT PROPHET, BUT HE SAW THAT MY MIND WAS MADE UP.
>
> —RICHARD NIXON

NO JEW DID AS MUCH TO SHAPE AND DETERMINE U.S. FOREIGN POLICY AS KISSINGER, WHO WAS SUBSEQUENTLY THE MOST POWERFUL AND INFLUENTIAL JEWISH CABINET MEMBER OR WHITE HOUSE ADVISER IN AMERICAN HISTORY.

president's most trusted speechwriters. One of the most highly visible aides was Leonard Garment, Nixon's former law partner and a registered Democrat, who had joined the White House staff when Nixon was elected president and who advised him on the selection of his cabinet. When the Watergate scandal was at its apex, Garment was appointed to replace John Dean as special counsel to President Nixon. It was Garment who advised Nixon to fire H. R. Haldeman and John Ehrlichman, the president's close White House assistants who were implicated in the Watergate cover-up.

A NEW NORMALITY: JEWS CONTINUE IN IMPORTANT ROLES

Assuming the presidency following Nixon's resignation, Gerald Ford retained Henry Kissinger as secretary of state. He quickly chose Alan Greenspan as chairman of his Council of Economic Advisers. Ford's first new cabinet appointment was that of Edward H. Levi, an eminent legal scholar and university administrator, as attorney general. When Levi was sworn in on February 7, 1975, he became the first American Jew to serve as attorney general. The descendant of one of America's most distinguished rabbinic families, Levi was the son, grandson, and great-grandson of rabbis.

Hailed by the American Bar Association as a "brilliant nomination," Levi's appointment was the first cabinet-level change of the Ford presidency. Unlike most of his predecessors at Justice, Levi's was a nonpolitical appointment. With his reputation for integrity and nonpartisanship and his impeccable legal credentials, Levi restored public confidence and professionalism in the Justice Department, which had been shaken by the Watergate scandals and the personal involvement of Attorneys General John Mitchell and Richard Kleindienst.

During his administration, President Jimmy Carter appointed four Jews to cabinet positions, more than had been appointed by any president until that time: Harold Brown at Defense, W. Michael Blumenthal at the Treasury, Philip Klutznick at Commerce, and Neil Goldschmidt at Transportation. During the 1976 presidential campaign and again in the period between his election and the inauguration, Carter promised a cabinet of new faces, rather than "old Washington hands" who had served in the government in earlier administrations. And yet, as Anthony J. Bennett has pointed out, Carter's choice of cabinet appointees "contained many who had seen service in the Kennedy–Johnson years and the 'crop of new faces' description never quite seemed to fit" (69). This was especially true of his Jewish appointees, three of whom had substantial prior experience in the federal government, having served under previous Democratic administrations.

Harold Brown, a prominent physicist, educator, and government official, had served as a member of the President's Science Advisory Committee during the Kennedy administration and, from 1965 to 1969, as secretary of the air force under President Johnson. Blumenthal was deputy assistant secretary of state for economic affairs at the start of the Kennedy administration. From 1963 to 1967, he served as ambassador and chairman of the U.S. delegation to the Kennedy Round of Tariff Negotiations. Klutznick, an influential lawyer, businessman, and Democratic Party fund-raiser, who had served as a federal housing commissioner under Presidents Roosevelt and Truman, was Adlai Stevenson's chief deputy at the United Nations and ambassador to the United Nations' Economic and Social Council during the Kennedy administration.

Of Carter's four Jewish appointees, only Goldschmidt, the youthful mayor of Portland, Oregon, could be considered part of Carter's "crop of new faces," with no previous "inside the beltway" government experience. Furthermore, in appointing Goldschmidt, in July 1979, as Nelson W. Polsby has noted, Carter was building on relationships established by the White House office of liaison with states and municipalities to reach out to the Democratic Party's traditional urban voting constituencies that the Carter White House had ignored during the first two years of his administration (40).

In appointing Klutznick, as the 1980 presidential elections were rapidly approaching, Carter was reaching out to another traditional Democratic Party constituency that he had heretofore ignored—America's Jewish voters. Carter's November 1979 appointment of Klutznick, one of the preeminent Jewish communal leaders and philanthropists of his generation, was widely acclaimed throughout the American Jewish community. Not since Theodore Roosevelt's appointment of Oscar Straus in 1906 had a Jewish cabinet appointee been able to boast such impressive credentials as a recognized and representative leader of American Jewry.

A growing number of Jewish Democrats, who had voted for Carter in 1976, were reassessing their support for the Carter ticket because of their dissatisfaction with the Carter administration's policies toward Israel. With the 1980 presidential election less than a year away, some political observers were already predicting that fewer Jewish voters would vote for the Democratic presidential candidate than in any election in recent memory; some said that President Carter might well receive less than 50 percent of the Jewish vote. The Carter White House, looking toward the campaign ahead, hoped that Klutznick in the cabinet, and thus part of the official presidential team, would reassure those Jewish Democratic voters who were wavering in their support for the president's reelection.

In addition to the four cabinet appointments and other subcabinet appointments, Carter also appointed Jews to important positions within the White House. Stuart E. Eizenstat served as a highly respected and especially influential member of the White House staff. A prominent young Atlanta attorney and Democratic Party activist, Eizenstat had been an early supporter of Jimmy Carter's presidential candidacy. In 1976, he joined the Carter campaign on a full-time basis and after the election was appointed President Carter's special assistant for domestic affairs and policy. In addition to his primary responsibilities as domestic policy chief, Eizenstat also held the "Jewish portfolio," serving as the administration's liaison to the Jewish community. Eizenstat was deeply interested in Holocaust-related issues and played an influential role in the creation of the President's Commission on the Holocaust. The first religiously observant Jew to serve on the White House staff, Eizenstat kept a kosher home and left work early on Fridays to observe the Sabbath.

THE FIRST RELIGIOUSLY OBSERVANT JEW TO SERVE ON THE WHITE HOUSE STAFF, EIZENSTAT KEPT A KOSHER HOME AND LEFT WORK EARLY ON FRIDAYS TO OBSERVE THE SABBATH.

Two prominent Washington attorneys, Lloyd Cutler and Alfred Moses, also served in the White House staff as special counsel to the president during the Carter years; Cutler would return in that role during the Clinton administration.

Although Presidents Ronald Reagan and George Bush did not nominate any Jews to their cabinets, the first American presidents since Harry Truman not to do so, both Reagan and Bush appointed several Jews to important policymaking subcabinet positions, especially in the State and Defense departments. President Reagan appointed Alan Greenspan, who had chaired the President's Council of Economic Advisers during the Ford administration, to head the Federal Reserve Board—a position he continued to hold into the new century.

In addition, several Jews did serve on the White House staff under these presidents. Among these was Marshall Breger, a law professor who became special assistant to the president and was the Reagan administration's liaison to the Jewish community. Breger, who would later be appointed solicitor of the Labor Department during the first Bush administration, was the first Orthodox Jew to serve on the White House staff. Jay Lefkowitz was the highest-ranking Jewish member of the White House staff during the first Bush administration, serving as secretary for cabinet affairs. William Kristol, a political scientist who had served as chief of staff to secretary of education William J. Bennett during the Reagan administration, served as chief of staff for Vice President Dan Quayle.

CONCLUSION: THE CLINTON ADMINISTRATION

During his eight years in the White House, Bill Clinton appointed more Jews to high-level positions than had any other president. Five Jews headed cabinet departments during Clinton's eight years; six others held portfolios with cabinet rank. The positions were of importance and covered the breadth of government activity. Robert E. Rubin and Laurence Summers each served as secretary of the treasury. Dan Glickman, formerly a nine-term Democratic congressman and a longtime member of the House Agriculture Committee, became secretary of agriculture, the first Jew ever to serve in that position. Robert Reich was secretary of labor, the third Jew in American history to head the Labor Department. Mickey Kantor became the third Jew to serve as secretary of commerce in a presidential cabinet; earlier he had served as special trade representative, with cabinet rank. In addition, Madeleine Albright, who was born a Jew but raised as a Roman Catholic, became secretary of state in 1997, after having served as United Nations ambassador (with cabinet rank) during the first Clinton administration.

After some controversy, Richard C. Holbrooke assumed the cabinet-rank position of ambassador to the United Nations in October 1998. Samuel "Sandy" Berger served as special assistant to the president for national security affairs. Charlene Barshefsky succeeded Kantor as special trade representative. Alice Rivkin and Jacob Lew were each named director of the cabinet-level Office of Management and Budget, and Gene Sperling served as assistant to the president for economic policy, also with cabinet rank.

> DURING HIS EIGHT YEARS IN THE WHITE HOUSE, BILL CLINTON APPOINTED MORE JEWS TO HIGH-LEVEL POSITIONS THAN HAS ANY OTHER PRESIDENT.

More Jews also served in prominent White House staff positions in the Clinton administration than at any time since the New Deal. Samuel (Sandy) Berger, who had served as deputy director of the State Department's Policy Planning Staff during the Carter administration, was appointed deputy assistant to the president for national security affairs. Following Clinton's reelection in 1996, Berger was elevated to special assistant to the president, thus becoming the third Jew to serve as the president's chief national security policy adviser on the White House staff. Three Jewish attorneys—Bernard Nussbaum, Lloyd Cutler, and former congressman and Federal Circuit Court Judge Abner Mikva—served on the White House staff as special counsels to the president. Numerous other Jews, including Rahm Emanuel, Ira Magaziner, Dick Morris, Ann Lewis, Maria Echaveste, and Sidney Blumenthal, served in a variety of advisory capacities on the White House staff. The number of Jews appointed to subcabinet positions or to ambassadorships is equally impressive.

In many respects, the 1990s were a historic—indeed, a golden—era for Jews in American politics and government. In that decade more Jews won election to the Congress and Senate than at any other time in American history. During the first four years of the 1950s, only one Jew was a member of the United States Senate; during the 1990s, eleven served at one time. For the first time in American history, a president, Bill Clinton, appointed two Jews to the United States Supreme Court. In the eight years of his presidency, Clinton appointed almost as many Jews to cabinet posts as had all of his predecessors combined. During the Clinton presidency, Jews received more ambassadorial appointments including the first appointment as ambassador to Israel, than in any other administration in American history. In 1997, President Clinton also appointed the first religiously Orthodox Jew as an ambassador to an Arab country, Egypt. Soon after Ambassador Daniel Kurtzer arrived in Cairo, moreover, a kosher kitchen was installed for him at the Cairo embassy. And, in August 2000, Senator Joseph Lieberman, an Orthodox Jew who does not campaign on the Sabbath, became the first Jewish candidate for vice president. Each of these developments would have been unimaginable during the 1950s. Collectively, they suggest that during the 1990s, as never before, Jews were politically at home in the United States.

Since the nineteenth century, American Jews have looked to the presidency and to individual presidents for political recognition and representation in the form of presidential appointments to cabinet and subcabinet positions, to the White House staff, and to diplomatic positions. And they have not been disappointed in their expectations of the White House. In the early years, the Jews who were appointed were friends and often financial supporters of their political benefactors. Often the positions to which they were appointed were those reserved for Jews. During the twentieth century, from President Theodore Roosevelt's historic appointment of Oscar Straus as secretary of commerce and labor in 1906 to the extraordinary and unprecedented number of Jewish appointments made by President Bill Clinton during the 1990s, American Jews have received ever-greater political recognition through presidential appointments, which have been one of the most important vehicles for Jewish representation and participation in American government and public life. Franklin D. Roosevelt named more Jews to appointive offices than any other president before him. The Jewish presence in the federal government grew enormously in the post–World

War II era, and especially beginning with the Kennedy administration, as presidents appointed more and more Jews to cabinet and subcabinet positions and to positions on the upper echelons of the White House staff. Presidents Kennedy through Carter made no less than twelve Jewish cabinet appointments, while naming two Jewish assistants to the president for national security affairs, two Jewish chairmen of the Council of Economic Advisers, three Jewish special counsels to the president and, for the first time, a Jewish ambassador to the Court of St. James.

Although it has been hardly remarked on, a distinctive legacy of the Clinton presidency was the extraordinary number of Jewish appointees in important policymaking and advisory positions throughout the executive branch of the federal government. Indeed, through appointments to his White House staff, cabinet, and a variety of subcabinet and diplomatic posts, President Clinton brought more Jews into high-level positions in government than had any other president. Through these presidential appointments, American Jews have received an unprecedented degree of political recognition and influence in American government and public life that would have been unimagined in any earlier generation.

THEY ARE NOT APPOINTED TO REPRESENT JEWS; THEY ARE APPOINTED AS AMERICANS WHO HAPPEN TO BE JEWISH.

And a full path has been navigated. As we enter the twenty-first century, Jews in government have been appointed because of their qualifications to whatever posts they are deemed qualified. They are not appointed to represent Jews; they are appointed as Americans who happen to be Jewish. The degree to which the Lieberman nomination was accepted by the American public, despite some concerns expressed shortly after his selection by Jewish leaders who feared an observant Jew would provide a convenient scapegoat, is ample testimony that Jews within the executive branch are now accepted according to their abilities without concern for the faith they profess or the background of their ancestors.

3

ON THE HILL

Jews in the United States Congress

CONNIE L. MCNEELY
AND SUSAN J. TOLCHIN

To the surprise of the nation, on August 7, 2000, Vice President Al Gore announced his choice of United States Senator Joseph I. Lieberman as his running mate for vice president on the Democratic ticket. As the first Jew to run for president or vice president on a major party ticket, Lieberman drew national and international attention. Reams of articles followed Gore's announcement, dissecting every detail of Lieberman's voting record, his religious faith, and his personal and political past. Despite the fact that Jews have served in public office for most of the nation's history, the Lieberman nomination clearly had the effect of raising questions among the general public about the influence of Judaism on public office. Would the country, the voters, and the Democratic Party accept a Jew, an Orthodox Jew who, as such, stood apart from many of his fellow Jews in Congress, as a candidate on his merits; or would Lieberman's faith become an issue in the campaign?

Notwithstanding some of the vitriolic antisemitism that appeared sporadically on web sites following the Lieberman announcement, the nation had risen dramatically in the last three decades above its history of intolerance. The Gallup polls of 1999 concluded that 92 percent of the American public would accept a Jew as president; only 6 percent said they would refuse outright to vote for a Jewish candidate for president. In 1965, a Gallup poll put the figure of those who would accept a Jew for president at 80 percent; in 1937, the figure had been 46 percent. (Polls also indicate that citizens are more willing to accept an African American candidate now than they have been in the past; however, other issues, particularly those associated with sexual preference, remain the same.)

> JEWS WHO HAVE SERVED THE NATION IN CONGRESS, WHILE TRUE TO THEIR CULTURAL IDENTITY AS JEWS, HAVE INVARIABLY RETAINED THEIR PRIMARY LOYALTIES TO THEIR DISTRICTS, TO THEIR PARTY, AND TO THEIR COUNTRY.

The public debate about Lieberman lacked a historical perspective. When John F. Kennedy ran for the presidency, opponents spread the rumor that the pope was building a tunnel from Rome. However, the nation has grown more sophisticated about the role that religion plays in the public life of elected politicians since that time. In the case of Jews who have served in public office, a long record exists. In this chapter, we look at the role of Jews in Congress, examining patterns of representation and congressional careers to understand the extent to which these senators and representatives have or have not acted in a way that systematically differentiates them from their non-Jewish colleagues. To anticipate our argument, we find that the Jews who have served the nation in Congress, while true to their cultural identity as Jews, have invariably retained their primary loyalties to their districts, to their party, and to their country.

JEWS IN THE SENATE

Jews have served in Congress since antebellum days. The first Jew in the Senate was David Levy Yulee, elected to the Senate as a Democrat from Florida; Yulee served from 1845 to 1851 and then again from 1855 to 1861. Ironically, Yulee did not publicly frame his identity as Jewish, referring instead to his "Moroccan parentage." Furthermore, in marked contrast to his twentieth-century Jewish counterparts, Yulee, like many other southern Jews at the time, was adamantly in favor of slavery. He was known for his fiery rhetoric in the Senate in support of secession. There have been claims that he was responsible for hatching a conspiracy against the government of Abraham Lincoln (Stone, 556–58).

The second Jew in the Senate, Judah Benjamin, one of the most important figures in Jewish and American history, was elected from Louisiana in 1852 as a Whig. Also a secessionist, he served until 1861, when the Civil War broke out. Benjamin remained loyal to the Confederacy throughout the Civil War, serving first as secretary of war and later as secretary of state in the administration of Jefferson Davis. He later fled to England after Davis's capture and the defeat of the South. Like Yulee, Judah Benjamin did not invoke his Jewish identity. While acknowledging his Judaism, however, Benjamin consistently claimed a closer affinity with America and the South than with the Jewish community. This "loyalty" did not spare him, however, from antisemitic criticisms from his opponents.

Only four more Jews served in the Senate from the time that Yulee and Benjamin left until 1949, when Herbert Lehman, a Democrat from New York and close ally of President Roosevelt, took office. During that nearly ninety-year period, there were long stretches of time—from 1861 until 1879, from 1885 until 1897, and for the thirty-six years after Republican Simon Guggenheim of Colorado left the Senate until Lehman took office—in which there were no Jewish senators. However, Jews became an important part of the New Deal coalition, contributing to the electoral success of Democrats, especially in states with relatively large Jewish populations, such as New York. In 1949, Lehman, a former New York governor who had run unsuccessfully for the Senate in 1946, became the first Jewish senator after that hiatus of nearly four decades when he won a special election over John Foster Dulles, who had been appointed by Republican Governor Thomas E. Dewey to fill a vacated seat. Lehman's special election victory allowed him to complete that unexpired term. He went on to win a full term in the election of 1950. Lehman was joined by Richard Neuberger (D-Oreg.) in 1955; after that time, the barriers against Jews in the Senate slowly eroded.

Twenty-one Jewish senators have served since Lehman was elected. (Three senators are excluded from this count: William Cohen [R-Me.], John Sanford Cohen [D-Ga.],

and Barry Goldwater [R-Ariz.]. Although they are in-
cluded in some studies of Jews in Congress because their
fathers were Jewish, all three declared their allegiance to
Christianity relatively early in their lives.) Reflecting
Jewish political views generally, most of the Jews elected to
the Senate in the last half of the twentieth century were
Democrats. Only five—Jacob Javits (N.Y.), Rudy
Boschwitz (Minn.), Warren Rudman (N.H.), Arlen
Specter (Pa.), and Jacob (Chic) Hecht (Nev.)—have been
elected as Republicans.

The career of Javits, who succeeded Lehman in the
Senate and served until his defeat in 1980, deserves special attention, not only because of his prominence but
also because of the difficult experiences he faced as a senator. For many of the years
that he served, Javits was one of only two or three Jewish senators, and he suffered a
fair measure of discrimination from some of his colleagues in the Senate. To cite one
example, during a debate on the Senate floor on welfare formulas for New York, Senator John McClellan (D-Ark.) turned on Javits in fury and frustration: "We don't
need your kind here," a thinly veiled reference to Javits's religion and ethnicity.

That someone as distinguished as Javits experienced such overt antisemitism on the
Senate floor explains in part why relatively few Jews chose to seek elective office at the
federal level for much of the twentieth century. Jews number
only 1 to 2 percent of the population; however, when their influence has been disproportionate to their numbers, antisemitism has tended to emerge. Fearing this reaction, many
politically active Jews have preferred, until very recently, to
exercise their power behind the scenes and not in the forefront of politics. More typically, Jews have occupied high-
ranking positions as advisers, financiers, publishers, and media figures.

MANY POLITICALLY
ACTIVE JEWS HAVE
PREFERRED TO
EXERCISE THEIR
POWER BEHIND THE
SCENES AND NOT IN
THE FOREFRONT OF
POLITICS.

After the 1992 election, for the first time in history, the
number of Jews in the Senate grew to ten, symbolically repre-
senting the first time that Jews in the Senate could form a *minyan,* the minimum number
required for a "prayer quorum." The Jewish senators elected in the last quarter-century remain mostly Democrats, but they show an interesting geographic dispersion. Some, like
Howard Metzenbaum (Ohio), Frank Lautenberg (N.J.), Charles Schumer (N.Y.), and
Barbara Boxer and Dianne Feinstein (both Calif.), are Democrats who represent traditionally liberal states with large Jewish populations. Others, like Edward Zorinsky (D-Neb.),
Rudy Boschwitz (R-Minn.) and Paul Wellstone (D-Minn.), or Herb Kohl and Russ Feingold (both D-Wis.), represent states with very few Jews and either more conservative or

mixed political traditions. It seems apparent in those cases that religion was not a significant factor in the eyes of the voters.

The most senior current member, Carl Levin (D-Mich.), was elected in 1978; the newest Jewish senator, Schumer, won his seat in 1998. Three of the newest members, Schumer, Boxer, and Ron Wyden (D-Oreg.), are the only three Jewish senators who rose to the Senate from seats in the House since Javits was elected in 1956, despite the fact that rising from the House to the Senate has been a common path for ambitious representatives. A tall, lanky man, Wyden says today that he is the "only Jewish Senator to have received a basketball scholarship" in college.

Two of the current senators, Feinstein and Boxer, are the first Jewish women to serve in that body. (As of 2000, California, Maine, and Washington each have two female senators.) Boxer, reflecting a new militancy about Jews and women in politics, talked about how religion and politics affected her campaign for the Senate in California when she and Feinstein were running for two seats that were open at the same time—and were competing with each other for attention and campaign contributions: "People would say, 'How could two women win in California?'" she recalled. "What they really meant was, 'How could two Jewish women win in California?' The pundits were wrong; they only thought that one of us would get elected. What you have to do with prejudice is turn it around. We should not stand still for one Jewish seat on the Supreme Court, or two Jewish women in California. That's [tokenism] all over. The momentum is continuing to build."

Boxer and Feinstein are interesting from several perspectives. Neither emphasized religion in the quest for office, and, for the most part, their religion turned out not to be much of a factor in their election from California—a large, heterogeneous state, with at

least half a dozen large urban areas. Both are liberal: Boxer is slightly more liberal, rating 95 percent, according to the Americans for Democratic Action (ADA) rating, which ranks lawmakers on a liberal scale, while Feinstein received a 90 percent rating.

According to former Senator Howard Metzenbaum, "There is less prejudice against Jews now; no one would claim there is antisemitism now." But he added another example of the subtle antisemitism that Jews like Javits and himself had encountered. Before his retirement, Senator Ernest Hollings (D-S.C.) referred to him on the floor of the Senate as the "Senator from B'nai B'rith." Hollings "apologized, but not too well," recalled Metzenbaum. "The Jews from South Carolina still voted for him. The remark was unprovoked. There was no issue on the floor at that time."

Unlike the House of Representatives, Jews in the Senate have never formed an informal or formal caucus—although they might ally with each other on specific issues. In fact, the Senate mores discourage the formation of groups that advocate their own interests, because their very existence would violate the long tradition of comity and collegiality in the Senate. "There is no Jewish Caucus," emphasized Metzenbaum. "If there were, I would not have tolerated it. If they had separated us, I would have resented it."

UNLIKE THE HOUSE OF REPRESENTATIVES, JEWS IN THE SENATE HAVE NEVER FORMED AN INFORMAL OR FORMAL CAUCUS.

Jews in the Senate do not stand out as an identifiable group. While most have been Democrats and many have come from states with large Jewish populations, others have been Republicans—and many have come from states with few Jews. Many of the Jewish senators have been liberals; as a group they have probably been more liberal than their partisan peers, but not overwhelmingly so. Of the senators elected in the last quarter century, few have emphasized the importance of their religion as a motivating factor for their commitment to public service or for the views that they have expressed and issues they have emphasized.

JEWS IN THE HOUSE OF REPRESENTATIVES

Since Lewis Charles Levin won his seat as an American Party candidate from Pennsylvania in 1844, only 155 Jews have served in the House of Representatives. Before the first large wave of Jewish immigration in the late 1840s, America had fewer than fifteen thousand Jews, and no distinct religious community existed as a political base from which potential Jewish lawmakers could get elected. Fewer than two dozen Jews were elected to the House before 1900. Those who were elected developed political followings often independent of their religious affiliation. However, with the wave of immigration from Eastern Europe from the 1880s until after the turn of the century, distinct Jewish communities grew up in urban centers; these began to form the base of support for Jewish candidates seeking elective office. Twelve Jews were elected to the House in the elections between 1884 and 1900; half of these came from New York, some clearly the products of political organizations. In retrospect, those lawmakers were very brave to run openly as Jews in the face of the nativist, anti-semitic, and anti-immigrant sentiments of the time. But they clearly represented their constituents in seeking a better life in America.

Some of the Jewish candidates of this period brought their politics from Europe into the U.S. political arena. The first two Socialists ever to serve in the United States House of Representatives were Victor Berger, an Austrian Jew who was elected from Wisconsin in 1910 and served five (nonconsecutive) terms, and Meyer London, a Russian Jewish immigrant, who was elected from New York in 1914. Berger's iconoclastic, socialist, and pacifist views continually got him into trouble; he was indicted five times and was convicted and sentenced to twenty-five years in prison. His conviction was overturned by the Supreme Court in 1921, and he was returned to Congress, where he served his final three terms (Stone, 25).

Despite a conservative and generally bigoted climate following World War I, more than a dozen Jews were elected to the House before Franklin Delano Roosevelt's (FDR) election to the presidency in 1932. Most of those first elected in this period were Republicans; and of the Republicans, only Florence Prag Kahn (R-Calif.), the first Jewish woman elected to the House, remained in office after the New Deal came to power in the important realigning election of 1932. Jewish representation in Congress was beginning to change during this period, as more and more Jews joined the Democratic Party.

Three of the Democratic members elected in 1922, Samuel Dickstein, Sol Bloom, and Emanuel Celler, all of New York, began what would be long and successful careers. Celler, who would become the powerful chairman of the Judiciary Committee, served his Brooklyn district for nearly fifty years. At the end of his long and distinguished career in the early 1970s, Celler engaged in a bitter confrontation over the Equal Rights Amendment (ERA) with another Democratic Jewish member of Congress, Bella Abzug. Celler opposed the ERA on the grounds that there were no women at the Last Supper. "There may have been no women at the Last Supper," retorted Abzug, "but you can be sure that there will be women at the next one." Ironically, Celler was unseated in 1972 by a Jewish woman, Elizabeth Holtzman, a thirty-two-year-old attorney.

Seventeen Jews served in Congress during the administration of Franklin Roosevelt. Ten of the eleven first elected during FDR's tenure were Democrats; the lone Republican, Daniel Ellison of Maryland, served only one term. These Jewish members of Congress reflected a party allegiance fostered by the New Deal that continued for the rest of the century. The candidacy and administration of FDR unified Jewish voters in their identification with the Democratic Party. In each of FDR's four presidential elections, he received between 80 and 90 percent of the Jewish vote. Jewish allegiance to Roosevelt and the Democrats can be attributed to his New Deal policies, to his leadership in waging war against Hitler, and to the visibility and prominence of Jews in his administration. It is clear that the Jewish members of Congress reflected many of these views.

> JEWISH ALLEGIANCE TO ROOSEVELT AND THE DEMOCRATS CAN BE ATTRIBUTED TO HIS NEW DEAL POLICIES, TO HIS LEADERSHIP IN WAGING WAR AGAINST HITLER, AND TO THE VISIBILITY AND PROMINENCE OF JEWS IN HIS ADMINISTRATION.

After World War II, the number of Jews elected to Congress slowly increased. As in the Senate, the vast majority were Democrats, with many from large, heterogeneous urban districts that appeared more congenial to voting for Jewish representatives. A number of representatives in the New York City delegation have represented districts with large Jewish populations. Almost 80 percent of the 163 Jewish

members who have served in the House through the election of
1998 have been Democrats: 120 were Democrats, and only 32
were Republicans. Sixty-eight of those 163 Jewish members,
including 46 of the 110 elected since 1932, have represented
districts in New York State. Of the 46 Jews elected to the
House during the time when the strength of the New Deal coalition was at its peak, between 1932 and 1968, 32 were from New
York State. In the last quarter-century, however, over one-third of the
Jewish members elected to Congress have come from California.

Patterns of party affiliation that began in the New Deal have continued unabated. Only
16 of the 110 Jews serving in the House since FDR's first election have been Republicans.

> "WALTER WINCHELL IS A SLIME-MONGERING KIKE!"
> —JOHN RANKIN (D-MISS.), ON THE FLOOR OF THE
> UNITED STATES HOUSE OF REPRESENTATIVES,
> CONGRESSIONAL RECORD, FEBRUARY 11, 1946

The 107th Congress in 2001 had twenty-seven Jewish members, up from twenty-four
in the 106th Congress. Four new Jewish representatives took their seats: Adam Schiff
and Susan Davis of California, Steven Israel of New York, and Eric Cantor of Virginia.
Jane Harman of California was reelected to a seat she had held previously but given up
to run for governor. Sam Gejdenson (D-Conn.) lost the seat in eastern Connecticut that
he had held since the 1980 election. Twenty-three of the twenty-six were Democrats;
Cantor and Benjamin Gilman of New York were the only Republicans; and Bernie
Sanders, the former Socialist mayor of Burlington, Vermont, continues in the House as
an Independent, though he is often allied with the Democrats.

Although there is no Jewish caucus in the Senate, an informal caucus of Jewish legislators operates in the House of Representatives. That caucus was originally convened
by Sidney Yates (D-Ill.), who retired in 1998 after having been elected continuously by
his Chicago constituents for fifty years—with the exception of one term he sat out after
a loss in a run for the Senate.

IDENTITY POLITICS AND JEWS IN CONGRESS

The boost that Lieberman's nomination gave to the Gore candidacy was rooted in
"identity politics"—namely, the Jewish identity that Lieberman embraced in the United
States Senate and in his personal, religious life. Lieberman's unique position as the vice
presidential candidate has in many ways thrust him into the public mind as a represen-

tative of Jewish identity politics, even though his public record has been atypical of Jews in Congress—especially those who have served in Congress in the last half-century. He is a moderate liberal; he has a record of opposition to affirmative action; and he was considered disloyal by some of his fellow Democrats when he became the first Democratic senator to denounce President Clinton during the impeachment trial in 1998—although he eventually voted to acquit the president.

In the House impeachment, as well as the subsequent Senate trial, Jewish members voted along party lines—as they tend to vote on most issues. In the impeachment vote, all twenty-one Jewish Democrats in the House voted against all four articles of impeachment; two Jewish Republicans each voted for two articles of impeachment. At the Senate trial, all ten Jewish Democratic senators voted with their party against conviction on both the perjury and obstruction-of-justice charges. One Jewish Democratic senator, Russell Feingold (D-Wis.), separated from his party earlier in the proceeding, voting with the Republican majority on several procedural motions. The one Jewish Republican senator, Arlen Specter (R-Pa.), broke with his party and voted against conviction. A former prosecutor, Specter explained his vote on the basis of early Scottish judicial practice: "Not proved, therefore not guilty." Some discomfort remained, however, during the Senate trial. Dianne Feinstein tried to introduce a resolution censuring the president, but, in a surprise development, was defeated by the same Republican lawmakers who had impeached the president and brought him to trial.

> IN THE HOUSE IMPEACHMENT, AS WELL AS THE SUBSEQUENT SENATE TRIAL, JEWISH MEMBERS VOTED ALONG PARTY LINES—AS THEY TEND TO VOTE ON MOST ISSUES.

Another factor sets Lieberman apart from his Jewish colleagues in the Senate: his campaign against violence and overt sexuality on television. To some extent, Lieberman's image as a pillar of morality helped inoculate Gore against the voters' subliminal identification of Gore with President Clinton's sexual escapades. But Lieberman's public quest for improved morality in popular culture did not help win over the Hollywood elites, many of whom were longtime backers of Democratic candidates. The distinctiveness of Lieberman's position on this issue does not mean that other Jewish senators were not concerned with morality issues. Rather, Jewish senators, Republicans as well as Democrats, traditionally avoided involvement in "First Amendment" issues, preferring instead to allow the movie and television industries considerable latitude with their own programming.

"Identity politics" is the stuff of democracy—the conglomeration of groups that derive their power from their origins—but do not remain limited to their narrow interests. "One's sense of identity should not be restricted to what one could not deny if questioned by a bigot of whatever denomination," wrote the well-known political psychologist Erik Erikson. "It should be based on what one can assert as a positive

ONCE WHEN CONGRESS HELD A LATE NIGHT SESSION TO
DEAL WITH A SCHOOL PRAYER AMENDMENT, CONGRESSMAN
[BARNEY] FRANK WAS DRAFTED TO CHAIR ONE OF THE SESSIONS
IN THE MIDDLE OF THE NIGHT. AT 6 A.M. IN THE MORNING,
CONGRESSWOMAN MARJORIE HOLT TOLD THE HOUSE: "MR.
CHAIRMAN, WE MUST HAVE SCHOOL PRAYER TO DEMONSTRATE
THAT THIS IS A CHRISTIAN NATION."

LATER, BARNEY FRANK RESPONDED, "IF THIS IS A CHRIST-
IAN NATION, WHY DO THEY HAVE TO GET A POOR JEWISH BOY
OUT OF BED SO EARLY IN THE MORNING TO CHAIR THE HOUSE
SESSION?" AFTER THE PRESS HAD PUBLICIZED THE INCIDENT,
THE CONGRESSWOMAN APOLOGIZED TO THE MASSACHUSETTS
LEGISLATOR: "I MEANT TO SAY THIS IS A JUDEO-CHRISTIAN NA-
TION." WITHOUT MISSING A BEAT, FRANK RESPONDED: "MAR-
JORIE, I'VE NEVER MET A JUDEO-CHRISTIAN. WHAT DO THEY
LOOK LIKE? WHAT DO YOU SEND THEM IN DECEMBER—WHAT
KIND OF CARD?"

—TIKKUN, 1989

core, and active mutuality, a real community. This would force fewer people to become . . . radical and religious caricatures. It would also force new standards on communities" (Coles, 181).

Jewish members of Congress fit the Erikson mold in that they typically defied stereotypes; they have not differentiated themselves beyond the narrow perspective expected of them in Congress. In 1998, for example, eleven Jews were members of the Senate. Arlen Specter, the only Republican, was considered moderate; the rest, liberal. Senator Lieberman had the lowest ADA score of the Jewish senators, but his liberal voting record was still 80 percent, according to the ADA.

VOTING PATTERNS AND ISSUES OF CONCERN

On a wide range of issues, including affirmative action and hate crimes, immigration, gun control, flag desecration, missile defense systems, and foreign aid to Kosovo, Jews have tended on the whole to vote to the left of center. All of the Jewish senators supported legislative initiatives relating to affirmative action and hate crimes. On two of the other issues, only one of the Jewish senators dissented from the others—Wellstone in the case of the missile defense system, and Wyden on a bill relating to temporary farm workers. On three of the issues—aid to Kosovo, the gun control vote, and the constitutional amendment on flag desecration—Specter dissented from the majority view. On two of those three votes Lieberman sided with Specter; on one of those two and one other, Feingold sided with Specter. The Jewish senators clearly did not vote as a bloc, and partisanship was not the only factor. In fact, the nine Jewish Democrats voted very much like the rest of their party on these issues, and Specter's record paralleled that of the other moderate Republicans.

The pattern of controversial House votes in the 105th Congress was remarkably similar. Benjamin Gilman, the lone Republican among the Jewish members of the House, dissented more frequently than any of the others from the majority view; but again, he was normally joined by a number of others who shared his stance. On six of the seven issues examined, the majority of the Jewish representatives voted on one side; only on the question of Internet gambling were they truly divided. On each of the issues the split or unanimity among the Democratic Jewish representatives reflected the extent of division within the Democratic caucus as a whole.

The issue that has most united Jews in Congress for most of the last half-century is American policy toward Israel. Their positions reflected the preferences of American Jews, in general, most of whom are strongly pro-Israel. Moreover, support for Israel among Jewish members is also compatible with Jewish members' identity as Americans, since Americans have traditionally supported the state of Israel—as the only true democracy in the Middle East. There is a clear nexus between the position that the Jews in Congress take as Jews, and the position they would also hold because support for Israel is seen as in America's strategic interest. The closeness of this connection—between interests as Jews and interests as Americans with certain views of geopolitical strategy—

THE ISSUE THAT HAS MOST UNITED JEWS IN CONGRESS FOR MOST OF THE LAST HALF-CENTURY IS AMERICAN POLICY TOWARD ISRAEL.

is reflected not only in the concern for Israel expressed by the Jews in Congress but also in their willingness, reflective of American views generally, to be critical of some specific actions of the Israeli government and of the views of some Israelis on how the peace process should evolve.

According to Sander Levin (D-Mich.), Jewish members have made it their business to keep themselves well informed on foreign policy relating to Israel and the Middle East. Among those most active today on Middle East issues are two California Democrats from Los Angeles, Henry Waxman and Howard Berman. Their California colleague, Democrat Tom Lantos, himself a Holocaust survivor, is the leading expert on legislative matters relating to the Holocaust. Yet Levin points out that Jewish members of Congress are not monolithic in their views or on their votes on Israel. In recent years when many members have not always agreed with the policies promoted by the government of Israel, they have not been hesitant to express their reservations.

In addition, the votes of Jewish members of Congress on issues relating to Israel have also been affected by partisan politics within Congress. In an article in the *San Diego Jewish Press-Heritage* in May of 1999, Congressman Robert Filner is quoted:

> Five or six years ago every Jew—almost by definition—would vote for the foreign aid bill because it had foreign aid for Israel, and you couldn't possibly want to undermine that. Well, now if there is something in the foreign aid bill that is a problem on some other issue, people may—to make a point—vote against it. If they [the Republicans] throw in something like anti-family planning—this is since the Republicans have been in the majority—then all of a sudden the bill is not so clear cut.

In the 106th Congress, all Jewish Democrats demonstrated unprecedented opposition to the original foreign aid legislation that passed in fiscal year 2000. Senator Specter and Representative Gilman, the only Jewish Republicans, voted with their party in supporting the legislation, which passed very narrowly (214–211 in the House; 51–49 in the Senate). The bill drew the ire of most major Jewish organizations because although it provided $12.6 billion in foreign aid funding, the amount was $2 billion short of the president's request, which included the funds to implement the Wye River accords between Israel and its partners in the peace process. Clinton vetoed the bill, and the American Israel Public Affairs Committee (AIPAC) organized a campaign to increase the funding for the Wye River accords. Congress acceded and increased the funding to almost $16 billion.

Although not afraid to use its clout in foreign aid controversies, AIPAC has seen its prominence decline slightly in recent years. Long considered among the most powerful lobbies in Congress, AIPAC has traditionally reflected the views of the Israeli government and the majority of the American Jewish community. The lobby's prominence has waned somewhat as the threats to Israel seemed to decline with the advent of the peace process in the 1990s, and as the same issues that divided Israel in the 1990s also seemed to divide American Jews. The decrease of monolithic voting among Jews in Congress on matters related to Israel reflects this division in the American Jewish community, and in the American political community as a whole.

THE DECREASE OF MONOLITHIC VOTING AMONG JEWS IN CONGRESS ON MATTERS RELATED TO ISRAEL REFLECTS A DIVISION IN THE AMERICAN JEWISH COMMUNITY, AND IN THE AMERICAN POLITICAL COMMUNITY AS A WHOLE.

The pro-Israel political action committees (PACs), which were formed as separate organizations in the early 1980s to oppose congressional candidates who were perceived to be anti-Israel, have shrunk in terms of the actual dollars contributed over the last fifteen years. This is largely a function of the fact that since the mid-1980s, with the defeat of such "nonfriendly" legislators as Congressman Paul Findlay

(R-Ill.), few United States legislators have taken such stridently anti-Israel positions. Moreover, over the last decade Republican legislators from areas of the country with few Jews have become somewhat more supportive of Israel because of the supportive Middle East stance of religious right. Federal Election Commission (FEC) data indicates that two-thirds of pro-Israel PAC dollars went to Democrats, in contrast to other political action committees, which tend to favor Republicans. In 1995, the National Jewish Democratic Council had created its own PAC to support Democratic candidates sympathetic to their issues. In 2000, the National Jewish Coalition announced the formation of its own Republican PAC at the same time that it decided to change its name to the Republican Jewish Coalition; the major function of this group is to raise money for Republican congressional and presidential candidates.

Despite some losses, Jews continue to occupy positions of leadership in Congress and are influential in maintaining American support for the state of Israel. In the 104th, 105th, and 106th Congresses, for example, Benjamin Gilman, the only Republican Jewish member, was chairman of the International Relations Committee, critical to a broad range of issues of paramount concern to the Jewish-American community. A strong advocate of close Israeli–U.S. relations, Gilman found his support for the foreign aid program in conflict with some groups within his own party. He found an ally on many Israel-related issues in Sam Gejdenson, who succeeded Lee Hamilton (D-Ind.) as the committee's ranking Democrat. Gejdenson, the son of Holocaust survivors, was born in a U.S. displaced persons refugee camp. The situation changed somewhat after the election of 2000, however, as Gejdenson lost his bid to return to the House. Gilman was forced to give up his chairmanship because of a Republican Conference rule on term limits for those heading committees, but as the likely head of the subcommittee on Europe and the Middle East, he will remain in a pivotal position. Gejdenson will be replaced as ranking Democrat by Tom Lantos, whose concern for Israel is as strong as his predecessor's.

RECENTLY ELECTED JEWS IN CONGRESS ESPOUSED A MORE UNIVERSALIST KIND OF IDENTITY POLITICS IN WHICH THEY REPRESENTED JEWISH INTERESTS BY SPEAKING MORE BROADLY TO ISSUES THAT AFFECTED JEWS, ALONG WITH OTHER GROUPS.

Concern for Israel is not the only issue area on which the record of Jewish members of Congress should be evaluated as a group. "American Jews acculturated, yet remained Jewish; most of them met the challenge of assimilation; in their Jewishness, they added to the richness and diversity of the American setting" (Marcus, 747). In other words, recently elected Jews in Congress espoused a more universalist kind of identity politics in which they represented Jewish interests by speaking more broadly to issues that affected Jews, along with other groups.

Jews in the Congress have traditionally voted in a bloc for antidiscrimination and antibias legislation, largely because they feared the effects of intolerance against them. On the issue of affirmative action, Senator Lieberman has taken a slightly different position. Lieberman's opposition to affirmative action echoed a view espoused by many Jews in the neoconservative movement. Their fear was that affirmative action, which some define as the selection of certain groups for special treatment, would be used as it was in the past to discriminate against Jews. Since it had taken so many years to erode those patterns of past exclusion, many Jews in public life feared that antisemitism would reappear to keep Jews out of the mainstream of American life.

> DURING A 1991 DEBATE ON THE HOUSE FLOOR, REPRESEN-
> TATIVE SAM GEJDENSON (D-CONN.) ARGUED WITH REP.
> NORMAN SISISKY (D-VA.) ABOUT THE NEED TO LOCATE A MAJOR
> SUBMARINE BUILDING CONTRACT IN THEIR RESPECTIVE DIS-
> TRICTS. WATCHING THE TWO LAWMAKERS FIGHT OVER THE VALU-
> ABLE CONTRACT, CONGRESSMAN FRANK QUIPPED THAT THE
> HOUSE WAS WATCHING A FASCINATING SPECTACLE: "TWO JEWS
> FIGHTING OVER PORK."
> —WASHINGTON POST, 1991

Identity politics also led Jews in Congress to oppose politically right-wing groups, since they had traditionally harbored antisemites, many of whom advocated the Christianization of the United States. The rise of the Christian Right, which gained considerable ground in the United States in the 1980s and the 1990s, worried many Jewish legislators, who had traditionally downplayed their Judaism in Congress for fear of this group, among others. The possibility that David Duke, a former member of the Ku Klux Klan, would run for Congress, for example, triggered a reaction among Jewish members of Congress, as well as the American Jewish Congress (AJCongress), which called on the Republican National Committee (RNC) to expel him. The RNC eventually assured the AJCongress that Duke would receive no assistance from them.

Jews in Congress have always advocated strong hate-crime legislation, since Jews have suffered disproportionately in the categories of "religion-related" crimes and as targets of "religious hate" crimes. Data compiled in 1998 by the Federal Bureau of Investigation (FBI) showed that while 13 percent of all hate crimes were committed against Jews, 80 percent of those labeled "religion related" were directed at Jews.

Jewish lawmakers from both houses supported the Hate Crimes Prevention Act, first introduced in 1997. Despite the increase in hate crimes, including the vicious, homophobic murder of Matthew Shephard in Wyoming, Congress has so far failed to pass legislation that would extend existing hate-crimes laws to those victimized by their gender, sexual orientation, and disability. That legislation would also remove barriers to the entry of federal authorities in those instances where local police have proved inadequate.

Frank Lautenberg has assumed a leading role on the issue of state-sponsored terrorism. He cosponsored an amendment in March 1998 that would have forced the Clinton administration to assist in the identification and location of assets of state sponsors of terrorism if a judgment had been won in court against that state. Known as the "Flatow amendment," after a New Jersey family that had sued Iran for its role in supporting terrorists who had murdered their daughter in an attack in Gaza, the bill contained a waiver that allowed the Clinton administration the leeway to reject its directives. One year later, in October 1999, Lautenberg cosponsored a bill, the Justice for Victims of Terrorism Act, that attempted to refine the Flatow amendment, but the administration also blocked this bill on the grounds that it would invite retaliation and jeopardize U.S. diplomatic property around the world.

The behavior of Jews in Congress reflects current research on social attitudes comparing Jews to non-Jews (similar in age, education, income, and residential patterns), which indicates that Jews tend to be more liberal than non-Jewish Americans. (See chap. 9 in this volume.) This pattern is reflected in their voting patterns in issue areas involving commitment to a welfare state, concern for oppressed groups, combating violence through legislation involving hate crimes or easy access to guns, and passion for individual freedom, especially freedom of speech. The Democrats in Congress have been strong party supporters; the Republicans, generally on the moderate side of their party.

> BARNEY FRANK: "[THE CONNECTICUT CONGRESSMAN] AND I SHARE A COMMON ETHNIC HERITAGE. IT IS AN ETHNIC HERITAGE WHICH HAS AN AFFINITY FOR CERTAIN FOODS. SO I WOULD NOT HAVE BEEN SURPRISED TO HAVE MY FRIEND DOWN HERE TALKING ABOUT PICKLED HERRING OR SCHMALTZ HERRING, BUT WHEN HE COMES DOWN HERE WITH A RED HERRING, I AM A LITTLE BIT DISAPPOINTED."
>
> —CONGRESSIONAL RECORD, 2000

THE FUTURE OF JEWS IN CONGRESS

Jews in Congress have always walked a fine line. Like Lieberman, they support their religious origins, yet proclaim that they are Americans first and that their primary loyalty rests with the United States. They are not completely homogeneous in their political opinions, their loyalties, and their party affiliation. Jewish members shirk "identity politics" in its negative forms: when it boxes them into narrow positions or forces them into alliances that they find unnatural. After all, Jewish Americans understand better than most groups how, in the wrong hands, identity politics can quickly turn negative, with disastrous consequences for minority groups. The Nazi experience is a prime example of an attempt to build a regime on racial identity that drove millions of Jews and others from Germany and Austria in the 1930s. Identity politics arising from misplaced chauvinism almost always results in discriminatory policies.

Jewish members of Congress reflect a more "universalist" kind of identity politics that represents "Jewish interests" by speaking more broadly to shared values and common societal needs. In other words, they believe that Jewish interests are best served by a more universalistic approach that seeks to improve all of society, not just their particular group, and embraces the principles of ecumenicism and inclusivity.

With Lieberman breaking down one more barrier in politics, there may in fact be a rise in the number of Jews running for and elected to Congress. "Jews have had a major impact on American politics. From their embrace of the religious freedom laid out in the United States Constitution to their contemporary participation in civil rights, social welfare, economics, and law, Jewish Americans have put tremendous energy into both local and national affairs" (American Jewish Historical Society, 166). This perspective has been reflected by Jews in the United States Congress.

4

ON THE BENCH

The Jewish Justices

ROBERT A. BURT

Of the 108 justices who have served on the United States Supreme Court since its founding, seven have been Jews. President Woodrow Wilson appointed the first, Louis D. Brandeis, in 1917. Benjamin N. Cardozo, the second Jew, joined Brandeis on the Court in 1931, having been appointed by Herbert Hoover. When Cardozo died in 1939, Franklin Roosevelt appointed Felix Frankfurter, the third Jew, to replace him; though Brandeis still remained on the Court, he resigned just three weeks later. When Frankfurter left the Court in 1963, he was succeeded by Arthur J. Goldberg, the fourth, at John Kennedy's appointment; and when Goldberg resigned two years later, Lyndon Johnson appointed Abe Fortas, the fifth, in his place. From Fortas's resignation in 1969 until 1993, no Jew served on the Court. In 1993 and 1994, Bill Clinton appointed the sixth and seventh Jewish Justices: Ruth Bader Ginsburg was followed by Stephen G. Breyer.

This quick chronology in itself points to several notable aspects of the Jewish presence on the Court. The first is the absence of any Jew until the early twentieth century (though a Jew, Judah P. Benjamin, was nominated by Millard Fillmore in 1853, he declined to serve). The second is the shift from the brief interregnum between 1931 and 1939, when two Jews served simultaneously, to the emergence of a single, informally designated "Jewish seat" occupied by Frankfurter, Goldberg, and Fortas in direct succession. This pattern was, however, broken by Richard Nixon in choosing Fortas's successor. It was not until twenty-four years later that another Jew joined the Court; and the quick accession of a second Jew, appointed by the same president, clearly denoted a new conception of the Jewish presence on the Court—not only the end of the apparent political understanding between 1939 and 1969 that there was room on the Court for only one Jew at a time but, more significantly, the disappearance of the Jewish seat as such.

There are two ways of looking at the progression of this Jewish presence on the Court: from the "outside, in"—that is, to see each Jewish justice as a mirror for the social position of Jews in the American society of his or her time; and from the "inside, out"—that is, to devote specific attention to the justice's own self-understanding and to examine the ways in which each saw his or her relationship to American society and role on the Court as distinctively affected by Jewishness. I will address these two different perspectives in turn.

FROM THE OUTSIDE, IN
The First Two

Brandeis and Cardozo, the first and second Jewish Justices, were atypical Jews at the time each was nominated to the Court. Brandeis was born in 1856 in Louisville, Kentucky, where his parents had settled after emigrating from Germany several years earlier. Few Jews lived in Louisville before the Civil War, and Brandeis was raised in a secular home with almost no sense of Jewish affiliation. His maternal uncle, Lewis Dembitz, was religiously observant, but this practice was viewed as exceptional and even peculiar within the family. In his mid-fifties, just before his accession to the Court, Brandeis stated, "I have been to a great extent separated from Jews. I am very ignorant in things Jewish" (quoted in Burt, 8).

Cardozo, by contrast, had a strong personal connection to Judaism. His family proudly traced itself to the Sephardic Jews who arrived in New York in 1654 during the last years of Dutch rule; born in 1870, Cardozo was bar mitzvahed in Congregation Shearith Israel, the synagogue founded by these early immigrants. The strength of this familial connection did not, however, sustain itself for Cardozo into his adult life; soon after his bar mitzvah, he abandoned any active religious practice, though he maintained his formal affiliation with Shearith Israel throughout his life.

Cardozo was not typical among American Jews in one obvious sense—he could trace his family's presence in this country back to the seventeenth century. By 1932, when Cardozo arrived at the Court, the overwhelming proportion of the three million American Jews had come here from Eastern Europe only after 1890. Cardozo was different, moreover, even among the American Jewish population immediately before this massive influx of Jewish immigrants. Of the three to four hundred thousand Jews then in America, all but about fifty thousand had emigrated from Germany after 1848. Cardozo's Sephardic background, as well as his extended American lineage, was entirely unrepresentative of American Jewry of his day.

When Brandeis came to the Court in 1917, his background was also unrepresentative of the numerical bulk of American Jewry. Even regarding the German Jewish community—a more highly visible segment of American Jewry than Cardozo's affiliations—Brandeis's connections were themselves somewhat unusual. Brandeis was in many ways a conventional product of that background: a well-educated, financially prosperous son of well-educated, commercially successful immigrants who had left Germany after the failure of the liberal revolutions of 1848. He was also representative of German American Jews in his connections to the Gentile community: he had a comfortable economic relationship with Gentiles (his law partner, in a firm established immediately following their graduation from Harvard Law School, was a member of a prominent Yankee Brahmin family), but he was more closely connected to fellow Jews (most of Brandeis's clients in the firm were commercially successful German American Jews); at the same time, Brandeis kept some visible distance from the Gentile community in activities such as club memberships and informal social gatherings.

Nonetheless, Brandeis was markedly—one might even say, ostentatiously—different from members of the German-American Jewish community in at least one particular way: his passionate, highly visible public identification with Zionism. Most German American Jews were openly hostile to Zionism; they had found their Zion—their economic success and social comfort—in America. In their view, any threat to their status in American society came from the open expression of Jewish separateness as such,

> Senator Roman Hruska (R-Neb.) on the nomination of G. Harold Carswell to the U.S. Supreme Court: "Even if he were mediocre, there are a lot of mediocre judges and people and lawyers. They are entitled to a little representation, aren't they, and a little chance? We can't have all Brandeises and Frankfurters and Cardozos and stuff like that there." To some, that there meant Jews. In any case, the remark was to go down as one of the greatest political blunders in the history of the Senate, and, in the opinion of those most intimately involved in the battle over the nomination, it contributed as much as any other factor to Carswell's defeat.
>
> —Richard Harris

especially visible in the insistently "un-American" appearance of their co-religionists newly arrived from the self-contained *shtetls* of Eastern Europe. These new immigrants were not equipped for easy American assimilation by education or prior experience of commercial and social interactions with Gentiles. By 1917, most German American Jews strove to distance themselves clearly from their Eastern European co-religionists, while some among them engaged in philanthropic activities designed to promote assimilation among these new immigrants. In either case, one underlying social motivation was apparent among almost all German American Jews: to stand apart from any identification with a distinctive separateness as Jews and thereby to protect themselves against the mounting antisemitism increasingly evident among Gentile Americans in response to the new presence of these visibly alien immigrants.

Brandeis, however, characteristically charted his own course in his public identification with the Jewish separatism implicit in the Zionist movement and in his relationship, through Zionism, with Eastern European Jewish immigrants. As late as 1912, Brandeis had taken no part in Jewish communal or religious affairs; in that year, however, when he was fifty-six years old, he met Jacob DeHaas, whom Theodore Herzl had dispatched to the United States to bolster the weak Zionist movement there. In a brief conversation, DeHaas ignited Brandeis's imagination about Zionism. DeHaas's opening salvo was to invoke Brandeis's uncle Lewis, who, until his recent death, had been an early Zionist exponent. From that moment, Brandeis was converted to Zionism. In 1914, he accepted election as head of the American Zionist organization—not as a figurehead but as an intensely committed activist with national stature, extraordinary organizational skills and energy, and a network of devoted associates who followed him into Zionist activism.

When Brandeis came to it, American Zionism was a feeble enterprise. His new leadership was an extraordinary social and financial coup for Zionism. Brandeis's public stature appeared to solve the problem of "dual loyalties" for American Jews; if he—by his own description, "one of the most American of Americans"—could be a committed Zionist, then so could any American Jew. Brandeis's accession to the United States Supreme Court in 1917 gave even greater credence to this proposition; and after his Senate confirmation, Brandeis remained publicly active in the Zionist movement, though he severed ties with virtually all of his extensive other organizational involvements. The intensity of Brandeis's continuing engagement and his public significance for the Zionist movement can be measured by the fact that in 1920, he considered resigning from the Court to accept the presidency of the World Zionist Organization.

For Brandeis, the establishment of a Jewish national home was much more than a philanthropic gesture for needy Jews; the goal of Zionism, as he saw it, was to create a state that would honor the biblical injunction to be a "light unto the nations"—to embody a set of values that would inspire Jews and Gentiles alike. The specific values that he identified for Zionism were the mirror image of his critique of American society—values of individual self-determination and self-respect that he saw threatened by the increasingly complex matrix of economic and social organization in America. Brandeis saw a realistic possibility in Palestine of a society based on small-scale economic activity, with special prominence for agricultural pursuits, which concretely exemplified his reformist vision for American society—his opposition to "bigness" in corporate and social life, his embrace of Jefferson's image of a nation of independent yeoman-farmers as the best and even only safeguard for democratic values. In ideological terms, this emblematic vision of Zionism permitted Brandeis to harmonize his "dual loyalty" to America. Brandeis believed that Palestine, organized on Jeffersonian principles, would serve as a beacon light for American democracy itself, recalling this country to its own best possibilities. As he put it in accepting the leadership of the American Zionist organization in 1914, "To be good Americans, we must be better Jews, and to be better Jews we must become Zionists" (quoted in Burt, 16).

However, just as he stood apart from mainstream opinion within the German-American Jewish community in embracing Zionism and by extension his Eastern European compatriots, Brandeis's vision of Zionism was too idiosyncratic for the leadership of the World Zionist Organization. In 1921, just one year after he turned down its presidency, a long-simmering conflict between the American and European Zionists publicly erupted, and Brandeis abruptly resigned from the entire enterprise (accompanied by the prominent American Jews who had been drawn into the organization by the force of his example). The specific issue in conflict was a seemingly trivial dispute about accounting procedures; but the deeper conflict was a different, and ultimately irreconcilable, vision of the goal of Zionism. For European leaders, the establishment of a Jewish national home had an all-consuming cultural and personal significance: its attainment necessarily implied the end of the Diaspora, the in-gathering of all Jews who truly viewed themselves as Jews. For Brandeis and his allies in the American organization, the goal of Zionism was to provide a home for those Jews who had no safe home elsewhere; for them, the Diaspora was not inherently unsafe or inappropriate for Jews, and America specifically could provide a home for Jews as Jews.

Brandeis and Cardozo were thus both hardly representative of American Jewry when each of them came to the Supreme Court. Brandeis's Jewishness was the basis for some considerable opposition to his nomination in 1917. There was much less opposition on this (or any) basis to Cardozo's nomination fourteen years later. The fact that Cardozo would join another Jew on the Court was apparently considered no more significant by President Hoover or his advisers than that Cardozo was a Democrat or that there were already two New Yorkers on the Court; that is, all of these elements were "problems" regarding Cardozo's nomination, but none were dispositive. And his Jewishness, in particular, did not appear to weigh more heavily than these other negative considerations. His considerable reputation for legal probity and personal integrity from his service on the New York State Court of Appeals counterbalanced all of these negatives, and were the basis for the virtually unanimous public approval of his nomination (Kaufman, 461–63, 467).

When both Brandeis and Cardozo joined the Court, the American Jewish community had no clear-cut, unitary public identity. The small group of "old family" Sephardic Jews and the larger group of prosperous, socially secure, "uptown" German Jews had little in common, beyond their formal identification as "Jews," with the "downtown," Eastern European, recent Jewish immigrants. Those "uptown" Jews who, unlike Brandeis or Cardozo, invested their Jewishness with religious content, were most likely to express this investment through the deracinated observance forms of Reform Judaism, while the "downtown" Jews held fast to the demanding, time-honored rituals of Orthodoxy. The fact that Brandeis's Jewishness essentially found expression only through his Zionism and that Cardozo was affiliated (and more by birth than by active engagement) with a minority group among American Jews reflected the absence of a distinctive Jewish identity at the time. American Jewry was a community in flux, unsettled by the vast numbers of more recent Eastern European immigrants but not yet coherently shaped into a clear social identification with or by these numerically dominant newcomers. The concurrent service of the first two Jewish justices speaks to an indeterminancy, even an incoherence, in the very idea of Jewishness as a social category in their day.

> WHEN BOTH BRANDEIS AND CARDOZO JOINED THE COURT, THE AMERICAN JEWISH COMMUNITY HAD NO CLEAR-CUT, UNITARY PUBLIC IDENTITY.

The Jewish Seat: First Occupant

Felix Frankfurter emigrated with his family from Austria in 1890 when he was twelve years old. The Frankfurters settled on the Lower East Side of Manhattan, the preferred destination for the largest proportion of the newly arriving Eastern European Jewish immigrants. Like their fellow immigrants, Frankfurter's family was financially strapped.

Frankfurter's climb to the Supreme Court followed the path chosen by most of his age-mates in his neighborhood, the path of educational achievement. Frankfurter attended the City College of New York (CCNY)—the "finishing school," one might say, for ambitious Jewish immigrant sons of the time. He was notable among his cohort in his demonstrated brilliance as a student; from CCNY, he was accepted at Harvard Law School in 1903 and, carried forward by his formidable intellectual gifts, joined its faculty in 1914, where he remained until Franklin Roosevelt appointed him to the Court in 1939.

For most of his tenure at Harvard, Frankfurter was the only Jewish faculty member, a badge he made no effort to conceal. By his own later account, Judaism had "ceased to have inner meaning" for him when he was a student at CCNY; at a Yom Kippur observance Frankfurter "left the service in the middle of it, never to return." In his subsequent career, however, he did not hold back from identification with Jewish causes (he took the leading role at Harvard in opposing quotas on Jewish students imposed during the 1920s) or from highly visible advocacy on behalf of immigrants

THE FIRST REPORTED USE OF THE WORD "CHUTZPAH" (IN A STATE JUDICIAL OPINION) WAS IN WILLIAMS V. STATE (1972), AN OPINION OF THE GEORGIA COURT OF APPEALS ADDRESSING AN INDIVIDUAL WHO BROKE INTO A SHERIFF'S OFFICE TO STEAL GUNS. THE DECISION IN WILLIAMS WAS WRITTEN BY JUDGE CLARK WHO WENT ON TO WRITE OPINIONS USING THE YIDDISH WORDS "SCHMOOZE," "TSORISS," "SHAMMES," AND "GUT GEZACHT." . . . IN A SUBTLER USE OF YIDDISH, A CALIFORNIA COURT OF APPEALS DECISION (1979), APPARENTLY REFERRING TO THE DISSENT, WROTE A FOOTNOTE IN WHICH THE FIRST LETTER OF EACH SENTENCE SPELLED OUT "SCHMUCK." . . . PERHAPS EVEN MORE UNEXPECTED IS THE USE OF THE WORD "CHUTZPAH" IN DECISIONS BY DISTRICT COURTS IN IOWA, ALABAMA, AND PUERTO RICO.
—JACK ACHIEZER GUGGENHEIM

(he was intensely active in contesting the convictions of Sacco and Vanzetti). He also followed Brandeis's lead to involve himself in Zionist affairs (and followed him in leaving the movement in 1921—though unlike Brandeis, Frankfurter never returned to Zionist affiliation).

If Brandeis and Cardozo were "exceptional Jews" in their time, Frankfurter was the "model Jew" (even though more socially successful than most) in his generation. Unlike his Jewish predecessors on the Court, Frankfurter was himself an immigrant (notwithstanding the socially insignificant detail that he was a German-speaking immigrant from Austria); and unlike his predecessors, he gained no impetus from his family's financial or social comfort in dealing with the American Gentile world. Frankfurter was a self-made man, a Jewish Horatio Alger. Like the very model of American individualism, Frankfurter had no discernible advantage beyond his intellect and personal energy; acting out the cherished fantasy of the immigrant children clustered in the Lower East Side of New York, Frankfurter parlayed this advantage to ascend to the highest peak of official social status in America.

Frankfurter occupied *the* Jewish seat on the Court in a way that Brandeis and Cardozo did not and could not; unlike him, they did not represent *the* American Jew. With Frankfurter's tenure, the Jewish seat on the Supreme Court assumed a representative character. As an idealized indicator of the social ambitions of Jews in America, Frankfurter played out the underlying logic of the designation of one and only one such symbol; when he joined the Court in 1939; that is, the "Jew in America" had come to have a single social meaning that had not been true for Brandeis's or Cardozo's time. Jews were no longer a polyglot assembly of old-family Sephardics, later German Jewish entrants, and subsequent *shtetl* immigrants; *the* Jew had become the Eastern European *shtetl* immigrant.

> JEWS WERE NO LONGER A POLYGLOT ASSEMBLY OF OLD-FAMILY SEPHARDICS, LATER GERMAN-JEWISH ENTRANTS, AND SUBSEQUENT SHTETL IMMIGRANTS; THE JEW HAD BECOME THE EASTERN EUROPEAN SHTETL IMMIGRANT.

The Jewish Seat: Successors

When Frankfurter retired from the Court in 1962, John Kennedy appointed Arthur Goldberg to succeed him; when Goldberg resigned in 1965, Lyndon Johnson appointed Abe Fortas as his successor.

By the mid-1960s, the numerically dominant Jews of Eastern European origin had solidified their dominance in defining, for themselves and for the broader society, *the* American Jew. The social experience of these Jews in America had, moreover, given them a special sensitivity to the symbolism of a Jewish presence on the Court. Felix Frankfurter's career had given perfect expression to the aspirations and preferred pathways of the Eastern European Jewish immigrants for more secure social status—from impoverished urban ghettoes via educational attainment and professional credentials (especially in law or medicine). By the mid-1960s, this aspiration was more extensively embodied in the experience of the American-born children of the immigrants of Frankfurter's generation.

Arthur Goldberg and Abe Fortas were virtual twins in this emblematic pursuit. Goldberg's family had come from Russia to Chicago, where he was born in 1908; notwithstanding his family's considerable financial difficulties, Goldberg worked his way through college and Northwestern Law School (the only one among his siblings to continue his education beyond grade school). Goldberg established a specialized practice in labor law, ultimately serving as general counsel for the newly merged AFL-CIO and as secretary of labor in the Kennedy administration. Fortas's Russian-born family came to Memphis in 1905, where he was born five years later. Though less financially strapped than Goldberg, Fortas followed a similar path for social mobility from a scholarship student at college and Yale Law School. He made such a strong impression on his law teachers that he was recruited to the Yale faculty in 1933 and then almost immediately enlisted for service in the New Deal, where he ascended within the federal bureaucracy to become undersecretary of the Department of the Interior in 1942. In 1946, he left government service to cofound a private law firm in Washington, D.C., one that ultimately brought him great financial success and influence as a back-stairs legal and political adviser, forming an especially close relationship with then-senator Lyndon Johnson.

These professional ascents of both Goldberg and Fortas were marked by direct encounters with antisemitism—from the most prominent law firms that would not consider hiring them, notwithstanding their strong academic records, to the social clubs from which they were openly excluded. In these encounters, both men shared the experience of their cohort of first-generation children of Eastern European Jewish immigrants. They had attained financial comfort and professional achievement almost beyond the fondest dreams of their immigrant parents, but these social accomplishments were marred by overt antisemitism that echoed, at least in a distant voice, the nightmares that had impelled their parents' flight to this country. This uneasy conjunction gave a special urgency, a deeply needed social salve, for American Jews in the preservation of the Jewish seat on the Supreme Court when Fortas succeeded Goldberg, who had succeeded Frankfurter.

At this same time, however, a new worry appeared for American Jews about the implication of a reserved place for Jews on the Supreme Court or anywhere in the higher reaches of American social status. By 1965, the black civil rights movement had taken a new turn—a turn that many Jews, who had been active allies in the campaign, found disturbing. In response to the stubborn white resistance to claims for an end to overt and covert racial segregation, many black leaders were demanding the adoption of race-based quotas in public and private enterprises; others ostentatiously embraced a new version of racial separatism, a voluntary turning away among blacks from the prior goal of inclusion in white social endeavors. These demands for social endorsements of racial categorization appeared to many Jews to be an abandonment of the ideological basis for their alliance with black aspirations; the new demands brought into sharp relief the extent to which this Jewish support had rested on the belief that Jews and blacks shared the same status (excluded from the American mainstream on the basis of racial or ethnic animosity) and therefore shared the same assimilationist strategies and goals (especially access to educational institutions for equal opportunities to develop and display their intrinsic merits). The new black demand for race-based social policies generally and racial quotas in particular also struck many Jews as a direct threat to their own social opportunities; numerically proportional representation in the higher reaches of American social life offered very little to Jews as such (a 3 percent participation, to be specific). The conflicting attitudes toward the preservation of a Jewish presence on the Supreme Court were captured in a 1965 memorandum to President Johnson from his attorney general, Nicholas Katzenbach, regarding the search for a successor to Justice Goldberg:

> The question of whether or not this appointee should be Jewish concerns me. I think most Jews share with me the feeling that you should not seek a Jewish appointment for the "Jewish seat" on the Court. It is somewhat offensive to think of religion as a qualification, and you will recall that after Mr. Justice Murphy's death [in 1948] there was not a Catholic on the Court for a period of eight years [until William Brennan's appointment in 1956]. At the same time, I think it undesirable for there to be no Jew on the Court for too long a period and I think it would be desirable if a Jew were appointed to the Court before 1968 [when Johnson would presumably seek a second term and would need Jewish electoral and financial support] . . . . On balance, I think, if you appoint a Jew he should be so outstanding as to be selected clearly on his own merits as an individual.

Katzenbach concluded this memorandum with the observation that Abe Fortas would be the perfect nominee: he had "every qualification for the Court. If you did not know him he would be my first recommendation—and still is" (Murphy, 107).

At least two elements of disingenuousness characterize this memorandum. First, it was almost certainly apparent to Katzenbach that President Johnson was resolved to appoint Fortas no matter what. Fortas had been Johnson's first choice for attorney general but had declined; they had been closely associated professionally and personally for many years, and Johnson had been open about his eagerness to appoint Fortas to the Court before any opening had presented itself (Kalman, 231, 241–44). At a deeper level, the memorandum displayed the same tangle of contradictory attitudes toward the "Jewish seat" that was common among American Jews generally: the idea of a religious quota was "somewhat offensive," but nonetheless it would be "desirable" to have a Jew on the

Court. Therefore, a perfect candidate should be found who was (who "happened to be"?) a Jew but nonetheless obviously would have been appointed (was "the only suitable candidate"?) based on his intrinsic merit even if he had not been Jewish. Enter Abe Fortas: *mirabile dictu*.

The internal strains apparent in these attitudes made the Jewish seat vulnerable to shifting political winds. In 1968 Johnson nominated Fortas as chief justice to succeed Earl Warren, but the nomination was blocked by Republican senators hoping to keep the position open for a possible Nixon presidential appointment; and when Richard Nixon did become president, his aides obtained information about Fortas's financial arrangements with a former client who had been imprisoned for securities violations and perjury (Kalman, 359–70). Fortas was forced to resign from the Court in 1969. Nixon, who had indeed won the presidency on a platform condemning both "liberal-activist" judges and racial quotas, did not appoint a Jew to succeed him. The Jewish seat fell vacant.

The Vanished Seat

Two Jews now serve on the Supreme Court, and both have personal links with prior occupants of the Jewish seat. Stephen Breyer's connection is close; after his graduation, with considerable distinction, from Harvard Law School, he served as law clerk to Justice Goldberg in 1964–65. Ruth Bader Ginsburg has an ironic connection; she was rejected as a law clerk by Justice Frankfurter on the ground that "he was not ready to hire a woman" notwithstanding her distinguished record at Columbia Law School in 1959 (Italia, 13). Neither Breyer nor Ginsburg can, however, be considered current occupants of the "Jewish seat." The striking aspect of their presence on the Court is that a Jewish seat as such no longer exists. This proposition finds support in the fact that both Ginsburg and Breyer were appointed, respectively, in 1993 and 1994 by the same president, Bill Clinton, successively filling the only vacancies that occurred during his two terms, and that the Jewishness of these two appointees received virtually no public attention as such. Further confirmation comes from the fact that Ronald Reagan had indicated his intention to nominate Judge Douglas Ginsburg to the Court in 1986; in the controversy surrounding the immediate withdrawal of Ginsburg's name because of revelations of his prejudicial marijuana use, his Jewishness was hardly noticed, and Reagan did not hesitate to replace him with Antonin Scalia, an Italian Catholic.

> THE STRIKING ASPECT OF THEIR PRESENCE ON THE COURT IS THAT A JEWISH SEAT AS SUCH NO LONGER EXISTS.

The personal success of Ginsburg and Breyer are, moreover, no longer unusual for Jews as in Frankfurter's time; and their ascents encountered no barriers on grounds of antisemitism as in Goldberg's and Fortas's time. Both Ginsburg and Breyer served on the faculties of elite law schools (Columbia and Harvard) in company with substantial numbers of Jewish colleagues; and both were engaged in highly visible public service activities in which their Jewishness was hardly noticed as such (Ginsburg as a public interest lawyer on behalf of women's rights, Breyer as general counsel of the Senate Judiciary Committee). Ginsburg did face discriminatory social barriers in the early stages of her career, but these were barriers erected against her as a woman, not as a Jew. The Jewish seat on the Supreme Court was no longer needed by Jews as a reassurance for their accepted social status; during the long interregnum from 1969 to 1993, from Fortas to Ginsburg, American Jews not only endured but prevailed by moving easily into positions of elite social authority.

The saga of the Jewish presence on the Supreme Court can be read as emblematic of the shifting character of the American Jewish community in the twentieth century—from the marginalized status of Eastern European Jews (signified by the German origins of Brandeis and the Sephardic background of Cardozo), to the recognition of the new immigrants in Frankfurter's appointment and the social solidification of the Jewish seat as such in the succession of Goldberg and Fortas (American-born children of Eastern European immigrants), to the disappearance of this demarcation in the accession of Ginsburg and Breyer (American-born grandchildren of Eastern European immigrants). Even more dramatically, the succession of Jewish justices can be read as an emblematic success story for the realization of the ideal of complete Jewish assimilation into the mainstream of American social life: from Jewishness as an obstacle to be overcome against overtly expressed antisemitism (Brandeis and Cardozo), to a qualification that was at the same time a limiting condition for the job (Frankfurter, Goldberg, and Fortas), to a virtually unnoticed and therefore irrelevant social characteristic (Ginsburg and Breyer).

> THE SUCCESSION OF JEWISH JUSTICES CAN BE READ AS AN EMBLEMATIC SUCCESS STORY FOR THE REALIZATION OF THE IDEAL OF COMPLETE JEWISH ASSIMILATION INTO THE MAINSTREAM OF AMERICAN SOCIAL LIFE.

FROM THE INSIDE, OUT

If the Jewish seat as such once had but no longer has strong social meaning, the question remains whether Jewishness has had any intrinsic significance for its occupants in their conception of their social role as (Jewish) justices. Two sentimentalized claims are often made for such significance: that Jews are inclined toward the legal profession because of the rabbinic tradition of close talmudic reading, and that Jews are inclined toward protection of all vulnerable minorities because of the Old Testament injunction to "remember that you once were slaves in Egypt." The causal connection is not, however, convincing. The Hebrew Bible expresses conflicting admonitions; alongside commandments for empathy with other socially vulnerable groups, there are directives for narrow self-aggrandizement as God's "chosen people" entitled to oust vulnerable others from divinely promised lands. The special affinity of Jews for the legal profession might well have some connection to rabbinic pursuits, but it is most plausible to see this Jewish concentration in the pursuit of professional credentials as "helpers" and "fixers" (whether in law, medicine, or accounting) as a secular strategy for self-protection and aggrandizement in a Gentile world offering limited social acceptance to Jews. It is less the rabbinic tradition than the hallowed social role of court Jew—as protected servant and financial facilitator of Christian kings in their struggles to exert centralized authority over feudal nobility—that marked the path leading so many American Jews to the legal profession (and seven of them to the Supreme Court).

> IT IS LESS THE RABBINIC TRADITION THAN THE HALLOWED SOCIAL ROLE OF COURT JEW THAT MARKED THE PATH LEADING SO MANY AMERICAN JEWS TO THE LEGAL PROFESSION.

It is, moreover, difficult in scanning the biographies of the seven Jewish justices to see ways in which their Jewishness definitively shaped their judicial philosophy or actions. From available documentary sources, at least four of the seven clearly did not view themselves as religiously engaged, even in a mild way. Brandeis was raised in an entirely secular home, with only a very remote connection to Jewish ritual through his uncle's religiosity; in his mid-fifties, as noted earlier, he described himself as "very ignorant in things Jewish." Cardozo was raised in a religiously observant family, but he self-consciously abandoned his family's observances immediately after his bar mitzvah. In his adult life he often referred to himself privately as a "heathen" and more gently in public as an agnostic (Kaufman, 45–46). Frankfurter definitively rejected his observant upbringing, as noted, when he was a college student and found that Judaism "ceased to have inner meaning" for him. For Fortas, according to his biographer, "Judaism never had much spiritual meaning. . . . He always identified himself as a Jew, but he viewed his religion as a handicap to disclose rather than as a heritage to claim" (Kalman, 8). Of all the Jewish Justices, Frankfurter took the most publicly adamant position that his Jewishness had no influence whatsoever on his judicial conduct. In a dissenting opinion to a Supreme Court decision that invalidated a local school board's requirement for Jehovah's Witness children to salute the American flag notwithstanding their religious objections, Frankfurter wrote:

> One who belongs to the most vilified and persecuted minority in history is not likely to be insensible to the freedoms guaranteed by our Constitution. Were my purely personal attitude relevant I should wholeheartedly associate myself with the general libertarian views in the Court's opinion. . . . But as judges we are neither Jew nor Gentile, neither Catholic nor agnostic. We owe equal attachment to the Constitution and are equally bound by our judicial obligations whether we derive our citizenship from the earliest or the latest immigrants to these shores. (*West Virginia State Board of Education v. Barnette*, 319 U.S. 624, 646–47 [1943])

Notwithstanding this adamance—or perhaps as a reflection of this "too much" protestation—Frankfurter's judicial conduct appeared to be more influenced by his Jewishness than any of the other Jewish Justices. This influence cannot be traced from the religious tenets but from the social significance of Judaism for Frankfurter, of what it meant to be Jew in America during his lifetime.

Frankfurter's position in the flag-salute case epitomizes this influence. His self-depiction of the judicial role—"neither Jew nor Gentile"—can be read as his personal celebration, as a "latest immigrant to these shores," of his attainment of the assimilationist ideal. But there is a more straightforward reading of this passage, as nothing more than a conventional restatement of the judicial impartiality, of the judge's obligation to stand above or outside any particularist, personal identifications. This conventional interpretation is, however, undermined by both the context and the emotion-laden language in which Frankfurter wrote. He did more than embrace the assimilationist ideal for judicial conduct; he generalized the application of that ideal to every American, even to Jehovah's Witness schoolchildren. He dismissed the children and their parents as "dissidents" demanding "exceptional immunity [for their] individual idiosyncracies [and] crotchety beliefs" (sic), whereas they were properly obligated to accept the "binding tie of cohesive sentiment" by saluting the American flag and acceding to the school board's "authority to safeguard the nation's fellowship."

This is the voice of the self-proclaimed, socially assimilated insider—a man who, as Frankfurter himself observed in a 1942 diary entry, "had to shed old loyalties and [thereby] take on the loyalty of American citizenship." This was also the rationale, as he explained in his diary entry, for Frankfurter's vote in another Supreme Court case to invalidate the citizenship of a Communist Party member who had not been asked about, and therefore neither affirmed nor denied, his membership at the time of his naturalization (*Schneiderman v. United States*, 320 U.S. 118 [1943]). This harsh rejection of "alien loyalties" also lay beneath his concurrence in upholding a congressional enactment that membership in the American Communist Party was in itself a criminal offense (*Dennis v. United States*, 341 U.S. 494 [1951]).

The one striking exception to Frankfurter's general unwillingness to favor minority claims against legislative majority impositions was in the race-relations cases that came to the Supreme Court throughout his tenure, most notably the unanimous 1954 decision in *Brown v. Board of Education* (347 U.S. 483 [1954]) invalidating racial segregation laws in public schools. This position itself, however, was consistent with Frankfurter's lifelong conception of the basic right and obligation of American citizenship: to transcend particularistic affiliations or self-identifications with a commitment to a unitary conception of communal membership. From this perspective, blacks had been wrongly denied this assimilationist right by racist segregation laws, whereas Jehovah's Witnesses or Communist Party members had wrongly denied their obligation to acknowledge the transcendent communal bond. From this perspective, the very model of the American constitutional ideal was in the passage of Jewish immigrants from the status of scorned immigrants at the beginning of the twentieth century whose Old World customs and affiliations marked them as such to a status of undifferentiated Americans by midcentury—a passage and the fulfillment of an ideal that Felix Frankfurter saw himself as epitomizing in his own career.

The linkage that can be seen between Frankfurter's Jewishness and his conception of his judicial role can also be discerned, though in a very different register, in Louis Brandeis's judicial career. Of all the Jewish Justices, Brandeis was the most actively involved in Jewish communal affairs before his entry on the Court and even for a time thereafter. Brandeis's involvement was limited to Zionism, the only Jewish affiliation that he ever clearly embraced. He became passionately engaged in Zionism, moreover, only in his fifties; his engagement did not arise from his prior involvement with Judaism, but, as best his midlife "conversion" can be understood, Zionism gave expression to some prior and, in this sense, deeper sense of himself and his relationship to American society. Brandeis's lifelong commitment to the protection of outsiders—his career of social activism, his virtual invention of the social role of "public interest lawyer" to advocate on behalf of economically vulnerable and socially excluded people—was also at the core of his Zionist engagement. In Zionism, as in his earlier advocacy for labor unions and consumers against the forces of corporate "bigness," Brandeis offered his prodigious energy, his considerable wealth, and his assimilated social status to protect vulnerable outsiders.

In his judicial career, Brandeis persisted in this commitment. It can be seen in his opinion in favor of protecting First Amendment free expression by reversing a state criminal advocacy conviction of a Communist Labor Party member (*Whitney v. California*, 274 U.S. 357 [1927]), his opinion to void a conviction based on government wiretapping in order to vindicate a constitutional "right to privacy" (*Olmstead v. United States*, 277 U.S. 438 [1928]), and his concurrence in the Supreme Court's invalidation of a New Deal economic regulation as an excessive exercise of centralized governmental authority (*Schechter Poultry Co. v. United States*, 295 U.S. 528 [1935]). This commitment can also be seen in his consistent dissents from Court rulings that overturned state and federal legislative measures supporting the claims of labor unions, of workers generally, and of consumers. Brandeis's commitment to the protection of economically and socially vulnerable people did not arise from his Judaism; like his late commitment to Zionism, his advocacy as a lawyer and as a judge were expressions of his previous commitment to, his empathic identification with the vulnerability of, these outsiders.

Possibly we can see these same strands of empathic advocacy for outsiders in the legal and judicial careers of Arthur Goldberg and Abe Fortas; and to see some impetus for this empathy, more directly than for Brandeis, in their social experience as victims of discriminatory exclusion as Jews. Ruth Bader Ginsburg's activism on behalf of women's rights, before her judicial appointment, can also be understood as a commitment to protection of vulnerable outsiders; but it is more plausible, on its face, to see the empathic sources of this advocacy arising from her personal experience as a woman rather than from social barriers that she encountered as a Jew.

No necessary link exists, however, between direct experience of bruising discrimination and empathic advocacy on behalf of other vulnerable outsiders, as Felix Frankfurter's judicial career reveals. The contemporary, comfortable social status of American Jews may suggest that, wherever the impulses in future Jewish Justices might originate for either empathic identification with or hectoring distance from vulnerable outsiders, their Jewishness will not be an important driving force.

5

MOVERS, SHAKERS,
AND LEADERS

Jewish Party Politicians

GERALD M. POMPER
AND MILES A. POMPER

Perhaps Jewish party politics began with the rivalry of Jacob and Esau. Each sought their father Isaac's blessing of political power: "Let peoples serve you, and nations bow to you" (Genesis 27:29). Jacob wins the prize, but he does so by making a deal for a bowl of porridge, by using the wily strategy of Rebecca (his mother and campaign manager), by pretending to the natural advantages of his first-born brother, and by deceptively imitating Esau's competitive skills as a hunter.

In America, party politicians descended from Rebecca and Jacob certainly have had less impact on world and Jewish history, but they, too, have demonstrated deal making, originality, ambition, occasional deceptiveness, and considerable success. We will discuss three kinds of American Jewish party politicians: machine leaders, reformers, and national party organizers.

These three types roughly trace the chronological development of Jewish politics—indeed, Jewish life—in America. Once large numbers of Jews arrived in the United States, they first settled in distinct areas, separated from Christians either by voluntary preferences or social barriers. This "ghettoization" provided the residential foundation for urban machine politicians. Soon, Jews began active involvement in their new nation's politics. They often took the stance of critics and reformers, at first from the socialist left, then from within the established parties, and later from the neoconservative right. Most recently, Jews have reflected their general assimilation into American life by assuming organizational leadership of the mainstream parties and even by becoming prominent candidates for public office.

The characteristic forms of Jewish politics in America are also broadly related to Lawrence Fuchs's classic description of fundamental Jewish values. Fuchs argues that three basic values provide the sources of American Jewish liberalism: learning (Torah), charity (*tzedakeh*), and nonasceticism, a celebration of life's pleasures. The emphasis on Torah made Jews receptive to intellectual designs for social reconstruction. The duty of *tzedakeh* stimulated Jews to support efforts toward redistributive justice. The emphasis on worldly pleasures made Jews seek improvements in their earthly life rather than patiently await redemption in a heavenly paradise.

THREE BASIC VALUES PROVIDED THE SOURCES OF AMERICAN JEWISH LIBERALISM: LEARNING (TORAH), CHARITY (TZEDAKEH), AND NONASCETICISM, A CELEBRATION OF LIFE'S PLEASURES.

We admittedly stretch these terms in the following three-part analysis. In the first section, we examine machine politics, an expression of materialist values—another possible meaning of nonasceticism. What Fuchs defined as an "emphasis on this-worldliness and the enjoyment of life here and now" can become manifest in Jewish striving toward the machine's material rewards of money, prestige, and power. In the second section, we discuss reform politics as an expression of *tzedakeh*. The commitment to social justice is particularly evident in socialist and other left-wing parties and can also be seen in reform movements both within and outside the major political parties. Another variety of reform is evident among contemporary neoconservative Jews. In the third section, we examine the group members' leadership in national party organizations. This leadership may be considered an expression of the bent toward order and planning embodied in the Torah.

MACHINE POLITICS

Jewish involvement in party machines was evident from the beginning of American political parties. At least five Jews were among the founders of Tammany Hall in 1794, and one of them, merchant Solomon Simon, became its president within three years. Jewish politicians would soon appear in cities across the growing nation, including Baltimore, Boston, Charleston, Chicago, Cincinnati, Cleveland, Philadelphia, San Francisco, and St. Louis.

The successful party machines were skilled in assimilating competing ethnic groups into vote-seeking coalitions. While less prominent and perhaps less politically adroit than the legendary Irish "pols," Jews evidenced a familiar pattern of ethnic political development. As Jewish immigration rose, first in a stream from Germany in the 1840s and then in a flood from Eastern Europe at the beginning of the twentieth century, ethnic representatives soon gained positions as election workers, patronage appointees, ward heelers, and ward leaders. Their number was certainly substantial but will never be known precisely.

The urban political machine flourished because it met some social needs of the time, of Jews as much as other groups. Cities teemed with poor and needy residents, but government provided few social services or welfare. Immigrants, driven by discrimination and attracted by economic opportunity, faced many problems in their new country—an unfamiliar language and strange customs, separation from family and known friends, dangerous and unhealthy living conditions, uncertain prospects for jobs and social life.

The machines met some of the needs of the poor and the new immigrants, even as the politicians were amply rewarded for their services through offices, contracts, and more than occasional graft. The poor gained some social welfare—the legendary Thanksgiving turkey or bucket of coal (and perhaps Passover matzoh?)—and many were helped with jobs on the public payroll or with utility companies doing city business. Individuals in trouble with the law received lenient sentences after the party precinct worker put in a good word with the judge. Immigrants found new friends who spoke their language at party rallies and learned, however crudely, the techniques and opportunities of electoral politics in a mass democracy. In these respects, Jews were little different from other ethnic groups, and their leaders in practice resembled their Irish, German, Polish, and Italian colleagues.

The character of Jewish machine leaders can be suggested by brief portraits of a few party politicians. One, Hymie Schorenstein, a Brooklyn ward leader, deserves mention as the author of a classic, perhaps apocryphal political tale, recounted by Theodore White. As legend has it, a local candidate in 1940 worried that his candidacy, and contributions, had yielded no election posters or other campaign efforts and that Schorenstein seemed to focus all of his attention on the head of the ticket, President Franklin D. Roosevelt. Schorenstein explained the simple electoral logic of machine politics:

> Ah, you're worried? Listen. Did you ever go down to the wharf to see the Staten Island Ferry come in? You ever watch it, and look down in the water at all those chewing-gum wrappers, and the banana peels and the garbage? When the ferryboat comes into the wharf, automatically it pulls all the garbage in too. The name of your ferryboat is Franklin D. Roosevelt—stop worrying!

Of course, Schorenstein was right. Roosevelt and the local "garbage"—surely including some Jews—were both elected as their co-religionists overwhelmingly voted for Roosevelt and the Democratic Party during the high tide of the New Deal.

Other Jewish party politicians surpassed Schorenstein, and not only in the elegance of their language. As they rose to higher positions, many demonstrated a broader understanding of politics, and selected candidates for public office more seriously.

Jack Pollack resembled Schorenstein but shined brighter, becoming the Democratic boss of Baltimore. The child of immigrants from Poland, Pollack left school in the fifth grade and never resumed his formal education. Although raised in an Orthodox home, he was not an exemplar of Judaism. He became a prizefighter, neglected religious rituals, loved Maryland's famed (and obviously nonkosher) crabs, and married a non-Jewish woman, although his children were raised as Jews. In the following years, he was arrested sixty times, including once for murder, but stayed out of jail.

Pollack first made his fortune on bootlegging during Prohibition, building a secret lower level to his home to hide illegal liquor. Laundering the proceeds, he developed insurance and real estate businesses, using his political contacts to win customers. With the cohesive support of the Jewish population in his ward, he came to dominate the Baltimore Democratic Party and to exert strong influence on the Maryland state party. One of his allies was Thomas D'Alesandro, who served as his family's "Shabes goy" (a Gentile who did manual labor on the Sabbath) before going on to become the local congressman and then mayor.

Politics consumed the Baltimore leader, so much so that his closest lieutenant described meetings at his party club as "political science lectures." Although a strong supporter of FDR and progressive Democrats, Pollack's interest was not in public policy but in political power itself. The key to this power was commonplace: handouts and intervention with the government for the poor, patronage distributed to election workers in keeping with their achievements in winning votes, payoffs from businesses that wanted city contracts and favors, and retribution for those who opposed him. Pollack established a frightening reputation for vindictiveness. "When you really got Jack angry and he wanted to dismiss you," his closest associate reported, "he would say goodbye to you by saying, 'Good luck and best wishes.' It was like he was sitting Shiva."

By the 1950s, Pollack began to lose his voter base, as Jews and other whites took flight from Baltimore, and blacks eventually become a majority of the city's population. A series of electoral battles ensued, with the first black success coming in 1954, as a young lawyer, Harry A. Cole, defeated the Pollack machine to become Maryland's first black state senator. Pollack grudgingly tried to accommodate, slating a small number of receptive black candidates along with predominantly Jewish candidates, while challenging new voters and bringing white voters to the polls in Baltimore even after they had moved to the suburbs. The population tides eventually could not be held back; by the 1960s, black leaders and machines replaced Pollack and took control of Baltimore's party organization and the city government.

Abraham Ruef of San Francisco came earlier. He was the first notable Jewish leader of a citywide machine. Intellectually distinguished, he graduated with high honors in classics from Berkeley before the age of nineteen and earned his law degree three years later. He spoke several modern languages and had a lifelong interest in philosophy and the arts. Beginning as an insurgent within the weak Republican Party, he led an unsuccessful reform movement at the turn of the twentieth century and then became a dominant major figure within the party.

Following the "general strike" of dock workers and teamsters in 1901, Ruef became active in the formation of the Union Labor Party and its successful campaign for Eugene Schmitz as an independent candidate for mayor. Ruef maintained his leadership of the Republicans, even as he served as the mayor's attorney and twice helped achieve his reelection. As he spun dreams of Schmitz's possible election as governor and even president, Ruef began to envision himself as a future United States senator.

These fantasies did not prevent him from gaining material advantages from his city position. Corporations seeking franchises, municipal contracts, or utility rate increases hired him at handsome fees to plead their case, and several provided bribes for him to pass on to city officials. In the liberal environment of San Francisco, brothels and gambling dens paid for protection from the police, and restaurants kicked in for liquor licenses. In a particularly licentious incident, the city built a "municipal lodging house," actually a house of prostitution, which paid Ruef and Schmitz a quarter of its profits.

Ruef came to the height of his power in 1906 when he won control of the state Republican convention. Soon after, however, he was indicted on sixty-five counts of bribery and other corrupt actions. After winning a promise of immunity, he testified against Mayor Schmitz, who was convicted and then released on appeal. Ruef was then newly prosecuted, convicted, and sentenced to nine years in prison, the only public official actually to serve time in prison for the civic corruption of his time. There, he wrote his autobiography and developed plans for reforming politics and eliminating the business sources of corruption. Eventually, with support from the Jewish community, Ruef was paroled, pardoned, and rehabilitated.

Jacob Arvey was a later, more prominent, and more honest machine leader, probably the most influential local Jewish machine leader in American politics. The son of immigrants from Poland, he began his political career in typical fashion, as a precinct party worker for the Democratic organization in a Jewish area on the western side of Chicago, quickly rising to the position of ward committeeman and city alderman. As Jewish support for Roosevelt and the Democrats rose, Arvey's ward produced the highest Democratic percentages of any local jurisdiction in the nation, and the party tradition continued even as blacks replaced Jews in the area.

> JACOB ARVEY WAS A LATER, MORE PROMINENT, AND MORE HONEST MACHINE LEADER, PROBABLY THE MOST INFLUENTIAL LOCAL JEWISH MACHINE LEADER IN AMERICAN POLITICS.

Although he dropped out of high school, Arvey later resumed his education, completed college, earned a law degree, and became a commissioned lieutenant colonel in the army during World War II. Soon afterward, he was chosen to lead Chicago's Democratic machine, the Cook County Democratic Committee, which carried with it effective control of the state party and a leading national party role. He moved against the former party leader and mayor, Ed Kelly, who had become tainted by corruption. Soon, he groomed Richard B. Daley for the mayor's office and as his successor as county chairman. Under Arvey and then Daley, Chicago achieved both a fair measure of civic development and political longevity, as the Democrats sustained the last of the powerful big-city machines.

By midcentury, Arvey's evident intelligence and skill made him one of the most respected local party politicians in the nation. He maintained the strength of the county and state party by selecting prestigious candidates to head the electoral ticket. His most notable success came in 1948, when he arranged for the nomination of Paul Douglas, a distinguished university economist, for United States senator, and Adlai Stevenson for governor. Arvey participated in the maneuverings that led to Stevenson's "draft" as the Democratic presidential candidate in 1952, after which Stevenson went on to unsuccessfully oppose Republican Dwight D. Eisenhower, and supported Stevenson's renomination in 1956. Four years later, however, the party organization spurned the former governor's try for a third nomination and threw its critical support to John F. Kennedy.

These individuals are not a full, or representative group, but they do suggest some general ideas about Jewish machine politicians. These machine leaders were rooted in their ethnic and religious communities, gaining support from fellow Jews and maintaining their connections to Jewish congregations and causes (although there surely were other Jews who were so thoroughly assimilated that they cannot be identified). Their Jewish heritage is reflected in some of their behavior.

At least two—Ruef and Arvey—of the more important citywide leaders show relatively high intellect, perhaps reflecting the basic Jewish value of learning and Torah. Perhaps, however, only Jews with exceptional intellect might have been able to overcome prejudices against their religion. Compared to other major examples of the species, leaders such as Arvey seem to approach politics with a somewhat greater theoretical understanding, a view broader than the mechanics of party organization or the pragmatic concerns of coalition building. While convicted of conventional corruption, Ruef also showed an unconventional intellectual approach to politics in his attempted creation of a social movement. Although Pollack was a more conventional machine leader, his devotion to the "political science" of party management also suggests a certain intellectual bent.

Perhaps the most notable feature of these politicians is the sheer scarcity of other Jewish party leaders at the top of urban machines. Beyond the three persons sketched here, it is difficult to name Jews who led the parties of major cities, even though millions of Jewish voters were often critically important at the polls. Many Jews held office in the big cities, including local and state legislators and representatives in Congress, and a disproportionate number of judges, as well as prominent policy advocates and generous campaign contributors. Yet, within the parties, Jewish activists rarely rose beyond positions in their home wards.

New York is conspicuous in this thinly populated portrait of big-city politicians. In the heyday of machines, New York had more Jewish residents than any city in the United States and possibly more than any city in the world. Jews, a fourth of New York's population, may have been the largest single ethnic group in the city. Yet no Jew of the time ever headed any of the five county Democratic organizations (although some were early county leaders of the minority Republican Party). In the Bronx, for example, where Jews were actually a majority of the total population, Irishman Ed Flynn ran the organization without challenge, while Jews were mollified by positions on a "balanced ticket" of nominees for public office. Only later, when the machines were in decline, did Jews rise to the top positions, including Stanley Friedman in the Bronx, Ruth Messinger in Manhattan, Claire Schulman in Queens, and Stanley Steingut and Sheldon Silver in Brooklyn.

The relative absence of Jewish machine leadership was probably not due to a lack of ambition or talent. Other reasons must account for this limited achievement among a population with a rich network of community organizations, where Jews strived mightily toward success in business, education, entertainment, and even in sports and crime. Jewish political success may have been undermined by the group's internal divisions, such as the conflicts of immigrants from Germany and Eastern Europe. A further explanation might be the diversion of Jewish political figures into radical politics and social causes. Combined with the disproportionate support of Jewish voters for these movements, third parties drew political talent that otherwise might have brought more Jews into leadership of the major party organizations.

THE DEMOCRATIC PARTY IN NEW YORK HAS TRADITIONALLY TRIED TO BALANCE ITS STATEWIDE TICKET ETHNICALLY. IN 1970, THE TICKET INCLUDED FOUR JEWS AND AN AFRICAN AMERICAN—ARTHUR GOLDBERG FOR GOVERNOR, BASIL PATERSON FOR LIEUTENANT GOVERNOR, ADAM WALINSKY FOR ATTORNEY GENERAL, ARTHUR LEVIT FOR COMPTROLLER, AND RICHARD OTTINGER FOR UNITED STATES SENATE.

WHEN DAN O'CONNELL, THE LONGTIME DEMOCRATIC BOSS OF ALBANY, WAS ASKED TO COMMENT ON THE TICKET, HE REPORTEDLY SAID, "AS FAR AS I'M CONCERNED, PATERSON IS THE ONLY WHITE MAN ON THE TICKET."

The contrast is striking between the scarcity of Jews and the dominance of the Irish in machine leadership. The Irish did begin with some natural advantages—early arrival, familiarity with the English language, experience with some English political practices, a cohesive group identity. Yet Jewish immigrants also brought some political assets with them—relatively high literacy, an urban heritage, close social bonds, and a knowledge of political combat extending back to the Bible. It may be that Jews were less disposed than the Irish to accept the hierarchical loyalties inherent in machine politics and less willing to subordinate internal conflicts.

More basically, Jews were often anathema to existing leaders, much more likely to face discrimination within political parties. Republicans would often support restrictions on citizenship, and Democrats were often uninterested in registering the new immigrants. The Irish who typically had established the machines were willing to seek Jewish votes when needed and to provide favors and jobs for Jewish workers. Yet, fearing the competition for patronage and power and sometimes tinged by antisemitism, they were far less willing to cede leadership to the newer arrivals. Instead, as Steven Erie describes Boston's machine leaders, the Irish practiced "minimalist" and symbolic politics. They dispensed food, loans, and licenses to the newcomers but not city jobs, nominations to office, or major party posts. James Michael Curley inaugurated a new era in symbolic politics. Elected to Congress in 1911, Curley crusaded against literacy tests, immigration restriction, and commercial agreements with Russia, where pogroms were raging. Elected mayor in 1913, Curley made symbolic "League of Nations" politics a regular feature at flag-bedecked city hall.

REFORM POLITICS

Irish leadership eventually declined, and power passed late, unwillingly, and often into Italian and black hands, not to Jews. For the most part, Jewish gains came outside the machines through independent parties or through reform movements that supplanted the old organizations. New York dramatically illustrated this change in 1977, when Abe Beame, the city's first Jewish mayor, lost to Ed Koch, a leader in the Democratic reform movement and perhaps New York's last Jewish chief executive. The succession marked the change from machine politics to the new politics of issues, media, and personalities.

Jews have been prominent in two different kinds of reform, ideological and organizational, although the goals of these two movements have often overlapped. Ideological reform includes efforts to promote a coherent policy agenda. For Jews this agenda has typically been of the left, toward liberalism, socialism, even communism—but modern conservatism also has prominent Jewish advocates.

Ideological reform of the left clearly stems from the basic Jewish values of *tzedakeh* and nonasceticism. The connection is underlined by the continuing Jewish identification of most leftists, who combined their political and religious faiths, rather than abandoning Judaism in their search for secular improvement. Liberalism and socialism, to many Jews, have been the worldly embodiment of the Yom Kippur admonition (Isaiah 58):

> This is the fast I desire: To unlock fetters of wickedness, And untie the cords of the yoke. To let the oppressed go free; To break off every yoke. It is to share your bread with the hungry, And to take the wretched poor into your home; When you see the naked, to clothe him, And not to ignore your own kin.

The leftism of Jews was evident in their creation and leadership of trade unions for the Jewish immigrant masses, leadership that went beyond demands of the workplace and developed a broad political agenda. Samuel Gompers came out of this tradition, although, as he rose to leadership of the American Federation of Labor, he came to epitomize its more cautious "bread and butter unionism." The radical tradition continued strong in the needle trades, where unions were created, led, and politicized by such Jews as Alex Rose and David Dubinsky.

Women were also active in the socialist and union organizations, including Pauline Newman, Fannia Cohn, and Rose Schneiderman. They faced additional obstacles in their political efforts, beyond the poverty and low status they shared with men. Not only did they lack the vote before women's suffrage, but they also confronted a Judaic tradition that restricted women's activism outside the home, as well as male domination and disrespect even from radicals, in an American society that would not become familiar with feminism for another fifty years.

Until the New Deal, socialist parties won extensive votes from Jews, and two New York Jews, Morris Hillquit and Congressman Meyer London, were nationally recognized "socialist" (labor) leaders. Although Roosevelt captured much of this vote for the Democrats, the unions maintained their influence in New York by forming independent parties. In 1936, they created the American Labor Party to give FDR a separate and nonmachine ballot line. In 1944, to combat communist infiltration, the unions created the Liberal Party, which held the balance of power in New York politics for decades.

Jewish proclivity for these parties of the left probably went beyond the implications of *tzedakeh*. Surely considerable self-interest showed in promoting welfare programs for a working class that at the time included most Jews and in building third parties that gave independent power to Jewish politicians. Yet self-interest cannot explain why Jews continued to vote for, and to lead, these parties even as Jews rose to middle-class status and wealth. An additional reason might well be that the coherence and apparent logic of ideological programs spoke to Jewish values of learning and intellect. That rationalistic appeal may also explain the latter-day appeal of more conservative programs to contemporary Jewish ideologues of the right, such as Norman Podhoretz and William Kristol.

The second kind of reform has been directed toward change in the structure of government and political parties, including efforts to diminish political corruption, establish universalistic practices in government such as merit systems of civil service, and increase popular participation within the parties. These Jewish goals often have been combined with policy objectives, usually liberal in character.

Jews have long been active in local reform movements. Jacob Shiff and Oscar Straus, for example, were prominent among early anti-Tammany leaders, often allied with old-line Protestants against the Irish Catholic organizations. Their co-religionists were notable supporters of the city's most prominent reform mayor, Fiorello LaGuardia, himself of mixed Jewish descent. The same ethnic alliance was evident when John Lindsay, a Protestant, was elected twice as New York mayor. In his second candidacy, Lindsay no longer had the support of his own Republican Party, but he won as the nominee of the Liberal Party, still led by Jewish trade unionists.

A broader reform movement came with the development of local Democratic "amateur" clubs, most prominently in Chicago and Los Angeles, as well as in New York. These organizations attempted to go beyond sporadic defeats of the established machine to institutionalize reform within the party by winning control of the organization. The effort was led by Jewish politicians and drew its greatest support from Jewish residents in such areas as Fairfax in Los Angeles, the neighborhoods near the University of Chicago, and the West Side of Manhattan.

The New York reform movement was the most successful. It took over the party leadership, literally tore down Tammany Hall when it sold the organization's building, and eventually accomplished the nomination and election of Koch as mayor. Ideological leftism has remained strong, with the reform groups breeding such candidates as Bella Abzug, Jerrold Nadler, and Ruth Messinger.

These reform movements were dedicated to a liberal policy agenda, but their distinctive characteristic was the emphasis on change in the party's processes. Reformers sought more open participation within the party, giving more power to the enrolled membership and less to the leadership. The reformers argued that members should be recruited, candidates selected, contracts awarded, and officials appointed because of their professional qualifications and policy positions, not on the basis of patronage or personal loyalties.

Jewish support for these movements is, again, partially rooted in self-interest. Machine rule has often blocked the rise of Jewish politicians, and corrupt contracts—although not unknown to Jews—were more likely to be given to other ethnic groups with closer friendships to the established politicians. Universalistic standards such as merit promotions would probably work to the benefit of Jews, given their educational achievements, as fair contracting would probably aid assertive Jewish businessmen. Control of machines by Catholics, first Irish and then Italian, made natural allies of excluded Protestants and Jews.

Beyond self-interest, however, basic values also probably come into play. The Jewish respect for intellect had some effect, gaining the group's support for abstract principles of reform. A personal example of this appeal could be seen in 1960, when many reformers preferred Adlai Stevenson to John Kennedy as presidential nominee, even though Kennedy was arguably more liberal in policy terms. As James Q. Wilson explains Stevenson's appeal:

> He was urbane and witty, he often uttered speculative rather than declamatory remarks, he keenly felt the ambiguity of the political situation and the complexity of public issues. He generalized and dealt in abstractions, and his generalities and abstractions were fresher, more polished, less obvious or chauvinistic, than those of his predecessors. . . . Beyond these elements was the belief he engendered that he was a true intellectual.

Another source of reform support came in Jews' apparent commitment to a "public-regarding" ethic, rooted in Torah ethics, and also reflected in Protestant conceptions of absolutist morality. According to this ethic, government should be structured to pursue policies that promote "the general welfare," however the term is defined, rather than the narrower self-interests of private groups. Jews often do show a willingness to vote against their particular interests, as in their support for redistributive social programs that will cost them taxes but provide little personal advantage; and often they will not reflexively vote for a Jewish candidate simply on the basis of his or her religion. Thus, Jews do ask Hillel's first question, "If I am not for myself, who will be?" But they also add his second question, "If I am only for myself, what am I?"

Reform activism by Jews also has extended to national politics, in both major parties and in both liberal and conservative ideological directions. Americans for Democratic Action (ADA) provides one important example of a group active in partisan politics. The group was founded in 1948 to provide a liberal but anticommunist voice, headlined by such prominent Democrats as Eleanor Roosevelt and Hubert Humphrey. Jews were among its most active founders, including Joseph Rauh, an early president, who was a distinguished labor and civil rights lawyer.

ADA won early attention when Rauh coordinated the successful effort of liberal Democrats to add a civil rights plank to the 1948 Democratic platform. Although supportive of Israel, the organization's agenda has gone far beyond causes particularly identified with Jews, and its annual ratings of members of Congress has become a scholarly index of liberalism. ADA has dealt with the broad spectrum of national issues, including economic programs, social welfare, civil rights including critical support for the 1960s Freedom Rides, and international policy. Jews continue to be important figures in the organization: Leon Schull was ADA's longtime national director. He was succeeded by the current director, Amy Isaacs, herself related by marriage to a founding Jewish member and rare Republican—Stanley Isaacs, Manhattan borough president in New York.

Another form of Jewish involvement in the political parties has come through influence on the party conventions and their nominations for national office. A notorious historical episode occurred in 1944, when Roosevelt was nominated for a fourth term. Recognizing FDR's failing health, party leaders gave unusual attention to the vice presidential candidate and sought to replace the quixotic incumbent, Henry Wallace. Roosevelt was persuaded to choose Senator Harry Truman of Missouri. He insisted, however, that the Democratic barons "Clear it with Sidney," meaning Sidney Hillman, president of the Amalgamated Clothing Union and a major figure in the labor movement.

Allard Lowenstein had a different effect on the Democratic Party. A student leader of protests against the Vietnam War, Lowenstein organized the 1968 campaign to deny the party's renomination to Lyndon Johnson. Unable to persuade Robert Kennedy or George McGovern to challenge the incumbent president, he successfully recruited Minnesota Senator Eugene McCarthy. When McCarthy came close to winning the New Hampshire primary, Johnson withdrew from the race, bringing Kennedy, and later McGovern, openly into the contest.

Lowenstein was himself elected to Congress for one term and continued his efforts to move the Democrats to the left for the next decade. Although party rules were changed to encourage more direct participation, he was generally unsuccessful in exerting influence on the nominations, as shown by the defeat of the liberal McCarthy in 1968 and Edward Kennedy in 1980. Lowenstein brought many young people into national Democratic politics, such as Representatives Barney Frank and Patricia Shroeder, but his reformist career ended violently with his assassination in 1980.

Jews are also active in the most recent, and successful, reform movement in the Democratic Party, the Democratic Leadership Council (DLC). Created in 1985, the group has worked to increase its party's electoral appeal by moving Democrats toward "the vital center" (interestingly, the title of a book by Arthur Schlesinger in the early period of ADA). The DLC provided a national stage and a policy program for Bill Clinton's successful presidential bid and for Vice President Al Gore's succession to party leadership. With Jews as significant leaders, notably its cofounder and current president Al From, the DLC has become a major source of advice and personnel for the national Democratic Party. Its most prominent Jew, clearly, was Senator Joseph Lieberman. His nomination as the Democratic candidate for vice president in 2000, and the success he achieved in the campaign, marked a definitive acceptance of Jewish politicians into American public life.

The Jewish impulse toward reform has not only been evident within the Democratic Party but also—a generation after Franklin Roosevelt—in direct opposition to it. In the social upheavals of the 1960s and 1970s, some Jews came to believe that the Democratic Party had been corrupted by narrow, special interests—too corrupted to be reformed. Dismayed by the weaknesses they perceived in the presidency of Jimmy Carter, they argued that the United States had lost its moral compass both internationally and domestically.

THE JEWISH IMPULSE TOWARD REFORM HAS NOT ONLY BEEN EVIDENT WITHIN THE DEMOCRATIC PARTY BUT ALSO IN DIRECT OPPOSITION TO IT.

Inheritors of the ADA tradition on international issues, they came to believe that the Democratic Party was increasingly "soft" on communism, indifferent to the Soviet Union's persecution of Jews, and acquiescent to third-world countries' domination of the United Nations on such issues as the notorious 1975 United Nations resolution condemning Zionism as racism. At home, they began to react against such conventional liberal policies such as affirmative action. Racial preferences were seen as contradictory to Jewish ideals of merit-based achievement and objective academic advancement. Not insignificantly, these programs were also seen as harmful to Jewish self-interests.

These "neoconservatives" had actually been slowly moving to the Republican Party since the 1950s: a half dozen Jews were among the founding members of *National Review*, the leading magazine of the intellectual right. But two events accelerated their movement to the Republican Party in the late 1970s: the defeat of their Democratic champion, Henry M. "Scoop" Jackson, in the 1976 Democratic Party presidential nomination and the emergence of Ronald Reagan as the GOP standard-bearer in the 1980 elections.

Reagan's moralistic voice in international relations struck a chord with these "neocon" Jews. They, too, regarded the Soviet Union as an "evil empire," and they welcomed Reagan's hard-line defense of Israel. More basically, Reagan's upbeat, optimistic view of the United States' role in the world resonated with these successful Americans, who felt that their fellow Jews had finally found a safe home in the United States, and angrily rejected the left's constant criticism. As one of their leaders, Irving Kristol, wryly said of American tolerance, Christians in the United States were less eager to persecute them than to have them marry their sons and daughters. Kristol's son, William, became an important player in GOP policy circles, serving as a key Republican strategist, editor of the Republican-leaning *Weekly Standard*, and as Vice President Dan Quayle's chief of staff.

The neoconservatives constituted a bridge between Jewish radical reform and contemporary conventional political involvement. Earlier, Jewish activists stood outside American society, often acting as virulent critics, such as 1960s Jewish radicals Jerry Rubin and Abby Hoffman. The newer Jewish intellectuals of the right accepted the worth of mainstream politics because they accepted the worth of American society itself. To them, foreigners, particularly communists, were the "other," the alien forces that merited criticism.

THE NEOCONSERVATIVES CONSTITUTED A BRIDGE BETWEEN JEWISH RADICAL REFORM AND CONTEMPORARY CONVENTIONAL POLITICAL INVOLVEMENT.

Norman Podhoretz personifies the change. In his recent book, *My Love Affair with America*, he traces his own personal journey from leftist social reformer to neoconservative as a reaction against the cultural left of the late 1960s and early 1970s. Podheretz's unique role as editor of *Commentary*, the magazine of the American Jewish Committee, gives this voyage a special resonance. Indeed, he links his current views to biblical tradition, remembering the Passover prayer of "Dayenu": "it would have been enough."

JEWS IN THE NATIONAL POLITICAL PARTIES

Podhoretz and Kristol were the intellectual vanguard of what has become a broader entry of Jews into Republican Party politics. For example, in the 2000 election cycle, GOP nominee George W. Bush boasted a Jew, Ari Fleisher, as his campaign spokesman, and Bush placed Jews in key policy roles from policy director to senior domestic policy adviser, as well as including them as his most prominent foreign policy advisers.

Yet, with a few exceptions, such as Senator Arlen Specter of Pennsylvania, who unsuccessfully sought the Republican presidential nomination in 1996, the Jewish role in GOP politics has been largely behind the scenes. But, aside from the major recent exception of Lieberman, that description is also true of the Democrats. In a role that harks back to the old "court Jew" tradition of hidden influence over political decisions and invokes Fuchs's description of Torah or "learning," Jews have served as key advisers to both political parties, using their intellect to influence leaders while largely remaining out of the limelight.

In both the Republican and Democratic parties, however, it is Jewish money and fund-raising ability, even more than intellect, that has spoken most loudly. For example, Matthew Brooks, executive director of the Republican Jewish Coalition, said he expected Republican Jews to raise $7 million for the Republican Party in the 2000 election cycle, and he noted that the finance chairman of the GOP, Max Sembler, was Jewish.

The GOP effort to tap Jewish money began in earnest with Reagan's 1980 election. On the other hand, the Democratic Party can trace its long relationship with Jewish financiers as far back as the beginning of the Civil War. At that time, August Belmont, the financial agent of the Rothschilds in America, was the best-known German Jew in this country. Belmont, now memorialized by the New York racing track he founded, was an active Democrat who eventually served as chair of the National Democratic Committee.

JEWS HAVE SERVED AS KEY ADVISERS TO BOTH POLITICAL PARTIES, USING THEIR INTELLECT TO INFLUENCE LEADERS WHILE LARGELY REMAINING OUT OF THE LIMELIGHT. IN BOTH THE REPUBLICAN AND DEMOCRATIC PARTIES, HOWEVER, IT IS JEWISH MONEY AND FUND-RAISING ABILITIES, EVEN MORE THAN INTELLECT, THAT HAVE SPOKEN MOST LOUDLY.

Three Jews chaired the Democratic National Committee near the end of the twentieth century: Robert S. Strauss, Steve Grossman, and, most recently, Edward Rendell. Though Rendell came to his leadership position through elective office, as mayor of Philadelphia, Strauss and Grossman followed Belmont's pattern of using their fund-raising and organizational savvy to work their way to the top of the national party. However, the role Judaism played in Grossman's life differed greatly from that role in Strauss's.

For Strauss, being Jewish has not been central to his political views or shaping his political career. He grew up in the tiny town of Stanford, Texas, where his mother and her sister headed the only Jewish families; his yearly visits to a Dallas synagogue were viewed more as family gatherings than religious occasions. "Education in anything Jewish was totally foreign to me," he said in a personal interview. When religious segregation forced him to join a Jewish fraternity at the University of Texas, he found the situation extremely uncomfortable and soon left.

Paradoxically, his mother instilled great pride in his religious affiliation: "My mother gave me so much pride in our faith, that I started feeling sorry for people who weren't Jewish," he remembers. While she would repeatedly boast at family occasions that "Bobby is going to be the first Jewish governor of the state of Texas," Strauss says that "my mother wanted me to be a political person, not a Jewish political person."

She soon got her wish. After a position as a clerk at the Texas state legislature, Strauss got his real start in politics by helping Lyndon Baines Johnson launch his first race for Congress in 1937. Johnson's campaign was centered on his support for President Roosevelt, and Strauss was an enthusiastic supporter of FDR.

From then on, Strauss's fortunes rose along with that of Johnson and another close friend, John Connally. After Connally was elected governor, he appointed Strauss to the State Banking Board and to the Democratic National Committee. A long succession of behind-the-scenes jobs followed, including chairman of the Democratic National Committee, U.S. trade representative, and U.S. ambassador to Russia. In the process, Strauss became known as a "fixer," someone who could cut difficult deals in Washington or overseas.

Indeed, despite his strong partisan background, Strauss's skills in courting favor with elected officials were so strong that it was a Republican president, George Bush, who named him ambassador to Russia, perhaps America's single most important diplomatic post. Even foreign officials were impressed. Despite Strauss's Jewish heritage, he played a crucial role at the original Camp David peace talks because he enjoyed the confidence of both Egyptian president Anwar Sadat and Israeli prime minister Menachem Begin.

In many ways, Strauss was the epitome of the modern "court Jew," with little interest in elective office. Twice in his life he considered but chose not to run for public office: in 1972 for the United States Senate against Republican John Tower, and in 1984 as a candidate for the Democratic presidential nomination, when there was an effort to draft him as a consensus alternative to former Vice President Walter Mondale and Senator Gary Hart. His reluctance to run for office was personal, not political. He discounted the potential electoral damage of his religion. In the 1984 campaign, his pollsters examined the possible effect of his Jewish heritage in upcoming primaries in New York, Illinois, and Texas, concluding that "it wouldn't have been a killer."

Steve Grossman is different. In his case, his political rise, his fund-raising savvy, and his Jewish identity were all closely linked. And he has been attracted to elective office. Grossman's serious involvement in politics began in 1977 when, as a thirty-one-year-old inheritor of a prosperous family business, he experienced a "Jewish epiphany" that led him to a new devotion to Jewish life and to participation in a young leadership program of the Jewish Federation of Boston. As he became more deeply involved in Jewish life in Massachusetts, Grossman began raising money for Jewish causes and eventually came to the attention of then Governor Michael Dukakis, a cochair of the U.S. Holocaust Memorial Museum. Dukakis eventually asked him to host a fund-raising event for the museum. That established a bond between Grossman and a rising politician; when Dukakis ran for president in 1988, Grossman became one of the cochairs of his finance committee.

That national access and Grossman's fund-raising ability would eventually lead him to develop relationships with such national figures as Bill Clinton and Ron Brown, later the Democratic national chairman. Grossman would play an important role in their crucial early efforts to win money and political support from the Jewish community. It would help him win election as chairman of the Massachusetts Democratic Party, which needed his help in getting out of a financial crisis. And it would help earn him the presidency of the politically powerful American Israel Public Affairs Committee.

All of these positions, in turn, offered him further access to key national political leaders such as Senator Ted Kennedy, Clinton, AFL-CIO President John Sweeney, House

Minority Leader Richard Gephardt, and Al Gore. That access proved crucial when Grossman successfully sought the chairmanship of the national Democratic Party after the 1996 election.

In addition to political smarts and fund-raising ability, Grossman said his interest in politics can be traced back to the Torah. In particular, he returns us to the prophetic promise of Isaiah (58:10) as the core of his political beliefs: "Then shall your light rise in the darkness, And your gloom shall be like noonday; The Lord will guide you always; You shall be like a watered garden, Like a spring whose waters do not fail."

Even more than Torah, however, Grossman traces his interest in politics to a long family tradition—he calls himself a "genetic Democrat"—a family tradition that mirrors the overall movement of Jews in American politics: from ghetto ward heeler to reform advocate to national power broker.

His grandfather, Max, the second-youngest of thirteen immigrant children, was the first to become involved in politics. As a thirteen-year-old shoeshine boy in the early years of the twentieth century, he was recruited into a political club in East Boston and worked on the mayoral reelection campaign of Honey Fitzgerald, John F. Kennedy's grandfather.

Max Grossman worked for decades in Boston's political clubs, eventually becoming a key fund-raiser and advocate in the Jewish community for the legendary mayor of Boston, Michael Curley. When Curley asked him to name a patronage position as a reward, Grossman responded that he wanted to become penal commissioner—hardly a typical response, but he had been convinced by social reformers that changes could be made in the prison system. He later surprised a newly elected Massachusetts governor by making and being granted the same request for a statewide position.

One of Max's sons, Jerome Grossman, was a radical social reformer, in an evolution characteristic of the Jewish community as a whole. Author of a book titled *Relentless Liberal*, Grossman was an originator of the Vietnam Moratorium effort in the late 1960s and a key political organizer for the presidential campaigns of Eugene McCarthy in 1968 and George McGovern in 1972. He was also the campaign manager for the campaigns of Father Robert Drinan, a four-term, strongly liberal Jesuit Massachusetts congressman.

For most of his career, Steve Grossman, Jerome's nephew, has personified the court Jew, the embodiment of Torah, the behind-the-scenes adviser who helps politicians, like the Kennedys and Clinton, carry out their agenda. But like Joseph Lieberman, Steve Grossman now hopes to take the next step in the evolution of Jewish politics. The former behind-the-scenes organizer is considering running for governor of Massachusetts in 2002. His election would make him the first Jewish governor of the Bay State.

CONCLUSION

JEWISH POLITICIANS
HAVE BEEN ABLE BOTH
TO ASSIMILATE
WITHIN AMERICA
AND TO MAINTAIN
THEIR ETHNIC
IDENTITY IN THEIR
PLURALISTIC NATION.

Any account of Jewish politics inevitably returns us to the great biblical narratives. The experience of Jews in America recalls the histories of Joseph and Moses. Joseph grew up in an isolated world of his brethren. Expelled to a foreign land, he became an eminent court Jew, an intellectual, a reformer, a political insider, and then a prominent leader, even as he consistently disguised his Hebraic ancestry. It was left to later representatives of the community, Moses and Aaron, to proclaim their heritage openly and to achieve independent power. Jewish politicians have been able both to assimilate within America and to maintain their ethnic identity in their pluralistic nation. Have Jews now found the political Promised Land?

6

WHO DOES WHAT?

Jewish Advocacy and Jewish "Interest"

JEROME A. CHANES

A merican Jewish advocacy is a reality. Over the past half-century, virtually all of the institutions in American Jewish life—social service, religious, public affairs, cultural, educational—have performed some sort of advocacy function.

What is advocacy? In the Roman world *advocare* meant to summon to one's assistance. The word itself suggests a mission that is singularly suited to a society organized on the principles of democratic pluralism, in which the agencies of the community conduct activity aimed at assisting the community. The natural extension of the delivery of direct services *internally* has been the relationships of Jewish groups with the *external* world in a communal effort to enhance the security and creative continuity of Jews, individually and as a community.

JEWISH ADVOCACY IS VIEWED AGAINST THE BACKDROP OF THE ASSOCIATIONAL AND VOLUNTARY NATURE OF THE AMERICAN JEWISH COMMUNITY.

Jewish advocacy is viewed against the backdrop of the associational and voluntary nature of the American Jewish community. The associational base of the community, and its federated structure, have permitted and, indeed, have depended on affiliation—with a synagogue, a federation, a community relations agency, a Zionist organization—to a degree far greater than at any other time in Jewish history. Any and all connections with Jewish organizational life in the United States depend on some degree of voluntary association. As Daniel Elazar has shown, the sum total of these associations determines, defines, and informs American Jewry's organizational structure and its approach to advocacy.

THE JEWISH COMMUNAL AGENDA IN THE TWENTIETH CENTURY

What is Jewish "interest"? What makes any given issue an issue of concern to the organized Jewish community—the Jewish polity—that must be addressed as a priority? To get a sense of why issues are selected for action by Jewish groups, one should survey the nature of the Jewish communal agenda along a historical "time line," to look at what it *was* in the past.

From the early twentieth century through the early 1950s, the primary agenda of the Jewish community was combating antisemitism at home and abroad and the corollary of antisemitism, discrimination, which was pervasive. From the early 1950s to the mid-1960s, the Jewish communal agenda was the civil rights movement, on the assumption that Jews would only be secure if all groups in American society were secure: again, a single issue to the exclusion of virtually everything else. Civil rights were *the* Jewish agenda. The separation of church and state played a significant role during these years as well. The great landmark cases were decided during this period, with essential participation—indeed, leadership—of the Jewish community. But the first priority was civil rights.

Two events occurred in the mid-1960s that radically changed American Jewish priorities: the emergence of the Soviet Jewry movement in the United States in 1963 and the Six-Day War in 1967. The crucial impacts of these two developments were that they led American Jews to become preoccupied with Israel and Soviet Jewry and to move away from the broad range of domestic advocacy issues that encompassed social and economic justice concerns. Issues on the domestic agenda were yet on the Jewish agenda, but they were no longer the *priority* issues for advocacy. Almost overnight the Jewish advocacy agenda became more particularistic, more "Jewish."

CIVIL RIGHTS WERE THE JEWISH AGENDA.

Beginning around 1980, the Jewish community started moving back to the broader agenda. The first Reagan administration, and the rise of an aggressive "religious right," led many in the Jewish community to point to a potential crisis with respect to constitutional protections, and a fearful consensus that economic justice could be undermined by the administration's restrictive policies. The Jewish community again engaged in a reordering of its priorities.

ALMOST OVERNIGHT THE JEWISH ADVOCACY AGENDA BECAME MORE PARTICULARISTIC, MORE "JEWISH."

Now, at the beginning of the twenty-first century, with radical changes in the communal agenda, American Jewry is once again reevaluating those issues it considers crucial to its survival and security. Levels of both behavioral and attitudinal antisemitism are very low, and in any case antisemitism poses no real threat to the ability of Jews to participate fully in the society. With the collapse of the Soviet Union a decade ago, the Soviet Jewry issue no longer constitutes an agenda for political and international advocacy but for social services. Finally, the Israel agenda, long the most critical for American Jews and Jewish advocacy groups, has changed radically. Whatever the serious problems and deep pitfalls in the peace process, the issues that have come to the fore are related more to the relationship between Israel and America's Jews than with the physical security of Israel.

The Jewish community, then, is clearly in a transitional period. One principle, however, remains the central organizing principle for issues on the public affairs agenda: The issues that the community addresses—that are "selected" for advocacy—are those in which *there is a consensus of the community that they affect Jewish security*. Debate grows within the Jewish community with respect to the parameters of the "Jewish security" rubric. I suggest that a set of concentric circles describes the priority of issues on the Jewish agenda.

At the center, some issues immediately and directly relate to Jewish security: antisemitism, Israel, and the security of Jewish communities abroad. These issues, tautologically "security" issues, lie at the core of advocacy.

We then move one concentric circle out. In the penumbra of Jewish concerns, the relationship to Jewish security remains absolutely central. The separation of church and state—the central guarantor of Jewish security in the United States—is the most obvious in this category. This circle includes First Amendment and other political freedom issues. Jewish communal leader Earl Raab suggests a construct: what government *cannot* do to an individual, and what one individual cannot do to another. Bill of Rights protections—the balancing of the interests of government, the state, the individual, majorities, and minorities—fall under this rubric.

DEBATE GROWS WITHIN THE JEWISH COMMUNITY WITH RESPECT TO THE PARAMETERS OF THE "JEWISH SECURITY" RUBRIC.

The next level of concentric circles includes issues that, while they are located at the periphery of Jewish concerns, are clearly important to the health of the society and are therefore important to Jews as enhancing the health of American Jewish society. The questions are not of restraint, as are those of political and personal freedom, but of positive beneficence: what government *can* and *should* do for a person. Social and economic justice, the environment, and other such issues fall into this category.

As the agenda expands, the inevitable question arises: "Why is this issue a priority for Jewish advocacy?" Issues are priorities for Jews when they implicate Jewish security. To take one dramatic example, the Jewish community became involved in civil rights not out of liberal philosophies but out of Jewish self-interest. As discussed later in this chapter, it was not without vigorous debate within the Jewish community over the question as to whether "relations with Negroes" was central to Jewish security. The Jewish advocacy agenda, therefore, ought not be refracted through the prism of the "liberal agenda"—and it never was in any case. The conventional wisdom that the "old-time religion" of 1950s and 1960s liberalism has driven the Jewish agenda is only partly right—and therefore mostly wrong. Jewish social and political tradition is neither liberal nor conservative; it is *Jewish*. American Jews have long understood that the advocacy agenda is the enabler of all of the other agendas of the community and is the vehicle by which a contemporary realization of the traditional imperatives of *kehilla* (community) and *tzedakeh* (justice and charity) is expressed.

JEWISH SOCIAL AND POLITICAL TRADITION IS NEITHER LIBERAL NOR CONSERVATIVE; IT IS JEWISH.

With the receding of the *exogenous* "security-and-survival" advocacy agenda, the concern of American Jews has turned increasingly *inward*, to its own values—indeed, to its very continuity. Concern over rates of intermarriage and massive Jewish functional illiteracy has brought about an *endogenous* agenda of identity, Jewish continuity, and Jewish "Renaissance." With the significant shift in priorities toward strategies aimed at guaranteeing Jewish continuity, Jewish advocacy organizations will be called on to rethink their missions and retool their operations. It remains to be seen whether the new emphasis on Jewish continuity can be effected without damage to the community's traditionally broad public-affairs advocacy agenda.

CONCERN OVER
RATES OF
INTERMARRIAGE AND
MASSIVE JEWISH
FUNCTIONAL
ILLITERACY HAS
BROUGHT ABOUT AN
INWARD-TURNING
AGENDA OF IDENTITY,
JEWISH CONTINUITY,
AND JEWISH
"RENAISSANCE."

A REVIEW OF JEWISH ADVOCACY GROUPS IN THE UNITED STATES

What was the genesis of the advocacy and interest groups? What were, and are, their missions? The American Jewish community of today is the repository of three and a half centuries of historical development. The evolution from "charity" to advocacy was a natural, albeit bumpy, one. In broad strokes, charitable societies under Jewish auspices were fashioned by German Jews beginning in 1844. Jewish hospitals were established in the 1850s and 1860s in the large cities, independently of the synagogues. Fraternal orders and educational institutions emerged, largely under German Jewish leadership. Finally, the increase in immigration from Eastern Europe, first in the 1860s and then, massively, after 1881, compelled the Jewish communities to expand their charitable and welfare services.

Accompanying this massive immigration was a stark social contrast between the new immigrants and the established Jewish community. However, most of the "uptown" German Jews, while they could easily divide the world they knew into "ours" and "theirs" from a *social* perspective, realized that the Eastern European Jews were, in a very real way, "theirs" as well. The leadership of the German Jewish "uptown" establishment acknowledged their communal obligation as brother and sister Jews. Out of this feeling of responsibility came the establishment of the network of social service agencies and, equally important, of the early "defense" agencies, which ultimately developed and implemented an advocacy agenda on behalf of American Jewry.

The forty years between 1920 and 1960 witnessed a proliferation of national Jewish organizations. The numbers are instructive: Nineteen such bodies were listed in 1900 in the *American Jewish Year Book*, 71 in 1914, 116 in 1925, and 247 in 1962. One community relations agency existed in 1900, twelve in 1962, and some thirty in 2000.

The "Defense" Agencies

During the nineteenth and early twentieth centuries, as Jewish communities around the country were gradually evolving in terms of their communal structures, national Jewish organizations developed to respond to advocacy needs. As early as 1859, the Board of

Delegates of American Israelites, a group arising, in large measure, out of the Reform Jewish movement and modeled after the Board of Deputies in Britain, was acting as the advocacy arm of the American Jewish community, responding to international anti-Jewish activity and some immigration issues. But the model of a central organizational structure was not one appropriate to the federated, voluntary nature of American Jewish society. In 1878 the Board of Delegates became part of the Union of American Hebrew Congregations, the congregational arm of the Reform movement in the United States.

Matters relating to advocacy in the public affairs arena are addressed by a number of community relations agencies—once known as "defense" agencies—which have multi-issued and multifaceted agendas.

The oldest "defense" agency, the American Jewish Committee (AJC), was formed as one of a number of responses to the search during the late nineteenth and early twentieth centuries for a basis on which a central representative organization of American Jews could be built. Established in 1906 in response to concerns about virulent anti-Jewish depredations in czarist Russia, particularly the 1905 Kishinev pogrom, the AJC initially consisted of a small group drawn from the established German Jewish community, these activists viewed their purpose as mobilizing American Jews to respond to matters of violent anti-Jewish concern.

For many years, the AJC was precisely what its name suggests: it was a committee with a membership of some fifty individuals; the group was small and self-selected. Enlarged after 1943, the AJC developed into a highly professional organization that was an effective voice for American Jews on public policy issues. The AJC has long had a special interest in ethnicity, pluralism, and Jewish family life, and its work in interreligious affairs and human rights over the decades is especially noteworthy. The AJC's orientation has long been that of a thoughtful and deliberative organization.

THE AMERICAN JEWISH CONGRESS HAS LONG HAD A SPECIAL INTEREST IN ETHNICITY, PLURALISM, AND JEWISH FAMILY LIFE.

During the 1990s, the AJC underwent a necessary process of redefinition of mission and function within the community; it has been significantly more active in the international arena, especially in Israel, than it had heretofore been. The fact of AJC's joining the Presidents' Conference in 1991 was more than merely symbolic; it was a statement of American Jewish solidarity, and, for AJC, it suggested an expanded role in international advocacy. Additionally, in recent years the AJC has become much more closely identified as a *Jewish* organization, in terms of enhancing Jewish organizational culture and programmatic commitment to Jewish continuity.

The origins of the American Jewish Congress (AJCongress), founded in 1918, provide an important lesson in how American Jewry responds to communal needs and to communal dissatisfaction. The AJCongress was established by a group, largely of Eastern European origin, that felt that the "aristocratic" German Jewish leadership of the AJC was a self-appointed, self-perpetuating body with no mandate from a majority of American Jewry. The debate, largely between Eastern European and German Jews, and between Zionists and anti-Zionists as well, centered primarily on the establishment of a "congress" that would represent *all* American Jewish interests at the peace conference following World War I; the result: an ad hoc congress for this purpose. While the AJC and other organizations wanted the "Congress" to go out of business—and indeed, it did formally dissolve itself in 1920—the pressure for a permanent representative organization resulted in the formation of the present AJCongress, established in 1922 as a council of agencies that devolved into a central and specific membership organization in the 1930s. The initial constituency of the AJCongress was mainly Zionist—indeed, the AJCongress was the only American Jewish organization that supported Zionism from its very beginnings.

The AJCongress has on a number of issues (including a boycott of German goods in the 1930s) been arguably more representative of the views of the grassroots than the other agencies. AJCongress, over the objections of many in the Jewish community at the time, pioneered the use of law and social action as tools in combating prejudice and discrimination. Many Jews voiced objections to this strategy, viewing such activity as unnecessarily exposing an American Jewry that felt vulnerable. However, the AJCongress has long viewed itself as being the "lawyer" for the American Jewish community; indeed,

THE AMERICAN JEWISH CONGRESS HAS LONG VIEWED ITSELF AS BEING THE "LAWYER" FOR THE AMERICAN JEWISH COMMUNITY.

it took a pioneering stance and leading role in Jewish involvement in landmark Supreme Court cases on First Amendment (especially church–state separation) and civil rights issues.

The Anti-Defamation League of B'nai B'rith (ADL) was originally created in 1913, in reaction to the highly publicized Leo Frank lynching, to combat antisemitism. Its focus on discrimination and Jewish security has remained ADL's most salient feature through the years. Unlike the AJCongress, the AJC, and other community-relations organizations, the ADL is not a membership organization. While the primary focus of the ADL has traditionally been combating antisemitism and discrimination, the league has over the years developed a broad agenda that includes Israel and international affairs, civil rights, church–state separation, interfaith activity, and Holocaust education. The ADL suggests that the threats to Jewish security come from an antisemitism that appears in new forms and guises, such as anti-Israel activity and radicalism of the right and left. Since 1981, the ADL has had a broad agenda of public affairs advocacy, particularly in church–state separation and in legislative initiatives involving individual freedom matters.

A FOCUS ON DISCRIMINATION AND JEWISH SECURITY HAS REMAINED THE ANTI-DEFAMATION LEAGUE'S MOST SALIENT FEATURE.

A number of other community relations and public affairs agencies, most established during the early decades of this century, are active in the American Jewish community. They include B'nai B'rith, an international fraternal and social organization that has become increasingly active in community-relations issues; Hadassah, a Zionist organization, now with an increasingly differentiated agenda; the National Council of Jewish Women, functioning both in the public affairs and in the social services arenas; Women's American ORT, a membership organization that functions as the support organization for the worldwide ORT network, and with an agenda that addresses a range of social concerns in the United States; and the congregational bodies of the Orthodox, Conservative, and Reform movements. Hadassah, the Women's Zionist Organization of the United States, is noteworthy as the largest Jewish membership organization in the United States (with a reported membership of 385,000). While in recent years Hadassah has had to address the dilemmas that come with an aging membership, it remains a potent force, able to mobilize a large cadre of members around issues advocacy, thereby enhancing its significance as a potential actor in the community relations sphere and on Israel-related matters.

> HADASSAH IS NOTEWORTHY AS THE LARGEST JEWISH MEMBERSHIP ORGANIZATION IN THE UNITED STATES.

Conference of Presidents of Major American Jewish Organizations

One of the most important—and least understood—advocacy groups is the Conference of Presidents of Major American Jewish Organizations, commonly referred to as the Presidents' Conference. The formal mandate of the Presidents' Conference is to express the collective voice of American Jewish organizations on international affairs—particularly those related to Israel—to the American administration.

The conference has also taken on the reciprocal function of carrying messages from the administration to the Israeli government. It consists of Jews belonging to more than fifty American Jewish organizations (the number fluctuates) representing all spheres of communal activity. It meets on a regular basis to get briefings from Israeli and American officials, the content of which are useful for advocacy efforts on the part of leadership and constituents of member agencies.

> THE FORMAL MANDATE OF THE PRESIDENTS' CONFERENCE IS TO EXPRESS THE COLLECTIVE VOICE OF AMERICAN JEWISH ORGANIZATIONS ON INTERNATIONAL AFFAIRS TO THE AMERICAN ADMINISTRATION.

A review of the genesis of this council of organizations is instructive. The Presidents' Conference was founded in 1954. Since Israel-related issues were not prominent on the American Jewish agenda—they did not become salient until the Six-Day War in 1967—and since no umbrella organization represented American Zionist interests, the Israelis were eager to have a table at which they could communicate with the American Jewish community. At the same time, the Jewish community came to recognize that executive-branch advocacy was no less important than congressional advocacy. For its part, the State Department was receptive to the idea of a single Jewish body that would represent the organized Jewish community, as opposed to many advocates conveying sometimes different messages from that community.

Additionally, international Jewish leader Nahum Goldmann, who was also president of the World Jewish Congress (which had no real base in the United States), wanted to be heard more forcefully on the American scene. He played a key role, together with Phillip Klutznick, then-president of B'nai B'rith, in the creation of the Presidents' Conference.

The conventional wisdom that the Presidents' Conference languished until the Six-Day War misrepresents the actual situation. In fact, the conference was launched at a time during which the Eastern bloc began shipping arms to Egypt, and arms sales became an issue for the first time. Activity of *fedayeen* across Israel's borders was also of increasing concern for the Jewish community and was on the conference's agenda. The 1956 Sinai Campaign, and the need to respond to the threat of sanctions from the White House, was the first critical issue facing the Presidents' Conference. Over the years, the Presidents' Conference has remained a significant vehicle for the Israeli government to communicate, through the American Jewish community speaking with one voice, with the administration.

Nonetheless—again contrary to conventional wisdom—for the most part the President's Conference is not responsible for the deliberative process of shaping strategy on public policy issues facing Israel. This is a function of the advocacy delivery agencies and, indeed, was in past years a central function of the National Jewish Community Relations Advisory Council's Israel Task Force. The federation system also views itself as a "player" in this area. In recent years, some have questioned the conference's expanding agenda, its finances, and the stances articulated by its professional leadership with respect to the peace process in the Middle East.

Community Relations Councils and the Jewish Council for Public Affairs: A Study in Coordination

The issue of the coordination of community relations within the Jewish community has long been a sensitive one and is worth exploring in some detail. Before the end of World War II, the American Jewish community did not play the role that it plays today as an advocate on public policy issues. Deep differences divided the community—between "Uptown" and "Downtown" Jew, between "Litvak" and "Galitzianer" and "Yecke," between Hasidim and Misnagdim, between Bundist and Zionist and religionist. These divisions did exist, but probably a more compelling reason for the relative inability of the Jewish community to act on public policy issues was the very real insecurity felt by Jews, essentially an immigrant community struggling to survive in a depression-racked society. Additionally, exacerbating the divisions within Jewish society was the fact that the Jewish community did not have a network of agencies, national and local, that was able to articulate the needs of the community and to act in a coordinated manner in addressing those needs.

IT WAS THE EVE OF THE FIFTH DAY OF THE PASSOVER FESTIVAL, APRIL 14, 1865. . . . JEWS WERE ON THEIR WAY TO SYNAGOGUE OR ALREADY WORSHIPPING WHEN TIDINGS OF THE ASSASSINATION [OF LINCOLN] REACHED THEM. BLACK DRAPERIES WERE QUICKLY HUNG ON THE ALTARS; YOM KIPPUR HYMNS AND CHANTS WERE SUBSTITUTED FOR PASSOVER MELODIES. . . . RABBI SAMUEL ADLER OF TEMPLE EMANU-EL, NEW YORK BEGAN TO DELIVER A SERMON, BUT HE WAS SO OVERCOME THAT HE COULD NOT CONTINUE. . . . THE GREATEST DEMONSTRATION OF ALL WAS HELD IN NEW YORK CITY. ABOUT THREE THOUSAND JEWS MARCHED IN THE CIVIC PROCESSION, REPRESENTING JEWISH MASONIC LODGES, THE B'NAI B'RITH AND OTHER JEWISH FRATERNAL ORDERS AND JEWISH SOCIAL AND LITERARY ORGANIZATIONS.

—BERTRAM KORN

Until the 1930s and the Nazi threat, federations had been more or less content to satisfy the community-relations needs of their communities by allocating funds to the three "defense" organizations: the AJC, the AJCongress, and the ADL. The viciousness of Nazi antisemitism, however, had an impact on every community and virtually every Jew, such that communities were no longer content to leave activity entirely to national organizations that rarely consulted with one another or with local leadership. The development of the local community relations council was the result.

Community relations councils (CRCs) have been for a half-century and more the central vehicles for advocacy in Jewish communities around the country. Contrary to a popular view, early CRCs were not spearheaded by the federations. Two parallel impulses were at work in the creation of CRCs: community councils were in large measure the outgrowth of grassroots democratic advocacy; and the view that each community should be able to respond immediately, in the manner of a fire brigade, to antisemitism. Indeed, a number of CRCs were organized as counterorganizations to their community federations, seen as more representative than their respective federations. In terms of resources, some of the early CRCs were funded almost in their entirely by the ADL and the AJC. An important result of this local coordination was a concomitant press for coordination on the national level. In 1938, the national agencies, responding to this pressure, formed the General Jewish Council. This short-lived agency, composed of the ADL, the Jewish Labor Committee, the AJC, and the AJCongress, was a failure. In 1944, the General Assembly of the CJF created the National Community Relations Advisory Council (NCRAC, after 1963 the National Jewish Community Relations Advisory Council [NJCRAC]; and after 1998 the Jewish Council for Public Affairs [JCPA]). In the agreement hammered out by the CJF, the absolutely crucial addition to NJCRAC membership was the membership of CRC representatives, who served for the first time, together with national agencies, on a coordinating and planning council. The NJCRAC/JCPA has grown from four national and fourteen community agencies to thirteen national and 120 local community agencies.

The creation of the NJCRAC was the first significant assertion of the federation world moving into the community-relations world. Indeed, following the creation of the NJCRAC, federations were charged with the responsibility of creating new CRCs. Over the years, the NJCRAC was a highly effective vehicle not only for fostering the sophisticated discussion of public policy and community-relations issues but for enabling the network of national and community agencies to bring the message of the Jewish community to the centers of power—in the United States Congress, by means of legislative advocacy; and in the federal courts, by submitting *amicus curiae* briefs. NJCRAC activity in community relations covered the spectrum of coalitional relationships, including the often tangled realm of interreligious relations; those issues relating to Jewish security and antisemitism; constitutional issues, especially those involving civil liberties and the separation of church and state; and issues of social and economic justice. The Israel Task Force of the NJCRAC was a significant vehicle for the coordinated shaping of strategy on issues involving Israel, including America's relationship with the state of Israel. The NJCRAC is the body that provided the first staffing of an agency that responded to the plight of Soviet Jews.

In the area of community relations the question of who acts as the voice for the American Jewish community is particularly sensitive. The JCPA is a planning and coordinating body, charged with coordinating the community-relations activities of its national member agencies and the CRCs, in an effort to reach consensus on the public policy issues facing the community. It also acts as a resource for the CRCs and federations. The NJCRAC's original "Statement of Purpose" barred the council from engaging in functional activity. The JCPA is an enabling mechanism and thus a vehicle for the coordinated activity of member agencies. In principle, the council's agencies jointly identify the critical issues before the Jewish community, determine the policies of the Jewish community, and shape the strategies on how these policies should be implemented. An umbrella body such as the JCPA is an instrumentality through which communities and national agencies speak collectively, thus maximizing the potential of these agencies to work together. Therefore, the old NJCRAC could be and was a significant force in the shaping and implementing of public policy, while maintaining a low profile. Consistent and constant tension resulting from the forces generated by the three actors complicated the process: national agencies, legitimately concerned about their institutional interests and prerogatives; CRCs, which regarded the NJCRAC/JCPA as their instrumentality and are impatient with the low profile that the JCPA usually maintains; and federations, particularly large-city federations, which also regard the JCPA as their instrumentality and feel that the council should be more responsive, especially on those issues the federations regard as of priority concern, including those related to fund raising, and which themselves occasionally enter the community-relations sphere. This friction notwithstanding, the coordinated activity of national and local community relations agencies resulted in the JCPA being a significant voice of the Jewish community in the public affairs arena and an effective platform for advocacy.

In recent years, the JCPA, beset by tensions with some key members of the federation system, its national member agencies, its own CRC constituency, and—most critically—its agenda, has been severely weakened. The JCPA no longer consistently functions as a consensus builder, as an advocate on a range of issues, or as a broker on behalf of the national community for joint action on issues. The JCPA's future will depend in large measure on whether the national advocacy agencies will reemerge at the forefront of the advocacy system, with the JCPA given a renewed mandate for its traditional role as "issues broker," to harness those agencies' expertise and influence for the grassroots resources of the community-relations councils.

"Single-Issue" Advocacy: AIPAC as Paradigm

The American Israel Public Affairs Committee (AIPAC), founded in 1950, has been over the years arguably the most influential voice in Washington advocating on behalf of the state of Israel. AIPAC is an officially registered lobby headquartered in Washington but maintains a network of regional offices, whose function it is to develop support for the state of Israel in the American government. Its activity includes research, legislative liaison, and public information. The weekly *Near East Report*, an autonomous publication, has very close ties to AIPAC. AIPAC's mission is a simple one: to lobby on behalf of legislation affecting U.S.–Israel relations and to make the case to Americans that a secure Israel is in America's interest. AIPAC, unlike most other Jewish organizations in America, is thus a single-issue agency. As is the case with a number of Jewish groups in the advocacy arena, however, AIPAC's activities, and its impact, have over the years moved beyond its original mission.

From its very beginning, AIPAC was a highly effective instrumentality even though in its earlier years it maintained a low public profile. Beginning in 1975, with a change in professional leadership and with the increasing salience of the Middle East crisis, AIPAC became a very high-profile agency. The lobby's growth accelerated during the late 1970s, but it was the campaign against the AWACS in the early 1980s that led the "defense" agencies and the coordinating bodies to accept a dominant role for AIPAC in the Israel advocacy arena. In the 1980s, AIPAC became a powerful advocacy force, moving beyond the legislative front to involve grassroots advocates that translated into a national agenda. Changes in the government of Israel in the 1990s, coupled with AIPAC's increasingly aggressive stance on some issues, gave some Jews pause. Nonetheless, AIPAC remains a formidable force on the advocacy front.

> AIPAC HAS BEEN OVER THE YEARS ARGUABLY THE MOST INFLUENTIAL VOICE IN WASHINGTON ADVOCATING ON BEHALF OF THE STATE OF ISRAEL.

Political Action Committees: The World of the Pro-Israel PAC

While advocacy organizations such as AIPAC and the defense agencies in the early 1980s conveyed their pro-Israel messages to the White House and on Capitol Hill, many American Jews, eager for more influence on who would get elected in the first place, turned to political action committees (PACs). PACs are organizations established by businesses, trade unions, and other interest groups to promote the interests of these organizations, primarily by channeling financial contributions to political campaigns. PACs solicit contributions, pool funds, and make donations to the campaigns of candidates for office at every level. PACs often coordinate their contributions, resulting in more money coming from the same set of interests contributed to a candidate.

Pro-Israel PACs first made their appearance in the 1980 congressional elections and have been a significant feature of the political landscape ever since. The 1981 struggle to defeat the AWACS sale ignited even more interest among American Jews in PACs, as both individuals and groups saw a way to engage in political advocacy in a way that was both legal and effective. In 1982, pro-Israel PACs were instrumental in bringing about the defeat of Paul Findlay (R-Ill.), one of Israel's harshest critics in the House of Representatives. Two years later, funds were directed successfully at an even bigger target, Senator Charles Percy (R) of Illinois, who at the time chaired the Senate's Foreign Relations Committee. In the 1984 elections, more than seventy Jewish PACs contributed $3.6 million to congressional candidates.

With the proven success of the numerous individual PACs, inevitably a "national PAC" had to be considered. Indeed, the establishment in 1982 of Nat PAC, a Washington-based, national pro-Israel PAC, raised concerns in many Jews, including some who had been instrumental in creating local PACs. Former AIPAC director Morris Amitay—the individual who was responsible for bringing AIPAC to a high level of visibility in the late 1970s—suggested that a national PAC would be counterproductive, indeed, serving as a whipping post for anti-Israel sentiment.

At present, most PAC money is directed not to defeat members of Congress deemed hostile to Israel but rather to elect or keep friends of Israel in office. Still, the question of how much impact pro-Israel PACs have is an important one. A high correlation between favorable voting records of members of Congress on Israel-related issues and the amount of financial support they receive from PACs and individual Jewish donors does suggest a connection. These lawmakers, however, may not necessarily be pro-Israel because of the contributions; their motivation probably has more to do with their perception of Israel's value to America's national interests, with Jewish financial support serving to reinforce these inclinations.

"Political" Advocacy

Two groups, the National Jewish Democratic Council (NJDC) and the National Jewish Coalition (NJC), promote Jewish involvement and participation in Democratic and Republican politics and parties, respectively. The NJDC was organized in 1990 for the purpose of encouraging Jewish candidates at all levels and of promoting greater Jewish involvement in the Democratic Party. The NJDC leadership hoped to maintain the pattern of a Jewish majority voting for Democratic candidates in presidential, congressional, and statewide elections. Republican Jews had already formed their own organization, the National Jewish Coalition, in 1985. In 1999, the NJC changed its name to the Republican Jewish Coalition (RJC). Both groups stressed that they were independent of their respective party's official organizations. Political observers suggested that the motivation for forming the NJDC was to prevent a recurrence of what happened in 1988, when seven state Democratic party conventions adopted resolutions supporting Palestinian "self-determination," and the issue was debated at the 1988 Democratic National Convention.

Evaluating the impact that the NJDC and RJC have had on voting patterns and other political behavior of American Jews is difficult. However, during Republican administrations, the RJC is one of the most important sources of Jewish community liaison with the White House. In 1999, the RJC also showcased all of the GOP presidential hopefuls at a one-day affair in Washington, D.C.

The NJDC has become recognized for a handful of targeted activities. During election years, the committee produces detailed information on the differences between Democratic and Republican candidates on such issues as Israel, separation of church and state, and abortion. This type of material is sent out to Jewish households in marginal districts in the form of voter guides and is widely disseminated to media outlets. The NJDC also works within the Democratic Party to advocate on behalf of these issues.

In 1996, an NJDC PAC was established to fund federal candidates. In 1999, the RJC formed a similar political action committee.

The Federation, the Federation System, and the United Jewish Communities

The federation is the central agency for the coordination of Jewish activities at the local level. While the federation is not primarily an advocacy organization, it plays a central role in the community and has, over the years, taken on some advocacy functions. And, although the federation is local, the collective influence of the federation system is broad and deep.

In America, Jews, like everyone else, relate to society as individuals. The choice to affiliate is voluntary, a fact that is crucial to understanding how the Jewish community is organized. The "federal" idea is that of a contact whereby individuals and institutions voluntarily link themselves to one another, creating partnerships that benefit all parties. The federation, a voluntary partnership of social service agencies in the community, has three functions, each of which developed along a historical time line: joint fund raising, allocations, and communal planning and coordination of social services. The advocacy function of the local federation is secondary; it consists of advocating on the local (and sometimes statewide) level for public-sector funding of services, but nonetheless an important function.

For more than a century, the umbrella body for the two hundred or so local federations in the United States and Canada was the Council of Jewish Federations (CJF), which viewed its basic mission as guiding federations in their community planning and budgeting. On the advocacy and "interest" front, the CJF represented the federation movement in the United States, Canadian, and Israeli capitals. In Washington, the Washington Action Office of the council was, and remains, an especially potent force for lobbying on behalf of federal reimbursement for social service programs and for support of legislative initiatives of concern to social service delivery agencies in the Jewish community. The potency of the CJF's Washington Action Office suggested to the community that the council could in fact deliver on federal funding and that it was a resource for coalition building on the national level.

For many decades, the CJF was one of the most significant voices in the community. Its influence derived from two sources: the CJF leadership, which was the top leadership of the community federations, and therefore the top leadership in the Jewish community; and the annual forum of the federations—the General Assembly ("the GA")— convened by the CJF. The GA was much more than just the annual convention of the federations. Held every November, the GA became *the* gathering place for individuals and groups at every level in the Jewish community locally, nationally, and internationally; it therefore was the nexus for communal planning and decision making at all levels.

After more than four years of discussion, the CJF and the United Jewish Appeal (UJA) became partners. The UJA had been principally responsible for receiving and disbursing funds from community campaigns for Jewish needs in Israel and in Jewish communities abroad. The impulse to integrate the principal federation and fund-raising structures came from the recognition of changing conditions. The fact is that an increasing portion of the funds raised by the Jewish community flows outside the federations, and in many cases these funds are specifically targeted to discrete projects of interest to donors. This system made communal leaders feel uneasy about effective functioning. The creation of a new entity out of the CJF and the UJA was seen as a step toward greater cohesiveness and coherence.

The discussions leading to a new partnership effectively put the two agencies out of business. The shift in Jewish communal ideology went from national to local (i.e., federation) "ownership" of decision making, in which intermediary agencies such as the UJA became irrelevant. Significant as well was the recognition of the increased role played in the Jewish polity by "megadollar" donors and family foundations. The new entity, the United Jewish Communities of North America (UJC), came into being in 1999. Will the UJC be the voice that the CJF was for many decades? Observers of the federation system suggest that it will be some time before the UJC has its structures in place in order that it can be the advocacy arm on behalf of the federations that it ought to be.

Other Advocacy Groups

On the international front, a number of agencies whose primary mission is social service continue to operate, but they have an advocacy function as well. Chief among these is the American Jewish Joint Distribution Committee (JDC, or "The Joint").

Reflecting the dynamism of American democratic pluralism, the American Jewish community is constantly creating new agencies to respond to new advocacy needs. The New Israel Fund, which uses innovative approaches to Israel-based philanthropy and advocacy; the Coalition on the Environment and Jewish Life; and Americans for Peace Now are examples. Not "advocacy" groups per se, notable is the growing significance of Jewish "family foundations," providing financial assistance for a range of initiatives, many of which are issues related.

Finally, the role of American Zionist groups in advocacy has been much diminished over the past fifty years as their role has been taken over by the Presidents' Conference, AIPAC, the national "defense" and community-relations agencies, and the JCPA. Most Zionist organizations are affiliated with Israeli political parties, either directly or through informal relationships.

Religious Bodies

The basic unit of American Jewish communal organization is the synagogue; the advocacy arm of American Jewish religion is the synagogue umbrella organization—the Union of Orthodox Jewish Congregations of America, the United Synagogue of Conservative Judaism, and the (Reform) Union of American Hebrew Congregations. These organizations have been most active on Israel and other issues on the international Jewish agenda and, in recent years, on church–state matters.

WHAT HAS BEEN THE INFLUENCE AND IMPACT OF JEWISH ADVOCACY ON THE AMERICAN POLITY?

Although observers perceive the Jewish community, with its multiplicity of organizations, as being chaotic, the reality is that the disparate forces do in fact work together. The resultant voice of American Jewry is an effective one and has had a significant impact on the public affairs agenda of the American polity—indeed, on the shaping of American society. It was the collective voice of American Jews that ensured U.S. support for Israel over the last half-century and secured administration and congressional backing for a tough stand in favor of the emigration of Soviet Jews. This voice immeasurably improved American society by helping shape the civil rights movement, to repeal the National Origins Quota System for immigration, to maintain and to strengthen the separation of church and state, and to provide a model for social service.

> THE VOICE OF AMERICAN JEWRY IS AN EFFECTIVE ONE AND HAS HAD A SIGNIFICANT IMPACT ON THE PUBLIC AFFAIRS AGENDA OF THE AMERICAN POLITY.

Two case studies—very different one from another—illustrate the impact that the organized Jewish community, via its advocacy agenda and activities, has had on American society.

The Struggle for Civil Rights

Contrary to conventional wisdom, the beginnings of Jewish involvement and leadership in civil rights came not in the 1950s but a decade earlier. In 1941, to avert a march on Washington threatened by union leader and civil rights activist A. Philip Randolph, who saw the expanding industrial base as a vehicle to alleviate discrimination against black employment, President Franklin D. Roosevelt issued Executive Order 8802, outlawing discrimination in certain defense industries and creating the Fair Employment Practices Committee (FEPC) to oversee enforcement. Plagued with serious employment discrimination in their own community, Jewish leaders saw their own opportunity and in turn created the Coordinating Committee of Jewish Organizations Concerned with Discrimination in the War Industries, which was incorporated in 1944 into the newly formed National Community Relations Advisory Council (NCRAC). Toward the end of World War II, as conservatives sought to abolish the FEPC—the one agency that gave "teeth" to Executive Order 8802—Jewish groups became involved with the National Council for a Permanent FEPC, started by Randolph. This coalition marked the beginning of what became known as the "civil rights movement."

Jewish groups hardly expressed unanimous support in the 1940s for making common cause with blacks. At an early NCRAC plenary session, the wisdom of coalition building with blacks caused stirring debate. Rabbi Stephen S. Wise, a leader in the AJCongress and National Association for the Advancement of Colored People (NAACP), made the case for continued involvement based not on "liberal" principles (although the Jewish community was a decidedly liberal one) but on Jewish self-interest. The Wise rationale, a rearticulation of the original reasons for involvement in civil rights issues, carried the day.

It was in the communities, with the growing Jewish community-relations council movement, that the black communities were seen as natural allies. During the 1940s, the community-relations councils were spearheads of the techniques of coalition, and CRCs established local human relations councils and committees that pioneered the technique of coalition building and that served as the primary vehicles for black–Jewish relations. A new strategy, the use of law and social action, emerged to fight discrimination. This strategy was spearheaded by Jewish community-relations agencies (particularly the AJCongress) and was embraced by the NAACP and the NAACP Legal Fund. The Leadership Conference on Civil Rights, founded by the NCRAC and the NAACP and staffed by the NCRAC, exemplified the joint activity of the NAACP and the Jewish community. Community by community, during the 1950s, featured local versions of the Leadership Conference arose around the country. The first pieces of civil rights legislation—local and state fair-housing laws—resulted from activity by local NAACPs and JCRCs.

With the growing success of the civil rights movement, the character of the relationship changed. The coalition expanded, and other groups came in. The relationship on the national level (less so locally) began to change. The *struggle* became a *movement*. As issues became more complex, we saw disillusionment and frustration on the part of many blacks that their daily lives did not change as their hopes and aspirations were stirred by the great—indeed, revolutionary—victories of *Brown v. Board of Education*, the Civil Rights Act of 1964, the Fair Housing Act, and the Voting Rights Act of 1965. Furthermore, with the emergence of the "black power" cry, black leaders rejected erstwhile allies, leading to a new perception that the ally was the enemy.

Whatever the causes and results of the broken alliance, the history is one of an alliance that was rooted in Jewish advocacy and—more to the point—national and local Jewish advocacy groups working together in a coordinated manner.

The Fight over AWACS: Advocacy on Behalf of the State of Israel

The period from the Six-Day War in 1967 to the Oslo peace process in 1983 represents a "golden era" of advocacy on behalf of the state of Israel. But the most significant event in pro-Israel advocacy—the point at which the organized Jewish community realized that it could mobilize a major national advocacy effort—was the struggle over AWACS.

The sharpest clash between Washington and Jerusalem in the fifty-plus years of their relationship arose in 1981 over the Reagan administration's plan to sell Saudi Arabia some $8.5 billion worth of highly sophisticated airborne warning and control system surveillance—AWACS—aircraft, together with advanced missiles, fuel tanks, and other equipment, in order to enhance the military capabilities of the sixty F-15s that the United States had originally agreed to sell the Saudis in 1978.

The task for opponents of the sale was to persuade Congress to express disapproval, requiring a majority vote in favor of disapproval in both houses of Congress following formal notification by the administration that it intended to sell military equipment overseas in order to prevent the sale from going forward. While the Jewish community's effort to stop the AWACS sale failed (the House voted for disapproval by a margin of 301–111, but the Senate voted in favor of the sale, 52–48), the ability of Jewish groups to act in a coordinated manner to develop a grassroots and national advocacy network left a deep impression both on the Hill and in the corridors of the administration. AIPAC played a leadership role in the struggle; indeed, AIPAC emerged as an advocacy force, perhaps *the* advocacy force, to be reckoned with. But a pivotal role was played by the NJCRAC (now the JCPA), which provided the grassroots mobilization that gave AIPAC the community underpinnings that it needed do its work on the Hill. Analysts suggest that the AWACS campaign led the defense agencies, heretofore unchallenged as the leaders in the Israel advocacy arena, to accept a dominant role for AIPAC in this arena.

The bottom line on the fight over AWACS: Even as the AWACS struggle was in the "loss" column for American Jewish advocacy groups, it was in this exercise in advocacy that the Jewish community overcame its fears of vulnerability and "exposure"—thereby discovering a critical mass of self-confidence—and proved that it could engage in a formidable coordinated advocacy effort among the grassroots, on the Hill, and in the administration around an issue on which there was communal consensus.

CONCLUSION

No self-identifying group in the United States offers as many institutions that provide opportunities for advocacy as does the American Jewish community. The multiplicity of Jewish organizations, however, is the strength, not the burden, of the Jewish community.

Moreover, the basic institutional format of the community, with its abundance of organizations, is one that provides for active debate on a range of issues.

NO SELF-IDENTIFYING GROUP IN THE UNITED STATES OFFERS AS MANY INSTITUTIONS THAT PROVIDE OPPORTUNITIES FOR ADVOCACY AS DOES THE AMERICAN JEWISH COMMUNITY.

The Jewish community consensus has been shaped over the years on the basis of pragmatic considerations, not as a direct result of conceptual frameworks. We have seen, of course, a high degree of consensus on general conceptual formulations that did define the debate. But questions of values and priorities, while they always underlay the community's approaches, were rarely at the forefront of the issue. These questions have been sharpened in recent years. To take but two examples, in 1988 the "Who is a Jew?" question forced Jews into defining and redefining themselves. The Soviet Jewry issue moved the American Jewish community to ask whether it ought to function on the basis of long-held freedom-of-choice positions or on the basis of the well-being of a Jewish national movement. These questions were about values rather than responses to the pure pragmatics of an issue. This defining of the debate on the basis of values in addition to pragmatics has added an important dimension to the question of consensus.

A number of approaches to the question of consensus and dissensus continue. But the core of the issue is not whether consensus is unraveling. The judgment of many observers is that consensus is a sign of increasing maturity. Thus, the American Jewish community can handle the degree of dissensus that exists on some issues without becoming defensive, as was the case in the past.

On the other hand, the Jewish community is not in danger of being "balkanized." Most Jews in America do not concede to any one organization the right to express their particular views; they may well look to a number of different organizations, and this dynamic is very important in shaping the voices of the community. American Jews are willing to accept a fair amount of elasticity on views and positions, as long as basic, elemental consensus positions (e.g., the security of the state of Israel) are at their core. These basic positions remain strong and secure.

Having said this, we might note that certain issues on the American domestic agenda, as we have entered the twenty-first century, could cause an unraveling of consensus. The funding of social welfare services is increasingly—and legitimately—a public sector function. The issues surrounding social service funding are likely to result in a widening gap between the federation world, which wants to protect the public funding to its facilities, even if many of those facilities are under sectarian auspices, and the community-relations sphere, which is committed to the pluralistic ideals of the separation of church and state.

The strength of the Jewish community—and, by extension, of Jewish communal advocacy—lies in the pluralistic structure of the community. The community does not seek unity merely for the sake of unity but in order for the community to achieve collectively

THE STRENGTH OF THE JEWISH COMMUNITY—AND, BY EXTENSION, OF JEWISH COMMUNAL ADVOCACY—LIES IN THE PLURALISTIC STRUCTURE OF THE COMMUNITY.

its shared goals. One perception has it that the American Jewish community, with its multiplicity of agencies, is chaotic. The reality is that the community possesses the mechanisms that are capable of getting these disparate, often cacophonous, voices to work together. This collective voice—an effective one in terms of its impact on public policy, as we have seen—is the envy of other groups. The vitality demonstrated by this coordinated activity bodes well for the future of the American Jewish polity.

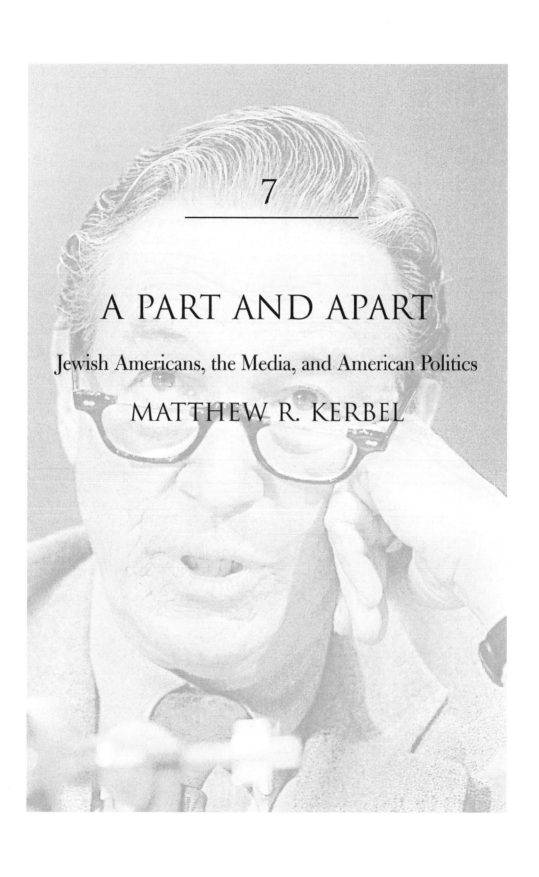

7

A PART AND APART

Jewish Americans, the Media, and American Politics

MATTHEW R. KERBEL

The enterprise of journalism in America, like the country of which it is part, has continually redefined itself over the decades, as a pencil-and-paper entity termed "the press" gradually morphed into the information and entertainment beast we call "the media." Partisan organs of nineteenth-century political parties yielded to the mass appeal of cheap newspapers, which later succumbed to the more immediate mass appeal of radio, then television, and now cyberspace. Anonymous reporters became correspondents, and correspondents became columnists, then pundits, then celebrities. Individual ownership of the arms of mass communication succumbed to massive octopus-shaped conglomerates, which sprouted an almost uncountable number of appendages in the form of cable stations, on-line magazines, radio and television networks, film studios, theme parks, and the like, nominally in competition with one another but in fact attached to the same body and head.

The story of this evolution parallels the movement of American economics from agrarian to industrial to high-tech; politics through a long period of increased franchise and diminished partisan attachment; and culture from the installment novel to vaudeville to the *Late Show with David Letterman*. At each turn, the press recorded and reflected these changes, invariably assuming a new shape better suited to the period it helped usher in.

From the beginning, the names of the people who witnessed and forged these changes were both Jewish *and* Gentile. They became publishers and editors, reporters and columnists—people with influence owing to their ownership of the press and those with influence owing to their skillful contributions to what was published and broadcast. For the Protestants among their ranks, it is safe to say that religious self-identification was not a universally important component of how they went about their work. But, for the Jews, it does not overstate the case to say that religious orientation—or, at least, those cultural aspects of being Jewish in a Christian world—was of overriding concern. Even for those like Walter Lippmann, who steadfastly avoided all mention of his Jewish heritage, it was throughout his life the five-ton elephant in the middle of the room.

The issue is a familiar one: how to handle the countervailing pressures of fitting in and being different. For some, like Lippmann and publisher Joseph Pulitzer, the question was how to assimilate into a society that considered them Jewish despite their best efforts to leave their heritage behind. For others, like RCA founder David Sarnoff, the dilemma was how to maintain a Jewish cultural identity while still claiming full participation in the elite strata of American society. As baby boomers came to power in a more open social climate, the question was often like the one faced by artist-turned-mogul Steven Spielberg: how to deal with the ambivalence produced by dual Jewish and American self-identification.

The issue of Jewishness even extended into policy decisions—for example, the decades-long refusal on the part of the House of Sulzberger to install Jewish managing editors at the *New York Times* for fear of being classified as a "Jewish" paper by a

Gentile establishment. Jewishness influenced political decisions, like the willingness of Louis B. Meyer and the first generation of film moguls to embrace the censorship of Will Hays in order to prove their devotion to the more conservative values of Protestant America. It shaped creative decisions, like Teddy White's novelization of politics—a model for a generation of political reporters that served to nudge journalism toward "infotainment"—rooted in his tendency to value compassion more than professional orthodoxy or, as Joyce Hoffman claims that White's immigrant grandparents put it, his tendency to be "a *mensch* first and a journalist second" (5–6).

To read the accounts of these and other prominent Jews in American media is to feel as if one were reading the same account over again. Variations abound, to be sure: some stories recount the experiences of immigrants; others, of immigrant children or grandchildren. Some stories are of the rags-to-riches variety; others tell of affluent beginnings in the suburbs or on Park Avenue. But these diverse details mask a common theme: the struggle between the values and customs of the Old World and the new, a conflict caused by competing pressures or desires to be simultaneously the same and different. The struggle inevitably includes encounters with open or latent antisemitism from the larger society and, not insignificantly, between Jews of Central and Eastern European backgrounds. It ultimately produces a strategy that allows individuals to accept their past, or to hide it, or modify it, or mollify it; to determine a livable boundary between being visible and invisible; to self-identify or assimilate.

THESE DIVERSE STORIES MASK A COMMON THEME: THE STRUGGLE BETWEEN THE VALUES AND CUSTOMS OF THE OLD WORLD AND THE NEW, A CONFLICT CAUSED BY COMPETING PRESSURES OR DESIRES TO BE SIMULTANEOUSLY THE SAME AND DIFFERENT.

Theirs is hardly a story confined to journalism, but if it is striking that many Jewish media notables were defined by their struggle with identity, it is noteworthy how well suited the field is for Jews seeking an assimilation strategy. Among owners—the publishers and movie moguls and network chiefs—fluidity in the media offered the prospect for swift upward mobility and social influence, a more rapid entry into the corridors of power than had been possible for many decades through electoral politics, big business, and other staid professions in which for decades Jews were simply unwelcome. For practitioners, the complex role of journalist as witness to history, simultaneously present and detached, nicely mirrors the predicament of being Jewish in a Gentile world. Journalism offered the enticing prospect of being able to gain real power in that world as a chronicler of its events, while remaining professionally and personally apart from it.

The battle with assimilation among Jews in the media tells half the story of their influence. The remainder is about the effect that their strategies had on their professional actions and journalistic judgments that, because they were so public, made their mark on the conduct of their profession and, on more than one occasion, on broader political and cultural developments. Throughout the twentieth century, as the media played an increasingly noisy role in the production of popular tastes, and

IT IS NOTEWORTHY HOW WELL SUITED THE FIELD OF JOURNALISM IS FOR JEWS SEEKING AN ASSIMILATION STRATEGY.

as journalism shifted from largely informing a readership to largely entertaining an audience, the options available for assimilation changed as dramatically as the culture into which Jews sought admission. But those cultural changes were themselves touched by the presence of the Jewish media owners and writers who came before. As ethnic and racial diversity became an uneasy agenda item in the politics of the latter half of the twentieth century, Jewish journalists (among others) were well placed to cover it and, by covering it, to embody it. The result was a different set of options for those who still struggled with what it meant to belong and be different simultaneously. If the dilemma hadn't changed, the possibilities for confronting it had.

The story of Jews in the media is an interesting one because it encompasses a fundamental human struggle, trades on matters of power and influence, and embodies the world of newspaper, television, and film that seems so glamorous to the uninitiated. The struggle has also been a long one, going back at least as far as the early nineteenth century, back when political parties owned the press and called the shots.

Although Jews represented a fraction of those who worked in the antebellum press, the tiny Jewish community that populated pre–Civil War America counted among its members the newspapermen Jacob Cardozo, Abraham Levy, Jacob I. Cohen Jr., Lewis Levin, Edwin DeLeon, Jacob DeCordova, and Naphtali Phillips. Perhaps the most celebrated member of this group was Mordecai Noah, who rose to political prominence as the editor of New York's Democratic-Republican newspaper, the *National Advocate*. His story reads like a prototype for Jews who would follow him in the next century.

> THE JEWISH RECORD COMPARED THE PASSING OF LINCOLN BEFORE HE COULD SEE THE FRUITS OF HIS WAR-YEAR LABORS WITH MOSES' DEATH ON MOUNT PISGAH IN SIGHT OF THE PROMISED LAND.
>
> —BERTRAM KORN

Noah was devoted to news management with flair. In an era when newspapers could rely on the party faithful to fork over their nickels for the privilege of reading juicy partisan attacks on the opposition, Noah recognized he could increase readership by writing in a lively style and broadening coverage to include entertaining features. In as much as he was interested in methods of appealing to a mass audience, Noah was ahead of his time, anticipating the penny press of the latter part of his century and, to no small degree, the mass media of the next. Part newsman, part showman, Noah combined the two most prominent characteristics of contemporary media—its informative and entertainment functions—a century before people recognized the amusement value of information.

This strategy made him something of an outcast (other editors thought his methods "indecent"), but it also won him attention from the Jacksonian establishment. Over the course of his career he became an important figure in politics and journalism, and as his influence grew, so did the antisemitic attacks against him. These slurs forced him to confront his Jewish identity as someone who wished to exercise power in America while maintaining his ties to his religious community. Again foreshadowing others who would follow in his path, Noah's dilemma proved to be a lifelong struggle and, ultimately, one without a satisfactory resolution. Squeezed by competing desires to find acceptance for his differences and to find peace through assimilation, Noah worked hard for both (even to the point of advocating a separate homeland for Jews in upstate New York)—but achieved neither.

By the end of his life in 1851, Noah had won respectability and influence in the Jewish community, but many Jews were uneasy about the way he moved through Christian society. Among Christians who accepted him, he was regarded as a Jew, which is to say as someone who was really of another world. Synthesis of the two spheres escaped him; neither group could accept the apparent contradictions in his desire to, as Jonathan Sarna has noted, "act as a good Jew, to be recognized as a 'good Christian,' and to identify as a good American—all at the same time" (142).

The poignancy of Noah's dilemma and the futility of his efforts to resolve it reverberate through the stories of Jewish publishers, studio heads, and network chiefs for a hundred years to come. The period from the late nineteenth century through the Great Depression was a time when newspapers were at the apex of their influence, and when moving pictures, forerunner of what would grow to be the "electronic media," were beginning their embryonic challenge to print. It was also a time marked by blatant antisemitism of the sort that touched Mordecai Noah, when Jews seeking acceptance in the larger society had to play down or renounce their ancestry. Against this backdrop, two of the most prominent Jewish publishers of the period did their utmost to assimilate: Joseph Pulitzer by joining the Episcopal Church and avoiding involvement with Jewish causes; and Adolph Ochs by embracing the look, politics, and work ethic of the elite stratum of Protestant America.

As Jews of Central European origin, their inclination to assimilate came rather naturally. Indeed, Ochs was from a family of pre–Civil War German immigrants of some stature in the old country, who had begun the process of assimilation in Europe. They settled in the American South at a time when the Reform movement gave Jews seeking to fit in a way to remain nominally Jewish while discarding those Orthodox practices that made Jews stand out as aliens. But Ochs retained his Jewish identity during his time in Knoxville and later in New York, marrying the daughter of a prominent Reform rabbi and maintaining cultural self-identification with Judaism even as he self-consciously made the *New York Times* appeal to upscale Christian sensibilities.

Accordingly, his newspaper carried all the marks of assimilation and the quest for elite acceptance. During his tenure as publisher of the *Times* from 1896 through 1935, while he was fashioning what would later be considered the "newspaper of record," Ochs rewarded cautious editorial decisions and dull writing and favored conservative morality. If his was a stilted approach to journalism, an audience for it existed at the turn of the last century, and Ochs parlayed his approach into an empire. He was fastidious about the possibility that, because of his background, the *Times* would be dismissed as a "Jewish paper," and he battled against this characterization with an unspoken rule that no Jew could become part of the senior editorial staff. His was a "policy" that continued for decades after the rabbi's son-in-law departed. Gay Talese recounts that during the 1930s, it was remarked that the *Times* was "owned by Jews and edited by Catholics for Protestants" (70).

Pulitzer's relationship to Judaism and journalism is a nice counterpart to Ochs's. A German-speaking Hungarian immigrant who embraced his new country by serving as an underage Union soldier in the Civil War, Pulitzer settled in the German immigrant enclave of St. Louis during Reconstruction. There, through early efforts in journalism and politics that included a stint in the Missouri legislature, he witnessed official corruption and was repelled by it. No less interested than Ochs in his status as an American, Pulitzer nonetheless saw journalism as a vehicle for challenging what was wrong in America: social inequity, abuse of power, and the plight of immigrants during a time of great anti-immigrant sentiment. These concerns followed directly from Pulitzer's Jewish heritage, his experience as an immigrant, and the virulent antisemitism he faced throughout his career.

> PULITZER SAW JOURNALISM AS A VEHICLE FOR CHALLENGING WHAT WAS WRONG IN AMERICA: SOCIAL INEQUITY, ABUSE OF POWER, AND THE PLIGHT OF IMMIGRANTS DURING A TIME OF GREAT ANTI-IMMIGRANT SENTIMENT.

But Pulitzer was not one to marry into a prestigious family of Reform Jews. If he didn't attend services at St. George's, his children were baptized there, and he did not attend synagogue or take part in Jewish activities. Unlike Ochs, who self-identified as a Jew even as he attempted to assimilate into high society, Pulitzer identified with an immigrant class and, subsequently, with the emerging urban middle class of the post–Civil War era, of which some of his fellow Jews were a part. Thus, Pulitzer's *St. Louis Post-Dispatch* and later his *New York World* took up the reformist causes heralded by these groups. Ochs's *Times* and Pulitzer's *World* were bookends of sorts, embodying the two great traditions of turn-of-the-century journalism: the *Times* chronicled for posterity the actions of the ruling class; the *World* challenged their abuses for a less affluent readership.

Not coincidentally, these differences parallel the assimilation choices made by their publishers. Perhaps because Pulitzer was not a practicing Jew, he did not feel the compunction to exclude Jews from the same important positions on his paper as Ochs did. Indeed, in the 1920s, at the peak of the *World*'s influence, Herbert Bayard Swope was executive editor, and Walter Lippmann presided over the editorial page. However, Pulitzer's sensitivity to social inequity came directly from his ethnic background. If reformist causes did not find a prominent place in the pages of Ochs's *Times*, it was because they were excluded from the package of cultural considerations that the publisher took with him as he sought a place as an assimilated Jew in early-twentieth-century society.

At roughly the same time, a child of impoverished immigrants from Minsk was finding his way in the world as a ragpicker and junk dealer, first in St. John, New Brunswick, where his parents had settled, then later in Boston and New York. Poor, unskilled, and "cursed" with the *yiddishkeit* demeanor of Russian Orthodox Judaism, Louis B. Mayer faced duel discrimination from poor Christian youths who would beat him up for his differences and from Ashkenazi Jews of the sort who aspired to identify with the *New York Times*.

This twin discrimination stirred in him an overpowering need for acceptance in his new land. Like many Jewish immigrants, Mayer (or perhaps his parents) Anglicized his name. When his real birthday was lost to immigration records, he created a new one for himself: Independence Day, the Fourth of July. But as a Russian Jew with a deep sense of self-identification, Mayer would for his entire life seek full acceptance without giving in to demands for full assimilation. He would marry (the first time) a cantor's daughter. His burial service would be in a fashionable Wilshire Boulevard synagogue. And in between marriage and death, people would tell numerous stories—some apocryphal, some true—in which his Jewish self-identification would come out in the most unlikely places. Crowther relates that he once instructed the singer Jeannette MacDonald to put more *schmaltz* into her presentation, demonstrating how to do it by getting down on his knees and performing "Eli, Eli" (6–7).

The conflict posed by the need for acceptance and the wish to retain a Jewish identity with links to the *shtetl* revealed itself in the lord of Metro-Goldwyn-Mayer through the types of films his studio produced and in the political agenda he pursued. As a filmmaker, Mayer was prudish, even puritanical, embracing scripts that embodied his version of conservative, small-town America: morality plays that emphasized the goodness of patriotism, community, and what in a later day would be dubbed "family values." These renderings of American life had nothing to do with his own history—certainly, they had no connection to the ruthless way he ran his studio. But they resonated with a middle-American audience who wished to see itself in these morals and with a movie mogul who craved acceptance by middle America.

If these values sound like something directly out of the Goldwater wing of the Republican Party, it should not be surprising that Mayer was personally involved in conservative Republican politics throughout his career. As a friend and confidant of President Herbert Hoover, Mayer found some of the social acceptance he badly needed. Nevertheless, his interests were economic as well as social, and he engaged in political action whenever it would render both economic self-benefit and affirmation by what he considered to be mainstream America.

THE CONFLICT POSED BY THE NEED FOR ACCEPTANCE AND THE WISH TO RETAIN A JEWISH IDENTITY WITH LINKS TO THE SHTETL REVEALED ITSELF IN THE LORD OF METRO-GOLDWYN-MAYER THROUGH THE TYPES OF FILMS HIS STUDIO PRODUCED AND IN THE POLITICAL AGENDA HE PURSUED.

The premiere example of this occurred in 1934: Mayer flexed his political muscle on behalf of California gubernatorial candidate Frank F. Merriam in an effort to stop the insurgent candidacy of Upton Sinclair, who had espoused a socialist agenda in a depression year while threatening to assess new taxes on the film industry. Mayer's success with what some called a smear campaign—featuring fake newsreels suggesting that Sinclair supporters were (ironically) unkempt, untrustworthy immigrant types—marked his entry into cutthroat politics. But for all his bluster and political success, Mayer could not completely eliminate the feeling that he was still one of those strange-sounding immigrants whom other, more secure forces could manipulate at will for *their* political purposes if conditions changed.

As the century progressed, American society presented Jewish media moguls with a new set of opportunities tempered by familiar restrictions. The generation who came to power following World War II operated in a world that was less outwardly hostile to Jews. But they had to deal with rough waters under the calm surface as well as the occasional roiling rapids, most notably the Red Scare of the 1950s that implicated many Jewish journalists and artists as communist sympathizers.

Under the tutelage of Arthur Hays Sulzberger, the wealthy son-in-law of Adolph Ochs who took control of the *Times* in 1935 and ran it for twenty-six years, there was a deep self-consciousness about the paper's place in the American establishment. A modest, soft-spoken man from a privileged background, Sulzberger would shepherd the *Times* through a period of diminishing fortunes for urban dailies, making changes to remain competitive (e.g., the introduction of more pictures) while remaining true to the careful reporting on which the paper had built its reputation. His policies generated a significant readership that remained loyal to the *Times* even as other papers found their circulation dwindling, and Ochs's background was well suited to his policies.

As publisher of an establishment paper whose family roots dated to some of the earliest Jewish settlements in America, Ochs was very sensitive to the truism that the *Times* would remain an icon of American journalism through the early Cold War days only if it downplayed its Jewish connections. If the times were a-changin' during the latter part of

Sulzberger's reign, the *Times* certainly was not—at least, not that much. Despite an increase in the number of qualified Jewish editors on the *Times* staff, Sulzberger maintained his father-in-law's record of not promoting any Jew to managing editor. Intentionally or not, editors and reporters with Jewish names often found their by-lines sporting innocuous first and middle initials: three Abrahams—Rosenthal, Raskin, and Weiler—were converted, respectively, to A. M., A. H., and A. H. Whether or not this "initialization" was a matter of policy was impossible to know at a shop like the *Times*, where such allegations could be whispered but never spoken and where official actions were shrouded in vagueness. But Jewish employees viewed the "policy" as an open secret.

Intentional or otherwise, Sulzberger's "sensitivity" to his paper's Jewish identity did serve to keep up appearances in an era when keeping appearances was critical to getting along at the level that the paper had achieved for itself in earlier days. If Sulzberger did not use his clout and influence to advance the place of Jews in American journalism, it was because he was more inclined to advance the place of his paper in American journalism, and that meant applying to his company the same assimilation strategies championed by Adolph Ochs. Metaphorically, the *Times* at midcentury played the role of the Ashkenazi Jew seeking parity with the Gentiles who shared its class sensitivities if not its country clubs.

> METAPHORICALLY, THE NEW YORK TIMES AT MIDCENTURY PLAYED THE ROLE OF THE ASHKENAZI JEW SEEKING PARITY WITH THE GENTILES WHO SHARED ITS CLASS SENSITIVITIES IF NOT ITS COUNTRY CLUBS.

For the Jewish barons of the new or emerging electronic media, for whom shepherding their product to a mass audience did not require the high level of elite acceptance sought by the *Times*, midcentury circumstances permitted a less desperate psychic struggle than that experienced by the moguls of earlier years. Not to say that conflict was not present, but, in keeping with the tenor of the period, one often had to look beneath the surface to find its cleavages.

Two mass media pioneers provide the paramount example of media giants from this period who chose different strategies to reconcile their Jewish identity with their professional roles. Bill Paley of CBS and David Sarnoff of RCA and later NBC were both of Russian ancestry, and although Paley was born in Chicago while Sarnoff was a young boy when his immigrant family settled on New York's Lower East Side, key similarities marked their backgrounds. Both families traced their roots to the *shtetl*, and both had experienced persecution in Russia and loss of status in the United States. Paley's grandfather had operated a successful lumber business, and Sarnoff's grandfather held an important place in the Jewish community of Minsk. But both found themselves starting over in America.

By the time Paley was born, his father had built a successful cigar business, and like many first-generation American Jews, he grew up in relative comfort one generation removed from the ways of the ghetto. In contrast, Sarnoff grew up in a home where tradition was still in place, a difference that may explain the contrasting strategies that they used to deal with their Jewish identities. Sarnoff lived in an Orthodox home, keenly aware of the striking contrast between his world and the broader life of Gentile America. Friends say the differences made an impression on the young boy, who was at times confused and even distressed by the different standards and actions of the two worlds. Sarnoff took this awareness of being an outsider with him on his professional journey, and as he rose rapidly to the top of his field, he continued to express the sense of being an outsider, at times speaking out publicly about the meaning he found in his Jewish heritage.

By contrast, Paley experienced mixed messages in his home, from a pragmatic father who had little interest in Jewish observances, to an Orthodox mother who held Shabbat services in Hebrew. Although he was confirmed at a Reform temple, by the time he was a teenager Bill Paley found little of relevance in the practice of his religion. A pragmatic individual like his father, the adult businessman Bill Paley found little practical value in being Jewish, especially since his Jewishness meant being barred from the more fashionable clubs and restaurants. But he could not escape his background or the prejudice he encountered because of it. The result was ambivalence about his identity. Paley would contribute generously to Jewish causes yet choose to vacation in a Protestant enclave on Long Island; he would intermarry and not attend temple but insist on a Jewish education for his children. Later in life, he would express resentment toward David Halberstam, who wrote of Paley's uncertainty about his heritage and what Halberstam regarded as efforts by Paley to be a social climber in WASP society.

Neither Sarnoff nor Paley fully appreciated how the other reconciled his relationship to Judaism, differences no doubt fueled by their professional rivalry but rooted in their different worldviews. Sarnoff thought Paley was pretentious, a WASP wanna-be yearning to jettison his past in order to enjoy social status commensurate with his wealth and power. Paley felt Sarnoff was something of the hypocrite to find meaning in his Jewish past if what it meant to be a Jew was to do little more than maintain membership in the heavily secular Reform congregation Temple Emanu-El.

But not too surprisingly, between the two, it was Paley who, as president of CBS, created the news organization that would be the electronic counterpart to the *New York Times*. Whether or not Paley's wish for acceptance was craven, it was consistent with his decision to create what for over two decades would be the gold standard of television news, and to do so at great cost. Year after year, CBS News would lose money for the network but pay dividends in prestige. Paley the businessman willingly picked up the check, cognizant that his news division was a shrewd investment, at the same time giving Paley, the irresolute Jew, a chance to take pleasure in the warm glow of elite praise.

Paley's was a monument worthy of Adolph Ochs, facilitated by a man whose desire for acceptance was on a par with his print counterpart. Paley didn't rebuff his Jewish identity as meticulously as Ochs did, because he didn't have to: the era in which he operated permitted room for the ambiguity he felt, provided he kept it to himself. But the drive for approval that fueled his actions was remarkably similar.

Perhaps the greatest challenge to the position of these powerful Jews came during the Red Scare. Among entertainers and writers were a number of Jews who had been drawn to the actions of the Soviet Union in the thirties, largely as a means of opposing Hitler. As these Jews were singled out or blacklisted, a virus of antisemitism pervaded the effort to purge the nation of communist sympathizers.

The response of Sulzberger, Sarnoff, Paley, and Mayer was equivocal. Although the *Times* pursued an editorial policy condemning McCarthyism, Sulzberger released employees, Jewish and Gentile, who took the Fifth Amendment in congressional testimony. Because Jews headed all three television networks (Leonard Goldenson was at ABC), the pressure to acquiesce to Washington was felt at the top, making the fifties an unpleasant time for lower-ranking executives of Jewish origin. Although at the time few CBS executives were Jewish, career advancement for those who were resembled the plight of their brethren who sought to be managing editor of the *Times*. As late as 1958, when Paley appointed Louis G. Cowan president of the CBS Television Network, he made it clear that the appointment would not have gone through had Cowan's family not had the foresight to change its name from Cohen.

For old-time immigrant conservatives like Mayer, the Red Scare proved to be another round in which he needed to finesse his loyalty to America while protecting his interests (at one point, testifying before Congress that there were communists in Hollywood, but the studio heads had everything under control). As blacklists persisted in the entertainment industry, the studio chiefs tried hard to maintain their distance from the proceedings playing out on the other side of the continent, hopeful that the hand of the inquisition would not touch them. Hardly a communist sympathizer, Mayer nonetheless held on through a period when his adopted country turned ugly in its treatment of his kinsmen.

But Mayer's time was about to come to an end, his cohort to be replaced by people like Lew Wasserman of MCA, the talent agency that would swallow Universal Studios—moguls for whom assimilation took on a more Ashkenazi touch. In the comparatively gentler period to come, Wasserman was able to borrow a page from Sulzberger and accomplish a level of assimilation his predecessors dreamed of.

Wasserman's biography looks more like Mayer's than Sulzberger's: an Orthodox upbringing, no formal education, a self-made self-starter, jealous for the approval of powerful Gentiles. But Wasserman operated in an era that enabled him to reach out beyond Hollywood to the WASP power centers of southern California, and he had the wherewithal to know how to do it and the inclination to try.

Thus, Wasserman's kingdom looked more like Sulzberger's than Mayer's. His strategy: appeal to Gentiles by appearing Gentile, or at least by appearing to embrace Wasserman's sense of dark-suited Gentile sensibilities. Brownstein has noted that at MCA, everything was "designed to suggest stability, continuity, discretion. . . . Agents were rarely fired, and rarely quit. 'It was like a Jewish Irish Republican Army,' said Jere Henshaw, a former executive" (184–85).

These efforts afforded Wasserman extraordinary political sway as a national power broker who could command Hollywood's money and glamor in concert with the Gentile establishment of Norman Chandler's *Los Angeles Times*. His was quite a combination and quite a coup for the Orthodox Jew from Cleveland who felt no qualms about assimilating to a degree that his more conflicted predecessors were unable to do.

If Wasserman felt secure in his ability to walk the corridors of Gentile power, he also didn't share Mayer's need for validation through the production of middle-American morality plays. So as the 1960s passed into the 1970s, Hollywood began producing a greater diversity of films acknowledging the social changes of the time. The Episcopalian version of Hollywood would feature a much wider array of voices, including, ironically, Jewish voices that were not explicitly treated as such in earlier times.

By the 1980s, tremendous change had come to the media. In film, Lew Wasserman had set the table for the next generation of moguls: Fox chairman Barry Diller; Disney's Michael Eisner whose empire would include ABC television; Steven Spielberg, the new-era film mogul whose power arose from commercial artistic success. At the *New York Times*, Arthur Sulzberger's son "Punch" was well on the way to preserving his family's dynasty by instituting changes that would produce a more up-tempo "newspaper of record" with a lively style that would have horrified his grandfather. By and large, these second-plus-generation Americans and baby boomer Jews were more secure than their predecessors, even if they weren't free of conflict about their identity. And why not? The culture they lived in and helped produce was far different than what had come before.

THE SECOND-PLUS-GENERATION AMERICANS AND BABY BOOMER JEWS WERE MORE SECURE THAN THEIR PREDECESSORS, EVEN IF THEY WEREN'T FREE OF CONFLICT ABOUT THEIR IDENTITY.

Punch Sulzberger didn't have to produce a button-down newspaper to win acceptance by Gentile America because cultural changes—produced in no small part by the media—made room for the colorful ways of immigrant groups and their descendants. There was a fair amount of irony in this modernization. The mass culture spun in Hollywood and New York by moguls and owners looking to assimilate played on the classical myth of the American dream. While those with power and money tried to live the dream by renouncing or reworking their pasts, the fruits of their labors permitted a later, more settled generation to embrace their differences in a way the previous group could not. Being an outsider was becoming mainstream.

Spielberg's story provides a good illustration of this phenomenon. As a second-generation American baby boomer, he was one generation removed from the persecution experienced by his religious Russian ancestors but quite familiar with prejudice experienced firsthand in the Protestant suburbs of Cincinnati, Camden, and Phoenix. Much like the moguls of an earlier day, the future creator of *E.T.* would feel, according to McBride, "like an alien" and "wanted to be a Gentile with the same intensity that [he] wanted to be a filmmaker" (18).

In the gray-flannel world of the 1950s, Spielberg tried to reject his Jewish roots in an effort to treat his ambivalence and his sense of being an outcast. In an earlier day, he would have probably pursued an assimilation strategy based on denial of his "otherness" and the desperate quest for acceptance by the American majority on their own terms. Indeed, during the early portion of his career, Spielberg did just that. But by the 1990s, other avenues were available for sorting out these conflicts, owing in no small part to a higher level of acceptance by mainstream America of some things ethnic. Against this backdrop, and wishing to reconcile his internal conflict, Spielberg began to embrace his Jewish past in a manner that previous moguls could and would not. Louis B. Mayer produced films celebrating an idealized midwestern Puritanism; Spielberg produced *Schindler's List*. And with it, he helped popularize the suffering that his predecessors felt that they had to deny in order to succeed.

Because of his experience as mogul and artist, Spielberg's story bridges the worlds of ownership and creativity, of power wielded through wealth and power earned through influence. During the century of Ochs, Sulzberger, Paley, Wasserman, and Spielberg, we see a parallel story of Jews who worked as editors, writers, reporters, and columnists. They, too, experienced some of the same doubts about their identity that the moguls and the owners did, and in much the same way, the climate of the times in which they lived shaped the resolution of their dilemmas. But as practitioners of a craft with the ability to influence society, they more than the owners were on the forefront of reinforcing, challenging, and shaping cultural expectations. Over the course of a century, they would change the art of journalism, the content of popular culture, and the place of traditional Jewish norms within that culture.

> BECAUSE OF HIS EXPERIENCE AS MOGUL AND ARTIST, SPIELBERG'S STORY BRIDGES THE WORLDS OF OWNERSHIP AND CREATIVITY, OF POWER WIELDED THROUGH WEALTH AND POWER EARNED THROUGH INFLUENCE.

Specifically, they would be involved in the century-long shift from journalism as an informative craft to news as an entertainment medium, calling on two sets of related skills deeply rooted in Jewish history: the ability to instruct and the ability to amuse. In the years before the Great Depression, when assimilating meant playing to Protestant tastes, reason and judgment were the hallmarks of good journalism. The midcentury transition to entertainment-oriented news saw the introduction of narratives to political coverage and commentary, as news became informative and enjoyable. With the arrival of the boomers, mass tastes had broadened and been transformed, and news had evolved into a source of entertainment that played on the ability to communicate and engage more than lecture or teach.

For Jewish practitioners, these changes influenced the skill sets that would be professionally rewarded as they shaped the various strategies available for dealing with a Jewish heritage. Many people could be addressed here: Izzy Stone and Irving R. Levine; Henry Anatole Grunwald at *Time*, Marvin Stone at *U.S. News & World Report*, Edward Kosner at *Newsweek*; columnists William Safire and Charles Krauthammer; Larry King, Mike Wallace, and Leslie Stahl. To name a few is simply to draw attention to those left out.

Several exemplify the journalism of their period in unique ways: Walter Lippmann, as one of the most influential voices of the first part of the century; Teddy White, the entrepreneurial journalist of the transitional middle years; Barbara Walters, the first Jewish and female television news anchor, during the century's close.

Lippmann was a man of ideas in a day when journalism's purpose was to inform and to open eyes. He wrote of the conflict and struggle of a world in flux, and in one important respect the political events he chronicled and influenced mirrored an internal struggle with self-acceptance and self-identification. His personal turmoil revolved around what to do with his Jewish identity—a commonplace conflict in the era of Adolph Ochs and Louis B. Mayer—although his rejection of his Jewish past was far more dramatic than either one.

Like Ochs, he was born to a Reform Jewish family of German origin. But the similarities end there. Lippmann lived in a privileged New York home, a second-generation American in 1889 whose father manufactured clothing and whose mother was a college graduate. As a child, he would regularly travel through Europe with his parents; as a small boy he would meet President McKinley. With other children of wealthy German Jews, he attended the Sachs School for Boys, in preparation for his undergraduate years at Harvard.

If these family and institutional cues pointed to assimilation, they were of a piece with Lippmann's religious upbringing. His family belonged to Temple Emanu-El, where successful nineteenth-century German Jews could distinguish themselves from their unassimilated and unsuccessful Russian counterparts living in less fortunate New York neighborhoods. Although Lippmann was confirmed, Steel asserts that he readily developed a perspective on religion as a "social convention" or an "act of bonding" that tied people of a class to one another and to the society at large (p. 7). Lippmann's was a deft act of reasoning that masked deep ambivalence about his religious heritage. In a world where being Jewish in fact meant being kept apart, Lippmann rationalized that if one removed all that was religious from the practice of Judaism and experienced it as just one more component of an upper-class life, one would be free to live that life without prejudice. Lippmann wanted others to see the Jewish component of his background as a matter of class rather than religion, as the difference between Temple Emanu-El and the Lower East Side. But he lived in a Protestant world that was more inclined to see Jews as Jews; in a personal portfolio with all the right credentials, Lippmann's religion would be the one thing to mark him as an outsider. He would battle against this part of himself his entire life.

Like many Jews who desperately sought to assimilate, Lippmann's semitic heritage was his demon. Those close to him sensed how tormented he was about it and knew not to bring it up. One friend even admitted to feeling dread over the possibility that she would draw the letters *J-E-W* when playing Scrabble with Lippmann, for fear that it would unearth feelings he could not control.

LIPPMANN WANTED OTHERS TO SEE THE JEWISH COMPONENT OF HIS BACKGROUND AS A MATTER OF CLASS RATHER THAN RELIGION.

Although he never converted, he submerged his Jewish heritage. Lippmann never talked about being Jewish—to the point where some who considered him a friend didn't know the great journalist was Jewish until they heard it from others. He did not support Jewish causes or even speak to Jewish groups. But, as Steel has noted, assimilation exacted a price in the form of "being cut off from one's origins and trying to fit into a society where one was never fully secure" (9).

As a public man, ignoring his Jewishness left a telling gap in his work. The great opinion leader who would comment on every major world event of his day was curiously silent about things Jewish. Before World War II, he wrote nothing about the plight of European Jewry. He did not criticize Franklin D. Roosevelt for failing to act against the Holocaust. He never mentioned the death camps. He had little to say about Zionism, short of endorsing an alternative that would have shipped all "surplus" European Jews to Africa.

When he did address Jewish issues, a rare phenomenon, it was in his private papers. In personal correspondence with the editor of the *Menorah Journal*, Lippmann blamed antisemitism on Jews who invited negative comment from Gentiles by virtue of their strange manners and ways. He had no sympathy for Jews who felt the bite of prejudice, and his recommendation to them was to assimilate as he had. Lippmann's was a cold, unfeeling sentiment, which stood in stark contrast to the public stand he had taken against the suffering experienced by other social groups as the editorial voice of Pulitzer's reformist *World*.

To harbor hostility toward and say little publicly about Jews makes sense in terms of Lippmann's personal strategy for dealing with his Jewishness. It explains why a commentator as worldly and prolific as Lippmann would ignore a group whose presence was so much a part of the events in his day. It speaks to his dilemma of trying to reconcile personal animosity with professional imperatives in an age when journalism was about ideas and influence, and Judaism was a delicate topic to approach.

Had Lippmann come of age later in the twentieth century when prejudice was less ferocious and overt, he might not have found the struggle with Jewish self-identification to be as tumultuous. But then he probably would not have found his far-reaching platform for the exercise of journalism as ideas. On both counts, he exemplified an era that began to change by midcentury.

As late as 1942, when the Jewish ownership of the *New York Times* still denied Jews top editorial posts, the paper of record devoted a mere two column inches to reports of the Nazi slaughter of seven hundred thousand Polish Jews—and buried the story inside the paper. However, as the century moved forward, the *Times*'s Jewish leadership would promote to managing editor Max Frankel, a Polish refugee whose remarkable story of escape from the Nazis barely spared him from inclusion in that nearly overlooked statistic. And Frankel, for his part, could embrace America as a patriot while embracing his Jewish identity. The opportunities and the options were simply different.

Similarly, as the *Times* began to lose its addiction to somber prose under Punch Sulzberger's leadership, and film messages became more diversified under Lew Wasserman and the second generation of film moguls, conditions supported a more experimental—and entertaining—style of journalism. By century's end, the *Times* would print color pictures and political reporters would expose every juicy detail of presidential misconduct. Into the period of transition between these two worlds marched Teddy White, the journalist/novelist who approached politics as a blend of fact and illusion, much the way he integrated the competing influences of his success-minded Orthodox Jewish mother and his cause-oriented socialist father.

In many respects, White's struggle for acceptance was more problematic than Lippmann's, because White did not begin with social advantages. But where Lippmann strove to eliminate his Jewish identity, White reached for synthesis. Accordingly, where Lippmann's journalism is neglectful and disdainful of Jews, White's writing is a tribute to the diverse and often contradictory influences in his Jewish home.

White was the son of poor Russian immigrants whose father abandoned the traditional ways of his own rabbi father as readily as he jettisoned the Vladefsky family name. White's boyhood home in Boston was an eclectic place, with his devout mother talking about the Talmud and his father talking of Karl Marx. Where Lippmann faced the prejudice of Protestant America, White experienced this discrimination and the disdain of Lippmann's wealthy German Jewish descendants (like Lippmann, White would attend Harvard, but with the dual outsider status of Jew and commuter student). Indeed, Lippmann's encouragement of Jews to avoid antisemitism through assimilation was aimed directly at Theodore White's family.

For their part, White's parents would not have disagreed with Lippmann's ends, and perhaps only his mother would have disagreed with his proscribed means. But the efforts of White's parents to find acceptance for their children through education and hard work, while successful, would instill in the future journalist a lifelong tension between the Old World influences of White's youth and the America of his adulthood. According to Hoffman, "despite his abundant success, the struggle for acceptance encumbered White's life—he would never forget that he was born Jewish and poor" and that, ultimately, White "would have to redefine what it meant to be a Jew" (15–16).

This exercise, in the context of the contradictory social messages White heard at home, meant navigating concepts that did not obviously go together: Old World and new, compassion and achievement, socialism and religious orthodoxy. It was a dilemma like the one that William Paley faced, but if Paley the businessman experienced ambivalence, White the journalist found synthesis, an approach he would apply with great success to his internal contradictions and to his work.

Writing as he did in a period of transition, White successfully synthesized information and entertainment, finding drama in political news and combining a novelist's appreciation of prose with a journalist's understanding of events. Earlier in the century, this combination might have put White out of favor in a profession that at times did not permit poetic license to its practitioners. Instead, White forever changed the practice of political reporting by injecting first-person observations and interesting, even "poetic" prose into his writing, in a manner that would influence the generation of political reporters that would come of age under the influence of his writing.

THEODORE WHITE FOREVER CHANGED THE PRACTICE OF POLITICAL REPORTING BY INJECTING FIRST-PERSON OBSERVATIONS AND INTERESTING, EVEN "POETIC" PROSE INTO HIS WRITING.

A harbinger of changes to come, his political reporting would take the reader behind the scenes to unmask the process by which a candidate becomes president. It would capture and embellish the feel of the campaign, with the victor seemingly elevated to a higher existence, as if touched by the mystical hand of his mother's God so as to advance (at least, in the case of John F. Kennedy) the benevolence of his father's social agenda. White's journalism was varying parts information, entertainment, historical record, and fiction. It was he who, writing as the mouthpiece for Jackie Kennedy, coined the term "Camelot" days after Kennedy's assassination to capture (inappropriately, some would argue) the meaning and flavor of the slain president's administration. It was he who would open the floodgates for the more interpretive and personalized journalism of the late twentieth century.

Because, by century's end, the term "infotainment" had entered the vocabulary. The ranks of journalists would expand to include White's fellow Bostonians Mike (Myron Leon) Wallace and Barbara Walters, who would bring a mix of journalism and show business to their craft in a manner inconceivable to Walter Lippmann. Their journalistic careers developed in the mold of the late-century "personality" whose identification was to a medium first, to journalism second. True, they were reporters, but they were *television* reporters: the medium afforded them celebrity status, and their great success made them stars.

Theirs was success born of the ability to master the performance requirements of the medium. Wallace, like White a child of Russian Jewish immigrants, would become famous for his hard-hitting investigative style that was in fact honed on celebrity interview programs. Before the respectability of *60 Minutes,* Wallace appeared on gossipy vehicles like *The Chez Show* and *Mike and Buff* with his second wife Buff Cobb.

Perhaps no one exemplifies the journalist–as–popular culture icon more than Barbara Walters, the sometimes compassionate, sometimes tough interrogator of the beautiful, rich, and powerful (television does not distinguish between movie stars and political stars). She would become the first Jewish and first female anchor of a network evening news program. Born to a show business family and an environment of social contradiction, Walters at an early age experienced some of the same cross-pressures felt by Jews in earlier periods, although with a distinctly show business cast. Her father's family, likely of Lithuanian origin, was artistic, intellectual, and colorful, in contrast to her mother's more earthy family of Russian immigrants. However, for all his refinement, her father was also a gambler, and during her childhood, Walters would experience dramatic reversals of fortune as her father built and gambled away fortunes, only to build new ones to gamble away.

Lou Walters made and lost his money at the margins of show business, as a nightclub owner. The glamor of his work conflicted with a sense of illegitimacy in the mind of a nice Jewish girl whose identity, like so many of her predecessors in journalism, was largely secular. Over the course of a childhood that followed her father from Boston to Miami to New York, back to Miami, then again to New York, Walters came to know the institutions of the Jewish well-to-do. She played at a Jewish summer camp in the Berkshires and was educated at upscale private schools catering to children of wealthy secular Jewish families.

Nothing in her early days suggests an interest in journalism. At Sarah Lawrence, Walters is described in her unauthorized biography as having been one of a group of nonpolitical Jewish students, who stayed away from campus activism while cultivating an interest in fashion. But if her background might not predict a career in show business, it is certainly not at odds with one. Observers struggle to know exactly what Walters made of the contradictions between her father's public life and his private dealings or of the Gentile trappings of her Jewish prep schools, for she has never authorized or written a biography and prefers conducting interviews to giving them. But the pattern of her upbringing as a secular Jew in a show business world provided Walters with excellent credentials for the television journalism of her time. Cultivating a smooth and elegant image while remaining personally distant and mysterious, Walters sculpted a persona that invited her audience to identify with her and encouraged her guests to open up to her. This technique worked well on the small screen, where skilled practitioners can selectively draw from their experience to decide what viewers will see, while downplaying or hiding the rest. If Barbara Walters's Jewish past is not a key part of her public persona, it is because she chooses not to make it so. That she could attain such a high level of success with a background that might have bedeviled others speaks to the nature of her industry and is a sign of her times.

By the end of the twentieth century, mass journalism had provided its practitioners with an imperfect solution to the dilemma faced by generations of Jewish publishers, moguls, and journalists. Television, with its emphasis on personalities, gives journalists a way to decide what they want their public profile to be. By adding a healthy dose of acting to a profession that was previously about writing, television added a new dimension to the age-old journalist's dynamic of being simultaneously separated from and intertwined with events. For the first time, the detached participant can be distinguished from the personality on the screen. From this perspective, it might not seem so ridiculous for a news personality to claim, like Mordecai Noah, to be a good Jew at home, a good Christian on the air, and a good American all the time. Acting makes possible a kind of compartmentalization between the public and private self, affording television journalists a solution to questions of Jewish self-identification not available to generations of practitioners whose words and actions were viewed by society or by themselves through the filter of Jewish identification.

THE PATTERN OF HER UPBRINGING AS A SECULAR JEW IN A SHOW BUSINESS WORLD PROVIDED BARBARA WALTERS WITH EXCELLENT CREDENTIALS FOR THE TELEVISION JOURNALISM OF HER TIME.

Critics have said that dwelling in the world of celebrities has generated an unfortunate lightness in journalism and undermined the solemnity of the profession. However, if television has taken the celebrity culture to previously unthinkable levels, we should still remember that some of the earliest American journalists brought a touch of the showman to their work. And while some among the generations of Jews in the media would no doubt be appalled by the extent of celebrity journalism in our culture, they would have to concede that having the ability to create a persona can short-circuit a lot of angst.

IT MIGHT NOT SEEM SO RIDICULOUS FOR A NEWS PERSONALITY TO CLAIM, LIKE MORDECAI NOAH, TO BE A GOOD JEW AT HOME, A GOOD CHRISTIAN ON THE AIR, AND A GOOD AMERICAN ALL THE TIME.

It's hard to know what Mordecai Noah would think of Barbara Walters. But the Jew who sought but never won the approval of his countrymen might well appreciate the way she resolved his biggest dilemma.

8

THE POLITICS
OF MINORITY
CONSCIOUSNESS

The Historical Voting Behavior of American Jews

IRA N. FORMAN

[T]he only difference between the Democratic Party and Reform Judaism [is] the holidays.

—Richard Brookheiser as paraphrased by J. J. Goldberg in *Jewish Power*

"The Jews: Forever Liberal Wherever They Are"

—Chapter title from *The Ethnic Factor* by Mark Levy and Michael Kramer

If an observer were to stand on the great millennial divide separating the twentieth and twenty-first centuries and gaze back into the mist of American Jewish political history, two landmarks would stand out most starkly: the Democratic Party and liberalism. But taking out binoculars and staring more intently, the landscape below would appear far more complex.

This chapter reviews the record of American Jewish political and voting behavior, a relatively easy exercise if readers are just interested in the recent past and the liberal Democratic nature of Jewish political behavior. But the task gets progressively more difficult as one extends that gaze further into the past, to times in which the data are far less complete and the details sketchier. Yet every period provides themes highlighting useful perspectives on not just the American Jewish experience but also on the nature of American politics.

METHODOLOGY

The American political system of 1800 was strikingly different from the system of 1900, which in turn was dramatically different from today's. Jewish demography is critical for understanding American Jewish voting in each case. The American Jewish community of 1800 was minuscule, a mere two thousand individuals, a bit less than 0.04 percent of the American population of 5,300,000. By 1950, the Jewish population had grown to 4.7 million Jews, 3.1 percent of the total. Moreover, Jewish Americans have long been concentrated in a number of urban areas. For example, during most decades, between one-third and one-half of the American Jewish population has resided in the greater New York City region.

The analysis of Jewish voting behavior in a historical perspective is made most difficult by the lack of reliable data sources. Before the mid–twentieth century, of course, no scientific public opinion surveys existed. The best set of surveys across time sampling a large number of Jewish voters on political matters are the exit polls done after each federal election since 1972. However, these surveys only register Jewish voter preference for president and Congress; they do not measure other political attitudes. Thus, this chapter relies largely on measures of partisan voting behavior to draw conclusions.

Top Five Jewish Population Centers, Selected Years

City	1860	1890	1910	1940	1970	2000
New York metro/NE NJ	35,000	205,000	1,173,000	2,310,000	2,440,000	1,886,000
Cincinnati	8,000					
Philadelphia	7,000	40,000	140,000	250,000	380,000	276,000
Baltimore	6,000	15,000				
Boston	2,300		70,000	160,000		
Chicago		50,000	135,000	290,000	253,000	261,000
San Francisco		16,500				
St. Louis			35,000			
Los Angeles				130,000	520,000	600,000
Southeast Florida					200,000	507,000
Total U.S. Jewish population	150,000	475,000	2,050,000	4,200,000	5,500,000	5,800,000
Percentage of total in top 5 cities	38.9	68.7	75.8	74.8	69.0	60.9

Before the 1880s and the influx of large numbers of refugees from Eastern Europe, precinct data do not exist at all. In these decades one has to rely on anecdotal evidence—descriptions in written sources of Jewish political behavior or analysis of the partisan attachments of Jewish officeholders and political party officials. For the purpose of trying to make educated guesses about Jewish partisan attachments before the New Deal, a database of approximately three hundred Jewish elected/party officeholders, their city of residence, and their political party was created.

In the period from the 1890s until the New Deal, the analysis of Jewish election districts offers some insight into Jewish partisanship in different elections. Clearly limitations with using these data to assess nationwide or even statewide Jewish voting does cause some difficulty. It is, for example, wrong to assume that a sample of Jews in neighborhoods that are exclusively Jewish are representative of the voting of Jews who lived in more "integrated" neighborhoods.

IT IS WRONG TO ASSUME THAT A SAMPLE OF JEWS IN NEIGHBORHOODS THAT ARE EXCLUSIVELY JEWISH IS REPRESENTATIVE OF THE VOTING OF JEWS WHO LIVED IN MORE "INTEGRATED" NEIGHBORHOODS.

From the New Deal until 1972, when exit poll data became available, one can only make educated guesses about Jewish voting for president or Congress. These educated guesses are probably fairly accurate for the presidential vote back to the 1930s. In this period ever more sophisticated polls in jurisdictions with large Jewish populations and analysis of precinct or election districts that were nearly 100 percent Jewish enabled analysts to make reasonable estimates of Jewish voting behavior.

Despite all these limitations, the existing information is still very rich and provides the curious with a great deal of insight on the political preferences of American Jews. We will examine this behavior separately in each of the periods designated as distinct party systems by those who study party history.

THE FEDERALISTS AND THE JEFFERSONIANS: 1789 TO 1828

During this period, Federalists battled Democratic-Republicans during a time in which political leaders still looked on parties as inherently dangerous to the health of the republic. After 1800, the Federalists were too weak in many areas of the new nation to pose a threat to Jeffersonian dominance. After the conclusion of the War of 1812, the Federalists outside New England ceased to exist as a political force altogether.

However, the Federalists, led by Alexander Hamilton and John Adams, advocated a stronger role for the federal government in the economy. The party was much more suspicious of such ideas as universal white manhood suffrage and the naturalization of immigrants. The Federalists believed that government should and could legislate in the area of morality. One such example was their support for Sunday closing laws—hereafter referred to as "blue laws."

The Democratic-Republicans were founded by Thomas Jefferson and James Madison in the early 1790s in opposition to Hamiltonian policies. The party was committed to states rights and deeply suspicious of all government power on the grounds that the rich and wellborn would use such central authority to further enrich themselves, their families, and their friends. Though men like Jefferson clearly did not believe in the rule of the uneducated mob, they were more democratic in their views toward political rights and much more welcoming of immigrant populations.

The few Jews of this era were concentrated in a handful of cities. Charleston, the city with the largest population of Jews in 1800, and New York City, with the second-largest number of Jews, accounted for nearly one-half of the Jewish population of America. The community was probably made up of a majority of Sephardic Jews, descendants of Dutch, Portuguese, English, and Spanish Jews, all of whom had been uprooted over the centuries by the Spanish and Portuguese Inquisitions. With such a small population, no electoral jurisdictions had majority Jewish populations. Therefore, one must rely on written accounts of Jewish partisan attachments.

Based on the two parties' very different issues agenda, most Jews in the 1790s and the first three decades of the nineteenth century probably identified with the party of Jefferson. Federalists' antagonism toward immigrants (they passed the Alien and Sedition Act), Federalist support for government enforcement of Christian morality, and Federalist attacks on Jefferson because of his insufficiently Christian religious beliefs all must have made postcolonial Jews suspicious of the party of Hamilton and Adams. Moreover, Jefferson argued for the disestablishment of the Anglican/

Episcopalian Church in Virginia, and Madison and Jefferson were vigorous proponents of the religious freedom provisions of the Bill of Rights. When, during the Adams administration, the parties split over foreign policy (Federalist sympathy for the British and Democratic-Republican support for France), Jews must have been reinforced in their pro-Jefferson proclivities by the anticlerical nature of the French republic.

> JEWS MUST HAVE BEEN REINFORCED IN THEIR PRO-JEFFERSON PROCLIVITIES BY THE ANTICLERICAL NATURE OF THE FRENCH REPUBLIC.

This account is not to argue that no Jews were Federalists. Given Federalist policies, any Jews who were significant creditors or those involved in manufacturing goods that competed with European wares would have had economic reasons for identifying with the party supporting a strong central government. In fact, the Jewish historian Jacob R. Marcus believed that in the first years of the Republic "a substantial number of the Children of Israel were Federalists" (527, 579).

However, the bulk of the evidence available regarding the tiny postcolonial Jewish population of the United States leads one to believe that most Jews were Democratic-Republicans. To begin with, in a number of known incidents the Federalists used antisemitism as part of their attack on the followers of Jefferson. In the 1800 election, the *Gazette of the United States,* one of the leading Federalist papers of the day, attacked the Philadelphia Jewish leader Benjamin Nones for being a Jew and a Republican. Arthur Hertzberg recounts that Nones shot back, "How then can a Jew but be a Republican?" (56).

Moreover, the vast majority of Jews who we know were active in politics appear to have been Democratic-Republicans. All twelve of the Jews who we identified as holding elective or party office between 1790 and 1818 identified with the party of Jefferson and Madison. Jews in this era held public office as Republicans in Maryland, Philadelphia, and Richmond; a number of Jews were early leaders of Tammany Hall in New York City; and Simon Snyder was actually the Republican Speaker of the Pennsylvania House at the beginning of the nineteenth century.

WHIGS AND JACKSONIAN DEMOCRATS: 1828 TO 1860

At the beginning of the 1820s, America was a one-party nation. The Democratic-Republicans had overcome all opposition. However, within the Jeffersonian Party divisions grew. By the end of the decade, the party had split into a Democratic faction attached to Andrew Jackson and Martin Van Buren, and a National Republican faction associated with John Quincy Adams and Henry Clay.

By the mid-1830s, the National Republicans had morphed into the Whig Party. The Whigs supported a stronger federal government and were devoted to high tariffs, a strong central bank of the United States, and internal improvements to aid in economic expansion. They were strong proponents of government playing a larger role in support of morality and/or religion. The Whigs were often also the party with an active nativist component. Whigs were strongest in parts of New England but did have significant voting strength in all sections of the country.

The Jacksonian Democrats combined a distrust of banks with a continued Jeffersonian dislike of strong central government and high tariffs. The Democrats were more enthusiastic in endorsing a politics of mass participation and more accommodating to naturalized American citizens, particularly Irish Catholics. They used populist ideology and rhetoric to attack strong central government as a threat to the common man. However, even though manufacturing and merchant interests were often Whigs, party identification was not strictly correlated with economic status during this period.

The Jews of Jacksonian America were still a very small minority, but in the 1840s and 1850s, their numbers rose dramatically with an influx of German immigrants. Between 1820 and 1840, the Jewish population multiplied by a factor of five (3,000 to 15,000) and it grew to 150,000 by the outbreak of the Civil War. During this period, New York became the preferred destination for immigrant Jews, while Philadelphia, Boston, and Cincinnati also became centers of Jewish population. Most Jews in this period lived in the Northeast, but approximately 20 percent of American Jewry lived in the South in the decades leading up to the Civil War.

As the party that had welcomed immigrants, the Democrats in the decades preceding the Civil War were a more natural home to the large number of Central European Jews pouring into New York and other East Coast port cities. The Democrats of this era were also more sympathetic to the notion that all white males regardless of religion had equal political rights, though they were often less concerned than the Whigs with the rights of blacks and Native Americans. The party that was opposed to government interference in the moral sphere was probably also a better fit than the Whigs, who were more likely to call for enactment or enforcement of blue laws. In addition, President Van Buren's strong denunciation of the Damascus blood libel in 1840 must have helped solidify Jewish identification with the Democrats. And as the revolutionaries fleeing the European revolutions of 1848 came to the United States, they found a party system in which the Democrats were still regarded as the more egalitarian and radical of the two parties.

Jews who were engaged in finance and large-scale commerce might have been more interested in the American system of Henry Clay and the Whigs. Though many businessmen of the era were Democrats, those who were less suspicious of banks and those convinced that government could play a positive role in economic development found the Whigs to be a congenial cohort.

In his study *Jacksonian Jew: The Two Worlds of Mordecai Noah,* the historian Jonathan Sarna found evidence that significant Whig support among Jews flourished in New York in the late 1830s, particularly among the older Sephardic Jews, who were probably more assimilated into American culture and materially better off than their

Ashkenazi brethren (100–01). Moreover, it is likely that some Jews resented the growing role Irish Catholic immigrants played in large urban, Democratic political machines. In the late 1850s, when Democratic President James Buchanan refused American Jewish demands to question the Vatican for kidnapping a Jewish Italian child in the Mortara affair, observers were quick to point out that in the last decade the Catholic vote had become a major source of support for the Democratic Party.

Nonetheless, at the eve of the Civil War most Jews remained in the Democratic constituency. J. J. Goldberg notes that Abraham Jonas, who had been a Whig state legislator from Illinois, a longtime friend of Abraham Lincoln and later a Republican partisan, wrote as late as the 1860 campaign that Jews had been voting Democratic by a two-to-one margin.

AT THE EVE OF THE CIVIL WAR MOST JEWS REMAINED IN THE DEMOCRATIC CONSTITUENCY.

The first Jewish members of Congress were elected in the Jacksonian era. In the Senate, David Yulee served as a Democrat from Florida; Judah Benjamin from Louisiana was a Whig who became a Democrat by the late 1850s. In the House, Emanuel Hart, a loyal Tammany supporter, served from 1851 to 1853; Henry Phillips, a Democrat from Pennsylvania, served from 1857 to 1859; and another Democrat, Philip Phillips from Alabama, served one term in the 1850s. Most surprising, one Jew from Philadelphia, Lewis Levin, was elected as a representative of the anti-Catholic/anti–Native American or Know-Nothing Party in the 1850s. Jewish officeholders and party activists from 1828 to 1859 may be not entirely representative of the era as most of the officeholders from this period were elected in the 1850s when the close Whig–Democratic competition had already disappeared. Nonetheless, this summary does point to the Democratic Party's majority status in the Jewish community. Twenty-eight of the Jews who served were Democrats; three, Whigs; one, an American Party officeholder; and three, Republicans, a party that only emerged after 1854.

REPUBLICANS AND DEMOCRATS REFIGHT THE CIVIL WAR: 1860 TO 1896

The 1850s witnessed the collapse of the Democratic–Whig Party competition over the issue of slavery. A new sectionalized system of Democrats and Republicans emerged. In the North, formerly Whig and Democratic voters flocked to the short-lived, nativist American Party and a new free-soil Republican Party. In the South, the Whig Party vanished, and the region became a one-party Democratic bastion.

With the end of Reconstruction and the de facto disenfranchisement of African Americans in the South, a new partisan alignment emerged. Americans voted as they fought. In the Upper Midwest, portions of Pennsylvania, and much of New England, the GOP was unchallenged. Similarly, in much of the South, the Republican Party faded into oblivion. In the border states, the mid-Atlantic, New York, Ohio, and Indiana, partisan fighting was intense. In the North, urban political machines organized the votes of European immigrants. In New York City, Democrats dominated; while in Philadelphia, the Republicans were the majority party. Once Reconstruction ended, the two parties were evenly matched in Congress, and presidential races were all closely contested.

At the beginning of this era the Jewish community continued to grow steadily, especially from an influx of German Jews. From 1860 to 1880, the Jewish population of the United States rose from about 150,000 to 250,000. By the 1880s and 1890s, the fallout from severe pogroms in the Russian Empire led to an explosion of immigration of Eastern European Jews. In the 1880s, the Jewish population nearly doubled and then doubled again in the 1890s to reach 1,000,000 in 1900.

New York was at the heart of this demographic explosion. Between 1860 and 1890, the city's Jewish population grew from 35,000 to 195,000. Throughout the period New York represented nearly 40 percent of American Jewry. At the same time, Philadelphia's Jewish population rose from 7,000 to 40,000; and Chicago's rose from 1,500 to 50,000. By 1890, other cities with 5,000 or more Jews included St. Louis, San Francisco, Boston, Cincinnati, Baltimore, Cleveland, Pittsburgh, and New Orleans. According to figures compiled by Simon Wolf at the turn of the century, about 20 percent of Jews who fought in the Civil War came from Confederate or slave states (143–144). By the 1890s, a much smaller percentage of American Jewry lived in the South.

Among Jews, Civil War loyalties played a major role in partisan attachments during this era. With few minor exceptions, the Jews of the South were passionate Democrats. Similarly, the German Jewish populations in Upper Midwest cities were likely to be Republicans.

> AMONG JEWS, CIVIL WAR LOYALTIES PLAYED A MAJOR ROLE IN PARTISAN ATTACHMENTS DURING THIS ERA.

For example, in the city of Chicago a Jewish Democrat and Douglas elector in 1860, Henry Greenbaum, turned to the Republican Party after 1860. He was typical of many German Jews from the Windy City. According to Edward Mazur's account of Jews in Chicago, the Jewish paper the *Occident* regularly pushed the Republican ticket and crowed that "the majority of our intelligent Israelites in Illinois were with the Republicans" (95). In the 1870s and 1880s, Yiddish-speaking Jews began to break with their German co-religionists and voted Democratic—especially on the local level. German Jews, who often attended Reform temples that met on Sundays, supported Protestant reformers who backed those local Republicans who wanted to close saloons on Sunday and forbid all commercial transactions on the Christian Sabbath. Meanwhile, their Yiddish-speaking brethren joined the Irish and Bohemians to vote for Democratic mayor Carter Harrison, who specialized in reaching out to his immigrant constituents.

Mazur explained this partisan split between Jews by postulating that "for post-war arrivals the [Civil War] had little if any direct meaning" (112).

During the Civil War, New York was a northern city that often demonstrated southern sympathies. That meant that after the war the city was largely Democratic, more often than not under the control of Tammany Hall. Some German Jews in New York supported the GOP, but some German Jewish businessmen were Democrats. They were anti-Tammany Democrats who followed reform Democratic governors like Samuel Tilden or Grover Cleveland; they were called "Swallowtails" for the long-tailed formal coats they often wore. The Jewish swallowtails were men like Henry Morgenthau Sr. and the Strauss brothers (who came from Georgia to New York with their partisan attachments intact). Jeffrey Gurock reports that the poor Yiddish immigrants who began pouring into the city in the 1880s were often Tammany voters (73–74). However, these Jewish immigrants sometimes broke with the machine to support non-Tammany reform candidates for New York mayor such as Henry George. These reformers appealed to the immigrant Jews with calls for clean municipal government; they were most often successful when they were sensitive to immigrant concerns like fighting antisemitism and not enforcing blue laws. In national elections, Tammany appears to have carried Jewish election districts more often than not for "the Democracy."

In this period nine Jewish Democrats (including one United States senator) and five Jewish Republicans were elected to Congress. Two of these congressmen came from New York City, and there were also representatives from Philadelphia, Boston, Chicago, and Baltimore. But most of these United States representatives came from such non-Jewish districts in Louisiana, California, Michigan, and rural Pennsylvania. The sixty Jewish officeholders and party officials identified in this period are evenly split among Democratic and Republican partisans.

Because of what is known about New York, Chicago, and southern Jewry, as well as what is known about the partisan attachments of Jewish officeholders, one can guess that the Jews of this era were evenly divided between the two main parties in America. Within the community, the older-stock German Jews in the North were decidedly more Republican than the more newly arrived immigrants.

POPULISTS, PROGRESSIVES, AND GOP MAJORITIES: 1896 TO 1932

The Depression of 1893 and the capture of the Democratic Party by the forces of agrarian populism insured the dominance of the Republican Party at the end of the nineteenth century and during the first three decades of the twentieth century.

At the beginning of this period the Democratic Party's new leader, William Jennings Bryan, turned the party's traditional opposition to governmental activism on its head. Unlike earlier Democrats who believed the activist government inevitably led to corruption, Bryan reasoned that in an era of rampant monopoly, the only power capable of protecting the public from the corruption of big business and big finance was government power. Bryan Democrats stood for inflation (the free coinage of silver) and low tariffs to help the agrarian South and West against the power of Wall Street and the industrial East. The Democratic Party of this period was often associated with the forces of rural fundamentalism. However, the party also adopted the mantle of progressive reform by championing antitrust measures, the eight-hour workday, and direct election of United States senators.

The Republicans of the era—from McKinley to Hoover—were also a mix of conservative and progressive forces. However, by the 1920s the forces of conservatism within the GOP had overwhelmed the progressivism of Theodore Roosevelt and Robert LaFollette.

By opposing Bryan's populism, the Republicans of this era cemented their hold on the electoral map of the country. States like Ohio and New York became Republican bastions, and the border area, which had once been Democratic, became highly competitive. In much of the Northeast and Midwest, the Democratic voting base was only among the immigrants of the large cities. Democrats controlled the South and were competitive in agricultural areas of the Plains states and the silver mining areas of the Mountain states, but that defined a losing coalition. The country became even more sectionalized by party than it had been in the immediate aftermath of the Civil War.

Meanwhile, the Jewish population grew as the stream of Russian, Polish, and Galician immigrant Jews continued unabated until the outbreak of World War I and also in 1919 until the change in immigration laws in the early 1920s. Nationwide, the Jewish population went from 1.0 million in 1900 to 3.9 million in 1930. New York's Jewish population jumped to nearly 500,000 in 1900, 1.1 million in 1910, and about 1.8 million in 1930. Other eastern and midwestern industrial centers saw similar growth in their Jewish population. The German Jews who had arrived in the mid–nineteenth century were largely wealthy or middle class fifty years later. However, the larger community was overwhelmingly poor and working class, as the number of Eastern European new arrivals overwhelmed the Germans.

The Jewish community did not follow the national trend to the GOP in this era. The older-stock Germans probably still voted their Civil War loyalties. However, the newly naturalized immigrants were much more fickle in their partisan attachments. To begin with, they did not evidence the strong party loyalties that had been a trademark of most American voters in the late nineteenth century. Moreover, many of these voters were more susceptible to the allure of the American Socialist Party.

At the beginning of the era, Jewish voters in the eastern and midwestern cities were undoubtedly affected by the fear of rural populism represented by Bryan in 1896. Some populists of the era bandied about antisemitic economic theories, and the GOP was also

In the eighteenth century, Catholics were disfranchised in five states and Jews in four. . . . New York City in 1908 took a swipe at Jewish voters, many of whom were Socialists, by holding registration on the Jewish Sabbath and on the holy holiday of Yom Kippur.
—Alexander Keyssar

quick to point out the dangerous economic consequences of Free Silver to an urban working class that was always concerned about unemployment. Moreover, Jewish businessmen, especially those who were large creditors, feared Democratic Free Silver.

Politicians of both parties appealed to Jewish voters by attacking antisemitism at home and abroad. Republican presidents of the era were quick to pledge opposition to attacks on the Jews by European despots. In New York, Tammany Hall politicians were quick to attack domestic discrimination policies.

On the local level, Jewish urban voters, unlike their urban Irish counterparts, were very open to calls for reform of municipal government. However, the same reformers who appealed for clean government often showed insensitivity to Jews and other immigrants by pushing enforcement of blue laws. While Jewish voters in cities like New York were capable of turning on the machine politicians, they were, more often, supporters of these machines. In New York, Tammany Hall struggled to keep Jewish voters loyal. Sometimes they used the same tactics they had used with the Irish—help with the city bureaucracy, lower-level patronage jobs, free pails of coal in the wintertime, and Passover baskets in the spring. By the turn of the twentieth century, Tammany was beginning to slate Jews for elective office as a means of keeping the Jewish vote in line.

On New York's Lower East Side, the Irish boss, John Ahearn, controlled the heavily Jewish Fourth Assembly District. Throughout the teens and twenties, Ahearn's precincts turned in higher Democratic percentages than other Jewish neighborhoods because Ahearn had perfected the practice of providing patronage, doling out favors, fighting discrimination, and slating Jewish candidates. However, in the nearby heavily Jewish Sixth Assembly District, the Republican leader Samuel Koenig ensured higher Republican percentages than other Jewish neighborhoods in the city by use of the some of the same methods.

By the second decade of the twentieth century, the success of the Socialists also convinced the Democrats of Tammany that they would have to adopt social welfare policies to keep this growing voting bloc in line. Tammany legislators in Albany, men like Al Smith and Robert Wagner, were perfecting this appeal by the end of the Progressive era.

Between 1896 and 1930, seventeen Jewish Republicans (including two United States senators), fifteen Jewish Democrats (including one United States senator), and two Jewish Socialists served in the United States Congress. The two hundred Jewish officeholders and party officials identified from the same years reveals similar ratios—slightly more Republicans than Democrats. One would guess that these Jewish officeholders were drawn proportionally more from the more established German Jews (normally Republican) than from the more numerous Yiddish-speaking Jews.

Voting data from heavily Jewish precincts, wards, and districts are accessible in some cities, especially after the turn of the century. From such figures in New York, Chicago, and Boston, a picture emerges of a Jewish electorate that was not solidly committed to any political party. Republican presidential candidates Theodore Roosevelt in 1904 and Warren G. Harding in 1920 won the Jewish vote. But Democrats Woodrow Wilson in 1916 and Al Smith in 1928 also enjoyed majority support among the Jews of the United States. In the other presidential contests of the era, the vote in Jewish precincts is somewhat closer. For example, a sampling of Boston Jewish precincts from 1908 until 1920 (see table) reveals the sometimes evenly split allegiances of the voters.

Presidential Votes in Heavily Jewish Boston Precincts, 1908–1920

Year	Democrat	Republican	Socialist	Progressive
1908	Bryan	Taft	Debs	
	48.5%	47%	4.5%	
1912	Wilson	Taft	Debs	Roosevelt
	36%	20%	8%	36%
1916	Wilson	Hughes	Benson	
	57%	35%	7%	
1920	Cox	Harding	Debs	
	18%	59%	24%	

Source: Data provided by Jonathan Sarna, Brandeis University, unpublished manuscript.

What is perhaps most striking about the Jewish vote of this period is the size of the Socialist vote from Jewish areas (especially in New York) from 1904 to 1924. Though the Socialists never attained a plurality of Jewish voters at the presidential level, Jewish voters gave a much larger proportion of their votes to Eugene Debs (in 1904, 1908, 1912, and 1920), Alan Benson (1916), and Robert LaFollete (running as a Progressive with Socialist support) than did their non-Jewish countrymen. For example, while Debs received about 3.4 percent of the national vote in 1920, it is estimated he received about 38 percent of the Jewish vote (see table).

Voting for lower-level office also reveals mixed partisan attachments. Tammany delivered a plurality of the Jewish votes for the Democratic nominee for governor of New York in most years. However, when in 1912 the Progressives ran a German Jew,

Jewish Voting Patterns in Presidential Elections, 1916–2000

Year	Democratic Candidate (percentage of Jewish vote)	Republican Candidate (percentage of Jewish vote)	Other Candidate (percentage of Jewish vote)
1916	55	45	
1920	19	43	38 (Debs)
1924	51	27	22 (LaFollette)
1928	72	28	
1932	82	18	
1936	85	15	
1940	90	10	
1944	90	10	
1948	75	10	15 (H. Wallace)
1952	64	36	
1956	60	40	
1960	82	18	
1964	90	10	
1968	81	17	2 (G. Wallace)
1972	64	34	
1976	64	34	
1980	45	39	15 (Anderson)
1984	67	31	
1988	64	35	
1992	80	11	9 (Perot)
1996	78	16	3 (Perot)
2000	79	19	1 (Nader)

Source: Data from 1916 to 1968 are reported in Stephen Isaacs (1974); data from 1972 to 2000 are drawn from Voter News Service exit polls as reported in the *New York Times* election analysis issues.

Oscar Strauss, Eastern European immigrants gave him a plurality over the Democratic nominee who had represented a Jewish district in Congress and who was a champion of keeping open the doors of immigration. In Chicago between 1896 and 1912, Republicans and Democrats split the Jewish vote, with each winning three of the six contests. The largest victory in Jewish precincts came in 1900 when a German Jew, Samuel Alschuler, was the Democratic nominee and the Jews of the city gave him 64 percent of the vote—even as he was losing statewide. In many of these gubernatorial races, especially in New York, Socialist candidates ran extremely well from the early years of the century to the mid-1920s.

In municipal elections, party was even a weaker predictor of Jewish voting. In New York City, Jews often backed Tammany-supported "gentleman mayors" (McClellan in 1903), periodically backed Fusion/Reform candidates (Low in 1901), and sometimes went Socialist (Hillquist in 1917). During the same years in Chicago, German

Jews usually voted Republican for municipal office, but the more numerous Russian
Jews more often voted Democratic. Still, this pattern was actually reversed in the

AFTER THE JEWISH
DISILLUSIONMENT
WITH WOODROW
WILSON AND THE
REPUBLICAN
LANDSLIDE OF 1920,
DEMOCRATIC VOTING
IN URBAN JEWISH
NEIGHBORHOODS
REBOUNDED
STRONGLY.

teens and twenties when Republican mayor Big Bill
Thompson made a career out of appealing to urban immigrant groups.

The most obvious trend in Jewish voting came in the
1920s. After the Jewish disillusionment with Woodrow Wilson
and the Republican landslide of 1920, Democratic voting in
urban Jewish neighborhoods rebounded strongly and Socialist
strength crumbled. In New York, Al Smith received upward of
80 percent of the vote for governor in Jewish neighborhoods in
1922, 1924, and 1926. In 1928, while he was decisively defeated in the rest of the country, urban Jewish neighborhoods
were providing him unprecedented Democratic presidential majorities. In the same year, a
non-Jewish Democrat, Franklin Roosevelt, overwhelmed a Jewish Republican, Albert Ottinger, in Jewish election districts across New York.

THE RISE AND DECLINE OF THE NEW DEAL COALITION:
1932 TO TODAY

The Great Depression enabled the Democratic Party to replace the GOP as the country's
majority party. Franklin Roosevelt finished the job that Bryan and Wilson had begun,
turning the Democrats into the party of progressive reform and government activism in
support of economic growth and the "common man." Voting in this new system often
broke down on class lines. Democrats could count on the votes of the poor, lower–
middle-class workers, and labor union members, while the rich and the upper middle
class became solidly Republican and disdainful of Roosevelt as a traitor to his class. The
Democrats maintained their hold on the solid South for three decades. States with larger
urban and immigrant populations such as New York, Pennsylvania, Ohio, Massachusetts, Illinois, and Michigan became either competitive or strongly Democratic.

By the late 1960s, this New Deal coalition was fraying. After 1964, Democrats
could no longer count on Electoral College victories in the South. Liberalism became
identified among many white voters with favoritism toward minorities. These shifts
in opinion enabled the Republicans to become the majority party at the presidential
level, while Democrats maintained their congressional majorities. Democrats in the
last two decades of the century could claim a small party registration advantage, but
no party could claim clear majority status. After Watergate, Vietnam, stagflation, and
the Clinton impeachment, most voters became increasingly independent and disillusioned with partisan politics.

During the last seventy years of the twentieth century, the Jewish community did not experience the type of explosive population growth of the previous seventy years, but other profound demographic changes emerged. The immigration laws of the 1920s were designed to maintain the white Western European character of the American population and to ensure a shut-off of "exotic" non–Anglo-Saxon immigration of such groups as the Jews of the Eastern European *shtetels*. Nonetheless, the Jewish population of the United States grew from 4.2 million in 1940 to roughly 5.8 million in 2000. As fertility rates plummeted and intermarriage rates soared in the last decades of the century, Jewish population maintained a very modest growth rate.

The transformation of this community was remarkable in other ways. The poor and working-class, immigrant population of the early Depression years gave way to the professionals and businesspeople of the 1950s and 1960s. As early as the Truman and Eisenhower years, the Jewish cohort of the U.S. population emerged as one of the best-educated, highest-income communities in the country. These trends as well as the economic and educational advances of Jewish women continued into the last years of the century.

In addition, a geographic migration of the population emerged. The first migration was out of the central cities in the 1950s, 1960s, and 1970s. As New York City's Jewish population declined, the Jewish populations of Long Island, Westchester County, and northeast New Jersey skyrocketed. Similarly, Jewish populations migrated out to suburbs, such as Montgomery County, Pennsylvania; Pikesville, Maryland; Skokie, Illinois; and Shaker Heights, Ohio. The second migration pattern moved away from the older metropolitan areas of the East and Midwest to the Sunbelt. Thus, the New York metropolitan area declined from roughly 50 percent of the total Jewish population in 1940 to 26 percent in 2000 at the same time that the Los Angeles (including Orange County) and southeast Florida communities each grew from about 3 percent to just less than 10 percent of the Jewish total. Other large new Jewish population centers in 2000 included San Francisco; Washington, D.C.; Atlanta; San Diego; Denver; Phoenix; Dallas–Fort Worth; Las Vegas; and Tampa–St. Petersburg.

The issues driving Jewish votes have evolved over the last two-thirds of the twentieth century. At the beginning of the 1930s, the largely working-class Jewish community was very concerned with the debates between Democrats and Republican over the level of social welfare responsibility that the federal government should shoulder. New Deal programs such as the Works Projects Administration and Social Security were extremely attractive to this Jewish constituency. Moreover, by the end of the decade, President Roosevelt was engaged in a bitter struggle with isolationist elements. Here, too, Jewish Americans were overwhelmingly supportive of the policies of the Democratic administration.

At the same time that a large majority of American Jews supported national Democratic public policy initiatives, Roosevelt was recruiting Jews in unprecedented numbers for federal service—from White House staff, to the Cabinet, to the Supreme Court, and throughout the bureaucracy (see chapters 1 and 2 in this volume). All of these actions led the most extreme right-wing elements in the country to attack Roosevelt's "Jew Deal." But the "moderate" Republicans in 1944 were not above making a campaign issue of the close relationship between the president and left-wing Jewish labor leader Sidney Hillman.

Following World War II, Jewish voters looked to American politicians to support the newly formed state of Israel. Support for Israel first became a major issue in 1948 when the state was created and quick U.S. recognition was vital. The issue became salient again in the late 1960s, 1970s, and 1980s when American financial and diplomatic help was crucial in Israel during a series of hot and cold wars with its Arab adversaries.

Jewish voting patterns since the Great Depression can be much more easily ascertained from widely available precinct data and, since 1972, from election-day exit polls. As the table presented earlier reveals, the Democrats have "owned" the Jewish vote at the presidential level since 1932. From 1932 through 1948, the portion of Jewish voters supporting Democratic presidential candidates was never less than 75 percent. During these early years of the New Deal party system, the American Labor Party and the Liberal Party made it easier for the Jews in New York to vote for Roosevelt and Truman without supporting what many former socialists and reformers felt was a Tammany-tainted Democratic Party.

In the Eisenhower years, these Jewish majorities for Democratic presidential nominees dropped a bit, only to return to the 80 to 90 percent level in the 1960s. In the 1970s and 1980s, George McGovern, Jimmy Carter, Walter Mondale, and Michael Dukakis all garnered between 65 and 70 percent of the vote. In the last decade, these Democratic victory margins climbed back up to the 80 percent level. The Democratic low point came in 1980 when economic problems, Carter's troubled relationship with the Israeli government, and John Anderson's Independent candidacy all combined to drop the Carter plurality among Jewish voters down to 45 percent.

The pattern is much the same for statewide and congressional office. The tables in roster L chart the Jewish vote for a sampling of gubernatorial and United States Senate races since midcentury. Throughout most of this period, Democratic majorities were quite lopsided. The most numerous exceptions to the rule took place when perceived liberal/moderate Republicans opposed relatively conservative Democrats (Maryland in 1966, Illinois in 1998) or when popular Republicans won lopsided victories against weak statewide Democrats (Ohio in 1966).

Many conservative Jewish commentators have predicted since the late 1960s the imminent rise of Republican fortunes among Jews. However, unlike the 1920s, when Jewish voting trends did presage the new Jewish Democratic majority, none of the most recent presidential data points to such a trend in the near future (see chapter 9 in this volume). Some evidence in those tables indicates that, though Democratic victory percentages in statewide races have remained the norm within the Jewish community at the end of the twentieth century, the stigma attached to the Republican label is not what it was at midcentury. For example, in New York's 1956 United States Senate race, a liberal Republican, Jewish candidate, Jacob Javits, could garner less than 20 percent of the Jewish vote. By 1968, Javits (with the assistance of the Liberal Party line) was able to capture 60 percent of that vote. In the 2000 United State Senate race in New York, Hillary Clinton was able to win a convincing statewide victory and only managed to carry less than 55 percent of the Jewish vote against a moderate Republican.

THOUGH DEMOCRATS HAVE DOMINATED THE JEWISH VOTE AT THE PRESIDENTIAL AND STATEWIDE LEVELS OVER THE LAST SEVENTY YEARS, THIS DOMINANCE HAS NOT ALWAYS BEEN THE CASE IN LOCAL ELECTIONS.

Though Democrats have dominated the Jewish vote at the presidential and statewide levels over the last seventy years, this dominance has not always been the case in local elections. In cities like Cleveland, the Jewish community voted solidly Democratic for higher-level offices by the mid-1930s but at the local level continued to elect Republican city council members up into the mid-1950s. Roster L highlights the support Republican mayoral candidates have received from the 1930s to the late 1990s. In New York City, just at the time that Al Smith and Franklin Roosevelt solidified the Jewish vote for Democratic presidential candidates, Fiorello LaGuardia (with help from the American Labor Party line) was winning solid support from Jewish voters in his three successful races for mayor. As recently as 1997, Republican mayor Rudolph Giuliani (with help from the Liberal Party line) was able to capture a commanding majority of the New York City Jewish vote against a liberal Democratic Jewish opponent. Throughout the twentieth century, Jewish voting for municipal office has been a poor predictor of Jewish partisanship for higher-level office.

CONCLUSION

To summarize, the available evidence is that:

- From the 1790s through the 1820s, the small Jewish community of the United States supported mostly Jeffersonian Democrats.
- In the 1830s, 1840s, and 1850s the majority of a community that was swelling with German immigrants probably gave its allegiance to the Jacksonian Democrats.
- From the Civil War to the Free Silver campaign of 1896, many northern Jews switched their allegiance to the new Republican Party, while southern Jews, and many of the newer immigrants (especially in New York), voted Democratic.
- During the period of massive Eastern European Jewish immigration, 1890 to 1930, the Jewish vote was split between the two major parties and the Socialists.
- Since 1930, the Jewish community has been a solidly Democratic constituency at the national and state levels of government.

This is a much more complicated picture than just saying that Jews have always been Democrats or that Jews have always been liberal. In fact, "Democrat" and "liberal" have not always been synonymous in American history.

So what do these voting patterns imply?

First, the same issues that non-Jewish voters responded to often swayed Jewish voters. The sectional divisions that characterized American politics from the Civil War until the end of the century also divided midwestern Jewish Republicans from southern Jewish Democrats. In the same way, the wealthy Jews of New York who had financed the Democratic Party in the age of Tilden and Cleveland were quick to abandon the national Democratic Party when it took up the standard of inflationary Free Silver, just as Wall Street abandoned the Democrats of 1896.

Nonetheless, the often distinctive partisan voting pattern of Jewish voters (as compared to their non-Jewish neighbors of similar socioeconomic backgrounds) leads one to speculate as to the particular motivation of this one ethnoreligious group. Obviously no single factor explains two hundred years of Jewish voting behavior, but a number of distinct patterns emerge.

For two hundred years, the issue of church–state separation and strict limits on the degree to which government should involve itself in moral matters have generated great support from American Jewish voters. Similarly, for two hundred years, one of the two major political parties has usually been more willing for government to legislate on "moral" questions, and one major party has been more libertarian in this regard. The impulse to accept a more puritanical role for government was, until the last part of the twentieth century, more pronounced in New England and in areas of the nation settled by New Englanders.

In postrevolutionary America, the Democratic-Republicans were on the side of church–state separation, and the Federalists were more likely to support church establishment, blue laws, and religious tests for voting. In the Jacksonian era, the Whigs, rather than the Democrats, were more likely to push for blue laws and were more sympathetic to the temperance movement. In post–Civil War America, the GOP was dominant in New England and the Upper Midwest, and Republicans, too, adopted the Whig's worldview. In many cities at the turn of the century, it was the WASP, mugwump, clean-government types (often Republicans) who opposed ethnic-dominated machines. On the issue of municipal reform, they could appeal to Jewish voters. But when these same reformers pushed for enforcement of Sunday closings, they lost their Jewish immigrant constituency.

In the twentieth century, this pattern continued, despite the fact that Democrats abandoned their libertarian impulses with regard to government's support for the social welfare state. Prayer in school was supported at midcentury by Democrats in the South as well as by the majority of Republicans. However, by the end of the century, the Christian Right had made school prayer an almost exclusively Republican issue.

Moreover, late twentieth-century Republican opposition to such issues as abortion rights also made Jewish support for the party problematic.

A second thread throughout American history is Jewish concern over the fate of their co-religionists abroad. Neither Democrats, nor Whigs, nor Republicans were consistently on the right side of this issue. In antebellum America, Jews both rewarded the Democrats for Van Buren's protest of the Damascus blood libel and punished Buchanan's Democrats for the president's refusal to criticize the pope in the Mortara affair. Post–Civil War Republican presidents won praise from Jews for criticizing Romanian or czarist antisemitism. But when President Taft opposed an attempt to abrogate a discriminatory Russian trade treaty, he paid a price in Jewish votes during his reelection campaign.

In the 1930s, Franklin Roosevelt's increasing antagonism toward Hitler's Germany created a loud uproar among isolationists in both parties. Yet, the lasting impression among American Jews was the contrast between Democratic antifascism and clear internationalism and Republican intransigent isolationism.

Support for or criticism of Israel has, of course, influenced Jewish voters. Truman's quick recognition of the Jewish state brought benefits to the Democrats in 1948. Eisenhower seemed not to have been hurt by his pressure on the Israelis in the 1956 Suez crisis, but the same cannot be said for Democrat Jimmy Carter in 1980 or Republican George H. W. Bush in 1992.

A third theme is twentieth-century Jewish reaction to the social welfare policies of the federal government. In the nineteenth century, the major parties—Democrats, Republicans, Whigs, and Federalists all supported only a very limited role for the national government in steering the economy and in providing income support, welfare, medical care, and other services for America's citizenry. When this consensus was broken in the 1930s by Roosevelt's New Deal polices, the American Jewish community was a poor and working-class community, a community that was in most need of government assistance to weather the economic storm. After World War II, when the community became one of the wealthier subgroups in the population, Jews maintained their support for the welfare state. Whether this support stemmed from classical rabbinical notions of social justice or from historical memory is beyond the scope of this chapter. Whatever the root cause for these attitudes, the Democratic Party has been the beneficiary over the last seventy years.

The final thread may be the most significant. Throughout the Jewish sojourn in America, the Jews have been a people who have always remained most cognizant of their minority status. Despite the relatively low levels of antisemitism in American society, despite the elimination of nearly all economic and social barriers against Jews in the late twentieth century, Jews have consistently viewed themselves as part of an out-group in American society. In many ways, despite historically high levels of assimilation, Jews are the one white ethnic group least susceptible to assimilation in the larger culture.

At the same time, the Democratic Party has been the party of the "outs" throughout its over two hundred years of history. In the early nineteenth century, this meant that the party supported the then radical notion that all white males were entitled to political equality—even Irish, German, and Jewish immigrants. In the late twentieth century this circle expanded to include women and racial minorities. In contrast, the Federalist, Whig, and later Republican parties have had more significant nativist sentiment within their ranks.

Democratic Party notions of political equality have not always helped with the Jewish vote. Clearly the long Irish domination of northern urban Democratic Party machinery caused resentment among other immigrant groups, including Jews. Some Jews supported the institution of slavery up to and during the Civil War. But during the conflict, the South's unrepentant support for "the peculiar institution" hurt the Democrats for a generation among the vast majority of American Jews who had fled Germany after the failures of the democratic revolutions of the 1840s. Even more recently, Democratic Party identification with some black political leaders (e.g., Reverend Jesse Jackson) who used antisemitic rhetoric also damaged the party with some Jewish voters in the 1970s and 1980s.

However, throughout most decades, Democrats seemed the most welcoming of political institutions for Jews. Jeffersonian Democrats opposed the Alien and Sedition Acts and welcomed Jews into their institutions, such as Tammany Hall. Jacksonian Democrats welcomed the Irish, the Germans, and the German Jews, while prejudice against immigrants within the Whig Party often plagued more tolerant Whigs, such as New York's Governor Seward. Upstate New York Republican legislators refused for years to pass legislation protecting Jews from discriminatory practices at resorts and hotels, but the Tammany-dominated Democratic Party passed such legislation as soon as it took control of the New York state legislature in 1913. Democrat Woodrow Wilson vetoed restrictions on immigration. Republican Warren Harding signed into law legislation all but ending Eastern European immigration. Democrats Wilson and Franklin Roosevelt appointed many more Jews to prominent federal office than their GOP predecessors. By the 1960s, the Democrats were the party of civil rights and that policy matched the prevailing sentiments within the Jewish community.

The Jewish historian Arthur Hertzberg has written profoundly of the peculiarly secular, nonreligious nature of American Jewish culture throughout American history. This secularism, he claims, combined with a stubborn loyalty to Jewish outsider status, has worked to shape the Jewish community's political behavior—most often, but not always, pushing the community into the Democratic Party coalition. Perhaps the recent trend toward increased religious observance and an ethnic pride among the segment of Jewry that is least likely to assimilate will change this political dynamic—at the same time lessening the support for church–state separation and lessening the need to cling to the party of the "outs." But until such change or some other unforeseen dramatic change manifests itself, American Jewry will remain an integral part of the Democratic Party coalition.

9

STILL LIBERAL AFTER
ALL THESE YEARS?

The Contemporary Political Behavior of American Jewry

ANNA GREENBERG
AND KENNETH D. WALD

From time to time, academic researchers have asked American Jews what qualities or traits make somebody a "good" Jew. If asked that question, rabbis would surely identify the most committed members of the Jewish community by their adherence to the 613 commandments enshrined in the Hebrew Bible. That kind of theological perspective has dominated the answers given by rank-and-file Roman Catholics when they are charged with distilling the essence of being a good Catholic. For them, it is clear, being a "good" member of the Catholic Church requires faithful performance of religious duties and loyal adherence to the teachings and moral authority of Rome. Do Jews understand their tradition in the same manner?

The clear answer is that they do not. As understood by ordinary members of the "tribe," being a "good" Jew seems to have little connection to religious behavior. By a two-to-one margin, in fact, the participants in Jewish surveys have rejected the notion that "good Jews" must do something as basically religious as believe in God or attend synagogue faithfully. Rather, most Jews define a "good" Jew as somebody who contributes to Jewish causes, supports civil rights for black Americans, favors generous social welfare benefits, and embraces other progressive social values. Asked explicitly about the qualities that most strongly define their own Jewish identity, Jews are four times as likely to mention a commitment to social equality as they are to choose either support for Israel or religious involvement. In other words, for many Jews, the values of their religion are understood to promote attachment to a liberal political agenda carried into public life.

> MOST JEWS DEFINE A "GOOD" JEW AS SOMEBODY WHO CONTRIBUTES TO JEWISH CAUSES, SUPPORTS CIVIL RIGHTS FOR BLACK AMERICANS, FAVORS GENEROUS SOCIAL WELFARE BENEFITS, AND EMBRACES OTHER PROGRESSIVE SOCIAL VALUES.

The attachment to liberal values and candidates is just one of the traits that make American Jewry such an interesting phenomenon in American public life. Jewish Americans represent an extremely small percentage of the population—2 to 3 percent, depending on how Judaism is defined; yet, as voters, donors, activists, leaders, and thinkers, they have had a profound impact on American political debate and the political process. The extent to which liberalism defines Jews' political attitudes is remarkable because it violates all the assumptions we make about the effect of upward mobility and assimilation on political behavior. Most immigrant groups move politically to the right as they become more integrated in American society. By contrast, American Jewry has retained a distinctive political identity and a liberal ideology, despite rapid social advancement and acceptance. We find relatively little political differentiation among Jews based on their economic or educational attainment. While other ethnoreligious groups are said to be dividing politically on the basis of religiosity, the link between religious commitment and political outlooks among Jewish Americans is much weaker.

Looked at from almost any angle, then, the political attitudes and behavior of American Jews are paradoxical. In this chapter, we explore the puzzling phenomenon by profiling contemporary Jewish beliefs about politics and elections. In most of the chapter, we present information about how Jews differ from non-Jews, taking advantage of a rare public opinion poll commissioned for this chapter. We also look for signs of internal political division among American Jews, emphasizing the role of religious commitment, age, gender, and other potential sources of disagreement. Before turning to the specifics of Jewish political behavior, we first summarize what scholars have written about Jewish politics in the United States, emphasizing in particular the explanations for Jewish distinctiveness and the claims that Jewish political cohesion will disappear in the near future.

JEWISH DISTINCTIVENESS AND ITS EXPLANATION

When he wrote that "Jews earn like Episcopalians and vote like Puerto Ricans," Milton Himmelfarb nicely captured the central paradox of Jewish politics in the contemporary United States. If politics is about economic self-interest, as so many observers believe, Jews should vote and think politically like Episcopalians, Presbyterians, and other high-status groups. Yet despite their affluence and status, Jewish voting patterns and attitudes are much closer to the norms for African Americans, Hispanics, and other groups who have the most to gain from progressive economic and social policies. This anomalous pattern has long perplexed scholarly observers and infuriated conservative activists like Irving Kristol who denounce what they call "the political stupidity of the Jews."

"JEWS EARN LIKE EPISCOPALIANS AND VOTE LIKE PUERTO RICANS."

In making sense of Jewish political patterns, one should start with the recognition that nothing is inevitable about the contemporary political alignment of American Jews. Although many Jews feel that their community's liberal political slant is nothing more than applied Judaism, the facts tell a different story. At other periods of American history, Jews were attached to a variety of political parties and causes. Although hard to know for sure, analysis of electoral data suggests that many Jews identified with Republican causes before Franklin Roosevelt came to the presidency. Moreover, a look at global and historical information reveals that Jews have been all over the political map. Unlike their counterparts in the United States, Jews in England, Australia, and Canada are often found politically divided or even on the conservative side in public debates. American Jews, who often blithely assume that Judaism by its nature compels support for human rights and progressive social values, are sometimes shocked to discover that Israeli Jews find very different political norms embedded in Judaism.

Judaism is philosophically compatible with a wide range of political outlooks. Because Jewish law has never produced a coherent or systematic philosophy of governance or politics, the tradition allows multiple interpretations of what Jews should do in the political realm. Consider the value of *tzedakeh*, the commandment that enjoins Jews to give assistance to the poorest members of the community. This value has commonly been invoked to explain the liberalism of American Jews. As most American Jews undoubtedly understand it, *tzedakeh* has meant support for government programs of income redistribution and food assistance. Yet political conservatives in the Jewish community maintain that Judaism has historically given the highest value to charitable acts that enable the poor to earn a living from their own labor. Under this interpretation, American Jews should be strong advocates of "workfare" rather than "welfare."

AMERICAN JEWS, WHO OFTEN BLITHELY ASSUME THAT JUDAISM BY ITS NATURE COMPELS SUPPORT FOR HUMAN RIGHTS AND PROGRESSIVE SOCIAL VALUES, ARE SOMETIMES SHOCKED TO DISCOVER THAT ISRAELI JEWS FIND VERY DIFFERENT POLITICAL NORMS EMBEDDED IN JUDAISM.

We do not mean to take sides in this debate but simply to note that it is a valid disagreement. The interesting question for us is not whether Judaism rightfully should be understood to command liberal political values, as so many American Jews believe. Rather, we are interested in why most American Jews understand their religious tradition to support political liberalism and long-term loyalty toward the Democratic Party.

That having been said, we need to consider the three major explanations for Jewish political behavior in the United States.

Values

Jewish support for liberalism and Democratic candidates is commonly attributed to social values associated with the religious tradition. In the fullest statement of this position, Lawrence Fuchs's classic *Political Behavior of American Jews* argues that Jewish political culture in the 1950s was anchored by two broad dispositions. *Internationalism*, the belief that the United States should play a leading role in world politics and that international cooperation should be emphasized, was a key value of the Democratic Party from the 1930s through the late 1960s. It contrasted with a strong strain of isolationism among Republicans for much of the same period. The other core political value, *liberalism*, was generally defined as a commitment to using government to address social problems like poverty and discrimination. Again, the Democratic Party was much more identified with this position, and Democratic candidates thus drew disproportionate support from Jews in the electorate.

Fuchs contends that these political lodestars are in turn anchored by three elements of Judaism. First, the Jewish emphasis on *learning* disposes Jews to support ambitious plans of social reconstruction under the aegis of government authorities. Jews have no trouble with the idea that experts ought to help plan society. Moreover, the commitment to education also makes Jews fierce defenders of intellectual freedom and hostile to restrictions on civil liberties. Such issues often divided Republicans and Democrats in the 1950s and 1960s.

Fuchs's second religious value, *tzedakeh,* is invoked to explain Jewish sympathy for the weak and oppressed and their commitment to social justice and compassion.

Third, Fuchs calls attention to the worldly, nonascetic nature of Judaism. Unlike some forms of Christianity, Judaism does not regard human pleasure as something separate from God but emphasizes the godliness of sensuality. Nor does Judaism believe that human beings should postpone gratification for an ideal heaven. Together, these values render Jews enthusiastic supporters of plans to remake the world in God's image. Thus, he concludes, the religious values of American Judaism account for the tight fit between Jewish political culture and the liberal political wing of the American political system.

History/Social Conditions

To explain Jewish political behavior, other scholars have paid less attention to values and given more emphasis to the particular social and historical circumstances of American Jewry. In Seymour Martin Lipset's account, the immigrant experience was the formative influence on the political outlooks of American Jewry. Most American Jews trace their ancestry to the great waves of immigration from Eastern Europe in the late nineteenth century. This experience sustained a commitment to political liberalism through several routes. As victims of oppressive regimes in the old country, the Jewish immigrants often brought with them sympathy for leftist political action—radicalism and various forms of socialism. While these movements waxed and waned in American politics, Jews came to see mainstream liberalism as the successor to the political impulses they carried across the ocean on their migration.

A left-wing style in politics also developed as a consequence of the living conditions faced by the newest Americans. Poor, crammed together in crowded slums, denied access to many opportunities for social advancement, Jews were natural recruits for trade unions and other movements seeking social change. When these movements coalesced into Franklin Roosevelt's New Deal Coalition in the 1930s, Jews were swept up into the new majority.

The Eastern European heritage left its mark on Jewish politics in another way. Vicious antisemitism forced many immigrants out of their homelands. More often than not, the most virulent antisemitism was found on the right wing of the political spectrum, among extreme nationalists, religious extremists, and monarchists. That left many Jews with a profound mistrust of movements that claimed to represent tradition. The Holocaust, the most systematic and horrific anti-Jewish movement, reinforced Jewish concern over antisemitism. Though antisemitism in the United States never reached a point even close to the levels it attained in Europe, its source was often found among people who were part of the right wing. The hostility of political conservatives to antidiscrimination legislation for blacks and other minorities appeared to reinforce the antipathy that Jews developed toward conservatism.

Jewish commitment to the left was also occasioned by the positive overtures that liberals and Democrats made toward Jews. Jews first attained high government positions through appointment by Democratic presidents. Wilson named Louis Brandeis as the first Jewish justice of the United States Supreme Court, and Franklin Roosevelt named more Jews to his cabinet and to other key positions than any president before him. Roosevelt also became the leader in the fight against Nazism abroad, earning enormous respect from Jews for his efforts to contain and then overthrow Hitler. The Democrats cemented their advantage when Harry Truman, another Democrat, overruled the State Department and threw the support of the United States behind the fledgling state of Israel in 1947. The hospitality of Democratic leaders thus helped maintain Jewish affinity for the Democratic Party, making it seem like the natural political home for Jews. That perception was certainly reinforced by the nomination of Senator Joseph Lieberman as the Democratic candidate for vice president in 2000.

Self-Interest: Liberalism as Good for the Jews

Scholars who are puzzled by Jewish liberalism and support for Democrats often assume that such behavior is contrary to Jewish interests. As an affluent community, surely American Jews have more to gain by *embracing* conservatism than by continued attachment to liberalism. These observers frequently wonder aloud why Jews do not follow their "interests" in politics. In response, some observers have asserted that Jews do indeed pursue their own interests in politics to the same degree as other ethnoreligious groups in the United States. Their behavior is puzzling only to people who assume that Jewish self-interest is defined solely by economic considerations. Looked at more broadly, advocates of this perspective contend, Jews remain liberal and Democratic because both alliances are good for them.

JEWS REMAIN LIBERAL AND DEMOCRATIC BECAUSE BOTH ALLIANCES ARE GOOD FOR THEM.

According to this view, Jews have thrived especially well in the liberal political and economic system of the United States. The low level of antisemitism and the easy breaking of barriers to advancement were possible for the Jews because of the pro–civil rights measures and policies pursued over the years by liberal politicians. Jews supported the efforts to make discrimination illegal because they benefited substantially from an open and fair competitive system. At the end of the day, nothing is very puzzling about Jewish political behavior because it simply reflects a rational calculation of the impact of public policies on Jewish existence.

Can It Last?

Many observers of American Jewish politics—both commentators and publicists—have doubted whether the tradition of Jewish liberalism can be sustained in the face of the progress made by Jews since the end of World War II. The Jewish community of the twenty-first-century United States bears little resemblance to the predominantly immigrant society that dated from the late nineteenth century. When they first arrived in large numbers, Jews were geographically segregated into big city ghettos, confined to blue-collar or lower–middle-class jobs, and kept out of many elite institutions by quotas and other devices. In contrast, Jews today are found distributed all over the country and have spread out from ghettos to the fringes of metropolitan areas. Given unrivaled opportunities with the end of the most egregious forms of discrimination, Jews have become one of the best-educated and economically most secure groups in the population.

A number of hypotheses have been presented to explain how these changes might undercut the traditional political patterns of American Jewry. First, Jewish economic progress may eventually undermine a commitment to liberalism and the Democratic Party. Jews may no longer see progressive taxation and aggressive social programs as important conduits to well-being. In the short run, for a generation or so, traditional Jewish political patterns may survive upward social mobility. The affluent lawyer whose parents struggled to provide her with opportunities may still regard herself as the beneficiary of liberal policies and retain a commitment to the Democratic Party. But her own children, raised in middle-class suburbs and religiously mixed schools, encountering virtually no signs of ethnic disadvantage, are less likely to pick up the partisan traits of their parents or grandparents. An understanding of Judaism as a force for progressive change may become less salient for subsequent generations that did not experience the conditions that produced a distinctive Jewish political ethos. Thus, in time, the old political patterns may become more tenuous.

The second consequence of social progress has been a striking decline in Jewish attachment and communal involvement. Jewish cohesion was in some respects easier to maintain when Jews felt themselves somewhat marginal and isolated in American society. The unprecedented openness of the last half-century has enabled Jews to choose whether or not they remain part of the community. Judging by low rates of organizational affiliation—barely half now join synagogues—and high rates of religious out-marriage, fewer Jews tie their own fate to the Jewish community. If liberalism and Democratic affiliation were once considered almost a part of Judaism itself, this "tribal knowledge" is less likely to be passed on to those who do not partake of tribal life.

The third change comes from the world of politics external to the Jewish community. With shifts in political tendencies since the Vietnam War, conservatives maintain, support for liberal policies and the Democratic Party are now not clearly good for the Jews. The historic Jewish commitment to civil rights has run headlong into the development of black nationalism in the 1960s and never since has been as comfortable for either group. Jews are less than enthusiastic about affirmative action, which many African Americans regard as essential to their progress, because such policies evoke memories of the anti-Jewish quotas that once blocked Jewish social progress. The development of a strong Muslim community among African Americans has also undermined close relations over the contentious question of Israel. Indeed, among liberals generally, support for Israel fell appreciably after it became the ruler of Palestinians as a consequence of the Six-Day War in 1967. Quick to seize on changing political circumstances, conservative Republicans have striven to make Jews feel welcome in their party.

The final factor that may undercut Jewish political cohesion is also a trend that developed apart from Judaism. For most of American history, religious conflict pitted Catholics against Protestants or Jews against Catholics. This type of antagonism was often rooted in high levels of residential segregation and reinforced by the presence of homogeneous ethnic communities. As Americans increasingly moved to religiously mixed suburban communities after World War II, this pattern began to disappear. In its place, some scholars have suggested, we have witnessed the internal fracturing of most religious groups on the basis of their commitment to religious observance and tradition. Within denominations, the more orthodox or traditional now fight on many issues against the more liberal or progressive. At the same time, the traditionalists from one denomination find they have more in common politically with traditionalists from other denominations than with the progressive members of their own religious community. If this pattern holds true for Jews, we should find increasing political tension between the most and least observant members of the community, further diminishing the distinctiveness of Jewish politics.

But we stress that these scenarios should be regarded as nothing more than hypotheses. Scholars have not yet produced the comprehensive and systematic research that would enable us to decide on the durability or change in Jewish political attitudes. Many anecdotes can be cited to show either continuity or transformation. In this chapter, we cannot comment authoritatively on changes over the long term, but we can determine how distinctive Jewish political views are today and how much they now vary by category within the Jewish community. This analysis will permit us to offer some informed guesses about the evolution of Jewish political behavior in the future.

JEWISH POLITICAL BEHAVIOR AT THE MILLENNIUM

In this chapter, we rely primarily on the Jewish Public Opinion Study, a national sample of Jewish Americans participating in an Internet-based panel study. We compared our sample with a similar sample of non-Jews. To look at voting and partisanship among Jews and non-Jews, we combine the Voter News Service exit polls from 1990, 1992, 1994, 1996, and 1998 to create a sample of 1,498 Jews. (See the appendix of this chapter for a discussion of the difficulty in studying Jewish political attitudes and for details of our data sources.)

Whatever the information source, we present analysis that answers three questions. First, are Jews still politically distinctive? To answer this question, we look for significant attitude differences between Jews and non-Jews ("statistically significant" refers to a difference that is unlikely to occur by chance because of the composition of the participants—typically differences that could occur by chance in less than five out of one hundred randomly drawn samples). We then ask the second question: What political characteristics are unique to Jews *because they are Jewish?* We examine the extent of Jewish distinctiveness by comparing Jewish positions with those of non-Jews who resemble Jews economically and sociologically. If Jews are politically different from comparable non-Jews, then it is safe to assume that something about the Jewish experience is responsible. Finally, we want to see whether Jews are cohesive or whether certain political issues divide them based on qualities such as age, gender, education, and religious observance.

This three-part strategy enables us to determine which of the scenarios about the evolution of Jewish political behavior fits the facts. That is, do Jews look distinctive on some issues because they have certain demographic characteristics such as high socioeconomic status or a propensity to reside in urban areas? If we find substantial political differences between Jews and other Americans, differences that cannot be reduced to economic disparities between Jews and others, that will suggest that Jews still look at the world in a distinctive manner. If those attitudes are largely the same among different types of Jews, that will tell us that Jews are much more politically cohesive than non-Jews. Because social scientists rarely find absolute consistency in human behavior, we should not expect to find precisely the same pattern among Jews on all political attitudes. Our goal is to discern the forest from the trees.

We begin by approaching Jewish political identity from multiple standpoints. First, we explore the general case of Jewish liberalism, considering to what extent Jews call themselves liberal and identify with groups on the left and the right of American politics. Then we consider voting in presidential and congressional elections primarily since 1980, to assess whether Jews actually vote as a bloc. Third, we discuss three important issue areas—social issues, race and affirmative action, and separation of church and state—on which Jews and non-Jews have differed. We find enduring differences between Jews and non-Jews on school prayer and religion in public life, abortion, and the death penalty, but fewer divisions around race and affirmative action. Finally, we examine Jewish attitudes toward international involvement and the Middle East peace process. We also use our data to compare Jewish levels of political participation with the behavior patterns of non-Jews.

The Endurance of Liberalism

Jews are clearly on the left of American politics in their partisan loyalties and voting preferences: they consistently support Democratic candidates and identify with the

Democratic Party at considerably higher rates than non-Jews. Jews strongly support the separation of church and state, abortion rights and the women's movement, gun control, civil rights, and environmental protection. At the same time, while Jews are more pessimistic than other Americans about the state of race relations in the United States, they share a similar hostility toward affirmative action. Moreover, they are no less likely to think of themselves as supporters of business interests. While Jewish Americans respond to the Democratic Party's commitment to the disadvantaged and a social welfare state, they are not anticapitalist or opposed to market solutions. Jewish Americans are more likely to support intervention in international conflict, but no less likely than non-Jews to consider themselves patriotic.

Clearly, Jewish liberalism, while strong, is by no means monolithic. But what is striking is how little variation shows within the Jewish community on most issues. The absence of internal political diversity distinguishes Jewish Americans from other citizens who are divided by class, religiosity, geography, and race. Certainly younger Jews are less partisan and more socially liberal than their elders, yet Jews overall are politically undifferentiated by class, geography, and, surprisingly, level of religious observance. In this high level of internal agreement, Jews resemble African Americans, Hispanic Americans, and other minority groups who exhibit a remarkable and enduring degree of internal political cohesiveness. Both in what they believe and how strongly they agree with one another, Jews continue to confound many of the commonplace assumptions about group political behavior.

How Jews See Themselves

What does it mean for Jews to be liberal in the context of American politics today? Debates rage in social science circles over the meaning of ideology and contemporary liberalism, about whether it constitutes a coherent set of beliefs or an affective orientation toward groups. Here we will examine both attitudes toward issues and groups, as well as Jewish self-identification, voting behavior, and partisanship.

Jewish Americans are more liberal in their self-image than non-Jews, though not by the same margins as is manifest in party identification or voting behavior. According to the Jewish Public Opinion Study, 35 percent of Jews call themselves liberal compared to 18 percent of non-Jews; 8 percent of Jews call themselves conservative compared to 26 percent of non-Jews. On the other hand, nearly an equal number of both groups call themselves moderate (50 percent of Jews compared to 44 percent of non-Jews).

Jews identify with groups in American politics traditionally found on the political left. Jewish Americans support the women's movement more than non-Jews; Jews are also far more likely to call themselves prochoice than prolife. Jews do not support groups traditionally allied with the Republican Party such as the National Rifle Association and the religious right.

Identification with Groups in American Politics

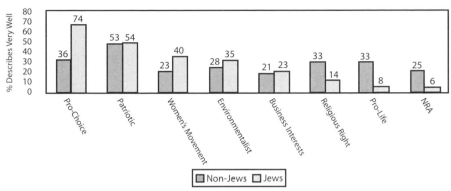

Source: Jewish Public Opinion Study/Knowledge Networks 2000

In the Voting Booth

Despite diversity on particular policy issues, American Jews constitute a fairly cohesive voting bloc in electoral politics. Since early in the twentieth century, Jewish Americans have associated themselves with the Democratic Party. They supported Woodrow Wilson and Al Smith, and lined up solidly behind Franklin Delano Roosevelt's candidacy for governor of New York and president of the United States. Through the early 1960s, Democratic presidential nominees generally followed in Roosevelt's footsteps by earning substantial majorities among Jewish voters. In the late 1960s, however, Jewish political patterns appeared to shift away from the Democrats, dropping from a 3-1 to a 2-1 ratio. The low point for Democrat fortunes occurred in 1980 when Jews deserted Jimmy Carter en masse, many voting for the independent John Anderson and some even defecting to the Republican Ronald Reagan.

Those who interpreted this erosion as a foretaste of partisan realignment among Jews were surprised by the resurgence of Democratic support thereafter. As the Republican Party became more closely identified in the public mind with Christian fundamentalists, Jews returned in large numbers to the party of FDR. Jewish Americans gave Democratic presidential candidates two-thirds of their votes in the 1980s, cast an astonishing 80 percent of their ballots for Bill Clinton in 1992 and, despite ongoing scandals, and cast 78 percent of their votes again for Clinton in 1996. In the most recent elections, 79 percent of Jewish voters threw their support with Al Gore. This Democratic loyalty is evident in congressional elections as well. According to the exit polls, two-thirds to three-quarters of Jewish Americans have supported Democratic candidates for the House since 1980. Thus, with the sole exception of the 1980 presidential race, Jews have supported Democratic candidates more than has the nation as a whole.

This constancy of Jewish support for the Democratic Party stands in stark contrast to the defection of other key elements of the New Deal coalition. Southern white

Jewish Support for Democratic Presidential Candidates

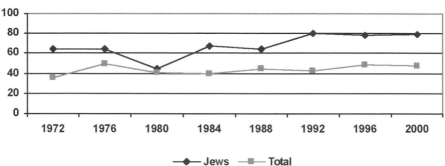

Source: Voter News Service, Exit Poll Data 1972–2000

Jewish Support for Democratic Congressional Candidates

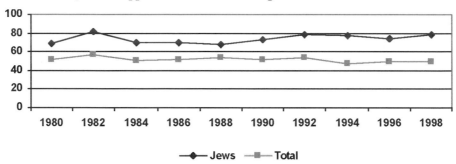

Source: Voter News Service, Exit Poll Data 1980–1998

Democrats, for example, fled the party in the aftermath of the civil rights movement and federal intervention in school desegregation and voting rights. Catholics, to a lesser degree, have come to resemble their Protestant counterparts, though a majority continue to vote Democratic. Only African Americans have remained as solidly in the Democratic camp as have Jewish Americans.

Over the 1990s, nearly 60 percent of Jews identified with Democrats, as did three-quarters of African Americans. These percentages remained relatively constant. In contrast, in the same period, fewer than half of Catholics and a third of white Southerners saw themselves as members of the Democratic camp. This shift represents a significant decline in Democratic identification among non-Jewish voters once considered at the heart of the New Deal coalition.

What accounts for the persistence of Jewish identification with the Democratic Party in the face of the flight of other white voters? While white Southerners began their flight from the Democratic Party in the early 1960s, Jews supported federal efforts to secure civil rights for African Americans and played a prominent, if at times controversial, role in the civil rights movement. Jewish Americans strongly identify the Democratic Party as

The Status of the New Deal Coalition in the 1990s (% Identify as Democrats)

	1990 (%)	1992 (%)	1994 (%)	1996 (%)	1998 (%)
Jewish	59	65	60	58	56
African American	72	75	76	72	76
Latino	56	51	49	61	49
White Catholic	38	41	35	40	38
White Southern	35	34	30	32	28

Source: Exit Poll Data, 1990–1998

the party of civil liberties and individual rights. Jewish Americans give the Democratic Party a strong advantage over the Republican Party, believing the Democrats do a better job of protecting individual rights by a forty-point margin.

After the upheavals of the 1960s, moreover, the parties polarized in a number of areas on which Jews and non-Jews exhibit important political differences. For instance, between 1972 and 1992, the parties and their adherents diverged sharply over cultural and social issues such as abortion, school prayer, and attitudes toward homosexuality. Christian Right leaders such as Pat Robertson and Pat Buchanan failed to appeal to Jewish Americans, despite the pro-Israel proclivities of the evangelical Christian community. Geoffrey Levey suggests that Democratic Jewish loyalty stems from precisely this association of the Republican Party with the Christian Right and with the Christian overtones of the "family values" agenda. According to the Jewish Public Opinion Study, non-Jews are twice as likely as Jews to call themselves supporters of the religious right, and 64 percent of Jews say this designation does not describe them well at all. Thus, Jewish Americans see the Democrats as better at "encouraging high moral standards and values," a conclusion that stands in stark contrast to non-Jews who see Republicans as better on that issue.

Overall, Jewish Americans believe the Democrats better represent "Jewish values" and "the interest of Jewish Americans." Consistent with arguments about the importance of *tzedakah* to Jewish political identity, Jews strongly prefer Democrats as the party with "compassion toward the disadvantaged." We should also note, however, that other non-Jewish Democrats give the Democratic Party the same advantage as Jewish Americans.

Jewish Americans do not exhibit the same political tendencies as other demographically equivalent groups. For instance, we might expect Jewish Americans to become more conservative in their beliefs and voting preferences as succeeding generations attain higher levels of affluence and education. In fact, Jewish Americans are among the

Views Toward the Parties

Which political party do you trust to do a better job at . . .

Democratic Margin over Republicans

	Jews	Non-Jews	Non Jewish Democrats
Compassion toward disadvantaged	+67	+29	+62
Protecting individual rights	+42	+9	+46
Encourage higher morals standards	+6	−19	+11
Promoting self-reliance	−4	−20	+10

Source: Knowledge Networks/Jewish Public Opinion Study 2001

most highly educated, professional, and affluent members of the population. In the Jewish Public Opinion Study, 58 percent of Jewish Americans have a college degree, compared to 22 percent of non-Jews. Twenty-eight percent of Jewish Americans describe themselves as professional, compared to 10 percent of non-Jews. Thirty-seven percent of Jews earn over $85,000, compared to 13 percent of non-Jews.

But when we compare these Jewish American voters to non-Jews with the same socioeconomic status, the Jews remain politically distinctive. White, college-educated, urban, middle-aged non-Jews, as we would expect, are not nearly so Democratic in their party self-identification nor in their voting behavior as are Jewish Americans. As the exit poll data show, 39 percent of comparable non-Jews identify as Democrats, compared to 60 percent of Jews; and 54 percent of comparable non-Jews supported Democratic candidates for the House, compared to 76 percent of Jews.

Even if Jewish Americans differ politically from non-Jews with similar socioeconomic and demographic characteristics, they may demonstrate internal political differentiation based on class, religiosity, geographic residence, and gender just as other groups do. In other words, affluent and well-educated Jews may exhibit more Republican tendencies than their poorer compatriots. Consistent with what we know about the "gender gap" in American politics, Jewish men may vote more conservatively than Jewish women. Urban residents may be more Democratic than suburbanites since central cities tend to be Democratic strongholds. Given the tensions within other religious communities based on level of orthodoxy, the deeply religious may be more politically conservative than their secular counterparts.

Unlike some of the differences we will see in certain issue areas, however, few divisions separate Jews from one another in their partisanship and voting behavior. While lower-income and high school–educated Jews look slightly more Democratic than higher-income

**Voting Behavior and Partisanship of Jews
and Non-Jews of Similar Socioeconomic Status**

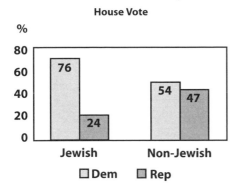

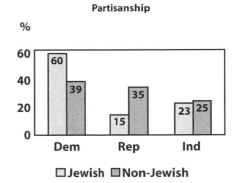

Source: Exit Poll Data, 1990–1998

and college-educated Jews, these differences are not statistically significant. Observant Jews do not have stronger Republican identification than less observant Jews, even though they are marginally more favorable toward Republican policies such as school vouchers and social conservatism. The vast majority of Jews live in urban or suburban areas rather than rural America, but they demonstrate few political differences based on geography.

Some speculate that Jews are increasingly likely to support Republican candidates, citing evidence such as Jewish support for Republicans Richard Riordan in Los Angeles and Rudolph Giuliani in New York. In the aggregate, Jewish Democratic loyalty appears solid, but this political hegemony may merely reflect the intense partisanship of older Jews, who tend to be more politically active and engaged than younger people. We know, moreover, that partisan change occurs as younger generations replace older generations in the electorate and that younger Americans are generally less partisan than older Americans. But Jews exhibit fewer differences related to age. Young Jews do appear less committed to the Democratic Party than older Jews, but they are *not* moving into the Republican Party. Instead, only 10 percent of Jews under thirty-five years old call themselves Republican, while 42 percent call themselves politically Independent, and 49 percent identify as Democrats. The lack of a strong partisan anchor among young Jews leaves them more open to Republican appeals than their elders, but the young have not yet moved in that direction. The vice presidential nomination of Senator Joseph Lieberman by the Democrats in 2000 may also have harnessed the young voters more closely to the Democrats, reducing their partisan difference from middle-aged and older Jews.

It is a truism of contemporary American politics that women are more Democratic and liberal than men in their political preferences and voting behavior. This gender difference achieved prominence after the 1980 presidential election but did not appear consistently and strongly until the 1990s. The 1996 presidential election witnessed the largest gender gap in modern politics, with 54 percent of women voting for Bill Clinton

Jewish Voting in Congressional Elections on the 1990s by Age Cohort

	18–29 (%)	30–39 (%)	40–44 (%)	45–49 (%)	50–59 (%)	60+ (%)
Democrat	70	73	69	74	80	82
Republican	30	27	31	26	20	18

Source: Exit Poll Data, 1990–1998

compared to 43 percent of men. Jewish women identify with the Democrats much more strongly than Jewish men. Interestingly enough, Jewish men are not drawn to the Republican Party but rather, like in the younger cohort examined earlier, migrate toward political independence. In spite of the gender difference in partisan identification, men (74 percent) and women (77 percent) support Democratic candidates for Congress equally strongly.

**Jewish Partisanship
in the 1990s by Gender**

	Men (%)	Women (%)
Republican	17	13
Independent	28	23
Democrat	56	64

Source: Exit Poll Data, 1990–1998

Social Issues

In the 1960s, when many social norms came under attack in American society, advocates of changing morality battled with those who believed in social tradition. This conflict over social issues became acute in the 1980s and 1990s as conservative Christians mobilized for political power through organizations like the Moral Majority and the Christian Coalition. Republicans embraced a package of issue positions known as "traditional" or "family" values while Democrats generally called for tolerance and inclusion.

We look at three of the social issues that divided the parties: abortion rights, the death penalty, and gay rights. Jewish activists were deeply involved in promoting both abortion rights and antidiscrimination protection for gays and lesbians, but they were less noticeable in the debate over the death penalty. To what extent do the views of activists mirror the rank and file?

Jewish law on reproduction has traditionally been interpreted to give priority to the life and health of the mother over the interests of the potential life represented by the fetus. In the numerically dominant Reform and Conservative denominations, the mother's "health" has been broadened beyond medical factors to incorporate social needs and mental condition. The Orthodox wing has tended to restrict the circumstances in which abortion is deemed permissible. When participants in the Jewish Public Opinion Survey were asked how well the "prochoice" and "prolife" labels fit them, we observed strikingly high levels of polarization between Jews and non-Jews. Whether compared to all non-Jews or just to highly educated whites, Jews stood out for their commitment to the prochoice label and their rejection of the prolife category. However, the high level of support for the prochoice position among Jews disguised significant gender and religiosity gaps. Jewish women and the least religiously observant were almost unanimous in their embrace of the prochoice label in comparison to support by "only" about two-thirds of Jewish men and the most religiously involved. Except for a tendency among the college-educated to reject the prolife marker more so than others, no comparable internal trait divided Jews on that question. Perhaps because the prolife cause has become so strongly identified with Christian conservatives, the most religiously involved Jews were no more likely than other Jews to accept it.

Views Toward Abortion

How well does each phrase describe you?

	Prochoice		Prolife	
	Jewish (%)	**Non-Jewish (%)**	**Jewish (%)**	**Non-Jewish (%)**
Very well	75	36	8	34
Somewhat well	17	29	12	29
Not very well	4	14	22	20
Not well at all	4	20	56	17

Source: Knowledge Networks/Jewish Public Opinion Study 2000

The most recent of the social issues, homosexuality, has become a debate over gay marriage. While gays have pressed for the opportunity to achieve some type of legally recognized union, their opponents have pushed through a "Defense of Marriage" act. On this question, Jews are decidedly with the gays and lesbians rather than the non-Jewish religious traditionalists, who regard the concept of gay marriage as blasphemy. Jews are twice as likely as non-Jews to believe that gay marriages should enjoy legal status. Although the difference is narrower, Jews still stand out as social liberals when they are compared to non-Jews who have high levels of education. In studies of the general population, the young, better-educated, and less religiously observant participants are considerably more sympathetic to gays and lesbians. Do such differences operate among Jews? As it does for non-Jews, age and education make a difference in Jewish positions on this issue. Younger and better-educated Jews are appreciably more likely to support gay marriage. But unlike the pattern for non-Jews, levels of religious observance do not

Views Toward Homosexuality

Do you think marriages between homosexuals should or
should not be legal, with the same
rights as traditional marriages?

	Jewish (%)	Non-Jewish (%)
Legal	55	26
Not legal	31	62
Don't know	14	12

Source: Knowledge Networks/Jewish Public Opinion Study 2000

matter among Jews. The most observant Jews are less in favor of this innovation, but the
difference is not statistically significant.

The death penalty is one of the issues on which some analysts have emphasized the absence of Jewish distinctiveness. The simple yes/no question traditionally used to assess
death penalty attitudes has produced overwhelming majorities in favor among both Jews
and non-Jews. Because the policy usually involves a choice between the death penalty and
life imprisonment, those two options were presented to participants in the Jewish Political Opinion survey. As expected, this better-balanced question produced greater division
among both Jews and non-Jews. Compared to all non-Jews, Jews were less supportive of
the death penalty and more likely to endorse the alternative of life in prison without parole. However, on this issue, social status appears to matter more than Jewish background.
When compared only to non-Jews with college degrees, Jews were not distinctive in their
death penalty attitudes. Given what we know about the factors that influence death
penalty attitudes in the general public, we expected age, education, and religious observance to divide Jews. More specifically, we anticipated that young, better-educated, and
less religiously observant survey participants would be more likely to favor life imprisonment over capital punishment. Of the background factors, however, only education affected Jewish opinion significantly. Jews with a high school education were 3–1 in favor of
the death penalty, while the college-educated were equally divided and much less certain
on this question. Again, level of religious observance did not divide Jews on this question.

Views Toward the Death Penalty

What do you think the penalty should be for someone convicted of murder?

	Jewish (%)	Non-Jewish (%)
Death penalty	50	58
Life imprisonment without parole	38	30
Don't know	12	13

Source: Knowledge Networks/Jewish Public Opinion Study 2000

In sum, then, Jews are more liberal than non-Jews by varying degrees on most social values. On some issues, Jewish cohesion is diminished by social traits, particularly education and age, which is not surprising given that younger people generally are more socially liberal and secular than their elders. But while these issues often divide the general public by gender and levels of religious commitment, that pattern did not show up consistently among Jews. On this set of issues, being Jewish appeared more powerful than competing social influences.

Church and State

We would expect to find substantial differences between Jews and non-Jews and, perhaps, among Jews on the question of the relationship between church and state. Jews are clearly less likely to consider themselves part of the religious right. As a tiny minority in an overwhelming Christian country, Jews have long been sensitive about government actions that appear to favor the dominant religious faith. Jewish organizations have taken the lead in pushing the boundaries of the Constitution's establishment clause to forbid governments at all levels from endorsing or promoting religion. This strongly separationist position—separationist in the sense of favoring a "strict separation" between religion and state—can be understood both in terms of the Jewish minority experience and as a form of collective self-interest. When the state promotes religion, the beneficiary is likely to be the faith of the majority at the expense of minorities.

Discrimination is the circumstance that appears to come to mind when Americans think about church and state in abstract terms. When we asked respondents in the Jewish Public Opinion Study to select between two philosophical alternatives—one that allows the state to advance religion and another that emphasizes the separation of religion and government—the Jews and non-Jews parted company. The non-Jews are closely divided between the options of positive government action on behalf of religion and a high wall of separation. Among the college-educated non-Jews, the division is almost exactly fifty-fifty. But, four out of five Jews are squarely in the separationist camp, endorsing the high wall of separation. This question unites Jews across all lines. No matter how the results were broken down—by gender, age, income, and education—no fewer than 80 percent of Jews embraced the "wall of separation." Interestingly, Jews who were most religiously observant were even more firmly committed to separationism than Jews as a whole. Even though personal religious commitment might be expected to translate into support for state endorsement of religion, as it does for non-Jews in other surveys, nine out of ten of the most observant Jews endorsed separation.

The polarization between Jews and non-Jews also shows up dramatically when the principle of church and state takes concrete form over the issue of school prayer. Religious conservatives have never accepted Supreme Court decisions that forbid public schools from promoting or endorsing public prayer by students. Since the

Views Toward Separation of Church and State

Which of the following two statements comes closer to your view?

	Jews (%)	Non-Jews (%)
The government should take special steps to protect American religious heritage	12	55
There should be a high wall of separation between church and state	88	45

Source: Knowledge Networks/Jewish Public Opinion Study 2000

decisions were reached in the 1960s, the opponents have tried a variety of ways to encourage prayer—a constitutional amendment overturning the Court's decision, "moment of silence" laws at the state level, student-initiated prayer at school events, even efforts to remove the issue from the Court's jurisdiction. The gap between Jews and Gentiles is dramatically revealed when respondents were asked about a constitutional amendment.

Attitudes Toward School Prayer

Would you favor or oppose an amendment to the U.S. Constitution that would permit prayers to be said in public schools?

	Jews (%)	Non-Jews (%)
Favor	14	70
Oppose	81	22
Don't know	6	9

Source: Knowledge Networks/Jewish Public Opinion Study 2000

Jews are dead set against such an amendment; non-Jews at all levels of education are committed to it. Jewish opposition is strong across the board. The least-hostile group, the relatively small proportion of Jews with only a high school education, opposes school prayer "only" by a 2–1 margin. On this question, too, the most religiously involved Jews do not cross lines to join with the religiously motivated advocates of school prayer in Christian denominations. Ninety percent of the most religiously observant Jews are against the proposed amendment.

These positions are not surprising considering that Jews believe a relaxation of the wall of separation would benefit the dominant faith and handicap Jews. But what if a policy that involved breaching the wall could be seen to enhance the position of Jews? That is the rationale for advocates of school vouchers, a policy that would permit the state to support religious education by funding attendance at religious schools. For example,

Jewish day school education has grown appreciably in the last decade amid concerns for what is described as "Jewish continuity." The National Jewish Population Study of 1990 rang alarms in the Jewish community with its report that half of Jews now marry non-Jewish partners. With evidence that the highest rate of marrying within the religion occurs among Jews who experienced a Jewish day school education, Jewish organizations have campaigned to increase these private enrollment opportunities. Vouchers would facilitate this goal by lowering the cost of sending children to Jewish day schools. Yet most American Jews remain committed to the public education system and see vouchers as a dangerous force that would divide Americans into competing camps.

We asked participants in the Jewish Public Opinion Study whether they approved or disapproved of a proposal "in which some of the education budget is devoted to school vouchers that allow parents to send their children to private and religious schools." Jews were against this proposal by a margin of 3–2, the same ratio by which non-Jews supported it. That is a much smaller gap than divides Jews and non-Jews on other church–state issues. Moreover, the gap eroded considerably, to less than 10 percent, when the comparison group was restricted to non-Jews with college degrees.

Vouchers might be an issue with the capacity to divide the Jewish community based on both self-interest and religious commitment. Those who would benefit from the policy financially and those who value traditional Jewish observance might well see vouchers as more attractive than other groups in the Jewish community. Level of observance does make a difference among Jews, but not so strongly as some might expect. The ten-point gap in support for vouchers for Jewish day school education between the least- and most-observant segments of the community is not statistically significant. The split within Judaism is related to age. A majority of those under forty-five support vouchers. Support drops off sharply over age forty-five; in fact, for those over fifty-five, support is only half that of those under forty-five.

At the present time, school vouchers remain hypothetical for the vast majority of American school districts. Although Jewish organizations have joined teachers'

Views Toward School Vouchers

Do you favor or oppose an idea now being tested in a few cities and states in which some of the education budget is devoted to school vouchers that allow parents to send their children to private and religious schools?

	Jews (%)	Non-Jews (%)	College Educated Non-Jews (%)
Favor vouchers	31	47	47
Oppose vouchers	51	29	41
Don't know	18	24	13

Source: Knowledge Networks/Jewish Public Opinion Study 2000

groups in challenging their constitutionality, the Jewish rank and file may not yet have understood the church–state implications of vouchers or considered the possibility that this innovation may hurt public school funding or permit state funds to flow to racist and antisemitic schools.

We envision two different scenarios on this issue. If vouchers become more politically salient, Jews may come to perceive them as an attack on church–state separation and move heavily into the opposition category. Yet the data also permit the conclusion that Jews approach this issue more from the perspective of self-interest than from constitutional values. Jews may be aware of the larger implications of vouchers but value them nonetheless because they put higher priority on facilitating Jewish education as a means of communal survival. The data presented here certainly raise the possibility that the voucher issue has the capacity to undermine Jewish political cohesion. Apart from vouchers, however, Jews continue to embrace the wall of separation with unalloyed enthusiasm.

Race/Affirmative Action

In the 1950s and 1960s, when liberalism was defined largely by positions on race relations, Jews were among the most ardent supporters of civil rights legislation for blacks. For a variety of reasons, the relationship between blacks and Jews weakened in time, never again achieving earlier levels. Much of the difference revolves around affirmative action, the policy of granting special assistance—what critics deride as special rights—to specific categories of people. Many black leaders regard this policy as essential to the progress of African Americans. Many Jews perceive it as a new form of the old quotas that once blocked Jewish social progress.

Despite the apparent estrangement, Jews remain more sympathetic than non-Jews to the claims of black activists. Jews perceive government as less responsive to black needs, believe that blacks will need assistance to escape poverty, and, most clearly, reject the notion that black welfare recipients are undeserving. On the last question Jews and non-Jews were not only deeply divided but also on opposite sides of the political fence. We found some tendency for education and religious observance to divide Jews on at least two of these questions. The best-educated and most religiously observant were most inclined to believe that blacks faced a different situation than previous white ethnic groups and that black welfare recipients were truly needy.

The participants in the survey were asked for their attitude toward employment preferences for four types of people. Jews are neither consistently more supportive nor consistently more opposed than Gentiles to affirmative action. On this issue, Jews appeared to be fairly cohesive. As income rises, so does opposition to hiring preferences for people with disabilities and women. The pattern is quite sharp. Support for giving preferences to people with disabilities dropped from 61 percent to

Views Toward Affirmative Action and Race

Do you agree or disagree with each of the following statements?

	Jews (%)	Non-Jews (%)
Government officials usually pay less attention to a request or complaint from a black person than from a white person. (% Agree)	43	29
Irish, Italians, Jewish, and many other minorities overcame prejudice and worked their way up. Blacks should do the same without any special favors. (% Disagree)	28	17
Most blacks who receive money from welfare programs could get along without it if they tried. (% Disagree)	53	34

Source: Knowledge Networks/Jewish Public Opinion Study 2000

Views Toward Affirmative Action

(%) favor

Do you favor or oppose giving preferences in hiring to . . .

	Jews (%)	Non-Jews (%)
The handicapped	50	45
Women	24	26
Blacks	18	22
Hispanics	15	20

Source: Knowledge Networks/Jewish Public Opinion Study 2000

40 percent from the poorest to the wealthiest group, and it was more than halved on the question about women. Looked at in total, Jews are probably not distinctive from non-Jews on affirmative action. Considering how Jews often part company with the college-educated non-Jews, the lack of a difference here is noteworthy.

Foreign Policy

The Six-Day War of 1967 galvanized American Jewry behind the cause of Israeli security. To this day, Israel is likely to be the first issue that comes to mind when somebody mentions Jews and American politics. Yet Israel has become not just a Jewish but also an American priority. Presidents from Nixon to Clinton have put the United States squarely behind Israel. Americans find it easy to embrace this cause because Israel is considered a pro-Western, democratic state in a region that is generally anti-Western and nondemocratic. So are American Jews massively more pro-Israel than other Americans?

Views Toward the Status of Jerusalem

As you may know, one of the issues being discussed in the negotiations between Israel and the Palestinians is the status of Jerusalem. Israel wants to keep control of all of Jerusalem. The Palestinians want East Jerusalem to be the capital of a Palestinian state. Which position do you agree with on this issue?

	Jews (%)	Non-Jews (%)
Israel should keep control of all of Jerusalem	69	31
East Jerusalem should be the capital of a Palestinian state	13	22
Don't know	19	47

Source: Knowledge Networks/Jewish Public Opinion Study 2000

Views Toward the Status of the Golan Heights

Do you think Israel should be willing to give up the Golan Heights if Syria agrees to demilitarize the area and recognize Israel?

	Jews (%)	Non-Jews (%)
Yes	36	36
No	43	17
Don't know	20	47

Source: Knowledge Networks/Jewish Public Opinion Study 2000

At first glance, Jews seem much more supportive of Israel than are other Americans. On two issues involving Israeli security—control over a unified Jerusalem and the Golan Heights—American Jews do register much higher levels of support than non-Jews for what are often considered hard-line policies. Yet on further inspection, the differences between American Jews and Gentiles do not involve the direction of attitudes but rather familiarity with the issue. Almost half the non-Jewish Americans surveyed did not have preferences on these two issues, while 80 percent of the Jewish sample selected a response other than "don't know." The distribution of opinion among those non-Jews who selected a preference, including those with college degrees, is close to the breakdown for Jews.

That same pattern holds when respondents were asked to provide an evaluation of the leaders of the two forces in peace negotiation. American Jews were much more favorable toward Israel's Ehud Barak and hostile toward Yasir Arafat of the Palestine National Authority than non-Jews. Rather than reflect a conflict with the opinions of other Americans, however, Jews differ primarily in their attentiveness to the negotiations. Simply put, most non-Jews, whether college educated or not, are much less likely than Jews to offer an assessment of Barak and Arafat.

Views Toward Leaders in the Middle East

Please rate your feelings toward (Israeli Prime Minister
Ehud Barak, Palestinian Authority President Yasir Arafat).
Is your overall impression of him . . .

	Jews (%)	Non-Jews (%)
View of Barak		
Favorable	53	17
Neutral/No opinion	40	78
Unfavorable	8	5
View of Arafat		
Favorable	6	9
Neutral/No opinion	21	52
Unfavorable	73	38

Source: Knowledge Networks/Jewish Public Opinion Study 2000

Does the Israeli cause still bind American Jews? In the 1960s and early 1970s, Israel was clearly the central item on the political agenda of American Jewry. Indeed, to some observers, Israel and the Holocaust had become the twin pillars of Jewish identity in the United States. Many of these same commentators believe that Israel became increasingly divisive among American Jews from the middle 1970s onward. Many liberal American Jews were upset about the dominant Likud Party's aggressive policy of planting Jewish settlements in the West Bank area and the religiously inspired position that all of the historical Land of Israel should be retained by the modern state of Israel. The Israeli Labor Party's embrace of the Oslo peace process, with its vision of Israeli's disengagement from most of the West Bank and the creation of an independent Palestinian state, further divided the community.

Jews were asked about the condition of Israel six years after the Oslo process began. Considering how much attention has been paid to this issue as a source of division among American Jewry, it is striking to observe how little polarization actually exists among the rank and file. Two-thirds of Jewish respondents report either that the process has not affected Israel's standing or that they don't know what the impact has been. Of the one-third who perceive a change, slightly more believe Israel is better off than it was before the Oslo process began. This conclusion hardly suggests massive divisions within the community. The extent of division may appear greater than it is because more attention is paid by the press to dissent rather than to harmony.

Looking over the entire range of questions about Israel and foreign policy, we observed only two tendencies toward internal division among Jews. One major difference was about who had opinions and who did not. As a rule, we found that the younger, less-educated, lower-income, and female members of the Jewish sample were more likely to

Views Toward Peace in the Middle East

It has been more than 6 years since Israel and the
Palestinians signed the Oslo Peace Accord. Do you think
Israel is now better off or worse off because of the accord?

	Jews (%)
Better off	22
About the same	39
Worse off	15
Don't know	24

Source: Knowledge Networks/Jewish Public Opinion Study 2000

respond with a "don't know" to the various questions. Nothing is particularly surprising about this finding; studies of Americans' political knowledge in general have identified the same patterns for the public at large.

We also considered how religious observance might affect foreign policy attitudes among Jews. As we saw, observant Jews appear to follow politics more closely. For many reasons we might expect observant Jews to pay attention to Israel despite the general tendency of Americans to ignore foreign policy. *Defending* Jerusalem is one of the commandments that the more religiously involved will hear in synagogue. Because Israel is the only country in the world with a Jewish majority, it is also likely to attract Jews who want to spend time in a pervasively Jewish environment. Taken together, these factors seem to promote a stronger tie to Israel and a harder line on the peace process.

As expected, Jewish attitudes were related to levels of religious observance. Compared to Jews with lesser ritual involvement, observant Jews were more committed to retaining the Golan Heights and Jerusalem, were more hostile to Yasir Arafat, and were more pessimistic about the Oslo process. They also differed by their greater levels of support for American intervention on behalf of threatened religious minorities abroad. We should not overstate the differences among Jews based on their level of religious involvement. As a rule, all three groups of Jews had the same majority or plurality position. The difference was that the most-observant group was even more enthusiastic in support of Israel than the other two groups.

This finding is also consistent with previous research suggesting that religiously observant Jews are more committed to Israel. As such, they tend to take the strongest position against giving up land or other policies that may threaten Israeli security. The source of this commitment is evident when we asked participants whether they had ever visited Israel or made a contribution to a pro-Israeli organization or cause recently.

Connection with Israel

Jewish Sample

In the last 12 months, has anyone in your household made a financial contribution to Israel, to an Israeli institution, or to any pro-Israel cause? Have you ever visited Israel?

	Visited (%)	Contributed (%)
Lowest observance	19	19
Intermediate observance	28	46
Highest observance	58	64

Source: Knowledge Networks/Jewish Public Opinion Study 2000

The more religiously involved Jews were three times more likely to have visited Israel as the least religious and twice more likely to have gone to the Middle East as those in the middle category on the religious observance scale. In line with that pattern, the most observant were also significantly more likely to have contributed funds to a pro-Israel cause.

Moving beyond the Israel question, surely the most salient foreign policy concern for many Jews, we wondered whether Jews were equally distinctive on other questions about America's role in the world. Because of the Holocaust and their own experience of oppression, we expected that American Jews would have strongly supported intervention abroad for humanitarian purposes. The participants in the Jewish Public Opinion Survey were asked whether the United States should send troops to help out an ethnic or religious minority group that was experiencing persecution. Such a question no doubt evoked recent memories of American intervention in *Kosovo* to defend Muslims and Croats against the *Bosnian* Serbs. A good many respondents refused to say yes or no to this hypothetical situation. Among those who did, however, American Jews were almost 2–1 in favor of intervention, while non-Jewish Americans were 2–1 against; college-educated non-Jews were split down the middle. Whatever the specifics of the Bosnian case, we suspect that the experience of Israel and the history of Jewish persecution abroad have made American Jews sensitive to the problem of religious persecution.

DO JEWS HAVE DISPROPORTIONATE INFLUENCE IN AMERICAN POLITICS? THE CASE OF POLITICAL PARTICIPATION

As interesting as these attitude differences are to Jews and students of political behavior generally, the general reader might wonder why they matter. If Jews constitute less than 3 percent of the American population, why should we care about their distinctive political habits? The answer is that Jewish Americans do have an important impact on American politics despite their small numbers. We know that Jews "overparticipate" in politics: they are more likely than other Americans to vote, contribute to campaigns, and embrace social activism. In a society in which politics is a spectator sport with an audience base that ranks somewhere below professional sports, Jews thus have a political impact beyond their numbers. But does this disparity stem from something distinctly Jewish or from the fact that Jews tend to have more resources than other Americans? As we know from studies of political participation, political engagement is closely related to the socioeconomic resources an individual possesses. For a variety of reasons that are beyond the scope of this chapter, highly educated and affluent citizens are much

JEWS "OVERPARTICIPATE" NOT BECAUSE THEY ARE JEWISH BUT BECAUSE THEY POSSESS CONSIDERABLE RESOURCES.

more likely than the disadvantaged to participate and exert influence in politics. But is Jewish participation higher or lower than we would expect after taking into account the social conditions of the Jewish community in the United States?

Comparing Jews with non-Jews of comparable socioeconomic status reveals that Jews "overparticipate" not because they are Jewish, but because they possess considerable resources. Overall, statistically significant differences exist between Jews and non-Jews on making campaign contributions, voter registration, and voting in the 1996 election. But high-status non-Jews' participation rate across a range of measures is nearly identical to Jewish Americans. The only exception is interest in politics—Jews are significantly more likely to be "very interested" in politics and public affairs than high-status non-Jews.

JEWS ARE SIGNIFICANTLY MORE LIKELY TO BE "VERY INTERESTED" IN POLITICS AND PUBLIC AFFAIRS THAN HIGH-STATUS NON-JEWS.

Political Participation

Which of the following have you yourself done during the year 2000 or do you expect to do in 2000?

| | High SES White | | |
	Jews (%)	Non-Jews (%)	All Non-Jews (%)
Volunteered	9	8	7
Contributed	23	26	17
Contact letter	34	38	31
Interest in politics	43	27	22
Registered to vote	84	85	73
1996 vote	89	87	71

Source: Knowledge Networks/Jewish Public Opinion Study 2000
SES: socioeconomic status

Like other Americans, Jews vary in their propensity to get involved in political life. Generally, more affluent, well-educated, and older Jews are more likely than their poorer, less-educated, and younger counterparts to participate in politics. The differences are rather small because, in general, few Americans engage in such demanding political activities as volunteering to work in a political campaign. Moreover, while generally the very least educated and least affluent Jews drop off in their political participation, they constitute a small part of the Jewish population. In some cases, however, the differences are larger. Older Jews are more interested in public affairs and more likely to participate in electoral politics than their younger counterparts. For instance, 29 percent of Jews over sixty-five years of age contribute to a campaigns compared to 11 percent of Jews between eighteen and thirty-five. Similarly, 39 percent of older Jews write to elected officials, compared to 27 percent of younger Jews.

Several recent studies emphasize the importance of social connection and networks to participation in politics. Members of voluntary associations and religious institutions are more likely to participate in politics than the socially disconnected. As Sidney Verba, Kay Scholzman, and Henry Brady argue in their important work *Voice and Equality,* members of associations and organizations acquire "transportable" civic skills that they find useful in the politics. Churchgoers, for example, who make speeches, organize activities, or write newsletters at church, may acquire the skills, confidence, and knowledge to volunteer on a campaign or participate in a local protest movement. They show quite clearly that even after considering the effect of socioeconomic resources, institutional membership leads to greater levels of activity across a variety of measures of participation.

The low levels of religious participation among Jewish Americans makes for an open question whether this relationship between organizational participation and civic engagement holds. In fact, this relationship exists quite strongly for Jewish Americans as well. Observant Jews are significantly more likely than secular Jews to participate in politics across a wide array of activities. Jews with the highest level of observance are three times as likely to volunteer for a political campaign, and twice as likely to contribute to a political campaign and contact an elected official than Jews with the lowest level.

CONCLUSION

As the discussion makes clear, the traditional liberal and Democratic tilt of American Jews endures. In fact, a number of economic, political, and cultural changes might have affected the cohesion of Jewish political identity. Contemporary Jewish Americans have assimilated to a greater degree than previous generations and are more dispersed geographically. The nature of American politics has changed. Newer generations of Jewish Americans have no direct experience with the upheavals of the 1960s and the civil rights, student, and antiwar movements. More distant still are the immigrant experience and the Holocaust. In the general public, we find less polarization among younger Americans around race and civil rights, changes in women's roles, sexuality, and homosexuality. Younger citizens generally are less partisan than their elders, and there is shrinking ideological differences between the political parties. These are powerful forces working against the maintenance of group political identity.

By almost any measure, however, Jewish Americans remain solidly Democratic and on the liberal side of the American political spectrum. Along with African Americans, Jews remain the most loyal members of the New Deal Coalition, and, in all likelihood, the nomination of Joseph Lieberman for vice president further cemented this connection. On issues such as abortion, the women's movement, gun control, civil liberties, the religious right, and the environment, Jewish Americans adopt liberal positions with little internal differentiation based on class, gender, level of religious observation, and geographic residence. Even in an area where Jews look more like other Americans such as affirmative action, Jews have a less rosy assessment of the state of race relations in the United States.

While the survey data employed in this chapter cannot directly address the competing explanations of the political distinctiveness of Jewish Americans, we can speculate about their contribution to an explanation for the durability of Jewish liberalism. Something is clearly distinctive about the Jewish community that creates a lasting sense of Jewish political identity. Scholars argue that African Americans maintain their political cohesion in the face of increasing internal differentiation because they think of their political interests in terms of group interests. They gauge their understanding of political and economic events by considering their effect on African Americans relative to other groups such as white Americans.

> SOMETHING IS CLEARLY DISTINCTIVE ABOUT THE JEWISH COMMUNITY THAT CREATES A LASTING SENSE OF JEWISH POLITICAL IDENTITY.

Similarly, we can speculate that a history of religious persecution and the immigrant experience, a distinctive religious tradition, and political self-interest may create a lens through which Jews view American politics. Public policies and political leadership could be key factors because of how they affect the standing of Jewish Americans in society and politics. At the current political moment, Jewish Americans see their interests as served by a particularly liberal political perspective. For instance, the association of the Republican Party and the religious right throughout the 1980s and 1990s engenders a resistance to Republicanism based on Jewish support for separation of church and state. Or Jewish secularism creates hostility toward the social conservatism often associated with the right in American politics. But this liberalism is by no means inevitable. We will have to wait and see whether broader political, cultural, and economic changes alter the enduring liberalism of Jewish Americans.

APPENDIX

Before the development of political polling, scholars used to infer Jewish political behavior from voting returns. They would identify small election districts—wards and precincts—known to have heavy concentrations of Jews and generalize about political loyalties from this information. Apart from concerns about the accuracy of the information, the technique has several important limitations. First, even if it was possible to discern Jewish voting patterns from so-called homogeneous voting districts, the data reveal only *how* Jews voted. Such information can say nothing about *why* Jews vote as they do or what they think about politics. Second, such data (again, assuming their accuracy) do not enable researchers to explore variations in political behavior among Jews based on religious commitment, socioeconomic status, ethnic origin, or other critical factors. Unless the researcher is lucky enough to isolate multiple districts with Jews and to know how those districts vary on these factors, there is no way to speak intelligently about political differences among Jews.

Many scholars doubt that the study of geographic areas can even reveal accurate information about group voting patterns. Researchers face a serious dilemma. Few districts can be said to contain only Jewish residents and voters. As the proportion of Jews in any single election unit declines, it becomes a challenge to isolate Jewish behavior from the influence of the other residents of the district. This has become a more serious problem as Jews took advantage of their mobility to move outside of Jewish "ghettos" and dispersed across the country. In districts that are overwhelmingly Jewish, researchers face the other horn of the dilemma. Jews who reside in homogeneously Jewish areas may not be typical of their less residentially clustered co-religionists. They may well be distinctive in terms of their religious commitment, ethnic background, or other social traits that influence voting and political opinion. It can be dangerous to generalize from these homogeneously Jewish environments to the behavior of Jews who live in more socially diverse surroundings.

Considering all these problems, specialists in the study of Jewish political behavior are more confident of conclusions drawn from public opinion polls that follow accepted scientific methods. Using random methods of selection, surveys can identify Jewish respondents who reside in a wide variety of geographic areas.

While surveys have so much potential, even this research tool presents the student of Jewish political behavior with its own set of problems. To really understand how Jews behave politically, it is necessary both to compare Jews to one another and to non-Jews. Studying internal differences among Jews requires a survey with a large number of respondents so there are plenty of individuals in each category. If we want to discover the effect of suburbanization on Jewish attachments to the Democratic Party, for example, we can do so only with a survey that includes a large number of Jews who live in urban, suburban, and rural environments. To determine what is unique about Jewry, the researcher also needs a comparison sample of non-Jews. Are Jews politically distinctive because they are Jewish, or do they hold essentially the same attitudes as non-Jews with comparable levels of education who reside in the same type of communities? Because they constitute at most 3 percent of the population, Jews seldom turn up in sufficient numbers in standard polls to offer firm generalizations or to conduct subgroup analysis. Only a very few surveys with large samples produce a requisite number of Jews, and those tend to be restricted to special topics.

To overcome these limitations, we rely on two sets of data about Jews. First, we conducted a survey using an Internet panel with a nationally representative sample of Jews, which we call the Jewish Public Opinion Study. Second, we pooled exit poll data from the 1990s to compile a sample size of sufficient size to analyze Jewish voting behavior.

The Jewish Public Opinion Study

The Knowledge Networks poll was conducted between July 21 and August 8, 2000, and includes 457 American Jews and 531 non-Jews eighteen years and older. The results among Jews are subject to a margin of error of approximately 5.0 percentage points at the 95 percent confidence level, while the results among non-Jews are subject to a margin of error of approximately 4.7 percentage points. Comparisons between Jews and non-Jews are subject to a margin of error of 6.9 percentage points. Sampling error is only one form of potential error in public opinion surveys.

The Knowledge Networks poll is one of the few nationally representative surveys of American Jews. Because Knowledge Networks collects demographic information on all of its respondents, the company can target surveys at specific groups that represent small portions of the U.S. population. Jews comprise less than 3 percent of the U.S. population.

Knowledge Networks employs a Random Digit Dialing (RDD) telephone methodology to develop a representative sample of households for participation in its panel. This form of selection makes it possible to reach every American household with a telephone. Knowledge Networks also employs a complex sample stratification design that incorporates the known probabilities of selection associated with geographic location, the number of phone lines, and whether the phone number is listed. Once a Knowledge Networks household is selected, members are contacted first by an express delivery mailing and then by telephone for enrollment in the Knowledge Networks panel.

Every participating Knowledge Networks household receives free hardware, free Internet access, free e-mail accounts, and ongoing technical support. Participants receive a short multimedia survey about once a week. Surveys are delivered by e-mail on the same standardized hardware, through the television set.

Exit Polls

Data for 1998 were collected by Voter News Service based on questionnaires completed by 10,017 voters leaving polling places around the country on election day. Data for 1994 and 1996 were collected by Voter News Service: 11,308 in 1994 and 16,637 in 1996. Data for 1990 and 1992 were collected by Voter Research and Surveys: 19,888 in 1990 and 15,490 in 1992.

The combined data set contain 1,498 Jewish Americans, based on the question "Are you: Protestant, Catholic, Other Christian, Jewish, Something else, None?" or "In what religion were you brought up: Protestant, Catholic, Other Christian, Jewish, Something else, None?"

10

RIGHT TURN?

Jews and the American Conservative Movement

EDWARD SHAPIRO

When I told a friend that I was writing an essay on the Jewish role in the American conservative movement for a volume on Jews and American politics, he jested that mine would certainly be the shortest one in the book. He meant by this that American Jewish conservatives were doubly marginalized, as conservatives living in the world's leading liberal nation and as Jews in a movement that historically has been seen as unfriendly to Jews and to Jewish interests. Conservatism seemed to have little relevance for a nation born in revolution and steeped in individualism, democracy, industrialism, and capitalism. It was this image of conservatism as an American irrelevancy that explains why Clinton Rossiter titled the second edition of his history of American conservatism *The Thankless Persuasion*. The United States, the political scientist Sheldon Wolin has argued, "presents a formidable challenge to the conservative imagination." Indeed, it was not so long ago that, to quote the conservative columnist George Will, conservatism "was widely considered, at best, an eccentricity and 'conservative' was an epithet." In the introduction to his 1950 collection of essays *The Liberal Imagination*, Lionel Trilling asserts, "In the United States at this time liberalism is not only the dominant but even the sole intellectual tradition. . . . [T]he conservative impulse and the reactionary do not, with some isolated and some ecclesiastical exceptions, express themselves in ideas but only in action or in irritable mental gestures which seek to resemble ideas." That same year a man was arrested in the Midwest for creating a public disturbance. A witness stated, "he was using abusive language, calling people conservative and all that."

There are few segments of American society in which conservatism has been so suspect than among Jews. Indeed, so pervasive has been the association of Jews with the political left, so widespread was the belief that the fate of Jews and the left were inextricably bound together, that the notion of a conservative Jew seemed almost oxymoronic. When Rabbi Dov Berush Meisels of Kraków, a member of the Austrian parliament in the mid–nineteenth century, was asked by the surprised speaker of the parliament why he sat with the left, he quipped, "Juden haben keine Rechte" (Jews have no rights). And when the Israeli Knesset first met, no political party wanted to sit on the right, and so a new parliamentary seating arrangement had to be devised.

This Jewish affinity toward the political left survived the mass migration of Jews to the Western Hemisphere. In his book *Jew vs. Jew*, Samuel G. Freedman notes that so deep was the commitment of America's Jews to Franklin D. Roosevelt and his New Deal that a Bronx mother insisted to the rabbi officiating at her son's bar mitzvah that he hold a portrait of FDR alongside the Torah scrolls during the procession through the sanctuary. Her attitude was not idiosyncratic. Rabbi William F. Rosenbloom of New York called FDR "the Messiah of America's tomorrow," while Rabbi Stephen Wise in his autobiography, published four years after Roosevelt's death, writes about his "immortality." Judge Jonah Goldstein, a New York Republican, asserted wryly that his fellow Jews appeared to have three *veltn: dei velt* (this world), *yene velt* (the other world), and Roosevelt. The hold of political liberalism on Jews has been so strong, write the sociol-

ogists Charles S. Liebman and Steven M. Cohen, that it has become "a major component of their understanding of what it means to be a Jew."

That Jews would identify politically with the left was not surprising. In Europe, the
left favored the emancipation of the Jews, opposed restrictions on Jewish economic and
social mobility, and supported the separation of church and state. Conservatism was also
identified with the defense of political and religious institutions that had been hostile to
Jewish interests. The modern Jewish attitude toward authority, both public and private,
was radically opposed to that of conservatism. Basic to modern Jewish political culture,
the sociologist Werner Cohn writes, is a "radical feeling of estrangement from the State,"
and this estrangement was found in the most insular and the most assimilated of Jews.
The alienation from politics was deeply rooted in the Jewish religious outlook. For Jews,
Michael Walzer notes, politics "was mostly a matter of war and conquest, killing and being killed, and . . . God had set Israel apart from all those hostile and fatal engagements,
destined it for a different existence. Politics was for the Gentiles." Politics would be legitimized only with the dawning of the messianic age.

Antisemitism intensified the Jewish suspicion of authority, whether private or public.
Authority was, more often than not, viewed as the source of Jewish problems. In *Fiddler
on the Roof,* the rabbi of Anatekva is asked to say a prayer for the czar. Puzzled by what
to say about an antisemite, he finally responds that he hoped the Almighty will keep the
czar . . . far away from us. This distrust of authority was intensified among nonreligious
Jews by the power of the Orthodox religious establishment. It is no coincidence that
Vilna, Lithuania, was the abode of the Vilna Gaon and the center of rabbinic Orthodoxy
in Eastern Europe, as well as the home of the radical and antireligious General Jewish
Workers' Union (the Bund).

Jewish immigrants carried these attitudes of distrust of authority and estrangement
from politics with them from Europe. Here in America, Nathan Glazer writes, Jews
"looked with a cold and hostile eye on the world of received things, traditional religion,
traditional culture, the traditional order of society. All these had historically meant for
Jews oppression, anti-Semitism, restriction. Freedom and fraternity and human possibility were for them bound up with the breaking of old forms and the letting in of
anything new and radical." Perhaps here is one explanation why Jews—including the
novelist Ayn Rand; Frank Chodorov, the founder of the Intercollegiate Society of Indi-
vidualists; and a slew of economists, including Alan Greenspan, Milton Friedman, Gary
Becker, Israel Kirzner, Murray Rothbard, and Ludwig von Mises—have been attracted to
libertarian economics and why anarchism was so important in the Jewish ghettos of New
York City's Lower East Side and London's East End before World War I. And here also
is a partial explanation why the New Left of the 1960s, which had a disproportionate
number of Jews in influential positions, saw authority, any authority, as its enemy. Today
the Jewish attitude toward state authority and individual power most clearly manifests itself in support for civil liberties and for freedom of choice concerning abortion.

Some American Jews have even argued that this estrangement from authority and distrust of power is what being Jewish is all about. The essence of Judaism, Michael Selzer writes, "involved a revolution to radicalize the world through Jewish powerlessness and suffering." Furthermore, as workers and inhabitants of large cities, Jews believed their economic and social interests were best nourished by socialism and urban liberalism. The Marxist slogan "Workers of the World Unite" was on the masthead of the *Forward,* the most popular and influential of American Yiddish papers, and it remained there long after the newspaper moved from socialism to liberalism.

American Jews were also attracted to the left because of its opposition to racial, ethnic, and religious discrimination, including antisemitism, and to the breaching of the wall of separation between church and state. Jews remembered the resistance within the Christian church in Europe to Jewish emancipation and that the church had been the most consistently antisemitic element in Europe for the past two thousand years. There is no more widely and deeply held political assumption among American Jews than that their security is threatened by the undermining of the secular basis of the polity and the intrusion by organized religion into what Reverend John Neuhaus has called the "public square," except when, as in the case of Martin Luther King Jr., it advances liberal goals. Jewish organizations such as the American Jewish Congress and the Anti-Defamation League of B'nai Brith have been in the forefront of opposition to governmental aid to parochial schools and to public efforts to accommodate the religious sensibilities of Christians (and Jews). "American Jews," Elliott Abrams writes, "believe simply as an article of faith that a more religious society threatens them—and this has been a much more powerful credo for the American Jew than any of the laws of Moses." This is not based on Jewish teachings, on any understanding of modern Christianity, or on "survey research, sociological analysis, or political science." It stems, rather, from a fear of Christians and Christianity based on memories with little relevance to contemporary American conditions.

This political love affair of American Jews with the left has persisted despite rapid economic and social mobility, suburbanization, and the changing focus of the left from economic issues involving taxes and the regulation of business to cultural issues concerning status and identity. In a famous comment on Jewish voting patterns voiced over three decades ago, Milton Himmelfarb said that Jews continued to vote like Hispanics even though they were now living like Episcopalians. Jewish political attitudes have not changed very much during the past thirty years, even though the Jewish advance up the economic and social ladder has continued. Jews, the sociologist Irving Louis Horowitz writes, "have proven to be a unique force in American politics in that, despite their class backgrounds or interests, they have exhibited the capacity to vote and act beyond their class and interest group constraints." This has befuddled observers, and there is a cottage industry of sociologists, historians, and political scientists researching this seeming anomaly. Words used to describe the voting patterns of American Jews include *paradoxical, dissonant, peculiar, strange, curious, contradictory,* and *idiosyncratic.*

Things were not always perceived this way. In the nineteenth century, Benjamin Disraeli remarked about the political conservatism of Jews. He once described himself as the blank page between the Old and New Testaments. In his book *Lord George Bentinck,* he calls Jews "the trustees of tradition, and the conservators of the religious element. . . . All the tendencies of the Jewish race are conservative. Their bias is to religion, property, and natural aristocracy; and it should be the interest of statesmen that this bias of a great race should be encouraged and their energies and creative powers enlisted in the cause of existing society."

Modern conservatives have eagerly anticipated the day when Jews would give up their abnormal attachment to the Left and return to their natural abode on the right. Russell Kirk's *The Conservative Mind* (1954), a landmark work in the postwar conservative revival in America, claimed that, had it not been for antisemitism, Jews would have been staunch conservatives. "The traditions of race and religion, the Jewish devotion to family, old usage, and spiritual continuity," Kirk writes, "all incline the Jew toward conservatism. It is exclusion from society which provokes the Jewish social revolutionary." Jews on the right have been continually predicting during the past forty years an imminent shift rightward of Jews to comport with their higher social and economic status and the decline in antisemitism in Europe and the United States. Thus, in his 1982 book *The Left, the Right and the Jews,* W. D. Rubinstein, an Australian political scientist, says that "the familiar left-liberal stance of most American Jews is undergoing a significant shift. . . . It may well be that American Jews are at last moving—as elsewhere in the West—to their natural political home." Irving Kristol has also been prophesying the imminent political metamorphosis of American Jews for the past three decades. Jewish political behavior, however, has continued to confound these predictions.

This most important contemporary manifestation of the addiction of American Jews to liberal politics has been their attachment to the left wing of the Democratic Party. By the 1960s, Jews were a major source of funds for the party, and, along with blacks, its most dependable source of votes. In 1960, a higher percentage of Jews than Roman Catholics voted for John F. Kennedy, himself a Catholic, and in 1988 more Jews than Greeks voted for Michael Dukakis, a second-generation Greek American. Not surprisingly, Jews on the left have virtually conflated Jewish identity with liberalism. Rabbi Arthur Herzberg warned Jews in the 1980s that they could vote for Ronald Reagan only by forsaking their Jewish political souls. Jews, he declared, knew instinctively that politics involved strengthening "democracy," creating "a world of justice," and opposing "selfishness," and they also knew (or should know) that Republicans were unsympathetic to such concerns. Jewish spokespeople for political conservatism, he avowed, reduce "the meaning of the Jewish struggle in America to a quest for success and abandons those who are still friendless and foreign to fend for themselves."

This belief that Jewish interests lay with the left and not with the right was reinforced by the popular interpretation of politics as a spectrum stretching from the far right to the far left. On the far right, according to this view, were reactionary and antisemitic elements, including Nazism and the Ku Klux Klan. On the left were the socialists and liberals. Hence the journey along the political spectrum from right to left was a passage from depravity to virtue. This belief that Nazism was an extremist conservative movement ignored the fact that the word *nazism* meant national socialism, that the Nazis sought to overturn the traditional social and political order in Europe, and that spokespeople for traditional European conservatism opposed the Nazis. The popular interpretation of Nazism also elided the similarities emphasized by Hannah Arendt and other students of totalitarianism between the various forms of fascism, including Nazism, and communism. In any case, the description of Nazism as a rightist movement made it difficult for any Jew to identify as a conservative.

In their 1977 essay "Are American Jews Turning to the Right?" Bernard Rosenberg and Irving Howe correctly note that "the overwhelming thrust of Jewish thought and writing in America . . . has been liberal and whatever radicalism we have had in America has found disproportionate support among Jews." It was not surprising when, beginning in the 1960s, a group of self-described conservative and neoconservative Jewish intellectuals appeared that their versions of conservatism should reflect the dominant liberal assumptions and values of the religious and ethnic community from which they came, or that some in this camp would abjure the term *conservative* and prefer to describe themselves as "liberal." There were good reasons for this initial reluctance to identify with conservatism. Without denying the conservative bona fides of an Irving Kristol, Norman Podhoretz, and other prominent Jewish thinkers generally thought of as conservatives, it is clear that in some crucial respects they and their most important magazines, particularly *Commentary* and *The Public Interest,* initially had more in common with their supposed liberal Jewish adversaries than with their presumed conservative allies.

If Jews such as Podhoretz were being described in the 1970s as "conservatives," it was not, they claimed, because they had changed but because liberalism itself had moved considerably to the left since the 1960s. As John Ehrman, a student of neoconservatism writes, the conservatism of Podhoretz "was rooted in its break with liberalism, not in the Burkean thinking that informs much of modern conservative thought." Jews had once been aided by a liberalism that stressed merit and individualism. They were now menaced by a new liberalism that, contrary to its predecessor, believed that considerations of race and ethnicity should be factored into political, economic, and social decision making in both the private and public sectors. The new liberal dispensation included affirmative action timetables, quotas, and other race-conscious policies. This "affirmative discrimination," to use Nathan Glazer's apt term, struck directly at Jews, who were an upwardly mobile white population, skilled at test taking and oriented toward higher education.

Quotas, Podhoretz said at the time, "are the most serious threat to Jews since World War II." Affirmative action evoked memories among Jews of the quotas that had limited their economic, social, and educational opportunities in Europe and America. Because of their overrepresentation in academia, Jewish neoconservative intellectuals were particularly concerned with the impact that affirmative action would have on academic standards and hiring practices, and they were among the founders of the Campus Coalition for Democracy, an organization dedicated to defending the merit principle and opposing political correctness in academia.

The new Jewish conservatives were also moved to rethink their political affiliations as a result of attacks on Israel and antisemitism emanating from the left. At one time liberals had staunchly defended the state of Israel. After the Six-Day War of 1967, however, some liberals now described the Jewish state as militaristic, imperialistic, capitalistic, and racist. Jews had once been in the forefront of the civil rights movement and had believed that Jews and blacks comprised a holy brotherhood of the oppressed. By the late 1960s, antisemitism had become an important staple of the rhetoric of black radicals, as, for example, in Harold Cruse's 1967 book, *The Crisis of the Black Intellectual,* and liberals seemed to be willing to overlook or excuse such talk out of fear of lending aid and comfort to the right. "Whatever the case may have been yesterday, and whatever the case may be tomorrow," Podhoretz said, "the case today is that the most active enemies of the Jews are located not in the precincts of the ideological Right but in the Radical Left."

"TODAY THE MOST ACTIVE ENEMIES OF THE JEWS ARE LOCATED NOT IN THE PRECINCTS OF THE IDEOLOGICAL RIGHT BUT IN THE RADICAL LEFT."

In a perceptive 1988 *Commentary* essay, Dan Himmelfarb, the managing editor of *The Public Interest,* stressed the differences between the traditionalist conservatives— or paleoconservatives, as they came to be called—and the neoconservatives, a group composed largely of Jews disaffected from contemporary liberalism. The traditionalists, Himmelfarb claimed, were part of the classic conservative tradition dating back to Edmund Burke and Thomas Carlyle, a tradition that valued religion, social hierarchy, and status. The neoconservatives, by contrast, were heirs to the liberal tradition of the eighteenth and nineteenth centuries, which favored free markets, democracy, individualism, and equality of opportunity. Himmelfarb doubted whether these neoconservatives should even be called conservatives. A better name for them, he said, would be "paleoliberals." But since liberal democracy was "the" American political tradition, these paleoliberals were actually America's most authentic conservatives. "Indeed," Himmelfarb wrote, "it might with some justification be argued that it is neoconservatism, and not paleoconservatism, that is both genuinely American and genuinely conservative."

Leading traditionalist intellectuals agreed with Himmelfarb that in crucial respects the neoconservatives were aliens to conservative orthodoxy. Russell Kirk, a revered figure with the American right, described the neoconservatives as a "little sect, distrusted and reproached by many leaders of what we may call mainline conservatives, who now and again declare that most of the neoconservatives are seeking place and preferment chiefly." The neoconservatives, Kirk avowed, were deficient "in the understanding of the human condition, and in the apprehension of the accumulated wisdom of our civilization." They preferred instead "to engage in ideological sloganizing, the death of political imagination." Kirk was correct that there were deep differences between the traditionalist conservatives and the neoconservatives.

The historian George H. Nash in his history of the post–World War II conservative intellectual movement describes neoconservatism as "right-wing liberalism." This was confirmed by the neoconservatives themselves. Neoconservatives, Irving Kristol claims in his 1983 book *Reflections of a Neoconservative,* simply wanted "to return to the original sources of liberal vision and liberal energy so as to correct the warped version of liberalism that is today's orthodoxy." Ruth Wisse, a professor of Yiddish literature at Harvard, notes that she became a conservative because "liberalism betrayed its principles when it yielded to leftist insurgencies and tactics." In his 1996 essay "Neoconservatism: A Eulogy," Podhoretz says that the neocons, at least in their own eyes, never became conservatives. "So far as they were concerned, they were indeed still liberals, fighting to reclaim the traditional principles of liberalism from the leftists who had hijacked and corrupted it." Neoconservatives had moved to the right as a result of the radicalization of liberalism, not because they had accepted conservative pieties. The differences between liberals and the neoconservatives, the sociologist Nathan Glazer avows, "do not have anything to do with deep underlying philosophical positions. They have to do with fact and common sense. Very often the people we disagree with, or who disagree with us, don't seem to have the facts."

> NEOCONSERVATIVES HAD MOVED TO THE RIGHT AS A RESULT OF THE RADICALIZATION OF LIBERALISM, NOT BECAUSE THEY HAD ACCEPTED CONSERVATIVE PIETIES.

The nonideological bent of Jewish conservatives was reflected in *The Public Interest,* the magazine founded by Daniel Bell and Irving Kristol in 1965. It soon became, along with *Commentary,* the leading voice of neoconservatism. "*The Public Interest,*" the quarterly declared on its founding, "is not some kind of preexisting, platonic idea; rather it emerges out of differences of opinion, reasonably propounded." The magazine strove to provide a rationale based on social science research for opposing the expansion of government during the 1960s, rather than to elucidate the philosophical and theological principles or assumptions of conservatism. The magazine was born during the political ferment of the Great Society, and while striving to maintain an aura of objectivity suitable for an organ of social science, its major role has been to challenge the new conventional liberal wisdom on crime, housing, race relations, welfare, health, education, the environment, and other public policy issues.

In contrast to paleoconservatives, the contributors to *The Public Interest* have argued that the left is naive and misguided, not evil, and that their proposals are counterproductive, rather than philosophically flawed. More articles by economists have appeared in the magazine than by any other group of social scientists, which is not surprising since, as Irving Kristol has maintained, economics "is the social science *par excellence* of modernity." This modernist bent did not prevent the journal from publishing articles on pornography, feminism, and sex education from a socially conservative perspective. But the arguments of these essays were derived from social science and not from the tenets of religion or traditionalist conservatism. Throughout, in Kristol's words, the tone of the magazine has been "skeptical, pragmatic, meliorist."

Traditionalist conservatives, by contrast, believed their differences with liberals did involve "deep underlying philosophical positions" involving human nature, the nature of society, and the role of government. The refusal of Jewish neoconservatives to break from the mind-set of liberalism more than anything else was responsible for the doubts of Kirk and other conservative true believers about the conservative credentials of their new associates. For them, the neoconservatives were simply chastened liberals. A good example of paleo suspicion of the neos was the complaint in 1986 of Clyde Wilson, a historian at the University of South Carolina, regarding the supposed attempt by neoconservatives to seize leadership of the American conservative movement. "The offensives of radicalism have driven vast herds of liberals across the border into our territories," he said. "These refugees now speak in our name, but the language they speak is the same one they always spoke. We have grown familiar with it, have learned to tolerate it, but it is tolerable only by contrast to the harsh syllables of the barbarians over the border. It contains no words for the things that we value. Our estate has been taken over by an impostor, just as we were about to inherit."

Among the things most valued by the traditionalists was religion. In the list of the six canons of conservative thought listed in Kirk's *The Conservative Mind,* the first is "the belief that a divine intent rules society as well as conscience, forging an eternal chain of right and duty which links great and obscure, living and dead. . . . Politics is the art of apprehending and applying the Justice which is above nature." The Jewish neoconservatives disagreed. Their most important role within the American conservative movement was to remind conservatives that politics and religion are separate categories and to encourage conservatism to remain hospitable to those who looked askance at religion in general and Christianity in particular. Jewish conservatives, by and large, have not shared the reverence of Edmund Burke and his modern acolytes such as Kirk for the premodern social order and its historic institutions, which included the Church, or their misgivings for such modern developments as capitalism, democracy, and bourgeois society. In premodern Europe, Jewish conservatives need not be reminded, Jews had been ostracized or marginalized. Jewish conservatives, in contrast, welcomed modernity, and neoconservatism, as Kristol pointed out, was "resolutely free of nostalgia" for preindustrial and predemocratic values and institutions.

Two essays by Charles Krauthammer and Jerry Z. Muller in *The Public Interest* illustrate the tendency of conservative Jews to sever conservatism from religion. Krauthammer, a political columnist, argues in "A Social Conservative Credo" (fall 1995) that religion is too weak a foundation on which to base a socially conservative revival. Our age of affluence and science is unsympathetic to the religious message. To reverse social decay and revitalize civil society depends on "the more coercive and less reliable agency of politics—a politics crucially capable of articulating cultural with structural reform."

Muller, a historian of European conservatism at Catholic University, maintains in "Dilemmas of Conservatism" (spring 2000) that a schism exists within American conservatism. On the one hand are those whom he calls the "orthodox," who stress that affirming the existence of a transcendent moral order is a fundamental tenet of conservatism. Opposing the orthodox are the "conservatives." The conservatives defend existing institutions not because they conform to ultimate theological or metaphysical truth but because they have worked well in the past and are preferable to any untried alternatives. Muller argues that there is no necessary link between conservatism and religion. He points out that many conservative thinkers have been agnostics and atheists. Also, conservatives have continually defended the existing social order against the revolutionary intentions of religious enthusiasts. (A good example of this is the sociologist Robert A. Nisbet's opposition to the antiabortion movement.) The true conservative, Muller avows, is concerned not with the truths of religion but with their usefulness in preserving traditional institutions and values. While conservatives are aware of the "partial contingency of moral norms," the orthodox believe "the admission of such contingency may seem tantamount to nihilism, if not heresy."

Traditionalists are not sympathetic to the secular emphasis of Muller. Jacob Neusner, a professor of Judaic studies and a paleoconservative, has accused Jewish neoconservatives of being tone-deaf when it comes to religion in general and Judaism in particular. Religion may serve valid instrumental purposes and it may even be beautiful, he said. But for Jewish neoconservatives "it forms no intellectual reality from which, or even against which, to mount sustained thought. . . . [W]hen it comes to the rich and sanctifying Judaic religious life, with its sophisticated intellectual heritage of reflection and rigorous thought, these people stand at one with the Left, in unity with the learned despisers of religion. Their conservatism has not yet fulfilled itself."

George A. Panichas, a professor of literature at the University of Maryland and the editor of the traditionalist journal *Modern Age,* protests that "the sanctities of tradition and the values of order" are being overwhelmed by the "tinsel, opportunistic, and hedonistic conservatism" of neoconservatism. The neoconservatives, Panichas charges, "lack a basic apprehension of the 'permanent things' and are responsive to the empirical ambitions that reflect the tastes and power-drives of a technologico-Benthamite world." Their conservatism "belongs almost exclusively to the world and is impervious to the primacy of God as the measure of the soul." To counter the modernity of neoconservatism, conservatism needs to be "lean, ascetical, disciplined, prophetic, unswerving in its censorial task, strenuous in its mission, strong in its faith, faithful in its dogma, pure in its metaphysic." The columnist Samuel Francis agrees. The neoconservatives, he complains, seek not to challenge liberalism "but simply to make it work more efficiently." Their watchwords are "moderation, gradualism, empiricism, pragmatism, and centrism," and they are unsympathetic to the critique posed by the traditionalists to the contemporary liberal state.

Jewish neoconservatives are concerned that so many of the traditionalist conservatives have sought to infuse conservatism with a Christian religiosity, and they wonder what role there would be for Jews in such a conservatism. Their response to the symposium "The End of Democracy" in the November 1996 issue of John Neuhaus's magazine *First Things* exhibits the neoconservatives' fear that religious enthusiasm could cause religion to overstep its proper bounds. The symposium was prompted by the failure of the political system to do anything about the spread of abortion and the devaluing of life, which the magazine considered to be the great moral question of the day. The symposium's contributors included Protestants, Roman Catholics, and Jews. Several speculated on the propriety of civil disobedience and on the need to deny legitimacy to a judiciary that seemingly sanctioned the murder of the unborn.

JEWISH NEOCONSERVATIVES ARE CONCERNED THAT SO MANY OF THE TRADITIONAL CONSERVATIVES SOUGHT TO INFUSE CONSERVATISM WITH A CHRISTIAN RELIGIOSITY, AND THEY WONDER WHAT ROLE WOULD THERE BE FOR JEWS IN SUCH A CONSERVATISM.

The historian Gertrude Himmelfarb was horrified by what she saw as the reckless and inaccurate rhetoric of the symposium, and she resigned from the magazine's editorial advisory board. The symposium, she claimed, has undermined the efforts of conservatives such as herself to introduce moral considerations into public discourse. "It can only confirm many Americans in their suspicion that cultural conservatism is outside the 'mainstream' of American politics, that it is 'extremist,' even subversive." Norman Podhoretz agreed. "I did not become a conservative," he wrote Father Neuhaus, "in order to become a radical, let alone to support the preaching of revolution against this country."

The *First Things* symposium prompted *Commentary* to run its own symposium, "On the Future of Conservatism," which appeared in its February 1997 issue. Here the economist Irwin M. Seltzer warns his fellow neoconservatives of the impossibility of working closely with the *First Things* crowd. The contributors to "The End of Democracy," Seltzer contends, long for a society "that derives its legitimacy solely from their divinely informed approval. . . . Jewish intellectuals may be useful exponents of some of the positions of *First Things* Catholics, but they should not expect to be partners in a governing theocracy." If for *First Things* the U.S. Constitution is a religious document embodying the principles of natural law, for neoconservatives such as Seltzer it is a secular document embodying the principles of classical liberalism and democracy. And if for the paleoconservatives the most fundamental conflict of modern life is between secularism and religion, for the neoconservatives it is between freedom and totalitarianism. "The End of Democracy," the neoconservatives believe, exhibits a religious fervor that threatened time-honored American political institutions and practices and that is inappropriate for anyone calling him- or herself a conservative. This is not to deny, however, the existence of a minority of Jewish conservatives, including rabbis such as Daniel Lapin and academicians specializing in Jewish studies such as Jacob Neusner and David Novak, who were sympathetic to Neuhaus's efforts to involve religion in the public square. They received a more respectful hearing in the 1980s and 1990s when increases in illegitimacy, divorce, sexual deviancy, and pornography seemed to indicate that America was in the midst of a pervasive moral breakdown.

Don Feder, a columnist for the *Boston Herald,* expresses the anxieties of these religiously oriented conservative Jews in his 1993 book *A Jewish Conservative Looks at Pagan America.* America, he laments, have ceased to be a Judeo-Christian nation, much less a Christian nation. Its reigning ethos is now paganism. "The gods of late twentieth century America," he writes, "include the doctrines of radical autonomy, of absolute rights divorced from responsibilities, of gender sameness, of self-expression which acknowledges no higher purpose, of moral relativism and sexual indulgence." His own conservatism, Feder continues, is "God-centered, premised on a passion to nurture to the best in human nature, which flows from our acceptance of divine injunctions. It is based on the ethical world view of the patriarchs and prophets, grounded in the heritage of a people who first taught humanity to think in moral terms." This religiously oriented conservatism was, nevertheless, a minority position among Jewish conservatives at the time.

Jewish conservatives, not surprisingly, are also more pluralist regarding American identity, culture, and immigration than traditionalist conservatives. The essence of America, the traditionalists have argued, had been formed before the massive waves of immigration from Southern and Eastern Europe during the late nineteenth and early twentieth centuries. Immigrants were desirable to the extent that they were willing to conform to an already-established Anglo-American culture. America, the paleo Thomas Fleming asserts, has "its own history, its own particular set of virtues and vices, its own special institutions," and it was the responsibility of conservatives to preserve these. This essentialist view of immigration and American culture is indicated by the word *the* in the title of *Immigration and the American Identity,* a 1995 collection of essays that originally appeared in the paleo magazine *Chronicles.*

Conservatives such as Fleming fear that if immigration from Western Europe does not increase and, conversely, immigration from the Third World does not diminish,

America will increasingly come to resemble a Third World country. Already southern Florida and California are moving in that direction. It is irrelevant, paleoconservatives claim, that immigration is an economic boon to the country. The most important question concerning immigration is not economic but its impact on the nation's culture, religion, politics, language, and, most important, values. "We have not lost control of our borders," Clyde Wilson complains. "Rather, in a sense we have lost control of our land." This generation is bequeathing to its descendants "a society intolerably lacking in moral, religious, political and cultural cohesion."

JEWISH CONSERVATIVES ARE ALSO MORE PLURALIST REGARDING AMERICAN IDENTITY, CULTURE, AND IMMIGRATION THAN TRADITIONAL CONSERVATIVES.

Jewish conservatives, not surprisingly, are cultural pluralists. They were born into an immigrant culture and religion that was hardly mainstream American. For them the essence of America is not the particularist history, institutions, vices, and virtues emphasized by Fleming but the universal political principles found in the Declaration of Independence, the Bill of Rights, and the Gettysburg Address. To them, American identity is less a matter of Anglo-American language and culture than of civic values and political ideology. In contrast to the traditionalists, Jewish conservatives do not oppose immigration from Asia and Latin America, since it brings to America a culturally conservative and entrepreneurially oriented population. The threat to American culture, as Norman Podhoretz's *Commentary* magazine repeatedly has emphasized, comes not from immigrants but from a native liberal elite that seeks to disseminate among immigrants a cult of victimization and ethnic entitlement.

The differences between the paleoconservatives and the neoconservatives—with one group stressing culture and the other ideology—accounts for their differences over foreign policy. The traditionalists are heirs to the isolationism and noninterventionism that marked American conservatism during the 1930s and 1940s. Their goal is not to spread American values but to protect American culture and borders, and this is compatible with a narrow view of the national interest. The neoconservatives, by contrast, conflate Americanness with liberal and democratic political principles, and they contend that American foreign policy should seek to spread these beliefs. This explains their support for the National Endowment for Democracy and their talk about the need for a global democratic revolution to counter the left. This view is anathema to the traditionalists. The paleo historian Paul Gottfried accuses the neoconservatives of seeking to create through land reform, democratic elections, and economic modernization "a worldwide, secular, politically egalitarian society with a mixed economy" in the image of America. John Lukacs, another conservative historian, agrees. The neoconservatives, he writes, "are not conservatives but global ideologues. What Is Good for America is Good for the World. Indeed, America Must Rule the Heavens, no matter what the cost."

Paleoconservatives also find it difficult to sympathize with the reflexive support of neoconservatives for Israel. They view the Jewish state as simply another foreign country with its own distinctive interests, and these interests frequently conflict with those of the United States. Russell Kirk, in a notorious crack, complained that neoconservatives such as Podhoretz and his wife, Midge Decter, frequently "mistook Tel Aviv for the capital of the United States." This statement deeply angered neoconservatives, particularly Decter, a staunch Zionist. By raising the old antisemitic canard of dual loyalty, Kirk had fostered doubts among the neoconservatives as to whether the conservative movement was truly sympathetic to legitimate Jewish concerns and whether it welcomed committed Jews to their ranks.

The final point of difference between Jewish neoconservative intellectuals and the traditionalist conservative thinkers concerns the welfare state. The Jewish neoconservatives do not share in that deep antipathy to the welfare state and Washington that has united the American right over the past six decades and that, more than anything else, was responsible for the emergence of the modern conservative movement after World War II. The neoconservatives, Irving Kristol writes, "felt a measure of loyalty to the spirit of the New Deal if not to all its programs and policies. Nor did we see it as representing any kind of 'statist' or socialist threat to the American democracy." The Jewish neoconservatives did oppose various elements of Lyndon Johnson's Great Society and welcomed many aspects of Ronald Reagan's administration. But this resulted from pragmatic rather than a priori reasoning. Kristol had no basic argument with the welfare state per se. He even suggests that conservatives should accept the inevitability of a welfare state, while working to shape it along less statist and paternalistic lines. Such a conservative welfare state, he says, will provide "the social and economic security a modern citizenry demands while minimizing governmental intrusion into individual liberties." For paleoconservatives, the notion of a conservative welfare state is a contradiction in terms, and they have been quick to decry the very concept. Paul Gottfried describes neoconservatives such as Kristol as "welfare state ideologues" dressed in conservative clothing.

One reason for the divergence between the paleoconservatives and the neoconservatives is their intellectual starting points. The most important paleoconservatives have been humanists—philosophers, historians, and students of literature and religion. Most of the leading neoconservatives, by contrast, have been social scientists—sociologists, economists, and psychologists. This accounts for their differing evaluations of contemporary liberalism. If the traditionalists spoke in terms of right and wrong, eternal verities, and moral certitudes, the neoconservatives talked in terms of good and bad and of what worked and what didn't. Neoconservatism, complains Melvin E. Bradford, a professor of English at the University of Dallas, seems to consist mainly of "opportunism, pop sociology, and a series of position papers."

These different starting points also help account for the different perceptions of the two groups regarding human nature. The traditionalists take a much bleaker view of human nature, with believing Christians, such as Kirk and William F. Buckley Jr., emphasizing the doctrine of original sin. For them, leftist attempts to remake the world and its faith in human progress stem from a secular hubris. Jewish conservatives, by contrast, have had a sunnier attitude; thus the subtitle of Podhoretz's book *My Love Affair with America* is *The Cautionary Tale of a Cheerful Conservative.* The term "cheerful conservative" struck some traditionalists as almost self-contradictory.

By the end of the twentieth century, the rift between the Jewish neoconservatives and their paleoconservative rivals had become muted. Kristol and Podhoretz, the two most important Jewish neoconservative intellectuals, emphasized during the 1990s that there were no longer any important substantial differences between the two groups. Kristol said then, "though the accents differ even to this day, there is more comity than friction." Neoconservatism, he stated, was "a generational phenomenon, and has now been pretty much absorbed into a larger, more comprehensive conservatism." In a 1996 *Commentary* essay titled "Neoconservatism: A Eulogy," Podhoretz also bid adieu to neoconservatism. Now that the neoconservative message had become absorbed by the conservative movement, he said, there was no longer any need for neoconservatives to see themselves as a distinctive group. Neoconservatives could take satisfaction in "a just war well fought, and a time for rejoicing in a series of victories that cleared the way and set the stage for other victories in the years to come." But now it was time to move on. Midge Decter agreed. "I am a neocon no longer," she said in 1999. "Since I can find no significant difference from the basic views of most serious conservatives, I have come to the conclusion that it is long since time for me to drop my original designation and call myself simply a conservative."

THE NEOCONSERVATIVE MESSAGE HAD BECOME ABSORBED BY THE CONSERVATIVE MOVEMENT.

This atrophying of neoconservatism was perhaps best seen in the willingness of some Jewish neoconservative intellectuals to break with the Jewish consensus regarding the danger of religious involvement in public life. Elliott Abrams, the son-in-law of Decter and Podhoretz, even wrote a book titled *Faith or Fear: How Jews Can Survive in a Christian America,* which criticizes the "high wall of separation" theory of church–state relations popular among Jews, praises Christian evangelicals, and asserts that believing Christians are not antisemites and do not threaten Jewish interests. In fact, he claims, Christians are now more respectful of Judaism than Jews are of Christianity. "Anti-Christian bias is apparently the only form of prejudice that remains respectable in the American Jewish community," Abrams declares. "The notion that the more fervent a Christian's belief the more danger he or she represents to Jews should be rejected outright."

Podhoretz echoed these sentiments. In an April 2000 *National Review* article titled "The Christian Right and Its Demonizers," he says that Jews have nothing to fear from Christian fundamentalists and evangelicals such as Jerry Falwell and Pat Robertson. Such fears are "atavistic" and "paranoid." Rather than being antisemites, Falwell and Robertson are actually highly supportive of Jewish causes, such as Israel and Russian Jewry. It would be wise, according to Podhoretz, for Jews to ally themselves with Christian conservatives and other Americans resisting cultural decadence, libertinism, hedonism, and moral relativism.

One ingenious and provocative attempt to bridge the gap between the emphasis of neoconservatives on economics and sociology and the stress of paleos and religious conservatives on culture and character was David Frum's 1994 book *Dead Right*. The most important enemy of all varieties of conservatism, Frum argues, is big government. Big government not only undermines economic growth but also weakens the virtues of prudence, orderliness, thrift, and self-reliance. Surely it is not accidental that higher rates of drug usage, crime, family dissolution, and illegitimacy accompanied the sharp increase in governmental welfare programs during the 1960s. These emancipated "the individual appetite from the restrictions imposed on it by limited resources, or religious dread, or community disapproval, or the risk of disease or personal catastrophe." Big government is not the only source of America's problems. "But without overweening government, none would rage as fiercely as it now does."

The influence of the Jewish neoconservatives on American conservatism and then the absorption of the neocons within the general conservative movement reflect the most important and fundamental fact of recent American Jewish history: the entry of Jews into the nation's social, political, economic, cultural, and intellectual mainstream. A movement once seen as unsympathetic to Jews and to Jewish issues now includes Jews within its highest ranks. It is true that Jews were present at the beginning of the postwar conservative renaissance. Of the thirty-one persons listed on the original masthead of William F. Buckley's *National Review* in 1955, for example, five were Jews. But there is a crucial difference between them and the Jewish conservatives of the 1980s and 1990s. The *National Review* conservatives were largely disaffected from Jewishness and Jewish affairs, and a few even converted to Christianity.

JEWISH CONSERVATIVES OF THE 1990s STRONGLY IDENTIFIED AS JEWS AND WITH JUDAISM.

Jewish conservatives of the 1990s, by contrast, strongly identified as Jews and with Judaism, and some even sent their children to Jewish parochial schools. For them being Jewish and being conservative are not mutually exclusive. Rather, they see Jewishness and conservatism as symbiotic, much as Jews on the left have seen Jewishness and liberalism as mutually reinforcing. The new prominence of Jewish Jews in the conservative movement is a product of the same forces that have resulted in Laura Schlessinger ("Dr. Laura"), an observant Jew, becoming the nation's leading apostle for conventional morality, and Senator Joseph Lieberman being selected as Al Gore's vice presidential running mate in 2000 because of his supposed appeal to conservative voters. Should things continue along these lines, the expectations of conservatives during the past four decades of a rightward political turn among Jews might well come to pass. But don't hold your breath!

11

FAMISHED FOR JUSTICE

The Jew as Radical

STEPHEN J. WHITFIELD

Only a fraction of American Jews have been radicals, but a conspicuous number of radicals have been Jews who have shaped the singularity of a certain Jewish style in politics. These radicals have contributed, however unwittingly, to the differentiation of Jews from others who have shared American citizenship, without agreeing about how its obligations ought to be met. This essay offers a brief historical overview of the relationship between American Jews and radicalism, to suggest its cultural and psychological texture, and to account for this relationship.

In the first two waves of Jewish immigrants to the United States, through the middle of the nineteenth century, political dissidents such as Ernestine Rose and the abolitionist David Einhorn were rare, and the fragmentary Jewish communities established in North America in the colonial and early national periods harbored few radicals. In the late nineteenth century, the first Marxist firebrand in the United States was Daniel DeLeon, whose origins Samuel Gompers of the American Federation of Labor (AFL) ascribed to "a Venezuelan family of Spanish and Dutch Jewish descent with a strain of colored blood. That makes him a first-class son of a bitch." Himself an immigrant Jew from London, Gompers got some of DeLeon's background wrong, including the canine ancestry, probably because DeLeon's Socialist Labor Party kept trying to undermine the AFL. But it is plausible, as Glen Seretan's scholarly biography of DeLeon claims, that he renounced his Jewish identity for the sake of shaping a future that would belong to the oppressed of all races and nationalities (102).

Among those groups were over two million Jews fleeing persecution and poverty in Eastern Europe. Only their arrival in the decades before the World War I fostered the rise of radicalism—a polysemous term, which in this essay is intended to encompass the varieties of Marxian, socialism, anarchism, and the more estranged forms of youth activism in the 1960s. The ideologies that the fin-de-siècle immigrants professed, the causes they espoused, and the institutions that they created established the standards against which subsequent versions of Jewish radicalism have been judged.

THE APPEAL OF SOCIALISM

Even after allowances have been made for the conventional, moderate politics and even indifference of perhaps the bulk of Jews, what was special about the first generation or so of Eastern European immigrants to the Northeast and Midwest was how authentically they consolidated political radicalism with other manifestations of Jewish life. On its masthead, the *Jewish Daily Forward* proclaimed slogans such as "Workers of the world, unite" and "The freeing of the working class must be the task of the working class itself." At its peak the circulation of this newspaper was a quarter of a million, making it the most widely read Yiddish paper on Earth. Sociologist Daniel Bell concludes that "the *Forverts* bound together the Jewish community and made it socialist" (98). The newspaper usually put ethnic claims above ideological loyalties, and honored such claims when socialism was mute, as when—early in its history—the *Forverts* supported bourgeois Dreyfusards in France and did not oppose the imperialist Spanish-American War. It was, after all, only four centuries earlier that Ferdinand and Isabella had expelled their Jewish subjects.

WHAT WAS SPECIAL ABOUT THE FIRST GENERATION OF EASTERN EUROPEAN IMMIGRANTS WAS HOW AUTHENTICALLY THEY CONSOLIDATED POLITICAL RADICALISM WITH OTHER MANIFESTATIONS OF JEWISH LIFE.

Socialism may have helped satisfy some of the idealistic yearnings of the Jewish community, but it did even more for the radicalization of the American labor movement and for the promotion of a more humane economic system. When the Lower East Side sent one of its own—Meyer London—to the United States House of Representatives, he had almost inevitably to be a member of the Socialist Party of America, which had been formed in 1901.

The garment trade unions were the backbone of the party: the International Ladies Garment Workers Union (ILGWU), the Amalgamated Clothing Workers, the Furriers and Millinery Workers. Their associated Workmen's Circle provided the Socialist Party of America with much of its organizational and financial strength. They maintained their allegiance to socialism long after other militant unions had fully reconciled themselves to the capitalist order. The ILGWU, historian John Laslett notes, "used its considerable vote at A F of L conventions on behalf of radical resolutions . . . more consistently than almost any other trade union." In opposing immigration restriction (more for ethnic than class reasons), in supporting women's suffrage and the rights of blacks, and in encouraging the growth of socialism in Europe, unions like the ILGWU exhibited "a humanitarian, idealistic, and

SOCIALISM MAY HAVE HELPED SATISFY SOME OF THE IDEALISTIC YEARNINGS OF THE JEWISH COMMUNITY, BUT IT DID EVEN MORE FOR THE RADICALIZATION OF THE AMERICAN LABOR MOVEMENT.

deeply held desire for equality and social justice." What made the ILGWU peculiar, Laslett adds, "was its various provisions for the health, education, and general welfare of its members, which went far beyond the sick, death, and other benefits provided by most other American trade unions. It was on the educational program of the union, however, that the greatest emphasis was laid" (99–100, 117, 119, 120–23, 129, 133–35). Even in the 1920s, despite the pressures of the open-shop movement and the bitter factional struggle with the communists, the ILGWU fostered the revival of postwar radicalism and continued to contribute to the coffers and the morale of the socialist movement.

Only when the *Forverts* endorsed Franklin D. Roosevelt for president in 1936 (as did its editor Abraham Cahan himself) did this relatively long chapter in radical history come to a close. Clearly other imperatives within the Jewish community sapped a sustained working-class militancy. The promises of the wider society and the impulses of upward mobility among its own membership weakened the ILGWU's commitment to class consciousness. Italian-Americans transmitted the skills of the needle trade to their children and therefore became increasingly important in such unions. But Jewish workers generally recommended educational advantages and property acquisition instead. Despite the stirring words of the *Forverts'* masthead, the Jewish working class did not free itself. Instead it taught its own children to free themselves *from* the working class. (For example, one son of Sol Chaikin, a president of the ILGWU, became a dress manufacturer.) Nevertheless, when the Socialist Party of America ran a national ticket for the last time, in 1956, the vice presidential nominee was Samuel H. Friedman.

THE APPEAL OF COMMUNISM

The allegiances of other Jews shifted to Bolshevism, which exerted a disproportionate appeal before that particular god failed. In the 1920s, the Communist Party of the U.S.A. (CPUSA) published nine daily newspapers, of which the one with the largest circulation was in Yiddish: the *Freiheit*. It even outsold the English-language *Daily Worker*. Though the Jewish membership in that decade probably did not exceed 15 percent, the proportion that constituted the leadership was much higher. Prominent comrades included Benjamin Gitlow, Jay Lovestone, William Weinstone, Bertram Wolfe, and Max Shachtman.

On the other hand, the policies of the party were hardly philosemitic. In the late 1920s, the Comintern supported Arab rioters against Jewish settlers in Palestine. In the 1930s, the Stalinist purges claimed uncounted numbers of innocent Jewish victims, and in 1939, Soviet Foreign Minister Vyacheslav Molotov proclaimed that fascism was "a question of taste." Early in World War II, the Soviet secret police (NKVD) handed Jewish prisoners over to the Gestapo, and after the war, Yiddish culture and its custodians were systematically extinguished under Stalin. Such antisemitism eventually caused the membership and support of the CPUSA to be depleted by the thousands of Jews who had cherished the promise of a militantly effective universalism and "progressivism."

Of the intellectuals who publicly proclaimed their support for the Communist Party ticket in the 1932 elections, almost a third were Jewish. Only later did most of them realize that they had been trying to thumb a ride on "the road to serfdom." Even philosopher Sidney Hook, probably the nation's first Marxist professor, explained to readers of *Modern Monthly* "Why I Am a Communist" in 1934. In that year, *Call It Sleep* was published, quite possibly the finest novel ever written by an American Jew. Its author, Henry Roth, was a communist. The Marxist group that had burrowed into the Department of Agriculture of the New Deal included John Abt, Lee Pressman, and Nathan Witt. The historian Daniel Boorstin, by 1953 a conservative who told the House Committee on Un-American Activities (HUAC) that his support of the Hillel Foundation at the University of Chicago demonstrated his hostility to communism, had been a party member for a year or so before the Molotov–Ribbentrop Pact undermined his reasons for joining—his opposition to Nazism and antisemitism. Boorstin's reasons were commonplace. Almost half of the communist leaders indicted under the Smith Act in 1948 were Jews, as was the editor of the *Daily Worker* in the 1950s, John Gates. Hollywood's "Unfriendly 10," who were summoned to testify before HUAC in 1947, were communists (or so close to the party that they were cheating it of dues). Most of those who were subpoenaed were also Jews, although, as, Victor Navasky quotes the director Billy Wilder as quipping, "only two had any talent; the other eight were just unfriendly." Even in the 1960s, when a Maoist splinter group, the Progressive Labor Party, challenged the anemic Communist Party, most of the PLP leaders were of Jewish birth.

Even more than Stalinism or Maoism, the movement led by Leon Trotsky won the loyalty of many Jewish radicals. The heresiarch himself was of course born Lev Davidovich Bronstein, provoking Colonel Raymond Robins, the U.S. military representative at Petrograd, to call this polyglot intellectual and man of action "a four-kind son of a bitch, but the greatest Jew since Jesus Christ." Trotsky's keen interest in literature and his fluency of expression were overshadowed by the flair for flamboyant engagement—political and even military—that his remarkable career exhibited. The American rank-and-file members of his movement, the Fourth International, were (apart from the truckers of Minneapolis) probably almost exclusively Jewish. Several of the younger members later rose to prominence as intellectuals, critics, and scholars, among them literary critics Leslie Fiedler and Irving Howe, historians Gertrude Himmelfarb and Marvin Meyers, political analyst Irving Kristol, sociologist Seymour Martin Lipset, and essayist and novelist Isaac Rosenfeld. It therefore made sense for Saul Bellow to send his fictional Augie March to Mexico intending to serve as Trotsky's bodyguard and to make Hyman Lustgarten, the black marketer in *Mosby's*

Memoirs (1968), a former Trotskyist. When a young historian interviewed for a job at Jewish-sponsored Brandeis University in the 1960s and was taken to its faculty club, he was astonished to be introduced to every variety of sectarian leftist, including two Shachtmanites (who were no longer speaking to one another). For all the effort primarily of Jews to keep the Trotskyist version of revolutionary Marxism alive, however, the verdict on it must be the same as that which Trotsky himself pronounced upon the Mensheviks led by Julius Martov (*né* Yurii Osipovich Tsederbaum). "You are miserable, isolated individuals" was Trotsky's curse in 1917. "You are bankrupt. You have played out your role. Go where you belong, to the dust-heap of history."

THE APPEAL OF AMERICA

That was generally the fate of radicalism in the United States, in no small measure because of the relative openness of the polity to governmental reform and social change. The American system often exhibited a capacity to roll with the punch. Such receptivity to alteration can be measured through Jewish biography. In his youth, Gompers had flirted with socialism, which, in the United States, he considered unnecessary and even dysfunctional; and his stewardship of the AFL had much to do with that systemic revision. He claimed to share the ideals of socialism, differing—at least initially—only over tactics. As a trade unionist here, Gompers asserted that he would have been a nihilist in czarist Russia, a socialist in Wilhelmine Germany.

KEEP SIDNEY HILLMAN
OUT OF
THE WHITE HOUSE

SIDNEY HILLMAN
Chairman of the Political Action Committee

VOTE FOR
DEWEY and BRICKER!

Or consider Sidney Hillman and David Dubinsky, both radicals in their native Russia. In America they were militant trade union leaders whose leadership of strikes did not land them in jail—or in the counterpart to Siberian exile. Abraham Cahan escaped from Russia because czarist police discovered his involvement in a revolutionary organization. By 1936 he, too, was supporting the squire from Hyde Park.

Another immigrant, Frank Tannenbaum, came to the United States in 1905, quickly becoming involved with the Industrial Workers of the World (known as Wobblies); in 1914, he was convicted of disturbing the peace when he tried to lead New York's unemployed and hungry in seeking refuge in churches. He was imprisoned. But the warden of Sing Sing encouraged Tannenbaum to go on to college. The result was graduation (Phi Beta Kappa) from Columbia, which eventually hired him for its faculty. And when Tannenbaum published a book about Sing Sing's warden, Roosevelt himself wrote the introduction.

THE PERSISTENCE OF PROTEST

But probably the most impressive radical among the immigrant Jews was not a socialist at all but an anarchist. Emma Goldman was a kinetic orator and polemicist, a labor organizer, a believer in both the necessity of individual freedom and the nobility of collective action, a scathing foe of capitalism and militarism, a champion of birth control and other rights for women, and a popularizer of avant-garde European culture. No wonder American parents tried sometimes to frighten their children by warning them that, unless they behaved, Emma Goldman would get them.

THE MOST IMPRESSIVE RADICAL EXAMPLE AMONG THE IMMIGRANT JEWS WAS NOT A SOCIALIST AT ALL BUT AN ANARCHIST: EMMA GOLDMAN.

Instead, the federal government got her, along with her anarchist comrade, Alexander Berkman. Primarily at the instigation of the head of the General Intelligence Division, J. Edgar Hoover (then only twenty-four), in 1919, Goldman was deported back to the Russia from which she had fled thirty-three years earlier. Goldman lacked any specific feelings of solidarity with the Jewish people. But it was a tribute to the integrity of her beliefs that she became as hostile to Bolshevism as she had been earlier to czarism. Unrepentant and incorrigible to the end, she died in exile in Canada in 1940.

With the prosperity and comity that pervaded so much of post–World War II America, with the embourgeoisement of much of the labor movement, and with the virtually complete integration of Jews into the polity and economy, dissidence could not have been expected to sustain itself. And "the end of ideology" was one way of writing its death warrant. No scholar or political analyst of the 1950s could have anticipated how dramatically the corpse of radicalism would be jump-started in the following decade. Many young Jews must still have felt a little like strangers in the land of Egypt, expressing their marginality through civil rights activism, antipoverty campaigns, the movement against the Vietnam War, feminism, and support of Third World causes. Most of the northern whites who participated in the fight against Jim Crow in the South were Jews. When the Students for a Democratic Society (SDS) needed a site for its 1965 convention, an SDS leader, Richard Rothstein, rejected New York. "The Midwest," Irwin Unger quotes him as arguing in a memo, would be "the only place where a more sociologically representative (you know what that means) and geographically representative conference can take place." More than enough showed up the next year to constitute a *minyan:* over half of the delegates to the national SDS convention were Jewish.

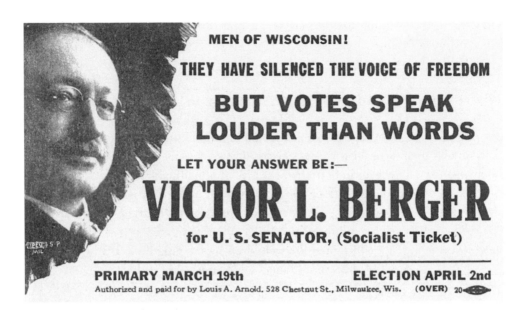

MEN OF WISCONSIN!

THEY HAVE SILENCED THE VOICE OF FREEDOM

BUT VOTES SPEAK
LOUDER THAN WORDS

LET YOUR ANSWER BE:—

VICTOR L. BERGER

for U. S. SENATOR, (Socialist Ticket)

PRIMARY MARCH 19th   ELECTION APRIL 2nd
Authorized and paid for by Louis A. Arnold. 528 Chestnut St., Milwaukee, Wis.   (OVER) 20

During the Great War and the Red Scare that followed, Jewish radicals such as Emma Goldman, Jacob Abrams, Victor Berger, Ben Gitlow, Rosika Schwimmer, and Yetta Stromberg had been unable to stay out of the line of fire, and their names became attached to important civil liberties cases. Jewish radicals in the 1960s and 1970s were no more successful in avoiding trouble. Captain Howard Levy was prosecuted for refusing to train Green Berets. The Chicago Seven, prosecuted for allegedly having crossed state lines to foment a riot at the Democratic Party's national convention in 1968, included Abbie Hoffman, Jerry Rubin, and Lee Wiener. President Richard Nixon nevertheless asked his aide H. R. Haldeman, "Aren't the Chicago 7 all Jews? [Rennie] Davis is a Jew, you know." Haldeman was doubtful, but the president at least got the next identification correct: "Hoffman, Hoffman's a Jew." According to Herblock, Haldeman agreed. (Indeed, so intertwined were leftism and ethnicity in Nixon's mind that he conjectured—wrongly—that Alger Hiss must have been half-Jewish.) The Boston Five, prosecuted for conspiring to advocate draft resistance, included Mitchell Goodman and Marcus Raskin.

The most embattled of the civil rights organizations in the South was the Student Nonviolent Coordinating Committee, whose second chairman was Chuck McDew, an undergraduate at all-black South Carolina State College in Orangeburg. During Religious Emphasis Week, McDew asked visiting Protestant ministers whether he would be permitted to worship in their churches. They all told him no. When a rabbi invited him to his synagogue, McDew became sufficiently intrigued that he converted to Judaism. In 1960, the news of the first sit-in, in Greensboro, North Carolina, spurred him to head a local movement of emulation. Later, when he was thrown into "the hole" of a Louisiana jail, he was tortured and lost thirteen pounds during his ordeal—and became the favorite display of right-wing groups touring the backwoods Bastille to stare at "the nigger

Communist." According to Howard Zinn, when two high school girls on such a tour whispered to him, "Say something Communist," McDew replied in Yiddish with a vulgar (and well-known) anatomical allusion.

THE PERVASIVENESS OF PROTEST

Even in other unexpected places, Jews cropped up. The Reverend Martin Luther King Jr., for all his militancy, was no radical. Yet one of his key advisers was Stanley Levison, a pivotal money manager for the Communist Party and a close associate of its leadership prior to his intimacy with King. Their friendship became one crucial justification for the FBI's squalid bugging campaign against the civil rights tribune. The organizing struggle of Cesar Chavez in the fields of California drew on the resources of Catholic commitment and Mexican American ethnic solidarity (*La Causa*). But Saul D. Alinsky, the son of immigrant Orthodox Jews, helped tutor Chavez in the tactics of peaceful but forceful confrontation. The pacifist and nonviolent mood of the folk music movement was much influenced by Joan Baez, who was in turn influenced by Ira Sandperl. And the letters from Folsom Prison that gave shape to Eldridge Cleaver's nascent militancy were addressed to his attorney, Beverly Axelrod, to whom *Soul on Ice* (1968) is dedicated. In the 1960s in then British Guiana, whose population was about evenly divided between East Indians and blacks, the leader of the People's Progressive Party was a Marxist dentist named Cheddi Jagan. His wife was a former member of the Young Communist League from Chicago, Janet Rosenberg.

In 1979, the last bloody clash of the civil rights movement took place in Greensboro, North Carolina, where the peaceful sit-ins had begun almost two decades earlier. Five members of the Communist Workers Party were murdered by the Ku Klux Klan and its associates. The dead included two Jews, and another Jew was seriously wounded. They were the last white victims in the struggle of solidarity with southern blacks, a chain of martyrdom that had begun with Andrew Goodman and Michael Schwerner, killed along with a local black, James Chaney, in Philadelphia, Mississippi, in 1964. Goodman had been in the state for only a few hours when he was abducted and killed by a group of whites who, according to William Bradford Huie, knew Schwerner as "the Jew-boy with the beard." The murderers even argued with one another of honoring of killing "the two Jews and the coon." Their deaths suggested the continuity of a certain dedication to social justice, even amid prosperity, reform, and the decline of antisemitism.

In some ways the most baffling aspect of that commitment involved the student power movement. Here the Jewish propensity for radicalism was most intriguing, because its militancy could not be explained as the immigrant working-class socialism of the New Leftists' grandfathers or in terms of the economic desperation that the Great Depression engendered. The student radicals who rebeled at Berkeley, Columbia, and Harvard and were also inclined to protest on other Ivy League and Big Ten campuses were privileged. They were not motivated by material self-interest, nor were they hampered by prejudice or discrimination. Jews constituted about a tenth of all college students in the 1960s, yet they were often half or more of the radicals on leading campuses. The American Council of Education concluded, after a survey of 1966–67, that the most accurate predictor of protest was the matriculation of Jewish students. Even during the Berkeley sit-in of 1964, *Hatikvah* was reportedly sung. Yet few of the Jews in SDS made their origins a source of self-consciousness or reflection about either their motives or their ideals.

JEWS CONSTITUTED ABOUT A TENTH OF ALL COLLEGE STUDENTS IN THE 1960S, YET THEY WERE OFTEN HALF OR MORE OF THE RADICALS ON LEADING CAMPUSES.

The most enduring of the protest movements to flourish in the 1960s, however, was the American women's drive for equality. Its main thrust was liberal, epitomized by Betty Goldstein Friedan, whose first book, *The Feminine Mystique* (1963), ignited a transformation of consciousness that also sparked political reverberations. For the rest of the century, law and policy would be expected to equalize the relations between the sexes. Friedan's best-seller betrayed no obvious political or intellectual antecedents. Yet her feminism was not created *ex nihilo*, in suburban kitchens and bedrooms. It was prepared in the 1940s, on factory floors and strikers' picket lines, which Friedan had sympathetically described for readers of the left-wing press. Virtually from the start of that decade, she had positioned herself on the far left, opposing "capitalism and its culture," championing labor militancy, warning of the dangers of a domestic "fascism," favoring close relations with the Soviet Union after World War II, and drawing the attention of the FBI. During the early phase of the Cold War, she was an *engagé* labor journalist and worked especially with the United Electrical Radio and Machine Workers (UE). One of the two unions that communists came closest to dominating, the UE was crippled during the Red Scare. Friedan wrote a 1952 pamphlet, *UE Fights for Women Workers*, which exposed the special plight of her sex and hinted at debts to Friedrich Engels's critique of the family.

Jewish women were so dedicated to fighting for equal rights that its provision in the postwar Japanese constitution was due to Beate Sirota Gordon, a Russian Jewish woman who moved to the United States in 1947 after ensuring that discrimination against women would henceforth be contrary to Japanese law. More explicitly radical feminists emerged in the United States later in the 1960s; among the most prominent were other Jews, such as Susan Brownmiller, Shulamith Firestone, and Naomi Weisstein. Earlier in the century their ancestors were Rose Pastor Stokes, Rose Schneiderman, and Rose Pesotta. They and other agitators were fighting the power and were organizing laundresses and seamstresses by telling them, "Don't iron while the strike is hot!"

THE REASONS WHY

But it is much easier to tabulate the impact of the Jews on radical movements and ideas than to account for such influence. Four theories have been devised to explain this historical propensity for the left, but none has the compass or ingenuity to compel unmodulated assent.

The Tradition of Judaism

One theory stresses Judaic culture itself, with its yearning for the repair of the world (*tikkun olam*), its commitment to social justice, and its insistence on speaking prophetic truth to power. "At Hebrew school," Robert Warshow quotes Julius Rosenberg, the executed spy, as writing, "I absorbed quite naturally the culture of my people, their struggle for freedom from slavery in Egypt." Hanukkah meant "the victory of our forefathers in a struggle for freedom from oppression and tyranny. [It] is a firm part of our heritage." The appeal for social justice is one strain in Jewish tradition, but it is certainly not the only one; and the long history of the Diaspora before Emancipation fails to disclose many antecedents for modern radicalism or even moderate liberalism. The early rabbis and sages would not have received high ratings from the Americans for Democratic Action, and they certainly would not have been vulnerable to red-baiting. The terrors of much of premodern Jewish life promoted a wary conservatism that cannot convincingly be invoked by Jews in a quest of sanctions for their radicalism.

Albert Einstein, himself a socialist, nevertheless believed in a connection between socialism and Judaism, for both are based on the sense of "solidarity of all human beings." But he could not claim a logically necessary connection between a radical ideology and a religious source. Even those who professed to find in holidays like Pesach and Hanukkah the inspiration for subsequent struggles against tyranny, as Julius Rosenberg did in his letters to his wife in Sing Sing, failed to acknowledge the nature of the despotism that they themselves freely chose to serve. They identified with the executioners, not the victims, of Stalinism, which means that one needs to explain how, say, leftist Jews selectively applied their religious heritage. Radicals in the post-Emancipation era distanced themselves from both pious and impious homes. But it is by now a commonplace that the most observant Jews are rarely radical, and the most radical are rarely observant. The more radical the Jew, the less he or she is likely to know (or care) about normative Judaic practice.

> THE MOST OBSERVANT JEWS ARE RARELY RADICAL, AND THE MOST RADICAL ARE RARELY OBSERVANT.

Still, the skepticism that this thesis engenders does not require its complete abandonment. For it allows us to take ideas and values seriously; and if what has distinguished the biblical Hebrews and their descendants from those around them has been their religion, then perhaps something in the value system of the Jews has made them susceptible to modern radicalism. Misery alone is an insufficient explanation, propelling neither American blacks nor Russian *muzhiks* to the varieties of Marxism. Among the Jews, as exemplified by the privileged partisans of the New Left, suffering is not even a necessary—much less a sufficient—cause of attraction to radicalism. That cause should be sought elsewhere. Denial of the importance of ideas in the formation of the Jewish people would defy common sense. Some tropes and values must have been transmitted in such a way that Jews even in the United States nourished more radicals than comparable groups. One does not have to be an intellectual historian to consider an analogy with Yogi Berra's description of baseball: "90 percent of this game is half-mental."

The observation that Orthodoxy coexists with radicalism far more rarely than religious ignorance and indifference is also problematic. Much depends on the implication that Talmudic law froze Judaism into an unchanging mold or that Reform Judaism on the other hand has placed undue weight upon certain prophetic ideals of social justice. It may well be the case that only this feature of Judaism—the emphasis on *tikkun olam*— got transmitted to emancipated Jewry. Such a stress should not be confused with the whole of Judaism, but reformist impulses may be the husk of what has remained for much of modern Jewry. In any event, scholarship does not require the acceptance of only an Orthodox definition of Judaism. Gershom Scholem, for one, rejects the "assumption that there is a well-defined and unvarying 'essence' of Judaism, especially . . . where the evaluation of historical events is concerned," and denies the possibility of knowing a priori which sorts of beliefs were tolerable within Judaism. The argument that ancient messianic hopes have been injected into modern politics therefore cannot be summarily scorned.

The hospitality of Judaism to diverse beliefs can be underscored by a contrast with Roman Catholicism. Papal encyclicals against socialism by Pius IX and Leo XIII may well have retarded the growth of socialism in the late nineteenth century. The Catholic Church was ideologically opposed to systematic political efforts to redistribute or abolish private property. So hostile was it (even in some cases to trade unionism itself), so frequent were the warnings uttered by parish priests all the way up the hierarchy, that ecclesiastical opposition helps account for the failure of socialism to sink deep roots in American soil. The movement was condemned as heretical, and to be both a Catholic and a socialist was often considered a contradiction. But even though some socialists were anticlerical and antireligious, even though Jewish radicals sometimes deliberately flouted traditional rituals and piety, American rabbis did not consistently oppose radicalism. Unlike rabbis, Catholic priests and Protestant ministers were occasionally radicals. But rabbis did not categorically stigmatize socialism, either, or make adherence to its creeds in any way incompatible with Judaism or with membership in the people of Israel. Indeed, a major strain of Zionism was based on a socialist ideology, and emphasized a natural affinity between the destiny of the Jewish people and an egalitarianism and collectivism pivotal to socialist doctrine.

The Sting of Bigotry

A second possible explanation is antisemitism, which provoked Jews to struggle to alter societies that denied their rights and disparaged their merits and dignity. And since Jews were the pariahs of Europe, radicalism and revolutions were intelligible responses to the frustration of full equality. In the United States, antisemitism has been far milder, especially by the time the New Left emerged in the 1960s. But the experience of discrimination and the fear of bigotry, abroad as well as in the United States, nevertheless motivated Jews to subscribe to and support radical causes, especially communism in the 1930s and 1940s. The advantage of this theory is that some Jews themselves explained the appeal of communism in the light of its militant opposition to Nazism. Boorstin's HUAC testimony, already cited, may be taken as representative.

One problem with this theory is its fudging of the distinction between liberalism and radicalism—quite apart from other reactions to antisemitism, such as Zionism. Nor is there any way of matching the extent of such deprivation in the popularity of radicalism among the Jews. The severity or scope of persecution does not correlate with the extent of adherence to radicalism, and those who have been turned down or turned away do not necessarily turn left as a consequence. The Lower East Side, which was the burnt-over district of American socialism, was probably far less aware of "status deprivation" and the incongruities of social and civic position than were the liberal and even conservative "uptown" Jews of the same era.

Moreover, if status deprivation were so decisive a motivating factor, one might have expected Jewish radicals to hope that the Jews themselves, so stung by bigotry, would become an important constituency for political change. This was rarely, if ever, the case. The "Jewish" garment workers unions were not consolidated along ethnic but rather economic and class lines, and Jews made a point of their alignment with others in the garment trades, like the Italians. A Jewish separatist labor socialist movement did not emerge in the United States; battles were conducted instead from the left flank of the AFL. Though Jewish sections of the Communist Party existed in the 1920s, it is not too hyperbolic to note how expert Jews became on the revolutionary potential of every oppressed group except their own. The party simply could not speak (even in Yiddish) in a special way to Jewish group interests. Agitator Israel Amter's famous salutation—"Workers and peasants of Brooklyn!"—was unlikely to rouse the masses. If such radicals thought that status deprivation made their fellow Jews embittered and indignant, such knowledge was successfully repressed.

Left or Right

A third explanation, originally propounded to account for liberalism (by political scientist Werner Cohn), has been extended (by another political scientist, W. D. Rubinstein) to incorporate radicalism as well. These scholars have argued that the leftist orientation of modern Jewry is due to the powerful historical circumstances of post-Emancipation Europe and beyond. The right was inhospitable and uncongenial because of its allegiance to tradition and hierarchy. The right was nostalgic for an era in which Christianity was preeminent; thus, it was no accident that the first Western thinker to uncouple religion from politics was a Jew, Spinoza. Rubinstein observes that, at least until recently, a certain set of historical conditions kept the Jews away from the right: its antisemitism, its association with elites that excluded them, its defense of privilege at a time when most Jews were impoverished and disadvantaged. The left was, by contrast, impelled to reduce the particularities of religion, tradition, and even class. Indeed, Karl Marx dared to imagine a world without Jews; his patrimony was the dream of universal solidarity, undivided by race or ethnicity or nation. By precept and example, Marx encouraged the sense that the Jews should renounce their sense of peoplehood, and could go first toward a utopia in which particularities would be obliterated.

This left–right axis—this set of historical circumstances—no longer prevails, at least not as sharply as it did in the nineteenth century. Until 1945 the lethal enemies of the Jewish people were on the right. Since then, Jewish interests and welfare, without which Jewish moral values cannot be sustained, have depended on a secure and thriving Israel, whose enemies in the world arena have generally emanated from the left. Anti-Zionism has been almost entirely a phenomenon of communism and of the putatively revolutionary regimes of the Third World. At the same time the Jewish proletariat largely disappeared, thus eliminating whatever class basis once existed for socialist ideology.

Yet, while the historical circumstances that might have produced the slant toward radicalism evaporated, the Jewish stance remains more tipped to the left than to the right. Wherever radicalism in the United States could still be found (apart from black separatism), Jews could be identified within its ranks. Leftist traditions—and perhaps even the Judaic value system—continued to block the reorientation of Jewish politics toward the Republican Party and toward conservatism. What caused immigrants to be socialists did not truly resemble what drew some of their grandchildren toward the New Left. But social and economic conditions neither changed so drastically nor overcame inertia to lead most Jews away from either their loyalty to liberalism or their tolerance for radicalism. If a particular historical setting alone produced a propensity for the left, the disproportionate number of Jews coagulating in the New Left could scarcely be explained.

Family Matters

Analysts have no reason to assume that the velocity of change since the industrialization of the West somehow skipped the Jewish family, whose dynamics have given rise to a fourth theory for the origins and perpetuation of radicalism. As religious authority yielded to the allure of secular culture, as some forms of traditional piety became more rigid and opportunities in business and the liberal professions widened, as ghetto walls tumbled down and the winds of modernity rustled through the *shtetl*, family was obliged to bear an increasing burden in reconciling the tensions and antinomies of Jewish life. The roles of fathers and mothers and children altered, sometimes subtly, sometimes searingly; and even when tensions ran silent, they ran deep.

As the Jewish family struggled to gain and restore its cohesiveness, political heterodoxy was sanctioned. "To other people, I'm a professional radical," Saul Alinsky once observed. But to his mother, he added, what mattered was that "I'm a professional." In Jules Feiffer's play *Grownups* (1981), a New York couple bubbles with pride that their son is a journalist for the *New York Times*. That is their emblem of making it, the certification of success. A jarring note is injected when the son informs them that he is writing a book blasting the political system as corrupt and immoral. The parents do not skip a beat in exuding *naches* (joy). That the system is rotten is irrelevant, so long as their son wins recognition for exposing it. Sociologist Nathan Glazer has argued that Jews were disproportionately attracted to the New Left simply because they had grown up in families that had already nurtured earlier dissidents: "Jewish political traditions, traditions of liberalism and socialism, open[ed] young Jews to the *possibility* of influence by liberal and socialist views" (232, 236, 243). He suggests that the presence in so many Jewish families of older radicals gave the young a sense of political alternatives. In such families upward mobility was encouraged, but Marxists (or ex-Marxists) were still hanging around. No character is more ambitious than Duddy Kravitz; but wealthy Uncle Benjy, who runs a dress factory, remains a Stalinist.

The phenomenon of the "red diaper baby" appears to be almost exclusively Jewish. The Rosenberg case was admittedly exceptional. But the couple's sons—Michael and Robert Meerepol—were themselves involved in SDS. For every Mark Rudd and Abbie Hoffman, whose fathers were somewhat conservative if not apolitical, there was a Bettina Aptheker, a Berkeley activist whose father was a communist historian and publicist; or a member of the Weather Underground like Kathy Boudin, whose father was prominently engaged in the legal defense of communists and fellow travelers. And even Rudd's parents made a point of supporting him during the Columbia insurrection of 1968, bringing him food and referring to him as their son, the revolutionary, though Rudd's father had pursued a military career before selling real estate. The ILGWU's Dubinsky had grown up in Lódz, where the Jewish working class toiled from twelve to fifteen hours a day. At thirteen David Dubinsky quit school;

at fourteen he was a master baker in his father's shop. At fifteen, as secretary of the bakers' union, he struck, helping shut down his father's own shop and source of livelihood. But when the police came to take the union secretary to jail, David Dubinsky's father gave him money and a prayer shawl.

How such families spawned radicals especially interested analysts of the New Left. For Glazer as well as for Seymour Martin Lipset, radical offspring wished to extend and make operational what liberal parents did not fully practice. Thus, the values of the two generations were continuous, with the young attempting to live up to the pieties of social justice that had been inculcated in the home (though not in the streets). The positive support of such parents gave New Leftists confidence in the rightness of their ideals and in the propriety of their engagement in the civil rights movement, in antipoverty campaigns, in battles for student power, and in their resistance to the military intervention in Indochina. The militant children of liberal parents thus discovered a fresh way to obey the Fifth Commandment. Social scientists like Kenneth Keniston, who investigated young radicals' attitudes toward their parents, found no hostility; and some of the young insisted on the compatibility of their politics with Jewishness and Judaism. The traditional cohesiveness of the Jewish family was undoubtedly decisive in shaping the identities of the rebels who emerged from homes that—unlike their grandparents' English— were rarely broken. Why such families produced radicals, and most others liberals, nevertheless remains an enigma.

Ideas Are Weapons

Another suggestion can be advanced, building on a fleeting glance in Lawrence H. Fuchs's early and influential study of liberalism, *The Political Behavior of American Jews* (1956), and on Glazer's reflections on the student radicals of the 1960s. In accounting for a penchant for radical ideologies and movements, scholars have given little attention to what sociologist Talcott Parsons considered the most distinctive characteristic of the Jewish people: its intellectuality. If Jews have been disproportionately radicals, it may be because they have been disproportionately intellectuals. Randolph Bourne and Thorstein Veblen were among the first Americans to recognize—during the era of the Great War—the spectacular impact that Jewish intellectuals were making on Western culture. But the remarks of Nikos Kazantzakis are even more to the point. "Ours is an age of revolution," the Greek writer says of the interwar period: "That is, a Jewish age." Modern life had become fragmented and decomposed, and "the Jews have this supreme quality: to be restless, not to fit into the realities of the time; to struggle to escape; to consider every status quo and every idea a stifling prison. This spirit of the Jews shatters the equilibrium." More than any other immigrant group, the Jews harbored intellectuals among their tired, huddled masses; and they fostered a radical spirit and outlook. According to Murray Polner, linguist Noam Chomsky, for example, has recorded his own indebtedness to the "radical Jewish working-class milieu" to which his family belonged: "It was a very unusual culture . . . . [It was] a mixture of a very high level of intense intellectual life, but at the same time it was really working class."

IF JEWS HAVE BEEN DISPROPORTIONATELY RADICALS, IT MAY BE BECAUSE THEY HAVE BEEN DISPROPORTIONATELY INTELLECTUALS.

That is why the Jews differed from other members of the proletariat and remained sympathetic to radicalism even when nestled in the middle class. To be sure, radical movements in the United States flunked the assignment of dialectical materialism and failed to appeal to their ostensible constituencies. Few of the wretched of the Earth agreed with radical agitators; they listened only in moments of crisis and then lapsed back into moderation or political indifference when special pressures were released. Because radicalism is an -*ism*—that is, a modern ideology—those groups most pervaded by intellectuals have been most likely to sustain it.

Nevertheless, not even most Jewish intellectuals have been radical. Such persons—and not serfs, or slaves, or peasants, or black sharecroppers—have nevertheless been overrepresented in revolutionary movements, almost as predictably as queens beat jacks in poker. In describing the homes of Jewish New Leftists, Glazer singles out the importance of books, lectures, and "cultural style" in promoting a greater responsiveness to the social environment. He isolates certain measurable indices, such as college attendance and choices of fields of concentration, but does not speculate on intellectuality itself as a susceptibility to radical impulses. Oddly enough, his own youthful radicalism was barely shaped by reading as such. Glazer's family—itself on the welfare rolls in Harlem during the Great Depression was so unfamiliar with his own vocation as a writer and an editor that his mother, once asked to describe his occupation, vaguely asserted that he was "in the pen business." Irving Howe also grew up in a working-class home devoid of a single book yet pursued the same inclinations. A hypothesis that emphasizes such vocations does not require the ascription of intellectuality to the Judaic faith, as the source of a certain tendency toward radicalism. That is another advantage of the theory.

A FINAL NOTE

One final note might be sounded. Radical movements have attracted the best as well as the worst of humanity; but however equivocal the record of socialism in the annals of human freedom, the pain of the dispossessed was common enough to spur remedies. Some advocates of systemic solutions dramatized the process of disenchantment, as they put into secular form longings for redemption that were once expressed in a religious idiom. What is so striking about this story is not how frequently such radicals abandoned such passions or how curiously some radicals would find their way to a set of values within their own religious tradition. What remains impressive in retrospect is how often the American Jew was willing to be a "security risk," challenging complacency and selfishness and indifference, urging others to live up more fully to democratic ideals, begging to differ with what Freud called "the compact majority." What is noteworthy is how this tiny ethnic minority distinguished itself by the disproportionate numbers of sons and daughters it produced who were famished for justice.

WHAT REMAINS IMPRESSIVE IS HOW OFTEN THE AMERICAN JEW WAS WILLING TO BE A "SECURITY RISK."

12

ACTIVISTS AND ORGANIZERS

Jewish Women and American Politics

JOYCE ANTLER

Although American politics have been largely dominated by men, with women relatively absent from centers of formal power, Jewish women have nonetheless played
a significant, sometimes crucial, role as political activists. Though their contributions
have been obscured in the historical record, Jewish women have generated political and
social change through their participation in a variety of secular and Jewish communal organizations and political movements. In the last generation,
as American women have moved from the margins to mainstream political life, Jewish women have staked out positions

JEWISH WOMEN
HAVE PLAYED A
SIGNIFICANT ROLE AS
POLITICAL ACTIVISTS.

of prominence and influence, holding elective and appointed
office at all levels of government.

Jewish women's political activism grew out of their daily
lives. When they felt unjustly treated, they organized, petitioned, lobbied, marched, and boycotted. Whether their targets were officials they considered unresponsive or manufac-
turers, landlords, grocers, or butchers they thought too greedy, Jewish women sought to
mold opinion and to reform, or sometimes to overturn, the political system. This kind of
activism marked Jewish immigrant women's lives even in the years before women received the vote. Middle-class Jewish women learned to exercise political power through
establishing their own organizations that fought to improve community life and, especially, to remedy those problems that impinged on the welfare of mothers and children
and the Jewish people as a whole.

In the nineteenth and early twentieth centuries, Jewish women participated in many
aspects of the women's movement, fighting for women's rights, birth control, and improved conditions for working women. In numbers disproportionate to their representation in the population, they joined labor unions and left-wing political movements.
Later, Jewish women activists led campaigns for civil liberties and civil rights, nuclear
disarmament, and peace. In the 1960s and 1970s, they became prominent leaders of
second-wave feminism.

Thousands of Jewish women exercised their social activism as members of temple sisterhoods or Jewish women's organizations, groups that most often devoted themselves
to meeting the social needs of women and children or promoting Jewish life and culture.
The National Council of Jewish Women (NCJW), founded in 1893, and Hadassah,
founded in 1912, were the largest of these Jewish organizations. Like the nineteenth-century female charitable associations that preceded them, these Jewish women's groups
helped shape the communal agenda through their provision of health and welfare services and their campaigns for social and political reforms. Often their interventions were
couched in the language of maternalism, yet there is no escaping the fundamental political nature of their activities. According to Henrietta Szold, Hadassah's dynamic
founder, Jewish women's "womanly" duty was to frame the central policies of Jewish life,
even when such assertion put them at odds with male groups. As historian Hasia Diner

argues, in seeing Jewish women merely as volunteers or "auxiliaries," scholars have "depoliticized" the fundamental political nature of their organizations. Following the lead of these early pioneers, successive generations of Jewish women have continued to play vital roles in political life.

The special circumstances that Jewish women experienced as Jews and Americans influenced their political activism in a variety of ways. In almost every case, their identity as women—particularly as *Jewish* women—shaped their political actions. Even when these women were unattached to or alienated from Judaism, Jewish values and traditions usually influenced the worldviews and ethical perspectives that drove their political contributions.

Some Jewish women sought to make political life a career rather than an avocation. Working as political consultants, campaign strategists, party leaders, administrators, and policymakers, they entered politics to solve community problems. They became municipal officeholders, state legislators, and governors, and won elections to the United States House of Representatives and Senate, influencing twentieth-century political life at every level. The great majority of these political professionals demonstrated substantial support for Jewish issues as well as liberal, feminist causes.

POLITICAL MOVEMENTS AND ORGANIZATIONS
Women's Suffrage

One of the earliest activists on behalf of equal opportunity for women was Ernestine Rose. Born in a *shtetl* in Poland, Rose, a rabbi's daughter, came to the United States in 1836. She quickly became a leader in the effort to reform married women's property rights acts and to give women the vote. At the first women's rights convention, Rose introduced the controversial resolution calling for "political, legal, and social equality with men." She worked with Susan B. Anthony and Elizabeth Cady Stanton to establish the American Equal Rights Association, and helped them transform that organization into the National Woman's Suffrage Association. Anthony named Rose, together with Mary Wollstonescraft and Frances Wright, as the most important women's rights leaders in history.

While Rose's outspoken rejection of religion troubled pious feminists, she took a "fighting stand" against antisemitism. She believed that her work on behalf of abolition and women's rights and against antisemitism demonstrated the "interrelationship between Jew and non-Jew, Negro and white, men and women." A committed pacifist, Rose argued that women had a special stake in crusades for peace.

In the next generation of feminist leaders, Maud Nathan, a descendant of one of the leading Sephardic families in the United States, became the suffrage movement's most significant Jewish leader. This "society woman in politics," as Nathan was called, came to suffrage through her work as president of the New York Consumer's League; lobbying for better protective legislation for working women, she understood that lawmakers ignored women since they lacked political status. One of the movement's most original tacticians, Nathan invented open-air automobile campaigns, "twenty-four-hour" speeches," using motorized placards, during which suffragists threw coins wrapped in literature to onlookers. Because suffragists were associated with aggressive, "masculine" women, Nathan dressed in her finest gowns when she spoke at mass meetings or participated in suffrage skits. After one of Nathan's speeches, President Woodrow Wilson commented, "When I hear a woman talk so well in the public interest, it almost makes me believe in woman suffrage." Nathan rooted her vigorous support of woman suffrage and her lifelong interest in promoting the welfare of working women in a prophetic Judaism that highlighted the individual's obligations to the social good. For Nathan, righteousness—the well-spring of all Judaic inspiration—meant the application of spiritual ideals to "social growth"; she often quoted biblical texts to show their applicability to contemporary society.

The organized Jewish community, including Jewish women's groups, did not openly support woman suffrage until relatively late in the campaign. A few Jewish women, such as Maud Nathan's sister, Annie Nathan Meyer, who founded Barnard College, even agitated publicly against suffrage. So strong was Meyer's opposition to the suffrage movement that she was often considered the "vice president" of the movement against votes for women.

The lack of organized Jewish support for suffrage led observers to believe, incorrectly, that Jewish women as a whole were uninvolved in rights for women. As evidence to the contrary, a contemporary history of the suffrage movement in the United States listed dozens of local Jewish suffrage leaders and indicated that thousands more were rank-and-file members of suffrage groups across the nation. Unlike Jewish women in Britain, where the lack of social mobility and integration of Jews within the general society led Jewish suffragists to organize a separate Jewish suffrage organization, American Jewish suffragists were well integrated into local groups and did not feel the need to establish an organization of their own.

Jewish women immigrants supported suffrage in particularly large numbers compared to native-born Americans and other ethnic women. Trade union activist Clara Lemlich Shavelson, the young woman who in 1909 urged her garment industry coworkers to go out on a general strike, was a cofounder of the Wage Earners' League for Woman Suffrage; other working-class leaders active in the suffrage fight were Rose Schneiderman, Pauline Newman, and Theresa Malkiel. In New York City, immigrant Jewish neighborhoods provided the strongest voting support of woman suffrage. The 1917 passage of a suffrage amendment in New York state, which served as a major catalyst to the 1920 federal amendment, was largely attributed to the Jewish vote—seventy-eight of the one hundred prosuffrage election districts were Jewish.

Support for Working Women, Birth Control, and the Campaign against "White Slavery"

Jewish women also led campaigns on issues such as the reform of women's working conditions, the promulgation of birth control, and the abolition of the traffic in women. Shavelson, Pauline Newman, Rose Schneiderman, Rose Pesotta, Fannia Cohn, and other immigrants went from laboring in sweatshops to championing causes of working women. Cohn, Pesotta, and Newman were among the handful of Jewish women who served as officers of the International Ladies Garment Workers Union (ILGWU). Often in conflict with male Jewish trade union leaders, they attempted to improve wages and working conditions from inside the industrial workforce. Shavelson's bases of operations were the Socialist, and later the Communist, parties, as well as neighborhood women's groups such as the United Council of Working Class Housewives (later called the United Council of Working Class Women). The United Council drew on the power of housewives in the 1920s and 1930s to agitate around such subsistence issues as the price of food and housing.

Union organizer Schneiderman found her way into the Women's Trade Union League (WTUL), an association of working women and middle- and upper-class allies. For many decades she worked both for traditional union drives and for the protective legislation supported by the WTUL, serving as president of the New York chapter and as national president. The efforts of Schneiderman and other working-class Jewish women on behalf of protective labor laws for women found ready congruence in the work of Maud Nathan and the New York Consumer's League.

For some Jewish women, sexual and reproductive freedom took precedence in the pantheon of women's issues. Anarchist leader Emma Goldman insisted that the denial of sexual freedom, not political or economic inequality, lay at the core of women's problems. She believed that the drive for suffrage and political rights, which imitated rather than dismantled male models of authority, would do little to alter women's subjugation. Goldman faulted suffragists for failing to attack the evils of marriage and for doing little to promote birth control, which she considered fundamental to women's liberation. She offered detailed birth control advice in her popular lectures, given in Yiddish and English. In 1916, she was arrested for distributing birth control pamphlets, but the conviction was overturned. After Goldman's arrest, Rose Pastor Stokes, another well-known Jewish radical, publicly proclaimed her willingness to break the law to help women obtain birth control. Jewish women such as Hannah Stone were among the pioneer founders and directors of birth control clinics in the United States.

While suffrage, labor reforms, and reproductive rights were issues pursued by individuals rather than by Jewish women's organizations, the campaign against enforced prostitution ("white slavery") became a major focus of the efforts of the National Council of Jewish Women. NCJW's program involved rescue homes, friendly visitors, employment guidance, and a worldwide campaign of prevention. Success in this work gave the NCJW an entrée into all levels of the secular women's movement and demonstrated the organization's political savvy.

That Jewish women were more likely than women of other immigrant groups to participate in strikes and other radical activities was well known to contemporaries. So prominent were Jewish women in the labor movement that others, especially American-born workers, often refused to participate in what they derisively called "Yiddish unions." According to labor historian Susan Glenn, the majority of Jewish women workers supported union activities, including strikes and protests, but those who were what she called "stalwart militants," deeply attached both to unionism and socialism, were probably a minority. Most important, however, was the fact that the ghetto community warmly encouraged its militant daughters, legitimating their strike activities and their presence in radical movements. Supported by their families and communities, women strikers' actions grew into wider community struggles for social justice and working-class dignity. When these militants left the workforce, as they often did after marriage, they frequently continued their political activities, joining tenant or other consumer committees, working for foreign relief groups, participating in Yiddish *shules* and other social and political societies spawned by the immigrant radical movement. While some women combined these activities with membership in the Socialist or Communist parties, for many others, participation in these cultural activities became what Glenn suggests was a "middle way," a means by which they could maintain their political voices while serving as primary caretakers of their families.

Watching their mothers struggle to provide for their families, much as they had in the *shtetls* and cities of Eastern Europe, gave daughters a sense of the primary importance of women's economic roles. As workers and partners, housekeepers and financial managers, Jewish wives had been central to their families' survival. When necessary, they took to the streets, waging bitter strikes to protest the high cost of housing and food. One of the most notable of these strikes took place in May 1902, when New York Jewish immigrant women launched a month-long campaign to bring down the inflated cost of kosher meat. Agitating in synagogues, they interrupted Torah readings to urge male congregants to support their boycott of expensive butcher shops; they also organized picket lines and open-air rallies and disrupted sales at stores that refused to close. These tactics taught their daughters the lesson that where family was concerned, political militancy was an acceptable, womanly trait.

The sources of Jewish women's radicalism were thus rooted at least in part in the traditional roles women played within the family. Some women, however, had been schooled in the revolutionary movements of Eastern Europe, such as the People's Will, the revolutionary populist movement of Russia, and especially the Bund, the Jewish socialist movement that spread rapidly through the big cities and small *shtetls* of Russia and Poland during the late nineteenth and early twentieth centuries. Others received their first taste of rebellion in the sweatshops and factories of the New World as they confronted the daily horrors of industrial capitalism.

Scholars have argued that Jews' attraction to socialism and other messianic movements sprang from deeper roots—from prophetic injunctions to social justice embodied in the Torah and Talmud. Although Judaism's messianic idealism called for a Zion on Earth at some future time, it also urged revolutionary changes in the here and now—*tikkun olam.* As "Judaism secularized," socialism and other radical American movements explicitly drew on such messages. Jewish activism may be seen as a response to this call to righteousness—or *tzedakeh,* which urged Jews to live their lives according to principles of justice. While many radicals formally rejected religion, they nonetheless incorporated Judaism's spiritual heritage into their political causes. Yet Jewish women in radical politics did not always acknowledge their attachment to Jewish ethics, apparently believing that such particularism conflicted with their more universalist class consciousness.

Antifascist Activism and Interwar Politics

Jewish women's connections to politics took new forms as members of the second generation made their way into American society. As the children of immigrants entered free municipal institutions such as Hunter and City colleges in New York City, they became, according to one Hunter official, "the most politicized [students] in the nation." Women were well represented among committed campus activists, serving as officers of political clubs, leading strikes, and marching in demonstrations. Vociferous opponents of fascism, they aided the cause of the Spanish Loyalists and protested Nazi persecutions of Jews as early as 1933. A 1935 study of New York youth found that twice as many young Jewish women as non-Jews participated in political or civic clubs.

The female Jewish activists who participated in these events carried over the radical tradition of their immigrant parents; for example, Bella Abzug, student council president at Hunter College, traced her pacifist views to the influence of her father, an Eastern European immigrant. Many Jewish women who engaged in student activism in the interwar years became teachers, social workers, or librarians. Although they often left the labor force when they became homemakers, their youthful concerns served as the matrix for lifelong commitment to social and political betterment.

The Politics of Jewish Women's Organizations

Working to improve conditions of daily life for families and local communities and to aid immigrants, refugees, and other Jewish needy, Jewish women's groups provided training ground for Jewish women's political skills. Some women used these opportunities to become leaders within the Jewish communal world, locally, nationally, and even internationally. In 1927, for example, Henrietta Szold was appointed to the three-member Palestine executive of the World Zionist Congress. For others, Jewish women's associations provided springboards to careers in American political institutions outside of the Jewish community.

JEWISH WOMEN'S GROUPS PROVIDED TRAINING GROUND FOR JEWISH WOMEN'S POLITICAL SKILLS.

The activities of Jewish women's organizations at times pitted them against other groups within the Jewish community or within the secular feminist movement. Szold complained that Zionist men "often made fun of Hadassah," criticizing it because it was "not political enough, or . . . it was too political." And while the NCJW joined other women's groups to form the Women's Joint Congressional Committee after the achievement of woman's suffrage, it disagreed with mainstream feminists over the 1924 Cable Act, which declared that foreign-born women could no longer become citizens by marriage to either naturalized or American-born men but rather had to take out citizen papers in their own right. While secular feminists welcomed this acknowledgment of women's independence, NCJW leaders feared that the Cable law would separate foreign-born women from their families and make it difficult for them to receive mothers' pensions, health benefits, and citizenship training. The paths that Jewish women's groups tread necessarily involved them in battles for power and influence, even when they themselves did not define their work as inherently political.

During the 1930s and 1940s, Jewish women joined Hadassah, NCJW, temple sisterhoods, and other Jewish women's groups in record numbers. These affiliations bolstered Jewish women's sense of sisterhood during a time of peril for Jews worldwide and allowed them to demonstrate their belief in a special mission for organized Jewish women. Directed variously toward preventive and ameliorative philanthropy, international peace, Zionism, and the education of women as citizens, Jewish women's organizations continued to influence community relations and the political agenda.

Second-Wave Feminism

The 1960s ushered in a vigorous grassroots protest against barriers to women's advancement and continuing discrimination. Betty Friedan's *The Feminine Mystique* (1963) had an enormous impact. In the book, Friedan exploded the myth of domestic contentment, which she argued had infantilized women, "burying them alive" in their suburban homes as if in a "concentration camp."

A *summa cum laude* 1942 graduate of Smith College, Friedan had gone on to a short-lived career as reporter for the *UE News,* the paper of the communist-led United Electrical, Radio and Machine Workers, before she lived the "feminine mystique" as a suburban wife and mother. Although Friedan attributes her sudden understanding of her own false consciousness to interviews with Smith alumnae from her own class, her earlier labor radicalism had also exposed her to an awareness of gender-based discrimination. Another factor in the making of Friedan's feminist consciousness was the anti-semitism she suffered growing up in Peoria, Illinois, as the only Jewish girl in high school. "Ever since I was a little girl," she acknowledged, "I remember my father telling me that I had a passion for justice. But I think it was really a passion against injustice which originated from my feelings of the injustice of anti-Semitism." Like Friedan, many of the leaders of the 1960s feminist movement—Bella Abzug, Phyllis Chesler, Letty Cottin Pogrebin, Karen DeCrow, and Vivian Gornick—as well as the half-Jewish Gloria Steinem—were Jews, although a good number were secular or unidentified Jews.

Jewish women were among the activists who had led campaigns for civil rights, nuclear disarmament, and peace. After a decade of militant antiwar struggles, activists such as Bella Abzug, leader of Women Strike for Peace, had also come to connect war with violence against women and to identify war as a feminist issue. These women's organizational know-how and skillful coalition building became essential tools in the development of feminism as a mass movement. While leaders such as Friedan and Abzug, who were then in their early forties, stimulated like-minded women to wage war on patriarchy, a group of younger women joined the antiwar and student movements. By 1967, many had become outraged at their treatment by male radicals whose beliefs in freedom and equality apparently only applied to men. After their attempts to introduce women's issues into the movement were met by ridicule, they began to organize groups of their own, identifying their cause as women's liberation. "The personal is political" became their slogan; and consciousness-raising, their primary tool. Among the Jewish leaders of the women's liberation movement were Robin Morgan, Shulamith Firestone, Meredith Tax, Andrea Dworkin, Alix Kates Shulman, and Naomi Weisstein.

> JEWISH WOMEN WERE AMONG THE ACTIVISTS WHO HAD LED CAMPAIGNS FOR CIVIL RIGHTS, NUCLEAR DISARMAMENT, AND PEACE.

Civil Rights

Jewish women also participated in the civil rights movement in numbers greatly disproportionate to their representation in the population. Working as fieldworkers, campus organizers, voter registration workers, and Freedom School teachers, Jewish women helped build the infrastructure of the civil rights movement. They played a critical coordinating role, managing and connecting people, money, resources, and information.

Among northern Jewish women activists who went South to participate in antiracist work led by the Student Nonviolent Coordinating Committee (SNCC) and other black groups during the summers of 1963 through 1965 were activists Florence Howe, who would later found the Feminist Press; Susan Brownmiller, who would write *Against Our*

Will, a groundbreaking analysis of rape as a feminist issue; and Rita Schwerner, the wife
of Michael Schwerner, one of the young men murdered in Mississippi during the 1964
Freedom Summer. While most of the Jewish women who
participated in the civil rights movement of these years did
not identify themselves as Jewish, many acknowledge in retrospect that a sense of marginality or "otherness" as Jews,
along with an inheritance of progressive familial values, stimulated their involvement in civil rights. Some were motivated
by direct experiences of antisemitism or family encounters
with the Holocaust; others grew up in poverty and circumstances of class conflict. For all these reasons, they em-
pathized with the black struggle in the South and were willing to risk their lives in dangerous work combating racism.

> JEWISH WOMEN
> PARTICIPATED IN THE
> CIVIL RIGHTS
> MOVEMENT IN
> NUMBERS GREATLY
> DISPROPORTIONATE
> TO THEIR
> REPRESENTATION IN
> THE POPULATION.

JEWISH WOMEN AND POLITICAL OFFICE
Political Consultants and Strategists

In the years after women won the vote, they gradually began the transition from outsiders
to insiders in American politics. Over the next decades, women emerged in leadership
positions at the local, state, and federal levels, often as the "first" females to occupy these
offices. Other women garnered power as campaign consultants, party leaders, and advisers to top officials.

Jewish women's routes to elective office varied. Sometimes they worked as community organizers and activists, volunteering at the local levels of government, often in areas of particular concern to women such as education, day care, peace, or women's
rights. In other cases, they moved to political office subsequent to professional careers
as lawyers, administrators, and executives. A good number of women officeholders were
motivated to enter politics by specific historical events in which they participated or
which they witnessed: the civil rights movement, feminism, the Vietnam War.

Advisers and Consultants: Belle Moskowitz and Anna Lederer Rosenberg

Born and educated in New York City, Belle Lindner Moskowitz worked at the Educational Alliance, a Jewish settlement on the Lower East Side, and then, after her first
marriage, joined the New York Council of Jewish Women, to work with delinquent
girls. The council provided role models, a focus on women and girls compatible with
Jewish family roles, and an opportunity to hone her leadership skills. After the death of
her husband, she worked as a labor arbitrator at the Dress and Waist Manufacturers Association. Moskowitz came to the attention of Governor Alfred E. Smith of New York

after organizing the women's vote for him in 1918; she soon became Smith's key adviser. In his 1928 race for the presidency, she directed campaign publicity as the only woman on the Democratic National Committee; in 1932, she organized Smith's unsuccessful bid for the Democratic presidential nomination. According to the *New York Times*, Moskowitz wielded "more political power than any other woman in the United States"; she was the first Jewish woman in America to hold an important political leadership post. Her granddaughter and biographer, Elisabeth Israels Perry, notes that Moskowitz was "the only woman of her time to achieve political power without holding office, inheriting wealth, or moving up through a husband's career."

BELLE MOSKOWITZ WAS THE FIRST JEWISH WOMAN IN AMERICA TO HOLD AN IMPORTANT POLITICAL LEADERSHIP POST.

With a political career extending from suffrage activism in the late teens through the 1950s, Anna Rosenberg occupied some of the highest government positions ever occupied by a woman. Born in Hungary and naturalized as a teenager, Rosenberg became active in local Democratic Party politics in Manhattan, managing several campaigns; she served in Roosevelt's New Deal in several posts, among them, regional director of the National Recovery Administration. Rosenberg advised New York City Mayor Fiorello LaGuardia, New York State Governor Herbert Lehman, and presidents Roosevelt and Truman. During World War II, she became assistant secretary of defense for military manpower requirements.

Political Officeholders: Jewish Women in the United States Congress

Florence Prag Kahn of San Francisco was the first Jewish woman to serve in Congress. Although she had opposed woman suffrage before it was adopted by California in 1911, Kahn later championed women's role in politics: "There is no sex in citizenship," she liked to say, "and there should be none in politics." Elected to the House in 1924 in a special election after the death of her husband, Julius, a Republican who had served two decades in the House, Kahn won reelection in her own right five times, serving from 1925 to 1937. Sharing her husband's views on military preparedness, she became the first woman to serve on the Military Affairs Committee and was responsible for introducing legislation that increased defense spending. Alice Roosevelt Longworth, the outspoken daughter of Theodore Roosevelt, perfectly portrayed Kahn's uniqueness on the national political scene: "Mrs. Kahn, shrewd, resourceful, and witty, is an all-around first-rate legislator, the equal of any man in Congress and the superior of most."

Roosevelt's portrait of Florence Prag Kahn captured many of the elements that came to characterize future Jewish women national legislators. Resourceful and shrewd, as a group they were responsible for a great many legislative accomplishments, following Florence Kahn's path in working in the so-called male areas of the economy and national defense. Later Jewish women legislators also led the nation as it dealt with such women's issues as women's political access, reproductive rights, health care, education, and child care. All of the Jewish women in Congress have shown strong support for Israel and related Jewish issues.

California has sent three other Jewish women to the House: Bobbi Fiedler, a Republican first elected in 1980; Barbara Boxer, a Democrat elected in 1982; and Jane Harman, a Democrat, elected in 1992.

Los Angeles born and bred, Fiedler entered politics in 1976 as the leader of a citywide antibusing crusade. She opposed forced busing because she believed it denied parents the right to choose their children's schools and because as a Jew, shaped by the Holocaust and her childhood experiences of antisemitism, she opposed identification of children by race or ethnicity. In Fiedler's words, "Being Jewish had a very strong impact on my political philosophy—not necessarily in the spiritual or religious sense—but in the sense of being a minority, of being the object of discrimination." After a single term in local office, Fiedler defeated a longtime Democratic congressman; she served three terms before leaving in 1987 to run, unsuccessfully, for the Senate. Fiedler considered herself an independent Republican who voted her conscience; a member of the House Budget Committee, she fought for tax and spending cuts and defense spending but broke with her party over her support for abortion rights and the Equal Rights Amendment (ERA). Her support for Israel was unswerving.

Barbara Boxer, a former stockbroker and journalist, experienced gender discrimination at Brooklyn College and upon entering the financial world. She became fully politicized during the Vietnam War and, in the late 1960s and early 1970s, helped establish community groups involved in issues of peace, women's rights, education, and child care. Moving to northern California, she lost her first bid for public office in 1972, when she failed to win a seat on the Marin County Board of Supervisors, but became a member of that board in 1977 and rose to become its first female president in 1981. Boxer went on to the House of Representatives, serving five terms before her election to the Senate in 1992. Her career has focused on feminist issues, including abortion rights and sexual harassment. With the appointment of Clarence Thomas to the Supreme Court, Boxer led a group of seven congresswomen to the Senate to demand that the Senate Judiciary Committee fully investigate charges of sexual harassment alleged against Thomas by Anita Hill.

Jane Harman was elected to Congress on a "prochoice" and "prochange" platform, with the slogan "This woman will clean House." Harman had extensive political experience as well as staff experience in both Congress and the executive branch before she ran for the House. Serving on the National Security Committee, the Science Space and Technology Committee, and the Intelligence Committee, she was a strong advocate for the defense and aerospace industries in her Los Angeles district. Harman was also an outspoken leader on women's issues, serving on the executive committee of the

Congressional Caucus on Women's Issues. The daughter of a physician father who fled Nazi Germany in the 1930s, Harman consistently supported pro-Israel policies and was a member of the Congressional Caucus on Anti-Semitism. She left Congress after her third term to run, unsuccessfully, for governor. In the 2000 congressional election, Harman recaptured her old seat in the House.

New York state has sent three Jewish women to the House: Bella Abzug, elected in 1970, served three terms before she left to run, unsuccessfully, for the Senate; Elizabeth Holtzman, elected in 1972, served four terms before she, too, ended her House career with an unsuccessful run for the Senate; Nita Lowey, elected in 1988, is currently serving her sixth term.

Abzug, the second Jewish woman elected to Congress (and the first not in a husband's wake) was elected to Congress as a leader of the women's rights and peace movements. According to Speaker Thomas O'Neill, she was the "hardest working member" of the House and one of its most skillful power players. A *U.S. News & World Report* survey named her as the "third most influential" member of Congress. She led the fight in Congress for the ERA and reproductive freedom, and she championed women's rights in all areas. As chair of the House Subcommittee on Government Information and Individual Rights, Abzug helped write and pass the Freedom of Information and Privacy Acts and the "Government in the Sunshine" Law, which opened up government agencies to public scrutiny; she also conducted inquiries into covert and illegal activities of government agencies and was the first to call for President Nixon's impeachment during the Watergate scandal.

Abzug's tenure in the House coincided with the intensification of the Soviet campaign of harassment against Jews. She became deeply involved in the campaign to win the right of Soviet Jews to emigrate, sponsoring legislation to issue visas for Soviet Jews and to provide aid to Israel for their resettlement. In April 1976, the House unanimously passed the Abzug Resolution, marking the first time it had explicitly called on the Soviet Union to permit free emigration and declaring its support for a massive public demonstration against the oppression of Soviet Jews. Abzug was a strong supporter of Israel. However, her support for arms for Israel placed her in direct opposition to pacifists and radical feminists who had become stridently anti-Israel after the 1967 war; she temporarily broke with New York chapter of Women Strike for Peace, which she had helped found.

Abzug's political career continued after she left Congress; she founded Women USA and then, in 1990, the Women's Economic Development Organization (WEDO), an international lobbying group for environmental, peace, and women's issues. According to Charlotte Bunch, director of the Center for Women's Global Leadership, Abzug was one of the few American women who transcended U.S. politics to understand the global nature of women's issues and to speak powerfully of the responsibility of the United States in the world.

Like Abzug, Elizabeth Holtzman came to the House fresh from her involvement in the civil rights and antiwar movements. During the summer of 1963, she went South and worked in Albany, Georgia, defending SNCC workers; with a few other law students she founded the Law Students Civil Rights Research Council, which sent hundreds more law students south the following summer. Her encounters in the South gave a new dimension to her family's experience of "pogroms and injustice" and fueled her determination whenever a political battle seemed "too perilous." Holtzman was active in the peace movement as well, working for "Take Brooklyn Out of the War Coalition." A Brooklynite who attended Radcliffe College and then Harvard Law School, Holtzman challenged the Democratic political machine in 1970 by opposing the machine candidate for Democratic state committeewoman; she won. Two years later, she defeated Brooklyn's fifty-year Democratic incumbent, Emanuel Cellar, a House icon thought to be invincible. Taking office at age thirty-two, Holtzman was the youngest woman ever elected to the House of Representatives.

One of Holtzman's first acts was to bring a suit in Brooklyn's federal District Court challenging the legality of the president's bombing of Cambodia without the consent of Congress. The District Court found in her favor, but after an Appeals Court ruling and several different Supreme Court opinions, the decision was overturned. As a member of the House Judiciary Committee, Holtzman played a highly visible role during the Nixon impeachment hearings. She also chaired the House Subcommittee on Immigration, Refugees, and International Law, writing and securing passage of the Holtzman Amendment, which authorized the deportation of Nazi war criminals. Holtzman coauthored the nation's first refugee law, which helped thousands of Jews from the Soviet Union enter the United States in the late 1970s and 1980s. In her four terms in the House, Holtzman showed a strong interest in women's issues, introducing a rape privacy act, helping extend the deadline for passage of the ERA, and introducing measures to bar sex discrimination in federal employment. After she ran unsuccessfully for the Senate in 1980, Holtzman was elected Kings County district attorney, the first female DA in New York City; in 1990, she became New York City comptroller.

Nita Lowey, elected from a district encompassing Westchester, Queens, and the Bronx, has been a leading voice for women's rights and pro-Israel positions. As chair of the Congressional Women's Caucus and later of the House Pro-Choice Caucus, Lowey has made women's health a priority, using her position on the House Appropriations Committee to fight for funding for breast and cervical cancer research and sponsoring legislation to combat domestic violence. She has been the Appropriations Committee's chief advocate of U.S. aid to Israel. Lowey was honored by Mothers against Drunk Driving (MADD) for her efforts to strengthen drunken driving laws and vigorously supports stricter gun control and public safety laws. A former PTA president who served as assistant secretary of state in New York, Lowey also maintains a strong interest in educational reform. Like several other Jewish women legislators mentioned to this point, Lowey thought of running for the Senate; she was poised to challenge for the seat vacated by Daniel Patrick Moynihan in 2000 but stepped aside in favor of Hillary Rodham Clinton; she was reelected to the House instead. In the 107th Congress, Lowey became chair of the Democratic Congressional Campaign Committee, the highest party post in Congress ever to be held by a woman.

In addition to these six Jewish congresswomen elected from New York and California, several other Jewish women have served in the House of Representatives. Gladys Noon Spellman, who had been a county official in Maryland and president of the National Association of Counties, was elected to Congress in 1975 and served six years before suffering a heart attack while campaigning for a fourth term. Marjorie Margolies-Mezvinsky from Philadelphia, Pennsylvania, served one term in Congress, from 1993 to 1995. During the critical budget debate in the first Clinton administration, Margolies-Mezvinsky cast a tie-breaking vote in favor of the president's program. While she earned the respect and gratitude of her fellow Democrats for that vote, it did not sit well with her constituents in suburban Philadelphia, who turned her out of office in the Republican landslide of 1994. In addition, Shelley Berkley from Nevada and Jan Schakowsky from Illinois were elected in 1998 and reelected in 2000, representing the Las Vegas area and the lakefront area of Chicago and its northern and northwestern suburbs, respectively.

Jewish Women in the Senate

In 1992, two Jewish women made political history by becoming the first pair of women to serve together as United States senators from a single state. What was more extraordinary, given California politics, was that Dianne Feinstein, California's senior senator, and Barbara Boxer, the junior senator, both came from San Francisco. Feinstein, the eighteenth woman ever elected to the Senate, joined six other women when she was elected to the Senate to the two years remaining in Pete Wilson's term; she was reelected to a full term in 1994 and to another in 2000. Boxer, the nineteenth female senator, was elected in 1992 and reelected in 1998.

Feinstein and Boxer took different routes to the Senate (although at one point each had served on local boards of supervisors) and emphasize different themes. Feinstein is a member of the moderate centrist coalition, while Boxer espouses more liberal views.

Feinstein had imagined a career in medicine, but her first course in American political thought at Stanford University whetted her appetite for politics. After interning for Governor Pat Brown of California and serving by his appointment on the California's Women Board of Terms and Parole (as its youngest member ever), Feinstein won a seat on the San Francisco Board of Supervisors, becoming its first woman president. After the assassinations of Mayor George Moscone and Supervisor Harvey Milk, Feinstein succeeded to the mayoralty, winning election twice in her own right before being term-limited out in 1987. As mayor, she was given credit for a steadying hand at the time of crisis following the assassinations in City Hall and was highly regarded for the effectiveness of her public safety measures and her handling of economic issues. She lost a close race for governor in 1990 before winning election to the Senate in 1992.

Feinstein's advice to women interested in political office derives from her own experience: "Start on the school board, go for a spot on the town council. *Earn your spurs.* . . . develop a portfolio of expertise." Her own special area was criminal justice, an interest she continued to pursue in the Senate where her consuming passion has been gun control. Feinstein also cites the Holocaust as a key influence on her activism. Because of the Holocaust, she grew up understanding that "terrible injustices could be inflicted on people because of hatred and bias. That awareness . . . instilled in me a commitment to the social good." Feinstein sponsored the Hate Crimes Sentencing Enforcement Act, increasing sentences for those convicted of hate crimes in a federal court. She has been deeply involved in health and medical issues, cochairing the Senate Cancer Coalition and working to increase funding for breast cancer research.

As senator, Barbara Boxer has continued to emphasize the issues she advocated in the House: abortion rights, education, health care, children's programs, environmental protection, the economy, and gun control. Among the legislation she has introduced are the Family Planning and Choice Protection Act, the Children's Environmental Protection Act, the School Safety Act, and the Child Safety Lock Act.

Local and State Politics

Jewish women have been leaders in state and local politics as well—holding office, serving in administrative posts, chairing or otherwise working with municipal or county commissions and committees, running campaigns, and participating in political parties or politically based interest groups and organizations. Although they have been active throughout the country, examples from New York City, Los Angeles, and Dallas will have to suffice as examples of the kinds of work Jewish women have done in different localities.

In New York, Ruth Messinger rose to prominence as a city council member and then as Manhattan borough president. After years as a teacher, school and college administrator, and social worker, Messinger entered local politics in 1977 and remained until she was defeated in the mayoral race of 1997 by Rudolph Giuliani. She now directs the American Jewish World Service, an organization that acts on Judaism's injunction to pursue justice by seeking to alleviate poverty, hunger, and disease. Throughout her career Messinger has pursued a social justice agenda, including promoting gay and minority rights, preservation of the environment, and education.

Rosaline Wyman has been a mainstay of California Democratic politics. Born in Los Angeles to New Deal Democrats, she was elected to the Los Angeles City Council the year after graduating from the University of Southern California, the youngest person ever elected to the council or, indeed, to any position in a major United States city. As the city's first female acting mayor, Wyman arranged for the move of the Brooklyn Dodgers to Los Angeles. After being defeated for a fourth term on the council in 1965, Wyman turned her energies to serving her fellow Democrats: she headed the party's fund-raising efforts, cochaired the 1984 Democratic National Convention, and cochaired the senatorial campaigns of Dianne Feinstein. Wyman has also led the Community Relations Committee of the Los Angeles Jewish Community Council.

Annette Greenfield Strauss became the first woman, and the first Jew, to be elected mayor of Dallas. When she could not find a paying job in Dallas, even with a master's degree, she volunteered for the United Jewish Appeal, becoming the organization's and the city's most effective fundraiser. Strauss was elected to the city council in 1983 and mayor in 1987. She has chaired the board of the John G. Tower Center for Political Studies at Southern Methodist University and the Dallas Council of World Affairs.

Jewish women's accomplishments in political life have not only taken place in areas with the highest concentration of Jews. On the state level, two of the most prominent examples of Jewish women's successful forays into politics occurred in Vermont and South Carolina. In Vermont, Madeline Kunin rose to the governorship, becoming the first woman to serve in that position and the first woman to be elected governor of any state three times. Kunin's identity as a feminist, immigrant Jewish woman infused her political career. Born in Switzerland, as a child she fled the threat of a German invasion with her widowed mother, immigrating to New York City in 1940. Many of her relatives died in the Holocaust, a factor that she says was "the source of my political courage." After graduating from the University of Massachusetts and the Columbia School of Journalism, she started work as a reporter with the Burlington, Vermont *Free Press*. She stopped working to raise her four children, but it was in this period that she also became a community organizer, gaining skills and learning lessons that she would utilize throughout her political career. First as a Democratic member of the State House of Representatives (1972–78), then as lieutenant governor (1978–84), and finally as governor (1984–91), Kunin used her offices as a way to promote leadership roles for women, appointing women in large numbers to various positions in her administrations. After serving as governor, Kunin played a major role in Bill Clinton's campaign and transition to the presidency; Clinton later appointed her deputy secretary of education and, in 1996, ambassador to Switzerland.

Harriet Keyserling, born in New York City, moved to South Carolina in 1944 after marrying Dr. Henry Keyserling, a native of that state. A liberal Jew in the conservative South, she became involved in community organizing while raising her four children and eventually was elected to the Beaufort County Council, the first woman to serve on that body. At the age of fifty-four, she was elected to the state legislature, joining with several progressive legislators in a so-called Crazy Caucus, which worked on such issues as control of nuclear waste, conservation, and education. Keyserling's interests in women's issues led her to start a woman's caucus as well, but she left the legislature after sixteen years, stymied by that body's partisanship and rancor.

Many Jewish women serve as mayors of municipalities of various sizes; notable among them is Vera Katz, former speaker of the Oregon legislature and current mayor of Portland, Oregon. Approximately seventy Jewish women are serving in state legislatures. Included in this number is Missouri legislator Harriet Woods, former lieutenant governor of the state who was defeated in a bitter United States Senate race. Woods had been a well-known figure in the women's political community in the 1980s and 1990s and served as former president of the National Women's Political Caucus.

CONCLUSION

Over the course of the last century, women have increasingly achieved political power. As seen in their success in the electoral sphere and in the ancillary endeavors of political life involved in electoral politics, Jewish women have been prominent in this achievement. Serving on boards of supervisors, city councils, mayor's offices, state legislatures, governor's mansions, as well as in the hallowed halls of the United States House and Senate, and even in far-flung diplomatic posts, these Jewish women political leaders have made a difference. As a group they have been bold and innovative, taking principled stands that they have struggled to translate into legislative or executive enactments. Most of these women have promoted liberal agendas; most have fought for the so-called women's issues of education and child care, health and reproductive rights, and women's rights more broadly; but they also champion economic and security issues that they consider to be significant "women's issues" as well. Jewish women in political office have shown strong support for Israel and other Jewish cultural and political interests; many have acknowledged the Holocaust as a motivating factor behind their activism. Continuing the tradition of community activism that characterized earlier generations of Jewish women, these officeholders often found their way into the political arena through participating in local civic and community life, secular and Jewish women's organizations, or political movements, including those concerning civil rights, poverty, social justice, women's rights, the environment, Soviet Jewry, and Zionism. Jewish women continue to be involved at the local level in these and other issues; new concerns such as genetic testing and breast cancer awareness may well stimulate new campaigns and another generation of leaders.

At the present time, the granddaughters and great-granddaughters of the immigrant women who fought sweatshop bosses and those of the wealthier Jewish women who organized to distribute food and clothing to needy newcomers have arrived front and center on the stage of American political life. Like the senior senator from California, who was frequently mentioned as a potential Democratic vice presidential candidate in the 2000 election, other Jewish women may be poised for highest office in years to come. They will take with them the inheritance of generations of Jewish women whose passion for political life and deep-seated commitment to social and moral values have been exercised in a variety of effective ways, both inside and outside conventional political channels.

13

ISRAEL AND BEYOND

American Jews and U.S. Foreign Policy

STEVEN L. SPIEGEL

The story of American Jews and U.S. foreign policy is one of weakness and tragedy, largely dominated by failure until the last third of the twentieth century. This chapter contends that the rising influence of the American Jewish community since the Six-Day War in 1967 is the result of Jews' increased interest in foreign policy, their more secure position in American society, and, most important, the enhanced power of Israel and its perceived value to the United States. One remaining question is whether the recent decades are an aberration or an indication of future trends.

THE RISING INFLUENCE OF THE AMERICAN JEWISH COMMUNITY IS THE RESULT OF JEWS' INCREASED INTEREST IN FOREIGN POLICY, THEIR MORE SECURE POSITION IN AMERICAN SOCIETY, AND, MOST IMPORTANT, THE ENHANCED POWER OF ISRAEL AND ITS PERCEIVED VALUE TO THE UNITED STATES.

The American Jewish experience in U.S. foreign policy can be divided into four periods, demarcated by three wars: pre–Civil War, the Civil War to World War II, World War II to the Six-Day War, and the post–Six-Day War period.

PRE-CIVIL WAR

In this period, only about 150,000 Jews were living in America. Jews were generally not formally organized, and when they were, their orientation was to synagogues and questions of religious reform. When American Jews did become engaged in U.S. foreign policy, it was in response to specific international incidents concerning the safety of other Jews abroad, and their involvement was largely unsuccessful and unsustained.

The first such incident occurred in 1840, when Jews in Damascus were accused of killing Christians to use their blood in the ceremony of the Passover Seder. The mysterious disappearance of a monk had triggered what ultimately became known as the Damascus Blood Libel. The American Jewish reaction was one of solidarity and support for the wrongly accused Jews. Jewish leaders like Mordechai Noah and Isaac Lesser made public appeals to their fellow American Jews to stand by their brothers in Damascus. American Jewish protest meetings helped mobilize a national and international response for Jewish self-defense, but in America it was largely symbolic. No evidence points to substantial financial aid from American families to the Jews in Damascus, and American Jews did not make a difference in the U.S. government's position. The U.S. diplomatic condemnation of the Damascus affair by President Martin van Buren was made in response to English protests. By the time the American Jewish community lodged its appeals, the State Department informed its representatives that action had already been taken.

In 1858, American Jews were unsuccessful in influencing President James Buchanan to intervene on behalf of Edgardo Mortara, a Jewish boy in Italy who had been baptized by his maid and forced to become Catholic (Hertzberg, 109–12). The

> ALTHOUGH HE WAS THE SON OF A LEBANESE-AMERICAN GRO-
> CER, AMBASSADOR PHILIP HABIB GREW UP IN AN AREA OF
> BROOKLYN DURING THE LATE 1920s HE DESCRIBED AS "99.9%
> JEWISH" AND WHERE HE REPORTEDLY LEARNED TO SPEAK YIDDISH.
> —JEWISH BULLETIN OF NORTHERN CALIFORNIA, 1992

case became a celebrated international affair, and Buchanan was suspected of being afraid that he would alienate American Catholics by taking action.

CIVIL WAR TO WORLD WAR II

The American Jewish community emerged from the Civil War both strengthened and weakened. On the one hand, the forty years after 1881 brought a huge increase in the number of Jews from Eastern Europe and Russia. On the other hand, the aftermath of the Civil War, including industrial growth, the continental expansion of America, new immigration, and a new interest in the field of eugenics, brought with it such developments as the Ku Klux Klan and the spread of social discrimination. Therefore, throughout the period Jews operated with strengthened numbers and enhanced organization, but with increased vulnerabilities.

With Eastern European immigration came new needs and attitudes. The first significant Jewish organization with a foreign policy orientation was the Hebrew Emigrant Aid Society (HEAS) founded in 1881, mainly to assist impoverished Eastern European Jews entering the United States, although its leaders were also alarmed by the burden impoverished and unskilled immigrants represented. HEAS was disbanded in 1883 in the misplaced expectation (perhaps hope) that the majority of immigrants had arrived. It was gradually replaced by a variety of makeshift organizations that united in 1902 to form the Hebrew Immigrant Aid Society (HIAS), which eventually became the senior society aiding Jewish immigration in the United States.

Eastern Europeans also brought with them a passion for culture, community, and social justice, leading to an enormous increase in the variety of Jewish organizations. This in turn led to a change in the stereotype of American Jews, from the peddlers and merchants of the earlier German immigrants, to the radicals and labor activists of the late nineteenth and early twentieth centuries. The absorption and integration of the influx was the main preoccupation of American Jewry before World War I. As larger numbers arrived in the United States, they naturally brought with them concern for relatives left behind. Once they were settled, it was common for Russian Jews to send funds back home. These concerns were a precursor to the founding of the

Joint Distribution Committee (JDC) in 1915, whose major purpose to this day is to assist Jews in distress around the world. The immediate impetus for the "Joint" was the horrendous condition of Jews caught on the Eastern Front between the Russian and German armies in World War I.

Given the increased suffering of Jews at the hands of the Russian government after 1881 and their resulting increased immigration to the United States, the issue became one of concern to the U.S. government. As early as December 9, 1891, President Benjamin Harrison addressed the plight of Russian Jews and demanded that the czar change his antisemitic policies. Even though he had indeed been approached by key community leaders, Harrison's action was not prompted by a desire to please American Jews, nor was it an indication of their influence. Rather, it arose out of his concern that America would not be able to handle the ever-increasing number of immigrants.

A decade later, a similar motivation prompted the Theodore Roosevelt administration to convey its concern about the persecution of Romanian Jews to the Bucharest government. In a period when Jews were still staunchly Republican, the Roosevelt administration was pleased to dispatch repeated, and largely ceremonial, protests to Russia over the rising suffering of Russian Jews in the early years of the twentieth century. It was in this context that the American Jewish Committee was founded in 1906 to bring together key individuals with strong contacts with the U.S. political leadership who might work on gaining American help in averting disaster for Russian Jewry.

It was, in turn, this group that shortly spearheaded a new successful campaign on the issue. When some Russian Jews became U.S. citizens and moved back to Russia, they were subjected to harsh treatment by the czar's government. A new campaign employed this indignity as a means of improving the lot of Russian Jews. After much public and congressional outrage, initiated by American Jewish organizations, in December 1912, a reluctant President Taft abrogated the commercial treaty with Russia that had been in operation since 1832.

Yet, if this incident suggested the potential of American Jewish clout in foreign policy, it was also, in many ways, a deceptively positive sign. Americans were really only being asked to protect their own citizens. Thus, when xenophobia, antisemitism, and anticommunism dominated American society after World War I, Jews were powerless to thwart the strict limits on immigration to America enacted in 1923. Indeed, this antagonism to immigration continued throughout the twelve years of the Nazi regime and even after World War II and the Holocaust.

The plight of Russian Jews was not the only foreign policy issue the fledgling American Jewish community confronted in the early part of the twentieth century. The other was the emergence of the Zionist movement, which at first garnered few American Jewish adherents. Most Russian Jews emigrating to America had rejected the Zionist alternative by coming to the United States; most thought the idea either wrong or hopeless. Socialists rejected Zionism, as did most Orthodox and Reform Jews. Rabbi Isaac Wise, the first leader of Reform Judaism and the founder of the Hebrew Union College, considered Cincinnati, Ohio, to be the new Jerusalem, and America the new Palestine; there was no need to return to the displaced center of Jewish life. Thus, in 1891, when a Presbyterian minister collected the signatures of a distinguished group of Americans on a document called the Blackstone Memorial, which advocated the return of the Jews to Palestine, he was opposed by many American Jews.

Influenced in particular by Theodor Herzl, Zionism did, however, gradually gain some support in the United States, leading to the foundation of the American Zionist Federation in 1897. Despite the continuing lack of enthusiasm, if not outright opposition, by many if not most American Jews before World War I, the movement did gain the support of one prominent Reform rabbi, Stephen S. Wise. Yet the major recruit to Zionism of the period was one of America's leading labor lawyers, Louis Brandeis, who was convinced to join the movement by a Zionist activist in 1913. The famous Brandeis soon became the leader of American Zionists, proclaiming, "[t]o be good Americans, we must be better Jews, and to be better Jews, we must become Zionists." The Americanization of the Zionist ideal had begun. As Brandeis proclaimed, "Let no American imagine that Zionism is inconsistent with patriotism" (Grose, 55).

As it happened, Wise and Brandeis had been major supporters of Woodrow Wilson in his successful campaign for the presidency. Thus, in the fall of 1917, when the British considered releasing the Balfour Declaration favoring a Jewish National Home in Palestine, they consulted with Wilson, and Wise and Brandeis—by now appointed by Wilson as America's first Jewish Supreme Court justice—tried to convince Wilson to support the effort. We now know that part of the initial motivation for the British in releasing the declaration was to maintain the support of both Russian and American Jews for the war effort to thwart a similar effort by the Germans. We also know that despite the intervention of Wise and Brandeis, Wilson made his own secret deal with the British to support the effort that was not directly related to any outside pressure.

The Balfour Declaration generated new enthusiasm for the Zionist cause, and American Jewish organizations became active in successful efforts to win congressional approval of the declaration, award the British mandate to Palestine, and enshrine the terms of the Balfour Declaration in international law. The American Jewish Congress, organized by Wise and supported by Brandeis, was also amply represented at the Versailles Conference to push the idea of a Jewish homeland forward.

Despite this increased prominence, however, American Jewish participation in the Zionist campaign would not be sustained. After the Balfour Declaration, Brandeis believed that it would now be necessary to devote the Zionist effort to the practical means of settling the land. His Zionism was uniquely American—a philanthropic effort devoted to helping other Jews, not to moving to Palestine. Chaim Weizmann, the leader of British Zionism and the hero of the Balfour Declaration who now became president of the World Zionist Movement, was a more traditional European Zionist and believed instead that the movement should also work for the political objective of a Jewish state. The differences between Weizmann and Brandeis proved irreconcilable. At the conclusive meeting of the Zionist Organization of America in Cleveland in 1921, the Weizmann forces defeated those backing Brandeis. The justice and his colleagues withdrew from active involvement with the Zionist movement, and its influence and impact in the United States declined.

The organization was revived by David Ben Gurion at the famous Biltmore Conference in New York in 1942, the first Zionist conference to declare explicitly that the aim of the movement was a "Jewish commonwealth" in Palestine. Ben Gurion was the first to see that Zionist hopes after the war would rest with the United States and, by extension, American Jewry.

Thus, in the interwar period, the American Jewish community was not able to influence U.S. immigration policy, and it did not take a leadership role in the world Zionist effort. But its greatest failing lay in its inability to do more for Jews trapped by Hitler. Many reasons account for this failure. First, the new prominence of antisemitism in American life frightened many American Jews. The flowering of such organizations as the Silver Shirts and the German-American Bund made many Jews feel that what was happening in Germany "could happen here." Second, the Depression dramatically amplified this insecurity, robbing organizations of personnel and causing many Jews to be preoccupied with simply earning a living.

IN THE INTERWAR PERIOD, THE AMERICAN JEWISH COMMUNITY WAS NOT ABLE TO INFLUENCE U.S. IMMIGRATION POLICY, AND IT DID NOT TAKE A LEADERSHIP ROLE IN THE WORLD ZIONIST EFFORT.

Third, some American Jews even miscalculated the extent of the threat that Nazism represented. There were those who argued that Hitler's views would be tempered by holding office. As Peter Grose points out, before Hitler took power in 1932, one major Jewish leader, Felix M. Warburg, wrote, "Even if the Hitlerites should get into power, the moment responsibilities rest on their shoulders and they are in the government, they will sober down, just as much as the Communists have in Russia and the Laborites have in England" (Grose, 107–08).

Fourth, as this quotation suggests, the American Jewish community was badly split in the 1930s, its membership divided by a proliferation of organizations and lacking a central arm for political action. It was also weakened by growing assimilation, ideological clashes over issues ranging from Zionism to socialism, and confusion about specific steps that might be taken effectively. Later in the 1930s, when it became clear Hitler would not change his policies, various segments of the community pursued different options, including attempts to boycott German goods, to convince the Roosevelt administration to press the British to permit an increase in immigration to Palestine, and to open doors for victims fleeing the Nazis to emigrate somewhere else. The latter pressure resulted in the pathetic Evian Conference in 1938 in which only the Dominican Republic offered sanctuary to Jews.

Fifth, Roosevelt proved to be a deceptively amicable president. Seen as being closely aligned with Jews on domestic affairs and strongly supported by them, he was often criticized by rightist elements for bringing Jews into government. This criticism increased his reputation for courage and reliability among Jews but made them less willing to press him on foreign policy issues. We now know that FDR was far more cautious and even deceptive on these issues than American Jews at the time realized. On both the refugee and Zionist questions, FDR tended to listen to advisers less sympathetic to Jews, and he often gave Jewish leaders the impression he was doing more and was more sympathetic to their aims than he really was.

Finally, Jewish dependence on Roosevelt must also be seen in the context of the times. Before Pearl Harbor, when the majority of Americans did not want to enter the war, FDR was more in tune with anti-Nazi objectives than most American politicians. American Jews were caught in the position of appearing to ask Americans to fight and die for foreign Jews. After America's entry into the war, Roosevelt's simple aphorism that the way to save European Jewry was to end the war seemed to make sense. No one seemed to understand the frightening implications for Hitler's victims of waiting that long. Those who dared to seek more active policies on behalf of European Jewry were left to battle the misrepresentations of administration officials, as well as the widespread public disbelief of the reports of atrocities. Both before and after American entry into the war, support for European Jewry was framed in a context in which urging activism or special efforts was made to appear unpatriotic.

FROM WORLD WAR II TO THE SIX-DAY WAR

The perspective of American Jewry was transformed by the end of the war and the horrifying knowledge of the true dimensions of the tragedy in Europe. The next few years were consumed by the twin projects of supporting the surviving victims of Nazism and aiding in the establishment of a Jewish state. Yet the insecurities and divisions that had led to Jewish ineffectiveness in the 1930s were still largely in place. In their efforts to overturn Truman administration decisions or guide its preferences, Jews were still largely tepid supplicants of politicians and diplomats. And they were still distrusted, their credibility compromised by a reputation for left-leaning sentiments in a period of growing anticommunism.

But two factors altered the failure syndrome of the 1930s. First, the knowledge of the Holocaust (and the widespread guilt at the inadequacy of the U.S. response) injected a powerful moral force into the policies American Jews were advocating. Second, American Jews were now being influenced—even guided—by Ben Gurion and his associates, who often provided the vision and focus that had been lacking in the 1930s. Despite these factors, however, some, like the American Jewish Committee and, much more vociferously, the American Council for Judaism, still opposed the newfound zeal for the Zionist cause.

Demonstrations and appeals to Truman notwithstanding, the results of American Jewish efforts were not as impressive as some historians would have us believe. Truman's recognition of Israel eleven minutes after it came into existence on May 14, 1948, was a dramatic act that gave the new state an immediate international legitimacy it otherwise would not have had. The timing of the decision was clearly influenced by the perceived importance of the Jewish vote to Truman's reelection hopes in November 1948. Moreover, in the preceding three years, American Jews had also played a role in several other U.S. moves, including pressuring Britain to admit more Jews into Palestine and urging American support at the United Nations for the partition of Palestine. As I have shown elsewhere, these achievements were impressive in light of the powerful bureaucratic forces within the administration that opposed support for a Jewish state as a fundamental threat to American interests (Spiegel, 16–38).

> TRUMAN'S RECOGNITION OF ISRAEL ELEVEN MINUTES AFTER IT CAME INTO EXISTENCE ON MAY 14, 1948, WAS A DRAMATIC ACT THAT GAVE THE NEW STATE AN IMMEDIATE INTERNATIONAL LEGITIMACY IT OTHERWISE WOULD NOT HAVE HAD.

Yet, there were also significant failures in this effort. American recognition of the Jewish state only assumed the significance it did because a host of U.S. diplomatic actions prior to that event indicated reluctant official support for partition. The State Department was searching for an alternative to partition that would prevent Jewish independence, and in the process it managed to convince the president to embargo arms to the Palestinian Jewish community.

While American Jews did ensure that Truman could not ignore the issue, he was brought to the decision to recognize Israel because the Israelis themselves had turned the tide of the battle for Palestine in the weeks before their state was declared. If Zionist fighters had not demonstrated in March and April 1948 that they might be able to survive, no amount of American Jewish pressure would have convinced Truman. In the end, the prime reason Truman ignored State Department advice and recognized Israel was his hope of upstaging an anticipated similar Russian act.

The ultimate proof of the weakness of American Jewish clout in foreign policy in this period lies in what happened after recognition. What is most striking about the nineteen-year period between Israel's War of Independence and the Six-Day War is the American Jewish community's singular ineffectiveness in influencing U.S. policy, in countering the Eisenhower administration's antagonism to Israel, and even in mounting a set of viable recommendations for American policy once the crisis erupted in May 1967. Whatever elements of the community were not politically and financially exhausted by the fight for recognition were subdued by the McCarthy era, with its Rosenberg spy case, loyalty oaths, and stifling intellectual atmosphere.

AMERICAN JEWS WERE BETTER KNOWN FOR THEIR OPPOSITION TO THE VIETNAM WAR THAN FOR ANY PARTICULAR POLICY TOWARD ISRAEL.

Growing Soviet support for the Arabs in the late 1950s led to increasing opposition to Russian policy by the Jewish establishment, but on Israel it was largely limited to efforts to gain measurable increases in economic and military aid to Israel and to oppose U.S. arms sales to Arabs, the Arab boycott, Saudi discrimination against American Jewish soldiers, and State Department Arabism. Indeed, in the years immediately prior to 1967, American Jews were better known for their opposition to the Vietnam War than for any particular policy toward Israel. On the eve of the Six-Day War, then, American Jewish influence on U.S. foreign policy could only be described as peripheral and limited, devoted mainly to increasing support to Israel.

FROM THE SIX-DAY WAR TO 2000

How is it that by comparison with the eve of the Six-Day War, by the year 2000 American Jews were incomparably more effective in their foreign policy influence? The pro-Israeli lobby, the American Israel Public Affairs Committee (AIPAC), was rated by *Fortune* magazine as the second and fourth most effective lobby in Washington in 1998 and 1999, respectively. The source of this transformation lies in the simultaneous evolution of the roles played by both American Jews and Israel itself in the U.S. foreign policy arena. In the years after 1967, Jews not only became more interested and active in foreign policy but were also more accepted as an integral part of the formulation of that policy. At the same time, Israel was increasingly being seen as more of a strategic asset to the United States.

When American Jews attempt to influence United States foreign policy, they do not operate in a vacuum. The Jewish role in American foreign policy must be viewed in terms of the evolving definition of American national interests. The most important determinant of the influence of American Jewish organizations and prominent figures is whether they are pressing the government in ways similar to or different from the direction in which the administration in power seeks to move. Indeed, often what is viewed as influence is simply receptivity on the part of the administration.

American policy toward Israel can be evaluated on the basis of three criteria: (1) the importance of the Middle East in an administration's global priorities, (2) whether Israel is viewed as a strategic asset or burden, and (3) whether key policymakers accept or reject the involvement of the Jewish community in foreign policy. Comparing the various U.S. administrations during the pre- and post-1967 periods across these three criteria demonstrates why American Jewish organizations were more successful in the foreign policy arena after 1967 but also shows how their influence has been inconsistent and is constrained by the reigning administration.

For differing reasons, the Truman and Eisenhower administrations were both characterized by a low receptivity to Jewish concerns. In the years immediately following World War II, when Jews were fighting in Palestine for a state, American leaders were focused on the effort to develop a global policy to combat the perceived Soviet threat. Arab–Israeli issues were peripheral. When the British announced their plans to leave Palestine, the administration gladly handed the unwanted issue over to the fledgling United Nations. In 1948, as violence escalated between the Arabs and Jews, Truman and his aides were more concerned about a possible communist victory in Italy, the future of Germany, and the Berlin blockade.

The national security bureaucracy was unanimous in its assessment that the concept of a Jewish state in the Middle East was a terrible idea and injurious to American interests. The State Department argued that a Jewish state would alienate the Arabs and large sectors of the Muslim world, endanger oil supplies to an impoverished Europe, and even threaten Jewish security in the United States when Americans realized the perils of U.S. support for a Jewish state. Most bureaucrats in the executive branch thought the Jews could not win after an inevitable Arab attack, and America's demobilized army would not be able to rescue them. Even if the Jews miraculously emerged victorious, the communists would benefit as the Arabs would hold the West, and especially the United States, responsible. Some even thought Israel would be an ally of the Soviets, as many of its leaders had emigrated from Russia and held socialist beliefs. In short, supporting a Jewish state was seen as either a disaster or at best a luxury America could not afford.

Eisenhower and Dulles went further, concluding the Arabs were essential to blocking the advance of international communism. True believers in the vision of a Middle East organized in the image of Europe, they proceeded to push for the Baghdad Pact—a Near East NATO—meant to contain the Soviets through cooperation with the "northern tier" of Turkey, Iraq, Iran, and Pakistan, and to promote "technical" solutions to the problems of the area, such as the equitable sharing of the waters of the Jordan river. Israel was seen as a burden, even an obstacle, because Eisenhower and Dulles knew they would have to resolve Arab fears concerning Israel in order to get Arab cooperation in their plans to contain Soviet influence in the region.

In the Kennedy era, the Arab–Israeli problem—now temporarily quiescent—was relegated to a back burner, although receptivity to Jewish concerns grew slightly. Policymakers concentrated on the flashpoints of Cuba and Berlin.

Under Johnson, America's vistas narrowed to a perilous preoccupation with Vietnam, but the president's personal foreign policy orientation increased interest in Israel and the Jewish leadership found more sympathy at the White House than ever before. Moreover, the Six-Day War reminded Washington that the Middle East was crucial to its strategic interests and that the region's instability could lead to a Soviet–American confrontation. Johnson, however, was too overwhelmed by the war in Indochina to deal with the implications of these conclusions.

The Six-Day War also represented a major emotional experience for most American Jews. The crisis leading up to the war was a period of fear, foreboding, and helplessness with the survival of the state seemingly at stake. The sudden Israeli victory created a powerful sense of triumph and relief. This combination of fear and triumph led to a new focus on Israel that would last for years.

In addition, the war coincided with a period of increased ethnic identification in American life, and many American Jews became more vocal in advocating Jewish causes. This tendency was heightened as many Jews became disillusioned when other groups with which they had been aligned the American left, the Christian ecumenical movement, blacks working for civil rights—did not share their newfound identification with

THE SIX-DAY WAR COINCIDED WITH A PERIOD OF INCREASED ETHNIC IDENTIFICATION IN AMERICAN LIFE, AND MANY AMERICAN JEWS BECAME MORE VOCAL IN ADVOCATING JEWISH CAUSES.

Israel and, indeed, often expressed sympathy for the Palestinians. The community's engagement in foreign policy was further intensified by the simultaneous occurrence of the Vietnam War, which prompted many Jews actively to oppose both the Johnson and Nixon administrations' policies.

While Jews were becoming increasingly interested in foreign policy in the early 1970s, their status in domestic politics was rising as well. The first real evidence of this shift can be found in the 1972 national election. On the one hand, many liberal Jews were active in the McGovern campaign. On the other hand, Nixon made an unprecedented effort to bring Jewish voters and contributors under the Republican umbrella. Although Jewish voters still tended to support Democratic candidates, individual Jews did become more prominent in Republican politics. The result was that the Democrats stopped taking the Jewish community for granted, the Republicans no longer ignored it, and Jews began to have more political influence.

United States policy toward the Arab–Israeli issue in Nixon's first term was inconsistent, and the administration's receptivity to Jewish concerns mixed. Nixon thought other matters, such as fostering relations with the Soviet Union and China and ending the Vietnam War, were more critical than addressing the Middle East. However, his administration was united in its determination to reassert American influence in the Arab world, perceived as having been lost in the wake of the Six-Day War, and thus embarked on a serious effort to reach an Arab–Israeli settlement. The Nixon policy team was, however, irreparably divided about how to achieve its objectives. On the one hand, Secretary of State William Rogers sought to improve American–Arab relations by pressuring Israel toward territorial and political concessions. On the other hand, national security adviser Henry Kissinger believed that before any pressure was placed on Israel, Egypt, and

> "ON FRIDAY NIGHTS I HAD A ROUTE," ONCE REMINISCED
> AMBASSADOR PHILIP HABIB, WHO LATER BECAME UNDER-
> SECRETARY OF STATE FOR POLITICAL AFFAIRS AND U.S. MIDDLE
> EAST MEDIATOR DURING THE REAGAN ADMINISTRATION. "I
> WOULD LEAVE MY HOUSE AT SUNDOWN AND I WOULD GO FIRST
> TO MOISHE'S HOUSE. I WOULD SHAKE UP THE GRATE, I WOULD
> BANK THE FIRE FOR THE NIGHT, AND I WOULD TURN OFF THE
> LIGHTS ALL OVER THE PLACE."

Syria, the major Arab states that remained clients of the Soviet Union must first turn to Washington for assistance in efforts to reach a settlement.

Rogers was weakened by the failure of his diplomatic efforts in the wake of the Egyptian and Soviet breach of the August 1970 cease-fire ending the 1969–70 Egyptian–Israeli War of Attrition and by the Jordan crisis one month later. Moreover, Israel's intervention to help save the Hashemite Kingdom of Jordan in September 1970 led Nixon and Kissinger to become the first high-level U.S. officials to see Israel as a strategic asset. The differences between Kissinger and Rogers on a wide range of policy conflicts ultimately led to Rogers's resignation in 1973; as a result, Kissinger became both secretary of state and national security adviser.

The October 1973 war marked a change in the administration's perception of the importance of the Middle East. The region was now viewed as central to relations with the Soviet Union, to the security of energy supplies and thus to the economic vitality of the West, and to amicable relations with America's allies. It was also seen as a model of the dangers of Third World instability and the potential for local conflicts to lead to superpower confrontation. However, while the perception of the importance of the Middle East increased after the 1973 war, Israel's prestige plummeted. The Jewish state's respected deterrent capability had not prevented an Arab attack, and its vaunted intelligence services had proven fallible.

Senator Henry Jackson, a Democrat from Washington state, was one of those most responsible for reversing the decline in Israel's status in U.S. foreign policy. One of the Senate's most respected leaders, Jackson became the chief spokesman for American Jewish causes. In a period of intensified attention to the Holocaust and of growing interest in human rights, the American Jewish community began to focus on how Moscow was treating its own Jews. Jackson mobilized the community and forced the Kremlin and the White House to concentrate on the problem through his efforts to link Soviet Jewish emigration to U.S.–Soviet relations. This strategy was codified in late 1974 with the passage of the Jackson–Vanik Amendment, which precluded the extension of most-favored-nation status for imported Soviet products until Soviet Jewish emigration was allowed on a wider scale. For the first time since the onset of the Cold War, a non-Israeli Jewish issue was tied directly to Soviet–American relations; Jewish leaders were thus involved in matters at the core of U.S. diplomacy.

Jackson's anticommunist, pro-Israeli positions legitimized Jewish analysts who offered alternative policy perspectives to those espoused by the State Department. Moreover, as the congressional leadership weakened and power on Capitol Hill became diffused in the 1970s, the influence of groups that were able to lobby the rank and file was enhanced. And the Jewish community was gradually becoming such a force. Evidence of the growing Jewish profile in U.S. foreign policy could also be found in the media as two of the most prominent journals contributing to the foreign policy debate, *Commentary* and the *New Republic*—one neoconservative and even Republican, the other moderate Democrat, but both pro-Israel—were accurately identified as being dominated by Jews.

This growing support for Israel came at a time of increased uneasiness in the American foreign policy elite about the situation in the Middle East and America's energy security in the face of the Arabs' newfound oil weapon. Since Jimmy Carter was a Democrat, his election in 1976 led to expectations of stronger support for Israel and greater Jewish involvement in the foreign policy process. Carter's perspective on the Middle East, however, was framed more by a concern for the Palestinians and a desire to improve relations with the Arab states. The 1950s view of Israel as a deficit to American interests resurfaced with a vengeance. At the same time, however, unlike Kissinger who had tried to avoid linking an Arab–Israeli settlement to problems such as the energy crisis and the shaky détente with the Soviet Union, the Carter team assumed that the resolution of the Arab–Israeli dispute would bring with it a resolution of the energy crisis and would lessen the potential for tensions with the Soviet Union, the allies, and the Third World.

Although Soviet Jews were an important focus of Carter's human rights campaign, and notwithstanding his successful mediation of the peace treaty between Egypt and Israel, American Jews found others of his actions, most notably his expressed empathy for the Palestinians, disturbing enough to prompt their continued high level of engagement in the foreign policy arena. Despite intense activity by Jewish organizations and lobbyists, however, the pro-Israeli forces suffered a major defeat in Carter's 1978 arms sale to Saudi Arabia.

Ronald Reagan entered office committed to righting what he viewed as Carter's wrongs. The Soviet Union would be confronted on all levels of potential competition—global and regional. In the Middle East, Reagan was determined not to repeat Carter's miscalculations; he viewed Israel as an important strategic asset in the confrontation with the Soviet Union, the fight against terrorism, and the protection of American interests in the area, especially in the wake of the Iranian revolution. The two secretaries of state of the period, Alexander Haig and George Shultz, believed that strategic cooperation with Israel would bring important benefits to the United States. Although Secretary of Defense Caspar Weinberger advocated the opposite approach, stressing the drawbacks of close collaboration with Jerusalem for U.S.–Arab relations, Reagan's strong commitment to strategic cooperation with Israel contributed to the ultimate victory of those who favored this policy direction.

Despite its general pro-Israeli orientation, however, the Reagan administration also completed a sale of AWACS jets to the Saudis in 1981, a bitter defeat for the American Jewish community that led to a significant expansion of Jewish lobbying efforts. The AIPAC flagship expanded dramatically. What began as a small office in Washington had, by the mid-1980s, become a national operation with a significantly enhanced capability for lobbying Congress, as well as hitherto untouched branches of government such as the Department of Defense. Other organizations such as the Anti-Defamation League, the American Jewish Committee, and the Presidents' Conference also increased their foreign policy involvement. Taking advantage of the post-Watergate election-funding reforms, pro-Israeli political action committees (PACs) were created around the country. As PACs made it easier for incumbents to win congressional elections, the strength of the pro-Israeli community was dramatically strengthened in the 1980s.

By the end of the Reagan era, the pro-Israeli community was in its strongest position ever. An increased number of Jewish legislators headed a bipartisan pro-Israeli coalition that included both liberals and conservatives, prominent representatives from all of the country's geographic regions and many of its ethnic groups. Impressive victories had become commonplace on issues such as foreign aid to Israel, arms sales, dealings with the United Nations, and the disposition of Palestine Liberation Organization (PLO) offices in the United States. Yet, despite these successes, when George H. W. Bush assumed the presidency, the Jewish community was unable to prevent him from returning to a modified Carter perspective marked by a willingness to pressure Israel for its own good and to improve America's relations with the Arabs.

The end of the Iran–Iraq War, the continuation of the Intifada (the Palestinian uprising against Israel), and a brief U.S. dialogue with the PLO all encouraged renewed attention to the Arab–Israeli peace process, but Bush saw the Shamir government as an impediment to successfully reaching a deal. The period of working together to reverse Saddam Hussein's invasion of Kuwait notwithstanding, Bush's approach to Israel was most notable for his decision in the fall of 1991 not to approve loan guarantees for Israel so long as the Shamir government continued to expand settlements in the West Bank. Jewish organizations protested vehemently, but Bush stood firm during the ensuing political firestorm. Even though his administration went on to arrange the pathbreaking Madrid peace conference in October 1991, the damage was done and American Jews turned against Bush and his secretary of state, James Baker, in passionate form in the 1992 election campaign.

Bill Clinton came to power with little foreign policy experience, planning to concentrate on domestic policy, celebrate the U.S.-Israeli relationship, and depend on the Arabs and Israelis to negotiate with each other. Surrounded by Jews and comfortable with Israel as a key U.S. ally, Clinton pursued a policy that was a Democratic version of Reagan's, and American Jewish influence blossomed. Given the Clinton administration's strong pro-Israeli leanings, the Democratic Congress was in the unusual position of cheering the president on. That situation would not last long, however, because the Republican revolution of 1994 brought both houses under the control of the Republicans. It is a largely unrecognized achievement of the pro-Israel community that it was rapidly able to gain the support for a new pro-Israel view from new Republicans with hitherto little experience in the Middle East.

The mid-1990s witnessed a sharp downturn in mass Jewish interest in foreign policy generally and in Israel in particular. The Oslo Accords seemed to suggest the end of Israel's conflict with the Arabs. Other factors also contributed to this downturn in concern: the dissension in Israel between religious and secular Jews, the assassination of Prime Minister Rabin, the settlement of Soviet Jews in Israel and the consequent removal of this issue from the political agenda, and the end of the Cold War, which resulted in a downturn in interest in foreign policy on the part of most Americans.

Nevertheless, Jewish lobbyists were still able to exercise considerable influence. The official Jewish organ supported and Congress passed additional aid to Palestinians after the signing of Oslo II in September 1995 and after the 1998 Wye agreement and its "Sharm El Sheikh" annex in 1999. Passage occurred despite conservative and right-wing protestations that the aid should be cut off due to what critics saw as the Palestinian Authority's failure to live up to previous agreements. Congress also approved legislation by huge margins in both houses that recognized a united Jerusalem as Israel's capital and required that the U.S. Embassy in Tel Aviv be moved to Jerusalem (although Clinton subsequently suspended the action).

In addition, although many in the Republican Congress of the late 1990s remained skeptical of foreign aid, American Jewish organizations were successful in retaining aid to Israel and Egypt and in gaining assistance for Jordan after it concluded its treaty with Israel in October 1994. Indeed, in an atmosphere of deep hostility to foreign aid, the American Jewish community's strong support was critical in salvaging a minimal foreign aid program worldwide.

Moreover, by the 1990s, Jews were also playing active roles in policies only indirectly related to Israel, including advocating the continuation of sanctions against both Iraq and Iran. Similarly, discussions of a National Missile Defense were colored by concerns over Israel's growing problem of preparing for the possibility of having to confront an Iran or Iraq in possession of weapons of mass destruction and the means to deliver them. That strategic defense might help not only the United States against such rogue regimes but Israel as well had become a legitimate factor in the discourse over U.S. security needs.

Thus, by 2000, the American Jewish community had become a major player in the coalition within the United States that advocated a global and internationalist perspective on foreign policy. As trusted members of the elite, Jews were in a position to express views that no longer seemed outrageous and outside the establishment consensus, as had been the case in 1948, 1956, or even 1967 and 1973. With 10 percent of the Senate being Jewish, with prime foreign policy advisers in both parties being Jewish, with Jews in government playing key roles even in dealing with Middle East policy, it was difficult to pretend that Jewish foreign policy views did not belong in the political establishment. Indeed, even the prime think tank for Middle East affairs in the nation's capital, the Washington Institute for Near East Policy, was clearly sympathetic to Israel despite its well-deserved reputation for academic quality and professionalism.

> BY 2000, THE AMERICAN JEWISH COMMUNITY HAD BECOME A MAJOR PLAYER IN THE COALITION WITHIN THE UNITED STATES THAT ADVOCATED A GLOBAL AND INTERNATIONALIST PERSPECTIVE ON FOREIGN POLICY.

From this brief review of the record of ten administrations, we can extract several lessons about the role of American Jews in the formulation of American foreign policy. First, when the priority of the Arab–Israeli issue is high due to American interest in gaining support in the Arab world, tensions with Jerusalem increase no matter what Jews do. We can see a large range of disputes between Jerusalem and Washington under Eisenhower, in the late Nixon period, and again under Ford, Carter, and Bush. When the priority of this issue is low, in the main because the United States is preoccupied with other, more pressing, global issues, as under Truman and Kennedy, it is difficult to gain the attention of high-ranking policymakers. This situation increases the influence of the national security bureaucracy, which works against close relations with Israel, since the bureaucracy tends to have a more geopolitical view of the issue. American Jews working on behalf of Israel seem to do best either when there is a president ideologically sympathetic to the Jewish state, such as Johnson, Reagan, or Clinton, or when a president sees Israel as playing a positive strategic role in the region, as with Nixon, Reagan, and Clinton.

ACCORDING TO HIS MEMOIR MY AMERICAN JOURNEY, SEC-RETARY OF STATE COLIN POWELL "EARNED A QUARTER BY TURNING THE LIGHTS ON AND OFF AT THE ORTHODOX SYNA-GOGUE" IN HIS SOUTH BRONX NEIGHBORHOOD.

Second, the political party of the president does not predict his attitude toward the Arab–Israeli issue. Thus, the greatest divergence in perspective between the American Jewish community and individual administrations occurred with two Republicans (Eisenhower and Bush) and one Democrat (Carter). The closest areas of agreement on Arab–Israeli matters occurred with one Republican (Reagan) and one Democrat (Clinton).

Third, the key factor affecting an administration's receptivity to American Jewish efforts is the fundamental approach of the key players—especially the president—while they are in office. Once he and his team have set the agenda, American Jews can only react. Thus, Jewish influence in U.S. foreign policy has mostly been on the margins and has often been more important in affecting the timing rather than the substance of policies. For instance, Zionist lobbying forced Truman to pay more attention to the Palestine issue than he would have preferred and led to an earlier de facto recognition of Israel than might have occurred otherwise. However, Truman continued to rely on the State Department rather than external authorities for advice, which resulted in major delays in actions supporting the Zionists and a host of anti-Israel policies.

The influence of the American Jewish community can also be seen in the timing of various arms deals. Kennedy approved the first major sale of arms to Israel in 1962; Johnson announced the sale of fifty Phantom jets in 1968; Nixon concluded the first long-term aid agreement with Israel in 1972. All three deals were concluded just prior to U.S. elections, congressional in 1962 and presidential in 1968 and 1972. In all three cases, however, there were solid national security grounds for reaching the agreements, even though the exact timing was hardly coincidental.

Another form of Jewish influence can be seen in the late 1970s when Carter was constrained in dealing both with the Russians on the Middle East and with the PLO by the pressure of Jewish organizations. But Carter was also limited by prior agreements (including Kissinger's 1975 assurance that the United States would not meet with the PLO until it recognized Israel's existence and accepted UN Resolutions 242 and 338) and by fears that Begin's Israel would not enter into negotiations if he went too far in pressing for Israeli concessions.

Thus, the Jewish community can try to restrain a president from doing what he wants to do, as it did with limited success under Carter. Sometimes Jewish groups can quicken a policy's pace (e.g., on aid for Israel) or slow it down (e.g., on arms for Arabs). It is not accidental, however, that supporters of Israel appeared particularly powerful under Reagan and Clinton: on most issues, they were preaching to the converted.

BEYOND 2000

Clearly the contemporary American Jewish community has vastly increased its role in U.S. foreign policy in comparison to the pre-1967 period. One of the ironies of the current situation, however, is that American Jews themselves are almost totally unaware of their new position. This explains the astonishment of most U.S. Jews when Senator Joseph Lieberman was selected as the Democratic candidate for vice president in 2000.

Signs by the end of the 1990s indicated, however, that the Jewish community's enviable position could change. A new president with a negative perspective toward

Israel would be a major challenge, as was the case with both Presidents Carter and Bush. The Republican Congress discovered a possible means of diminishing foreign aid to Israel when it attempted unsuccessfully in 1999 and 2000 to split off Middle East aid from the entire package, highlighting the disproportionate amounts provided to the Middle East. In the spring of 2000, a huge conflict erupted in Washington over the proposed Israeli sale of Phalcon jets to China. The opposition in the Pentagon and among most in Congress was so vehement that many in the pro-Israeli community found themselves trying to convince the Israelis to cancel the sale (which they eventually did) because of the harm done to Israel's position. This incident suggests that the pro-Israeli forces are certainly not all-powerful in Washington. Quite the contrary, it reinforces the conclusion that their strength lies in the widespread perception that support for Israel is consistent with American interests.

AMERICAN JEWS THEMSELVES ARE ALMOST TOTALLY UNAWARE OF THEIR NEW FOREIGN POLICY POSITION.

The key question asked earlier was whether the success of American Jewish influence between 1967 and 2000 was an aberration or an indication of future success. It was clearly triumphal when compared with the inefficacy of the Jewish community in the period before 1967. Whether it will also lead to future success depends on how well the Jewish community adapts to its current situation. First, in the 1990s, American Jewish unity, which had been a source of American Jewish strength since World War II, was shattered. In a sense, the Likud–Labor conflict was exported to the United States, with some Jews taking the Likud perspective, focusing on the dangers of the peace process and the errors of Oslo, and others vehemently supporting Oslo and peace efforts. Although the polls show that the overwhelming majority of American Jews were supportive of the peace process, the more intense partisans were clearly on the right.

As the 1990s wore on, many U.S. politicians became confused as to where the American Jewish community actually stood. The disunity among American Jews was reflected in the emergence of new organizational players. On the right, the Zionist Organization of America, long dormant on the political scene, reemerged under the dynamic leadership of Morton Klein to become a major player lobbying against peace diplomacy. On the other side of the political spectrum, Americans for Peace Now emerged as a passionate and vocal organization favoring a settlement between Israel and the Palestinians. Surveying the continued fracturing of the American Jewish community, Yitzhak Rabin influenced the founding of a group called the Israel Policy Forum. The organization gradually emerged in the 1990s as a powerful and effective arm for promoting American Jewish support for the peace process.

These new organs of the American Jewish community often challenged the better-known and more established institutions such as AIPAC and the Presidents' Conference, at times accusing them of leaning either too far left or too far right. These internal divisions and disputes accurately reflected the state of the community, but they also were bound to diminish the effectiveness of American Jewish influence over U.S. foreign policy.

But the larger question of where the American Jewish role in foreign policy is heading remains uncertain. Concentrating on lobbying activities, Jews still see themselves as supplicants and largely react to events. While individual American Jews have become major figures in U.S. foreign policymaking, the organized Jewish community has never seen itself as a participant in the serious discourse about the content and future of American foreign policy globally. In part this is because American Jews have themselves not understood their new establishment role.

Certainly, in domestic policy, Jews have for decades expounded clear positions and pursued a vision of American society that encompasses guaranteeing the separation of church and state, advocating social justice, and protecting minorities and the poor. Yet in foreign policy, Jews have tended overwhelmingly to concentrate on issues of special concern such as the Middle East and the plight of Soviet Jews. They have never delineated a global vision of the direction of American foreign policy. There is little consideration in American Jewish community circles of the relevance of Russia, China, or Europe, or economic or Third World policy for an American worldview that Jews can support. This lack of attention is in part because disagreement exists within the American Jewish community between neoconservatives and liberal internationalists, but it also reflects an inability to conceive of a global picture that would include support for Israel in particular and Jewish interests more generally. Moreover, this lack of a philosophical underpinning has exacerbated differences within the community and weakened the ability of American Jews to speak for Americans as a whole.

Thus, at the dawn of the twenty-first century, American Jewish influence on U.S. foreign policy is profound and has never been so important. At the same time, however, we can question whether this influence will remain intact as new groups in American society emerge to seek a similar role or whether an unsympathetic administration comes to power. Having celebrated the special relationship between the United States and Israel but also often having presented themselves as a special interest, American Jews are left with a unique position in the discussion of American foreign policy. It is a successful position today, but it is likely to be sorely tried if and when American perspectives change.

14

HOSTS, NOT VISITORS

The Future of Jews in American Politics

DAVID M. SHRIBMAN

The most remarkable aspect of this chapter has already appeared. It is not in the body of the essay but in the title, implicit but not explicit, inferred but not implied. Its presumed boldness—its cavalier, upbeat sweep, its breezy assumption of promise—represents one of the most extraordinary statements in the entire history of the Jewish people. For centuries, from the military struggles of the biblical Saul and David to the brittle prospects of European Jews in the charnel house that was Europe at the end of the last millennium, the political issue facing Jews was not success but survival. Yet here, at the beginning of the new millennium, American Jews have such a curious mix of security and audacity that they can contemplate a future in the politics of the sole remaining superpower that is active, unapologetic—and unabashedly optimistic.

The status of Jews in America today represents both the attainment of a gift and the achievement of a goal. The gift, of course, is a birthright that differs substantially from the one granted in Genesis to Esau and later sold to Jacob. In America, the birthright goes to the second-born (and to the third-born, and the fourth, etc.) as well as to the first-born; and, in modern times at least, it belongs to the females of the line as much as it does to the males. The great American birthright is possibility, and if American Jews share one quality at this period, it is the conviction that possibility, not ideology, is the defining element of this ancient people in this new land. Here all things are possible: not only security and, in many cases, unimaginable material wealth but also responsibility for assuring those elements for others, not only for fellow Jews. For Jews, the American difference goes beyond the achievement of safety and prominence for a people that has lived at the very edge of extinction since biblical days. For Jews, the American difference is the assurance of safety and prominence—and, above all, possibility—for others as well. Here we have enough security to go around. Here we have enough prosperity to go around.

The point of departure for any effort to contemplate the future of Jews in American politics must be the unique position of Jews in contemporary life. From the very start, even in colonial days, the quality that set America apart was its openness to Jews as immigrants. So startling was this development that it has remained front and center in the Jewish American consciousness, shaping the folklore of the Jewish people, molding the vision of Jews for generations to come. The Jewish people were strangers in this strange land, yet they were accepted, given a chance to survive, to be fruitful, and to multiply. So overwhelming was this notion, celebrated in fable and song, that the more significant and the more astonishing truth has almost always been overlooked. The period of the great modern Jewish immigration movements, principally the flood of Jews from oppression between 1890 and 1910 and then the flood of Jews from embattled Europe beginning with the ascendancy of Hitler in the winter of 1933 and continuing well after the end of the Third Reich in the spring of 1945, is over—and it has been for several decades. Since then a far more surprising and enduring event has happened: Jews have been comfortable in their American home not as visitors but as hosts.

The emergence of Jews as part of the host population of the United States is one of the signal and least remarked on qualities of this remarkable land and this remarkable people. Clearly American society is no longer being shaped by waves of Jewish immigration. Instead, a broader society, of which American Jews are but one part, is itself being shaped by waves of immigrants that no longer include substantial numbers of Jews. As the new immigrants reach American shores (or, more precisely in this age of air travel, American airport arrival lounges), they are confronting the challenges of assimilation into a nation in which Jews and Jewish culture indisputably are a part.

This status as part of the host population is reflected in many indicators, some of which have been ably noted in earlier chapters, some of which often appear in books celebrating Jewish achievements in American life. Books such as *The Jewish Americans*, for example, sold, pointedly, at the Ellis Island bookstore, set out many of these achievements, all of which are evidence that in America, Jewish culture is no longer apart from but is, instead, a part of the broader culture. Al Jolson, Fanny Brice, the Marx Brothers, Vladimir Horowitz, Bob Dylan—all are known as American cultural icons. They are, of course, all Jews. Even a figure like Isaac Bashevis Singer, who wrote in Yiddish, occupies a place in the American cultural pantheon.

But the greatest indicator of the place of Jews among the host population of this country is their place in the political life of the country, not only as agents of change (which is the traditional role of newcomers seeking to shape a nation to their inclinations and interests) but also, unavoidably and significantly, as agents of the status quo. It is in the latter role, prominent primarily in the more recent past, that American Jews seal their place in the host community of the nation.

THE GREATEST INDICATOR OF THE PLACE OF JEWS AMONG THE HOST POPULATION OF THIS COUNTRY IS THEIR PLACE IN THE POLITICAL LIFE OF THE COUNTRY.

The American story is, to be sure, preeminently the story of change—the winning of new rights, the assertion of new prerogatives. Jews have always been at the forefront of change on this continent; their very presence here was, for a time, proof enough of change in the nation. Indeed, the appearance of Jews in the labor movement at the end of the nineteenth century, in progressivism in the early twentieth century, in American socialist movements and the American Communist Party in the 1920s and 1930s, and in the civil rights and youth rebellion protest days of the 1960s, stands as a symbol of Jews' effort to change American culture and to make it compatible with the impulses and inclinations of Jews. Though this notion was not broached publicly, Jews embraced many of these reform and revolutionary movements as a key means to make the nation safe for Jews. But one of the great truths is that these movements, especially when they were accepted by the broader American establishment, as they were in the case of civil rights and the struggle against American involvement in Vietnam, themselves provided a path to the comfortable high ground of the host community.

Yet, tellingly and ironically, not until American Jews felt so vested in the way things already were did they begin to assert themselves as conservatives and thus as bulwarks against radical change. In that role, especially, they established themselves as important elements of the host community and, in political terms, of the host coalition.

By numbers, Jews account for ten members of the Senate, and twenty-seven members of the House in the 107th Congress—10 percent of the upper body, 6 percent of the lower. By any measure, these are remarkable figures considering that Jews constitute only 2.3 percent of the nation's population. This prominence is even more striking when contrasted to the period between 1960 and 1967; during those years, only three Jews (Jacob K. Javits, the New York Republican, and Democrats Abraham A. Ribicoff from Connecticut and Ernest H. Gruening from Alaska) sat in the Senate.

But what is most indicative of Jews' place in the host community is that half of the ten senators serving in 1996 were elected from states where Jews accounted for less than 1 percent of the electorate. Indeed, two Jewish Democrats, Russell D. Feingold and Herb Kohl, now serve in the Senate from Wisconsin, where Jews constitute 0.5 percent of the population. And for the past twenty-one years, a Jewish senator has represented Minnesota, a state where Jews account for 0.9 percent of the population and a state once widely known as an island of antisemitism. When Republican Senator Rudy Boschwitz, who was elected in 1978, was defeated in 1990, he was beaten by Democrat Paul Wellstone, providing the remarkable situation of one Jew succeeding another Jew in the Senate. In the 1990 race, an unusually bitter contest, Senator Boschwitz attempted to win favor among Minnesotans by suggesting that Wellstone, a political scientist, was an insufficiently observant Jew.

With two Jews on the Supreme Court and with one Orthodox Jew, Democratic Senator Joseph I. Lieberman of Connecticut, serving in the Senate (and refusing to work on the Sabbath), most of the hurdles to Jewish service in American civic life seem to be eliminated. (Jews have played prominent roles in the cabinet for years, symbolized in modern times by the ascension of Henry A. Kissinger to the position of secretary of state in the Nixon administration.) The final barrier remains the White House.

Even that seems closer than ever. The nomination of Lieberman as the Democrats' vice presidential candidate in 2000 represented the shattering of one of the last stained-glass ceilings in America. Lieberman spoke openly and proudly of his religion, and after a week hardly anyone remarked on his practice of refusing to campaign on the Sabbath. He campaigned vigorously in areas where Jewish voters were concentrated, accounting in large measure for the Democratic ticket's strong performance in Florida, which ordinarily would have been regarded as Republican territory in a year in which the state's governor was the brother of the GOP nominee. Lieberman's selection prompted enormous speculation over whether there would be a backlash against the ticket, but as the campaign proceeded, that talk receded. If anything, Lieberman's presence on the ticket assisted the Democrats, in the critical state of Florida and elsewhere.

> VICE PRESIDENT AL GORE SERVED AS A SHABBOS GOY FOR SEN-
> ATOR JOSEPH LIEBERMAN, ONCE INVITING HIM TO STAY IN HIS
> PARENTS' NEARBY WASHINGTON, D.C., TOWNHOUSE DURING A
> LATE FRIDAY NIGHT SENATE SESSION. VICE PRESIDENT GORE
> TURNED ON THE LIGHTS IN THE HOUSE.

Governor Michael S. Dukakis, who is married to a Jewish woman, won the Democratic presidential nomination in 1988; his wife's religion was seldom remarked upon.
Republican Senator Arlen Specter of Pennsylvania mounted a legitimate campaign in
1996, entering early contests in Iowa and New Hampshire, and his religious identity
never emerged as a major, or even a minor, factor. Though Specter's Judaism might have
raised more attention had he been a more competitive candidate for the nomination, we
have ample reason to conclude that Jews should no longer regard the giddiest heights of
American political life as being beyond their attainment. Indeed, a Gallup Organization
poll in 1937 found that 46 percent of Americans said they would vote for a Jew for president. Now the figure has doubled—to 92 percent.

Strikingly, the difficulty that Senator John F. Kennedy faced as a Catholic in his
1960 campaign now seems part of a long-ago, vanished world. That year, commonly
regarded as the beginning of the modern period in American politics, Kennedy's
campaign seemed haunted by the experience of Alfred E. Smith, the Catholic New
York governor who was defeated by Herbert Hoover in 1928. Today no one seriously
doubts that a Catholic could again win the presidency, and the corollary to that conviction is the notion that a serious Jewish candidate would also be given a fair chance
at the office. In truth, the possibility that a Jew might someday win the presidency
was sealed by Kennedy's deft handling of the religious issue, particularly the persua-
sive speech he delivered in the fall campaign to the Greater Houston Ministerial Association. Similarly, the ability of a Jew to win the highest office in American civic life
depends on the ease (or the necessity) with which it is possible to imagine a serious
Jewish presidential candidate delivering an analogue to the Kennedy speech: "If this
election is decided on the basis that six million Americans lost their chance of being
president on the day they were Bat or Bar Mitzvahed, then the whole nation is the
loser in the eyes of Jews and non-Jews around the world, in the eyes of history and in
the eyes of our own people."

In recent years, Dianne Feinstein of San Francisco has twice been considered a Democratic vice presidential nominee, and neither time was her religion a particularly important part of the calculation. A former mayor, Democratic gubernatorial nominee, and
later a senator, Feinstein is one of two Jewish women to represent California in the Senate. The other is Barbara Boxer of Greenbrae. In one year, 1992, California voters filled

two Senate seats with two women and two Jews—as sturdy a measure as there is of the openness of the American political system.

While the future for individual Jews seeking individual political office seems bright, the future of Jewish impact on American politics is far less certain. As Jews become more intimately woven into the American fabric (and as intermarriage rates remain high), their coloration becomes less distinctive. That, of course, may help explain why the prospects for Jewish candidates are so bright. But it also may help explain why it is harder than ever to define a distinctly Jewish brand of politics for the contemporary period—and for the future. And with changing demographics, many of the old rules governing the places where large groups of Jews can as a group make an impact are being altered.

In the recent past, Jewish influence was strongest in eight states where Jews provided a critical mass of voters to attract interest and attention and, in turn, to project power. These states were California, Florida, Illinois, Maryland, Massachusetts, New York, New Jersey, and Pennsylvania, all of which had vibrant, sophisticated, and politically active Jewish populations. (Nearly 5 percent of all voters in the District of Columbia are Jewish, making the nation's capital another redoubt of potential Jewish influence.) Even today, one voter out of eleven in New York is Jewish; in New Jersey, one voter in seventeen is Jewish.

Demographic movements are altering the geography of American politics, and no less so where Jews are concerned. These alterations in population patterns affect Jews in several complex, interrelated, ways, creating several new circumstances, including the effect produced by an influx of non-Jewish voters into areas where a large Jewish population already is in place. These changes are caused by the movement of Jews from areas where they once were a substantial voting bloc into areas with large non-Jewish populations and the transformation of areas where Jews were once concentrated and, as a result of out-migration, now are less prominent.

This three-dimensional movement of people makes it difficult to project the "hot spots" for Jewish power in the decades ahead, but some broad contours nonetheless can be discerned. In Arizona, for example, where Jews now constitute less than 2 percent of the population, the recent robust influx of Jews in Phoenix (a net gain of ten thousand in 1998 alone) raises the possibility that Jews might someday be an important voting group there. Jews still account for less than 1 percent of the population of Texas, but the suburban sprawls around Houston and Dallas have become magnets for Jews, raising the possibility that Jews might become an important political factor in those metropolitan areas if not in the state at large. Jews have moved in greater numbers than ever into California and Florida and once within those states have settled in areas where they were not previously prominent; the growth of the Jewish population along the west coast of Florida (a growth of five thousand Jews in Tampa in 1998 alone) is a signal example. But Jews are not the only people flooding into Florida and Texas, and the net result of all the migration and immigration, particularly among Hispanics, may well be to dilute rather than to enhance Jewish influence in those two states.

Georgia remains a state with scant Jewish population and political power, but the movement of Jews into the Atlanta suburbs makes it possible to contemplate rising influence for Jews there. Nevada, seldom considered one of the power centers of American life, nonetheless now has about sixty thousand Jews—more than Alaska, Arkansas, Hawaii, Idaho, Iowa, Maine, Mississippi, Montana, Nebraska, New Hampshire, North Dakota, South Dakota, Vermont, and Wyoming combined. And because the population of the entire state is so small (1.7 million), the concentration of Jews in Nevada has greater potential force than it would have in, say, California, a far larger state that ordinarily is considered one of the leading states politically for Jews.

Two other unavoidable demographic truths bear mentioning. Because the population of Jews is stable at a time when the national population is growing, the percentage of Jews in the population is necessarily decreasing—a trend that may accelerate as high intermarriage rates produce lower smaller replacement populations. And with a stable Jewish population, the movement of Jews to new areas of high-octane growth, including Phoenix and the Atlanta suburbs, means a diminished impact for Jews in the places they left (primarily northeastern states and larger Industrial Belt cities) and an only slight impact in the places they are settling in (primarily Sun Belt centers). One startling figure makes the point: in 1998, the number of Jews in Syracuse, New York, dropped by 17 percent, bringing the number of Jews in that city to 7,500. The overall effect of migration, Jewish and otherwise, might thus be to reduce the importance of Jewish voters overall. Moreover, this potential reduction comes at a time when we are less certain than ever that Jews will vote as a bloc or—an important and sometimes overlooked factor— that Jews will vote in a higher proportion than other groups.

Throughout most of the modern political era, Jews have been a reliable part of the Democratic coalition, especially in New York. Jews were drawn into the orbit of Al Smith in part by the presence of such figures in the Smith circle as Rose Schneiderman of the Women's Trade Union League and Belle Moskowitz, the incomparable strategist and Smith confidante. Herbert Lehman, the New York banker/politician, was in many ways the link between Smith, who won Jews' hearts, and Franklin Roosevelt, who won their heads.

Jews' affinity for the Democratic Party, especially in presidential politics, grew ever deeper during the Roosevelt years (some Jewish areas gave FDR more than 90 percent of the vote in 1944) and was sealed by President Harry Truman's willingness to recognize Israel shortly after it declared statehood. Jewish majorities for Democrats often topped 80 percent, except during the two candidacies of Dwight Eisenhower (who had a special place among Jews as a liberator of Nazi death camps) and Ronald Reagan (whose brand of anticommunism and his strong support for Israel appealed to many Jewish neoconservatives). Even so, no Republican has won a majority of the Jewish vote in the modern era. The Democratic low point came in 1980, when Jimmy Carter won only 45 percent of the Jewish vote; independent John B. Anderson received 15 percent, while President Ronald W. Reagan won about 37 percent. Four years later, Walter F. Mondale took the Jewish vote, 68 percent to 32 percent, the largest margin the Minnesotan recorded among white voters. In both 1992 and 1996, Bill Clinton captured the same portion of the Jewish vote: 78 percent.

The return of the Jewish vote to levels approaching the New Deal margins suggests that Jews likely will remain part of the Democratic coalition for some time to come. The Washington-based Republican Jewish Coalition tried to stoke doubts about the 2000 Democratic nominee, Albert Gore Jr. of Tennessee, by pointing out that the vice president met twice with the Reverend Al Sharpton, who has often been accused of anti-semitism, and by suggesting that Gore, a Southern Baptist, demonstrated a "pattern of insensitivity to matters of religious intolerance, bigotry and anti-Semitism." These efforts to move Jews away from their traditional political moorings were generally unavailing; in the spring before the election, Gore appeared before the B'nai B'rith Anti-Defamation League and won rousing approval for his policies and for a southern-fried version of a Borsch Belt routine that included mock country-western tunes such as "I Was One of the Chosen People—Until She Chose Somebody Else" and "The Second Time She Said 'Shalom' I Knew She Meant Goodbye."

Even so, modern Jews do show an openness to Republican and conservative ideas to a degree that they did not in earlier generations. "The political conservatism of American society today fully coincides with the Jewish values of justice, fairness, respect for the dignity of man, and the punishment of those forces of evil who would seek to destroy us," wrote Alan. J. Steinberg in *American Jewry & Conservative Politics: A New Direction.* "That is why the time is right for American Jewry to enter into a new covenant, a covenant with political conservatives." Indeed, Jews have shown a willingness to support some Republicans at the state and local levels; in the 1998 election, Peter Fitzgerald won more than 30 percent of the Jewish vote in the Illinois senate race.

MODERN JEWS DO SHOW AN OPENNESS TO REPUBLICAN AND CONSERVATIVE IDEAS TO A DEGREE THAT THEY DID NOT IN EARLIER GENERATIONS.

Republicans, moreover, have made important inroads among Jews at the elite level of American politics. This trend began at the end of the Carter years and accelerated during the Reagan years; such leading Jewish figures as Norman Podhoretz, the editor of *Commentary,* and Irving Kristol, the writer and critic, expressed their disapproval of what they considered Democratic dogma (especially on areas such as race and foreign policy) and became prominent members of the Reagan coalition. As the new millennium began, a number of Jews occupied prominent positions in Republican politics, including Mel Sembler, the Republican National Committee finance chairman in 2000; Stuart Bernstein, the cochairman of Team 100, consisting of those who donated $100,000 to the Republican National Committee; Eric Javits, head of the Republican Eagles, another group of major donors; Sheldon Kamins, chairman of

GOPAC, an important Republican political action committee; Clifford May, communications director of the Republican National Committee; and many prominent advisers and consultants such as William Kristol, who was Vice President Dan Quayle's chief of staff, and Frank I. Luntz, who has done polling work for Senate Minority Leader Trent Lott and former House Speaker Newt Gingrich.

American politics are a curious mixture of policy and personality, and so the prospects for a realignment among Jewish voters could be affected by either. The appearance, for example, of a compelling national Republican figure with special appeal to Jews might help sever Jews from their traditional ties. Under a model of political behavior where the elites move first, the underpinnings of such a realignment certainly are present. But American Jews are motivated above all by issues, and the future of Jews in American politics is as much a story of Jewish views on important issues as it is on Jewish party alignment.

The issues that Jews have cared about have varied over time, mostly with the condition of Jews in the United States and with the prospect for Jews around the world. In the beginning of the last century, for example, Jews worried about urban working conditions, a concern that was heightened in the wake of the 1911 fire in New York's Triangle Shirtwaist Co., which in a quarter of an hour killed 146 people, many of them Jewish girls between the ages of thirteen and twenty-three. The fire led Jews to fight for, and help win, the passage of progressive labor laws, fire safety codes, and workers' compensation plans. During the 1930s, Jews were consumed with economic questions and with worries about the fate of Jews in Nazi Germany. In the 1960s, Jews turned to the struggle for civil rights and, later, to a bitter struggle within New York, often with blacks, over the destiny of the public schools and the public colleges that had been a laboratory for reform, a petri dish for assimilation and a ladder of social mobility for many Jews.

The issues that will occupy the concerns of Jews in the future surely will be tied no less to the tensions and pressures of the time. Some of those tensions and pressures, of course, will inevitably come from inside the Jewish community rather than from outside it: cultural, religious, and political divisions among Jews may produce issues, or differing views on issues, for the future. These tensions include, but will not be limited to, differences among Orthodox, Conservative, Reform, and other movements. And though it is not possible to identify with certainty the issues that will dominate debate among Jews in the years and decades to come, some broad contours are nonetheless visible from our perspective here at the hinge of the new century and millennium.

Israel

The founding of Israel and its struggle for international recognition and regional survival are events that occurred far from American shores, yet they are an intimate part of the internal Jewish landscape in the United States.

In many ways, American Jews regard the security of Israel as an issue with much of the urgency and moral force that they reserve for the security of the United States. Such has been true in the past and almost certainly will be true in the future. Though American Jews have preferred some Israeli governments to others—the government led by Benjamin Netanyahu in the very last years of the last century was particularly unpopular among American Jews—their allegiance to the Jewish state remains strong and is probably unshakable. The most recent American Jewish Committee (AJC) annual survey found that three out of four American Jews said they felt "very close" or "fairly close" to Israel, with the same rate agreeing with the statement, "Caring about Israel is a very important part of my being a Jew." The AJC poll found that about half of American Jews believe the relationship between Jews in Israel and Jews in the United States will remain about the same, but, tellingly, about a third of those polled said they thought that Israeli Jews and American Jews actually would grow closer.

Though Jews in America worry considerably about the state of the peace process in Middle East, and though some Jews worry about Israel's vacating the moral high ground in the region, concern about Israel and its viability remain vitally important for American Jews. Jewish commentators have worried that as the Holocaust and the 1967 Arab–Israeli War receded into memory and as intermarriage rates grew, the urgency surrounding Israel's survival would diminish, but that has not been the case. Jews in the next several years will still push for strong backing for congressional support for Israel and for foreign aid to Israel, much of it military. Strong Jewish lobby groups such as the American Israel Public Affairs Committee can be expected to continue to play a big role in Washington, and the prominence of Jews in major-party fund-raising operations can be expected to keep the issue in front of political leaders. American Jews in the future are as likely to say as they have in the past, "Israel isn't out of the woods yet."

Foreign Policy Issues

Jews have always had strong feelings about foreign affairs and foreign aid, not limited to their concern over the survival and security of Israel. Even commentators outside the Jewish community believe that Jewish support for the foreign aid account, for example, is one of the essential lifelines for a corner of the budget that has been under attack in recent years. Perhaps because they believe that the brand of isolation practiced by the United States in the interwar years of 1918–39 contributed to the rise and power of Hitler, American Jews have always believed in a strong American influence abroad.

In recent years, American Jews have taken pride in the fact that the United States, even as a single superpower, is engaged in world affairs. American Jews, moreover, were a major voice in the debate over NATO's involvement in the former Yugoslavia during the 1999 Balkan war, with Jews raising humanitarian concerns that had antecedents in the Holocaust in Europe. Almost every major Jewish organization deplored the human rights violations in the Balkans and urged American action to halt "ethnic cleansing," a phrase that holds a particular horror for American Jews.

In future years, American Jews almost certainly will call for the United States to play a prominent role in foreign affairs and almost certainly will encourage the nation to assert itself in defense of human rights. A leading indicator is the spring 2000 decision by the Simon Wiesenthal Center of Los Angeles to create a new $130-million facility in Jerusalem. Its emphasis: global issues of peace and tolerance.

Immigration

This is one of the preeminent issues in American life, occupying the minds not only of Jews but also of other groups, including many of the Jewish people's colleagues among the host population. This issue is so difficult for Americans because it involves a conflict between two important values: the political value, important in contemporary times, of national control of borders; and the cultural value, important in the American heritage, of open borders.

Jews on the whole are more open to immigration than are many other groups in the United States, in part because they are slow to recognize their status as part of the host community and still regard themselves, in spirit if not in reality, as part of the immigrant community. To Jews, America was and is the golden land. American University sociologist Rita Simon, who has written widely on Jewish life in America, believes that Jews living in America are experiencing what she calls "the Golden Age of Jews." For that reason, Jews in the future will be reluctant to close the immigration doors. The people who are proud to have been part of the wretched refuse that found earthly redemption in the Great Hall on Ellis Island are likely to work to offer that redemption to others.

Civil Rights

The story of the Jewish people is the story of the struggle for civil rights, and so it was natural that Jews took a large role in the black struggle for civil rights, not only in the late 1950s and 1960s but also as early as the 1930s. Jews provided early support for the National Association for the Advancement of Colored People (NAACP). Jewish activists were prominent in the boycotts, marches, and arrests that roiled American waters in the civil rights era, and many leading Jewish figures, including Abraham Joshua Heschel, the Hasidic rabbi and expert on Jewish ethics and mysticism, accompanied the Reverend Martin Luther King Jr. on his 1965 march between Selma, Alabama, and Montgomery. King once said that "it would be impossible to record the contribution that the Jewish people made toward the Negro's struggle for freedom—it has been so great."

American Jews and blacks were allies in the fight for freedom at midcentury, yet tensions between the two groups have provided one of the most heartbreaking developments in American Jewish history. The causes and origins of this tension still are not well understood, but they are also undeniable, especially in New York, where housing, crime, and education issues have combined to produce a sometimes incendiary environment. (One factor, to be sure, was Jewish skepticism over quotas designed to insure the inclusion of blacks in important American social, political, and cultural institutions. Though the word *quota* signaled opportunity to some African Americans, it was regarded as a synonym of *barrier* to some Jews, who themselves had battled quotas designed to keep people out, not to invite them in.)

The recent contentiousness aside, the basic inclination of Jews is to support any group's efforts to win a place in the mainstream even as it struggles to maintain its identity. Overall, Jews in the future can be expected to have an open mind and, just as important, an open heart with regard to civil rights struggles.

The attention in the meantime almost certainly will be on how to repair the damage between two communities that over the years have worked very closely together in the most American of causes—to redeem the promise, set out in the Declaration of Independence, of creating a society in which all men and women are treated equally, in which they have unalienable rights, and in which the purpose of the government is to assure freedom and equality.

Education

As a people of the book, Jews have always had a reverence for learning. Long before they made landfall on the American continent, Jews conferred respect and status on the educated, and inculcated among their people the conviction that learning was a great Jewish value. It is no surprise, therefore, that, from the start, Jews in America have supported public education—first, because they regarded education as a value in its own right; second, because they regarded secular education as an avenue for Jewish advancement. Although Jews have maintained private schools for centuries, they elevated the notion of the secular public school to a pedestal: here Jews, unencumbered by the religious doctrines of the majority culture, could pursue knowledge and their destiny. Moreover, Jews who (still) regarded themselves as an immigrant community believed that outsiders get their start—a fair start—in public schools.

A decade ago observers found little support among Jews outside the Orthodox community for school vouchers and tuition-tax credits. But in recent years a number of new Jewish private schools, and not only those Orthodox in orientation, have grown and prospered, with prominent examples in Atlanta and Washington. Many of these schools draw students from the children of secular Jews; among the reasons are a growing sense of spirituality among these Jews and their growing skepticism over the rigor, discipline, and curriculum in the public schools. Thus, vouchers and tuition-tax credits, once regarded as anathema among all but the most observant Jews, have become major issues within the Jewish community. The most recent annual survey of American Jewish public opinion by the American Jewish Committee found that 57 percent opposed a school voucher program—but that 41 percent favored it. This debate almost certainly will heat up in coming years.

Separation of Church and State

This issue is related to the school issue but has its own footing as well—and it will certainly be one of the leading issues of the next decade. Many Jews, the victim of state-sponsored religious persecution, were drawn to the United States in the first place because of the nation's heritage of separating church and state.

Generally Jews hew to the strict separation doctrine as espoused by such groups as People for the American Way and the American Civil Liberties Union. But signs of a new debate are emerging within Jewish circles relating directly to one of the basic themes of this chapter: the emergence of Jews as part of the American host community. Increasingly significant voices within the Jewish community do not accept the orthodoxy of the traditional view of the separation of church and state, which looks askance at any official or governmental expressional of religious identity. The appearance of a large menorah near the White House, for example, has shattered the consensus that opposed religious symbols in public places. Some Jews regard the menorah as a symbol of pride, a statement that Jews have arrived.

Remaining, however, is a signal opposition among Jews to the notion of prayer in public schools. Many of today's parents remember with real discomfort the days before the Supreme Court decision against prayer in the schools. The prospect of reviving such worship has little support among Jews, and continuing efforts, mostly by religious Christian conservatives, can be expected to be fought strenuously by American Jews.

Relations with Religious Conservatives

Many of the tenets of the religious right strike a responsive chord with American Jews, particularly the emphasis on strong families, family values, and support for Israel. A few Jews have turned up in religious conservative organizations, including the 1988 presidential campaign of the Reverend Pat Robertson. And Ralph E. Reed Jr., the onetime executive director of the Christian Coalition, eased many Jews' fears in his celebrated 1995 address to the Anti-Defamation League of B'nai B'rith during which he acknowledged that "religious conservatives have at times been insensitive and have lacked a full understanding of the horrors experienced by the Jewish people," and when he vowed to "move beyond the pain of the past and the uneasy tolerance of the present to genuine friendship."

Nonetheless, genuine friendship between the two groups has been elusive. Jews, for example, are wary of statements like one from Reverend Robertson, who said on his *700*

Club television broadcast that the United States Constitution was "a marvelous document for self-government by Christian people," adding, "But the minute you turn the document into the hands of non-Christians and atheistic people they can use it to destroy the very foundation of our society."

One indication of the tensions between the two groups comes from the AJC's survey of Jewish public opinion. When respondents were read a list of various groups, 51 percent said that "most" or "many" members of the religious right were antisemitic. That figure compares with 46 percent for Moslems, with whom many Jews believe they are involved in a geopolitical struggle in the Middle East, and 26 percent for blacks, in which case tensions between the groups have received enormous media attention. The continued prominence of Christian religious conservatives in American life almost certainly means that relations between them and Jews will remain a major issue for the next decade.

Social Security, Medicare, and Housing

With a high percentage of elderly and with medical advances assuring longer life spans, secular issues involving the economic condition of older Americans have become "Jewish issues." The future of Social Security and Medicare, hardy perennials in the American political landscape, are now important issues to Jewish groups.

In recent years, housing has emerged as a significant Jewish issue. Many Jewish social service agencies sponsor retirement homes and programs for the aging. B'nai B'rith itself works with the federal Department of Housing and Urban Development to build senior housing. Currently, Jewish agencies are working to refinance many of the elderly housing projects in eastern cities, particularly New York. Much old-age housing stock, of course, is already in place; the emphasis in years to come will be in rehabilitating much of that housing, in converting some of it to assisted-living facilities, and in constructing new stand-alone assisted-living units. Much of that work will require tax credits from Washington or new legislation.

In the last decade and a half, Jewish immigrants from Russia have been using much of the existing subsidized housing stock, some of it originally intended for aging Jews, and new funding will be required to build additional units in areas affected by high rates of Russian immigration, including New York and the North Shore of Greater Boston. At the same time, Great Society subsidy programs that have been used to house Jews at or below the poverty level are expiring, and Jewish agency officials worry that unless these subsidies are renewed by Congress, some of the privately owned, publicly subsidized housing stock will be converted to condominiums and market-rate housing.

Secular Social Issues

A number of social issues that are part of the broader political debate have special resonance for Jewish voters. Crime, for example, is a secular social issue that has become a

"Jewish issue"; crime is a growing concern of older Jews and of the Orthodox community. In recent years important Jewish groups have fought to support legislation to put more police officers on the streets. Jews have also been prominent in efforts to broaden opportunities for women and for gays, and though there are strong feelings on both sides of the abortion issue, Jews generally have been open to abortion rights.

Emerging New Issues

New foreign policy issues are even now developing. In coming years, Jews and their representatives in Washington can be expected to take interest in "encryption" (part of Jewish groups' vigilance against terrorism, both in the Middle East and against Jews in the United States) and to step up the battle for legislation to fight religious persecution around the world (part of Jewish groups' efforts to insure the freedom to worship for Jews and others). At home, Jewish groups may fight zoning regulations that target religious institutions, local laws that may make it illegal to wear religious symbols such as the Star of David, and legislation forcing members of the clergy to give state's evidence against confessors.

The process of speculating about the future of any people is fraught with danger. It is impossible to know, for example, what foreign or domestic events will occur in the years to come. It is impossible to know what issues will be created by continued economic prosperity or by the onset of an economic downturn. It is impossible, moreover, to know which issues of interest to Jews may become national issues. And it is impossible to know which issues may recede in importance.

But the future will be shaped at least in part by the interaction between two utterly unpredictable elements: what happens to the United States and what happens to the Jewish people. Any alteration in the one will almost certainly produce an alteration in the other.

The main factor in considering the future of Jews in America is the character of the Jewish people themselves in America. If further assimilation and continued high rates of intermarriage, for example, produce a decline in Jewish identity—if Jews relinquish their remaining distinction as they remain part of the host community in America—the question of Jewish prospects in American politics could become one of survival, not merely of success. There is the danger of a loss of Jewish identity at a time when American politics increasingly consists of identity politics.

> THERE IS THE DANGER OF A LOSS OF JEWISH IDENTITY AT A TIME WHEN AMERICAN POLITICS INCREASINGLY CONSISTS OF IDENTITY POLITICS.

Yet the richness of American Jewish life is still one of its defining characteristics, still one of its most admired qualities, still one of its most revered marks of distinction. Jews are, to be sure, part of the host community—not reluctant hosts here in America, but proud hosts. But the Jewish people are an ancient people, taught by long history and bitter experience to cultivate memories, not to efface them. Jews know that they cannot forget their heritage. And they know, moreover, that, with the abiding power of antisemitism, elements of the broader society would not permit them to forget even if they wanted to. In recent years, many of the Jews who turned from their culture and faith have returned, often with enthusiasm, often with a sense of wonder, always with a sense of freshness and discovery. Jewish identity applies even, or perhaps especially, to the millions who have intermarried. The flowering of Orthodox life and the resurgence of serious spirituality among many Jews have contributed to an immensely healthy community—and an immensely healthy part of the American mosaic.

And so we return to the question, so full of implicit optimism: What are the prospects for Jews in American political life? The question is complex, the answer perhaps simple. Jews no longer consider themselves visitors in the American mansion. They believe they belong here. As part of the host community, Jews can be expected to play an important role in every aspect of American life—in sports, in entertainment, in letters, and in politics. Full participation in all of these realms—not the least of which is politics, in which the character of a people is molded—is, after all, the obligation of a host.

ANNOTATED
SOURCES AND
SUGGESTED READINGS

The following bibliography provides the references for some of the works cited in the preceding essays and briefly annotates selected works thought to be of particular interest to those pursuing this topic further.

American Jewish Historical Society, ed. *American Jewish Desk Reference*. New York: Random House, 1999.

Antler, Joyce. *The Journey Home: Jewish Women and the American Century*. New York: Free Press, 1997. This work combines social history with biographical portraits of notable American Jewish women.

Appelbaum, Paul. "The Soviet Jewry Movement in the United States." In *Jewish American Voluntary Organizations,* ed. Michael Dobkowski. New York: Greenwood, 1986. This historical survey was written by a longtime Soviet Jewry activist.

Auerbach, Jerold. *Unequal Justice: Lawyers and Social Change in Modern America*. New York: Oxford University Press, 1976. A social history of elite lawyers, this volume "explores the efforts of these lawyers to mold their profession to cope with the forces that have transformed our national life: industrial capitalism, urbanization, immigration, war, economic depression, and social ferment."

Baltzell, E. Digby. *The Protestant Establishment: Aristocracy and Caste in America*. New Haven, Conn.: Yale University Press, 1987. Written by the distinguished University of Pennsylvania sociologist, this frequently cited work analyzes the WASP establishment and popularizes use of the acronym.

Bean, Walton. *Boss Ruef's San Francisco*. Berkeley: University of California Press, 1967. This is the definitive scholarly work on the first big-city Jewish boss and politics at the turn of the twentieth century.

Bell, Daniel. *Marxian Socialism in the United States*. Princeton, N.J.: Princeton University Press, 1967. This is an analysis of socialist ideology written by the famous Harvard sociologist.

Bennett, Anthony J. *The American President's Cabinet: From Kennedy to Bush* (New York: St. Martin's, 1996).

Bernheimer, Charles S., ed. *The Russian Jew in the United States*. Philadelphia: Winston, 1905.

Bone, Hugh A. "Sol Bloom: Supersalesman of Patriotism." In *Public Men in and out of Office*, ed. John T. Salter. Chapel Hill: University of North Carolina Press, 1946. This essay describes the very colorful career of the New York congressman who earlier worked as a theater producer, music publisher, and real estate developer.

Brawarsky, Sandee, and Deborah Mark, eds. *Two Jews, Three Opinions: A Collection of Twentieth-Century American Jewish Quotations*. New York: Perigee, 1998. This volume includes an eclectic range of more than two thousand quotations on both Jewish and non-Jewish topics.

Brownstein, Ronald. *The Power and the Glitter: The Hollywood–Washington Connection*. New York: Pantheon, 1990. The author, a Washington journalist, searched archives and interviewed personalities to find the special connection between politicians and movie stars since Herbert Hoover's administration.

Burt, Robert A. *Two Jewish Justices: Outcasts in the Promised Land*. Berkeley: University of California Press, 1988. This work analyzes the influence Judaism had on Justices Brandeis and Frankfurter in both their personal lives and Supreme Court decisions.

Cassedy, Steven. *To the Other Shore: The Russian Jewish Intellectuals Who Came to America*. Princeton, N.J.: Princeton University Press, 1997. This volume examines the influential Jewish group—mostly secular Jews raised in Orthodox homes—who immigrated to the United States between 1881 and the early 1920s and who frequently propagated the radical political theories that circulated in nineteenth-century Russia.

Cauthen, John K. *Speaker Blatt: His Challenges Were Greater*. Columbia: University of South Carolina Press, 1965. Written by a friend, this privately published biography recounts the life of a Jewish South Carolina representative who was the longest-serving state legislator in American history.

Celler, Emanuel. *You Never Leave Brooklyn: The Autobiography of Emanuel Celler*. New York: Day, 1953. In this memoir, the longtime New York congressman discusses his strong advocacy for immigration reform, labor laws, and support for Israel, among other issues.

Chafe, William H. *Never Stop Running*. Princeton, N.J.: Princeton University Press, 1998. This insightful biography of Allard Lowenstein details the life of the political activist who played an important role in the Vietnam War protests and the effort to deny Lyndon Johnson renomination as president in 1968.

Chanes, Jerome A. "The Voices of the American Jewish Community." In *Survey of Jewish Affairs*. London: Institute of Jewish Affairs, 1989.

———. *A Primer on the American Jewish Community*, 2d ed. New York: American Jewish Committee, 2000.

Chanes, Jerome A., Norman Linzer, and David Schnall, eds. *A Portrait of the American Jewish Community*. Westport, Conn.: Praeger, 1998. In these publications, a veteran Jewish community leader discusses the sociology and organizational structure of the multifaceted American Jewish community.

Cohen, Edwin S. *A Lawyer's Life: Deep in the Heart of Taxes*. Arlington, Va.: Tax Analysts, 1994. An expert on tax reform who served as undersecretary of the treasury during the Nixon administration, Cohen anecdotally writes about his life and personal involvement in milestone tax legislation.

Cohen, Michael J. *Truman and Israel*. Berkeley: University of California Press, 1990. This book is an important examination of the relationship between President Truman and the nascent Jewish state, including his decision to recognize the new country.

Cohen, Naomi W. *A Dual Heritage: The Public Career of Oscar S. Straus*. Philadelphia: Jewish Publication Society of America, 1969. This is the definitive biography of the first Jewish cabinet member, who also served as the U.S. ambassador to Turkey.

——. *Not Free to Desist: The American Jewish Committee, 1906–1966*. Philadelphia: Jewish Publication Society, 1972. This is an institutional history of the AJC during the first half of the twentieth century.

Cohen, Steven M. *The Dimensions of American Jewish Liberalism*. New York: American Jewish Committee, Institute of Human Relations, 1989.

——. *American Assimilation or Jewish Revival?* Bloomington: Indiana University Press, 1988.

——. *American Modernity and Jewish Identity*. New York: Tavistock, 1983. Cohen's work includes extensive analysis of community and national surveys of the social and political values of American Jews.

Coles, Robert. *Erik H. Erikson: The Growth of His Work*. Boston: Atlantic, Little, Brown, 1970. The prolific Harvard professor examines the theories of one of the most famous psychiatrists since Freud.

Crowder, David Lester. "Moses Alexander: Idaho's Jewish Governor," unpublished Ph.D. dissertation, University of Utah, 1972. This is the only monograph on the first Jewish governor of the Gem State.

Crowther, Bosley. *Hollywood Rajah: The Life and Times of Louis B. Mayer*. New York: Holt, 1960.

Cutler, Irving. *Jews of Chicago: From Shtetl to Suburb*. Urbana: University of Illinois, 1996. A social history of Jews in the Windy City, this volume includes much biographical information on notable residents, including Democratic Party activist Jacob M. Arvey.

Dalin, David G., and Alfred J. Kolatch. *The Presidents of the United States & the Jews*. Middle Village, N.Y.: David, 2000. This fascinating survey provides little-known information on the attitudes of American presidents from Washington to Clinton toward the American Jewish community.

Dershowitz, Alan M. *The Vanishing American Jew*. New York: Simon & Schuster, 1997. This somber work predicts a bleak future for American Judaism with the rise in intermarriage and the lessening of religious involvement and identification.

Donin, Hayim Halevy. *To Raise a Jewish Child*. New York: Basic Books, 1977.

Drinnon, Richard. *Rebel in Paradise: A Biography of Emma Goldman*. Boston: Beacon, 1961.

Elazar, Daniel J., ed. *The New Jewish Politics*. Lanham, Md.: University Press of America and Jerusalem Center for Public Affairs/Center for Jewish Community Studies, 1988.

Elazar, Daniel. "Developments in Jewish Community Organization in the Second Postwar Generation." In *American Pluralism and the Jewish Community*, ed. Seymour Martin Lipset. New Brunswick, N.J.: Transaction, 1990, pp. 173–92. A leading political scientist and specialist in the study of federalism, political culture, and the Jewish political tradition, the late Professor Elazar examines the complex interactions between Jewish organizations and the secular political culture.

Erie, Steven P. *Rainbow's End*. Berkeley: University of California Press, 1988. Erie's work is an outstanding analysis of the urban machine, concentrating on the Irish, but with important insights into Jewish political life.

Evans, Eli N. *Judah P. Benjamin, The Jewish Confederate*. New York: Free Press, 1989. Written by a leading southern Jewish historian, this volume provides a massive amount of biographical information on the most prominent Jew in the Confederacy.

Fackenheim, Emil L. *What Is Judaism?* New York: Summit, 1987.

Farber, Roberta Rosenberg, and Chaim I. Waxman, eds. *Jews in America*. Hanover, N.H.: Brandeis University Press, 1999.

Featherman, Sandra. *Philadelphia Elects a Black Mayor: How Jews, Blacks and Ethnics Vote in the 1980s*. The American Jewish Committee: Philadelphia, 1984.

——. *Jews, Blacks and Urban Politics in the 1980s: The Case of Philadelphia*. The American Jewish Committee: Philadelphia, 1988.

Featherman, Sandra, and John Featherman. *Race and Politics at the Millennium: The 1999 Mayoral Race in Philadelphia*. The American Jewish Committee: Philadelphia, 2000.

Featherman, Sandra, and Allan B. Hill. *Ethnic Voting in the 1991 Philadelphia Mayoral Election*. The American Jewish Committee: New York, 1992.

Frankel, Jonathan. *The Damascus Affair*. New York: Cambridge University Press, 1997. Professor Frankel, a Hebrew University historian, analyzes the profound historical impact of a Jewish ritual murder accusation when an Italian monk and servant disappear in Damascus in 1840.

Fraser, Steven. *Labor Will Rule: Sidney Hillman and the Rise of American Labor*. New York: Free Press, 1991.

Freedman, Samuel G. *The Inheritance*. New York: Simon & Schuster, 1996. This premier journalist follows decline of New Deal loyalties, including extensive insights into Baltimore politics.

——. *Jew vs. Jew: The Struggle for the Soul of American Jewry*. New York: Simon & Schuster, 2000. A journalist portrays of the severe cleavages dividing American Jews over questions of identity, pluralism, gender, Israel, and other issues.

Friedman, Murray. *What Went Wrong? The Creation and Collapse of the Black-Jewish Alliance*. New York: Free Press, 1994. Friedman examines the contentious relations between blacks and Jews since the 1960s.

Fuchs, Lawrence H. *The Political Behavior of American Jews*. Glencoe, Ill.: Free Press, 1956. In this classic study, Brandeis University professor Fuchs provides an analysis of American Jewish political activity and political values, with an emphasis on the mid–twentieth century.

Ginsberg, Benjamin. *The Fatal Embrace: Jews and the State*. Chicago: University of Chicago Press, 1998. This is a political account of the role of anti-Jewish prejudice from the Civil War to the 1992 presidential election.

Glazer, Nathan. *Remembering the Answers: Essays on American Student Revolt*. New York: Basic Books, 1970.

Glazer, Nathan, and Daniel P. Moynihan. *Beyond the Melting Pot,* 2d ed. Cambridge, Mass.: MIT Press, 1970. This is a classic study of ethnic politics in New York City, focusing not only on Jews but also on blacks, the Irish, Italians, and Puerto Ricans.

Goren, Arthur A. *The Politics and Public Culture of American Jews*. Bloomington: Indiana University Press, 1999. The author describes how "Jews transplanted, changed and invented their social institutions and ideologies and created over time an impressive organizational culture."

Gornick, Vivian. *The Romance of American Communism*. New York: Basic Books, 1977. Gornick offers a sympathetic account of the lure of leftist politics to a generation of secular Jews.

Grose, Peter. *Israel in the Mind of America*. New York: Knopf, 1983. Former editor at the journal *Foreign Affairs,* Grose traces the long history of American interest in the establishment of a modern Jewish homeland.

Guggenheim, Jack Achiezer. "The Evolution of Chutzpah as a Legal Term." *Kentucky Law Journal* 87, no. 2 (1998–99). This fascinating article documents the use of *chutzpah* and other Yiddish words in federal, state, and local judicial decisions.

Gurock, Jeffrey S. *When Harlem Was Jewish, 1870–1930.* New York: Columbia University Press, 1979.

Ha-am, Ahad. *Al Parashat Derakhim*. Tel Aviv: Dvir & Hotzaah Ivrit, 1964.

Halperin, Samuel. *Political World of American Zionism*. Detroit: Wayne State University Press, 1961. This is one of the most cited works on the influence and power of U.S. Zionist organizations.

Hand, Samuel. *Counsel and Advise: A Political Biography of Samuel I. Rosenman*. New York: Garland, 1979. Counsel to Presidents Roosevelt and Truman, Rosenman assisted Truman in preparations for the Nuremberg trial and worked with Chaim Weizmann in discussions with the State Department on the establishment of a Jewish state.

Heilman, Samuel. *Portrait of American Jews*. Seattle: University of Washington Press, 1995.

Henderson, Thomas M. *Tammany Hall and the New Immigrants*. New York: Arno, 1976.

Hertzberg, Arthur. *The Jews in America: Four Centuries of an Uneasy Encounter.* New York: Columbia University Press, 1997. The author traces the history of Jews in America since colonial times and their complex attitudes toward religion and ethnicity.

Higham, John. *Strangers in the Land: Patterns of American Nativism, 1860–1925*, 2d ed. New Brunswick, N.J.: Rutgers University Press, 1988. This is a major historical "investigation of American attitudes and policies toward foreign-born minorities."

Hoffmann, Joyce. 1995. *Theodore H. White and Journalism as Illusion*. Columbia: University of Missouri Press.

Hoover, Kenneth R. (with J. Marcia and K. Parris). *The Power of Identity: Politics in a New Key*. Chatham, N.J.: Chatham House, 1997.

Horowitz, Daniel. *Betty Friedan and the Making of* The Feminine Mystique. Amherst: University of Massachusetts Press, 1998. Smith College graduate analyzes the pathbreaking work on modern American feminism written by the Peoria-born author originally named Bettye Naomi Goldstein.

Howe, Irving. *World of Our Fathers*. New York: Harcourt Brace Jovanovich, 1976. Howe presents a major work on the history of Jewish immigration to the United States from Eastern Europe during the nineteenth and early twentieth centuries.

Huhner, Leon. "Some Jewish Associates of John Brown." In *Publications of the American Jewish Historical Society*, vol. 23: 55–78 (New York: Jewish Historical Society, 1915). This classic essay documents the activities of Jewish abolitionists, including August Bondi.

Isaacs, Stephen D. *Jews and American Politics*. Garden City, N.Y.: Doubleday, 1974. This was one of the first works to examine the different roles played by American Jews in political life, especially during the 1950s and 1960s.

Italia, Bob, and Paul Deegan. *Ruth Bader Ginsburg*. Minneapolis: Abdo & Daughters, 1994.

Johnson, Paul. *A History of the Jews*. New York: Harper & Row, 1987.

Juergens, George. *Joseph Pulitzer and the* New York World. Princeton, N.J.: Princeton University Press, 1966. Juergens details how after purchasing the *New York World,* newspaper magnate Joseph Pulitzer turned it into a journal that concentrated on investigative reporting, human interest stories, scandal, and sensational material.

Kalman, Laura. *Abe Fortas: A Biography*. New Haven, Conn.: Yale University Press, 1990. This is a sympathetic study of the Supreme Court justice, appointed by President Johnson in 1965, who resigned from the bench amid controversy in 1969.

Karkhanis, Sharad. *Jewish Heritage in America: An Annotated Bibliography*. New York: Garland, 1988. This useful annotated bibliography provides access to a wide range of books, monographs, and popular magazine articles on American Jewish life, from 1925 to 1987.

Kaufman, Andrew L. *Cardozo*. Cambridge, Mass.: Harvard University Press, 1998. Among the half dozen biographies of the "hermit philosopher" who was a Supreme Court justice, this work provides unique information on his ethnic background and attitudes toward Judaism and the Jewish community.

Kaufman, Jonathan. *Broken Alliance: The Turbulent Times Between Blacks and Jews in America*. New York: Mentor, 1988. Former *Boston Globe* reporter provides a journalistic overview of the bittersweet encounter between African Americans and American Jews.

Keyssar, Alexander. *The Right to Vote: The Contested History of Democracy in the United States*. New York: Basic Books, 2000. This is a historical survey of the struggle to win suffrage for minority groups, women, and others. It also includes historical incidents such as the 1908 New York voter-registration date scheduled for Yom Kippur, to exclude Jewish voters.

Kisch, Guido. *In Search of Freedom: A History of American Jews from Czechoslovakia*. London: Goldston, 1949. This well-documented work provides little-known historical and biographical information on Jews from this Eastern European country.

Klutznick, Philip M. *Angles of Vision: A Memoir of My Lives*. Chicago: Dee, 1991. This is a memoir of the influential lay Jewish leader and major real estate developer.

Kohler, Max J., and Simon Wolf. "Benjamin F. Peixotto's Mission to Rumania." In *The Jewish Experience in America,* ed. Abraham J. Karp, vol. 2. Waltham, Mass.: American Jewish Historical Society and KTAV, 1969.

Korff, Baruch. *The President and I: Richard Nixon's Rabbi Reveals His Role in the Saga That Traumatized the Nation*. N.p.: Baruch Korff Foundation, 1995. In this self-published memoir, Rabbi Baruch Korff—a strong Nixon supporter—discusses his encounters with the president before his resignation.

Korn, Bertram Wallace. *American Jewry and the Civil War*. Philadelphia: Jewish Publication Society of America, 1951 (also published 1961). Although written a half century ago, this work is still considered the preeminent historical account of Jews—in both the Union and Confederacy—during the American Civil War.

Lash, Joseph. *Dealers and Dreamers*. New York: Doubleday, 1988. Lash presents a revised look at the New Deal by the biographer of the Roosevelts.

Laslett, John. *Labor and the Left: A Study of Socialist and Radical Influences in the American Labor Movement, 1881–1924*. New York: Basic Books, 1970.

Lebow Richard N. "Woodrow Wilson and the Balfour Declaration." *Journal of Modern History* 40 (December 1968): 501.

Levey, Geoffrey Brahm. "Toward a Theory of Disproportionate American Jewish Liberalism." In *Values, Interests, and Identity: Jews and Politics in a Changing World*, Studies in Contemporary Jewry, ed. Peter Y. Medding, vol. 11: 64–85 (1995). New York: Oxford University Press, 1995.

——. "The Liberalism of American Jews—Has It Been Explained?" *British Journal of Political Science* 26 (July 1996): 369–401.

Levitan, Tina. *First Facts in American Jewish History.* Northvale, N.J.: Aronson, 1996. This popular reference work contains a wide range of fascinating facts, ranging from the first Jewish Medal of Honor winner to the first Jew to die in the American Revolution.

Levy, Mark R., and Michael S. Kramer. *The Ethnic Factor: How America's Minorities Decide Elections.* New York: Simon & Schuster, 1973. Levy and Kramer provide a statistical analysis of ethnic group contributions to various mid-twentieth century American elections.

Liebman, Arthur. *Jews and the Left.* New York: Wiley, 1979.

Liebman, Charles S. *The Ambivalent American Jew: Politics, Religion and Family in American Jewish Life.* Philadelphia: Jewish Publication Society of America, 1973.

Liebman, Charles S., and Steven M. Cohen. *Two Worlds of Judaism: The Israeli and American Experiences.* New Haven, Conn.: Yale University Press, 1990. This work finds large differences in the ways American and Israeli Jews understand their faith and its social implications.

——. "American Jewish Liberalism: Unraveling the Strands." *Public Opinion Quarterly* 61 (Fall 1997): 405–30.

Lipset, Seymour Martin, ed. *American Pluralism and the Jewish Community.* New Brunswick, N.J.: Transaction, 1990.

Lipset, Seymour Martin, and Earl Raab. *Jews and the New American Scene.* Cambridge, Mass.: Harvard University Press, 1995. This is a thorough account of Jewish political values in the contemporary United States.

Luskin, John. *Lippmann, Liberty, and the Press.* Birmingham: University of Alabama Press, 1972.

Mackenzie, G. Calvin. *The Politics of Presidential Appointments.* New York: Free Press, 1981.

Marcus, Jacob Rader. *United States Jewry, 1776–1985.* Detroit: Wayne State University Press, 1993.

——. *To Count a People: American Jewish Population Data, 1585–1984.* Lanham, Md.: University Press of America, 1990.

Mazur, Edward Herbert. Minyans *for a Prairie City: The Politics of Chicago Jewry, 1850–1940.* New York: Garland, 1990.

McBride, Joseph. *Steven Spielberg: A Biography.* New York: Simon & Schuster, 1997.

McNickle, Chris. *To Be Mayor of New York: Ethnic Politics in the City.* New York: Columbia University Press, 1973. McNickle undertakes a careful analysis of the contributions of ethnic minorities to New York City mayoral campaigns in the mid–twentieth century.

Medoff, Rafael. *The Deafening Silence: American Jewish Leaders and the Holocaust.* New York: Shapolsy, 1987.

Miller, Sally M. *Victor Berger and the Promise of Constructive Socialism, 1910–1920.* Westport, Conn.: Greenwood, 1973. Miller's work is a biography of the first socialist mayor of Milwaukee.

Murphy, Arthur W. "Jack Pollack," 1996. www.politicomcreative.com/archives/pollack. This political consultant's description of Jack Pollack of Baltimore includes extensive personal interviews.

Newport, Frank. "Americans Today Much More Accepting of a Woman, Black, Catholic, or Jew as President: Still Reluctant to Vote for Atheists or Homosexuals." *Poll Releases*, Gallup News Service, March 29, 1999.

Nodel, Julius J. *Ties Between: A Century of Judaism on America's Last Frontier.* Portland, Oreg.: Temple Beth Israel, 1959. This is a history of one of the oldest synagogues in the western United States.

Novick, Peter. *The Holocaust in American Life.* New York: Houghton Mifflin, 1999. In this controversial work, University of Chicago historian Peter Novick critically analyzes the role of the Holocaust in defining American Jewish identity and political views.

Oren, Dan. *Joining the Club: A History of Jews and Yale.* New Haven, Conn.: Yale University Press, 1985. Oren, a 1979 Yale graduate, documents attitudes toward Jews at Old Eli, including antisemitism expressed by both fraternity brothers and members of the board of trustees.

Parrish, Michael. *Felix Frankfurter and His Times.* New York: Free Press, 1982.

Podhoretz, Norman. *My Love Affair with America.* New York: Free Press, 2000. Podhoretz tells of his rise from poverty in New York, his disillusionment with the left, and his eventual alliance with Republican conservatives.

Polsby, Nelson W. "The Democratic Nomination." In *The American Elections of 1980,* ed. Austin Ranney. Washington, D.C.: American Enterprise Institute for Public Policy Research, 1981.

Rakove, Milton. *Don't Make No Waves . . . Don't Back No Losers.* Bloomington: Indiana University Press, 1975. This is a revealing description of Mayor Richard Daley and the Chicago Democratic organization, the last of the great urban machines.

Rapoport, Louis. *Stalin's War against the Jews.* New York: Free Press, 1990.

Raskin, Jonah. *For the Hell of It: The Life and Times of Abbie Hoffman.* Berkeley: University of California Press, 1996.

Rothman, Stanley, and S. Robert Lichter. *Roots of Radicalism: Jews, Christians, and the New Left.* New York: Oxford University Press, 1982.

Rubinstein, W. D. *The Left, the Right and the Jews.* New York: Universe Books, 1982.

Salzman, Jack, and Cornel West, eds., *Struggles in the Promised Land: Towards a History of Black-Jewish Relations in the United States.* New York: Oxford University Press, 1997.

Sampson, Edward E. "Identity Politics: Challenges to Psychology's Understandings." *American Psychologist* 48 (1993): 12.

Sarna, Jonathan D. *Jacksonian Jew: The Two Worlds of Mordecai Noah.* New York: Holmes & Meier, 1981.

Sarna, Jonathan D., and David G. Dalin, eds. *Religion and State in the American Jewish Experience.* Notre Dame, Ind.: University of Notre Dame Press, 1997. This work contains documents and essays on the Jewish approach to church–state relations.

Schwarz, Jordan. *The Speculator: Bernard M. Baruch in Washington, 1917–1965.* Chapel Hill: University of North Carolina Press, 1981. This is a major biography on the adviser to several U.S. presidents and special World War II adviser on war mobilization.

Seltzer, Robert M., and Norman J. Cohen, eds. *The Americanization of the Jews.* New York: New York University Press, 1995. Seltzer and Cohen have brought together a first-rate series of essays on the trends and developments in American Jewry at the end of the twentieth century.

Seretan, L. Glen. *Daniel DeLeon: The Odyssey of an American Marxist*. Cambridge, Mass.: Harvard University Press, 1979.

Shefter, Martin. "The Electoral Foundations of the Political Machine: New York City, 1884–1897." In *The History of American Electoral Behavior*, eds. Joel Silbey et al. Princeton, N.J.: Princeton University Press, 1978.

Silver, Abba Hillel. *Where Judaism Differs*. New York: Macmillan, 1956.

Snyder, Jill Donnie, and Eric K. Goodman. *Friend of the Court, 1947–1982*. New York: Anti-Defamation League, 1983. This work examines the legal strategies pursued by the ADL.

Sorin, Gerald. *The Prophetic Minority*. Bloomington: Indiana University Press, 1985. This is a learned and readable study of Jewish immigrant radicals in the formative period of 1880–1920.

Spiegel, Steven L. *The Other Arab-Israeli Conflict*. Chicago: University of Chicago Press, 1985. UCLA professor Spiegel examines the attitudes and policies of recent presidents and their major advisers and how each administration dealt with the Arab-Israeli conflict in the light of international, regional, and local concerns.

Stadtler, Bea. *The Holocaust: A History of Courage and Resistance*. New York: Behrman House, 1974.

Stanton, Bill. *Klanwatch: Bringing the Ku Klux Klan to Justice*. New York: Grove Weidenfeld, 1991.

Steel, Ronald. *Walter Lippmann and the American Century*. Boston: Little, Brown. 1980.

Stone, Kurt F. *The Congressional* Minyan: *The Jews of Capitol Hill*. Hoboken, N.J.: KTAV, 2000. This superbly researched work includes biographies of 179 Jewish men and women who have served in the United States House and Senate.

Svonkin, Stuart. *Jews against Prejudice: American Jews and the Fight for Civil Liberties*. New York: Columbia University Press, 1997. Svonkin's work describes the role of Jews in controversies over the Bill of Rights.

Swanberg, W. A. *Pulitzer*. New York: Scribner, 1967.

Synott, Marcia Graham. *The Half-Opened Door: Discrimination and Admissions at Harvard, Yale, and Princeton, 1900–1970*. Westport, Conn.: Greenwood, 1979.

Talese, Gay. *The Kingdom and the Power*. New York: Ivy Books, 1981. This is one of the early critical works on the history and workings of the *New York Times*.

Tedlow, Richard S. "Judah P. Benjamin." In *"Turn to the South": Essays on Southern Jewry*, eds. Nathan M. Kaganoff and Melvin I. Urofsky. Charlottesville: University Press of Virginia, 1979. This is a fine essay on the precarious position of the most prominent Jew in the Confederacy, who was loathed by northerners as a rebel leader and scorned by his fellow southerners because of his religion.

Tolchin, Susan. *The Angry American—How Voter Rage Is Changing the Nation*, 2d ed. Boulder, Colo.: Westview, 1998. Tolchin examines the views of voters at a time of electoral repercussions against incumbents.

Tolchin, Susan, and Martin Tolchin. *Clout—Womanpower and Politics*. New York: Coward, McCann & Geoghegan, 1974. The Tolchins provide a close-up look at the increased power of women in politics during the second women's movement.

Wald, Alan M. *The New York Intellectuals: The Rise and Decline of the Anti-Stalinist Left from the 1930s to the 1980s*. Chapel Hill: University of North Carolina Press, 1987.

Walker, Samuel. *In Defense of American Liberties: A History of the ACLU.* New York: Oxford University Press, 1990. This is a sympathetic treatment of the oldest civil liberties organization in the United States.

Ward, Geoffrey C. *A First-Class Temperament: The Emergence of Franklin Roosevelt.* New York: Harper, 1989.

Waxman, Chaim I. "Center and Periphery: Israel in American Jewish Life." In *Jews in America,* eds. Roberta Rosenberg Farber and Chaim I. Waxman. Hanover, N.H.: Brandeis University Press, 1999.

Wells, Leon Weliczker. *Who Speaks for the Vanquished? American Jewish Leaders and the Holocaust.* New York: Lang, 1987.

Wertheimer, Jack. "Religious Movements in Collisons: A Jewish Culture War?" In *Jews in America,* eds. Roberta Rosenberg Farber and Chaim I. Waxman. Hanover, N.H.: Brandeis University Press, 1999.

West, Cornel. *Prophetic Reflections: Notes on Race and Power in America: Vol. 2. Beyond Eurocentrism and Multiculturalism.* Monroe, Maine: Common Courage Press, 1993.

Weyl, Nathaniel. *The Jew in American Politics.* New Rochelle, N. Y.: Arlington House. 1968. The author, a political conservative, offers his critique on the problems of Jewish liberalism.

Wilson, James Q. *The Amateur Democrat.* Chicago: University of Chicago Press, 1962. This is the first thorough study of modern urban reform politics, including Jewish participation, covering New York, Chicago, and Los Angeles.

Woocher, Jonathan. *Sacred Survival: The Civil Religion of American Jews.* Bloomington: Indiana University Press, 1986. Former Brandeis University sociologist attempts to "document, describe and interpret American Jewry's civil religion."

PART II

BIOGRAPHICAL PROFILES

INTRODUCTION

As so many Jews have played prominent roles in American politics over the more than two hundred years of our country's history, the task of deciding whom to include in this listing was most arduous.

Of course, the first question we faced dealt with the age-old query, Who is a Jew? Our answer was a pragmatic one. For historical figures, we included as Jews those politicians who were treated as Jews in their own time. Thus, for example, the publisher and congressman Joseph Pulitzer, who for most purposes was not Jewish but who clearly faced discrimination as a Jew, is included. On the other hand, Martin Behrman, the New Orleans political boss, who was born a Jew but formally converted to Roman Catholicism as a teenager, is not. For contemporary figures, to the extent possible, we used self-identification. Those who consider themselves to be Jewish—whether observant or not, whether they meet the matriarchal test or not—are included. Those who might meet formal tests but do not consider themselves Jewish are not. We have thus excluded some whom others might include—Madeleine Albright, Bill Cohen, Barry Goldwater, David Sholtz, among others. We do not claim virtue for our test, only utility. And if we have erred, we hope readers of this book will let us know, so that we might make corrections in later editions. The editor can be contacted at lsmaisel@colby.edu.

Having defined "Jews" for the purpose of this book, we turned to the next question: What do we mean by "in American politics"? We defined the term broadly to include appointive as well as elective politics, government officials in addition to partisan politicians, and those participating in government and politics from the outside, such as journalists and interest group leaders, as well as those on the inside.

Even with these decisions made, drawing up a list for inclusion was most difficult. Our criteria varied according to the position an individual held. All Jews who have served in a president's cabinet are included, as are all of those who have served in the

United States House of Representatives or Senate, all Supreme Court justices, and all governors. Beyond that, we attempted to draw distinctions that were as objective as possible. Mayors of large cities have been included, as have some early mayors whose cities did not qualify as large, but contemporary mayors of smaller cities have not. Noncareer ambassadors were included, as were career foreign service officers who reached ambassadorial rank, if the embassy they served was in a major country. Most noncareer subcabinet officers are included, though we could not include them all; civil servants who served in subcabinet positions are included if their assignment was considered political in nature. Statewide constitutional officers whom we have been able to identify are included if they were elected by the public, not if they were chosen by legislatures or appointed by governors. Party leaders have been included if they have had an impact on national campaigns over a period of years or if they dominated the politics of their region. Political consultants and pollsters who have had significant impact on national campaigns have been included; those who have worked more locally have not. We included prominent publishers and Washington bureau chiefs of major newspapers, but not local journalists.

Our goal was to be inclusive, but space limitations forced us to make judgments. When objective criteria were not available, the Editorial Advisory Board was consulted and reached decisions, not always by consensus. Again, we do not claim to have been infallible. We ask readers who believe someone has been excluded to let us know; we will try to make amends in later editions.

A series of scholars—younger and older, more experienced and less so—contributed these sketches. Their initials appear after each of the sketches they have written: Donald Altschiller (DA), Sarah Barclay (SB), John Beaudoin (JB), Ben Brown (BB), Marni Davis (MD), Amanda Epstein (AE), Beth Festa (BF), Yoel Finkelman (YF), Cathy Flemming (CF), Ira Forman (IF), Kade Jubboori (KJ), Jonathan Koppel (JK), L. Sandy Maisel (LSM), Jeanna Mastrodicasa (JM), Brooke McNally (BMcN), Marlene Pomper (MP), Oliver Sabot (OS), David Sandak (DS), Jeremy Shere (JSh), Jennifer Steen (JS), Larry Tye (LT), Theresa Wagner (TW), Jocelyn Wilk (JW), and Miranda Winer (MW). They have the thanks of all who have been involved with this project. Any questions for the authors of these sketches should be directed to them through the editors.

The material for these sketches has been drawn from many sources. The only sources cited directly after individual sketches are works specific to an individual and of particular interest. Other than those sources, the sketch authors drew on the following standard reference works:

Almanac of American Politics. Editors, Michael Barone and Grant Ujifusa. Washington, D.C.: National Journal, biennial editions.

American National Biography. General editors, John A. Garraty and Mark C. Carnes. New York: Oxford University Press, 1999.

Biographical Directory of the American Congress, 1774–1996. Alexandria, Va.: CQ Staff Directories, 1997.

Biographical Dictionary of American Labor Leaders. Editor, Gary M. Fink. Westport, Conn.: Greenwood, 1984.

Biographical Dictionary of the American Left. Editors, Bernard K. Johnpoll and Harvey Klehr. Westport, Conn.: Greenwood, 1986.

Biographical Dictionary of American Mayors, 1820–1980. Editors, Melvin G. Holli and Peter Jones. Westport, Conn.: Greenwood, 1982.

Biographical Directory of the Governors of the United States, 1789–1978. Editors, Robert Sobel and John Raimo. Westport, Conn.: Meckler, 1978.

Biographical Directory of the Governors of the United States, 1978–1994, Editor, Marie Marmo Mullaney. Westport, Conn.: Greenwood, 1994.

Congressional Quarterly's Politics in America. Washington, D.C.: CQ Press, biennial editions.

Encyclopedia Judaica, CD ROM edition. Editor, Thomas J. Tobias. [Israel]: Judaica Multimedia, 1997.

Jewish Justices of the Supreme Court Revisited: Brandeis to Fortas. Editor, Jennifer M. Lowe. Washington, D.C.: Supreme Court Historical Society, 1994.

Jewish Woman in America: An Historical Encyclopedia. Editors, Paula E. Hyman and Deborah Dash Moore. New York: Routledge, 1997.

National Cyclopedia of American Biography. New York: James T. White, annual editions beginning in 1893.

Supreme Court Justices: Illustrated Biographies, 1789–1995. Editor, Clare Cushman. Washington, D.C.: Congressional Quarterly, 1995.

Who's Who in America. Chicago: Marquis Who's Who, annual editions.

Who's Who in American Politics. Editors, P. A. Theis and E. L. Henshaw. New York: Bowker, annual editions.

A

ABRAMOWITZ, MORTON

U.S. Ambassador to Turkey, 1989–1991;
Assistant Secretary of State for Intelligence
and Research, 1985–1989

Morton Abramowitz was born January 20, 1933, in Lakewood, New Jersey. He received a B.A. from Stanford University in 1953 and an M.A. from Harvard University in 1955.

In 1960, Abramowitz joined the Foreign Service as a consular/economic officer. In his early career, he served as a political officer at the United States Consulate General in Hong Kong, an international economist and foreign affairs analyst in Washington, and an adviser to the commander in chief of the Pacific Command in Honolulu.

From 1974 to 1978, Abramowitz was the deputy assistant secretary of defense for Inter-American, East Asian, and Pacific Affairs. In 1978, he became U.S. ambassador to Thailand, a position he held until 1981. Between 1983 and 1984, Abramowitz served as U.S. ambassador to the Mutual and Balanced Force Reduction Negotiations in Vienna. He then became assistant secretary of state for intelligence in 1985. Finally, in 1989, Abramowitz was named U.S. ambassador to Turkey, a position he held for two years.

After leaving the State Department, Abramowitz became president of the Carnegie Endowment for International Peace in 1991. In 1997, he was named acting president of the International Crisis Group, Inc., and senior fellow at the Council on Foreign Relations in 1998. (TW)

ABRAMS, ELLIOTT

Assistant Secretary of State for Inter-American
Affairs, 1985–1989; for Human Rights
and Humanitarian Affairs, 1981–1985;
for International Organization Affairs, 1981

Elliott Abrams was born in New York City on January 24, 1948. In 1969, he received a B.A. from Harvard College; in 1970, a master's degree from the London School of Economics; and in 1973, his J.D. from Harvard Law School. He has used his expertise in pursuit of human rights throughout his lengthy career.

Abrams worked in the U.S. Senate for four years—as assistant counsel to the Senate Permanent Subcommittee on investigations (1975), as special counsel to Henry M. Jackson (D-Wash.) (1975–1976), and as Senator Daniel Patrick Moynihan's (D-N.Y.) chief of staff (1977–1979).

He served in the Reagan administration State Department as assistant secretary for international organization affairs (1981), assistant secretary for human rights and humanitarian affairs (1981–1985), and assistant secretary of state for inter-American affairs after 1985.

He has been a member of the U.S. Commission on International Religious Freedom, a fellow at the Hudson Institute, in 1996, and was named president of the Ethics and Public Policy Center in Washington, D.C. An expert on Latin American Affairs and the American Jewish community, Abrams is a contributing editor to the *National Review* and the author of *Faith or Fear: How Jews Can Survive in Christian America* (1997), *Security and Sacrifice* (1995), *and Undue Process* (1993). (MP)

ABRAMS, ROBERT

Attorney General of New York, 1979–1995

Robert Abrams, a Democrat, spent nearly three decades serving the people of New York City and New York state. He was elected in 1965 to represent the Bronx in the state assembly at the age of twenty-seven. There, he led legislative efforts for election law reform, protecting victims of child abuse and changing New York's abortion laws. After three terms in Albany, he was elected Bronx borough president in 1969. In that capacity, he was a member of New York City's Board of Estimate, which made many of New York City's most important policy and spending decisions. He also helped bring new housing, schools, and libraries to the Bronx during his three-term presidency.

In 1978, Abrams was elected to the first of four terms as state attorney general, the first Democrat elected to that post in forty years. Among his achievements as New York's top law enforcement officer were criminally prosecuting organized crime figures, improving consumer protections, enforcing environmental laws, and protecting victims' rights. Abrams was a national leader among state attorneys general, serving as president of the National Association of State Attorneys General, and was recognized by his peers by receiving the coveted Wyman Award as the outstanding attorney general in the nation.

In 1992, Abrams won a hard-fought battle for the Democratic nomination for the U.S. Senate, only to lose narrowly to Republican incumbent Alphonse D'Amato in the general election.

After leaving office in 1995, Abrams became a member of the boards of several corporations and philanthropies and a partner in the law firm of Stroock & Stroock & Lavan in New York City. (IF)

ABRAMSON, JERRY EDWIN
President, U.S. Conference of Mayors, 1993–1994; Mayor of Louisville, Kentucky, 1986–1998

Jerry Abramson was born September 12, 1946, in Louisville, Kentucky. He graduated from Indiana University in 1968 and from the Georgetown University School of Law in 1973.

Abramson served in the United States Army between 1969 and 1971; he received a commendation medal for meritorious service. After graduation from law school, he began a career at the Louisville law firm of Greebaum, Doll & McDonald in 1973. Abramson became a partner before leaving the firm in 1985. Between 1975 and 1979, he served as a member of the Louisville Board of Aldermen; he was the chairperson of their finance committee at the same time. In 1979, he became general counsel to Kentucky governor John Y. Brown Jr., a post he held until 1981. From 1986 to 1998, Abramson served as mayor of Louisville. He also served as the president of the U.S. Conference of Mayors from 1993 to 1994. Abramson was vice chair of the Democratic Platform Committee and the City Task Force of the Democratic National Committee in 1992. During the 1996 presidential campaign, he chaired the Clinton–Gore effort for the state of Kentucky.

Abramson currently practices law with the firm of Brown, Todd, and Heyburn in Louisville. (TW)

ABZUG, BELLA SAVITSKY
Member of Congress, 1971–1977

Born on July 24, 1920, in the Bronx, New York, to Emanuel and Esther Savitsky, Bella S. Abzug was raised in a home that encouraged political activism and Judaism. Her Hebrew school teacher convinced Abzug to join a left-wing labor Zionist group, which became the center of her young life. From this group, raising money for a Jewish homeland, she learned about the power of alliances, unity, and alternative movements.

Abzug attended Hunter College as a political science major and served as student government president. She graduated Columbia Law School in 1947, where she was an editor of the *Law Review*. Immediately after law school she joined a labor law firm. As an attorney, she represented a variety of union groups and worked for civil rights and civil liberties litigants. It was at this time, often overlooked as she entered an office, that she decided to wear her trademark hats.

In 1971, Abzug was the first woman elected on a women's rights/peace platform to the House of Representatives. She opposed the Vietnam War and military conscription, cast her first vote for the Equal Rights Amendment, had some success in steering federal public works funds to New York City, actively supported Israel and Israeli-Palestinian peace efforts, and was the first member to demand Richard Nixon's impeachment. As chair of the Subcommittee on Government Information and Individual Rights, she coauthored three important pieces of legislation: the Freedom of Information Act, the Government in Sunshine Act, and the Right to Privacy Act. She advocated for women, helping organize the National Women's Political Caucus, and served as chief strategist for the Democratic Women's Committee. In 1975, she introduced an amendment to the Civil Rights Act to include gay and lesbian rights.

Defeated in a 1976 bid for the Senate, Abzug completed her congressional term and turned her energies to the United Nations (UN) and the international women's movement. She led the fight against the UN's Zionism Is Racism resolution passed in 1975, which was finally repealed in 1985. Continuing to champion women's causes, she became cochair of the Women's Environment and Development Organization and was a prominent participant in the United Nation's Beijing conference on women in 1995.

She married Albert Abzug in June 1944. Bella Savitsky Abzug died in Manhattan on March 31, 1998. (JW)

Source: Doris Faber, *Bella Abzug* (New York: Lothrop, 1976).

ACKERMAN, GARY L.
Member of Congress, 1983–present

Gary Ackerman was born November 19, 1942, in Brooklyn, New York. He grew up in Flushing, Queens, graduated from Queens College, and published a newspaper, the *Queens Tribune*, before his election to the New York Senate in 1979. In 1983, Ackerman won a special election for the congressional seat then covering the eastern part of Queens; since the 1992 redistricting, he has represented the north shore of Long Island in addition to his home borough.

A senior Democrat on the House International Relations Committee, Ackerman is a former chair of the subcommittee on Asia and the current ranking minority member of the Western Hemisphere Subcommittee. He has been a strong advocate of foreign aid programs and, especially since the Republicans assumed the House majority in 1995, an opponent of dismantling the foreign policy agencies.

Ackerman has been active on aiding victims of the Ethiopian famine and on helping Ethiopian Jews emigrate to Israel. He has also secured funding to investigate whether German veterans living in the United States were war criminals. In the 1990s, Ackerman sponsored the "Baby AIDS" bill, requiring that newborns be tested for HIV and mothers informed of the results.

Ackerman is the leader of House opposition to a constitutional amendment banning flag desecration. During each iteration of the debate, he has brought to the House floor novelty items decorated with the stars and stripes—napkins, hats, even pantyhose—and asked whether using them would constitute flag desecration. His colorful, entertaining displays carry a serious message: "You cannot destroy a symbol unless you destroy what it represents." (JS)

ALEXANDER, MOSES
Governor of Idaho, 1915–1919

Some historians dispute whether Moses Alexander was the first Jew to be popularly elected governor of any state in the Union (see the entry on David Emanuel). However, there is no doubt that this Bavarian-born immigrant was the first Jewish governor of Idaho.

Born on November 15, 1853, in Obrigheim, Rheinpfalz, Bavaria, Moses Alexander came to the United States at age fourteen. According to an unpublished manuscript, his mother refused to let him leave until he was bar mitzvahed. After a brief stay in New York City, he moved to Chillicothe, Missouri, where he was first elected to the City Council and later, mayor, in 1887.

In 1891, Alexander moved to Boise, Idaho, where he established a men's clothing business, later expanding the stores throughout the state and into Oregon. When Alexander came to Boise, an estimated one hundred Jews lived in the city, without a synagogue. He helped establish the Reform Beth Israel Congregation in 1896 and was its first vice president. In 1905, he represented the state of Idaho at the 250th anniversary conference on the settlement of Jews in the United States, held in New York City.

Alexander's political ambitions, first nurtured in Missouri, spurred him on to seek and become mayor of Boise in 1901. After a failed first bid for the Idaho governorship, Alexander, a Democrat, was later successful in his 1914 campaign.

Responding to the enthusiastic acclaim from both Jews and non-Jews greeting his election, Moses Alexander wrote about his fervent hope that "others will rise and point toward the Northwest, to Idaho, as the spot where the Star of equality, fraternity and the brotherhood of mankind has begun to set."

Before speaking at a national Jewish gathering in Boston's Faneuil Hall in 1915, Alexander offered some harshly critical remarks about his fellow Jews in an interview published in the August 25, 1915, issue of the *Christian Science Monitor*. He criticized Jews for a tendency to view themselves as a "distinct religious nation" and urged them to "become true citizens of the United States on a broad basis of Christian brotherhood." Finally, he condemned Jews as the "most priest-ridden people in the world . . . they have no other literature but the prayerbook." The article quickly created a stir among the three thousand people attending the conference, expecting to hear from Governor Alexander a public repudiation of the views published in the *Monitor* article.

Despite the increasing uproar, including angry shouts from the audience, the Idaho governor would not comment on the article. Alexander, however, subsequently wrote an article in the August 31 *Monitor*, claiming he "did not intend to make reflections against the Jewish people" and charging the reporter's account was mistaken. He did apologize for using the term "priest-ridden people."

During Alexander's two gubernatorial terms, his administration helped reduce the tax rate and supported liquor prohibition and also a progressive workers' compensation act. At the end of his second term, he returned to his Boise business and was a delegate to several Democratic national conventions. Although he was nominated to run again for governor in 1922, he came in a distant third in the election. Alexander never again ran for office and died in Boise on January 4, 1932. (DA)

ALSCHULER, SAMUEL
Judge, U.S. Court of Appeals, 1916–1939

Born November 20, 1859, in Chicago, Samuel Alschuler read law in 1881 and went on to private practice in the Chicago area until 1915. From 1896 until 1900, he was a member of the Illinois House of Representatives. In 1900, he received the Democratic nomination for governor, the first Jew to run for that office in Illinois; he was defeated by Richard Yates. He remained active in Democratic politics, serving as a delegate to the 1912 Democratic National Convention.

In 1916, Alschuler was nominated by President Woodrow Wilson to a seat on the U.S. Court of Appeals for the Seventh Circuit. In early 1918, Judge Alschuler heard testimony offered by packinghouse workers, their wives, and children when he served as a binding arbitrator in the decision that was described as the "Magna Carta for packinghouse workers," granting them an eight-hour day, a guaranteed forty-eight-hour week, time and a quarter for overtime, the full dollar-a-week raise demanded by the union, a proportional increase for all piece-rate workers, and equal pay for men and women.

During his tenure on the bench, impeachment proceedings were initiated amid charges of abuse of powers, favoritism, and judicial misconduct, but they never moved beyond the committee stage. Alschuler assumed senior status in 1936, and he died in 1939. (TW)

ANNENBERG, WALTER H.
U.S. Ambassador to Great Britain, 1969–1974

Born March 13, 1908, Walter Annenberg, publisher, diplomat, and philanthropist, attended the Peddie School in Hightstown, New Jersey, before studying business at the Wharton School of the University of Pennsylvania. Following his graduation, Annenberg entered the family publishing business, becoming the president of Triangle Publications, Inc. in 1940 and later its chairman of the board. Triangle publishes several magazines, including *Seventeen* and *TV Guide*. In addition to pursuing his own business interests, Annenberg became a leader in providing educational television programming; for his efforts in this field, he received the Marshall Field Award, the Alfred I. Dupont Award, and the Ralph Lowell Medal

An active supporter of Republican candidates, Annenberg was appointed to be the ambassador to the Court of St. James, Great Britain, by President Nixon in 1969. He served in that post for five years.

Annenberg is a trustee for the Winston Churchill Traveling Fellowships. He is a founder and trustee of the Eisenhower Exchange Fellowships. In 1986, he received the Medal of Freedom. (DS)

ANSORGE, MARTIN CHARLES
Member of Congress, 1921–1923

Born in Corning, New York, on January 1, 1882, Ansorge attended public schools and the College of the City of New York. He transferred to Columbia College, graduating in 1903 and moving on to Columbia Law School, from which he graduated in 1906.

Following the outbreak of World War I, Ansorge enlisted in the army, serving in the Motor Transport Corps. His early political career was marked with three successive unsuccessful bids to be elected to Congress in 1912, 1914, and 1916. Despite the fact that he had been unable to win the election, the Republican Party nominated Ansorge in 1918 to run again, which he declined.

In that same year, Ansorge became the chair of the Triborough Bridge Committee. In 1920, he decide to run for Congress once again and was elected to the Sixty-seventh Congress. Ansorge served only one term, being beaten in 1922 by the Democratic candidate Royal H. Weller.

Directing his attentions in a different direction, in 1924, Ansorge unsuccessfully tried to gain a seat on the bench on the Court of General Sessions of New York City. He made a second attempt to enter the judiciary, failing to become a justice of the Supreme Court of New York City. Following these defeats, Ansorge entered the private sector, becoming the director of United Airlines, serving at that post from 1934 to 1961.

Ansorge died on February 4, 1967. (DS)

ARONSON, BERNARD W.
Assistant Secretary of State, 1989–1993

Born May 16, 1946, Bernard William Aronson graduated from the University of Chicago with honors in 1967 and served in the U.S. Army Reserves. From 1973 to 1977, Aronson was assistant to the president of the United Mine Workers. In 1977, he moved to be special assistant and speechwriter for Vice President Walter Mondale, a post he retained through the Carter administration. For the next two years, he worked at the Democratic National Committee before he founded the Policy Project, a consulting firm located in Washington, D.C.

In 1989, President George H. W. Bush nominated Aronson to be an assistant secretary of state for inter-American affairs, a post he held until 1993. In that position, he was the principal coordinator of U.S. foreign policy toward the thirty-four nations of the Western Hemisphere and was the principal foreign policy adviser to the president and the secretary of state on relations with Mexico, Central and South America, and the Caribbean basin. In particular, Aronson is known for his expertise on U.S.-Cuban relations.

Since leaving government, Aronson has concentrated on business dealings, including serving as international adviser to Goldman Sachs & Co. and as a member of the boards of the Liz Claiborne company and Royal Caribbean Cruise Lines. He is also a member of the Council on Foreign Relations and serves on the board of directors of the National Democratic Institute for International Affairs. (TW)

ARVEY, JACOB M.
Political Party Leader

Affectionately known as "The Colonel" because of his U.S. Army rank during World War II, Jacob M. Arvey was a major mover and shaker in local Chicago and national politics.

One of seven children from Russian parents, Arvey was born on November 3, 1895, and grew up in a Jewish neighborhood on Chicago's West Side. After attending the Jewish Training School and the John Marshall Law School and passing the Illinois bar, Arvey became active in the powerful world of Second City politics, serving from 1923 to 1941, first as a precinct captain and then alderman—at age twenty-eight—from the mostly Jewish Twenty-fourth Ward. Running a very tight political machine that garnered up to 97 percent of the vote, Arvey once confidently asserted that "the only ones who voted Republican were the Republican precinct captains, election judges, and their families."

Although small in stature, Arvey soon loomed large in the wily world of Chicago politics. In 1946, his endorsement helped a local businessman, Martin Kennelly, become the city's mayor. Arvey is also credited with aiding the nomination and later the election of both economist Paul Douglas as United States Senator and lawyer Adlai Stevenson as Illinois governor. In 1950, however, his support for a losing Democratic Party official charged with corruption resulted in Arvey's resignation as the chair of the Cook County Democratic Central Committee. Although Arvey still maintained his position as a member of the Democratic National Committee, Richard J. Daley, a new and powerful rival, was emerging as the major force in Chicago politics.

Partly as a result of his declining political fortunes, Arvey focused his interests and talents on a variety of Jewish causes. In 1951, he helped originate the Israel bond sale program in the United States, which has raised hundreds of millions of dollars for the state of Israel. He served on the board of directors of numerous Jewish and Zionist institutions, including the American Israel Public Affairs Committee, the World Jewish Congress, the American Friends of the Hebrew University, and Brandeis University. Jacob M. Arvey died on August 25, 1977. (DA)

B

BACHARACH, ISAAC
Member of Congress, 1915–1937;
New Jersey State Representative, 1911–1915

Born in Philadelphia on January 5, 1870, Isaac Bacharach moved to Atlantic City, New Jersey, with his parents and attended the local public schools. He became involved in various business and financial activities, including real estate, lumber, and banking. A member of the Atlantic City Council from 1905 to 1910, he subsequently was elected to the New Jersey state legislature in 1911. Starting in 1915, he was the Republican congressman, representing the Second District, serving from the Sixty-fourth to the Seventy-fourth Congress. After an unsuccessful reelection bid in 1936, he resumed his business activities in real estate and insurance in his native Garden State, until his death on September 5, 1956. (DA)

BAMBERGER, SIMON
Governor of Utah, 1917–1921

Simon Bamberger was the first non-Mormon governor of Utah and also the first Democrat to serve in that office. Born in Eberstadt, Hesse-Darmstadt, Germany, on February 4, 1846, Bamberger came to the United States in 1861 and arrived in Utah nine years later. He soon became involved in a variety of business enterprises, including hotels, coal mines, railroads, and an amusement park.

In 1898, he started his electoral career, first serving as a member of the Salt Lake City Board of Education and then state senator from 1903 to 1907. In 1916, at the age of seventy, he ran as the Democratic candidate for governor, decisively defeating his Republican opponent, Nephi Morris, a prominent Mormon churchman. During the campaign, some anti-Jewish literature was circulated, but apparently these tactics offended most Utah voters.

In one perhaps apocryphal incident, a voter in this heavily Mormon state, where many residents consider themselves the true children of Israel, approached Bamberger and called him a "damn Gentile." Bamberger looked aghast and responded, "As a Jew, I have been called many a bad name, but this is the first time in my life I have been called a damn Gentile!" While he was a strong supporter of Prohibition and oversaw the passage of temperance legislation, Bamberger also pursued a progressive agenda. During his administration, he helped establish a Public Utilities Commission and a Department of Public Health and helped pass a Workmen's Compensation Act.

Despite his popularity among voters, he chose not to seek reelection. After his retirement, Governor Bamberger resumed his position as the director of some railroad companies. He died on October 6, 1926. (DA)

BARSHEFSKY, CHARLENE
U.S. Trade Representative, 1996–2001

Charlene Barshefsky was born in in Chicago on August 11, 1950. At the beginning of her life in the United States, she was a non-English-speaking Polish child. However, she went on to receive a B.A. from the University of Wisconsin and a J.D. from Catholic University.

From 1975 until 1993, Barshefsky was a partner at the law firm of Steptoe and Johnson in Washington, D.C., specializing in international trade law and policy. In 1993, she accepted President Bill Clinton's request that she serve as deputy U.S. trade representative. In April 1996, when Mickey Kantor became commerce secretary, Barshefsky was promoted to acting U.S. trade representative until her appointment was confirmed in December 1996. The appointment was controversial because it violated a 1995 law barring the appointment of anyone who has been employed by a foreign government in trade proceedings. However, Barshefsky was approved, and she remained in the position of trade representative until the end of the Clinton administration.

As trade representative, she achieved many trade agreements and investment treaties, most notably with China, Japan, and various countries in Latin America. As an example, Barshefsky was able to convince the Chinese to crack down on piracy of U.S. compact discs, computer software, and movies. (TW)

BARUCH, BERNARD
Financier and Statesman

Although he considered himself an agnostic, Bernard Baruch never joined any Jewish organizations and married an Episcopalian woman who raised their children in her faith, He still felt his Jewish background would not allow him to succeed in an elected public office in the United States.

Born in Camden, South Carolina, on August 19, 1870, Baruch was the great-grandson of the cantor at Charleston's historic Reform synagogue, Beth Elohim. His father Simon, a prominent medical doctor, moved the family to New York City when his son was young. Nevertheless, Bernard later retained his ties to the Palmetto State and entertained major political figures on the family plantation, "Hobcaw."

After graduating from the College of the City of New York, Baruch made a fortune on Wall Street from 1891 through 1912 by his shrewd stock and commodity investments. He soon became one of President Woodrow Wilson's top financial supporters. After the United States entered World War I, Baruch became chairman of the influential War Industries Board and achieved public acclaim for his supervision of this crucial government agency. As the war was coming to an end, he joined Herbert Hoover at the Paris Peace Conference.

Baruch became a major power in the Democratic Party, financially supporting its Senate and presidential candidates. His financial support of Franklin D. Roosevelt assured him of influence during the New Deal. During World War II, Baruch chaired the Rubber Survey Committee, recommending huge development of this vital war-related product. He became known as the "Park Bench Statesman" because he claimed his office was a Lafayette Park bench across from the White House.

Although he was an assimilated Jew, he attended Yom Kippur services and would not trade on the stock market on the major Jewish holidays. Biographer Jordan Schwarz notes that Baruch "liked to remind people that his name meant 'blessed' in Hebrew which led some to conclude that he attended services only to hear his name mentioned frequently."

Bernard Baruch died on June 20, 1965. (DA)

Source: Jordan Schwarz, *The Speculator: Bernard M. Baruch in Washington, 1917–1965* (Chapel Hill: University of North Carolina Press, 1981).

BAZELON, DAVID LIONEL
Judge, U.S. Court of Appeals, 1949–1993

The legacy of David Lionel Bazelon lives on through the Judge David L. Bazelon Center for Mental Health Law, which is the leading national nonprofit legal advocate for persons with mental illness and mental retardation, honoring the judge's landmark decisions in the field of mental health law.

Born September 3, 1909, in Superior, Wisconsin, Bazelon attended Northwestern University and practiced law in Chicago, both in private practice as well as for the U.S. government, until 1949. Bazelon was then nominated by Harry S. Truman as judge for the U.S. Court of Appeals for the D.C. Circuit, on which he served as chief judge from 1962 to 1978 and assumed senior status in 1979.

Famous decisions that Bazelon made included upholding the order to President Richard M. Nixon to produce the Watergate tapes and other decisions in support of individual rights. Most prominent in Bazelon's legal career were his decisions that declared that patients confined in public mental institutions have a right to treatment and those expanding the scope of the insanity defense.

When U.S. Supreme Court Justice Frankfurter became seriously ill in 1962, Judge Bazelon was one of two Jewish men who were suggested as his replacement. However, President John F. Kennedy instead nominated Arthur Goldberg. In 1988, Bazelon published *Questioning Authority: Justice and Criminal Law*, which exemplifies his reputation as a judge seeking honest disclosures from those in his presence.

Judge Bazelon died February 19, 1993, in Washington, D.C. (JM)

BEAME, ABRAHAM DAVID
Mayor of New York, 1974–1978

Born on March 20, 1906, in London, Abe Beame emigrated to the United States one year later. He attended city schools and the College of the City of New York, from which he earned a degree in accounting in 1928. After graduating, Beame became a teacher, working in public schools before opening an accounting firm.

Beame became involved in city government early in his professional career, serving in a variety of positions, including assistant budget director. Eventually he was promoted to budget director under Mayor Vincent Impellitteri. Beame won his first election, as city comptroller, in 1962. Following an unsuccessful candidacy for mayor in 1965, he was once again elected comptroller in 1969. In a campaign that focused on his qualifications to address the city's financial crisis, Beame was elected mayor of New York in 1973, receiving nearly seven hundred thousand votes.

As the first Jewish mayor of New York, Beame acknowledged the uniqueness of his position by stating shortly after being elected, "I hope to be a matchmaker in the years of my administration, wedding our people to their city, encouraging them to identify with this great metropolis that is their home." Beame entered office with the city of New York on the verge of bankruptcy. He was able to arrange annual federal loans of $2.3 billion to avert the crisis. Seeking reelection, Beame was defeated in the Democratic primary by Edward Koch, who went on to become the second Jewish mayor of the city.

Abraham Beame died in New York City on February 9, 2001. (DS)

BEILENSON, ANTHONY
Member of Congress, 1977–1997

Born in New Rochelle, New York, on October 26, 1932, Anthony Beilenson received a B.A from Harvard University in 1954 and an LL.B. from Harvard Law School in 1957. After his admittance to the California Bar in 1957, Beilenson began to practice law in Beverly Hills.

Beilenson served as a member of the California State Assembly from 1963 to 1967 and then in the State Senate from 1967 to 1977. His first run for federal office was a failed attempt as a peace candidate to the United States Senate in 1968. He was elected to the United States House of Representatives in 1976 from Los Angeles's Twenty-third District—known for being one of the most liberal and heavily Jewish parts of L.A. Early in his career, Beilenson was instrumental in the creation of the Santa Monica Mountains National Recreation Area. While in Congress, he served on both the Budget Committee, for which he chaired the Subcommittees on Budget and Process and on Reconciliation and Enforcement, and the Rules Committee, on which he chaired the Subcommittee on Rules of the House. His leadership of the Select Intelligence Committee was so widely praised that Speaker Thomas Foley extended his term during the 101st Congress. During the Persian Gulf War, President George H. W. Bush asked Beilenson to serve on an eighteen-member committee advising him on U.S. policy—a policy of which Beilenson became very critical. Throughout his career Beilenson also sought to protect elephants through banning ivory imports from countries without effective elephant conservation programs.

On his retirement in 1997, Beilenson's colleagues praised his avoidance of partisan confrontation. He and his wife Dolores Martin have three children. (AE)

BELMONT, AUGUST
Chair, Democratic National Committee, 1860–1872

Born the son of a wealthy Jewish landowner in the Rhenish Palatinate on December 8, 1816, August Belmont went to work for the House of Rothschild at age fourteen. Seven years later, he moved to New York and opened his own investment firm, serving as the Rothschild's American agent.

Naturalized as an American citizen in 1844, Belmont was a committed Democrat. His financial contributions to Franklin Pierce's 1852 presidential victory led to a diplomatic posting in Holland. After returning to the United States, Belmont backed Stephen A. Douglas for the 1860 presidential nomination and was named chair of the Democratic National Committee. When Douglas died in 1861, Belmont became the titular head of the party.

Belmont supported the Union in the Civil War and discouraged European financiers from investing in the Confederacy. He recruited General George B. McClellan to run for the presidency in 1864 and directed his unsuccessful campaign. After the war, Belmont favored reconciliation and split with many Democrats, especially midwesterners, because of his opposition to inflationary policies. He resigned as party chair in 1872 because of his dissatisfaction with the candidacies of Horatio Seymour in 1869 and Horace Greeley in 1872.

Belmont died at the age of seventy-four in 1890, a fabulously wealthy financier but no longer the political power behind the scenes he had been at mid-century. (LSM)

BENJAMIN, JUDAH PHILIP
Confederate Attorney General, Secretary of War, Secretary of State, 1861–1865; United States Senator, 1853–1861

"The most important American-Jewish diplomat before Henry Kissinger, the most eminent lawyer before Brandeis, the leading figure in martial affairs before Hyman Rickover, the greatest American-Jewish orator, and the most influential Jew ever to take a seat in the United States Senate," wrote historian Richard S. Tedlow about this remarkable American statesman.

Born on August 6, 1811, in Christiansted, St. Croix, West Indies, Judah Benjamin was the son of Philip Benjamin, a shopkeeper, and Rebecca de Mendes, of Portuguese Sephardic descent. Growing up in Charleston, South Carolina, he later attended Yale and then moved to New Orleans, where he studied law and was admitted to the bar. In 1833, Benjamin, a nonobservant Jew, married Natalie St. Martin, a Creole Catholic, and they had one child. They became estranged, and his enemies would later refer to him as "the Jew whose wife lives in Paris."

His career, nevertheless, rapidly progressed; he was elected to the Louisiana state legislature and by the legislature to the United States Senate. He helped write two state constitutions, and in the winter of 1852–1853, he was the first Jew to be offered a seat on the United States Supreme Court, which he declined.

After Louisiana seceded from the Union, Confederate President Jefferson Davis appointed him attorney general of the Confederacy. Soon after, he assumed the position of secretary of war, making him the second most important officeholder in the Confederacy. The military loss of Roanoke Island in 1862—a complicated story in which he was unjustly blamed—made him the most "unpopular and hated man in the Confederacy," and Benjamin was subjected to fierce anti-Jewish vitriol. Since Davis still considered him a valued adviser, he appointed Benjamin as secretary of state, his third portfolio.

In a public meeting in 1865, Benjamin advocated freeing the slaves, evoking additional anti-Jewish comments from his detractors. Using several disguises, Benjamin was able to flee the country during the last days of the Confederacy, finally arriving in England. He soon became a British barrister and wrote some brilliant legal works. Although he had not lived with his wife for forty years, Benjamin spent his final days with her in Paris. He died on May 6, 1884, and is buried in a Catholic cemetery.

Few Northern Jews have sought to defend Benjamin, a slaveholder, who was once termed an "Israelite with Egyptian principles." Ironically, Judah Benjamin, who had little interest in Jews and Judaism, as one historian noted, was a lightning rod for the growth of nineteenth-century American anti-semitism. (DA)

Source: Eli N. Evans, *Judah P. Benjamin: The Jewish Confederate* (New York: Free Press, 1989).

BERGER, SAMUEL (SANDY)
Presidential Adviser, 1993–2001

A *Washington Post* columnist once called Sandy Berger "an unheralded but central figure" in the Clinton White House. Sandy Berger first met Bill Clinton while serving as a speechwriter during George McGovern's 1972 campaign, and they developed a lifelong friendship that would eventually lead Berger not only to be central but very much heralded as one of the architects of Clinton's national security policy.

Born in Sharon, Connecticut, on October 28, 1945, Samuel Richard Berger grew up in Millerton, New York, a small upstate town. After graduating from Cornell and Harvard Law School, Berger worked as a legislative assistant for both Senator Harold E. Hughes (D-Ia.) and Congressman Joseph Resnick (D-N.Y.). He helped investigate the American Farm Bureau Federation and wrote a book critical of this powerful agricultural lobby, *Dollar Harvest: The Story of the Farm Bureau* (1971).

Berger later served as a legislative aide to New York City Mayor John V. Lindsay and then joined a Washington, D.C., law firm. He was soon recruited to the administration of President Jimmy Carter, to serve as deputy director of the policy planning staff at the Department of State. He helped write speeches for Secretary of State Cyrus Vance and was involved in a wide range of international economic and security matters.

After Carter lost the 1980 election, Berger returned to his law practice and then was among those who urged Bill Clinton to run for president. Berger served as a senior foreign policy adviser in the 1992 campaign and worked as part of the presidential transition team. He served as the deputy national security adviser during Clinton's first term. After Clinton's 1996 reelection, Berger became the chief national security adviser to the president and was generally regarded as his top adviser in crisis situations. (DA)

BERGER, VICTOR L.
Member of Congress, 1923–1929, 1911–1913

A founder of the American Socialist Party and the first socialist to be elected to the United States Congress, Victor Berger was forbidden from taking the oath of office after two victories because of his opposition to U.S. involvement in World War I.

Born on February 28, 1860, in Nieder Rebbah, Austria-Hungary, Berger emigrated to the United

States with his innkeeper parents, Ignatz and Julia, first settling near Bridgeport, Connecticut, and later moving to Milwaukee. From 1880 until 1890, Berger taught in the Milwaukee public schools and B'nai Jeshurun synagogue.

After meeting German-American socialists in the city, he pursued a career as a socialist journalist, serving as the editor and/or publisher of the *Wisconsin Vorwaerts, Social-Democratic Herald*, and the *Milwaukee Leader* from 1892 to 1929.

Joining with noted socialist Eugene V. Debs, Berger became active in local and national socialist circles, helping build a powerful radical movement in Milwaukee. He was successful as a Socialist Party candidate for Congress in 1910, after having lost one previous bid for that seat. As a United States Representative, he strongly supported labor and a wide range of social reforms, including old age pensions, unemployment insurance, women's suffrage, public works, and health insurance.

In 1919, Berger was convicted of violating the Espionage Act of 1917 because of his published antiwar writings. In November that year, the House adopted a resolution declaring that Berger was not entitled to take the oath of office. He was reelected during the same Congress and again excluded on January 10, 1920. The United States Supreme Court reversed his conviction, and Berger was elected three more times and seated without opposition.

Victor Berger primarily identified himself as a German-American who was born Jewish. Like many socialists he rejected both religion and nationalism; but, after learning about the pogroms against Jews throughout Europe, he modified his views and supported a Jewish homeland in Palestine.

On August 29, 1929, Berger was killed in a streetcar accident. His funeral was attended by thousands of Milwaukee residents. (DA)

Source: Sally M. Miller, *Victor Berger and the Promise of Constructive Socialism, 1910–1920* (Westport, Conn.: Greenwood, 1973).

BERKLEY, SHELLEY
Member of Congress, 1999–present

Shelley Berkley was born January 20, 1951, in South Fallsburg, New York, and moved to Las Vegas at age eleven. She was the student-body president at the University of Nevada–Las Vegas. In 1982, she was elected to the Nevada State Assembly, serving one term. Governor Bob Miller appointed Berkley to the Nevada University and Community College Board of Regents in 1990; she was subsequently reelected twice. Berkley won election to the United States House of Representatives as a Democrat from Nevada's First District in 1998. She was reelected in the 2000 elections. In Congress, she serves on the Small Business, Transportation, and Veterans' Affairs Committees.

Berkley is married to Larry Lehrner. (JS)

BERKMAN, ALEXANDER
Anarchist

Probably most known as the man who shot steel executive Henry Clay Frick, Alexander Berkman was a major leader of the American anarchist movement during the early years of the twentieth century.

Born in Vilna, Russia, on November 21, 1870, to a wealthy Jewish merchant family, he was raised in St. Petersburg. Although the city was normally barred to Jews, his father—who died when Alexander was thirteen—was allowed to stay because of his economic status. After his mother died a few years later, Berkman emigrated to the United States.

He quickly affiliated with an American Jewish anarchist group and met Russian immigrant Emma Goldman. They were involved with a campaign to free the men convicted in the Chicago Haymarket bombing and together studied anarchist writings.

In 1892, Berkman became enraged at the strikebreaking activity against Pittsburgh steelworkers, attacking Frick in that effort. Frick survived the attack, but the twenty-two-year-old Berkman was imprisoned for fourteen years.

After his release, Berkman was still an anarchist but became disillusioned with violence. He spent the next decade helping Emma Goldman publish her book and journal and also founded the Modern School in New Jersey. He helped raise money for striking workers in Lawrence, Massachusetts, and the families of union miners in Colorado.

After moving to San Francisco in 1916, Berkman edited his own anarchist newspaper, *The Blast*. When the United States entered World War I, Berkman was convicted of violating the Espionage Act and sentenced to two years in prison. When he was released in 1919, both Berkman and Goldman were deported to Russia. He quickly became disillusioned with the totalitarian Bolshevik government and published a book entitled *The Bolshevik Myth* (1925), one of the earliest critiques of Russian communism. After leaving Russia, he spent time in Sweden and Germany and later settled in France.

The Jewish Anarchist Federation of New York asked Berkman to write a primer on the anarchist movement. His work, *Now and After: The ABC of Communist Anarchism,* attacked capitalism, socialism, and communism.

Suffering from prostate cancer and chronic pain, he committed suicide on June 28, 1936. (DA)

BERMAN, HOWARD L.
Member of Congress, 1983–present

Born April 15, 1941, in Los Angeles, Howard Berman is highly regarded as both a legislator and a politician. The *Almanac of American Politics* has noted, "There are few House members who have made such an imprint on legislation in so many areas as Howard Berman." He has been an active and productive member of the Committees on the Judiciary and International Relations, and in 1997, he became the ranking minority member of the Committee on Standards of Official Conduct, better known as the Ethics Committee. Berman's first elective office was the California State Assembly, where he was elected majority leader in his freshman term.

For many years Berman served as the Democrats' chief whip on foreign aid bills. While he consistently scores near 90 percent on *Congressional Quarterly*'s Party Unity index of roll-call votes, Berman has coauthored measures with Republicans. Among his bipartisan efforts are a law authorizing embargoes on nations that condone terrorism (with Representative Henry Hyde), the False Claims Acts Amendments (with Senator Chuck Grassley), and an amendment to the 1996 immigration bill that would have stricken restrictions on legal immigration (with Representative Dick Chrysler). Berman's seat on the Judiciary Committee has made him an important player on immigration policy.

Berman and his brother Michael, a Los Angeles political consultant, lend their name to the "Berman–Waxman machine." Berman–Waxman is not a machine like those dominated by old-time political bosses; rather, it is an informal association of liberals whose tactics rely on modern political consulting and fund-raising instead of traditional patronage. (JS)

BERNAYS, EDWARD L.
Political Consultant

Born November 22, 1891, in Vienna, Austria, and moving to the United States as a youth, Edward Bernays, Sigmund Freud's nephew, began putting his uncle's theories to work in the marketplace soon after he graduated from Cornell University in 1912. When he went to work for America's biggest book publishers, he rejected the conventional advice, which suggested cutting prices to boost sales. Rather, he reasoned that "where there are bookshelves there will be books." So he got respected public figures to endorse the value of books, then persuaded architects and decorators to build shelves to store the precious volumes, which is why homes from that era have built-in bookshelves.

Hired to sell a product or service, Bernays sold whole new ways of behaving that reaped huge rewards for his clients and redefined the very texture of American life. Sometimes he appealed to consumers' best instincts; at other times he willfully deceived the public. In his most famous campaign, in the 1920s, Bernays recast smoking as an act of liberation for women, helping convince a generation of women to light up cigarettes that he suspected were deadly. Always, he displayed the brash, big thinking that was part P. T. Barnum and part J. P. Morgan, blended in a way that was uniquely E. L. Bernays. Bernays' techniques worked so well with corporate America that politicians could not resist trying them. America's number-one salesman helped Calvin Coolidge transform his image from sourpuss to sweet guy and worked with a series of other candidates over eighty years old, helping them pioneer scientific polls and use marketing methods to win over a skeptical public.

Bernays died on March 9, 1995, in Cambridge, Massachusetts. (LT)

Source: Larry Tye, *The Father of Spin: Edward L. Bernays and the Birth of Public Relations* (New York: Crown, 1998).

BERNSTEIN, CARL
Journalist and Author

Carl Bernstein was born on February 14, 1944, in Washington, D.C. While attending the University of Maryland, he worked as a copy boy for the *Washington Star* and eventually moved up through the journalistic ranks to the position of reporter with the *Washington Post.*

On June 17, 1972, a break-in occurred at the Watergate Hotel headquarters of the Democratic

National Committee. Teaming with fellow *Post* reporter Bob Woodward, Bernstein followed leads and compiled sources, regularly contributing front-page articles under a joint byline. Although their working relationship was often stormy, Bernstein and Woodward pursued the story for almost a year. Receiving the bulk of their information from lower-level government employees, Bernstein and Woodward hit pay dirt when a high-ranking government official, known to the public only as "Deep Throat," emerged as a major source. The Woodward and Bernstein articles in the *Post* were considered major factors in ending Richard M. Nixon's presidency.

By the time the full story of the scandal broke in March 1973, Bernstein and Woodward were working on a book about their investigations. Published in 1974, *All the President's Men* received critical acclaim and was followed up in 1976 by a book about the last fifteen months of the Nixon presidency entitled *The Final Days*. Bernstein and Woodward won numerous awards for their coverage of Watergate, including the Pulitzer Prize.

Bernstein currently lives and writes in Washington, D.C. (JSh)

Source: Adrian Havill, *Deep Truth: The Lives of Bob Woodward and Carl Bernstein* (Secaucus, N.J.: Carol, 1993).

BETTMAN, GILBERT
Attorney General of Ohio, 1928–1932

Born in Cincinnati, Ohio, on October 31, 1881, Gilbert Bettman graduated from Harvard College and Harvard Law School and was the commencement speaker at his Law School graduation. During World War I, he was assigned to the United States Army military intelligence division and subsequently worked for an American Legion committee on war insurance. Bettman helped draft congressional legislation to consolidate government benefits for veterans with disabilities, and he wrote an early draft of a bill that culminated in the establishment of the U.S. Veterans Bureau.

After many years as a partner in a Cincinnati law firm, Bettman became active in Republican Party politics and was elected the city's vice mayor in 1921. A law professor and later dean at the YMCA

Law School in Cincinnati, he was active in the local, state, and national bar associations. He served two terms—from 1928 until 1932—as attorney general of Ohio. In 1932, he was the Republican candidate for the U.S. Senate but was defeated. Bettman was elected judge of the Ohio Supreme Court in 1940 and served until his death on July 17, 1942. (DA)

BLATT, SOLOMON
South Carolina State Legislative Leader, 1933–1986

Serving in the South Carolina legislature for more than a half century, Solomon Blatt was recognized by the Council of State Governments as the longest-serving legislator in the United States. First elected to the state house in 1933, he was still a member when he died fifty-three years later. Blatt served as the House speaker of South Carolina from 1937 to 1947 and from 1951 to 1973.

Born on February 27, 1895, Solomon Blatt spent his entire life—except for World War I service in France—in South Carolina. His father, a Russian Jewish peddler, moved to Charleston, South Carolina. Aided by Jewish charitable organizations, his father soon opened a store in the railroad town of Blackville.

Blatt attended the University of South Carolina Law School and became a partner in a law practice in nearby Barnwell. He soon ran for the state legislature and was later elected to the House speakership, even though he was the only Jew in the General Assembly. When a derisive editorial about the "Barnwell Jew" appeared in a local newspaper, Blatt's colleagues and even political adversaries rallied to his defense, passing a resolution attacking religious intolerance.

Although urged to seek a state Supreme Court position, Blatt preferred to remain in his office as speaker of the House of Representatives. Generally conservative, he supported both right-to-work legislation and private power companies against the government-sponsored Rural Electrification Administration.

Solomon Blatt, who considered himself just a "darn good country lawyer," died on May 14, 1986. (DA)

Source: John K. Cauthen, *Speaker Blatt: His Challenges Were Greater* (Columbia: University of South Carolina Press, 1965).

BLITZER, WOLF
News Correspondent and Anchor

Wolf Blitzer, who holds a bachelor's in history from the State University of New York–Buffalo and a master's in international relations from Johns Hopkins University, has covered many groundbreaking international news events. He began his career as a journalist with the Reuters News Agency in Tel Aviv in 1972. He then served as the Washington correspondent for the *Jerusalem Post* before moving to television and joining the nascent Cable Network News (CNN) in 1990.

From 1990 until 1992, Blitzer was the military affairs correspondent for CNN at the Pentagon. He served as White House correspondent during the entire Clinton presidency.

Blitzer has been the host of CNN's *Late Edition* since 1998 and the senior anchor of *The World Today* since 1999. He won an Emmy Award for his coverage of the Oklahoma City bombing in 1996. Blitzer is also the author of two books: *Between Washington and Jerusalem: A Reporter's Notebook* (1985) and *Territory of Lies* (1989). The latter book is the story of Jonathan Jay Pollard, an American accused of spying on the United States for Israel. It received a Most Notable Book Award from the *New York Times Book Review* in 1989. (TW)

BLOOM, SOL
Member of Congress, 1923–1949

Congressman Sol Bloom served as the chair of the powerful House Foreign Relations Committee during and after World War II, after a very colorful earlier career as a theater producer, music publisher, and real estate developer.

Born in Pekin, Illinois, on March 9, 1870, Sol Bloom was the third of six children of Gershon and Sarah Bloom, Polish Jewish immigrants. His schooling was limited, and he was taught to read Hebrew and English by his religious mother. After his family moved to San Francisco, he began working in a factory at the age of seven. Ambitious and enterprising, he became interested in show business and was the assistant treasurer of a local theater while still a teenager.

After visiting the 1889 Paris Exposition, he arranged an American tour for a variety of show acts, including sword swallowers, scorpion eaters, and belly dancers. Four years later, he directed an amusement section of the Columbian Exposition in Chicago and is credited with originating the tune for the "Hootchy Kootchy." Bloom progressed in the entertainment business, moving with his wife, songwriter Evelyn Hechheimer, and their newborn daughter Vera to his business headquarters in New York in 1897. Quickly amassing a fortune in various business ventures, Bloom invested his money in Manhattan real estate development, building and renovating many theaters.

Having succeeded in the business world, Bloom changed course at age fifty, declaring his desire "to devote his life to public service." Asked by a Tammany Hall leader to run for Congress to fill the vacancy caused by the death of Samuel Marx, Democrat Bloom was elected in a January 1923 closely contested special election in the traditionally Republican "silk stocking" district.

Early in his career, Bloom was not an active legislator, though he was an ardent supporter of the New Deal. However, his relative lack of activity changed when he assumed the chairmanship of the House Foreign Relations Committee in 1939. Working closely with the Roosevelt administration, he managed a congressional compromise to ensure passage of the Lend-Lease Act. He also helped pass military draft extension legislation and the creation of the United Nations Relief and Rehabilitation Administration. As a result of his chairmanship and support for the president, he was given access to confidential war plans decided at the Casablanca conference. Some critics dubbed him "a Jewish warmonger." He was also criticized for not speaking out against the Holocaust. A strong supporter of Zionism, Bloom supported aid to the nascent Jewish state and opposed British policies in Palestine. Congressman Bloom was a delegate to the San Francisco conference that drafted the United Nations Charter, and he also lobbied for passage of the Marshall Plan.

Sol Bloom died of coronary thrombosis on March 7, 1949. (DA)

BLUMENTHAL, RICHARD
Attorney General of Connecticut, 1991–present

Richard Blumenthal was born February 13, 1947, in New York City. He graduated with honors from Harvard College (Phi Beta Kappa; magna cum laude) and Yale Law School, where he was editor in chief of the *Yale Law Journal*.

Blumenthal served as United States attorney for Connecticut from 1977 through 1981. An effective prosecutor, he was involved in successful prosecution of many major cases against civil rights violators, consumer frauds, organized crime, and environmental polluters. Blumenthal, a Democrat, was elected to the Connecticut state legislature in 1984. As a state representative, he was the chair of the Housing Committee and the Regulations Revenue and vice chair of the Judiciary Committee. In 1986, he was elected to the first of two terms in the state senate, and in 1990, he was elected Connecticut's attorney general. He was reelected in 1994 and again to an unprecedented third term in 1998. As attorney general, Blumenthal has been an advocate for consumers, the environment, children, and the civil rights of the citizens of Connecticut. (BMcN)

BLUMENTHAL, WERNER MICHAEL
Secretary of the Treasury, 1977–1979

W. Michael Blumenthal was born January 3, 1926, in Oranienburg, Germany. His family fled the Holocaust by escaping to China, where they stayed for eight years before moving to the United States in 1947. In 1951, Blumenthal graduated Phi Beta Kappa from the University of California–Berkeley. Subsequently, he received three graduate degrees from Princeton University: a master's in economics, a master's in public affairs, and a doctorate in economics.

Between 1954 and 1957, Blumenthal taught economics at Princeton University. After working in private industry for several years, he joined the Kennedy administration as deputy assistant secretary of state for economic affairs in 1961. He held that position until 1963, when he became the president's deputy special representative for trade negotiations. In 1967, Blumenthal began work for Bendix, a manufacturer for automotive and aerospace–electronics markets. Within five years, he was the chief executive officer of the corporation. In 1977, Blumenthal joined President Jimmy Carter's cabinet as secretary of the treasury, a post he held until 1979. Returning to private industry, he eventually engineered the creation of UNISYS, a communications systems company, from the merger of two smaller firms in 1986.

After retiring from business, Blumenthal moved to Berlin, Germany, to become the director of Berlin's new Jewish museum, which opened in 1999. (TW)

BOGGS, DANNY JULIAN
Judge, U.S. Court of Appeals, 1986–present

Danny Julian Boggs was born October 23, 1944, in Havana, Cuba. After coming to the United States, he graduated cum laude from Harvard College in 1965 and received a J.D. from the University of Chicago Law School. After spending time in private practice and serving as legal counsel to elected officials in Kentucky, he moved to Washington, D.C., to continue his career as an attorney for the government.

Boggs became assistant to the solicitor general of the United States in 1973 and was named deputy secretary of the United States Department of Energy in 1983. He was appointed to the U.S. Court of Appeals for the Sixth District by President Ronald Reagan in 1986. He is known for his support of judicial restraint and minimal governmental intervention.

Boggs lives in Arlington, Virginia, and is married with three children. (JM)

BONDI, AUGUST
Abolitionist

More than a century before young Jews joined in fighting for civil rights for African Americans in the Deep South in the 1960s, an Austrian Jewish immigrant joined with noted abolitionist John Brown in Kansas to help end slavery in the United States.

Born in Vienna on July 21, 1833, August Mendel Bondy (later changed to "Bondi") studied at the public secondary school, the Gymnasium, and became a member of a student revolutionary organization, the Vienna Academic Legion. The failure of the 1848 revolution convinced his parents to take the family to the United States, settling first in St. Louis. There he met Jacob Benjamin, a Bohemian immigrant, and they traveled to Kansas in 1855 to set up a trading post.

An adamant opponent of slavery, Bondi joined forces with John Brown and his followers. For more than two years, Bondi—along with his two Jewish compatriots, Jacob Benjamin and Theodore Weiner—fought against slavery in "Bleeding Kansas," in battles that were the precursor to the American Civil War. He took part in the Battle of Black Jack, fighting side by side with John Brown.

When the Civil War began, Bondi joined the Fifth Kansas Cavalry and fought for more than three years, achieving the rank of first sergeant. After the war, he settled in Salina, Kansas, becoming an attorney and businessman, and was involved in local civic affairs. A director of the Kansas State Historical Society, he presented the organization with the musket given to him by John Brown. Bondi died in 1907. (DA)

BOOKBINDER, HYMAN H.
American Jewish Committee Leader

Hyman H. Bookbinder, son of Louis and Rose Bookbinder, was born March 9, 1916. He earned a bachelor's degree at City College in New York in 1937. Bookbinder was an economist for the Amalgamated Clothing Workers (1938–1943 and 1946–1950). He served as a labor advocate for the Production Authority (1951–1953) and as a legislative representative for the Congress of Industrial Organizations (CIO; 1953–1955) and for the American Federation of Labor (AFL-CIO; 1955–1960). He was an assistant to the secretary of commerce (1961–1962) and served on the President's Committee on the Status of Women (1961–1963). Bookbinder was director of the Eleanor Roosevelt Memorial Foundation (1963–1964), executive officer of the President's Task Force on Poverty (1964), assistant director of the Office of Equal Opportunity (OEO), and special assistant to the vice president of the United States (1964–1967). He was named Washington, D.C., representative to the American Jewish Committee (1967) and representative emeritus in 1986, a position he continues to hold.

Bookbinder, who was chair of public policy advocates for the Corporation for Public Broadcasting (1972–1977), was a member of the Commission on the Holocaust (1979–1980) and the U.S. Holocaust Memorial Council (1980–1985), Washington chair of the ad hoc Coalition for the Ratification of the Genocide Treaty (1970–1987), and special adviser to Governor Michael Dukakis (1988). He was one of the founding members of the National Jewish Democratic Council.

Bookbinder has received numerous awards, including honorary degrees from the New School for Social Research and Hebrew Union College, the National Brotherhood Citation (1977), and the Franklin Delano Roosevelt Four Freedoms Medal (1990). (MP)

BOSCHWITZ, RUDOLPH ELI
United States Senator, 1978–1991

Rudy Boschwitz was born in Berlin, Germany, on November 7, 1930. He came to the United States as a child, after fleeing Nazi Germany. He attended Johns Hopkins University but then transferred to New York University, from which he earned his B.A. in 1950

and his law degree in 1953. After practicing law in New York City and serving in the Army Signal Corps, Boschwitz moved to Minnesota in 1963 and founded Plywood Minnesota, Inc., serving as its chairman.

Boschwitz was a member of the Republican National Committee from 1971 to 1978. In 1978, he was elected to a six-year term in the United States Senate, replacing Wendell Anderson, the former governor who had appointed himself to fill an unexpired term. Boschwitz, who served on the Agriculture, Nutrition, and Forestry Standing Committee, the Budget Committee, and the Foreign Relations Committee while in the Senate, won reelection in 1984. In 1990, he was challenged by a relatively unknown liberal college professor, Paul Wellstone, in the rare occurrence of one Jew running against another in a state with relatively few Jews. Though outspent six times, Wellstone narrowly defeated Boschwitz. Boschwitz challenged Wellstone again in 1996 but did not come close to regaining his former seat. (MW)

BOXER, BARBARA
United States Senator, 1993–present;
Member of Congress, 1983–1993

Though born in Brooklyn, New York, on November 11, 1940, and educated in that borough, right through her graduation from Brooklyn College, Barbara Boxer has represented the citizens of California throughout her entire political career. Moving to California in 1965, Boxer worked on civic and local campaigns before seeking a seat on the Marin County Board of Supervisors. Initially unsuccessful, she was elected to that board in 1976 and served six years.

Boxer moved up to the House of Representatives when John Burton, for whom she had worked, unexpectedly retired in 1982. During her five terms in the House, she frequently provided headline material for national news, especially with her vigorous opposition to the Persian Gulf War and when she led a group of female House members to the Senate to protest the treatment of Anita Hill during the Clarence Thomas confirmation hearings.

Boxer was elected to the Senate in 1992, on the same day that Dianne Feinstein was elected to fill the remaining years of the other seat from California; thus, the state elected two Jewish women from northern California to the Senate at the same time. Along with Paul Wellstone of Minnesota and Edward Kennedy of Massachusetts, Boxer has been among the most outspoken liberal Democrats in the Senate throughout her service. She earns a near-perfect rating from Americans for Democratic Action and is outspoken on many of the issues liberals hold most dear.

Following her feminist instincts, Boxer received national attention when she led a caucus of female members against Oregon senator Bob Packwood, who had been accused of sexual harassing his female staff. She has also garnered attention in fighting the Republican effort to ban so-called partial birth abortions. Active in the legislative arena, she has sponsored a wide range of legislation, including environmental protection laws, the Family and Medical Leave Act, the Freedom of Access to Clinic Entrances Act, and a bill to protect worker pensions. She has consistently opposed balanced-budget amendments and tax cuts for the wealthy. She remains most recognized for her pugnacious style and unabashed liberalism. (JK)

BRANDEIS, LOUIS DEMBITZ
Associate Justice of the Supreme Court, 1916–1939

The first Jewish Supreme Court justice and probably one of the most brilliant jurists to serve on the high court, Louis D. Brandeis was an avowed secularist who had virtually no involvement in organized Jewish religious life but eventually became a leader of the American Zionist movement.

Born on November 13, 1856, in Louisville, Kentucky, Brandeis was the son of Adolph, a successful grain merchant, and Frederika Dembitz. His mother disdained religious activities and taught her children to respect the ethical teachings of all faiths. Although lacking a college degree, Brandeis entered the Harvard Law School at the age of eighteen and graduated in 1877 with the highest grades in the law school's history at that time.

A successful Boston lawyer, Brandeis became sympathetic to the plight of the working person and argued many cases on the side of labor without compensation. The press soon dubbed him the "people's attorney." His "Brandeis briefs,"

which used social data to buttress legal arguments, presaged a new direction in American jurisprudence. Impressed with Brandeis's brilliance and integrity, President Woodrow Wilson nominated him to the Supreme Court in 1916 on the death of Justice Lamar.

The Senate debate on Brandeis's confirmation was often bitter. One supporter characterized the opposition as due to the fact that "Mr. Brandeis is an outsider, successful and a Jew." His opponents were among the most powerful individuals in the country, including former president William Howard Taft. He was finally confirmed by a 47–22 margin on June 1, 1916.

For more than two decades on the bench, Justice Brandeis wrote prolabor opinions and adamantly defended the rights of the individual against the government. In a famous wiretap case—*Olmstead v. United States*—Brandeis asserted Americans had the "right to be left alone," a phrase that has now become a venerable part of American jurisprudence.

Despite his nonreligious upbringing, Brandeis developed a strong kinship to his fellow Jews after serving as a mediator in a New York garment workers' strike. He later became active in the nascent American Zionist movement. In 1914, he became chair of the Provisional Committee for General Zionist Affairs. Some historians believe that his close relationship with President Wilson helped secure U.S. support for the Balfour Declaration. Brandeis fervently believed that love of America and Zionism were mutually compatible ideals. "To be good Americans we must be better Jews, and to be better Jews, we must become Zionists," he stated.

Feeling the burden of serving on the Court was too great, Louis Brandeis resigned at the age of eighty-three. He died two years later of a heart attack on October 5, 1941. (DA)

BREYER, STEPHEN GERALD
Associate Justice, United States Supreme Court, 1994–present; Judge, Court of Appeals, 1980–1994

Stephen Gerald Breyer was born on August 15, 1938, in San Francisco. He earned two bachelor's degrees, both with honors, one from Stanford University (1959) and another from the University of Oxford (1961, as a Marshall Scholar).

Following his graduation from Harvard Law School in 1964, Breyer served as a clerk for United States Supreme Court Justice Arthur J. Goldberg. Between 1965 and 1967, he worked as assistant to the assistant attorney general, focusing on antitrust regulations. In 1967, he began teaching at Harvard Law School, also serving as professor at Harvard's John F. Kennedy School of Government beginning in 1978.

In addition to his teaching duties, Breyer served in various government posts. In 1973, he worked as assistant special prosecutor for the Justice Department during the Watergate scandal. He was special counsel to the United States Senate Judiciary Committee from 1974 to 1975 and became its chief counsel in 1979, working on federal criminal law and on the deregulation of the airline and trucking industries.

In 1980, he was appointed to the U.S. First Circuit Court of Appeals in Boston, becoming chief judge in 1990. Following Justice Harry Blackmun's retirement, President Bill Clinton appointed him associate justice of the Supreme Court in 1994. He is known for his pragmatic judicial approach and his opposition to direct government intervention into business.

Breyer is the author of a number of books, including *The Federal Power Commission and the Regulation of Energy* (1974), *Regulation and Its Reform* (1982), and *Breaking the Vicious Circle: Toward Effective Risk Regulation* (1993). (YF)

BRODER, DAVID SALZER
Journalist and Columnist

Born September 11, 1929, in Chicago Heights, Illinois, David Broder earned a bachelor's and a master's from the University of Chicago in 1946 and 1951, respectively.

His Washington career began in 1955 at *Congressional Quarterly*, where he worked until 1960. From 1960 until 1965, he was a reporter with the *Washington Star*. Broder then moved to the Washington bureau of the *New York Times*. In 1966, he joined the staff of the *Washington Post*. He was promoted to associate editor of the *Post* in 1975, a position he continues to hold today.

In 1973, Broder was awarded a Pulitzer Prize in journalism. He received the Elijah Parrish Lovejoy Award for excellence in journalism from Colby College in 1990 and a Lifetime Achievement Award from the National Society of Newspaper Columnists in 1997. (TW)

BROWN, HAROLD
Secretary of Defense, 1977–1981

Harold Brown was born September 19, 1927, in New York City. He was educated at Columbia University, receiving his B.A. in 1945, an M.A. in 1946, and a Ph.D. in physics in 1949.

Brown began his career as a physics lecturer at Columbia and the Stevens Institute of Technology. He moved on to E. O. Lawrence Radiation Lab between 1950 and 1960. From 1952 to 1960, Brown served as the director of the Lawrence Livermore National Laboratory. For the next four years, he was the director of defense research and engineering at the Department of Defense. President Lyndon B. Johnson appointed Brown secretary of the Air Force in 1965. Throughout the 1960s, he was a United States delegate at the Strategic Arms Limitation Talks (SALT).

Brown, a Democrat, became president of the California Institute of Technology in 1969; he stayed there until 1977, when he accepted President Jimmy Carter's invitation to return to Washington as secretary of defense, a post he held throughout the Carter administration. With Carter's defeat, Brown returned to the private sector, holding several positions with private corporations and serving on the boards of directors for several companies, including IBM and Mattel.

In 1993, he was awarded the prestigious Enrico Fermi Award for his contributions to science and technology in America. Since 1990, Brown has been the managing director of Warburg Pincus and a member of the Washington, D.C.–based Center for Strategic and International Studies. (TW)

BROWNSTEIN, RON
Political Correspondent and Analyst

Ron Brownstein was born in New York City on April 6, 1958. He received a B.A. in English literature from the State University of New York–Binghamton in 1979.

Following graduation, Brownstein began his writing career as a senior staff writer for Ralph Nader. He left that position in 1983 to become White House correspondent for the *National Journal*.

Beginning in 1987, Brownstein served as a contributing editor for the *Los Angeles Times*. In 1989 he left the *National Journal* to report full time for the *Times*. Between 1989 and 1993, he was a national correspondent for the paper. He then was named national political correspondent. He left the *Times* in 1997 to serve as chief political correspondent for *U.S. News & World Report* but returned to the paper within a year. Currently, he serves as a national political correspondent and also writes the "Washington Outlook" column.

After serving as a regular panelist on CBS's *Face the Nation* from 1995 to 1997, Brownstein became a political analyst with CNN's *Inside Politics* in 1997. Brownstein has written several books and has appeared on *Meet the Press, Nightline, Good Morning America, The Today Show,* and *Larry King Live.* (TW)

BURNS, ARTHUR F.
Chair, Federal Reserve Board, 1970–1978;
Chair, President's Council of Economic Advisers,
1953–1956

On April 27, 1904, Arthur Frank Burns was born in Stanislau, Austria. His family moved to Bayonne, New Jersey, when he was ten. In 1925, Burns graduated Phi Beta Kappa from Columbia University, receiving his master's degree that same year. Burns later also received a Ph.D. from Columbia University.

Burns taught economics at Rutgers from 1930 until 1944, when he moved to Columbia University. In 1953, President Dwight D. Eisenhower brought Burns to Washington as the chairman of the President's Council of Economic Advisers. Burns improved the reputation of the council by removing it from politics and running it as an advisory panel of professional economists. In 1956, however, he returned to teaching at Columbia. President Richard M. Nixon convinced Burns to return to Washington in 1969 as a White House counselor with the condition that Burns would succeed William McChesney Martin as chair of the Federal Reserve Board. After assuming the position in February 1970, the conservative Burns supported the independence of the board and warned against the dangers of inflation. Burns's chairmanship ended in 1978 when President Jimmy Carter declined to renominate him. Between 1981 and 1985, Burns served as President Ronald Reagan's ambassador to West Germany. Throughout the 1980s, Burns was active in the American Enterprise Institute, where he continued to deal with public policy issues.

Arthur Burns died in Baltimore on June 26, 1993, at the age of eighty-three. (TW)

BURTON, SALA GALANT
Member of Congress, 1983–1987

Born on April 1, 1925, in Bialystok, Poland, Sala Galant and her parents fled to the United States ahead of Nazi occupation forces in the late 1930s. In San Francisco, she attended public schools and eventually San Francisco University. She began her career working as associate director for the California Public Affairs Institute.

Politics became her primary concern after she met her husband, Philip Burton, in 1950. A Democrat and political activist, he spent nearly two decades in Congress, championing liberal causes. Sala Burton helped organize the California Democratic Council in the 1950s and served as its vice president between 1951 and 1954. From 1957 to 1959, she served as president of the San Francisco Democratic Women's Forum.

Burton was elected to fill the vacancy caused by her husband's death, in a special election in June 1983. She was reelected on her own in 1984 and 1986. A member of the Education and Labor Committee and the House Rules Committee, she continued to carry on her husband's liberal policies. Previously viewed as the "shy wife," once in Congress she became one of the strongest supporters of national Democratic Party policies, advocating for poor people, education, the environment, and arms reduction.

Less than a month after being sworn in for her third term of office as part of the 100th Congress, Sala Burton died of complications from cancer on February 1, 1987. (JW)

C

CAHAN, ABRAHAM
Newspaper Editor

One of the most influential Jewish journalists of the twentieth century, Abraham Cahan edited *The Forward,* the leading Yiddish newspaper in the world. His turn-of-the-century novels are currently taught in college and university American literature courses throughout the country.

Born in Podberezy, Lithuania, on July 7, 1860, Cahan attended the Vilna Teachers Institute before emigrating to the United States in 1882. Soon after arriving on Manhattan's Lower East Side, he began writing for Yiddish newspapers. He then briefly became a reporter for the *New York Commercial Advertiser* under the editorship of the famous muckraker, Lincoln Steffens. After cofounding *The Forward* in 1897, Cahan became the editor in chief, a position he held for the next half century. Described by historian Ronald Sanders as the "immigrants' friend and confidant," *The Forward* attained an astonishingly high circulation of 250,000 and was published in eleven cities. The newspaper was a vigorous advocate of both organized labor and democratic socialism and also published a wide range of intellectual, cultural, and social features. The *"Bintl briv,"* a personal advice column, was hugely popular among its immigrant readership.

Cahan was also a fiction writer and deemed the "new star of realism" by the noted literary critic, W. D. Howells. His popular novel *The Rise of David Levinsky* (1917) describes the life of a successful garment manufacturer who became alienated with materialism.

Abraham Cahan died on August 31, 1951. (DA)

CANTOR, ERIC
Member of Congress, 2001–present

Eric Cantor was born June 6, 1963, in Richmond, Virginia. He received his undergraduate degree from the George Washington University in 1985. He eared a law degree from William and Mary in 1988 and a master's degree in real estate development from Columbia in 1989.

Cantor, a Republican, was elected to the House of Representatives from Virginia's Seventh District after Thomas J. Bliley Jr.'s retirement. Cantor had cut his teeth on politics by interning for Bliley in 1982; he maintained the connection and served as campaign chair for Bliley's most recent reelections. Cantor's personal political career began with election to the Virginia House of Delegates in 1991; he was reelected four times before leaving to run for Congress. Cantor, a successful lawyer and real estate developer, is regarded among House leadership as one of the brightest political stars of the GOP 2001 freshman class. He comes to Washington advocating limited government, lower taxes, and a stronger military.

Cantor is a member of the board of directors at the Jewish Community Center in Richmond as well as member of the board of trustees of the Virginia Holocaust Museum. (BMcN)

CANTOR, JACOB AARON
Member of Congress, 1913–1915

Born in New York City on December 6, 1854, Jacob Aaron Cantor attended the local public schools and University Law School, the law division of the College of the City of New York. After working as a reporter on the *New York World* and practicing law in the city, he was elected to the New York State Assembly (1885–1887) and then served as president of the state senate and also acting lieutenant governor of New York (1893–1894).

After leaving the state legislature, he was elected on a reform ticket as president of the borough of Manhattan. In 1913, the Democrat Cantor was elected to the Sixty-third Congress to fill the va-

cancy in the Twentieth District in New York City. After failing to win reelection, he served as president of the New York City Tax Commission until his death on July 2, 1921. (DA)

CARDIN, BENJAMIN L.
Member of Congress, 1987–present

Benjamin Cardin was born in Baltimore on October 5, 1943. At age twenty-three, he was elected to the Maryland House of Delegates and served from 1966 until his election to Congress in 1987. In the Maryland House, Cardin chaired the Ways and Means Committee from 1974 to 1979 and was speaker from 1979 until his departure in 1986.

In the United States House of Representatives, Cardin sits on the Ways and Means Committee. He is the ranking Democratic member of the Subcommittee on Human Resources. Cardin's legislative record has focused on health care and Social Security. He has been especially active in the area of managed care reform, and his proposal to reinstate the self-employment tax deduction for health insurance premiums passed the House with strong bipartisan support.

Concerned about the ethical standards of public servants, Cardin has served as the chair of the Special Study Commission on Maryland Public Ethics Law, on the Committee on Standards of Official Conduct during the 1996 investigation of then-Speaker Newt Gingrich, and as cochair of the Bipartisan Ethics Task Force in the House of Representatives. (JS)

CARDOZO, BENJAMIN
Associate Justice, United States Supreme Court, 1932–1938

Descended from Sephardic Jews, Benjamin Cardozo occupied the so-called scholar's seat on the

United States Supreme Court. His predecessor was Oliver Wendell Holmes Jr., and he was succeeded in turn by Felix Frankfurter, Arthur Goldberg, and Abe Fortas. Prominent personalities illuminated his life: Cardozo was tutored before college by the legendary writer Horatio Alger Jr., and he was a cousin to Emma Lazarus.

Born on May 24, 1870, in Manhattan, Benjamin—both of whose parents died by his teenage years—was mostly raised by his older sister, Ellen. At age fifteen, he was admitted to Columbia University and graduated with honors in four subjects. After studying at Columbia's School of Law, he was admitted to the New York Bar and began a brilliant legal career in the Empire State, serving as a New York State Supreme Court judge, a Court of Appeals judge, and then the Chief Judge of the New York State Court of Appeals. An elegant prose stylist, he wrote more than five hundred opinions from 1913 to 1932.

On February 15, 1932, President Herbert Hoover nominated Cardozo to the United States Supreme Court, and he received quick Senate confirmation. The *New York Times* described the unanimous support as "quite without precedent." Although he served on the Court for only six years, Cardozo wrote many liberal opinions on a largely conservative court. He supported the constitutionality of New Deal legislation and the liberal view of First Amendment protections.

A bachelor known as "the hermit philosopher," Cardozo was a lifelong member of Shearith Israel, the venerable Spanish-Portuguese synagogue in Manhattan. Although he was nonobservant, he was deeply proud and respectful of his heritage. During a synagogue controversy, he spoke eloquently and persuasively in favor of maintaining separate seating for men and women.

After a long illness, Benjamin Cardozo died on July 9, 1938, in Port Chester, New York. (DA)

Source: Andrew L. Kaufman, *Cardozo* (Cambridge, Mass.: Harvard University Press, 1998).

CELLER, EMANUEL
Member of Congress, 1923–1973

One of the longest-serving members of Congress in U.S. history, Emanuel Celler, known as "Pro labor,

New Dealer, Trustbuster Celler," represented his district for almost fifty years, serving under nine presidents and for many years as chair of the powerful House Judiciary Committee.

Born in Brooklyn, New York, on May 6, 1888, Celler attended Columbia College and Law School. After practicing law in the city, he ran for and was elected to Congress from Brooklyn's Tenth District, beginning his first term in 1923. Although this first election was an upset victory, his campaigns in subsequent decades resulted in huge winning margins over his opponents.

Beginning in his first term, Celler supported liberal causes, the whole gamut of New Deal legislation: prolabor laws, Social Security, the Tennessee Valley Authority, and so forth. He was a longtime critic of immigration quotas and helped pass displaced-persons legislation following World War II. Celler was also a key figure in the passage of the liberal Immigration and Naturalization Act of 1965, known as the Hart–Celler Act.

Celler was a vigorous and vocal opponent of Senator Joseph A. McCarthy and spoke out against the House Un-American Activities Committee and its investigations. Under the House seniority system, Celler became a ranking Democrat on the House Judiciary Committee and was a major supporter of civil rights legislation from the 1950s through the height of the movement in the next two decades.

From the age of twenty-five, when he first read Herzl's *Jewish State,* Celler, a Reform Jew, was an active and vocal supporter of Jewish statehood. *Time* once termed him "Zionist Celler." During World War II, President Franklin D. Roosevelt confided in him about Churchill's support for a Jewish homeland in Palestine after the end of the war.

Celler attended the United Nations sessions on the partition of Palestine and visited the country shortly before statehood was declared, meeting with David Ben-Gurion. While Celler supported President Harry S. Truman's Marshall Plan and foreign aid, he opposed a loan to Great Britain because of its policy toward Palestine.

As a powerful member of the Judiciary Committee, he coauthored the Celler–Kefauver Anti-Merger Act of 1950, barring business mergers achieved through acquisition of assets.

In later years, his support of the Vietnam War and his conservative opposition to the Equal Rights Amendment antagonized a growing number of his constituents. In an upset victory in 1972, young attorney Elizabeth Holtzman defeated him in the Democratic primary. After serving twenty-five terms in the United States House of Representatives, Celler returned to New York to resume his law practice. He died on January 15, 1981. (DA)

Source: Emanuel Celler, *You Never Leave Brooklyn: The Autobiography of Emanuel Celler* (New York: Day, 1953).

CHOTINER, MURRAY
Adviser to Richard Nixon, 1946–1974

One of the first paid political consultants, Murray Chotiner was born in Pittsburgh on October 4, 1909. He graduated from the University of California–Los Angeles in 1926 and earned his law degree at Southwestern University. Chotiner practiced law in California and in 1944 was elected president of the California Republican Assembly. As president, Chotiner sent letters to all county unit presidents with suggestions for helping Republicans get elected.

From the beginning of Richard Nixon's political career, Chotiner was a key adviser. Nixon first won a seat in the House in 1946; Chotiner set his political strategy. In 1950, Nixon sought to move up to the United States Senate. In California at the time, one could run in both parties' primary elections at the same time, a process know as cross-filing. Chotiner had Nixon cross-file in the Democratic primary and sent campaign leaflets to registered Democrats during the primary with the message "As One Democrat to Another." The leaflet never disclosed Nixon's true party identity but referred to him as Congressman Nixon and as "The Man Who Broke the Hiss Espionage Case." On primary eve the *Los Angeles Daily News* accused Nixon of misrepresenting himself. In his letter to Democrats, Chotiner had Nixon imply that Helen Gahagan Douglas was a communist; she consequently became known as the "Pink Lady." Nixon was successful in the campaign; the effect of Chotiner's strategy was to taint Nixon's reputation among Democrats for the rest of his political career.

Chotiner stayed on as a Nixon adviser as he rose to vice president and eventually president. His tactics caused controversy again in the 1972 election. In that campaign, Chotiner planted paid spies in the McGovern campaign organization so that Nixon would understand its mechanics, an action possibly related to the Watergate break-in. Prosecutors considered charging Chotiner with criminal intent, but Chotiner's death on January 30, 1974, as a result of an auto collision, ended their investigation.

When some suggested that Nixon get Chotiner, his longtime Jewish friend, to defend him during Watergate, Nixon's tapes reveal him saying, "It's the Jew business. I don't want to be soft on the Jews. That's one problem. But he won't, I don't think." (MP)

CHUDOFF, EARL
Member of Congress, 1949–1958

Earl Chudoff was born November 15, 1907, in Philadelphia, where he would remain most of his life. Educated in the local public school system and the Wharton School of the University of Pennsylvania, Chudoff earned his law degree from the University of Pittsburgh Law School, was admitted to the bar in 1933, and returned to Philadelphia to practice law.

From 1936 to 1939, Chudoff acted as the building and loan examiner for the Pennsylvania State Department of Banking. Voters elected him to the Pennsylvania House of Representatives as a Democrat in 1940; he held that seat through 1948; simultaneously, he served in the United States Coast Guard Reserve from 1942 to 1945. Chudoff was elected to the United States House of Representatives in 1948 and won reelection four times. He resigned his seat upon his election to the position of justice on the Philadelphia Court of Common Pleas, on which he served until his retirement in 1974.

Chudoff died on May 17, 1993, at the age of eighty-five. (CF)

CITRON, WILLIAM MICHAEL
Member of Congress, 1935–1939

Born in New Haven, Connecticut, on August 29, 1896, William Citron attended grammar and high school in the Nutmeg State. He was commissioned an army second lieutenant before graduating from Wesleyan University and Harvard Law School. After being admitted to the bar and starting his law practice in Middletown, Connecticut, Citron was elected to the State House of Representatives, serving as Democratic minority leader during two sessions. While he was an unsuccessful congressional candidate in 1928, he later was elected as a Democrat to both the Seventy-fourth and Seventy-fifth Congresses. After losing a third election bid, Citron became chair of the Housing Authority of Middletown from 1940 to 1942.

During World War II, Citron rose to the rank of major in the Corps of Military Police, serving in Africa until a physical disability forced him into retirement. In his later years, he was a commander of the Connecticut Disabled American Veterans and a member of the Connecticut Veterans Reemployment and Advisory Commission.

William Citron died in Titusville, Florida, on June 7, 1976. (DA)

COHEN, BENJAMIN VICTOR
Presidential Adviser, 1933–1952

A brilliant disciple of Supreme Court Justice Felix Frankfurter, Ben Cohen became part of President Franklin D. Roosevelt's celebrated "brain trust," crafting major domestic legislation during the New Deal; he later served as an international relations expert during the Truman administration.

Born in Muncie, Indiana, on September 23, 1894, Benjamin Cohen was the son of Polish immigrant Moses Cohen, a successful ore dealer, and Sarah Ringold. Cohen received his college degree from the University of Chicago at age fifteen and a law degree from that university one year later. He went on to Harvard Law School and obtained a doctorate in law.

Cohen became an expert on corporate reorganization, and his clients included some of the nation's largest corporations. But he also served as a volunteer counsel for the National Consumers' League and worked on a draft model minimum-wage law for women.

Encouraged by Frankfurter's mentor, Justice Louis D. Brandeis, Cohen served as a counsel for the American Zionist movement from 1919 to 1921 and went to the Paris Peace Conference to help negotiate the Palestine Mandate.

During the New Deal, Cohen helped draft major legislation, including the Securities and Exchange Act of 1934 and the Fair Labor Standards Act of 1938. From 1943 to 1945, he served as general counsel to the Office of War Mobilization and then became a close adviser to Secretary of State James F. Byrnes. During the Truman administration, Cohen continued his interest in foreign policy, serving as a member of the U.S. delegation to the United Nations from 1948 to 1952 and also to the UN Disarmament Commission.

A shy and self-effacing bachelor who delivered few speeches and avoided the public eye, Benjamin Cohen died on August 15, 1983, in Washington, D.C. (DA)

COHEN, EDWIN S.
Undersecretary of the Treasury, 1972–1973

An expert on tax reform, Edwin Cohen was a major author of the Tax Reform Act of 1969, a milestone in tax legislation.

Born in Richmond, Virginia, on September 27, 1914, Cohen was the son of LeRoy S. and Miriam Rosenheim Cohen. His great-grandfather, Maximilian J. Michelbacher, had arrived in the city in 1846 and had been the first rabbi of Congregation Beth Ahabah.

A graduate of the University of Richmond, Cohen received his law degree from the University of Virginia in 1936. While working as a tax law expert for a prominent New York law firm, Cohen consulted for both the House Committee on Ways and Means (1956–1958) and the Advisory Group to the Commissioner of Internal Revenue (1967–1968). He was appointed the assistant secretary of the treasury for tax policy in 1969 and promoted to undersecretary of the treasury from 1972 to 1973.

After leaving government, Cohen was a partner in the prestigious Washington, D.C., firm of Covington and Burling and also taught at the University of Virginia Law School, Cardozo Law School, Chicago–Kent College of Law, and the University of Miami School of Law.

A bespectacled, diminutive man, Cohen was friendly with many Washington power brokers during the Nixon administration. He and his wife, Helen Herz, reside in Charlottesville, Virginia. (DA)

COHEN, HERMAN J.
Assistant Secretary of State for African Affairs, 1989–1993

Although Ambassador Herman Cohen held only a subcabinet position, he was a most influential diplomat on African affairs during the George H. W. Bush administration.

Known as "Hank," Herman Cohen, the son of Morris Cohen and Fannie Zauzner, was born in New York City on February 10, 1932. After graduating with high honors from CCNY in 1953, he served in the United States Army. He then joined the Foreign Service and became a labor attaché at various African U.S. embassies. Growing up in a working-class New York Jewish family, Cohen found the African labor movements more democratic than their governments.

From 1977 to 1980, he was the United States ambassador to Senegal and Gambia. After returning to the United States, he served as deputy assistant secretary for intelligence and research at the State Department (1980–1984) and deputy assistant secretary for personnel (1984–1986).

After a stint as the senior director of African Affairs at the National Security Council during the last years of the Reagan administration, Ambassador Cohen became the assistant secretary of state for African affairs in 1989. In this role, he played a major role in American responses to crises in many trouble spots, including Ethiopia, Liberia, Mozambique, Somalia, and Zaire. He was closely involved with South African officials during the historic period culminating in black African majority rule. The

United States State Department has awarded Herman Cohen the personal rank of career ambassador, an honorary designation accorded to only about a dozen other distinguished diplomats. (DA)

COHEN, WILBUR JOSEPH
Secretary of Health, Education, and Welfare, 1968–1969

Known as both the architect of Medicare and an expert on Social Security, Wilbur Cohen was an influential policy official during both the Kennedy and Johnson administrations.

Born in Milwaukee, Wisconsin, on June 10, 1913, Cohen was the son of Aaron Cohen and Bessie Rubenstein, managers of a grocery store. After graduating from the University of Wisconsin in 1934, he worked with the Committee on Economic Security, a New Deal agency that helped create the Social Security Act. Cohen was involved for the next two decades in both legislative and executive branch efforts to expand Social Security coverage and health insurance. In the mid-1950s, he left the government to teach public welfare administration at the University of Michigan School of Social Work. He continued to advise both government and elected officials about Social Security and medical assistance for the elderly. His book *Retirement Policies in Social Security* helped establish his national stature as an expert on the subject.

During the Kennedy administration, Cohen was appointed assistant secretary of health, education, and welfare (HEW) and was instrumental in creating Medicare legislation, which was finally passed after Lyndon Johnson's landslide election in 1964. President Johnson appointed Cohen as HEW secretary, a post in which he served from March 23, 1968, to January 20, 1969. Among Cohen's most significant accomplishments were the creation of community health programs and an increase in medical research funding. After leaving government, he served as the dean of the University of Michigan School of Education and was president of the American Public Welfare Association.

Cohen married Eloise Bittel, a Baptist raised in the Texas hill country, and they had three children. While attending a gerontology conference in Seoul, South Korea, Wilbur Cohen died on May 18, 1987. (DA)

COHEN, WILLIAM WOLFE
Member of Congress, 1927–1929

Born in Brooklyn on September 6, 1874, William Wolfe Cohen attended the New York City public schools. After working in his father's shoe business, he started his own stock brokerage firm and became a member of the New York Stock Exchange and a director of both the New York Cotton Exchange and the Chicago Board of Trade. Active in Democratic Party politics, he was chair of a Tammany Hall finance committee. In 1926, he was elected to the Seventieth Congress from the Seventeenth District in New York, serving only one term. He was not a candidate for renomination to Congress in 1928 and resumed his former business activities on his return to New York.

Cohen was also very involved in Jewish philanthropies and civic organizations, serving as a trustee of the Home of the Daughters of Jacob and a director of the Federation of the New York Guild for Jewish Blind. In addition, he was president of the Jewish Council of Greater New York and of the New York chapter of the American Jewish Congress.

William Cohen died on October 12, 1940. (DA)

COPPERSMITH, SAMUEL
Member of Congress, 1993–1995

Samuel Coppersmith was born in Johnstown, Pennsylvania, on May 22, 1955. He attended Harvard University, graduating with an A.B. degree in 1976. From 1977 until 1979, Coppersmith served as a Foreign Service officer with the United States Department of State, with postings in Spain, Trinidad, and Washington, D.C. He left the Foreign Service to attend law school at Yale, receiving his J.D. in 1982 and practicing law in Phoenix, Arizona, for the next decade.

Though active in the political campaigns of others, Coppersmith had not seriously considered running for office himself during this time. Indeed, he decided to run for Congress only one week prior to the primary filing deadline. Running in a historically Republican district, Coppersmith won an upset victory by a margin of six percentage points, thus becoming the first Democrat elected from his district since 1950.

While in the House, Coppersmith served on the Committee on Science, Space, and Technology. He was an economic conservative who took more liberal positions on social issues. For example, his prochoice position on the abortion question reflected a longtime commitment to that stance; earlier he had served as president of Planned Parenthood in northern and central Arizona.

Coppersmith left the House in 1994 to run for an open Senate seat. Hampered by a close primary in which his fifty-nine-vote victory was not confirmed until the completion of a recount only six weeks before the general election, he lost to fellow House member, Republican John Kyl. (MW)

D

DASH, SAMUEL
Chief Counsel, Senate Watergate Committee, 1973–1974

Best known as chief counsel during Watergate from 1973 to 1974, Samuel Dash was born on February 27, 1925, and raised in Philadelphia. While in college, he enlisted as an Army Air Corps bombardier, served in Italy during World War II, yet managed to graduate first in his class at Temple University. After graduating from Harvard Law School, he taught at Northwestern University and joined the Chicago Crime Commission. An undercover investigator, he discovered widespread corruption in the lower courts, resulting in his *Illinois Law Journal* report, "Cracks in the Foundation of Criminal Justice."

Dash served in the Criminal Division of the United States Department of Justice during the McCarthy-era investigations and took the unpopular anti-McCarthy position. The youngest lawyer to be elected district attorney of Philadelphia, he earned a national and international reputation as an advocate for human rights in South Africa, Russia, Britain, and Ireland. His wife, Sara, often assisted him.

While director of the Institute of Criminal Law and Procedures at Georgetown University Law School, Dash was asked by Senator Sam Ervin to serve as chief counsel to the Watergate Commission, charged with investigating the break-in at the Democratic headquarters. The investigation resulted in the House Judiciary Committee's call for President Richard Nixon's impeachment.

In a synagogue appearance, as reported in a 1998 interview in *Bar Report*, Dash argued that Nixon had abused his executive power. "American Jews," he said, "regardless of our love of Israel, have to love America and our constitutional system" [and be first] "to protect that system." (MP)

DAVIDSON, IRWIN DELMORE
Member of Congress, 1955–1956

Irwin Delmore Davidson was born in New York City on January 2, 1906. He graduated from Washington Square College of New York University in 1927 and from that university's law school a year later.

While practicing law, Davidson served as counsel for New York's Legislative Bill Drafting Commission and Special Counsel for the New York State Mortgage. In 1936, Davidson was elected as a Democrat to the state assembly; he served six terms, resigning to accept an appointment as special session court justice for the City of New York.

In 1954, Davidson was elected to the United States Congress, where he served one term, before leaving to return to the bench. Davidson sat on the Court of General Sessions, County of New York, until his appointment to the New York State Supreme Court in 1963, on which bench he sat until his retirement in 1974.

Irwin Davidson died August 1, 1981. (MW)

DAVIS, SUSAN
Member of Congress, 2001–present

Susan Davis was born on April 13, 1944, in Cambridge, Massachusetts. She received her bachelor's degree from the University of California–Berkeley in 1965 and her master's in social work from the University of North Carolina in 1968.

For three years, she was the executive director of the Aaron Price Fellows Program, which seeks to teach leadership and citizenship skills to multiethnic high school students. Davis served on the San Diego City School Board for nine years, five of them as president or vice president. The League of Women Voters of San Diego also elected Davis to serve as its president.

In 1994, Davis was elected to the California State Assembly, representing the Seventy-sixth District. She served for three terms in the Assembly, forced to retire by a state term limitation. During her six years in the legislature, Davis played an integral role in the formation of the Select Committee on Adolescence and authored legislation to protect medical privacy rights, to allow women direct access to obstetric-gynecological care, and to reduce school class sizes. Among her committee assignments were Appropriations, Economic Development, and Education.

Davis was elected to the United States House of Representatives in 2000 to represent California's Forty-ninth District. She and her husband, Steve, have two sons and currently reside in San Diego. (SB)

DE LEON, DANIEL
Socialist Leader

Daniel De Leon was born on December14, 1852, on Curaçao, a Dutch-owned island off Venezuela. Although Jewish, he always claimed to be descended from a prominent family of Spanish Catholics. He received his education in Europe in the 1860s and 1870s and later attended Columbia College, after he arrived in the United States in 1874. He began a promising career as a professor of international law at Columbia but chose to sacrifice his academic career to dedicate himself to the socialist cause.

In 1890, he joined the Socialist Labor Party, quickly moving up the ranks and becoming the editor of its newspaper, *The People,* a position he held until his death. He was generally dissatisfied with American labor unionism, which struggled merely to patch up local problems and improve conditions for workers. Thus, in 1895 he worked to found the Socialist Trade and Labor Alliance (STLA), the first labor union in the United States to advocate the overthrow of capitalism and its replacement with a socialist structure.

In 1905, De Leon helped found the Industrial Workers of the World (IWW), members of which were called Wobblies, with which the STLA merged. In 1908, he lost most of his influence in the IWW, when that group split over the political function of the trade union, and he founded the short-lived Worker's International Industrial Union. Eventually, the IWW lost most of its influence during World War I, when it was suppressed by the U.S. government due to its wartime strikes. To this day, the Socialist Labor Party considers De Leon its ideological leader.

De Leon died in New York City on May 11, 1914. A number of his lectures were published in a book, *Socialist Landmarks: Four Addresses* (1952). (YF)

DE LEON, EDWIN
American Consul General in Egypt, 1853–1861

Born in Charleston, South Carolina, in 1828 to a prominent early American Sephardic family, Edwin De Leon attended South Carolina College (now the University of South Carolina). After graduation he became a journalist and editor of several southern papers, in which capacity he supported slavery in the South.

After helping Franklin Pierce gain the presidency in 1853, De Leon was appointed American consul general in Egypt, where he served for eight years. With the start of the Civil War in 1861, he resigned his post and reported to Confederate President Jefferson Davis. Davis sent De Leon to Europe to drum up support for the Confederacy in England and France. Failing to gain European support, he returned to the United States in 1862.

After the Civil War, De Leon worked as a freelance writer in New York and eventually returned to Egypt as a private citizen. While in Egypt, he helped install the Bell telephone system there and wrote several books, including *The Khedive's Egypt* (1870) and *Thirty Years of My Life on Three Continents* (1878).

Edwin De Leon died in 1891 in New York. (JSh)

DEUTCH, JOHN M.
Director, Central Intelligence Agency, 1995–1996; Deputy Secretary of Defense, 1994–1995

John Deutch was born July 27, 1938, in Brussels, Belgium. He came to the United States in 1940 and was naturalized six years later. In 1961, Deutch received a bachelor's degree from Amherst College, as well as a bachelor's degree in chemical engineering from the Massachusetts Institute of Technology (MIT). He earned a Ph.D. from MIT in 1965.

Deutch began his government career as a systems analyst with the Office of the Secretary of Defense in 1961 but left for academia after receiving his doctoral degree. After spending 1967 to 1970 as an assistant professor at Princeton, Deutch moved to MIT, serving not only as a chemistry professor but also as provost from 1982 until 1990.

In 1993, Deutch became undersecretary for acquisitions and technology at the Department of Defense. After being promoted to deputy secretary of defense in 1994, he left the department to become director of the Central Intelligence Agency (CIA), serving until the end of President Bill Clinton's first term.

Deutch's post-CIA career has been extremely controversial. His security clearance was revoked, and investigations into criminal proceedings were undertaken because he stored top-secret information on unsecured computers in his home and improperly kept a private journal detailing his experiences at the Defense Department and the CIA. President Clinton pardoned Deutch before leaving office in January 2001. (TW)

DEUTSCH, PETER R.
Member of Congress, 1993–present

Born on April 1, 1957, in New York City, Peter Deutsch was elected to the Florida House of Representatives at the age of twenty-five, just a few months after graduating from Yale Law School and moving to Florida. Deutsch was reelected four times, three times without Republican opposition, before moving up to the United States Congress in the 1992 election.

Deutsch represents Broward County and Fort Lauderdale, home to many Jewish retirees and, more recently, young Jewish families. The *Almanac of American Politics* reports that Deutsch is "an expert at using procedural rules to advance or torpedo." There is no doubt that Deutsch has represented the seniors of his district well on Medicare issues, opposing an increase in the participation age and means-testing to determine premiums, but working to tie reimbursement rates to local costs. Deutsch's congressional district also includes the Florida Everglades, and he treats them like an important constituent, seeking funds for restoration. (JS)

DIAMOND, M. JEROME
Attorney General of Vermont, 1975–1981

Jerome Diamond was born March 16, 1942, in Chicago. He graduated from the George Washington University in 1963 and subsequently received his M.A. and J.D. from the University of Tennessee.

Diamond passed the Vermont Bar in 1968 and clerked for Chief U.S. District Court Judge Ernest Gibson from 1968 to 1969. After working in Gibson's office, Diamond served as state attorney for Windham County from 1970 until 1975, when he was elected attorney general of Vermont. During his tenure as Vermont's chief legal officer, he also served as president of the National Association of Attorneys General.

Diamond left political office and founded the law firm of Diamond & Robinson in 1981. Originally a local, general trial practice, the firm soon attracted a statewide clientele, providing a wide variety of litigation services as well as working on legislative policy and governmental relations. (BMcN)

DICKSTEIN, SAMUEL
Member of Congress, 1923–1945

Samuel Dickstein was born in Russia on February 5, 1885. His family emigrated to New York City in 1887. After attending public and private schools in the city, Dickstein graduated from City College of New York and New York City Law School. He was admitted to the New York State Bar in 1908.

From 1911 until 1914, Dickstein was special deputy attorney general for New York City. In 1918, he was elected as a Democrat to the state assembly. He left the state house to run for the Congress in 1922, holding his seat through eleven successful reelection bids. During his time in Congress, Dickstein most notably served as chair on the Committee of Immigration and Naturalization and sponsored legislation to admit European refugees who were being held at Camp Oswego, New York, pending their acceptance to a country. Dickstein helped create Camp Oswego as a haven for those seeking to escape war-torn Europe. In addition, Dickstein was responsible for much of the immigration legislation from 1930 until 1945.

Dickstein left the House to accept an appointment to the New York State Supreme Court, on which bench he served until his death, in New York City, on April 22, 1954. (MW)

DINE, THOMAS
Director of American Israel Public Affairs Committee, 1980–1993

Tom Dine was born in Cincinnati, Ohio, on February 29, 1940. He attended Colgate University, receiving his B.A. in 1962. He earned his M.A. from the University of California–Berkeley in 1966. He also attended Johns Hopkins University and served in the Peace Corps in the Philippines.

Dine was the foreign affairs assistant for Idaho's Democratic senator Frank Church and served as the national security staff director for the Senate Budget Committee. He was also the deputy foreign policy adviser to Massachusetts senator Edward Kennedy and personal assistant to Chester Bowles, United States ambassador to India.

From 1980 until 1993, Dine was the head of the American Israel Public Affairs Committee (AIPAC). After leaving AIPAC, Dine went to the United States Agency for International Development, where he served as the assistant administrator for Europe and the Newly Independent States from 1993 until 1997. Using his breadth of involvement in foreign issues, Dine then went to serve as the president of Radio Free Europe/ Radio Liberty, his current position.

Tom Dine currently lives in the Washington, D.C. (MW)

DOLLINGER, ISIDORE
Member of Congress, 1949–1959

Isidore Dollinger was born in New York City on November 13, 1903. He received his undergraduate degree from New York University in 1925 and his law degree from New York Law School in 1928.

After a time in the private practice of law, Dollinger was elected as a Democrat to the New York State Assembly in 1936; eight years later he moved up to the state senate. Following a somewhat typical career path for that time, Dollinger was nominated and won election to the United States House of Representatives in 1948. He served two terms in the House.

After leaving Congress, Dollinger was the district attorney for Bronx County, New York, from 1960 until 1968. In 1968, he was appointed to the New York State Supreme Court, where he remained until his retirement in 1975. (MW)

DRYFOOS, ORVIL E. *See* Adolph Ochs.

DUBINSKY, DAVID
President, International Ladies Garment Workers Union, 1932–1966

David Dubinsky was born on February 22, 1892 in Brest Litovsk, which was then part of Russia. At the age of eleven, he became a baker's apprentice and eventually joined the bakers' union in Lodz, which was also then part of Russia but is now in Poland. After participating in a strike against Jewish bakeries, Dubinsky was arrested as a labor agitator and sentenced to eighteen months in prison. Later exiled to Siberia, he bribed his way to freedom and emigrated to the United States in 1911.

Settling in New York, Dubinsky worked as cloak cutter in the garment district and joined Local 10 of the International Ladies Garment Workers Union, eventually becoming its chair. In 1932, Dubinsky was elected president of the union. He inherited an organization hit hard by the Depression: it was financially strapped, mired in debt, and plagued by internal tension between communists and anticommunists. Spurred by the election of Franklin Roosevelt to the presidency and the subsequent New Deal funds made available to the union, Dubinksy undertook its resurrection.

During his tenure as president, Dubinsky instituted widely adopted workers' benefits such as a health and welfare fund, a workers' retirement fund, and severance pay. In 1977, he wrote an autobiography entitled *David Dubinsky: A Life with Labor*.

Dubinsky died on September 17, 1982, in New York City. (JSh)

DUBROW, EVELYN
Labor Leader

Evelyn (Evy) Dubrow was born in Passaic, New Jersey, in 1912. She earned a journalism degree from New York University in the late 1930s.

Dubrow began her career in the labor movement as a secretary in the Textile Workers Union in New Jersey. She went to Washington briefly in 1947 to help organize Americans for Democratic Action (ADA), a liberal lobbying organization. The next year, she returned to New Jersey to do political organizing for unions, but she stayed with broader political organizing as she was named New York state director for the ADA in 1948.

In 1956, Dubrow wished to return to the labor movement, so she joined the staff of the International Ladies Garment Workers Union. The union opened up a Washington office in 1958, and Dubrow went to the capital to work as a lobbyist. She later lobbied for the Union of Needletrades, Industrial, and Textile Employees (UNITE) and was a founding member of the Coalition of Labor Women. She was an advocate for laws that would improve domestic labor conditions and came to be highly respected by members of Congress. Speaker Tip O'Neill actually gave Dubrow her own chair outside the door of the House Chamber. In 1997, at the age of eighty, Evy Dubrow retired as vice president, legislative director, and executive secretary of the political department at UNITE.

In August 1999, President Bill Clinton awarded Dubrow the Medal of Freedom, the highest civilian honor in the United States, for her dedication to improving the lives of working families. (TW)

E

EDELSTEIN, MORRIS MICHAEL
Member of Congress, 1940–1941

Michael Edelstein was born in Meseritz, Poland (then part of Russia), on February 5, 1888, coming to the United States with his parents three years later. He attended Cooper Union College and graduated in 1909 from Brooklyn Law School of St. Lawrence University in New York City.

Edelstein practiced law until he was elected as a Democrat to the United States House of Representatives in a special election to fill the seat vacated by the death of William I. Sirovich. He was subsequently reelected to a full term in the 1940 general election but served only until June 4, 1941. On that day, Representative John Rankin (D-Miss.) accused "Wall Street and a little group of our international Jewish brethren" of leading America into war. In response, Edelstein strenuously denounced making Jews scapegoats, declaring such attacks "unfair and un-American." Five minutes after delivering his passionate speech, Edelstein collapsed and died of a heart attack in the House cloakroom. (MW)

EILBERG, JOSHUA
Member of Congress, 1967–1979

Joshua Eilberg was born on February 12, 1921, in Philadelphia. After receiving his B.S. degree from the Wharton School of the University of Pennsylvania and his LL.B. from Temple University School of Law, he practice law in Philadelphia as a partner in the law firm of Eilberg, Meshon, and Brener.

Eilberg served as the assistant district attorney for Philadelphia from 1952 to 1954 before his election as a Democrat to the Pennsylvania House of Representatives, a seat he held for six terms (1954–1966). Eilberg was elected to the United States House of Representatives, from a predominantly white-collar district, in 1966.

While in the House, Eilberg earned a reputation for a liberal, antiwar critic of the Nixon administration. He served on the Merchant Marine and Fisheries Committee and the Judiciary Committee. As a member of the latter committee, he voted for the impeachment of President Richard Nixon. While Eilberg's first four elections to the House had been won by extremely narrow margins, in the post-impeachment years he won handily, with 71 percent of the vote in 1974 and 74 percent in 1976. (MW)

EINSTEIN, EDWIN
Member of Congress, 1879–1881

Edwin Einstein was born in Cincinnati, Ohio, on November 18, 1842. He and his family moved to New York City in 1846. Einstein attended the College of the City of New York, as well as Union College but received no degree.

Einstein was a successful New York businessman. In 1878, he was elected as a Republican to the United States House of Representatives but served only one term. He reentered politics briefly in 1892, running unsuccessfully for the mayor of New York City. He also served as dock commissioner in 1895.

Edwin Einstein died in New York City on January 24, 1905. (MW)

EIZENSTAT, STUART E.
Undersecretary of the Treasury, 1999–2001;
Undersecretary of State, 1997–1999;
Undersecretary of Commerce, 1996–1997;
Ambassador to the European Union, 1993–1996;
Assistant to the President for Domestic Affairs and Policy, 1977–1981

Born in Chicago on January 15, 1943, Stuart Eizenstat, formerly undersecretary of state for economic, business and agricultural affairs, served at the end of the Clinton administration concurrently as undersecretary of the treasury and special envoy for property claims in Central and Eastern Europe. After graduating with honors in political science from the University of North Carolina and spending three summers as a political intern for the federal government, he received his law degree from Harvard University in 1967. From 1967 to 1968, he worked as White House staff aide to President Lyndon Johnson and in 1968 as a research director in Hubert Humphrey's presidential campaign. He practiced law from 1968 to 1993, first as a clerk to U.S. District Court Judge Edenfield in Georgia and later as an attorney, partner, and vice chair in the firm of Powell, Goldstein, Frazer and Murphy. For four years, from 1976, when he worked on the Carter presidential campaign, until 1981, when he took a break from his law practice to serve as President Jimmy Carter's assistant for domestic affairs and policy, he was executive director of the White House Domestic Policy staff. From 1996 to 1997, Eizenstat served as undersecretary of commerce for international trade.

Eizenstat's special interest and experience in Jewish causes made him a likely candidate at the beginning of the Clinton administration for the ambassadorship to the European Union to settle the claims of Holocaust victims. He served as a board member in many nonprofit organizations both in the United States and in Israel. For his civic dedication, he has received numerous awards, including the Israeli Bond and Jewish Leadership awards. (MP)

ELLENBOGEN, HENRY
Member of Congress, 1933–1998

Henry Ellenbogen was born in Vienna, Austria, on April 4, 1900, and attended law school in that city before emigrating to the United States. In this country, Ellenbogen resumed his education, receiving both undergraduate and law degrees from Duquesne University. He was admitted to the bar in 1926 and began practice in Pittsburgh. He served as arbitrator and public panel chair for the War Labor Board during World War I and wrote extensively on economic, social, and legal problems.

Ellenbogen served three successive terms in the United States House of Representatives, from 1933 until 1938. An avid New Deal Democrat, he was a cosponsor of legislation that established the federal public housing program. He resigned from Congress to serve as judge of Common Pleas Court in Allegheny County, Pennsylvania, continuing his service on that bench until his retirement in 1966.

Ellenbogen was very active in philanthropic and volunteer work, including raising funds for the Jewish National Fund and the United Negro College Fund.

Henry Ellenbogen retired to Miami, Florida, where he died on July 4, 1985. (MW)

ELLISON, DANIEL
Member of Congress, 1943–1945

Daniel Ellison was born on February 14, 1886, in Russia, emigrating to the United States with his parents while still an infant. Ellison received his undergraduate degree from Johns Hopkins University in 1907 and his law degree two years later from the University of Maryland at Baltimore, beginning the practice of law in that city.

Ellison soon became involved in city politics. He served on the Baltimore City Council from 1923 until 1942. In 1942, he was elected to the United States House of Representatives as a Republican, but he lost his reelection bid two years later. He returned to practicing law and to participation in state and local politics. He served as a member of the Maryland State Senate from 1946 until 1950.

Daniel Ellison died on August 20, 1960, in Baltimore. (MW)

ELLSBERG, DANIEL
Political Activist

Born on April 7, 1931, in Chicago, Daniel Ellsberg changed the course of America when he gave the *New York Times* a copy of a secret history of the Vietnam War in 1971. That report, commonly known as the Pentagon Papers, revealed that the government deliberately misled the American people about the escalation of the war. After charging Ellsberg with crimes against the government, White House officials broke into the office of Ellsberg's psychiatrist in pursuit of discrediting information. The charges against Ellsberg were dropped, however, as the Watergate affair began to unravel. Negative comments made by President Richard Nixon about Ellsberg's Jewish background were released when the tapes from the Oval Office became public.

Ellsberg received both a B.S. and a Ph.D. from Columbia University in the 1960s. After serving as a first lieutenant in the United States Marine Corps in Vietnam, he worked for the RAND Corporation on defense issues and became an influential adviser to Secretary of Defense Robert McNamara. In the course of studying American policy toward Vietnam, Ellsberg came to question his own views on the war in that region, eventually becoming a vocal critic of U.S. policy. His committed opposition to the Vietnam War led to his decision to leak the Pentagon Papers.

Ellsberg has continued his political activism in Washington, D.C., and northern California, where he shares his time. He focuses on the prevention of nuclear arms proliferation and has been jailed numerous times in antinuclear protests. (JM)

EMANUEL, DAVID
Governor of Georgia, 1801

Some historians claim that David Emanuel was the first Jew to hold the office of governor in any U.S. state. Others, however, refer to him as Presbyterian. The most current scholarship indicates that he was in fact Jewish by birth, although he does not seem to have maintained any ties to Jewish life.

Emanuel was born in 1743 or 1744 in Pennsylvania, to German immigrant parents. The large family—eight children in all—moved to Georgia in 1768, where Emanuel's father became a successful planter. Emanuel eventually did the same.

Emanuel served in the Revolutionary War. Legend has it that he was captured by British forces; stripped almost naked and placed before a firing squad, he escaped into a swamp and made his way back to his commanding officer, General

John Twiggs. Twiggs was also Emanuel's sister's husband.

After the war, Emanuel returned to his wife, Ann Lewis, and resumed management of his Georgia plantation. He was elected to the state senate and was that body's president; he also served in Georgia's constitutional conventions in 1789 and 1795. In March 1801, when Governor James Jackson resigned to become United States senator, Emanuel succeeded to that position, serving until November of that year, when a new governor was elected.

Emanuel died on February 19, 1808, and was survived by his wife and their six children. Georgia's Emanuel County is named after him. (MD)

EMERICH, MARTIN
Member of Congress, 1903–1905

Martin Emerich was born in Baltimore, Maryland, on April 27, 1846, and attended public schools in that city. Emerich, who was engaged in the import business, was involved in Democratic politics throughout his career. He was a ward leader and appointed ward commissioner of the poor at the age of twenty-four. From 1881 to 1883, he served a term in the Maryland legislature. He was also an aide to Governor William Hamilton from 1880 to 1884 and to his successor, Elihu Jackson, until Emerich moved to Chicago in 1887.

In Chicago, he also mixed business and politics. He ran a brick manufacturing business but also served on the Cook County Board of Commissioners and as assessor for South Chicago. In 1902, he was tapped as the party candidate for Congress and won election. He was not a candidate for renomination in 1904. Emerich returned to Chicago and retired shortly thereafter.

Martin Emerich died while visiting New York City on September 27, 1922. (LSM)

ENGEL, ELIOT L.
Member of Congress, 1989–present

Born February 18, 1947, in the Bronx, Eliot Engel began his elective career as a member of the New York State Assembly, in which he served for five terms. In 1988, Engel challenged ten-term incumbent, Mario Biaggi, who had been convicted of bribery and extortion, in the Democratic primary. He unseated the incumbent and has held the safely Democratic seat since. Engel's main competition has come in two primary elections in which the challengers, one a Latino and the other an African American, sought to dislodge him from his seat in what is now a majority minority district.

In the House, Engel has devoted a great deal of energy to foreign policy concerns as a member of the International Relations Committee. He has focused on issues of interest to his ethnically diverse constituency. For example, Engel played a leading role in congressional discussion of U.S. policy in the Balkans. He pressed for U.S. participation in Bosnia and decried Serbian policies of ethnic cleansing. He also advocated American intervention in Haiti. Engel is one of the most outspoken pro-Israel advocates in the House. He has urged administrations to move the U.S. embassy to Jerusalem and has advocated taking a hard line with Palestinian terrorists.

Engel is also recognized for his consistent appearance among members of Congress who position themselves to be seen on television, shaking the hand of the president prior to the State of the Union address. (JK)

ERDREICH, BEN
Member of Congress, 1983–1993

Ben Erdreich was born on December 9, 1938, in Birmingham, Alabama. Educated in the Jefferson County public schools, Erdreich graduated from Yale University before returning to Alabama to attend the University of Alabama School of Law.

After service in the United States Army as a first lieutenant from 1963 until 1965, he practiced law before his election to the Alabama House of Representatives in 1970. He held that office for four years before becoming Jefferson County Commissioner, a position he held until his election to the United States House of Representatives in 1982. During his ten years in Congress, Erdreich was a moderate on most national issues, though he tended to be more liberal on cultural issues to reflect the nature of his urban constituency. After his unsuccessful bid for reelection in 1992, President Bill Clinton appointed Erdreich to a seven-year term as chair of the United States Merit Systems Protection Board. (CF)

F

FARBSTEIN, LEONARD
Member of Congress, 1957–1971

Leonard Farbstein was born in New York City on October 12, 1902, and educated in the city's public school system. During World War I, he served in the United States Coast Guard Reserve. After the war, he continued his studies at the City College of New York, Hebrew Union Teachers College, and New York University School of Law; he was admitted to the bar in 1925.

After several years of practicing law, Farbstein became a member of the New York State Assembly as a Democrat in 1932. He would continue to serve the community in this capacity until 1956, when he was elected to represent the Nineteenth District in the Eighty-fifth United States Congress. An establishment Democrat, Farbstein supported President Lyndon Johnson, not only on his domestic initiatives but also on his Vietnam War policy. Despite representing an overwhelmingly Democratic district, Farbstein often had to be concerned about reelection chances as he was repeatedly challenged by liberal, antiwar activists in his own party's primary elections. Farbstein withstood these challenges until the 1970 primary in which Bella Abzug defeated him. (KJ)

FEINGOLD, RUSSELL
United States Senator, 1993–present

Russ Feingold, Democrat of Wisconsin, is best known for his work on campaign finance reform. The bill he first cosponsored with Senator John McCain of Arizona in 1996 was killed by Senate Republicans but remained the focal point of all discussions concerning the possible solutions to the perceived problems of money in American politics; the McCain–Feingold bill finally passed the Senate in 2001.

Born in Janeville, Wisconsin, on March 2, 1953, Feingold earned his B.A. from the University of Wis-consin, won a Rhodes Scholarship to England, and earned a law degree from Harvard. At age twenty-nine, Feingold began to serve ten years in the Wisconsin State Senate, earning a reputation as a political reformer and rising to become chair of the Committee on Aging, Banking, Communications, and Taxation.

In 1992, he challenged incumbent senator Robert Kasten and won one of the major upsets of that political year, despite being outspent nearly three to one. Feingold countered Kasten's heavy spending and staid image with humorous commercials, such as a famous one in which he opens a closet door and merely states, "No skeletons."

In the Senate Feingold has taken consistently liberal positions and displayed his willingness to champion unpopular causes. He was one of only eight senators who voted against an antiterrorism measure because he objected to its restrictions on appeals for death row inmates. He fought efforts to amend the Constitution to prohibit burning of the American flag. Campaign finance remains his enduring legacy, however. In 1998, Feingold was narrowly reelected, despite being a prime target of the Republicans and one of the few incumbents outspent by his challenger. (JK)

FEINSTEIN, DIANNE
United States Senator, 1992–present;
Mayor of San Francisco, 1978–1988

A politician of considerable stature, Dianne Feinstein will always be remembered for the dramatic fashion in which she became San Francisco's first female mayor. After Mayor George Moscone was assassinated, Feinstein, who was then president of the city's Board of Supervisors and among those to discover the grim shooting of Moscone and Supervisor Harvey Milk, assumed his office. She served from 1978 until 1989. After winning the Democratic nomination for governor in 1990, Feinstein was defeated by Republican Pete Wilson. In 1992, however, Feinstein won a special election to fill Wilson's abandoned Senate seat. Feinstein turned back a serious challenge from millionaire Michael Huffington in 1994. That extremely close race was notable for its nastiness and cost, standing at the time as the most expensive Senate race in U.S. history.

As a senator, Feinstein has displayed an independence that surprises many who assumed the former mayor of San Francisco would be a reliable partisan Democrat. She has sided with Republicans who have wanted to restrict immigration and amend the Constitution to prohibit flag burning. She also supports the death penalty. With Arizona Republican John Kyl, she has proposed a "Crime Victim's Bill of Rights," a constitutional amendment that would "give victims of violent crime fundamental rights protected under law."

On other issues, however, she has taken positions typically associated with her Democratic colleagues. She authored and passed the 1993 legislation banning many types of assault weapons. During the debate on this measure, Feinstein famously invoked her own firsthand knowledge of the dangers posed by guns. She fought to preserve California's Mojave National Preserve as part of the National Park System and has supported legislation to ban discrimination based on sexual preference.

Born in San Francisco on June 22, 1933, and educated at Stanford, Feinstein has been consistently mentioned as a possible candidate for the vice presidency prior to each Democratic National Convention since 1984. In 2000, she was reelected to a second full term in the Senate, defeating Congressman Tom Campbell. (JK)

FELDMAN, SANDRA
Labor Leader

Sandra Feldman was born on October 14, 1939, and grew up in the Coney Island section of New York City. Her family lived in a housing project, and she attended public schools. Feldman studied English at Brooklyn College and received an M.A. in literature from New York University while teaching first and fourth grades at a Manhattan public school.

Feldman's early years in the New York public schools led her to a career in schools and teachers' unions. She became a field representative for the United Federation of Teachers (UFT), the New York local branch of the American Federation of Teachers (AFT). Feldman held that position between 1966 and 1983. She served as executive director and secretary of the UFT from 1983 to 1986. In 1986, Feldman became the president of that organization. She succeeded the late Albert Shanker as president of the national AFT in 1997 and resigned from the UFT post in early 1998. Currently, Feldman serves as AFT president and is a member of the

national executive board of the AFL-CIO. Under her leadership, the AFT has gained more than one hundred thousand members, bringing the total membership to more than one million.

Feldman lives near Gramercy Park in New York City and commutes to the union offices in Washington, D.C. (TW)

FIEDLER, BOBBI
Member of Congress, 1981–1987

Bobbi Fiedler was born Roberta Frances Horowitz in Santa Monica, California, on April 22, 1937. She attended Santa Monica Technical School from 1955 to 1957 and Santa Monica City College from 1955 to 1959.

A businesswoman and housewife, Fiedler organized BUSTOP, a movement against the Los Angeles busing order, in 1976. To promote this cause, Fiedler ran and was elected to the Los Angeles (City) Board of Education, on which she served from 1977 to 1980. In 1980, she defeated the Democratic incumbent, James Corman, for a seat in the House of Representatives from California's Twenty-first District. A moderate Republican, Fiedler was a member of the House Budget Committee. She served from 1981 to 1987, when she gave up her seat in the House to run unsuccessfully for a seat in the United States Senate. (TW)

FILNER, BOB
Member of Congress, 1993–present

Born September 4, 1942, in Pittsburgh, Bob Filner grew up in New York City. At the age of nineteen, he went to Mississippi to work for civil rights and was jailed for two months for integrating a lunch counter.

Filner originally went to Congress as an aide to Hubert Humphrey, when Humphrey returned to the Senate after his service as vice president. Filner left Washington for the West Coast where, as a history professor at San Diego State, he directed the Lipinsky Institute for Judaic Studies. In San Diego he became involved in local politics, serving on the local school board and city council.

Elected to Congress in 1992, Filner sits on the Transportation and Infrastructure Committee and the Veterans' Affairs Committee and is active on both. His district is home to a large population of military retirees, and his position as the second-ranking Democrat on Veterans' Affairs has allowed him to pursue veterans' interests doggedly. One of his pet projects has been securing benefits for Filipino veterans who served in World War II. Filner has also supported other San Diego interests, including the regulation of San Diego's wastewater treatment facility and issues surrounding the Miramar Naval Air Base. (JS)

FINE, SIDNEY ASHER
Member of Congress, 1951–1956

Born on September 14, 1903, in New York City, Sidney Fine attended public schools before graduating from the College of the City of New York in 1923. Three years later he graduated from Columbia Law School and was subsequently admitted to the bar.

Fine practiced law in New York City before being elected in 1944 to the New York State Assembly. He served for two years before being elected to the state senate in 1946.

In 1950, he was elected as a Democrat to serve in the House of Representatives. He served there until his resignation in 1956. He returned to New York from Washington to gain a seat on the bench of the New York State Supreme Court, serving from 1956 to 1975.

Fine died on April 23, 1982. (DS)

FINGERHUT, ERIC DAVID
Member of Congress, 1993–1995

Born in Cleveland, Ohio, on May 6, 1959, Eric David Fingerhut has spent his professional life serving the people of Ohio. A graduate of Northwestern University in 1981, Fingerhut went on to receive his law degree from Stanford University in 1984. After graduating, he returned to his hometown to accept a position as a staff attorney in the Older Persons Law Office of the Legal Aid Society of Cleveland. He went on to became the associate director of a welfare-recipient job training program entitled Cleveland Works, chair of Common Cause Ohio, and campaign manager for Michael R. White's successful campaign for mayor of Cleveland.

In 1990, Fingerhut began his own political career when he was elected as a Democrat to the Ohio State Senate. In his one term in the senate, he was an active reformer, helping oust the Democratic leader and advancing gun safety laws. After the decennial redistricting, Fingerhut aggressively sought election to the House of Representatives, winning a newly drawn seat when the two incumbents whose districts had been merged decided to retire. Fingerhut's victory would be short-lived, however, as he, like many incumbent Democrats, fell victim to a Republican landslide in 1994.

After leaving the Congress, Fingerhut served as the director of the Cleveland Federation for Community Planning. In 1998, he reentered politics and was once again elected to the Ohio State Senate. (KJ)

FINKELSTEIN, ARTHUR
Political Pollster, Consultant, and Campaign Director

Known as the man who made "liberal" a four-letter word, Arthur Finkelstein was born in 1945 in Brooklyn to Eastern European immigrants. Finkelstein earned a bachelor's degree from Queens College in New York in 1967.

Finkelstein has made a name for himself as a highly successful, but reclusive, political consultant, working almost exclusively for conservative Republicans. After a brief stint at *NBC News*, he began his career as a political consultant and pollster. During the 1970s, he worked for the reelection of President Richard Nixon and helped Jesse Helms secure his first Senate seat in 1978. He designed a poll question for a Republican congressional candidate in South Carolina, testing voter reaction to the Democratic opponent's Jewish background. After a third candidate used language similar to that in Finkelstein's poll to attack the Democrat's Jewish beliefs, Finkelstein was criticized for his methods. As a successful consultant, he orchestrated an important North Carolina primary win for Ronald Reagan in 1980.

During the late 1970s, Finkelstein met Alfonse D'Amato, who would become one of Finkelstein's most consistent clients and loyal supporters. Finkelstein led D'Amato to a narrow victory in the 1980 New York race for the United States Senate, one of the most brutal Senate campaigns ever. This campaign showed what has become Finkelstein's trademark style: poll extensively, use opposition research (particularly to expose an opponent's liberal tendencies), use incendiary language, and repeat slogans and commercials relentlessly. With Finkelstein's help, D'Amato was reelected in 1986 and 1992. Among Finkelstein's other successful clients were United States Senators Don Nickles (R-Okla.) and Connie Mack (R-Fla.) and New York governor George Pataki. In 1996, Finkelstein exported his talents to Israel, serving as an adviser to Benjamin Netanyahu in his campaign for prime minister of Israel. Finkelstein's strategy of focusing on national security worked—Netanyahu won by a slim margin. In 1998, D'Amato lost a bid for reelection in what was to become a series of defeats for Finkelstein clients.

Finkelstein has guarded his privacy, thinking of himself as "the director, not the actor." He maintains an office in Irvington, New York, and a home in Ipswich, Massachusetts, where he lives with his companion and their two children. (AE)

FISCHER, ISRAEL F.
Member of Congress, 1895–1899

Israel Frederick Fischer was born in New York City on August 17, 1858, and attended the Cooper Institute. In 1879, after studying law, he was admitted to the bar of New York and practiced law in New York City from 1880 to 1895.

Fischer was elected to the United States House of Representatives as a Republican in 1894, where he remained until losing the election in 1898. In 1899, President William McKinley appointed Fischer to the U.S. Board of General Appraisers, which became the U.S. Customs Court in 1926. In 1927, President Calvin Coolidge appointed him chief justice of the Customs Court. Fischer served until his retirement in 1933; he died in New York City on March 16, 1940. (JM)

FISHER, LEE
Attorney General of Ohio, 1991–1995

Lee Fisher was born August 7, 1951, in Ann Arbor, Michigan. He graduated from Oberlin College in 1973 and received his J.D. from Case Western Reserve University in 1976.

Fisher began his political career as an Ohio state representative. After serving for one year, Fisher served as Ohio state senator from 1983 to 1991. In 1990, Democrat Fisher and Republican Paul Pfeiffer finished in a virtual dead heat for the office of Ohio

Attorney General. Out of the 3.3 million votes cast statewide, only 1,234 votes separated the two candidates. It was the closest statewide election in Ohio history, and after a laborious process of settling numerous and lengthy challenges, Fisher was declared the winner. After four years as Ohio attorney general, Fisher narrowly lost his reelection bid in the GOP landslide of 1994. Four years later, Ohio Democrats nominated Fisher for governor, but he lost the general election to Ohio secretary of state Robert Taft.

Fisher has been a member of board trustees for the Legal Aid Society in Cleveland since 1980 and of the American Jewish Committee since 1981. Fisher is currently the president and CEO of the Center for Family and Children. (BMcN)

FISHER, MAX MARTIN
GOP Fundraiser

Max M. Fisher was born in Pittsburgh, Pennsylvania, on July 15, 1908. He attended Ohio State University, where he received his B.S. in 1930. Over many decades, Fisher received many honorary degrees from universities such as Michigan State University (1971), Hebrew Union College (1975), Eastern Michigan University (1973), and Yeshiva University (1976).

From 1932 until 1959, Fisher served as the chairman of the board for Aurora Gasoline Company, of Detroit. From 1957 until 1974, he was the director of Memorial American Petroleum Institute. He served as chair for Fisher–New Center Company, also of Detroit. In 1973, Fisher became the director of Comerica Bank Incorporated, a position he continues to hold. He also serves on the board at Comerica, which is an elected position. Since 1983, Fisher has also been the auction group director for Sotheby's Auction House.

Politically, Fisher has always supported the Republican Party, having been adviser to President Richard Nixon from 1969 until 1970. He has been a financial source for the GOP, from both his personal support and his ability as a fundraiser. In the Detroit community, Fisher has served on many boards of directors for varied agencies and businesses. He has also been a strong supporter of United Way.

Max Fisher lives in the Detroit area and in Florida. (MW)

FLEISCHER, ARI
White House Press Secretary, 2001–present

Ari Fleischer was born in New York City and grew up in Pound Ridge, New York. He graduated from Middlebury College in 1982.

Immediately on graduating from college, Fleischer worked as press secretary for the unsuccessful congressional campaign of Republican Jon Fossel in New York. Despite his candidate's loss, Fleischer moved to Washington; he has been involved in politics ever since. From 1989 to 1994, Fleischer was press secretary for Republican senator Pete Domenici of New Mexico. For the next five years, he was communications director for the Republican majority on the House Ways and Means Committee. He left that position in 1999 to serve as spokesperson and communications director for Elizabeth Dole's brief presidential campaign. When the Dole campaign folded in the fall of 1999, Fleischer joined George W. Bush's presidential campaign as senior communications adviser and spokesman. On Bush's election, Fleischer was named White House press secretary. (TW)

FLEISCHMANN, JULIUS
Mayor of Cincinnati, 1901–1909

Julius Fleischmann was born on June 8, 1872, in Riverside, Ohio. He received his education at Franklin, a private school in Cincinnati, and began to work at his father's yeast and distilling business in 1889.

Fleischmann became the president of Fleischmann & Co. after his father's death and was also the president of the bank his father founded, Market National Bank of Cincinnati. He was elected mayor of Cincinnati in 1900 and served for two terms before refusing a third nomination. In 1904, 1908, and 1912, he served as a delegate to the Republican National Conventions. He also served as aide-de-camp for Governors William McKinley, Asa Bushnell, and George Nash.

Cincinnati has benefited from Fleischmann's patronage of the arts and music. He was the president and director of the Cincinnati College of Music for many years. A sports fan as well, Fleischmann was an owner of the Cincinnati National League Baseball Club, played polo, and was commodore of the Port Washington, New York, Yacht Club.

Julius Fleischmann died on February 5, 1925, while playing a polo game. (SB)

FORTAS, ABE
Associate Justice,
United States Supreme Court, 1965–1969;
Undersecretary of Interior, 1942–1946

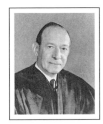

Abe Fortas was instrumental in changing the course of American criminal justice system as the attorney arguing *Gideon v. Wainwright* in 1963, which established the right of counsel to those charged with a criminal violation, regardless of their ability to pay.

Born June 19, 1910, in Memphis, Tennessee, Fortas was the son of an Orthodox Jew who had emigrated to the United States from England. After earning a bachelor's degree from Southwestern College, Fortas graduated from Yale Law School in 1933 at the head of the class.

A protégé of future Supreme Court Justice William O. Douglas, Fortas taught at Yale with Douglas and then followed him to the Securities and Exchange Commission (SEC), where he served as assistant director of divisions of the SEC. Fortas served the U.S. government in various capacities during the Roosevelt administration, culminating his early public service career as undersecretary of the interior from 1942 to 1946. Fortas then practiced law privately until 1965, when President Lyndon Johnson nominated him to the United States Supreme Court. Three years later, Johnson nominated Fortas to replace retiring Chief Justice Earl Warren. However, Fortas's support of the liberal court majority led to a filibuster in the Senate, and he eventually withdrew his consideration for the position. He remained on the court as associate justice.

Fortas was later a target of inquiry for a previous business relationship with a financier who was subsequently imprisoned for securities violations. Impeachment proceedings seemed imminent, and Fortas resigned in May 1969 to return to private practice.

Abe Fortas died on April 6, 1982, in Washington, D.C. (JM)

FOX, JON D.
Member of Congress, 1995–1999

Born on April 22, 1947, in Abington, Pennsylvania, Jon Fox grew up in the same district he later represented in Congress. He received his B.A. from Pennsylvania State University in 1969 and his J.D. from the Delaware School of Law in 1975 before entering the practice of law.

Early in his career Fox worked as an assistant district attorney for Montgomery County. From 1976 to 1980 and again from 1991 to 1994, he served on the Abington Township Board of Commissioners. Between the two stints in local government, he served three terms in the Pennsylvania House of Representatives. He first attempted to be elected to Congress in 1992, barely losing to the Democratic candidate, Marjorie Margolies-Mezvinsky. Fox reversed that result and was swept into Congress in 1994 as part of the "Republican Revolution."

Unlike many of his colleagues, in the House Fox adopted a number of moderate positions. While he reflected the views of the new Republican majority's efforts to balance the budget, reform the welfare system, and institute a middle-class tax cut, he diverged from the position of party leaders on issues such as gun control, abortion, and environmental issues. In 1998, Fox was defeated for reelection by Democrat Joe Hoeffel.

Fox has been a member of the GOP/Israel Caucus and of B'nai B'rith. In addition, he was a guest lecturer for the Presidential Classroom for Young Americans. (DS)

FRANK, BARNEY
Member of Congress, 1981–present

Born March 31, 1940, in Bayonne, New Jersey, Barney Frank began his political career as the chief assistant to former Boston mayor Kevin White. After working for Mayor White from 1967 to 1971, Frank became administrative assistant to United States Representative Michael Harrington. Frank's first elective office was the Massachusetts House of Representatives, in which he represented the Back Bay of Boston as a Democrat from 1973 to 1981.

In 1980, Frank ran for and won the race in Massachusetts's open Fourth Congressional District. He was promptly voted "outstanding freshman" in a public television survey. His formidable

debating skills and acerbic wit quickly became apparent to his colleagues; in 1998, these traits brought him public attention as he played a prominent role defending President Bill Clinton in the impeachment proceedings. More than just an accomplished speaker, Frank has been a hard and productive worker in the areas of immigration, housing, and intellectual property, among others.

Despite his impressive legislative record, Barney Frank is best known as the first openly gay member of the Congress. Frank came out to his constituents in 1987; he has been viewed as a national leader on gay and lesbian rights since that time. His personal sexuality has not hurt him in his home district, which has reelected him by wide margins each time he has run. (JS)

FRANK, JEROME NEW
Judge, U.S. Court of Appeals, 1941–1957

Jerome N. Frank was born in New York City on September 10, 1889. He received a Ph.B. in 1909 from the University of Chicago and a J.D. from the University of Chicago Law School in 1912. He remained in Chicago to practice law, until moving to New York City in 1930 to continue his practice.

Frank joined the New Deal after Franklin D. Roosevelt's election in 1932. He served as general counsel to the Agricultural Adjustment Administration from 1933 to 1935 and as special counsel in 1935 for the Reconstruction Finance Corporation in railroad reorganization. He spent the next two years back in private practice in New York City, until Roosevelt appointed him commissioner of the Securities and Exchange Commission (SEC) in 1937. Frank was named chair of the SEC in 1939, where he remained until FDR nominated him to the U.S. Court of Appeals in 1941. He served on the appellate court until his death on January 13, 1957, in New Haven, Connecticut.

Frank's relationship with Yale Law School began in 1932, when he was a research associate at the law school. Today, the Jerome N. Frank Legal Services Organization at Yale Law School matches law students with individuals in need of legal assistance who cannot afford private counsel. (JM)

FRANK, NATHAN
Member of Congress, 1889–1891

Nathan Frank was born in Peoria, Illinois, on February 23, 1852. After attending local schools in Peoria and receiving his undergraduate degree from Washington University in St. Louis, Nathan graduated from Harvard Law School at the age of nineteen and returned to St. Louis to practice law.

In 1886, Frank unsuccessfully challenged John M. Glover in a race for Congress. Two years later, he reversed that decision and was elected to the Fifty-first Congress, in which he served as a Republican and a Union Labor member. Refusing renomination in 1890, Frank returned to St. Louis and founded the *St. Louis Star,* which he combined with the *St. Louis Chronicle* in 1905. In 1910, 1916, and again in 1928, Frank sought to return to public service, running unsuccessfully for the United States Senate in each year.

Nathan Frank died on April 5, 1931, in St. Louis, Missouri. (BB)

FRANKFURTER, FELIX
Associate Justice, United States Supreme Court, 1939–1962

Born November 15, 1882, in Vienna, Austria, Felix Frankfurter emigrated to the United States in 1894. He attended the City College of New York and later Harvard Law School, where he returned as a law professor in 1914.

During his twenty-five years at Harvard, Frankfurter gained a reputation as a liberal, helping found the American Civil Liberties Union and the *New Republic* magazine. In a 1927 article, he argued against the conviction of Sacco and Vanzetti, anarchists sentenced to death after a widely publicized case. Throughout World War I, Frankfurter served as a counsel to government agencies, and he was President Woodrow Wilson's legal adviser at the Versailles conference in 1919.

In 1939, President Franklin Roosevelt appointed Frankfurter to the Supreme Court. Due to his liberal reputation, Frankfurter became the first Supreme Court nominee called to appear before the Senate Judiciary Committee during confirmation hearings. As a justice, Frankfurter toned down his liberalism. In 1940, he held that West Virginia had the right to punish Jehovah's Witness students who refused to salute the flag in school. He did, however, support the majority rule that held segregated

schools unconstitutional in *Brown v. Board of Education* in 1954.

The author of many books and articles on law and the Supreme Court, Frankfurter received the Presidential Medal of Freedom in 1953. He died on February 22, 1965. (JSh)

Source: Michael E. Parrish, *Felix Frankfurter and His Times* (New York: Free Press, 1982).

FRIEDAN, BETTY NAOMI GOLDSTEIN
President, National Organization for Women, 1966–1969; Author

Born on February 4, 1921, in Peoria, Illinois, to Harry and Miriam Horowitz Goldstein, Betty Friedan attended Smith College, where she majored in psychology and was the award-winning editor of her college newspaper. She graduated in 1942 with honors and received a fellowship to the University of California–Berkeley, where she studied for one year. She married Carl Friedan in 1947 and spent the next number of years caring for their three children in their suburban New York home and writing articles for women's housekeeping magazines.

In 1957, dissatisfied with her life, Friedan sent a questionnaire to other Smith graduates in which she found out she was not alone in suffering from "the problem with no name": a feeling of personal worthlessness and lack of self, arising from women's attempts to live through their husbands and children. The results of this inquiry were published in the best-selling book *The Feminine Mystique* (1963), which became a rallying point for American women and made Friedan their most prominent spokesperson.

In 1966, Friedan and other concerned women founded the National Organization for Women (NOW) to bring women into full participation in the mainstream of American society. Friedan served as NOW's president until 1969, advocating passage and ratification of the Equal Rights Amendment, legal abortion, child care and maternity leave policies, and increased job opportunities for women. After her resignation from NOW, she organized the Women's Strike for Equality (August 26, 1970) to demand increased rights for women.

In 1976, Friedan published *It Changed My Life: Writings on the Women's Movement* in which she voiced her concerns about the direction of the women's movement. Friedan next urged men and women to work together to find an equitable balance between domestic life and public achievement in *The Second Stage* (1981). *The Fountain of Age* (1993) explores the issue of age discrimination as well as the great potential of later life. Continuing to work and fight, Betty Friedan is now divorced from her husband and resides in New York City. (JW)

Source: Betty Friedan, *Life So Far* (New York: Simon & Schuster, 2000).

FRIEDEL, SAMUEL NATHANIEL
Member of Congress, 1953–1971

Born on April 18, 1898, in Washington, D.C., to Phillip and Rose Friedel, Samuel Friedel attended public schools in Baltimore and later graduated from Strayer Business College. Starting in the business world as a mailing clerk, Friedel eventually founded and served as president of Industrial Loan Company.

Friedel's political career began with two terms in the Maryland legislature. He was elected to House of Delegates, serving from 1935 to 1939. Immediately following his service in the legislature, he was elected to the Baltimore City Council, where he served until his election to the Congress in 1952. In the House, Friedel served as the chair of the Committee on House Administration, the Joint Committee on Printing, and the Joint Committee on the Library. He lost his bid for reelection to a tenth term in 1970.

Samuel Friedel died on March 21, 1979, in Towson, Maryland. (DS)

FRIEDMAN, STANLEY M.
Democratic Leader, Bronx County, New York

Stanley Friedman was born in New York City on March 18, 1936. He attended City College of New York, where he received his B.A. in 1958. He then attended Brooklyn Law School, where he received his LL.B. in 1961. From 1961 until 1964, Friedman worked at the New York field office of the Federal Trade Commission. In 1964 and 1965, he was as-

sistant district attorney for Bronx County, New York, and from 1966 until 1973, he served on the New York City Council.

Friedman served as the deputy mayor of New York City under Mayor Ed Koch from 1975 until 1977. In 1978, he became the chair of the Bronx County Democratic Executive Committee. He served in that position until 1988, when he surrendered to authorities under suspicion of racketeering.

Brought to trial for illegally using his influence to sell portable computers to New York City's Parking Violations Bureau, Friedman was overwhelmingly reelected to Bronx Democratic Leader five days before his trial began. Barred from politics forever by the federal judge, and given what was viewed by many as an oppressively long prison term, Friedman was later found guilty on similar state charges. Friedman served four years of the twelve-year sentence. While in prison, he worked with AIDS patients and taught fellow convicts about the relationship between business and government. In an interview with the *New York Times* after his release, Friedman gave a nod to his wrongdoing when he said, "Everybody else was doing it, but that doesn't make it right." (MW)

FROM, ALVIN
Founder, Democratic Leadership Council

Alvin From was born in South Bend, Indiana, on May 31, 1943. He attended Northwestern University, where he received his B.S.J. in 1965 and his M.S.J. in 1966. From 1966 until 1969, From was an inspector in the Office of Economic Opportunity, in Washington, D.C. He also served as counsel for the D.C. Committee in the United States Senate from 1969 until 1970. In 1971, From became the staff director on the Intergovernmental Relations Subcommittee, a position he held until 1978. In 1979 and 1980, he was the deputy adviser to the president on inflation. He moved back to the Hill as the staff director for the Democratic Caucus in the House of Representatives from 1981 until 1985.

From left that position to become the first president of the Democratic Leadership Council (DLC), a position he continues to hold. The DLC has pushed for policy innovation within the Democratic Party, defining the agenda for the so-called New Democrats. From was instrumental in convincing Arkansas governor Bill Clinton to run for president as a New Democrat in 1992 and served as a domestic policy adviser during Clinton's two terms.

Al From lives in Maryland. (MW)

FROST, (JONAS) MARTIN
Member of Congress, 1979–present

Born January 1, 1942, in Glendale, California, Martin Frost grew up in Forth Worth, Texas, and now represents the Dallas–Fort Worth area in Congress.

A moderate Democrat, Frost was first elected in 1978 after defeating incumbent Democrat Dale Milford in the primary. Then-Majority Leader Jim Wright, also from Fort Worth, helped the freshman Frost secure a coveted seat on the House Rules Committee. Frost is now the second-ranking Democrat on Rules.

Noted as a prodigious fund-raiser, Frost assumed the helm of the Democratic Congressional Campaign Committee (DCCC) after the disastrous midterm election of 1994. During Frost's tenure as chair, the DCCC helped Democrats pick up seats in both 1996 and 1998. In the 106th Congress, Frost became the chair of the Democratic Caucus, the first Jew ever elected to a House leadership position.

Frost's legislative agenda has focused on the interests of his Texas constituency, including the expansion of the Dallas–Fort Worth airport, construction of a new highway interchange, and funding projects at local Bell Helicopter. He has been especially active on defense conversion issues.

Martin Frost is married to Brigadier General Kathryn George Frost, the Adjutant General of the United States Army. (JS)

G

GARIN, GEOFFREY
Political Analyst, Pollster, and Campaign Strategist

Geoffrey Garin, one of the nation's leading political polling and campaign experts, was born in New York City on July 8, 1953. He received a B.A. in social studies from Harvard University in 1975. On graduation he went to work for Senator John Heinz (R-Pa.), eventually becoming Heinz's legislative director. In 1978, Garin joined Peter D.

Hart Research Associates as a senior research analyst, becoming president of Hart Research in 1984. He also heads the firm's political division, Garin-Hart-Yang Research Group. The American Association of Political Consultants awarded Garin-Hart-Yang "Pollster of the Year" for the 1997–1998 election cycle.

Garin has devised winning campaign strategies and directed polling for approximately one-third of the Democrats in the United States Senate, a dozen House members, and several governors. He has also done work for many nonpolitical organizations, including the AFL-CIO, the Children's Defense Fund, MTV, and the United Nations Foundation. His essays on politics have been published in several prominent newspapers, such as the *New York Times* and the *Christian Science Monitor*. Garin has appeared as a guest on *Nightline*, *Meet the Press*, and *The News Hour with Jim Lehrer* and served as an on-air analyst for CBS during the 1990, 1992, 1994, 1996, and 1998 elections. (AE)

GARMENT, LEONARD
Presidential Adviser, 1969–1975

Although he describes himself as a "birthright Democrat and lifelong liberal," Leonard Garment was an influential policy adviser to both Presidents Richard Nixon and Gerald Ford.

Born in Brooklyn on May 11, 1924, Garment attended Brooklyn College and Brooklyn Law School. After receiving his law degree, he spent the next two decades working as a litigation specialist for the influential Manhattan law firm of Mudge, Rose, Guthrie and Alexander. When Richard Nixon joined the firm in 1963, Garment became friendly with the former vice president. During Nixon's 1968 presidential bid, Garment served as the head of the media division. After the Republican victory, Nixon appointed him as special counsel to the president, a position in which he served from 1969 through the Watergate affair. He later was appointed the United States representative to the United Nations Human Rights Commission during the Ford administration. At the latter post, he defended Israel and fought against the notorious "Zionism is racism" UN resolution.

During the Nixon administration, Garment dealt with many civil rights issues and persuaded the president not to veto the Voting Rights Act of 1970. He also served as the president's adviser on the American Jewish community and as an unofficial link to the state of Israel.

A former jazz musician, Garment wrote a colorful autobiography, *Crazy Rhythm: My Journey from*

Brooklyn, Jazz, and Wall Street to Nixon's White House, Watergate, and Beyond (1997). The *Wall Street Journal* noted that "Mr. Garment's eloquent book reminds us that the classic tale of a child of immigrants—especially one with its own spirit—can still provide inspiration." (DA)

GARTH, DAVID L.
Political Consultant

One of America's best-known political consultants, David L. Garth was born on March 5, 1930 in Hewlett, New York, to Russian immigrants, Leon, a tailor-turned-manufacturer, and Beulah, a former vice president of the American Jewish Congress. He graduated from college in the 1950s, after having dropped out to fight in the Israeli war for independence and to join the United States Army Security Agency. He later attended Columbia Graduate School in clinical psychology. Before turning to politics, Garth worked as a weekly ABC-TV sports and public affairs broadcaster, winning awards for both shows. However, his enduring legacy will be as an innovative political consultant. He has run more than 150 political campaigns beginning in 1960, when he campaigned jointly with Eleanor Roosevelt to draft Adlai Stevenson for president. For more than forty years he has backed Republicans, Democrats, and Independents.

Garth's first major political victories came with the election of New York mayor John Lindsay (1965, 1969) as a result of successful media campaigns. Other notables he helped elect to office include Tom Bradley of Los Angeles as the city's first black mayor (1973, 1977, 1982), New York governor Hugh Carey (1974, 1978), and mayors Edward I. Koch (1977, 1981, 1985, 1989) and Rudolph Giuliani (1993). In Pennsylvania, he succeeded in the elections of Philadelphia mayor Bill Green (1979) and United States senators John Heinz (1976, 1982, 1988) and Arlen Specter (1988, 1992). In 1978, he backed Connecticut's first female to become governor, Ella Grasso.

For his important campaigns efforts here and abroad, the *Wall Street Journal* and the *Los Angeles Times* called him the "best" and the "hottest political consultant." His expertise and reputation extend beyond this nation's borders, as he has served as consultant to the United Bermuda Party of Bermuda (1979, 1980), to Luis Herrera Campins's campaign for president of Venezuela (1978), and to Menachem Begin's campaign for reelection as prime minister of Israel (1981). (MP)

GEJDENSON, SAMUEL
Member of Congress, 1981–2001

Born in an American displaced persons camp in Eschwege, Germany, on May 20, 1948, Gejdenson is the first child of Holocaust survivors elected to the United States House of Representatives. His parents moved to the United States where they established a dairy farm in Bozrah, Connecticut. Gejdenson received his B.A. from the University of Connecticut in 1970.

Gejdenson began his career in Connecticut's state house of representatives, serving two terms from 1975 to 1979. From 1979 through 1980, he was legislative liaison for Connecticut's governor, Ella Grasso.

In 1980, Gejdenson won election to the United States House from Connecticut's Second District, in the eastern part of the state. In his two decades in Congress, he focused on boosting American exports of goods and services. He has also fought for sanctions against foreign companies that aid the oil industries in Iraq and Libya, a law pushed by the American Israel Public Affairs Committee (AIPAC). Although his record was generally liberal, Gejdenson was a defender of military spending, in large part because of his district's reliance on defense contracts.

Gejdenson rose through the committee system to be the ranking Democrat on the International Relations Committee; he also served as cochair of the Democratic Task Force on Retirement Security charged with creating a sweeping package of pension reforms.

Gejdenson's electoral history was rocky at best. In the 1980s, he won reelection without much difficulty. In the early 1990s, however, he faced three serious challenges, twice barely surviving. After a convincing win in 1998, Gejdenson seemed more secure, but he was surprised by Robert Simmons in 2000, one of the small number of House incumbents who lost reelection bids in that election. (JK)

GELB, LESLIE H.
Assistant Secretary of State, Director of the Bureau of Politico-Military Affairs, 1977–1979

Leslie H. Gelb, son of Max and Dorothy Gelb, was born in New Rochelle, New York, on March 4, 1937. He received his B.A. and M.A. degrees from Tufts University (1959, 1961) and his Ph.D. from Harvard University (1964). After working as an assistant professor at Wesleyan University (1965–1966), he was executive assistant to United States senator Jacob K. Javits, the director of Policy Planning and Arms Control for International Security Affairs at the Department of Defense and director of the Pentagon Papers project (1967–1969). He is the recipient the Pentagon's Distinguished Service Award.

Gelb left the Pentagon in 1969 and became a senior fellow at the Brookings Institution and a visiting professor at Georgetown University. In 1973, he began his journalistic career at the *New York Times*. Gelb took leave from the *Times* to serve as assistant secretary of state for political-military affairs in the Carter administration. In 1979, he returned to the *Times*, resuming an awarding-winning career as a journalist and prolific author.

In all, Gelb, spent nearly twenty years with the *New York Times* as diplomatic and national security correspondent, a columnist, and an editor. In 1985, he earned a Pulitzer Prize for Explanatory Journalism. He is the author of four books: *The Irony of Vietnam: The System Worked* (1980), which earned him a Woodrow Wilson Award; *Our Own Worst Enemy: The Unmaking of American Foreign Policy* (1984); *Anglo-American Relations 1945–1950: Toward a Theory of Alliances* (1988); and *Claiming the Heavens: Star Wars* (1988).

Since 1993, Gelb has been president of the Council on Foreign Relations, a member of the International Institute of Strategic Studies, and a fellow at the American Academy of Arts and Science. In addition, he serves as a trustee and board member of various academic establishments. (MP)

GELBARD, ROBERT S.
State Department Official and Ambassador, 1967–present

Robert S. Gelbard was born March 6, 1944, in Brooklyn. In 1964, he received a B.A. in history from Colby College. He also earned an M.P.A. in economics from Harvard University in 1979.

Gelbard joined the Foreign Service in 1967 after serving for two years in the Peace Corps in Bolivia. After serving in junior-level positions in Brazil, Washington, and Paris, Gelbard has been assigned a series of increasingly sensitive posts in a varied State Department career. In 1985, he was named deputy assistant secretary of state for South Africa. After holding that position until 1988, Gelbard was named ambassador to Bolivia by President Ronald Reagan. In 1991, he returned to Washington as the principal deputy assistant secretary of state for inter-American affairs.

From 1993 to 1997, he served as assistant secretary of state for international narcotic and law enforcement affairs. From 1997 to 1999, he served President Bill Clinton and Secretary Madeleine Albright as special representative for implementation of the Dayton Peace Accords, frequently shuttling between Washington and the Balkans. In 1999, President Clinton nominated Gelbard to be ambassador to Indonesia. He began his tenure in Jakarta in October 1999. (BMcN)

GILBERT, JACOB H.
Member of Congress, 1960–1971

Born June 17, 1920, Jacob Gilbert grew up in New York City. He graduated from St. John's College and St. John's Law School.

After practicing law for several years, Gilbert was appointed as assistant corporation counsel for the city of New York in 1949. In 1950, he was elected to a seat in the New York State Assembly, a seat he held for two terms, before moving up to the state senate. In 1960, he was elected in a special election to the House of Representatives to replace Isidore Dollinger, who had resigned. A Democrat representing New York's Twenty-second District, Gilbert was reelected until 1970. In the 1970 Democratic primary, Gilbert was defeated by James Scheuer. Both men were incumbents competing for the same seat as a result of redistricting. When his term ended in 1971, Gilbert returned to the legal profession.

Gilbert moved to the Bronx, where he resided until his death on February 27, 1981. (TW)

GILMAN, BENJAMIN A.
Member of Congress, 1973–present

Benjamin A. Gilman was born in Poughkeepsie, New York, on December 6, 1922. As a boy he traveled to

Nazi Germany with his father; nine years later he served in the Army Air Corps in World War II, earning the Distinguished Flying Cross and the Air Medal with Oak Leaf Clusters. After the war, Gilman attended law school and practiced law until his election to the New York State Assembly in 1966. Gilman represented Orange County in the assembly for three terms; in 1972, he was elected to the United States House of Representatives.

For many years the ranking minority member on the Select Committee on Narcotics, Gilman has been a strong advocate against drug trafficking. When the Republicans gained the majority in the 104th Congress, Gilman took over the chair of the House Committee on International Relations. Always a strong supporter of Israel and foreign aid generally, Gilman has sometimes been at odds with his copartisans in the House. While still in the minority, Gilman was noted for his efforts on human rights issues. He is often described as a "Rockefeller Republican" and compiled a moderate to liberal voting record on social issues such as family planning and abortion funding.

In the 106th Congress, Gilman had exhausted the three-term limit on committee chairs imposed by Republican Conference rules. In 1999, he announced that he would retire from the House, but he reconsidered and won reelection in 2000. (JS)

GINSBURG, DOUGLAS HOWARD
U.S. Court of Appeals, 1986–present

Born May 25, 1946, in Chicago, Douglas Ginsburg currently holds a seat in the U.S. Court of Appeals for the District of Columbia. He received a B.S. in 1970 from Cornell University and a J.D. from the University of Chicago Law School in 1973. Ginsburg clerked for Carl McGowan in the U.S. Court of Appeals, D.C. Circuit, immediately after graduation, and then for U.S. Supreme Court Justice Thurgood Marshall from 1974 to 1975.

Ginsburg became a professor of law at Harvard University in 1975, where he taught until 1983 when he became a deputy assistant U.S. attorney general for the Antitrust Division in Washington. He spent a year as an administrator for information and regulatory affairs for the U.S. Office of Management and Budget before returning to the Antitrust Division in the same capacity. President Ronald Reagan nominated him to the U.S. Court of Appeals in 1986. In 1987, after the failed nomination of Robert Bork, President Reagan nominated Ginsburg to a seat on the United States Supreme Court. Ginsburg withdrew his nomination after public disclosures about past use of marijuana.

Since then, Ginsburg has also maintained his commitment to legal education by teaching law at various institutions, including Columbia University, Harvard University, George Mason University, and the University of Chicago. He is the author of books and articles on antitrust and economic regulation, and in 1991 he published the second edition of his casebook, *Regulation of the Electronic Mass Media.* (JM)

GINSBURG, RUTH BADER
Associate Justice, United States Supreme Court, 1993–present; Judge, U.S. Circuit Court of Appeals, 1980–1993

Ruth Joan Bader was born on March 15, 1933, in Brooklyn. She received a B.A. with high honors from Cornell University in 1954. Shortly after graduation, she married Martin D. Ginsburg. Although Ginsburg began Harvard Law School in 1956, she transferred to Columbia Law School after two years. She was elected to the law review of both schools and graduated tied for first in her Columbia class in 1959. Despite her stellar academic record, she still had trouble finding work in the male-dominated legal profession.

After two years as a clerk for U.S. District Judge Edmud L. Palmieri, Ginsburg began teaching at Rutgers University Law School in 1963, moving to Columbia Law School in 1972, where she became the first tenured female faculty member. During the 1970s, she cofounded the American Civil Liberties Union's Women's Rights Project, also serving as the project's director and legal counsel. During this period, she won five of the six women's rights cases that she argued in front of the Supreme Court.

In 1980, Ginsburg was appointed to the U.S. Circuit Court of Appeals for the District of Columbia, on which she served until 1993, when President Bill Clinton appointed her associate justice of the Supreme Court. As a judge, she is generally considered a moderate liberal; she places a premium on consensus among judges. She is a coauthor of *Civil Procedure in Sweden* (1965) and *Text, Cases, and Materials on Sex-Based Discrimination* (1974). (YF)

GLICKMAN, DAN
Secretary of Agriculture, 1995–2001; Member of Congress, 1977–1995

On March 30, 1995, Dan Glickman was sworn in as the country's twenty-sixth secretary of agriculture. During his tenure, Glickman focused his energies on, among other things, the situation of small, family farms, by promoting legislation aiding farmers and monitoring the increase of large farming corporations. He has also supported the development of genetically enhanced foods by pushing for strict, scientifically sound biotechnology regulations.

A native of Kansas, born on November 24, 1944, Glickman received a B.A. from the University of Michigan in 1966 and his law degree from George Washington University three years later. His subsequent career as a Democratic congressman from Kansas (1977–1995) presaged his appointment of secretary of agriculture. Glickman served on the House Agriculture Committee and for six years was chair of the Subcommittee on Wheat, Soybeans, and Feed Grains.

Alongside his agricultural activities, Glickman served as chair of the House Permanent Select Committee on Intelligence, in which capacity he oversaw the investigation of Aldrich Ames, a former FBI agent convicted for espionage. Glickman sponsored the legislation creating the United States Institute of Peace and promoting alternative energy use.

At the end of the Clinton administration, Glickman joined the Washington law firm of Akin, Gump, Strauss, Hauer, and Feld. (JSh)

GOLDBERG, ARTHUR JOSEPH
Ambassador to the United Nations, 1965–1968; Associate Justice, United States Supreme Court, 1962–1965; Secretary of Labor, 1961–1962

Arthur Joseph Goldberg was born August 8, 1908, in Chicago, the son of Russian immigrants. He attended the Northwestern University School of Law, earning a J.D. in 1929, and passed the bar exam at the age of twenty.

Goldberg first gained prominence as counsel for the Chicago Newspaper Guild during its 1938 strike. He continued to serve the labor movement and was a major influence in merging the American Federation of Labor (AFL) and the Congress of Industrial Organizations (CIO) in 1955. He was general counsel to the United Steelworkers, the CIO, and the AFL-CIO until he was appointed to be the U.S. secretary of labor in 1961. In 1962, President John F. Kennedy nominated him to the United States Supreme Court, where he served until 1965 when he resigned. Goldberg was known for his decision in *Escobedo v. Illinois*, which held that a criminal suspect must have counsel when the police interrogate him to elicit a confession.

In 1965, at President Lyndon Johnson's request, Goldberg gave up his seat on the Supreme Court and became the U.S. ambassador to the United Nations. In 1968, he resigned his post in opposition to the escalation of the Vietnam War. He returned to private practice in New York City and was defeated as a candidate for governor of New York by Republican incumbent Nelson Rockefeller in 1970. Goldberg moved to Washington, D.C., where he continued his private practice and also served as U.S. ambassador-at-large twice during the Carter administration. He focused on human rights issues in his later years.

Arthur Goldberg died January 19, 1990, in Washington, D.C. (JM)

GOLDER, BENJAMIN MARTIN
Member of Congress, 1925–1933

Born on December 23, 1891, in Cumberland County, New Jersey, Benjamin Golder moved to Philadelphia to attend public schools. In 1913, he graduated from the University of Pennsylvania Law School, and he was admitted to the bar one year later.

Golder began to practice law, but at the commencement of World War I, he enlisted in the Naval Aviation Service. He was honorably discharged as an ensign after the armistice. On his return, he was elected to the Pennsylvania House of Representatives in 1916. He served in the state legislature until 1924 when he was elected as a Republican to the Sixty-ninth Congress. Golder was a member of Congress until he lost his reelection bid along with many other Republicans in the Democratic landslide of 1932. He made one more unsuccessful attempt to return to the Congress in 1940.

Golder enlisted in the army as a captain in World War II and was promoted to lieutenant colonel by the war's end. Following the war, he returned to Philadelphia, where he resumed his law practice and engaged in the banking business until his death on December 30, 1946. (DS)

GOLDFOGLE, HENRY MAYER
Member of Congress, 1919–1921, 1901–1915

Born on May 23, 1856, in New York City, Henry Goldfogle attended public schools before being admitted to Townsend College. Following his graduation, he began to read law and was admitted to the bar in 1877. Goldfogle practiced privately for ten years until being appointed in 1887 and again in 1893 to serve on the Fifth District Court of New York. In between these two terms, he was a judge on New York City municipal court.

An active Democrat, Goldfogle was elected to Congress in 1900. He was reelected six times, before losing in 1914 and again in 1916. Goldfogle ran again in 1918, serving but one term before returning to New York to resume the practice of law. He was appointed to be president of the New York City Board of Taxes and Assessments, which he served until his death on June 1, 1929. (DS)

GOLDMAN, EMMA
Anarchist

Emma Goldman was born on June 27, 1869, to an orthodox Jewish family in Kovno, Russia (now Lithuania). After attending school in Germany, she immigrated to Rochester, New York, in 1886. Deeply influenced by the execution of anarchist leaders falsely connected to the Haymarket Square bombings in Chicago in 1887, Goldman moved to New York City to begin her career as an anarchist.

In New York Goldman met leading anarchists, among them Russian émigré Alexander Berkman. Together they plotted to assassinate Henry Clay Frich, a Carnegie Steel boss responsible for the deaths of striking workers at a Pittsburgh plant. The attempt failed, and Berkman was sentenced to twenty-four years in prison. Although Goldman escaped indictment, she was jailed one year later for inciting workers to riot in a speech given at New York's Union Square.

Released from prison, Goldman, known as "Red Emma," traveled for several years in the United States and abroad lecturing on anarchism, women's rights, birth control, and modern drama. In 1917, Goldman and Berkman, set free after serving fourteen years, agitated against U.S. participation in World War I and were promptly imprisoned for violating the Espionage Statue. After serving two years, both were deported to Russia.

Disillusioned by the Bolshevik regime, Goldman left Russia and lectured throughout Europe during the 1920s and 1930s. She died at the age of seventy in Toronto, Canada, in 1940. (JSh)

GOLDSCHMIDT, NEIL
Governor of Oregon, 1987–1991; Secretary of Transportation, 1979–1981; Mayor of Portland, Oregon, 1974–1979

Long considered a rising political star, Neil Goldschmidt, at thirty-four, was featured in the 1974 *Time* magazine essay "200 Faces of the Future." In 1980, he received the International B'nai B'rith Sam Beber Award for Outstanding Leadership.

A fifth-generation Oregonian, Goldschmidt was born on June 16, 1940. After graduating from the University of Oregon in 1963, he served as a congressional staff fellow and then went to Mississippi to help with the statewide voter registration drive. His experience in the civil rights movement inspired him to attend the University of California's Boalt School of Law.

After graduation, he worked in the Portland Legal Aid Society and was soon elected to the city council. In 1973, he became the youngest major in Portland's history and also the youngest mayor of a major American city. During his tenure, he helped revitalize the city's downtown and improve the public transportation system. Impressed with his knowledge of urban transit, President Jimmy Carter selected him as the U.S. secretary of transportation in 1979.

After Ronald Reagan was elected president, Goldschmidt returned to Oregon and became a business executive. In 1986, he was elected Oregon governor and ushered in the "Oregon comeback," a revival of the state's floundering economy. Although he was a popular and respected figure in Oregon politics, he felt the need to devote more time to his personal life after his twenty-five-year marriage was breaking up and he decided not to seek reelection. Currently, Goldschmidt works as a lobbyist and consultant.

Once appearing at a city council meeting dressed in a clown suit, Goldschmidt is known for his love of pranks. Nevertheless, the divorced father of two was a serious advocate for the poor and disadvantaged. According to the former director of the Portland Urban League, Goldschmidt's social concerns had its roots in his minority experience as a Jew. (DA)

GOLDSTEIN, LOUIS L.
Maryland State Comptroller, 1958–1998

Considered to be the longest-serving statewide elected official in the United States and the longest-serving state official in Maryland history, Louis Goldstein was often just known as "Mr. Maryland."

Born on March 14, 1913, Goldstein earned bachelor's and law degrees from Washington College in Chestertown, Maryland. He first entered politics by being elected to Maryland's House of Delegates in 1938. He served in the United States Marine Corps from 1942 to 1946, returning to Maryland state politics and winning a seat in the state senate in 1946.

Goldstein was majority leader of the Maryland state senate from 1951 until 1955 and president from 1955 to 1958. He was elected comptroller of the treasury in 1958 and was subsequently reelected continuously. Goldstein worked hard to improve the efficiency of the office and was an early advocate of advanced technology. Shortly before the stock market crash in 1987, Goldstein recommended that the state retirement system switch $2 billion from stocks to bonds, saving the state from a near calamity. Known for his strong handshake and fake gold coins that he gave out, Goldstein was a popular personality who became legendary in Maryland politics.

Louis Goldstein died while seeking his eleventh term of comptroller at the age of eighty-five in 1998. After his death, he lay in state in Maryland's state house, the first person to be so honored by the state. (JM)

GOLDSTEIN, NATHANIEL L.
Attorney General of New York, 1943–1954

Nathaniel L. Goldstein was born in 1896 in New York City. He received his B.S. degree in commercial science from New York University in 1915. Goldstein also received his J.D. and LL.D. from New York Law School.

After serving as an infantry private in World War I, Goldstein became an aide to state legislative committees investigating housing in New York City. He was elected attorney general of New York in 1942 and served three four-year terms. While in office, Goldstein worked to improve rent-control laws and addressed the growing narcotics problem. He was an adviser to United States representatives in United Nations drug-control negotiations.

After retiring in 1954, Goldstein formed the law firm of Goldstein, Shames and Hyde. He became the first chairman of the board of overseers of the Albert Einstein Medical College of Yeshiva University. Goldstein was also active in the Israel bond organization, Hebrew University of Jerusalem, Brooklyn Hebrew Orphan Asylum, National Conference of Christians and Jews, and the United Jewish Appeal. He was also the chairman of the board of overseers of the Harry S. Truman Research Institute for the Advancement of Peace at Hebrew University.

Nathaniel Goldstein died in New York in March 24, 1981. (BMcN)

GOLDZIER, JULIUS
Member of Congress, 1893–1895

Julius Goldzier was born in Vienna, Austria, on January 20, 1854. After attending the public schools of Vienna, he emigrated to the United States in 1866. While living in New York, he studied law and was admitted to the bar.

In 1872, Goldzier moved to Chicago, where he began his legal career. After practicing law for eighteen years, he served as a member of the city council of Chicago from 1890 to 1892. Goldzier was elected as a Democrat in 1892 to the House of Representatives. He lost his bid for reelection in 1894 and resumed his practice of law. The people of Chicago elected him again to their city council in 1899.

Julius Goldzier died on January 20, 1925, in Chicago. (SB)

GOMPERS, SAMUEL
Labor Leader

A child of working-class parents, Samuel Gompers was a seminal figure in the history of the American labor movement.

Born on January 27, 1850, in London, Gompers was the son of Solomon, a cigar maker, and Sarah Rood, a Dutch Jewish immigrant. He attended Jewish Free School, where he studied both Hebrew and French. Suffering economically, the family emigrated to the United States in 1863. By the age of fifteen, Samuel was working as a skilled cigar maker in New York, where he was introduced to the nascent and exciting world of labor organizing at his workplace.

From 1864 through the 1870s, Gompers was a leader of the Cigarmakers International Union. In 1886, he helped found the American Federation of Labor (AFL)—an umbrella organization of skilled craftspeople—and he served as its leader for almost forty years. During his tenure, the AFL grew from a quarter million to a high of more than four million members, although it leveled off to under three million during his last year as union head.

Although considered by many labor activists as too conservative because of his support for World War I and his unyielding opposition to socialism, Gompers helped prevent one local union from joining the AFL because of its whites-only membership requirement.

Samuel Gompers died of a heart attack on December 13, 1924, in San Antonio, Texas. (DA)

GOODWIN, RICHARD
Presidential Adviser, 1961–1969

Richard Goodwin was born in Boston on December 7, 1931. In 1953, he graduated summa cum laude from Tufts University and then went on to Harvard Law School, from which he also graduated summa cum laude in 1958.

After graduation from law school, Goodwin clerked for Supreme Court Justice Felix Frankfurter. In 1960, he joined the presidential campaign of then-senator John F. Kennedy, writing many speeches used in the race for the White House. President Kennedy appointed Goodwin assistant special counsel to the president in 1961; he served briefly as deputy assistant secretary of state for inter-American affairs and then, from 1962 until 1964, Goodwin as director of the International Peace Corps Secretariat. While working for the Kennedy administration, he helped create the Alliance for Progress. Goodwin returned to the White House as special assistant to President Lyndon B. Johnson and helped design the Great Society domestic agenda.

Goodwin is the author of many books, including *The American Condition* (1974), *Remembering America* (1989), *Triumph or Tragedy: Reflections on Vietnam* (1966), and *Promises to Keep: A Call for a New American Revolution* (1992). (SB)

GRADISON, WILLIS DAVID JR.
Member of Congress, 1975–1993;
Mayor of Cincinnati, 1971–1975

Born on December 28, 1928, Willis D. Gradison Jr. grew up in Cincinnati, Ohio. He received a B.A. from Yale University, an M.B.A. from Harvard Graduate School of Business Administration, and a D.C.S. from Harvard University.

Gradison began his career in government in the Eisenhower administration, working in the departments of Treasury and Health, Education, and Welfare for two years. Returning to his hometown, he served on the Cincinnati City Council from 1961 to 1975, as mayor for the last four years of that period. In 1974, Gradison lost to Thomas Luken in a special election for the United States House of Representatives. In the 1974 general election, however, he defeated Luken to win the seat. In the House, Gradison rose to become a high-ranking Republican on the Ways and Means Committee and the ranking Republican on the House Budget Committee. Continuously reelected by large margins, Gradison's congressional career lasted until his relinquished his House seat in

1993 to enter the private sector as president of the Health Insurance Association of America.

Gradison currently resides in McLean, Virginia. (TW)

GREEN, SEDGWICK WILLIAM (BILL)
Member of Congress, 1978–1993

Congressman William (Bill) Sedgwick Green, a Republican who served from 1978 to 1993, was born in New York City on October 16, 1929. He received his bachelor's degree from Harvard College in 1950 and his law degree from Harvard Law School in 1953. In 1953 he was admitted to the D.C. bar, and in 1954 to the New York bar. From 1953 to 1955, he served in the United States Army and from 1955 to 1956 was a law secretary to Judge George T. Washington of the U.S. Court of Appeals in D.C. His special interest was housing.

From 1961 to 1964, Green was chief counsel to the New York Legislative Committee on Housing and Urban Development; from 1965 to 1968, he was a member of the New York State Assembly; and from 1970 to 1977, he was regional administrator from New York to the United States Department of Housing and Urban Development.

After Edward I. Koch resigned his House seat to become mayor of New York in 1978, a special election was held, and Green was elected to the Ninety-fifth Congress to fill Koch's vacancy. After having won seven successive elections to Congress, Green was defeated in 1992. Thus, Green never was able to serve in the majority and to gain the influence his seniority would have earned him when his party took control of the House two years later. (MP)

GREENE, HAROLD
U.S. District Court Judge, 1978–1998

Harold Greene was born Heinz Gruenhaus in Frankfurt, Germany in 1923. He fled the Nazis with his parents in 1939. Arriving in the United States in 1943, Greene was drafted and returned to Europe as an Army intelligence officer. After the war, he received a B.S. in 1949 and a J.D. in 1952 from George Washington University.

Between 1953 and 1957, Greene served as the assistant U.S. attorney for Washington, D.C. In 1957, he moved to the Civil Rights Division of the Department of Justice. While there, he helped draft the historic Civil Rights Act of 1964 and the Voting Rights Act of 1965. In 1965, President Lyndon Johnson appointed Greene to the D.C. Court of General Sessions, the predecessor of the D.C. Superior Court. In 1966, Greene was promoted to chief judge. When many people were arrested for the rioting that occurred in response to Martin Luther King Jr.'s death, Greene ordered local judges to work around the clock so those people could receive individual hearings. President Jimmy Carter nominated Greene to U.S. District Court in 1978. While district judge, Greene oversaw the breakup of the AT&T telecommunications monopoly and the creation of the Baby Bells in 1984. He stopped hearing court cases in 1998.

Harold Greene died at his home in Washington on January 29, 2000. (TW)

GREENSPAN, ALAN
Chairman of the Federal Reserve Board, 1987–present

Born on March 6, 1926, in New York City, the only child of Herman Herbert and Rose (Goldsmith) Greenspan, Alan Greenspan was raised in New York City, where he attended public schools and then enrolled in the Juilliard School of Music. After a year at Juilliard, he left to play tenor saxophone and clarinet on the road with Henry Jerome's swing band. At age nineteen, Greenspan put his musical career aside and entered New York University where he received a bachelor's in economics in 1948 and a master's in economics in 1950. He studied for a doctoral degree at Columbia University but left in 1953 before completing his degree requirements. In 1977, based on his impressive career, New York University awarded Greenspan a Ph.D. in economics without a formal dissertation.

Greenspan cofounded the economic consulting firm of Townsend-Greenspan & Co., Inc. with William Townsend. The very successful company provided industrial and financial institutions with forecasts and other business-elated services.

Greenspan's political career started in 1968 when he was recruited to serve as an adviser to the presidential candidate Richard Nixon. In 1974, his friend from his days at Columbia, Arthur Burns, then chairman of the Federal Reserve Board, convinced Greenspan to join the administration as chair of the President's Council of Economic Advisers, to work with him to combat inflation. During the next

three years, under Greenspan's leadership, inflation dropped from 11 percent to 6.5 percent.

In 1987, President Ronald Reagan nominated Greenspan to chair the Federal Reserve Board. Greenspan has gone on to be considered the best chairman in the Fed's history. From 1989 to 1992, he tightened lending practices but also injected cash into the U.S. economy to ensure recovery from the post–Cold War economic downturn. He maintained price stability when he refused to inflate the money supply in reaction to a temporary worldwide price hike for oil. In 1994, Greenspan raised interest rates several times in a successful effort to avoid possible inflation. Under his leadership, the United States has had a booming economy, a balanced federal budget, and an inflation rate below 2 percent.

Sometimes described as the second most powerful person in the world, Greenspan is known as one of the most politically savvy government officials. His ability to look beyond partisan infighting has endeared him to both Democrats and Republicans, including four presidents. In 2000, the Senate voted eighty-nine to four to confirm Greenspan to a fourth four-year term as Fed chair. Alan Greenspan is married to NBC News correspondent Andrea Mitchell. (JW)

GROSSMAN, STEVEN
National Chairperson, Democratic National Committee, 1997–1999

A graduate of Princeton and the Harvard Business School, Steven Grossman has long been active in Democratic politics. As chair of the Massachusetts Democratic Party in the early 1990s, he led the campaign in which the Democrats won every congressional race, the first such occurrence for either party since 1872. In 1992, Grossman helped the Democratic presidential candidate Bill Clinton achieve victory in Massachusetts by nearly twenty points. In the course of that election, Democrats gained enough seats in both houses of the Massachusetts legislature to negate the effect of the Republican gubernatorial veto.

Based on his success in Massachusetts, Clinton tabbed Grossman to chair the Democratic National

Committee (DNC). A member of the DNC since 1989, Grossman had also served on the Democratic Platform Committee and the Platform Drafting Committee.

President of the Massachusetts Envelope Company, a business founded by his grandfather in 1910, Grossman has been a leader of the Jewish community in the nation, as well as in his home state. He has served as a trustee of Brandeis University and of Beth Israel Hospital and as director of the Combined Jewish Philanthropies of Greater Boston. As president of the American Israel Public Affairs Committee (AIPAC), Grossman supported the Middle East Peace process; the centrality of his role was recognized by the administration when Grossman was asked to attend the funeral of Israeli Prime Minister Yitzhak Rabin as a member of the American delegation.

Grossman has established a campaign organization to pursue the Democratic nomination for governor of Massachusetts in 2002. (JSh)

GRUENING, ERNEST HENRY
United States Senator, 1959–1969

Ernest Gruening was born February 6, 1887, in New York City. He entered Harvard College at the age of sixteen and received his bachelor's degree in 1907 and an M.D. in 1912.

Although Gruening's degree was in medicine, he began a career in journalism. Between 1911 and 1918, he worked as reporter and managing editor for several Boston publications, including the *Herald* and the *Journal*. He then moved to New York as managing editor of the *Tribune* in 1918. Gruening was the publicity manager for Robert M. LaFollette's unsuccessful presidential campaign in 1924.

After traveling to the Seventh Pan American conference in Montevideo, Uruguay, Gruening persuaded Cordell Hull and Franklin Roosevelt to adopt a Good Neighbor Policy with the Latin American states. In 1934, Roosevelt appointed Gruening the director of the Division of Territories and Island Possessions. Gruening was elected provisional United States senator of Alaska in 1956; he became a bona fide senator when Alaska gained statehood in 1958. Despite his many accomplishments, Gruen-

ing is most often remembered for being one of the two senators who voted against Lyndon Johnson's Gulf of Tonkin Resolution in 1964. In 1968, Gruening lost the Democratic primary for reelection to the Senate. Despite his loss, Gruening remained active politically by opposing the Vietnam War and campaigning for George McGovern during the 1972 presidential election.

Ernest Gruening died at his home in Washington, D.C., on June 26, 1974. (TW)

GRUNWALD, MANDY
Political Consultant

Mandy Grunwald, White House consultant and director of advertising for Bill Clinton and Al Gore in their presidential races and for Hillary Clinton in her senatorial race, was born in Morristown, New Jersey, on January 21, 1963.

For twenty years, Grunwald has been a Democratic media consultant; she is now president of Grunwald Communications. A consultant to Senator Daniel P. Moynihan for three of his campaigns, he referred to her as "a joy to be with in person, a wonder to watch on the tube, and a great creator of commercials. . . . In 1988, with a campaign staff of eleven and a treasury not all that much greater, she helped produce the largest turnout for a single candidate—4.1 million—in the history of the United States Senate."

Grunwald sheds some light on her own preferences when discussing Hillary Clinton's preference for freedom of choice. She, too, believes that women should be free to choose to work or to stay at home, to have or not to have children; she has championed Hillary Clinton's interests in health care and education, interests close to the hearts of many Jewish voters.

Like those she supports, Grunwald has combined a career with motherhood. Married to Matthew Stanley Cooper, she is the mother of Benjamin, born in 1998. She has served as a political adviser in other races, including those of Governor Roy Romer of Colorado and Harvey Gantt, in his unsuccessful bid to unseat Republican senator Jesse Helms of North Carolina. (MP)

GUGGENHEIM, SIMON
United States Senator, 1907–1913

Simon Guggenheim was born on December 30, 1867, in Philadelphia. He was educated in the Philadelphia public school system and attended the Pierce Business School. After graduating, Guggenheim traveled to Europe for two years where he studied various languages. On returning from Europe, he became involved in the mining and smelting business in Mexico and the United States. In 1888, he moved to Pueblo, Colorado, where he joined his brothers in managing the Philadelphia Smelting and Refining Company. Four years later, he moved from Pueblo to Denver.

It was from Denver that Guggenheim launched his successful bid for the United States Senate. He was elected in 1906 and served one term, choosing not to run for reelection. During his tenure in office, Guggenheim was chair of the Committee on the University of the United States and also served with the Committee on the Philippines.

On leaving public life, Guggenheim moved to New York City, where he worked as a member and later chairman of the board of the American Smelting and Refining Company. He was elected president of that company in 1919. During this period, Guggenheim shared his wealth charitably. Notably, he established the John Simon Guggenheim Memorial Foundation to award scholarships for advanced study abroad.

Simon Guggenheim lived in New York until his death on November 2, 1941. (KJ)

H

HAHN, MICHAEL
Member of Congress, 1885–1886, 1862–1863; United States Senator, 1866; Governor of Louisiana, 1864–1865

Michael Hahn is one of three individuals, along with David Emanuel and Moses Alexander, who has a claim on being the first Jewish governor of an American state. Hahn was born in Bavaria, Germany, on November 24, 1830, and emigrated to the United States with his parents as a child. Around 1840, the Hahns moved from New York

City to New Orleans, where Michael was educated. Hahn studied law at the University of Louisiana and practiced in New Orleans in the years preceding the Civil War. After the capture of New Orleans in 1862, Hahn was elected as a Unionist to the Thirty-seventh Congress, serving from December 3, 1862, to March 3, 1863.

After serving his brief term, Hahn returned to New Orleans and engaged in newspaper work. On February 22, 1864, he was elected governor of Louisiana, serving until March 4, 1865. Hahn could thus be considered the first Jewish governor elected in the United States. However, because of the Civil War, the entire state of Louisiana did not participate in the election. He was elected by that portion of Louisianans who were supporting the Union at that time, not those in the state who had seceded. In the winter of 1866, Hahn was elected to the United States Senate by the Reconstructionist legislature in Louisiana, but he never served, forgoing service due to differences with President Andrew Johnson's view of how the Reconstruction of the South should proceed.

Returning to New Orleans, Michael became manager and editor of the *New Orleans Daily Republican* from 1867 to 1871; he later founded the village of Hahnville, Louisiana. Hahn returned to public service as member of the State House of Representatives from 1872 to 1876, serving as speaker in 1875. He was appointed superintendent of the United States Mint at New Orleans in 1878 and district court judge in 1879. Hahn resigned his judgeship when he was elected as a Republican to the Forty-ninth Congress, assuming office in 1885 and serving until his death in Washington, D.C., on March 15, 1886. (BB)

HALBERSTAM, DAVID
Journalist

Born on April 10, 1934, in New York City, David Halberstam is a Pulitzer Prize–winning journalist and best-selling author. His nonfiction works include *The Children* (1998), about the civil rights movement; *The Best and the Brightest* (1972), an ironic title for the Johnson administration's conduct during the Vietnam War; *The Fifties* (1993); *Summer of '49* (1989), recounting a memorable baseball season; and *Playing for Keeps* (2000), a biography of Michael Jordan.

Halberstam served for a number of years as a reporter and contributing editor. After graduating from Harvard University in 1955, where he was managing editor of the *Harvard Crimson*, he worked briefly as the only reporter on the *Daily Times Leader* in West Point, Mississippi. From

1956 to 1960, he was a reporter for the *Nashville Tennessean,* responsible for stories on the lunch counter sit-ins and on Martin Luther King Jr.'s crusades. As *New York Times* foreign correspondent from 1960 to 1967, he covered the Congo, Vietnam, and Eastern Europe. Halberstam won the Pulitzer Prize in 1964 for his reports on Vietnam. From 1967 to 1971, he was a contributing editor to *Harper's* magazine.

In his praise, the *Boston Globe* described Halberstam as "this generation's equivalent of Theodore White and John Gunther." His observations as a reporter form the bases of several of his books, ranging from the civil rights struggle to international relations, and reveal broad interests in sports and music. Echoing a recurring theme of Jewish authors, his books highlight the dignified struggle of oppressed people in their search for freedom and equality. (MP)

HALPERIN, MORTON H.
Special Planning Assistant and Deputy Assistant Secretary of Defense, 1966–1969

On June 13, 1938, Morton H. Halperin was born to Lillian and Harry Halperin in Brooklyn. With degrees from Columbia (B.A., 1958) and Yale (M.A., 1959; Ph.D.,1961), he taught and conducted research at Harvard University's Center for International Affairs from 1961 through 1966. During that time he wrote two books, *Limited War in the Nuclear Age* (1963) and *China and the Bomb* (1965), and supported policies favoring disarmament and "limited warfare."

Testifying before the Foreign Relations Committee (1966), Halperin argued for recognition of communist China and its admission into the United Nations. Later that year, he joined the Defense Department as a special planning assistant; and from 1967 to 1969, he served as deputy assistant secretary of defense. When the Johnson administration ended and President Richard Nixon came to office, Halperin was named senior assistant to Henry A. Kissinger, the national security adviser to the president. Halperin resigned in 1970 to protest Nixon's decision to enter Cambodia and bomb Haiphong Harbor in North Vietnam. Later, he was a fellow at the Brookings Institution and the Council on Foreign Relations and a consultant to the RAND Corporation, Hudson Institute, and the Institute for Defense Analyses.

Since 1974, Halperin has directed the Center for National Security Studies and sought to expose those national policies that might threaten civil liberties and security. As a Jew, liberal, and author or coauthor of more than twelve books, he has been widely recognized for his work, including as a recipient of a MacArthur Foundation fellowship. (MP)

HALPERN, SEYMOUR
Member of Congress, 1959–1973

Seymour Halpern was born in New York City on November 19, 1913. He graduated from Richmond Hill High School and attended Columbia University from 1932 to 1934, working as a newspaper reporter while in college. He later engaged in the insurance business.

Halpern's political career began as a staff assistant to Mayor Fiorello LaGuardia in 1937; he served as an assistant to the president of the New York City Council from 1938 to 1940. In 1941, Halpern was elected as a Republican member of the New York State Senate, where he served until 1954. As a state senator, Halpern served as a member of the Temporary State Commission to Revise the Civil Service Laws, from 1952 to 1954. From 1956 to 1958, he served on the Mayor's Committee on Courts. While achieving political goals, Halpern remained active in his business life; he was vice president and later chairman of the board of the Insurance Corporation of America.

In 1954, Halpern left the state senate and ran unsuccessfully as a candidate for election to the Eighty-fourth Congress. Four years later, he was elected to the Eighty-sixth; he was reelected six times, before his retirement in 1973.

Seymour Halpern died on January 10, 1997. (BB)

HAMBURG, DANIEL
Member of Congress, 1993–1995

Daniel Hamburg was born in St. Louis, Missouri, on October 6, 1948. He earned his B.A. from Stanford University in 1970 and his M.A. from the California Institute for Integral Studies in 1992. Hamburg founded an alternative school in Ukiah, California. He also began and directed a program of cultural study in China.

Hamburg was active in local politics, serving as a member of the Ukiah city planning commission from 1976 to 1980 and as a Mendocino County supervisor from 1981 to 1985. In 1993, he was elected as a Democrat to the 103d Congress, winning as President Bill Clinton carried California with ease. In 1994, however, he fell victim to the Republican landslide and lost his seat in the House. (BB)

HARMAN, JANE F.
Member of Congress, 2001–present, 1993–1999

Jane F. Harman, a Democrat from California's Thirty-sixth District, was born in New York City on June 28, 1949. She graduated from Smith College (1966) and Harvard Law School (1969). Harman worked as a Washington, D.C., lawyer and as a Senate subcommittee staff director prior to moving to California and her eventual election in 1992.

With the help of her husband Sydney, a business executive, she raised $2.3 million to fund her 1992 campaign, the nation's third-largest congressional campaign chest in that election year. Her narrow 1994 reelection benefited from the large number of absentee ballots; her 1996 victory, from the election of Democratic president Bill Clinton.

Representing a constituency largely employed in the aerospace industry, her liberal views on abortion and gun control are tempered by more conservative defense policy views. Unlike most Democrats, she staunchly supports the B2 bomber, for which Hughes Electronics supplies the radar. Harman sits on both the Select Intelligence Committee and the Energy and Commerce Committee, the jurisdiction of which matches the economic and environmental concerns of her district. A member of the House bipartisan task force on immigration, Harman opposes restrictions on legal entry to the United States. As the daughter of Jews who fled Nazi Germany, she views immigration as both culturally and economically advantageous to America.

In 1998, Harman ran unsuccessfully for the Democratic nomination for governor. She successfully sought to regain her seat in the House in the 2000 election. (MP)

HARRIS, LOUIS
Pollster

Louis Harris was born on January 6, 1921, in New Haven, Connecticut. After graduating from the University of North Carolina in 1942, he served in the United States Navy during World War II.

Harris is best known for the Harris Polls that were for many years leading arbiters of American public opinion. In 1956, Harris founded Louis Harris and Associates, a firm specializing in marketing and public opinion research that became widely known for its association with John F. Kennedy's 1960 primary and general election campaigns. Harris left Louis Harris and Associates in 1992 to form a new firm, LH Research.

Harris has written syndicated columns for newspapers and magazines on politics and business and has published several books, including *Black-Jewish Relations in New York City: The Anguish of Change* (1970) and *Confidence and Concern: Citizens' View of American Government* (1974). (JSh)

HART, EMANUEL BERNARD
Member of Congress, 1851–1853

Emanuel Bernard Hart was born in 1809 in New York City. His political career began in 1832 when he joined the Tammany Society as a Jacksonian Democrat. From 1845 to 1846, he served two terms as a member of New York City's municipal legislative body. Although he lost in his first attempt to gain a seat in the United States House of Representatives, he was successful in the 1850 election, serving one term.

A career civil servant after leaving Congress, Hart held a long if not particularly remarkable series of posts, including surveyor of the Port of New York (1857–1862), a commissioner of immigration (1870–1873), and disbursing agent at the New York customs house (1885–1889). He was also active in Jewish organizations, including Shearith Israel Congregation and Mount Sinai Hospital, for which he served as president from 1870 until 1876.

Emanuel Hart died in 1897 in New York. (JSh)

HART, PETER
Pollster

Peter Hart was born in San Francisco on January 3, 1942. He received a B.A. from Colby College (ME) in 1964.

In 1971, Hart founded Peter D. Hart Research Associates, one of the leading survey research companies in the United States. He has provided valuable strategies for more than thirty-five senators and thirty governors, including former senators Hubert Humphrey and Lloyd Bentsen and current senators Robert Byrd and Jay Rockefeller. In 1988, he played a pivotal role in the NO campaign's defeat of General Pinochet of Chile and has worked on Colombian and Czech presidential campaigns as well. Before the first multiracial elections in South Africa in 1993, Hart's firm originated focus-group research for Project Vote.

Along with his political analyses, Hart has also produced studies of the media, employee attitudes, housing, economic development, tourism, and American consumerism. Well regarded for his focus-group research, Hart has used this methodology for his work with the Democratic National Committee, Greenpeace, and the National Cable Television Association.

Hart is currently a consultant to NBC News and can often be seen on *This Week with David Brinkley* and *The Today Show*. Along with Robert Teeter, Hart also conducts all of the public opinion polls for NBC News and the *Wall Street Journal*. (SB)

HECHT, JACOB (CHIC)
*Ambassador to the Bahamas, 1989–1993;
United States Senator, 1983–1989*

Former Republican senator from Nevada, Jacob Chic Hecht was born in Cape Girardeau, Missouri, on November 30, 1928, and graduated from Washington University in St. Louis in 1949. From 1951 to 1953, he served in the United States Army Intelligence Corps. After working as a businessman who owned a clothing store and as part owner of a hotel, he was named director of the Nevada State Bank. In his first foray into elective politics, he was elected to the Nevada State Senate, a position he held from 1967 to 1975. In 1982, he won election to the United States Senate.

The Senate committees on which he served drew on his earlier work experience and service: Banking, Housing, and Urban Affairs; Energy and Natural Resources; and the Select Committee on Intelligence. He served only one term in the Senate, losing a 1988 reelection bid to Richard Bryan in a campaign that centered on Hecht's inability to keep the nation's major nuclear-waste site out of Nevada.

Hecht's nomination as ambassador to the Bahamas, and his confirmation for that position, followed his unsuccessful reelection bid. President George H. W. Bush chose him for the ambassadorship as a result of his experience as an intelligence agent in the army. The Bahamas' seven hundred islands are considered not only prime vacation spots but also key drug-smuggling sites between South and North America. The majority of cocaine and marijuana entering the United States are shipped through the Bahamas, which made Hecht's position vital to U.S. interests. His ambassadorial service ended with President Bush's defeat in 1992. (MP)

HELLER, LOUIS B.
Member of Congress, 1949–1954

Louis Benjamin Heller was born in New York City on February 10, 1905. He attended the public schools of New York and graduated from Fordham University School of Law at the age of twenty-one. Heller was admitted to the bar in 1927 and commenced the practice of law in Brooklyn, serving as special deputy assistant attorney general in election fraud cases in New York from 1936 to 1946.

Heller served as a member of the state senate from 1943 to 1944. In 1944, Republican governor Thomas E. Dewey appointed Heller, a Democrat, as secretary of the New York State Temporary Commission against Discrimination. From 1944 to 1954, Heller served as the Democratic state committee member and executive member (leader) of the Sixth Assembly District of Kings County, New York. In 1949, as party leader he was nominated and elected to fill the vacant seat in Congress caused by the death of John J. Delaney. Heller was reelected to the Eighty-second and Eighty-third Congresses, but he resigned on July 21, 1954, to accept an appointment as a judge of the Court of Special Sessions of New York City. He served on that bench until December 1958, when he again resigned, this time to move to the City Court of the City of New York, to which he had been elected the previous November. In 1966, Heller became a judge of the Supreme Court of the State of New York, sitting until his retirement in 1977.

On his retirement, Louis Heller moved to Florida, where he resided until his death on October 30, 1993. (BB)

HERSH, SEYMOUR M.
Investigative Reporter

Seymour Hersh first became known in 1969 for his freelance reports on the army cover-up of the My Lai massacre in Vietnam, which he later compiled in two books. During the 1970s he worked primarily for the *New York Times* in Washington and New York; he later returned for special assignments.

Continuing his investigative reporting, Hersh targeted the foreign policy of the Nixon administration during the 1970s, exposing the Central Intelligence Agency's (CIA) actions in Chile and the secret bombing of Cambodia. In the 1980s, Hersh revealed the CIA's illegal sale of weapons to Libya and the misinformation of the 1983 invasion of Grenada. He has won more than a dozen major awards for journalism, including a Pulitzer Prize in 1970 and four George Polk Awards. He is the author of six books, including *The Dark Side of Camelot* (1997), which looks deeper into the life of John F. Kennedy. He has been at the fore of investigating Gulf War Syndrome and published the book *Against All Enemies: Gulf War Syndrome* (1998). Hersh is considered one of the foremost but also most controversial investigative reporters for his constant persistence in revealing the secrets of American foreign policy. (OS)

HILLMAN, SIDNEY
Presidential Adviser

Sidney Hillman, adviser to Franklin Delano Roosevelt, was born in Lithuania on March 23, 1887, to Samuel and Judith Hillman. His father, trained in the rabbinate, had expected his son to follow him in his religious training. However, Sidney rebelled against his talmudic training, joined the Bund, the outlawed socialist movement, and was imprisoned in 1904.

Following the revolution and his release, Hillman emigrated first to England and then to the United States. He settled in Chicago in 1909 and worked for Hart Schaffner & Marx, a garment company whose low wages led to an employee walkout and bitter strike that spread to the entire garment industry in Chicago. Hillman was a leader among the strikers. He then moved to New York. His Bund training, sensitivity to diverse ethnic groups, and marriage to striker Bessie Abramowitz helped him be elected president of the Amalgamated Clothing Workers in 1914.

By 1920, his union, a supplier of World War I army uniforms, represented 85 percent of the men's clothing industry. Under his leadership, the Amalgamated Clothing Workers offered loans, insurance, social programs, and cooperative housing. In 1933, he led his union into the American Federation of Labor (AFL) but soon switched their allegiance to the Congress of Industrial Organizations (CIO), becoming its vice president under John L. Lewis from 1935 to 1940. He organized the steel, auto, and textile industries and led them to support FDR in 1936 and 1940. Roosevelt appointed Hillman to a number of New Deal and wartime commissions, including the Labor Advisory Board, the National Recovery Administration, and the Office of Production Management.

He became a close adviser of the president. Despite splitting with Roosevelt over some of the president's "conservative" business policies, Hillman's influence remained strong enough that at the 1944 Democratic National Convention, when Harry S. Truman was under discussion as Roosevelt's running mate, the president told the party's inner circle, "Clear it with Sidney."

Prior to his death in 1946 at Point Lookout, New York, Hillman had helped found the World Federation of Trade Unions, which then included both communist and noncommunist countries. His greatest impact, however, was in bringing Jews and unions into the Democratic Party. (MP)

HILLQUIT, MORRIS
Socialist Leader

Morris Hillquit was a major U.S. Democratic Socialist leader and was internationally known for his opposition to Russian communism.

Born in Riga, Latvia, on August 1, 1869, Hillquit was the son of Benjamin Hillkowitz, a schoolteacher, and Rebecca Levene. After emigrating to the United States in 1886, the family changed its name to Hillquit. Morris started working in a shirt factory and became interested in the Jewish labor movement. He also began to learn Yiddish and served as a staff member of the *Arbeiter Zeitung*, the first Yiddish-language socialist newspaper in this country.

Dissatisfied with the policies of the Socialist Labor Party, Hillquit helped found the Socialist Party of America, serving as its lifelong leader and theoretician. Although he unsuccessfully ran for Congress in 1906, 1908, 1916, 1918, and 1920, Hillquit received substantial support from the Jewish immigrants in his district.

A skilled orator, he once debated Samuel Gompers about unions and socialism. An author of the first major book on socialism in the United States, Hillquit was an active opponent of U.S. entry in World War I.

Hillquit was a graduate of New York University Law School and served as the general counsel for the International Ladies Garment Workers Union (ILGWU), defending the rights of workers and socialists. He twice sought election as mayor of New York; after his second unsuccessful campaign in which he received more than a quarter million votes in 1932, Hillquit's health deteriorated, and he died on October 7, 1933. (DA)

HIRSCH, SOLOMON
U.S. Ambassador to Turkey, 1889–1892

Probably one of the only U.S. ambassadors who ever served as president of his synagogue, Solomon Hirsch was the U.S. ambassador to Turkey, a country known at the time of his appointment for its hospitality to Jews.

Born in Wurtemburg, Germany, on March 25, 1839, Hirsch was the son of Samson and Ella (Kuhn) Hirsch. After emigrating to the United States in 1854, he briefly lived in New Haven, Connecticut; New York City; and Rochester, New Hampshire, before moving to Oregon. In Portland, he and his partners formed a wholesale dry goods business that soon became one of the largest concerns on the West Coast. He became active in Oregon Republican Party politics and was elected to the state legislature in 1872. He moved up to the state senate in the 1874 election, serving five terms and, for a period of time, as that body's president. He also was chair of the state Republican central committee and helped elect the Republican governor. In 1885, he ran for United States Senate and came within one vote of election by the state legislature to that position.

President Benjamin Harrison appointed Solomon Hirsch as U.S. ambassador to Turkey in 1889; he served in the Court of the Sultan until 1892. After leaving his post, he resumed his business activities in Oregon. In 1897, President William McKinley offered Hirsch the ambassadorship to Belgium, but he declined.

Ambassador Solomon Hirsch was the president of Temple Beth Israel in Portland, Oregon, from 1900 to 1901 and was active in Jewish and communal affairs. He died on December 15, 1902, in Portland. (DA)

HOFFMAN, ABBIE
Political and Environmental Activist

Abbot (Abbie) Hoffman lived a fascinating life as an American political activist. Born November 20, 1936, in Worcester, Massachusetts, Hoffman received degrees in psychology from both Brandeis University and the University of California–Berkeley. He became active in the civil rights movement and eventually founded the Youth International Party (Yippies) in 1968. The Yippies focused on protesting the Vietnam War and the state of the political and economic system in the United States. During the Democratic National Convention in Chicago in 1968, Hoffman became famous for being one of those arrested and charged with crossing state lines with intent to riot. As part of the Chicago Seven who were put on trial for those charges, Hoffman was convicted, but the ruling was later overturned.

Hoffman was arrested for selling cocaine in 1973, leading to his decision to go underground and to alter his identity through a name change to Barry Freed and plastic surgery. Freed was an environmental activist in New York until his identity was revealed seven years later. As such, Hoffman served a year in prison before continuing his environmentalism.

Hoffman was the author of *Revolution for the Hell of It* (1968), *Steal This Book* (1971), and an autobiography, *Soon to Be a Major Motion Picture* (1980). Hoffman died by his own hand on April 12, 1989, in New Hope, Pennsylvania.

Source: Raskin, Jonah, *For the Hell of It: The Life and Times of Abbie Hoffman* (Berkeley: University of California Press, 1996).

HOFFMAN, JULIUS JENNINGS
Judge, U.S. District Court, 1953–1983

Julius J. Hoffman was born in Chicago on July 7, 1895. He received a Ph.B. in 1912 from Northwestern and his LL.B. from the Northwestern University School of Law in 1915. He practiced law in Chicago from the time of his graduation until 1947, when he was named a Superior Court judge of Cook County, Illinois.

President Dwight Eisenhower nominated Hoffman in 1953 to a newly created U.S. District Court seat for the Northern District of Illinois, and he was quickly confirmed. He assumed senior status in 1972. His most famous case was when he presided at the age of seventy-four over the conspiracy trial of the

Chicago Seven, in which he issued more than two hundred citations for contempt of court against the defendants and their attorneys. The courtroom antics of the trial provided colorful drama for the media.

Julius Hoffman served until his death on July 1, 1983, in Chicago. (JM)

HOLBROOKE, RICHARD CHARLES ALBERT
United States Ambassador to the United Nations, 1999–2001

Born in New York City, April 29, 1941, Richard Holbrooke received a B.A. from Brown University in 1962. He spent some time as a postgraduate at Princeton between 1969 and 1970.

Holbrooke joined the Foreign Service in 1962 and served in Vietnam from 1963 to 1966. After returning to the United States, he served on the White House staff until 1967. Between 1968 and 1969, Holbrooke was assigned to the State Department and attended the Paris peace talks as a staff member. He then functioned as the director of the Peace Corps in Africa from 1970 until 1972.

In 1972, Holbrooke left the foreign service to become the managing editor of *Foreign Policy* magazine, where he stayed until 1977. He was also the director of publications for the Carnegie Endowment for International Peace during that period. During the Carter administration, Holbrooke returned to government service as the assistant secretary of state for East Asian and Pacific affairs. In 1981, he became the vice president of the Washington organization Public Strategies, where he remained until 1985. Between 1981 and 1984, he also worked as a senior adviser at Lehman Brothers.

In 1993, President Bill Clinton appointed Holbrooke ambassador to the Federal Republic of Germany. He then moved to Washington to serve as assistant secretary for European and Canadian affairs at the Department of State. Between 1996 and 1999, Holbrooke served as the vice chair with Credit Suisse First Boston in New York City. He was called back to government service to serve President Clinton as special envoy to the Bosnia peace talks. He remained prominent in efforts to implement the results of the Dayton accords.

Holbrooke's nomination to succeed Madeleine Albright as United States ambassador to the United Nations was held up for almost a year by North Carolina's Republican senator Jesse Helms, then chair of the Senate Foreign Relations Committee. He was finally confirmed and assumed the New York post in 1999, serving until the end of the Clinton administration. (TW)

HOLTZMAN, ELIZABETH
Member of Congress, 1973–1981

Born August 11, 1941 in Brooklyn to Sidney Holtzman, a criminal lawyer, and Filia (Ravitz) Holtzman, a professor and former chair of the Russian Department at Hunter College, Holtzman attended Abraham Lincoln High School in Brooklyn and earned her bachelor's degree at Radcliffe College. She received her law degree from Harvard Law School in 1965.

Holtzman started her career at a private law firm in New York and then joined Mayor John V. Lindsay's administration in 1968. Having become increasingly active in local Democratic Party affairs, in 1972 she won the Democratic nomination representing Brooklyn's Sixteenth Congressional District, upsetting the fifty-year incumbent, Emanuel Celler, to become, at age thirty-two, the youngest woman ever elected to the House of Representatives.

As a member of the House Judiciary Committee, she took part in the Watergate hearings. As chair of the House Subcommittee on Immigration, Refugees, and International Law, she challenged the Immigration Service and the Justice Department with regard to former Nazi war criminals admitted to the United States. In Congress, the Holtzman Amendment authorized the deportation of such war criminals and led to the establishment of a special investigative unit at the Justice Department. She coauthored the country's first refugee law, ultimately helping thousands of Jews from the Soviet Union enter the United States as refugees in the late 1970s and 1980s. Additionally, she authored a rape privacy act and worked to increase public benefits for the aged and the poor and to bar sex discrimination in federally funded employment programs.

She ran, unsuccessfully, for United States Senate in 1980. In 1981, she was elected district attorney for Kings County (Brooklyn), becoming the first woman DA in New York City. She left that office in 1990 to become New York City comptroller, one of the three most important municipal offices. She ran unsuccessfully for the Senate again in 1992, losing a Democratic primary, and was also defeated in a primary in her bid for reelection as comptroller. She has since resumed her practice of law and currently resides in Brooklyn. (JW)

Source: Elizabeth J. Holtzman with Cynthia L. Cooper, *Who Said It Would Be Easy? One Woman's Life in the Political Arena* (New York: Arcade, 1996).

HOLTZMAN, LESTER
Member of Congress, 1953–1961

Lester Holtzman was born in New York City on June 1, 1913, and attended the public schools of New York. He graduated from St. John's Law School in 1935 and began the practice of law in Middle Village, Queens.

Active in local politics, Holtzman was elected as a Democrat to the Eighty-third and the four succeeding Congresses, serving from January 3, 1953, until his election to the New York State Supreme Court in 1961. He served on that bench from 1962 until 1973, at which point he became the president and chief executive officer of Central Queens Savings and Loan Association. (BB)

HORNER, HENRY
Governor of Illinois, 1933–1940

Henry Horner was born in Chicago in 1878, attending public school in Chicago and graduating from Kent College of Law in 1898. Horner's political career began when he ran successfully for probate judge of Cook County, Illinois, in 1914. Horner was reelected four times. As judge he introduced numerous changes in probate procedures. One of his more important innovations was the Horner Plan for handling the estates of war veterans without legal costs to the beneficiaries. His court was the "busiest court in the world." Judge Horner had sixty-five assistants under him.

In 1932, Horner was elected governor of Illinois. He was reelected easily in 1936, despite the opposition of the Cook County Democratic machine. During his governorship, he introduced the sales tax as a means of raising funds to meet unemployment needs and an expanding public school program. Throughout his career as governor, Horner fought corruption and supported the New Deal.

Horner gathered one of the world's greatest Abraham Lincoln libraries, consisting of more than six thousand volumes. In 1933, Horner presented his library to the Illinois State Historical Library. Horner was also active in Jewish affairs, being a leader of various philanthropic organizations. He was involved with the National Conference of Jewish Social Welfare and the Jewish Charities of Chicago, was director of the Young Men's Jewish Charities of Chicago, and was an honorary chair of the Joint Distribution Committee. (BB)

HOUSEMAN, JULIUS
Member of Congress, 1883–1885

Julius Houseman was born in Leckendorf, Bavaria, on December 8, 1832. After attending schools in Leckendorf and in Munich, Bavaria, he emigrated to the United States in 1848 and settled in Battle Creek, Michigan. In 1852, he moved to Grand Rapids and began what would be a forty-year career in the mercantile and lumber manufacturing businesses.

As a businessman, Houseman became prominent in community affairs; he was a member of the Board of Aldermen of Grand Rapids from 1861 until 1870, represented the city in the state legislature in both 1871 and 1872, and was elected mayor in 1873. In 1876, Houseman ran unsuccessfully for lieutenant governor. That political defeat, however, did not end his career of public service. In 1882, he was elected as a Democrat to the Forty-eighth Congress. After serving one term, Houseman returned to Grand Rapids and resumed his business pursuits.

Julius Houseman died in Grand Rapids on February 8, 1891. (BB)

I

INDYK, MARTIN
U.S. Ambassador to Israel, 1995–1997, 2000–present

Only a short time after becoming a U.S. citizen, Martin Indyk became the first Jewish U.S. ambassador to Israel. He was once reportedly also offered the post of ambassador to Syria.

The son of a prominent surgeon, Indyk was born in London on July 1, 1951, but was raised and educated in Australia. With degrees from Sydney University and the Australian National University, he worked on Middle East issues for the Australian prime minister. Indyk studied in Israel and at the behest of his mentor, Middle East expert Steven Rosen, moved to Washington to work at the American Israel Public Affairs Committee (AIPAC). In 1985, Indyk helped found the Washington Institute for Near East Policy and served as its first executive director.

During both the 1988 and 1992 presidential campaigns, Indyk served as a valued foreign policy adviser to the Democratic campaigns. At the beginning of the first Clinton administration, he was appointed as special assistant to the president and senior director for Near East and South Asian affairs at the National Security Council. In 1995, he was nominated and approved as the U.S. ambassador to Israel, serving as an influential negotiator during the Oslo peace process. Indyk subsequently served as assistant secretary for Near Eastern affairs and in January 2000 was reappointed ambassador to Israel.

According to one journalist, Indyk's initial ambassadorial appointment may have surprised the American embassy staff in Tel Aviv: they had a Jewish boss with an Australian accent who had never before been a professional diplomat. (DA)

IRVING, THEODORE LEONARD
Member of Congress, 1949–1953

Born March 24, 1898, in St Paul, Minnesota, Theodore Leonard Irving moved with his parents to North Dakota, where he attended public schools.

Irving held a variety of jobs in several locations during his early life. After working for the railroad during World War I, he moved to Montana, then to California. In 1934, he relocated to Jackson County, Missouri, and became a construction worker. He also served as a representative of the American Federation of Labor. A Democrat, Irving was elected to the Eighty-first Congress in 1948. He won reelection in 1950 but lost his 1952 reelection bid. He also lost the 1954 Democratic primary for the same seat. Irving later served as a labor organizer and president of a Kansas City, Missouri, labor union.

Irving died on March 8, 1962, while on a business trip to Washington, D.C. (TW)

ISACSON, LEO
Member of Congress, 1948–1949

Leo Isacson was born in New York City on April 20, 1910. He attended public schools in New York and graduated from New York University in 1931 and its law school in 1933. Isacson was admitted to the bar in 1934 and commenced practice in New York City.

He was elected as a member of the state assembly in 1944, serving one term. In 1948, he was elected as an American Laborite to the Eightieth Congress in a special election to fill the vacancy caused by the resignation of Benjamin J. Rabin. However, his bid to win a full term failed.

After his defeat, Isacson resumed the practice of law. In 1970, Isacson moved to Florida and became a professor of political science at Nova University. He died September 28, 1996. (BB)

ISRAEL, STEVE
Member of Congress, 2001–present

Steve Israel was born May 30, 1958, in Brooklyn, New York, and grew up in Levittown, Long Island. He received an A.A. degree from Nassau Community College. He attended Syracuse University from 1978 to 1979 and received his bachelor's degree from George Washington University in 1982.

After college, Israel went to work on Capitol Hill. He worked first as an administrative assistant to Robert Matsui (D-Calif.). In the early 1980s, he worked for Richard Ottinger (D-N.Y.) as an adviser on foreign policy and national security issues. In 1993, Israel returned to Long Island and won a seat on the Huntington Town Council. In the 2000 election, Israel ran for the congressional seat vacated by Rick Lazio, who gave up a safe Republican seat to challenge Hillary Rodham Clinton in New York's Senate race. Israel handily defeated Republican Joan Johnson. A fiscal conservative, Israel headed to Washington with health care as a top priority.

Israel is the president of the Institute on the Holocaust and the Law, a think tank based in Huntington, New York. There he and his colleagues explore what happened to lawyers and judges during the Holocaust and how their counterparts in Nazi Germany used the law to take away the legal rights of citizens. (BMcN)

J

JACOBSTEIN, MEYER
Member of Congress, 1923–1929

Meyer Jacobstein was born in New York City on January 25, 1880. At the age of two, his family moved to Rochester, New York. Jacobstein attended the public schools and the University of Rochester and then moved to New York, graduating from Columbia University in 1904. Jacobstein pursued graduate study at Columbia, studying economics and political science, receiving his Ph.D. in 1907. That same year Jacobstein was hired as a special agent in the Bureau of Corporations in the U.S. Department of Commerce.

In 1909, Jacobstein returned to academia. He was an assistant professor of economics at the University of North Dakota at Grand Forks for four years and professor of economics at the University of Rochester from 1913 until 1918.

In 1922, Jacobstein was elected as a Democrat to the Sixty-eighth Congress. He was reelected in 1924 and 1926. In 1925, Jacobstein declined the nomination of mayor of Rochester.

After serving in Congress, Jacobstein engaged in banking in Rochester from 1929 to 1936. In 1936, he became chairman of the board of the Rochester Business Institute and a member of the Brookings Institution staff. In 1942, Jacobstein also served as a member of the board of governors of the Hebrew

Union College. He was also economic counsel in the Legislative Reference Service of the Library of Congress from 1947 until his retirement May 31, 1952.

Jacobstein retired to Rochester, where he lived until his death there on April 18, 1963. (BB)

JAVITS, JACOB KOPPEL
United States Senator, 1957–1981;
Attorney General of New York, 1954–1956;
Member of Congress, 1947–1954

Born in New York City on May 18, 1904, Jacob Javits graduated from Columbia University and New York University Law School. He practiced law in New York City until 1941, when he joined the Chemical Warfare Service as a commissioned officer during World War II. He served in both Europe and the Pacific and was discharged as a lieutenant colonel in 1945.

In 1946, Javits was elected from New York to the United States House of Representatives, where he served until 1954, when he became New York's attorney general. In 1956, he was elected to the United States Senate, where he remained until 1981. A liberal or moderate Republican, Javits supported a government role in welfare programs and sponsored legislation to enforce civil rights and did not support the presidential candidacy of Republican Barry Goldwater in 1964. In 1980, he lost the Congressional Republican nomination to Alphonse D'Amato; though he remained on the ballot as the Liberal Party candidate, he was defeated in the general election.

Javits later served as an adjunct professor of public affairs at Columbia University's School of International Affairs. In his honor, the U.S. Department of Education sponsors the Jacob K. Javits Fellowships for graduate students of superior ability in the arts, humanities, and social sciences.

Jacob Javits died on March 7, 1986, in West Palm Beach, Florida. (JM)

JOELSON, CHARLES S.
Member of Congress, 1961–1969

Charles Samuel Joelson was born in Paterson, Passaic County, New Jersey, on January 27, 1916. Joelson attended public school and graduated from Montclair Academy. He graduated from Cornell University with a bachelor's degree in 1937 and a law degree in 1939. After admission to the bar in 1940, Joelson practiced law in Paterson, New Jersey. In 1942, Joelson enlisted in the United States Navy and served in the Far Eastern Branch of the Division of Naval Intelligence.

After his discharge, Joelson returned to Paterson and was elected to city council, serving from 1949 to 1953. He then served as deputy attorney general for the state's criminal investigation division from 1954 to 1956 and for the Passaic County Prosecutor's Office from 1956 to 1958. Joelson served as the director of criminal investigation for the state of New Jersey from 1958 to 1960.

In 1960, he was elected as a Democrat to the Eighty-seventh Congress; he was reelected four times, serving from January 3, 1961, until his resignation on September 4, 1969, when he assumed a seat on the bench of the Superior Court of New Jersey.

Joelson was a resident of Paramus, New Jersey, until his death on August 17, 1999. (BB)

JONAS, BENJAMIN FRANKLIN
United States Senator, 1879–1885

Benjamin Franklin Jonas was born in Williamstown, Kentucky, in 1834. He was the son of Abraham Jonas, the Cincinnati pioneer, and the nephew of Joseph Jonas, the first Jew to settle in Cincinnati. In 1853, Jonas moved to New Orleans, where he studied law at the University of Louisiana. During the Civil War, he fought for the Confederacy and served as a member of the Louisiana Legislature.

Jonas was politically active as a Democrat. In 1872, he was elected to the Louisiana State Senate and, in 1874 and again in 1878, as city attorney of New Orleans. In 1878, Jonas was chosen by the legislature to represent Louisiana in the United States Senate. Returning to his home after one term in the Senate, Jonas was collector of customs in New Orleans from 1885 until 1889.

Benjamin Jonas died in New Orleans in 1911. (BB)

K

KAHN, ALFRED EDWARD
Chair, Council on Wage and Price Stability, 1978–1980; Chair, Civil Aeronautics Board, 1977–1978

Born October 17, 1917, in Paterson, New Jersey, Alfred Kahn received a B.A. in 1936 and an M.A. in 1937 from New York University. He earned a Ph.D. from Yale in 1942.

Kahn's academic career took him to the Brookings Institution, the Twentieth Century Fund, and Ripon College before he began a long career at Cornell University in 1947, eventually holding the university's Robert Julius Thorne chair in political economy. He also served as dean of the College of Arts and Sciences from 1969 to 1974. Between 1943 and 1944, Kahn was an economist on the Palestine surveys.

Kahn has served the government in many capacities. He was a senior staff member of the Council of Economic Advisers from 1955 to 1957 and served in the Justice Department. During the Carter administration, Kahn was assistant secretary of state for economic affairs, chair of the Civil Aeronautics Board, and a member of the Council on Wage and Price Stability. He was also a court-appointed expert for the U.S. District Court between 1993 and 1994 and has served on the committee for studying the U.S. airline industry at the National Research Council since 1999.

Kahn is best known for his role in the deregulation of the airline industry. His two-volume *The Economics of Regulation: Principles and Institutions* (1970, 1971) is the seminal work in that field. (TW)

KAHN, FLORENCE PRAG
Member of Congress, 1925–1937

Born November 9, 1866, in Salt Lake City, Utah, but raised in San Francisco, Florence was the only daughter of Conrad and Mary (Goldsmith) Prag, Polish Jews and early settlers of California. She grew up in a household that emphasized both secular and Jewish education. Educated in the public schools of San Francisco, she graduated from the University of California—Berkeley in 1887. She taught high school English and history until she married Julius Kahn in March 1899. Florence served as Julius's secretary throughout his career in the United States House of Representatives, starting in 1899—a position he would hold almost continuously until his death in 1924. Upon his death, Florence Kahn was elected, as a Republican, to fill his seat. In so doing, she became the first Jewish woman to serve in the Congress.

She continued her husband's support of military preparedness and devotion to her congressional district. Believing military might was the only means of ensuring national security, she consistently supported increasing the size of the military, even when it was opposed by President Calvin Coolidge. As the first woman to serve on the Military Affairs Committee, she successfully supported the creation of several military bases in the San Francisco area and the building of the Bay Bridge, linking Oakland and San Francisco. Kahn also promoted the interests of the Federal Bureau of Investigation so successfully that J. Edgar Hoover dubbed her "the mother of the FBI." While in Congress, she was noteworthy for opposing Prohibition and motion picture censorship as government intrusions.

She lost her seat in the 1936 Democratic landslide victory but remained involved in the Republican Party. She was active in Hadassah, the National Council for Jewish Women, the Association of University Women, and the Congressional Club and was a member of Congregation Emanu-El in San Francisco.

Florence Prag Kahn died in San Francisco on November 16, 1948. (JW)

KAHN, JULIUS
Member of Congress, 1905–1924, 1899–1903

Julius Kahn was born in Kuppenheim, Grand Duchy of Baden, Germany, on February 28, 1861, and emigrated with his parents to the United States, settling in San Francisco in 1866. Kahn attended the public schools of San Francisco and then followed the theatrical profession for ten years. In 1890, Kahn studied law in San Francisco. Two years later, he was elected a member of the state legislature.

In 1898, Kahn was elected as a Republican to the Fifty-sixth Congress; he was reelected in 1900. Following a two-year hiatus, Kahn returned to the House after the 1904 election, the first of ten in a row that he won. Kahn died in office on December 18, 1924; his wife, Florence, won a special election to fill the seat he left vacant, thus becoming the first Jewish woman to serve in the House.

Although Kahn was a Republican, he was a leading supporter of President Wilson's foreign policy. During World War I, Kahn served on the House Committee on Military Affairs. In 1921, he was elected chair of that committee and was instrumental in the development and adoption in the House of what became the National Defense Act, which reorganized and modernized the military.

Kahn was active in Jewish affairs as well, helping found the Jewish Educational Society, the first organization of its type on the Pacific Coast. He was a member of Congregation Emanu-El of San Francisco. An anti-Zionist, Kahn rejected the concept of a revived Jewish nationalism, believing instead that mission of the Jewish people was religious rather than political. (BB)

KALB, BERNARD
Journalist; Assistant Secretary of State for Public Affairs, 1984–1986

Born in New York City on February 4, 1922, Bernard Kalb's reputation as a journalist has grown immensely during his almost fifty years of work in that profession. Starting in the mid-1950s as a news correspondent in Southeast Asia for the *New York Times* and later CBS, Kalb covered events leading up to and during the Vietnam War. His CBS documentary based on his experiences in Vietnam, "Viet Cong," won an Overseas Press Club Award.

From 1984 to 1986, Kalb served as assistant secretary of state for public affairs and was a spokesperson for the State Department. In that capacity he accompanied President Ronald Reagan to the 1985 Geneva Convention. Kalb is best known, however, for traveling the world as a moderator, lecturer, and reporter. He journeyed with President Richard Nixon to China in 1972 as a television correspondent and participated in a conference with former USSR president Mikhail Gorbachev days before the Soviet leader stepped down.

Currently, Kalb moderates *Reliable Sources*, a weekly CNN news program scrutinizing the media. He has coauthored two books with his brother and fellow journalist, Marvin Kalb: *Kissinger* (1974), a biography of former secretary of state Henry Kissinger, and *The Last Ambassador* (1981), a novel set in Saigon in 1975. (JSh)

KALB, MARVIN LEONARD
Journalist

Marvin Kalb was born on June 9, 1930, in New York City. Educated at the City College of New York (B.S.S., 1951) and Harvard University (M.A., 1953), Kalb served in the United States Army from 1953 to 1955.

Kalb began his career in journalism in 1955, when he was appointed by the U.S. State Department as press attaché, stationed at the American Embassy in Moscow. In 1957, Kalb took a job as the CBS news correspondent in Moscow, a post he held until 1963, when he returned to the United States to work as a diplomatic correspondent for CBS in Washington, D.C. In 1980, Kalb switched networks, becoming a D.C. diplomatic correspondent for NBC News. He became the director of the Joan Shorenstein Barone Center for Press, Politics and Public Policy at Harvard in 1987; he currently serves as the director of the center's Washington office.

Alongside his work as a network political correspondent, Kalb has written several books, including *Roots of Involvement: The U.S. in Asia, 1784–1971* (1971) and *Kissinger* (1974), a biography, written with his brother Bernard, that was praised as a detailed study of American diplomacy in the post–Cold War era and also criticized as too worshipful of its subject.

Kalb has received several awards, including the Overseas Press Club Award (1961) and the International Cinema Society Award (1967). (JSh)

KANTOR, MICKEY
Secretary of Commerce, 1996–1997;
United States Trade Representative, 1992–1996

Mickey Kantor grew up in Nashville, Tennessee, and graduated from Vanderbilt University before serving in the United States Navy for four years. In 1968, he received a law degree from Georgetown University.

After graduating from law school, Kantor helped establish South Florida Migrant Labor Services, a legal aid program for farm workers. He also helped create the Legal Services Corporation in Washington, where he met Bill and Hillary Rodham Clinton. In the early 1970s, Kantor moved to Los Angeles and practiced law at the firm of Manatt, Phelps, Phillips and Kantor.

He also became very active in Democratic Party politics. In 1976, he chaired former governor Jerry Brown's unsuccessful presidential campaign; in 1984, he ran Walter F. Mondale's presidential campaign efforts in California. Kantor helped manage his friend Bill Clinton's presidential campaign in 1992 and advised Clinton as he dealt with Gennifer Flowers's claim that she and Clinton had had an affair.

During the first Clinton term, Kantor served as the United States trade representative. In that capacity, he used extraordinary pressure to force Europe, Japan, and China to open their markets and played an instrumental role in gaining congressional approval of the North American Free Trade Agreement (NAFTA). When Commerce Secretary Ron Brown was killed in a plane crash, Kantor was promoted to replace him in April 1996. He left the administration in 1997, declaring that hard work had taken its toll on his personal life.

In 1998, President Clinton hired his friend Kantor and his firm, Mayer, Brown, and Platt, to aid in fighting Kenneth Starr's investigation of the allegations in the Monica Lewinsky scandal.

Kantor is married to former NBC correspondent Heidi Schulman; they have a daughter, Alix. He was named senior adviser to the investment banking division at Morgan Stanley Group in 1997 and continues to serve as a partner at the Washington office of Mayer, Brown, and Platt. (TW)

KAUFMAN, DAVID SPANGLER
Member of Congress, 1846–1851

David Spangler Kaufman was born in Boiling Springs, Pennsylvania, on December 18, 1813. After graduating with high honors from Princeton College in 1830, he studied law under General John A. Quitman in Natchez, Mississippi, and began his legal career in Natchitoches, Louisiana, in 1835. Two years later he settled in Nacogdoches, Texas, where he practiced law and participated in military campaigns against the Cherokee Indians.

Kaufman served as a Democrat in both houses of the Congress of the Republic of Texas from 1838 to 1845; he was speaker of the lower house for the Fourth and Fifth Congresses of the Republic. After annexation to the United States, Kaufman represented the Eastern District of Texas in the United States House of Representatives for three terms. While in Congress, he argued unsuccessfully that Texas owned lands that are now parts of New Mexico, Colorado, Kansas, Wyoming, and Oklahoma and encouraged Governor Peter H. Bell to have Texas troops seize Santa Fe. Kaufman also played a prominent role in the compromise of 1850, in which the national government assumed the debts of Texas. No other Jewish Texan served in Congress until the 1970s.

Kaufman died in Washington, D.C., on January 31, 1851, and was buried in the District of Columbia Congressional Cemetery. In 1932, his remains were moved to the Texas State Cemetery in Austin. Kaufman County and the city of Kaufman in Texas are both named for him. (BB)

KAUFMAN, IRVING ROBERT
Judge, U.S. Court of Appeals, 1961–1992; Judge, U.S. District Court, 1949–1961

Born June 24, 1910, in New York City, Irving Kaufman graduated at eighteen from Fordham College and was twenty when he finished law school there, a year before he was eligible to take the bar exam. In the 1930s, he was a special assistant and then assistant U.S. attorney for the Southern District of New York. He returned to private practice in 1940, returning to public service as special assistant to the U.S. attorney general from 1947 to 1948.

In 1949, President Harry S. Truman gave him a recess appointment to the U.S. District Court in the Southern District of New York; he was nominated and confirmed in 1950. He presided over the Rosenberg case, which marked the first time that American civilians were put to death for espionage in the United States, after they were found guilty of conspiring to deliver atomic-bomb secrets to the Soviet Union.

In 1961, President John F. Kennedy nominated Kaufman to the U.S. Court of Appeals for the Second Circuit, where he served as chief judge from 1973 to 1980, and assumed senior status in 1987. His career was noted for liberal rulings. He wrote the order for the first desegregation of a predominately black school in the North in 1961 and was the lone dissenting vote in 1971, when the court ruled not to allow the *New York Times* to publish the Pentagon Papers. However, his harsh sentencing of the Rosenbergs likely kept him from a seat on the Supreme Court.

Irving Kaufman died on February 1, 1992, in New York City. (JM)

KENEN, I. L. (SI)
Founder and Director, American Israel Public Affairs Committee, 1954–1974

Born in St. Stephens, New Brunswick, Canada, in 1904, Si Kenen began his career as an actor on Canadian stages before moving to Cleveland, Ohio, as a journalist; in that role he was among the founders of Local One of the American Newspaper Guild.

But Si Kenen made his mark as a tireless advocate of Israel. He moved to New York in 1943 and became the director of the American Emergency Committee on Zionist Affairs. He remained part of the Zionist lobby through the period of Israeli independence. In 1951, he moved to Washington; the Zionist lobby was reorganized as the American Zionist Committee, to avoid allegations that it was an agent of a foreign government. In 1954 that committee became the American Israel Public Affairs Committee (AIPAC) under Kenen's leadership. Three years later Kenen established and became editor of the *Near East Report*, in an effort to counter anti-Israel propaganda emanating in part at least from American diplomats. Throughout his career, he strove to disseminate accurate information to counter myths that opponents spread about developments in Israel.

When Kenen formed AIPAC to lobby the Congress on behalf of the new Jewish state, the goal was to gain $150 million in U.S. aid. Despite State Department fear of alienating the Arab states and consequent objections to any aid, Congress did eventually grant Israel an initial package of $15 million. Kenen was not to be deterred. A congenial and understated man, he worked closely with legislators, won and returned their respect, and built an impressive group of strong advocates for aid to Israel. AIPAC came to be one of the most powerful and successful lobbies on Capitol Hill under his guidance. At the time of Kenen's retirement from AIPAC in 1974, United States aid to Israel exceeded $1 billion.

Si Kenen died in Washington on March 23, 1988, at the age of eighty-three. (LSM)

KEYSERLING, HARRIET
Member of South Carolina House of Representatives, 1977–1993

Harriet Keyserling was born on April 4, 1922, in New York City; both of her parents were immigrants from Eastern Europe. In 1943, she graduated cum laude from Barnard College.

After marrying Dr. Herbert Keyserling, she moved to Beaufort, South Carolina. Elected to the Beaufort City Council in 1974, she was the first woman ever to hold a seat there. During her two years on the council, she helped create a library consortium of three local libraries, thus increasing the resources and their availability to the public. Keyserling served in the South Carolina House of Representatives from 1977 to 1993. A prominent member of the legislature, she was a mainstay on the House Judiciary Committee, the Education Committee, the Joint Legislative Committee on Energy, and the Joint Legislative Committee on Cultural Affairs, which she chaired. Keyserling played an integral role in the passage of many pieces of major legislation, including the South Carolina Energy Conservation and Efficiency Act of 1992, the Energy Tax Credit Bill, the Prohibition of Nuclear Waste from Foreign Countries Act, and the Education Improvement Act. The Joint Legislative Committee on Cultural Affairs that seeks to enhance cultural activities and awareness across the state resulted from Keyserling's vision.

Also committed to the advancement of women's issues, Keyserling was the chair of the Women's Legislative Caucus from 1991 to 1992 and of South Carolina Women in Government.

In 1998, Keyserling published her autobiography, *Against the Tide: One Woman's Political Struggle.* (SB)

KEYSERLING, LEON
Council of Economic Advisers, 1946–1953;
Chair, 1949–1953

Born on January 22, 1908, in Beaufort, South Carolina, to William Keyserling and Jenni Hyman, owners of varied agricultural and mercantile enterprises, Leon Keyserling was the eldest of four children. A very bright child who finished public high school at age sixteen, Keyserling enrolled at Columbia University in 1924, graduated with a B.A. in economics in 1928, and went on to study at Harvard Law School, receiving his LL.D. in 1931. Keyserling returned to Columbia as a Ph.D. student in economics and by 1933 had completed his doctoral program.

Keyserling joined his Columbia mentor, Rexford Tugwell, in the U.S. Department of Agriculture when Franklin Roosevelt came to power. Shortly after settling in Washington, D.C., Keyserling moved to the Congress as Senator Robert Wagner's (D-N.Y.) legislative assistant. In that position, he helped draft a number of famous New Deal laws, most significantly Section 7A of the National Labor Relations Act of 1935, providing governmental encouragement for workers to organize unions.

In 1944, Keyserling wrote a prize-winning essay on the future of the American economy, advocating balanced economic growth. Parts of the legislation creating the Council of Economic Advisers (CEA), a new economic advisory unit in the Executive Office of the President, emanated directly from his essay. Appointed to the CEA by President Harry S. Truman in 1946, Keyserling became chair three years later. In that role, he supported a policy of economic growth sustained by joint planning and cooperation between private business and the federal government. Keyserling left the CEA after Dwight D. Eisenhower's election, believing that the chair should reflect the views of the administration in power.

In 1953, Keyserling founded the Conference on Economic Progress, a nonprofit foundation concerned with public policy, which he directed until 1972. During this period, he consulted widely in the United States and with the governments of France, India, and Israel. From 1972 until his death in Washington on December 13, 1988, he lobbied for a broad range of liberal causes. (JW)

KING, LARRY
Talk-Show Host

Born Larry Harvey Zeiger on November 19, 1933, in Brooklyn, New York, the well-known broadcaster and radio personality is now known as Larry King.

King began his career as a disc jockey for several radio stations in Miami, Florida, from 1957 to 1971. For three years, beginning in 1972, he worked as a freelance broadcaster and author. King returned to radio broadcasting in 1975 for three years, before joining the staff of the *Miami Herald*'s entertainment section. In 1978, he became host of *The Larry King Show* on the Mutual Radio Network and in 1984 began writing columns for *USA Today*.

King's career made its biggest leap in 1987 when he became host of *Larry King Live* on CNN. He has become the most popular talk-show host in the world and one of the most respected talk-show personalities in the industry. His high-profile guests have included Bill and Hillary Clinton, H. Ross Perot, and Colin Powell, as well as many other actors, politicians, and influential personalities in America.

King chairs the Larry King Cardiac Foundation, a charitable organization devoted to providing grants for life-saving cardiac procedures for individuals who would otherwise be unable to pay for them. He is also an honorary trustee of the American Women in Radio and TV Committee and a member of the Washington Center for Politics and Journalism. (BMcN)

KISSINGER, HENRY ALFRED
Secretary of State, 1973–1977; Assistant to the
President for National Security Affairs, 1969–1975

Henry Kissinger is often regarded as the most influential player in American foreign policy throughout the second half of the twentieth century.

Undoubtedly, he has been the most influential Jew to hold a cabinet position. Some critics fault Kissinger for his personality, but none can deny his brilliance in the field of international relations.

Kissinger was born Heinz Alfred Kissinger in Fuerth, Germany, on May 27, 1923. In 1935, he and his brother were expelled from school because of the Nuremberg Laws. They were sent to an all-Jewish secular school. As conditions worsened for German Jews, the Kissinger family fled to London in 1938 and then to the Washington Heights section of New York. Kissinger was a straight-A student at George Washington High School and worked at Leopold Ascher, a shaving-brush factory in Manhattan. In 1941, Kissinger continued working and enrolled in night school at the City College of New York (CCNY). He moved to CCNY's business school in 1942 but left school after receiving a draft notice in 1943. He was inducted into the United States Army and departed for Germany in 1944, serving in the counterintelligence corps.

After returning to the United States, Kissinger was accepted at Harvard University and awarded a Harvard National Scholarship. He received a B.A. in 1950 and went on to earn an M.A. and a Ph.D. in 1952 and 1954, respectively. Between 1951 and 1969, while serving on the faculty of the Government Department, Kissinger served as the director of the Harvard International Seminar, a position that allowed him to develop a large network of contacts worldwide.

In 1969, Kissinger joined the Nixon White House as assistant to the president for national security affairs. He became the first American government official to visit the People's Republic of China in more than twenty years; his secret 1971 trip to Beijing opened the doors for communication between the United States and China, paving the way for Nixon's historic visit in February 1972. Kissinger also played an instrumental role in negotiating the Strategic Arms Limitation Talks (SALT I) with the Soviet Union and negotiated a cease-fire with the North Vietnamese in early 1973. This action earned Kissinger a Nobel Peace Prize that year, although some critics deem the award inappropriate because of his assertive role earlier in the war.

His brilliance as a negotiator enabled Kissinger to arrange a cease-fire between Israel and Egypt following the Arab-Israeli war of 1973. The same year, he replaced William P. Rogers as secretary of state. Kissinger was the first Jew to serve in that post and was the only secretary of state to continue in the capacity of special assistant to the president for national security affairs. Although Richard Nixon resigned the presidency in 1974, Kissinger continued as secretary of state under Gerald Ford until 1977.

Since 1977, Kissinger has been a lecturer and consultant for international affairs. President Ronald Reagan appointed Kissinger as chair of the National Bipartisan Commission on Central America, a position he held between 1983 and 1985. Kissinger was also a member of the President's Foreign Intelligence Advisory Board between 1984 and 1990.

Kissinger is the founder and chair of Kissinger & Associates, an international consulting firm based in New York City. He is councillor to Chase Manhattan Bank and has served on the boards of directors for several companies. (TW)

KLEIN, ARTHUR GEORGE
Member of Congress, 1946–1956, 1941–1945

Arthur George Klein was born in New York City August 8, 1904. He attended the public schools and Washington Square College of New York, ultimately graduating from the law department of New York University in 1926. In 1927, Klein was admitted to the bar and commenced practice in New York City.

Klein was elected to the Seventy-seventh Congress as a Democrat in a special election to fill the vacancy caused by the death of M. Michael Edelstein and was reelected to the Seventy-eighth Congress, serving from July 29, 1941, to January 3, 1945. Klein was not a candidate for renomination in 1944. However, he was elected to the Seventy-ninth Congress, again in a special election, this time to fill the vacancy caused by the resignation of Samuel Dickstein; Klein was then reelected in 1946 to the Eightieth and to the four succeeding Congresses, serving from February 19, 1946, until his resignation December 31, 1956.

Klein resigned from the House to assume a seat on the New York State Supreme Court on January 1, 1957; he served until his death on February 20, 1968. (BB)

KLEIN, HERBERT CHARLES
Member of Congress, 1993–1995

Herbert Klein was born in Newark, New Jersey, on June 24, 1930. He attended Rutgers University, where he received a B.A. in 1950. Klein received his J.D. from Harvard University School of Law in

1953, and his LL.M. from New York University in 1958. Klein also served in the United States Air Force from 1954 until 1956. He was admitted to the New Jersey Bar in 1953 and proceeded to practice law in Clifton, New Jersey.

Klein's career in political life began in 1972, when he became a member of the New Jersey State Assembly, a position he held until 1976. He then returned to practicing law until he ran for United States Congress in 1992. Klein ran as a Democrat for the seat vacated by the retiring Robert Roe, who had held the seat for twenty-three years. Klein promised new job growth to the economically depressed area of North Paterson, New Jersey. On a liberal campaign against Republican state senator Joseph Bubba, Klein supported universal health care, gun control, and abortion rights. Klein defeated Bubba by a margin of six percentage points.

Klein served one term in Congress, before losing by 1 percent to Bill Martini in a race that was often driven by harsh rhetoric. (MW)

KLUTZNICK, PHILIP M.
Secretary of Commerce, 1979–1981

Once joking that he had a B'nai B'rith membership card before he owned a razor, Philip Klutznick was an important figure in both the U.S. government and American Jewish life. He served seven U.S. presidents from Roosevelt to Carter. "He is considered to be the leading Jew in the U.S.," declared Rabbi Seymour Siegel in 1985.

Born in Kansas City, Missouri, on July 9, 1907, Klutznick grew up in an Orthodox Jewish home. After attending the University of Kansas and the University of Nebraska, he received a law degree at Creighton University in 1930. He held several government posts in the city of Omaha before he became the first commissioner of the U.S. Federal Public Housing Authority from 1944 to 1946.

During World War II, President Franklin D. Roosevelt put him in charge of building temporary housing for defense workers, and he was later involved in the building of Oak Ridge, Tennessee, the center for major research on the atomic bomb. An influential American Jewish leader, Klutznick served as president of B'nai B'rith and the World Jewish Congress; he was a founder and chair of the Conference of Presidents of Major American Jewish Organizations and general chair of the United Jewish Appeal. After the war, Klutznick became one of the major real estate developers in the country, building shopping malls and suburban planned communities. In 1979, President Jimmy Carter appointed him secretary of commerce.

A generous philanthropist who had decidedly dovish views on Israel, Klutznick expected that the recipients of his generosity would freely express their own views regardless of whether they conflicted with his own.

Philip Klutznick died at age ninety-two on August 14, 1999. (DA)

KOCH, EDWARD IRVING
Mayor of New York City 1978–1989;
Member of Congress, 1969–1977

Edward Irving Koch was born in the Bronx on December 12, 1924. The son of Polish Jewish immigrants, Koch was raised as a Conservative Jew and enlisted in the army during World War II to fight the spread of Nazism. During the war, he earned two battle stars for his service as a front-line soldier. After the war, he received his LL.B. from New York University in 1948 and entered private practice as an attorney in New York in 1949.

In 1963, Koch decided to enter politics when he successfully challenged powerful New York Democratic chair Carmine de Sapio for the position of district Democratic leader for Greenwich Village. He held this position until 1965, when he returned to private practice as a senior partner in a New York City law firm. However, just two years later, Koch reentered politics, successfully running for a seat on the New York City Council. In 1968, he defied the political odds again by becoming the first Democrat since 1934 elected to Congress from New York City's silk stocking district. Koch remained in Congress for nine years and served as an active member of the House Appropriations Committee.

In 1977, Koch defeated Mario Cuomo in a runoff to become the 105th mayor of New York City. During his twelve-year tenure as mayor, Koch's major achievement was the restoration of fiscal stability to the city. Koch failed to become the first four-term mayor of New York City when he lost to David Dinkins in 1989.

Since leaving office, Ed Koch has been remarkably active. He has served as a judge on the television show *The People's Court*, conducted his own daily radio show, written articles and books, provided commentary on cable news programs, taught at New York University, and given speeches in every part of the country. A lifelong bachelor, at the age of seventy-six, Koch shows no signs of slowing down. (KJ)

KOHL, HERB
United States Senator, 1989–present

Born in Milwaukee on February 7, 1935, Democratic senator Herb Kohl is best known for his relentless pursuit of a balanced budget. His criticism of unnecessary spending earned him high regard from the Concord Coalition and other groups concerned with deficit reduction. Although Kohl has generally sided with the Democrats on policy matters, he has joined Republicans to support a constitutional balanced-budget amendment, term limits, and the line-item veto.

In Wisconsin, Kohl, a graduate of the University of Wisconsin and the Harvard Business School, is probably best known for his family's ownership of the Kohl's grocery store chain. His personal fortune is derived from the sale of this company. He has used the proceeds to purchase the Milwaukee Bucks basketball team, to fund numerous charitable ventures, and, most notably, to finance his own campaigns for United States Senate with millions of his own dollars. Herb Kohl is one of a few so-called self-financers who has personally financed not only his initial bid for office but also his reelection campaign.

In the Senate, Kohl has taken an extremely active role on antigun legislation. He used his position on the Judiciary Committee to sponsor the Gun-Free Schools Act, and, when this law was struck down by the Supreme Court, he reinserted its provisions into another law once the Court's concerns had been addressed. Along with Wisconsin's junior senator, Russ Feingold, Kohl has also represented the concerns of his state's dairy industry, successfully opposing the New England Dairy Compact, an arrangement that would allow dairy farmers in the New England region to band together and effectively keep Wisconsin dairy products out of the market.

Kohl was reelected to a third term in the Senate in the 2000 election. (JK)

KOPPEL, TED
Journalist

Ted Koppel was born in Lancashire, England, on February 8, 1940. His parents had emigrated to England from Germany in 1936 to escape the Nazis. Moving to the United States in 1953, he earned a bachelor's degree from Syracuse University and a master's degree in mass communications research and political science from Stanford University.

Koppel worked at WMCA Radio in New York City before joining ABCNews in New York in 1963. After general assignment correspondent's work for five years, he became the Miami bureau chief for ABCNews. From 1969 to 1971, he was the Hong Kong bureau chief. Koppel served as the chief diplomatic correspondent for ABCNews from 1971 to 1980, where his coverage included special attention to former secretary of state Henry Kissinger's "shuttle diplomacy." He also anchored the *ABC Saturday Night News* from 1975 to 1977.

Koppel has reported in every presidential nominating convention since 1964. In 1980, he coanchored ABC's coverage of the Democratic and Republican National Conventions.

When ABCNews introduced *Nightline*, the first late-night news program, Koppel was named the anchor. The show brought him to the national limelight with its coverage of the Iran hostage crisis. For twenty years, Koppel has been a leader in innovative broadcasting and in-depth reporting on major news stories. For his excellence in broadcasting and journalism, he has won twenty-five Emmy Awards and five George Foster Peabody Awards, among other honors. (SB)

KOPPLEMANN, HERMAN PAUL
Member of Congress, 1945–1947, 1941–1943, 1933–1939

Born in Odessa, Russia, in 1880, Herman Kopplemann emigrated to the United States with his parents in 1882, settling in Hartford, Connecticut. He began his political career on the state level in 1904, when he was elected to the Hartford City Council, a position he held for four consecutive terms. In 1913, Kopplemann won election to the Connecticut House of Representatives; in 1917, he moved up to the state senate.

His career on the federal level began in 1933 when he became the first Jew from Connecticut to serve in the United States House of Representatives. He served three terms as an active supporter of the New Deal. Kopplemann failed in his bid for reelection in 1938 but triumphed once again in 1940, returning to the Seventy-seventh Congress. His checkered career in electoral politics continued, however. He lost a bid for reelection in 1942, won in 1944, and lost his final run for office in 1946.

An active Jew, Kopplemann held a number of posts in Jewish agencies, including chair of the

United Jewish Appeal, vice president of the United Synagogue of America, and secretary of the Board of Overseers of the Jewish Theological Seminary.

Herman Kopplemann died in Hartford on August 11, 1957. (JSh)

KOZINSKI, ALEX
Judge, U.S. Court of Appeals, 1985–present

Born July 23, 1950, in Bucharest, Romania, Alex Kozinski came to the United States at the age of eleven. He earned an A.B. in 1972 and his J.D. at University of California—Los Angeles in 1975. Immediately after law school, Kozinski clerked for Judge Anthony Kennedy on the Ninth Circuit of the U.S. Court of Appeals and then for Chief Justice Warren Burger on the U.S. Supreme Court from 1976 to 1977.

Kozinski practiced privately in Los Angeles until 1979 and then in Washington, D.C., until 1981. The election of President Ronald Reagan in 1980 provided Kozinski the opportunity to serve as deputy legal counsel in the Office of the President-Elect from the election through the inauguration and as assistant counsel in the Office of Counsel to the President in 1981. Kozinski was also special counsel for the Merit Systems Protection Board from 1981 to 1982. He was then named as chief judge for the U.S. Court of Claims, where he served until 1985, when Reagan nominated him for the U.S. Court of Appeals in the Ninth Circuit.

Trivia about Kozinski includes the distinction of having appeared on the *Dating Game*, where he was selected for the date as Bachelor 2. He ran for high school class president against Lance Ito, who defeated him soundly. Finally, he also was the only federal judge to admit to having been a member of a communist youth organization, an affiliation he ended when he emigrated to the United States. (JM)

KRAFT, JOSEPH
Journalist

Born in South Carolina on September 4, 1924, Joseph Kraft began his career as a journalist at the age of fourteen as a stringer covering high school sports for the *New York World-Telegram*. Kraft served as a cryptographer during World War II and afterward attended the Sorbonne, Columbia, and Princeton Universities.

In 1950, Kraft joined the *Washington Post* as an editorial writer. Several prestigious jobs followed, including staff writer for the *New York Times* Sunday edition (1952–1957), Washington correspondent for *Harper's* magazine, and a syndicated columnist for more than two hundred papers until his death in 1986.

An award-winning contributor to the *New Yorker* and speechwriter for John F. Kennedy's presidential campaign, Kraft was celebrated by his colleagues as one of the most gifted journalists of his time, renowned for his scrupulous research and sensitive insights into a wide variety of topics, domestic and international. Despite a heart condition, Kraft traveled extensively in search of facts and stories.

During his career Kraft received numerous honors and awards, including the Overseas Press Club award (1958, 1973, 1980), the John Jay Award for Distinguished Professional Achievement (1983), and the French Legion of Honor Chevalier Award (1983).

Joseph Kraft died on January 10, 1986, in Washington, D.C. (JSh)

KRAMER, KENNETH BENTLEY
Member of Congress, 1979–1987

Kenneth Kramer was born in Chicago on February 19, 1942. He attended the University of Illinois, receiving his B.A. in 1963. In 1966, he earned his J.D. from Harvard and was admitted to the bar in 1966.

From 1967 to 1970, Kramer served in the United States Army. On his discharge, he settled in Colorado and became deputy district attorney for the Fourth Judicial District in 1970, holding that position until 1972. Kramer was in private practice law from 1972 until 1978. He also served as state representative to the Colorado General Assembly from 1973 until 1978.

In 1978, Kramer ran for an open congressional seat that was vacated by William Armstrong, who left to run for the Senate. Though experiencing a tough primary race against Bob Eckelberry in the heavily Republican district, Kramer prevailed and went on to win election to the Fifth District of Colorado by a margin of twenty-six percentage points against Democrat Gerry Frank.

Kramer served four terms in the House before running unsuccessfully for the Senate. After his defeat, President Ronald Reagan appointed him assistant secretary of the army. After two years in that position, he was tapped by President George H. W. Bush to be associate judge of the United States Court of Veterans Appeals. (MW)

KRAUS, MILTON
Member of Congress, 1917–1923

Milton Kraus was born in Kokomo, Indiana, on June 26, 1866. He attended the University of Michigan, where he graduated with a law degree in 1886. He was admitted to the Indiana Bar in 1887. Kraus began to practice law in Peru, Indiana. Kraus organized a volunteer brigade of soldiers for the Spanish-American War.

A Republican, Kraus was elected to Congress from Indiana in 1917 and served three successive terms until he was defeated in the election of 1922. Afterward, he resumed manufacturing activities.

Milton Kraus died in Wabash, Indiana, on November 18, 1942. (MW)

KREBS, JOHN HANS
Member of Congress, 1975–1979

John Krebs was born in Berlin, Germany, on December 17, 1926. In 1933, he moved with his family to Israel. He emigrated to the United States in 1946 and became a citizen in 1954. Krebs graduated from the University of California–Berkeley with an A.B. degree in 1950. After serving two years in the United States Army, he entered the University of California, Hastings College of Law, in San Francisco, from which he graduated in 1957. He then began practicing law in Fresno, California.

Krebs began his political career in the Fresno County government. In 1974, he was one of the Democrats elected to the United States House of Representatives in his party's post-Watergate sweep. Krebs was reelected once, but lost his second bid for reelection in 1978.

John Krebs is retired and lives in Fresno, California. (MW)

KRISTOL, WILLIAM
Editor, The Weekly Standard, *1995–present; Chief of Staff to Vice President, 1989–1993*

William Kristol was born December 23, 1952. He is the son of Irving Kristol, one of the founding editors of the conservative publication *The Public Interest.* William received his bachelor's degree in 1973 and a doctorate in 1979 from Harvard University. Between 1978 and 1983, Kristol taught political science at the University of Pennsylvania. He returned to Harvard as an assistant professor of public policy, a position he held until 1985.

During President Ronald Reagan's second term, Kristol was a special assistant to the chief of staff in the Department of Education in Washington. In 1988, he was campaign manager of Alan Keyes's Senate campaign in Maryland. After that election, he

joined the Bush administration as Vice President Dan Quayle's chief of staff. Following Bush's defeat in 1992, Kristol founded and became chair of the Project for a Republican Future, a Washington think tank. Since 1995, he has been the editor and publisher of *The Weekly Standard,* an important publication for conservative viewpoints. (TW)

KRIVOSHA, NORMAN
Chief Justice, Nebraska Supreme Court, 1978–1987

Norman Krivosha was born August 3, 1934, in Detroit, Michigan. He attended the University of Nebraska at Lincoln, receiving his bachelor's degree in 1956 and his law degree in 1958.

Krivosha began his political career as the city attorney of Lincoln, Nebraska, from 1969 to 1970. He was general counsel for the Lincoln Electric System and Lincoln General Hospital from 1969 until 1978. In addition to practicing law, Krivosha also taught at the University of Nebraska College of Law as an adjunct professor. In 1978, Krivosha returned to public life, serving as chief justice of the Nebraska Supreme Court until he retired in 1987. Krivosha then went on to work for the Ameritas Insurance Corporation of Lincoln (formally Bankers Life Insurance). He was the company's executive vice president for law and government affairs, secretary, and general counsel. In 1999, Krivosha left Ameritas Insurance Corporation to head the new Kutak Rock Law Firm in Omaha.

Krivosha is the past president of the United Synagogue of Conservative Judaism and currently is a member of the United Synagogue of America. He was also the elected chair of the Nebraska State Historical Society Board of Trustees. (BMcN)

KROCK, ARTHUR
Washington Bureau Chief, New York Times, *1932–1953*

Arthur Krock was born November 16, 1886, in Glasgow, Kentucky. He was accepted by Princeton in 1904 but was only able to attend for a year because of financial problems. Instead, he earned a junior college degree from the Lewis Institute in Chicago. Krock began working in Washington in 1910 as a reporter for the *Louisville Times.* He soon moved on to work at the *Louisville Courier-Journal and Times* and then at the *New York*

World as a personal assistant to the powerful publisher Ralph Pulitzer.

In 1927, Krock accepted a job with the *New York Times* in Washington, and he was put in charge of reorganizing the Washington bureau in 1932. As the Washington bureau chief, he was given virtual autonomy by the *Times's* New York office, and he resisted all later attempts by the main office to assert control over his reporters. His strict administration and numerous contacts turned the newspaper's Washington bureau into a professional and highly respected institution. He also wrote editorials, and—as a conservative southern Democrat—he was best known for his scathing critiques of President Franklin Roosevelt. During his twenty-one years with the *Times,* he was considered one of the most powerful journalists in the country. In 1953, at age sixty-six, he retired and passed the bureau's leadership on to his successor, James Reston.

Arthur Krock died in 1974. (OS)

KUNIN, MADELEINE MAY
Ambassador to Switzerland and Liechtenstein, 1996–1999; Deputy Secretary of Education, 1993–1996; Governor of Vermont, 1985–1991

Born on September 28, 1933, in Zurich, Switzerland, Madeleine was the second child of a German father and Swiss mother, Ferdinand and Renée Bloch May. After her father died in 1936, money pressures and a growing fear of the Nazis prompted her family to emigrate to the United States, arriving in New York City in June 1940. Although her immediate family was safe, several relatives died in concentration camps, leaving a lasting impression on Kunin. She wrote in her autobiography, "I believe I transformed my sense of the Holocaust into personal political activism. This was the source of my political courage. I could do what the victims could not: oppose evil whenever I recognized it."

Kunin graduated from the University of Massachusetts in 1956 with a B.A. in history, earned an M.S. from the Columbia University School of Jour-

nalism, and received an M.A. in English from the University of Vermont. She began her career as a journalist in Burlington, Vermont, where she met her husband, Dr. Arthur S. Kunin, whom she married in June 1959. When she had their first child in 1961, she put her career on hold but remained active in community affairs.

In 1972, she followed an initial political defeat by winning a seat in the Vermont House of Representatives, where she served for six years. After serving two terms as lieutenant governor, Kunin secured the Democratic gubernatorial nomination in 1982. She lost the first campaign but two years later emerged victorious as the first Jew and first woman elected governor of Vermont. While in office, Kunin led the fight for increased educational funding, the creation of a state venture capital corporation, and tough new environmental laws. She also managed to erase a large budget deficit inherited from her predecessor.

After her third term, Kunin returned to private life, lecturing and writing at Radcliffe, Harvard's Kennedy School of Government, and Dartmouth. She became very active in Bill Clinton's presidential campaign in 1992 and helped select his running mate. President Clinton named Kunin deputy secretary of education, a position she held until 1996, when she became United States ambassador to her native Switzerland and simultaneously nonresident ambassador to Liechtenstein. She returned to the United States in 1999, accepting a position as scholar in residence at Middlebury College. (JW)

Source: Madeleine Kunin, *Living a Political Life* (New York: Knopf, 1994).

KUNSTLER, WILLIAM
Lawyer for Radical Causes

William Kunstler was born on July 7, 1919, and grew up in New York City. He attended Yale for his undergraduate degree and Columbia Law School. Serving in the United States Army during World War II, he was stationed in the South and was appalled by the state of social justice. This experience shaped his career as a defender of civil rights and lawyer for accused radicals.

Kunstler earned a name for himself as a high-profile lawyer. He defended Jack Ruby, who killed Lee Harvey Oswald, President John F. Kennedy's accused assassin, in a Dallas police station before a national television audience. But he was most renowned as one of the premier civil rights lawyers of his generation, representing clients such as Martin Luther King Jr. and Malcolm X.

In 1968, Kunstler undertook his most famous case, the defense of the Chicago Seven, accused of conspiracy to incite rioting at the Chicago Democratic National Convention. His scathing (and intemperate) criticism of the government and the American legal system during that trial earned him a jail term for contempt of court.

In 1970, he organized the defense of those arrested for protesting the Vietnam War at Kent State; in 1971, he represented the prisoners at the Attica prison rebellion. Kunstler's radicalism earned him the hatred of many, but his role in some of the most important cases during a particularly turbulent time in American history made him a controversial figure to many and one of the foremost champions of social justice in the eyes of his supporters.

William Kunstler died of a heart attack September 3, 1995. (OS)

KURTZER, DANIEL CHARLES
U.S. Ambassador to Egypt, 1997–present

As the first Jewish U.S. ambassador to serve in an Arab country, Daniel Kurtzer's appointment to Egypt evoked a rash of anti-Jewish commentary and cartoons in the Egyptian press. One article, headlined "A Rabbi in the Robes of a Diplomat," mocked the plan of the Orthodox Jewish diplomat to make the ambassador's kitchen kosher.

Born on June 16, 1949, and raised in Elizabeth, New Jersey, Kurtzer received his B.A. from Yeshiva University in 1971 and two master's degrees in 1974 and a doctorate in 1976 from Columbia University. After beginning a career in the foreign service in the Bureau of International Organizational Affairs in 1976, he left Washington briefly to serve as dean of Yeshiva College, the men's undergraduate division of the university.

In 1979, he was appointed the second secretary for political affairs at the American Embassy in Cairo. Three years later, he became first secretary for political affairs at the U.S. Embassy in Israel.

After returning to Washington in 1986, Kurtzer served successively as deputy director for Egyptian Affairs, speechwriter for the policy-planning staff, deputy assistant secretary for Near Eastern affairs, and principal deputy assistant secretary for intelligence and research.

Confirmed by the United States Senate in 1997, in 2001 Kurtzer was still serving as the U.S. ambassador to the Arab Republic of Egypt. (DA)

L

LANTOS, TOM
Member of Congress, 1981–present

The only Holocaust survivor to serve in the United States Congress, Tom Lantos was born February 1, 1928, in Budapest. Just sixteen years old when the Nazis invaded Hungary, Lantos was active in the underground resistance before he was imprisoned in a Nazi labor camp in Hungary. Lantos first came to the United States in 1947 to attend the University of Washington on an academic scholarship. He became a citizen in 1953 and twenty-seven years later was elected to Congress from San Mateo County, on the San Francisco peninsula. Lantos was one of only two new Democrats elected to the House in the Republican landslide of 1980.

Lantos holds a Ph.D. in economics from the University of California–Berkeley and was a professor at San Francisco State University prior to his election to Congress. In the House of Representatives, he is the ranking Democrat on both the International Relations and Government Reform committees. In 1983, he cofounded the Congressional Human Rights Caucus.

Lantos is married to the former Annette Tillemann, a fellow Holocaust survivor and his childhood sweetheart. (JS)

LAUDER, RONALD STEPHEN
Chair, Conference of Presidents of Major Jewish Organizations, 1999–present; U.S. Ambassador to Austria, 1986–1987

Ronald Lauder, the son of Estée Lauder, the famous cosmetics executive, was born February 26, 1944, in New York City. He received a degree in French literature from the University of Paris in 1964 and a B.S. from the University of Pennsylvania in 1965.

Lauder worked with Estée Lauder, Inc., in Brussels, Paris, and New York City between 1965 and 1983. He was on the company's board of directors from 1980 until 1983.

In 1983, Lauder accepted the position of deputy assistant secretary of defense. President Ronald Reagan appointed him U.S. ambassador to Austria in 1986, a post he held for two years. His time in Europe influenced Lauder's dedication to the revitalization in communities that had been devastated by the Holocaust. He created the Ronald S. Lauder Foundation to foster Jewish education and outreach programs in nations such as Austria, Germany, and Slovakia.

Lauder is active in many other Jewish and professional organizations as well. In 1997, for example, he became president of the Jewish National Fund, after more than ten years of activity with that organization. He is also the treasurer of the World Jewish Congress, and he became chair of the Conference of Presidents of Major Jewish Organizations in June 1999. (TW)

LAUTENBERG, FRANK
United States Senator, 1982–2001

Born on January 23, 1924, in Paterson, New Jersey, Frank Lautenberg was the son of a working-class immigrant father who died when Lautenberg was nineteen. To support his mother, Lautenberg worked evenings and weekends at a sandwich shop owned by his sister Mollie, before leaving to serve in the Army Signal Corps during World War II. The GI Bill of Rights enabled him to attend Columbia University after his discharge; he graduated with a B.S. in business in 1949.

In 1952, Lautenberg started a company called Automatic Data Processing. The firm has been tremendously successful and has made Lautenberg an extremely wealthy man. He has always viewed public service as an important obligation of those who have benefited from the promise of the American dream. Between 1978 and 1982, he served as a commissioner of the New York and New Jersey Port Authority.

In 1982, he sought election to the United States Senate from New Jersey, running against Republican congresswoman Millicent Fenwick for a seat vacated by Democrat Harrison (Pete) Williams Jr., who was under indictment as part of the ABSCAM scandal. Lautenberg defeated Fenwick, spending $5 million of his own money in the effort. Williams resigned the seat before his term expired, after his conviction on bribery and conspiracy charges. Lautenberg was appointed to fill the unexpired term about a week early, on December 27, 1982, and thus became senior to other senators elected at the same time as he was. Lautenberg was reelected quite easily in 1988 but faced a significant challenge from Republican Chuck Haytaian in 1994, winning by a margin of only 3 percent.

In the Senate, his voting record has been consistently liberal, in part because he believes that the government was a key factor in his own success. Lautenberg has been a supporter of issues of concern to Jews, not only those involving Israel but others such as the 1989 bill that sought to give persecuted Jews and evangelical Christians in the Soviet Union eased access to refugee status in the United States.

Lautenberg announced his retirement prior to the 2000 election, resisting efforts by President Bill Clinton and others to dissuade him by noting that, at the age of seventy-six, he desired to spend time with his grandchildren. (TW)

LAWRENCE, M. LARRY
United States Ambassador to Switzerland, 1994–1996

M. Larry Lawrence rose from poverty during the Great Depression to become a wealthy entrepreneur and United States ambassador to Switzerland.

Lawrence began his career as an advertising salesperson in Chicago but soon moved to California and became a highly successful real estate developer. Through construction, real estate, and insurance, he acquired enormous wealth and was among the four hundred wealthiest Americans listed by *Forbes* magazine. Lawrence was not only an entrepreneur but also a philanthropist. He contributed generously to the arts, education, and Jewish charities. Lawrence, the patriot, was also a prominent donor to the Democratic Party.

Lawrence was appointed ambassador to Switzerland in 1994. His confirmation was held up in the Senate for two months because of claims of military service that investigators were unable to verify. He assumed his post in March, however, and served two years before dying of leukemia in January 1996 at the age of sixty-nine.

His ambassadorship was controversial at times, but his final place of rest proved most contentious. Despite the fact that State Department officials were still unable to substantiate evidence of Lawrence's supposed claims of heroic wartime service in the U.S. Merchant Marine, he was buried in Arlington National Cemetery for his status as ambassador. However, reports surfaced in 1997 that he had, in fact, fabricated the story of service during World War II. His body was promptly exhumed from Arlington Cemetery and reburied in San Diego. (BMcN)

LEFKOWITZ, LOUIS
Attorney General of New York, 1957–1978

A liberal Republican, Louis Lefkowitz was the longest-serving New York attorney general in this overwhelmingly Democratic state.

Born in New York City on July 3, 1904, he was the son of Samuel and Mollie Isaacs. After graduating from Fordham Law School, he practiced law and then was elected to the New York State Assembly at the age of twenty-three. He later served as a judge in the New York City Municipal Court.

After being nominated for attorney general in 1956 to replace Senator-elect Jacob Javits, Lefkowitz was subsequently elected to the office in 1958, 1962, 1966, 1970, and 1974. His only electoral defeat was in 1961 when he ran for New York City mayor against Democrat Robert F. Wagner.

Unapologetic about his old style of politics, Lefkowitz once remarked that "people complain now about the old clubhouses, but they served the people, especially in the minority neighborhoods. Where I came from [the Lower East Side], there were the Jews and the Italians and the Irish, and we helped them to become citizens."

In 1978, he retired from politics and returned to his law practice. A close confidant of Governor Nelson Rockefeller, he was one of the few people ever invited to stay in the Executive Mansion in Albany. He reportedly taught Rockefeller how to eat blintzes.

Louis Lefkowitz died on June 20, 1996, at the age of ninety-one. (DA)

LEHMAN, HERBERT H.
United States Senator, 1949–1957;
Governor of New York, 1933–1942

Herbert H. Lehman was born on March 28, 1878, the son of Meyer Lehman, one of the original partners of Lehman Brothers and a founder of the Cotton Exchange. In 1899, Herbert Lehman received an A.B. from Williams College. He served as colonel in the United States Army in World War I.

In 1928, Lehman was elected lieutenant governor of New York, while his friend Franklin D. Roosevelt was elected governor. Four years later, Lehman was elected governor, and he was reelected three times. The Lehman era in New York was marked by progressive policies often called the "Little New Deal," including a social security program, the largest public housing project ever attempted by a state, and an extensive park system.

In 1942, FDR asked Lehman to run the United Nations Relief and Rehabilitation Administration, where he remained until 1946, when he ran for and lost a bid for the United States Senate. In 1949, at the age of seventy-one, he was tapped to finish an unexpired term in the Senate; he won a special election over John Foster Dulles to complete the term and was elected to a full term in the 1950 election. While in the Senate, Lehman was an early foe of Senator Joseph McCarthy's ideas. He died December 5, 1963, as he prepared to go to Washington to receive the Presidential Medal of Freedom.

In 1968, the Bronx campus of Hunter College became an independent college of the City University of New York and named itself for Lehman. Today, Lehman College is a public comprehensive liberal arts college enrolling nearly ten thousand students. (JM)

Source: Robert P. Ingalls, *Herbert H. Lehman and New York's Little New Deal* (New York: New York University Press, 1975).

LEHMAN, WILLIAM
Member of Congress, 1973–1993

William Lehman was born in Selma, Alabama, on October 4, 1913. He attended the University of Alabama, where he received a B.A. in 1934. From 1936 until 1972, Lehman was an auto dealer. Lehman was also an instructor in the public schools in the Miami–Dade area of Florida from 1966 until 1972; he served as a school board member during those years as well.

Lehman was elected as a Democrat to Congress in 1972. Running in a district heavily populated with Jews from the North, Lehman maintained a firm hold on his seat until he left Congress after two decades. Known as a liberal Democrat who voted more with his northern counterparts than his southern, Lehman supported generous assistance to Israel, higher subsidies for public transit, child care assistance, and increases in Social Security payments.

Lehman was also very instrumental in the fight for refugee resettlement aid for Cuban and Haitian refugees into Florida in the 1980s. In a similar vein, he traveled on a "mercy mission" to the Soviet Union in 1984 to deliver an artificial heart valve to a twenty-two-year-old Soviet woman who needed the valve for a life-saving surgery.

Despite several health issues in his later congressional career, including a stroke, Lehman continued to remain active and successful with his constituency, maintaining a strong hold on his seat until his retirement in 1993. (MW)

LERNER, MAX
Columnist and Author

Born December 20, 1905, in Minsk, White Russia, Maxwell (Mikhail) Alan Lerner was the son of Benjamin, a teacher, and Bessie (Podell). His father emigrated to the United States in 1906, followed by Max, his mother, and siblings in 1907. Benjamin moved the family to New Haven, Connecticut, in 1913 and entered the dairy business. Lerner attended Yale University on a scholarship for local Jewish students, earning his B.A. in 1923. He studied law for one year at Yale, leaving to earn an M.A. in economics at Washington University, St. Louis, and, in 1927, a Ph.D. at the Brookings Graduate School of Economics and Government in Washington. Lerner took a job with the editorial staff of the *Encyclopedia of the Social Sciences.*

During the 1930s, Lerner started publishing book reviews and essays. He was soon able to give voice to his liberal, progressive thinking on a regular basis as a member of the editorial staff of *The Nation* magazine (1935–1937). In 1938, he published his first book, *It's Later Than You Think: The Need for a Militant Democracy,* which supported the social goals of the New Deal while criticizing American capitalist society. With the onset

of World War II, Lerner reentered political journalism, contributing to the *New Republic,* which was very supportive of an active American role in Europe during the war.

In 1943, he became editorial director for *PM* and established his column, which would continue in newspapers for the rest of his life. As a correspondent at the front in 1945, Lerner drew on contrasts between the ruins of war-torn Europe and the industrial might of America to begin work on his most famous book, *America as a Civilization* (1957). *PM* folded in 1948, and his column moved in 1949 to its eventual home, the *New York Post.*

Lerner was also an educator, teaching at Sarah Lawrence College, Harvard, Williams, and, for most of his career, Brandeis as a professor of American civilization. After his retirement from Brandeis in 1973, Lerner taught at the United States International University in San Diego until shortly before his death from cancer on June 5, 1992 in New York City. (JW)

Source: Sanford A. Lakoff, *Max Lerner: Pilgrim in the Promised Land* (Chicago: University of Chicago Press, 1998).

LESSLER, MONTAGUE
Member of Congress, 1902–1903

Born in New York City on January 1, 1869, Montague Lessler graduated from the College of the City of New York in 1889 and went on to Columbia Law School. He practiced law in New York after admittance to the bar in 1891.

Lessler's political career was short and relatively uneventful. When New York representative Nicholas Muller resigned, Lessler was elected as a replacement to the Fifty-seventh Congress as a Republican. He held the post from January 7, 1902, to March 3, 1903.

When Lessler lost his reelection bid in 1902, he returned to New York and continued to practice law until his death on February 17, 1938. (JSh)

LEVI, EDWARD HIRSCH
Attorney General, 1975–1977

Born June 26, 1911, in Chicago, Edward Levi was the son and grandson of rabbis. He attended a special kindergarten, elementary school, and high school at the University of Chicago. He also received Ph.B. and J.D. degrees from Chicago in 1932 and 1935, respectively. In 1938, Levi attained his J.S.D. degree from Yale.

Levi returned to the University of Chicago in 1936, as an assistant professor of law. He remained at the university until 1940, when he became a special assistant to the United States attorney general. In 1945, he returned to the Law School with the rank of full professor. He was named dean in 1950, the first Jewish dean of a major American law school. In 1962, Levi became the university provost; and, on November 14, 1968, he was appointed president of the University of Chicago, again setting a precedent as the first Jewish leader of a large American university.

As with many educational leaders, Levi was also active in government service. Between 1966 and 1967, he served on the White House Task Force on Education. In 1969 and 1970, he was a member of the President's Task Force on Priorities in Higher Education.

But his government service took a sharp turn when, in 1975, in the aftermath of the Watergate scandal that shook the nation's confidence in the integrity of the Justice Department, President Gerald Ford appointed Levi as attorney general. His performance in that job is credited with restoring not only integrity but also professionalism to the office of the attorney general and to the department that had come to be viewed as a political arm of a discredited president.

After leaving the presidency of the University of Chicago, Levi returned to teaching. He was elected president of the American Academy of the Arts and Sciences in 1986.

Edward Levi died on March 7, 2000, in his beloved Chicago. (TW)

LEVIN, CARL
United States Senator, 1979–present

Born on June 28, 1934, in Detroit, Michigan, Carl Levin received a B.A. from Swarthmore College in 1956 and a law degree from Harvard University in 1959. He returned to his native Detroit and began practicing law in 1959.

Between 1964 and 1967, Levin served as special assistant attorney general for the State of Michigan. From 1968 to 1969, he was the chief appellate defender for the City of Detroit. He became a member of the Detroit City Council in 1969 and was elected president of the council in 1974. In 1978, Levin, a liberal Democrat, was elected to the Senate. He had challenged incumbent Robert Griffin and benefited from Griffin's uncertainty about remaining in the Senate; Griffin entered the race, withdrew, and then reentered, allowing Levin to raise the issue of the incumbent's continued dedication to his job. Levin was reelected by wide margins in 1984, 1990, and 1996.

Levin has been among the most liberal members of the Senate. A strong defender of organized labor and of the automobile industry in particular, Levin also has been concerned with congressional ethics. He was the sponsor of the Senate gift rule, which set a $50 limit on gifts to senators and staffers. He also played a large role in the enactment of the special counsel law. Levin's brother, Sander, is a member of the House of Representatives. (TW)

LEVIN, LEWIS CHARLES
Member of Congress, 1845–1851

Lewis Charles Levin, the first Jew to serve in the United States House of Representatives, was born in Charleston, South Carolina, on November 10, 1808. He graduated from South Carolina College (now the University of South Carolina) with a degree in law. In 1838, Levin moved to Philadelphia and, in 1842, became one of the founders of the Native American Party. To advocate the positions of the Native American Party, Levin published and edited the *Philadelphia Daily Sun.*

In 1844, Levin was elected as a candidate of the American Party to the Twenty-ninth Congress; he was reelected twice but defeated when seeking a fourth term in the election of 1850. In the House, Levin chaired the Committee on Naval Affairs.

After his 1850 defeat, Levin resumed the practice of law in Philadelphia, until his death on March 14, 1860. (BB)

LEVIN, SANDER M.
Member of Congress, 1983–present

Sander M. Levin was born in Detroit on September 6, 1931. He represented Oakland County for six years in the Michigan State Senate, serving as Senate minority leader in his final term (1969–1970). In 1970, and again in 1974, Levin was the Democratic candidate for governor of Michigan, narrowly losing both contests to William Milliken. During the Carter administration, Levin served as assistant administrator of the Agency for International Development.

Levin was elected in 1982 to the United States House of Representatives. At that time his brother Carl was already serving as a United States senator from Michigan. He sits on the Ways and Means Committee and is the ranking minority member of the Trade Subcommittee. He has used this position to support the auto manufacturers and workers based in his district. Levin was one of the leading House opponents of the North American Free Trade Agreement, and he has consistently worked to remove barriers to American exports. (JS)

LEVINE, MELDON EDISES
Member of Congress, 1983–1993

Mel Levine was born on June 7, 1943, in Los Angeles. He received a B.A. from the University of California–Berkeley in 1964, an M.A. from Princeton University in 1966, and a law degree from Harvard University in 1969.

Levine was elected to the California State Assembly in 1976 and served four terms. He was elected to the United States House of Representatives in 1982. While in Congress, he sat on the Foreign Affairs and Judiciary Committees. He was an early advocate of an investigation into President Ronald Reagan's Central American policies and an early supporter of the Brady Bill. Throughout his career, Levine specialized in U.S. foreign policy, particularly around issues of international trade and Middle East policy—always cautioning against relationships with anti-Israeli states. In 1987, Levine founded Rebuild America, an educational foundation focused on improving American competitiveness by increasing support for high-technology industries. Levine gave up his seat in the House in 1992 to run for the Senate but lost the Democratic primary to Barbara Boxer.

Between 1993 and 1997 Levine served as co-president of Builders for Peace, an effort by the private sector to aid the Middle East peace process. He is currently a partner in the law firm of Gibson, Dunn, and Crutcher. He also currently serves as the U.S. chair of the U.S.-Israel-Palestinian Anti-Incitement Committee. (AE)

LEVITAS, ELLIOT HARRIS
Member of Congress, 1975–1985

Elliot Harris Levitas was born in Atlanta on December 26, 1930. He attended the public schools of Atlanta and earned his B.A. from Emory University in 1952 and his law degree from Emory Law School in 1956. After law school, Levitas received a Rhodes scholarship and studied at Oxford University, earning a master's of law degree in 1958.

Levitas commenced practice in Atlanta, after serving in the United States Air Force from 1955 to 1958. He was elected to represent Atlanta in the Georgia House of Representatives from 1965 to 1974. In 1974, he was one of many freshmen elected to the Ninety-fourth Congress, as part of the reaction to the Watergate scandal. A liberal Democrat, Levitas was reelected to four subsequent congresses. He was, however, unsuccessful in his bid for a sixth term, losing in the 1984 election.

Levitas remains a resident of Atlanta. (BB)

LEVITT, ARTHUR
New York State Comptroller, 1955–1979

Born on June 28, 1900, Arthur Levitt grew up in Brooklyn. He served as a private in World War I and then went on to Columbia University, graduating in 1921. He went on to receive his law degree from Columbia in 1924.

After his admission to the New York State Bar, Levitt began legal practice and played an active role in Brooklyn's civic and charitable affairs. His political career began as campaign manager for Assemblyman Irwin Steingut in a primary election. Mayor Vincent R. Impellitteri appointed Levitt to the New York school board in 1952. He was elected board president in 1954.

Levitt became the Democratic nominee for state comptroller in 1954 under unusual circumstances; the original candidate had been involved in a public scandal and had to step aside. Levitt went on to serve as state comptroller for an unprecedented six terms before his retirement. During his tenure, his office became an aggressive auditor not only of state and local money but also of the way the government did its job. Levitt established a standard of responsibility. He even endorsed his Republican successor instead of the Democratic candidate because his regard of trust transcended partisan politics.

Arthur Levitt died at the age of seventy-nine, working at his desk in his office at the Lincoln Savings Bank, on May 6, 1980. (BMcN)

LEVY, DAVID A.
Member of Congress, 1993–1995

Born in Johnson County, Indiana, on December 18, 1953, David Levy attended Hofstra University on Long Island, receiving a B.A. in 1973 and his J.D. in 1979. He was admitted to the New York State Bar in 1980 and began practicing law. He also was involved in local politics, serving on the Hempstead town council from 1989 until 1993.

Levy ran as a Republican for an open seat in the 1992 congressional election. His opponent, Democrat Philip Schiliro, was a strong candidate, despite having recently returned to the area after a ten-year absence. Levy prevailed, however, and defeated Schiliro by a margin of five percentage points.

While in office, Levy maintained votes with his party, with the exception of President George H. W. Bush's loan-guarantee restrictions for Israel. While Levy received the party organization's endorsement in the 1994 campaign, he lost in the Republican primary election to Daniel Frisa, whom he had narrowly beaten in the primary two years earlier. Levy remained on the November ballot as the Conservative Party candidate but finished a distant third as Frisa won handily over Levy and their Democratic opponent. (MW)

LEVY, JEFFERSON MONROE
Member of Congress, 1911–1915, 1899–1901

Jefferson Levy was born in New York City on April 16, 1852. He received a law degree from New York University Law School in 1873. He was admitted to the New York Bar and began practicing law in New York City.

At the age of nineteen, Levy had inherited Monticello, Thomas Jefferson's estate, from his uncle, Commodore Uriah P. Levy. Jefferson Levy spent much time and effort to maintain and improve Monticello and also opened the estate for public view on several occasions.

In 1898, Levy was elected as a Democrat to the United States Congress. He served one term in office and did not run for reelection. He returned to his law practice, where he specialized in real estate law.

In 1910, Levy successfully ran for Congress for a second time; this time he served two terms. While in office, he was the leader of the gold Democrats, who advocated for the maintenance and parity of all forms of currency issued by the government. He also obtained an increase in wage for postal clerks and advocated an enlarged navy. He retired from Congress in 1915 and resumed practicing law in New York City.

Jefferson Levy died on March 6, 1924. (MW)

LEVY, WILLIAM MALLORY
Member of Congress, 1875–1877

William Mallory Levy was born in Isle of Wight, Virginia, on October 31, 1827. A graduate of the College of William and Mary, Levy served in the Mexican War as second lieutenant. In 1851, he was accepted to the Virginia Bar, but the following year he moved to Natchitoches, Louisiana, and established a practice there.

In 1860, Levy became the editor of the *Natchitoches Chronicle;* that same year, he served as a presidential elector on the Democratic ticket. He fought in the Confederate infantry during the Civil War, commissioned first as captain and then as major.

Levy was elected to Congress in 1874, but his bid for reelection was not successful. He was appointed associate justice of the Louisiana Supreme Court in 1879 and served until his death on August 14, 1882. (MD)

LEW, JACOB
Director of Office of Management and Budget, 1998–2001

Jacob Lew was born August 25, 1955, in New York City. His father was a Polish immigrant. In 1978, he received a B.A. from Harvard University; he was awarded a law degree from Georgetown in 1983.

Lew became involved in politics at an early age. When he was twelve, he took to the streets of New York City to campaign in Senator Eugene Mc-

Carthy's effort to unseat President Lyndon Johnson. At the age of eighteen, he began working as an aide to Bella Abzug. After graduating from college and while attending law school, he served as the principal domestic policy adviser to House Speaker Thomas P. "Tip" O'Neill. Lew practiced private law between 1987 and 1991. Recognized for his expertise in the political implications of policy proposals, he was chosen in 1988 as the issues director for the Democratic National Committee during Michael Dukakis's presidential campaign.

When President Bill Clinton took office, Lew joined the White House staff as special assistant to the president at the Office of Management and Budget (OMB). In 1995, he assumed the position of deputy director. When OMB director Franklin D. Raines resigned to head Fannie Mae, Lew was appointed as his successor, a position that holds cabinet rank. A tough negotiator, Lew frequently served as the point man in Clinton administration budget conflicts with the Republican Congress. (TW)

LEWIS, ANN
Presidential Adviser, 1997–2001

Ann Lewis was born in Jersey City, New Jersey, on December 19, 1937. She attended Radcliffe but left without receiving a degree. After assisting in campaigns in Indiana in the 1960s, she returned to Boston and served on the staff of Mayor Kevin White until 1975. Throughout the 1970s, Lewis served as administrative aide for several politicians from Indiana to New York. She also participated in the founding meeting of the National Women's Political Caucus in Houston in 1971.

In 1981, Lewis became the political director of the Democratic National Committee, a post she held until 1984. In 1985 she served as the executive director for Americans for Democratic Action, a liberal political action group. She also served as adviser to Reverend Jesse Jackson's 1988 bid for the Democratic presidential nomination. In the 1990s, Lewis was very active in Planned Parenthood, serving as vice president for public policy, director of the campaign for human rights, and executive director.

During the 1996 presidential campaign, she served as Bill Clinton's chief campaign spokesperson and as his deputy campaign manager. After Clinton's reelection, Lewis served in the White House, first as director of communications (1997–1999) and later as counselor to the president (1999–2000).

Ann Lewis is the sister of Democratic congressman Barney Frank. (MW)

LEWIS, ANTHONY
Newspaper Columnist

Born in New York City on March 27, 1927, Anthony Lewis earned a bachelor's degree from Harvard College in 1948.

Lewis began his career in journalism immediately after college. From 1948 to 1952, he was a deskman for the Sunday department of the *New York Times*. In 1952, he served as a staff member for the Democratic National Committee and became a reporter for the *Washington Daily News*, where he remained until 1955. From 1955 until 1964, Lewis worked with the Washington bureau of the *New York Times*. In 1965, he became chief of the *Times*'s London bureau, serving there until 1972. Since 1969, he has also been an editorial columnist for the *Times*.

Between 1979 and 1984, Lewis was a lecturer on law at Harvard University. Since 1983, he has been the James Madison visiting professor at Columbia. He has written several books on the Supreme Court, including *Gideon's Trumpet* (1964) and *Make No Law: The* Sullivan *Case and the First Amendment* (1991), and is a frequent contributor to numerous journals. Lewis received the Pulitzer Prize for national reporting in 1955 and 1963 and the Elijah Parrich Lovejoy Award for distinguished journalism in defense of the First Amendment in 1983.

Lewis is married to Margaret H. Marshall, the chief justice of the Massachusetts Supreme Judicial Court. (TW)

LICHT, FRANK
Governor of Rhode Island, 1969–1973

Frank Licht was born on March 13, 1916, in Providence, Rhode Island, the son of Russian immigrants. He attended Brown University, where he founded a branch of the Menorah Society, a Jewish cultural organization.

After attending law school, Licht won election to the Rhode Island State Senate, where he served until 1956. He left the senate to accept a position as associate judge of the Rhode Island Superior Court. In 1968, Licht left the bench to run for governor of

Rhode Island as a Democrat, a race he won over the favored Republican incumbent, John Chafee. In 1970, he ran for reelection and defeated another Republican challenger, Herbert F. DeSimone, by a slim margin. By most estimates a cautious governor, Licht was nonetheless active in creating a board of regents to oversee statewide public education, reorganizing the district court system, and initiating a Department of Social Rehabilitation Services and a Department of Mental Health, Retardation, and Hospitals.

Choosing not to run for a third term, Licht returned to private life and practiced law in Providence. An active member of the Rhode Island Jewish community, Licht served as chair of the Rhode Island campaign for Bonds for Israel and in 1969 received the Hervert H. Lehman Ethics Award of the Jewish Theological Seminary of America.

Frank Licht died on May 30, 1987. (JSh)

LICHT, RICHARD
Lieutenant Governor, Rhode Island, 1985–1989

Born on March 25, 1948, in Providence, Rhode Island, Richard Licht graduated from Harvard College in 1968 and from Harvard Law School in 1971. In 1975, he graduated from Boston University with an L.L.M. in taxation.

Licht's political career has been extensive. When only twenty-six years old, he was elected to the Rhode Island State Senate; he served five terms in that body, from 1974 to 1984. In 1984 Licht was elected lieutenant governor of Rhode Island; he was reelected in 1986.

In 1988, Licht ran unsuccessfully for the United States Senate against the powerful incumbent, John Chafee. He then became the managing partner in the Rhode Island law firm of Tillinghast, Licht & Semonoff; he was also appointed to the Board of Governors of Higher Education in 1991.

Licht left his law firm in 1999 to run once again for the United States Senate. He lost the Democratic primary to Congressman Robert Weygand, who in turn lost the general election to John Chafee's son Lincoln, who had been appointed to the seat on his father's death.

Active in the Rhode Island Jewish community, Licht sat on the board of directors of Temple Emanuel, a Rhode Island synagogue, and is a member of the Jewish Federation of Rhode Island. He was rewarded the State of Israel Bonds David Ben Gurion Award in 1977 and given an Outstanding Public Service Award by Temple Yorat Yisrael in 1985. (JSh)

LIEBERMAN, JOSEPH I.
United States Senator, 1989–present;
Attorney General of Connecticut, 1983–1988

Jews throughout the country reacted with both astonishment and pride when Vice President Al Gore, the Democratic nominee for president, named Connecticut senator Joseph Lieberman as his running mate in August 2000. No Jew had ever sought such a lofty office. Jews in American politics were breaking yet another perceived barrier.

Joe Lieberman was born in Stamford, Connecticut, on February 24, 1942. The son of Orthodox Jews who raised him in that tradition, Lieberman attended public schools in Connecticut before going on to Yale and Yale Law School.

Lieberman began his political career in Connecticut's state senate, serving five terms, including three as majority leader. He ran unsuccessfully for the United States House but then was elected attorney general, a position he used to gain attention as he went after various ne'er-do-wells, including polluters, deadbeat parents, and public utilities. In 1988, Lieberman upset liberal Republican Lowell Weicker to win his seat in the Senate. He was easily reelected in 1994; in 2000, he ran simultaneously for reelection and for election as vice president, a possibility in only two states, and thus retained his Senate seat even while the Gore–Lieberman ticket lost the presidential election. Lieberman impressed politicians throughout the nation in his campaign and clearly enhanced his stature of a politician to be reckoned with in the future.

As a senator, Lieberman received a great deal of national attention for the verbal chiding he gave

President Bill Clinton during the Monica Lewinsky scandal. His outspokenness, which was particularly telling as Lieberman was a friend as well as a supporter of the president, struck a familiar chord for many who have seen Lieberman take positions guided by his own moral conservatism. Earlier he had formed an odd alliance with conservative Republican William Bennett and attacked the television, music, and video-game industries for producing material that is offensive and undermines the moral education of children. He was a proponent of the "v-chip" and has pushed the entertainment industries to take their own self-policing responsibilities seriously.

Despite his reputation for social conservatism, Lieberman voted consistently with the Democrats and in support of President Clinton's programs in most areas. These positions reflect Lieberman's active role in the Democratic Leadership Council, an organization created to cultivate moderate Democratic officials. He has also shown a willingness to work with moderate Republicans—for example, collaborating with the late Rhode Island senator John Chafee to bring greater environmental protection to the Long Island Sound.

Clearly Vice President Gore chose Lieberman for a variety of reasons, not the least of which were his reputation for high moral standards and his ability to mute criticism of Gore as too closely connected to the Clinton scandals. But the net effect of the nomination has been to change the perception of what is possible for Jewish candidates for public office for all time. (JK)

LIPPMANN, WALTER
Syndicated Columnist; New Republic *and* New York World *Editor, 1914—1931*

Born on September 23, 1889, in New York City to Jacob Lippmann, an investor, and Daisy Baum, into a family of wealth and leisure, Walter Lippmann attended private schools in New York City and entered Harvard as part of the class of 1910. He studied philosophy, political science, and economics. He wrote his first book, *A Preface to Politics,* in 1913; this publication led Herbet Croley to recruit him in 1914 as editor for the influential *New Republic.* While editor, he often wrote on the issues of World War I, particularly on whether the United States should be drawn in or not.

Lippmann joined the *New York World,* the city's leading liberal newspaper, in 1922, becoming editorial page editor and then editor. As head of the editorial page, he set the newspaper's position on the leading issues of the day, such as prohibition, disarmament, the financial crash, the Sacco–Venzetti affair, and the Scopes Trial. His editorials reached a large audience and established his reputation as a leading opinion maker. While working as editor, he continued to write books. Although born into a Jewish family, Lippmann rejected this religious and cultural identity. He wrote about ethics and morals in *A Preface to Morals* (1929), aimed at people, like himself, who had lost their faith but not their search for meaning in life.

The *World* shut down in 1931, and Lippmann joined the *New York Herald Tribune* as a columnist. His column "Today and Tomorrow" quickly became widely syndicated, made him an international figure, and won him two Pulitzer Prizes. His influential views would change with the times and with his own reading of events. From 1963 to 1971, he contributed an occasional column for *Newsweek.* The author of nearly two dozen books on politics, ethics, philosophy, perception, and governance as well as countless newspaper columns, Lippmann wrote about nearly every major event that touched Americans in his adult lifetime.

He married Faye Albertson in 1917. Walter Lippmann died in Manhattan on December 14, 1974. (JW)

Source: Ronald Steel, *Walter Lippmann and the American Century* (New York: Vintage, 1981).

LIPSHUTZ, ROBERT J.
Presidential Adviser, 1977–1979

Born December 27, 1921, Robert J. Lipshutz received his J.D. from the University of Georgia School of Law in 1946. An early supporter of Jimmy Carter, Lipshutz served as Carter's campaign treasurer for both the gubernatorial election in Georgia and the 1976 presidential race. President Carter named him to serve as White House counsel when he took office in 1977. Lipshutz's outsider status as an attorney from Atlanta put him in constant conflict with the insiders of Washington; he was considered a weak link in the Carter White House staff. In 1979, Lipshutz was replaced by longtime Washingtonian Lloyd N. Cutler.

Lipshutz returned to law practice in Georgia and was involved in the establishment of the Carter Presidential Library and the administration of the Jimmy Carter Personal Assets Trust. He continues to serve as counsel to Carter with regard to the documents from his tenure in the White House that are located in the Carter Center library. These include human rights documents and documents concerning the innocence of Dr. Samuel Mudd (the physician who set John Wilkes Booth's broken leg after the assassination of President Abraham Lincoln). (JM)

LISAGOR, PETER L.
Washington Bureau Chief, Chicago Daily News, *1959–1976*

Peter L. Lisagor was born August 5, 1915, in Keystone, West Virginia. In 1933, he studied at Northwestern University. He then enrolled at the University of Michigan, where he received a B.A. in 1939.

Lisagor's journalism career began in 1939 when he went to work for the *Chicago Daily News,* writing about sports. In 1941, he went to the United Press to work as a general assignment news reporter but left the next year to enlist in the army. During World War II, he was managing editor of the London edition of *Stars and Stripes,* from 1944 to 1945, as well as editor of *Stars and Stripes* in Paris in 1945. He was news editor of the *Paris Post* for a brief period in 1945 but then returned home to the *Chicago Daily News.* He became the paper's United Nations correspondent in 1949 and from 1950 to 1959 was its diplomatic correspondent in Washington. He served as the Washington bureau chief from 1959 until his death on December 10, 1976.

Lisagor is probably most remembered for his frequent appearances on *Meet the Press* and *Washington Week in Review.* He also wrote a syndicated newspaper column and was coauthor, with Marguerite Higgins, of *Overtime in Heaven* (1964), a collection of stories of heroism among American Foreign Service officers. (MP)

LITTAUER, LUCIUS NATHAN
Member of Congress, 1897–1907

Lucius Nathan Littauer was born on January 20, 1859, in Gloversville, New York. After graduating from Harvard with a bachelor's degree in 1878, Littauer entered his father's glove business. Littauer assumed control of the company in 1883; under his direction, it became the largest manufacturer of gloves in the United States.

Littauer's political career began in 1896 when he was elected the Republican representative from upstate New York. During his tenure in Congress, Littauer, a close friend of President Theodore Roosevelt, was a leader of the House Appropriations Committee. A practicing Reform Jew, he pushed legislation to revise immigration laws to help Jewish victims of religious persecution in Eastern Europe.

After leaving Congress in 1907 to oversee his various businesses, Littauer embarked on a philanthropic career. He donated funds for the construction of a hospital in his hometown of Gloversville and later oversaw the creation of a Jewish community center there. Among a number of generous endowments, his most prominent gift was funding the Littauer Center of Public Administration and the Graduate School of Public Administration at Harvard.

A proud and devoted Jew, Littauer endowed the Nathan Littauer Professorship of Hebrew Literature and Philosophy of Harvard in 1925 and created the Lucius N. Littauer Foundation in 1929, which gives grants to the advancement of Jewish studies and learning.

Lucius Nathan Littauer died on March 2, 1944, in New York. (JSh)

LONDON, MEYER
Member of Congress, 1921–1923, 1915–1919

Born on December 29, 1871, in Gora Kalvaria, Poland, Meyer London emigrated to the United States in 1891. He settled in New York and, after graduating from law school and being admitted to the bar, represented various unions and labor organizations.

Initially a member of the Socialist Labor Party, he joined a movement opposed to its leader, Daniel De Leon, and eventually switched to the Socialist Party of America. In 1910, London led the garment workers' strike and helped create the Protocol of 1910, trying to create collective bargaining and arbitration in the women's garment trade.

It was as a socialist that London won election to Congress in 1914. Representing a largely Jewish constituency from New York's Lower East Side, he was reelected for a second term in 1916 but lost in 1918. Campaigning successfully in 1920, London regained his seat for one term, losing for a final time in 1922.

As a congressman, London fought for reform of immigration laws and for naturalization of the coal industry. Although he opposed U.S. involvement in World War I, his refusal to condemn all wartime actions made him an outcast in the American socialist movement.

Meyer London died in a car accident in New York on June 6, 1926. (JSh)

LOWENSTEIN, ALLARD KENNETH
Member of Congress, 1969–1971

Allard Lowenstein was born in Newark, New Jersey, on January 16, 1929. He graduated from the University of North Carolina in 1949 and received his law degree from Yale in 1954.

Lowenstein served a short stint as a special assistant to Senator Frank Porter Graham in 1949. After graduating from Yale, he served in the United States Army before joining the staff of Senator Hubert H. Humphrey in 1959 as his foreign policy assistant.

Lowenstein rose to prominence as a liberal activist in the 1960s. He organized protests in Mississippi and at Stanford and North Carolina State universities. But he was best known for leading the "Dump Johnson" movement in protest to the war in Vietnam. After failing to persuade Senator Robert Kennedy to make the race, he was among those who convinced Senator Eugene McCarthy to challenge the sitting president. That campaign eventually led to Johnson's withdrawal from the Democratic nominating contest. Lowenstein earned the reputation of being a charismatic leader who inspired young people to get involved in the political system.

In 1968, running on an antiwar platform with the support of many in the movement with whom he had worked, Lowenstein was elected to the House of Representatives from a highly Republican district on Long Island. He was defeated in a bid for reelection in 1970 and lost three subsequent elections to return to the House. Reflective of his vision of equal-

ity for all people, he was appointed by President Jimmy Carter to lead the United States delegation at the United Nations Commission on Human Rights in Geneva, Switzerland, in 1977.

On March 14, 1980, Lowenstein was assassinated by Dennis Sweeney, a former protégé he met while working at Stanford University. He was fifty-one years old. (SB)

Source: William H. Chafe, *Never Stop Running: Allard Lowenstein and the Struggle to Save American Liberalism* (New York: Basic Books, 1993).

LOWEY, NITA M.
Member of Congress, 1989–present

Born on July 5, 1937, in the Bronx, Nita Lowey began her political career in 1975 as an aide to Mario Cuomo, then New York's secretary of state. She continued as an aide in the Department of State until 1988, when she ran for Congress from Westchester County. In her first election, she defeated a political scion in the Democratic primary and a two-term incumbent congressman in the general election. Both victories were considered upsets.

During her second term in Congress, Lowey was appointed to the House Appropriations Committee. From this powerful position, she has become one of the leading advocates of women's issues, particularly family planning and reproductive rights, in the House of Representatives. Chair of the House Pro-Choice Task Force, Lowey led the effort to include abortion coverage in the 1994 health care reform package. In 1998, she was successful in having her provision requiring federal prescription-drug plans to cover contraceptives passed by the House. She has also been a proponent of funding for breast- and cervical-cancer research.

Lowey was considered a potential candidate for the United States Senate in both 1998 and 2000. Actively laying the groundwork to succeed retiring Senator Daniel Patrick Moynihan, Lowey withdrew from the race in 1999, when it was clear that First Lady Hillary Rodham Clinton would enter the race. In 2001, she was named to chair the Democratic Congressional Campaign Committee, the first woman to hold that post. (JS)

M

MACK, JULIAN W.
U.S. Court of Appeals, 1911–1943

Julian William Mack was born in San Francisco on July 19, 1866, the son of the cousin of Henry Mack, the businessman. Julian graduated from Harvard Law School in 1887, where he and Louis Brandeis founded the *Harvard Law Review*. Harvard awarded him a Parker Fellowship to the Universities of Berlin and Leipzig after graduation.

Mack practiced law in Chicago until 1895, when he became a professor of law at Northwestern University. In 1902, he moved to the University of Chicago to teach law. Two years later, he became a judge for the Cook County Circuit Court in Illinois; and, in 1905, he was named to the Illinois State Court of Appeals.

In 1910, President William Howard Taft named Mack to the U.S. Court of Appeals and to the Commerce Court. Although the latter court was abolished in 1913, Mack remained a judge of the circuit court until his death on September 5, 1943.

Mack served as president of the American Jewish Congress and was part of its delegation to the Versailles Peace Conference in 1919, where it passed a plan ensuring the right for minorities to establish their own schools and speak their own languages, while retaining full citizenship. In 1936, Mack was named honorary president of the first World Jewish Congress in Geneva. (JM)

Source: Harry Barnard, *Julian Mack: The Forging of an American Jew: The Life and Times of Judge Julian W. Mack* (New York: Herzl, 1974).

MANDEL, MARVIN
Governor of Maryland, 1969–1979

Born April 19, 1920, in Baltimore, Marvin Mandel eventually evolved into an important figure in the politics of his home state. He graduated from the Baltimore City College in 1937 and received his law degree from the University of Maryland in 1942. After serving in the army during World War II, Mandel returned to Baltimore to practice law.

In 1952, Mandel was appointed to the Maryland House of Delegates to fill a vacancy; he was reelected for four more terms. He became speaker in 1963 and remained in that position until 1969 when he was elected to complete the unexpired term of Governor Spiro T. Agnew, who had been elected vice president of the United States. Mandel was reelected governor in 1970 and in 1974. Accomplishments during his gubernatorial leadership included a major reorganization of government, creating agencies to manage public transportation, developing subway systems in Baltimore and the Maryland suburbs of Washington, and implementing public defenders in the court system.

In 1977, after two long and sensational jury trials, Mandel and five codefendants were convicted in federal court on mail fraud and racketeering charges. Mandel was ordered jailed in 1979 and served his sentence in Florida, until President Ronald Reagan cut his original four-year sentence down to the nineteen months served and granted a full pardon in 1982. Mandel continued to profess his innocence and support for his cause continued; in 1989, the matter finally concluded, with the U.S. Supreme Court upholding a lower court decision that overturned Mandel's original conviction. After this decision, he was readmitted to the Maryland Bar. Before retiring, Mandel practiced law in Annapolis. (JM)

Source: Bradford Jacobs, *Thimbleriggers: The Law v. Governor Marvin Mandel* (Baltimore: Johns Hopkins University Press, 1984).

MARCUSE, HERBERT
Philosopher, Social Theorist, and Political Activist

Herbert Marcuse was born July 19, 1898, in Berlin. After serving with the German army during World War I, he studied at Freiburg, receiving his Ph.D. in literature in 1922, returning in 1928 to study philosophy with Martin Heidegger.

In 1933, Marcuse joined the Institut für Sozialforschung in Frankfurt, identifying with its critical theory. That same year, Marcuse, a Jew and radical, fled from Nazism and emigrated to the United States, becoming a citizen in 1940. He worked at Columbia University (where the institute was granted offices and academic association during the Nazi period), until 1940. Leaving Columbia in 1941, he worked in the U.S. State Department for ten years, a personal contribution to the fight against fascism. In 1958, Marcuse became a professor of politics and philosophy at Brandeis University. Though one of most popular and influential members of the faculty, Marcuse was denied a new teaching contract in 1965 because of his radical beliefs. He found a position at the University of California—San Diego, remaining there until his retirement in 1970.

Throughout his life, Marcuse was faithful to his revolutionary vision. Defending Marxist theory and libertarian socialism until his death, he generated fierce controversy. His critique of both capitalism and communism and support of revolutionary change won him the contempt of establishment and respect of the new radicals. Important works by Marcuse include *Reason and Revolution* (1941), *Eros and Civilization* (1955), and *One-Dimensional Man* (1964).

Herbert Marcuse died July 29, 1979, in Starnberg, Germany. (JM)

MARGOLIES-MEZVINSKY, MARJORIE
Member of Congress, 1993–1995

Marjorie Margolies-Mezvinsky was born on June 21, 1942, in Philadelphia. She earned her bachelor's degree from the University of Pennsylvania in 1963 and was a CBS News Foundation Fellow at Columbia University.

Margolies-Mezvinsky was a television journalist at WCAU-TV in Philadelphia from 1967 until1971, when she became a correspondent for NBC, first in Washington, D.C., and later in New York City. Between 1971 and 1991, she won five Emmys for her reporting.

Margolies-Mezvinsky was elected as a Democrat to the House of Representatives from Pennsylvania's Thirteenth District in 1992. In her first year in office, she cast the deciding vote that allowed President Bill Clinton's economic package to pass. That vote, favored by Democrats nationally but opposed by her constituents, was used prominently by her opponent when she ran unsuccessfully for reelection in 1994.

She stayed active in politics after her defeat. President Clinton appointed her deputy chair of the United States delegation to the United Nations Fourth World Conference on Women. She was president of the Women's Campaign Fund from 1996 to 1998. In 1998, she was the unsuccessful Democratic candidate for lieutenant governor of Pennsylvania. She also considered a race for her party's nomination for the United States Senate in 2000 but dropped out of the race when she could not raise enough money to compete.

Margolies-Mezvinsky married Edward Mezvinsky (a member of Congress from Iowa, 1973–1977) in 1975. They have a combined family of eleven children. (SB)

MARKEL, LESTER
Editor, New York Times Sunday Edition, 1939–1964

Lester Markel was born on January 9, 1894, in New York City. After growing up in New York, he attended City College and the Columbia School of Journalism. Following his graduation in 1914, he began his career at the *Bronx Home News*. He soon moved on to *the Evening Post* and then to the *New York Tribune*, where he spent nine years.

In 1923, Markel accepted a job with the *New York Times*, and he worked at various positions in the organization before assuming the role of editor of the Sunday edition. During his twenty-five years of leadership, Markel transformed the Sunday edition into a highly praised institution and increased circulation by more than half a million copies. An extremely demanding editor, Markel offended many top writers and frequently surrounded himself in controversy. Due to his ability to manage the Sunday edition with little interference from the rest of the organization, Markel was considered one of the "Dukes" of the *Times*. He is best known for his development of the "Week in Review" section, which received a special Pulitzer Prize citation. In 1964, as he reached the *Times*'s mandatory retirement age, Markel was removed from the position of Sunday editor and made an associate editor. (OS)

MARKS, MARC LINCOLN
Member of Congress, 1977–1983

Marc Marks was born in Farrell, Pennsylvania, on February 12, 1927. After high school, he served two years in the United States Army Air Corps at the end of World War II. He then attended University of Alabama, receiving his B.A. in 1951. After completing his law degree at the University of Virginia in 1954, he returned north and began practicing law in Farrell, Pennsylvania. From 1960 until 1966, Marks served as the solicitor for Mercer County, Pennsylvania. Afterward, he resumed his private law practice.

Elected to the United States House of Representatives as a Republican in 1976, Marks was immediately outspoken and controversial; he also frequently found himself exercising more influence than many freshmen, as his vote was often the "swing vote" on the Commerce Committee. Reelected to the Ninety-sixth Congress, Marks announced his candidacy for the Senate and was accused of moving to the left to attract votes from a statewide constituency. Marks's Republican colleagues were displeased; support for his candidacy was not forthcoming, and he dropped out of the race. Marks decided to seek reelection to the House; his winning margin in 1980 was fewer than one thousand votes. He retired at the end of his third term. (MW)

MARX, SAMUEL
Member of Congress, elected 1922
but never served

Samuel Marx deserves a footnote, if not a place, in Jewish American history. Marx, born in New York City in 1867 and educated in the city's public schools, is the only Jewish American to have been elected to Congress but never to have served.

Marx was one of the premier auctioneers in New York City in the early twentieth century, but he was also an active Democrat. A loyal son of Tammany Hall, he served as alderman from his West Side district and as appointed internal revenue collector, but his most important position was as Tammany district leader for the Thirty-first Assembly District, the distributor of great patronage.

In 1916, Marx sought appointment as postmaster of New York, one of the most lucrative patronage position in the city. Denied that position, he remained active in local politics and eventually ran for Congress, unseating a five-term Republican in 1922. However, barely three weeks after his election and before he was sworn in, Sam Marx died of a massive coronary, on November 30, 1922. (LSM)

MASCHKE, MAURICE
Party Leader

Maurice Maschke was born on October 16, 1868, in Cleveland to Joseph and Rosa Salinger Maschke. He received his A.B. from Harvard University in 1890, returned to Cleveland, studied law, and was admitted to the Ohio Bar in 1891.

In 1897, Maschke was a precinct worker for Republican mayor Robert E. McKisson, who appointed Maschke deputy county recorder. Maschke formed a political alliance with Albert "Starlight"

Boyd and became a very close associate of Republican congressman and later United States senator Theodore Burton.

In 1909, Maschke engineered the defeat of Cleveland's celebrated reform mayor Tom L. Johnson. Maschke was the master of ethnic politics. He upset Johnson by finding a prominent German-American candidate to run, thus undermining the reformer's own ethnic base.

In 1911, he was appointed collector of customs by President William Howard Taft, serving until 1914, when he became the head of the Cuyahoga County Republican Party; his power was at its peak from 1914 until 1928. During that time, he was the dominant figure in Cleveland politics and a force to be reckoned with in Ohio and national Republican circles. He engineered the selection of Harry Hopkins as Cleveland's city manager, and when Hopkins broke with Maschke, he arranged for his removal. With the ascendancy of the Democratic Party in the 1930s, Maschke saw his influence begin to wane, and he retired as county Republican chair in 1933.

Maurice Maschke died in Cleveland on November 19, 1936. (IF)

MASSELL, SAM JR.
Mayor of Atlanta, 1971–1973

Sam Massell experienced antisemitism firsthand when he awoke to see a cross burning in his yard during the course of his ultimately successful campaign to become the first Jewish mayor of Atlanta.

Born in Atlanta on August 26, 1927, Massell was educated in the Atlanta public school system. Later he gained a law degree by attending night school in Atlanta.

In 1961, he entered public life as the vice mayor of Atlanta. This position had previously been a largely ceremonial role; however, Massell transformed this office into an active full-time job. In 1970, he ran for mayor. With a large outpouring of support from the African American community, he was able to become not only the first Jewish mayor but also the youngest mayor in Atlanta's history. However, Massell failed to win reelection in 1973, when he lost to Maynard Jackson, the city's first black mayor.

Massell has remained an active member of the Atlanta community. In recent years, he served as president of the Buckhead Coalition, which is an influential business group in Atlanta. (KJ)

MAY, MITCHELL
New York Secretary of State, 1913–1914; Member of Congress, 1899–1901

Born in Brooklyn, New York, on July 10, 1870, and educated at Brooklyn Polytechnic Institute and Columbia University School of Law, from which he graduated at the age of twenty-one, Mitchell May was a one-term congressman who went on to a distinguished career on the New York state judicial bench.

As a young lawyer active in politics, May was offered the Democratic nomination for Congress, tantamount at the time to election, in 1898. During his one term in the House, May broke with his party—and its leader William Jennings Bryan—over the party's policy favoring a silver standard; he was thus denied renomination in 1900.

Returning to Brooklyn, May worked his way back into party favor, serving first on the county board of education, then as counsel to the county clerk and assistant attorney general. In 1913, he was elected New York's secretary of state, again serving one term. In 1915, he began what would become a twenty-five-year judicial career, with election as judge of the King County Court. He was elected in 1921 to the first of his two fourteen-year terms on the New York State Supreme Court. He retired in 1940, having reached the mandatory retirement age of seventy. For the next two decades, May returned to the practice of private law with the Brooklyn firm long associated with Congressman Emanuel Celler.

May was quite active in Jewish affairs, serving as president and eventually director of the Brooklyn Federation of Jewish Charities and working for the Jewish Hospital of Brooklyn and the Hebrew Educational Society.

Mitchell May died in Brooklyn at the age of ninety on March 24, 1961. (LSM)

MEIER, JULIUS L.
Governor of Oregon, 1931–1935

President of the Federated Jewish Societies of Portland and the Jewish shelter home, director of the B'nai B'rith center, and 1932 president of Congregation Beth Israel, Julius L. Meier was a religious man who cared deeply for his country and his state. During World War I, Meier served his country as the Northwest regional director of the Council of National Defense and as regional director in Portland for Liberty Loan drives. He served the state of Ore-

gon as one of the original proponents of the Columbia River Highway, an advocate for improving airplane landing fields, director of the state chamber of commerce, and, most important, governor.

Born on December 31, 1874, in Portland, Oregon, Meier was educated in both the Portland public schools and Bishop Scott Military Academy. he continued his education and gained his LL.B. at the University of Portland in 1895. He joined with George W. Joseph to form a small law firm; however, this partnership lasted only one year, when Meier left to join his father's department-store business. During the next several decades, Meier's business grew, and he became president of the corporation in 1930.

For many years his former law partner, Joseph, had been actively involved in state politics and had served as the regular Republican nominee for governor. On his death in 1930, the state Republican Party refused to nominate candidates who adhered to the same platform as had Joseph. Meier believed in Joseph's platform and independently ran for governor, pledging to eliminate machine politics from state government. He was elected by a large majority. Meier's term in office was noted for reducing government expenditures and providing schoolchildren with free textbooks. After serving one four-year term, Meier reentered private life. Nearly two years after leaving office, Julius L. Meier died on July 14, 1937. (KJ)

MELLMAN, MARK
Democratic Pollster

Mark Mellman was born in Hampton, Virginia, on September 13, 1955. After graduating from Princeton, he went on to receive graduate degrees from Yale.

Mellman is the CEO of The Mellman Group, which is one of the leading Democratic polling and consulting firms. Among his clients are Senate Majority Leader Tom Daschle, House Democratic leader Dick Gephardt, former Vice President Al Gore, Senator Barbara Boxer, Governor Barbara Roberts, and Congressmen Bob Etheridge and Sander Levin. Mellman also advises the Democratic National Committee, the Democratic Senatorial Campaign Committee, and the Democratic Congressional Campaign Committee.

Mellman has played a critical role in devising Democratic strategies on the environment, education, health care, the budget, and Medicare. His clients extend well beyond Capitol Hill. The American Cancer Society, AFL-CIO, League of Women Voters, Janus mutual funds, and Bankers Trust are some of the public interest organizations and corporations that Mellman represents.

A highly sought-after consultant and analyst, Mellman regularly offers his knowledge and expertise to the public. He has taught political science at Yale University, has been a consultant to CBS News, and has served as a presidential debate analyst for PBS. (SB)

MESSINGER, RUTH
Manhattan Borough President, 1990–1997

Ruth Messinger was born in New York, New York, on November 6, 1940. She completed her bachelor's degree at Radcliffe College and received a master's of social work degree from the University of Oklahoma.

For more than twenty years, Messinger was involved in New York City politics. She was elected to the New York City Council in 1977 and was the Manhattan Borough president from 1990 to 1997. In 1997, she was the first woman to be nominated as the Democratic Party candidate for mayor of New York. Messinger fought an unsuccessful campaign against Mayor Rudolph Guiliani.

Judaism is a central force in Messinger's life and is always at the heart of her work. Messinger's Jewish commitment to social justice is most recently translated in her job as the president and executive director of the American Jewish World Service (AJWS). This not-for-profit organization provides emergency relief, humanitarian aid, and technical support to communities around the globe regardless of race, religion, or nationality. AJWS is rapidly expanding its programs and visibility under Messinger's guidance. She is also a member of the Society for the Advancement of Judaism.

Messinger has been a visiting professor at Queens and Hunter Colleges. She has taught in numerous New York Master of Social Work programs as well. (SB)

METZENBAUM, HOWARD
United States Senator, 1976–1995, 1974

Howard Morton Metzenbaum was born June 14, 1917, in Cleveland, Ohio, and earned a bachelor's degree in 1939 and a law degree in 1941 from the Ohio State University. After practicing law in his hometown, he was elected to the Ohio House of Representatives in 1943 at the age of twenty-three as the youngest member of that body. Four years later, he was elected to the Ohio State Senate as one of four Democrats. Just two years later, he became a party leader as the Democrats took the majority; he remained in the state senate until 1951. On leaving the state legislature, Metzenbaum returned to the Cleveland area to practice law and direct a group of suburban weekly newspapers.

Metzenbaum was active in politics, running the campaigns of others, but he himself did not seek elective office again until 1970. In that year, he ran for the United States Senate, defeating John Glenn in the primary, but losing to Robert Taft in the general election. In 1974, the other United States Senate seat for Ohio became open, when William Saxbe resigned to accept appointment as attorney general of the United States during the Watergate affair. Metzenbaum was appointed to the seat and served to the end of that year, but he lost a primary election to Glenn. Two years later Metzenbaum ran for the Senate once again; with a united party behind him, he defeated Taft in 1976. He was reelected twice but chose not to run for a fourth term in 1994.

Highlights of Metzenbaum's service in the Senate include his key roles in passage of the Brady Bill, which called for a mandatory waiting period prior to the sale of handguns; the Multiethnic Placement Act, which bars discrimination in the adoption process; the Food Labeling Bill; and the act creating the Cuyahoga Valley National Park.

On his retirement, Metzenbaum, known throughout his career as a liberal who backed legislation aiding average citizens against corporate society, became chair of the Consumer Federation of America. (JM)

MEYER, ADOLPH
Member of Congress, 1891–1908

Adolph Meyer was born in Natchez, Mississippi, on October 19, 1842. He attended college at the University of Virginia but left school to join the Confederate Army in 1862. He attained the rank of adjutant general.

After the war, Meyer returned to Natchez, where he engaged in cotton and rice planting. He also established himself in banking in New Orleans and married Rosalie Jonas, the sister of a Louisiana senator, in 1868. Meyer held several high-ranking positions in the Louisiana militia between 1879 and 1891.

In 1890, he was elected to Congress as a Democrat, despite the antisemitic rhetoric that was used against him. Meyer served as a Louisiana representative until his death on March 8, 1908. (MD)

MEYER, ANNIE NATHAN
Antisuffragist Leader

Annie Nathan was born on February 19, 1867, in New York City to an orthodox Sephardic Jewish family. She received her early education in Green Bay, Wisconsin, before her family returned to New York.

Nathan wished to receive a higher education, but not many options were available for women. She participated in Columbia University's Collegiate Course for Women between 1885 and 1886, before leaving to marry Dr. Alfred Meyer. Annie Nathan Meyer then fought for the creation of a college specifically for women, helping assure the creation of Barnard College in 1889. Meyer became a lifelong trustee of the college. Although she supported women's education, and although her sister, Maud Nathan, was an active suffragist leader, Annie was an antisuffragist. She believed that women should be educated to influence their husbands' votes but should not vote themselves. Meyer and her sister also differed in their view toward Judaism. While Maud Nathan was active in many Jewish organizations, Annie Meyer believed that American Jews should be assimilated into the mainstream. Meyer wrote novels, plays, and short stories dealing with women's issues.

Annie and Alfred Meyer had one child. Meyer died in New York City on September 23, 1951. (TW)

MEYER, EUGENE ISAAC
Publisher, Washington Post, *1933–1946;*
Governor of Federal Reserve Board, 1930–1933

Born October 31, 1875, in Los Angeles, the son of Marc Eugene Meyer, a French Jewish immigrant, and Harriet Newmark, Eugene Meyer grew up in San Francisco. He attended the University of California for one year (1892–1893) and, when his family moved to New York, transferred to Yale, earning an A.B. in 1895. He spent the following year studying languages and banking in Europe and then was employed as a clerk in his father's firm, Lazard Frères. Despite his father's wishes that he take a place there, Meyer left in 1901 to establish his own brokerage business. Shrewd investment of $600 (given to him by his father for not smoking) yielded $50,000 with which Meyer bought a seat on the New York Stock Exchange. He made his fortune by buying stocks others were dumping in a panic and later reselling them at their true value. By the age of forty, these tactics earned him a estimated fortune of $40 million to $60 million.

When the United States entered World War I in 1917, Meyer closed down his business and became an adviser to the military for the nominal salary of a dollar a year. His unpaid government service continued after the war and reached a pinnacle in 1930, when President Herbert Hoover appointed Meyer governor of the Federal Reserve Board. Meyer tried to institute reforms of the banking system; however, the Great Depression disrupted these attempts, and Meyer spent his time struggling through one financial emergency after another. He left government work in 1933 due to disagreement with President Franklin D. Roosevelt's New Deal.

In June 1933, Meyer bought the troubled *Washington Post* at public auction. He had no publishing experience but led the paper as it grew into one of the great newspapers of the nation. He built his paper around the idea that journalism is a form of public service, encouraging fair and trustworthy reporting and vigorous editorial comment separated from politics and ideologies. In June 1946, Meyer turned over the management of his paper to his son-in-law, Philip L. Graham, to accede to President Harry S. Truman's request that he become the first president of the World Bank. He remained at the bank only long enough to establish its organization and then returned to the *Post* as chairman of the board.

Eugene Meyer died in Washington, D.C., on July 17, 1959. (JW)

MEZVINSKY, EDWARD MAURICE
Member of Congress, 1973–1977

On January 17, 1937, Edward Mezvinsky was born in Ames, Iowa. He attended the University of Iowa, where he received his bachelor's degree in 1960. He went on to earn his master's degree in political science and a law degree at the University of California–Berkeley.

Mezvinsky began his political career as a legislative assistant to U.S. Representative Neal Smith (D-Iowa), before he himself was elected to the Iowa House of Representatives in 1968. After serving one term in the state house, Mezvinsky was elected to the United States House of Representatives in 1972. He won his campaign for reelection in 1974 but was defeated in 1976. During the Watergate investigation, Mezvinsky served on the House Judiciary Committee. Appointed to the United Nations Commission on Human Rights by President Jimmy Carter after losing his House seat, Mezvinsky served as the United States representative from 1977 to 1979. Continuing his work in the political arena, Mezvinsky was elected as the Democratic Party state chair of Pennsylvania in 1981. He ran unsuccessfully for lieutenant governor of Pennsylvania in 1990.

Mezvinsky married Marjorie Margolies (member of Congress, Pennsylvania, 1993–1995) in 1975. Between them, they have eleven children. (SB)

MICHAELSON, JULIUS COOLEY
Attorney General of Rhode Island, 1975–1979

Julius C. Michaelson was born January 26, 1922, to Carl and Celia (Cooley) Michaelson, in Salem, New Hampshire. Michaelson served in the army for three years, entering as a private in 1943 and being released as a first lieutenant in 1946. After his wartime service, he received his law degree from Brown University in 1947.

Michaelson began his public service career in 1957, serving as public counsel in utility rate cases and as a delegate of the State Constitutional Convention of Rhode Island. In 1962, he was elected to the Rhode Island State Senate, a position he held for eleven years. During that time, he was the deputy majority leader (1969) and a member of the Committee on State-Urban Relations and the Rhode Island Commission on Interstate Cooperation. In 1974, Michaelson was elected attorney general of Rhode Island, a position he held for four years. Following his term as attorney general, Michaelson returned to practicing law. He ran unsuccessfully for the United States Senate in 1982. (BF)

MIKVA, ABNER J.
White House Counsel, 1994–1995;
Judge, U.S. Court of Appeals, 1979–1994;
Member of Congress, 1969–1973, 1975–1979

Born January 21, 1926, in Milwaukee, Wisconsin, Abner Joseph Mikva served in the U.S. Army Air Corps from 1944 to 1945. He was educated at the University of Chicago, receiving his law degree cum laude in 1951. After graduation, Mikva clerked for Justice Sherman Minton of the U.S. Supreme Court and then moved to private practice in Chicago, beginning in 1952.

Mikva was a state representative in Illinois from 1956 to 1966, earning several "Best Legislator" awards. He was elected to the United States House of Representatives in 1968. Reelected twice in a hotly contested district, Mikva lost in the Republican landslide of 1972 after his seat had been redistricted. He returned to the House after the 1974 election, when many Democrats won in the post-Watergate congressional election. While out of office, Mikva practiced law in Chicago and also became a professor at the Northwestern University School of Law during that time.

In 1979, President Jimmy Carter appointed Mikva to the U.S. Court of Appeals for the District of Columbia Circuit. He served as chief judge from 1991 until 1994, when he left the bench.

Mikva served President Bill Clinton as White House counsel in 1994 and 1995; he has been a visiting professor at the University of Chicago since 1996. Mikva is the coauthor of *An Introduction to Statutory Interpretation and the Legislative Process* (1997) and a political science textbook entitled *The American Congress: The First Branch* (1983). In 2000, Mikva was selected to serve the American Bar Association as an honorary cochair of the Commission on Public Financing of Judicial Campaigns. (JM)

MILK, HARVEY
Gay Rights Activist, 1973–1978

Born on May 22, 1930, in New York City to Jewish Russian immigrants, Harvey Milk graduated from Albany State Teachers College in 1951 and returned to New York to become a financial analyst on Wall Street. In 1969, he left New York for San Francisco, first to continue in the investment business and then to open his own camera shop.

Like many others, Milk was disgusted by the picture of politics implied by the Watergate scandal. By this time, he was openly gay. In 1973, he ran for the San Francisco Board of Supervisors, the first openly homosexual candidate to run in the United States. Although he won only a few votes in 1973 and lost again in 1975, Milk began to build a political base and won a seat on the board in 1977, defeating sixteen other candidates and winning over 30 percent of the vote.

Milk, a liberal Democrat, was assassinated along with Mayor George Moscone in 1978. However, through his courage and conviction, he broke important barriers for homosexuals despite the brevity of his career. Milk knew his open homosexuality threatened others. In a taped message that he asked to be read in the event he was assassinated, Milk urged "all to work toward . . . constructive pursuits" and pleaded with other homosexuals not to conceal their sexual preference. (LSM)

MILLER, JOHN RIPIN
Member of Congress, 1985–1993

John Miller was born in New York City on May 23, 1938. A 1959 graduate of Bucknell University, he served in the United States Army in 1960 and remained in the Army Reserves from 1961 until 1968. He earned a master's and a law degree at Yale while in the reserves. In 1965, he moved to the state of Washington, where he began the practice of law in Seattle.

From 1965 until 1968, Miller served as the assistant attorney general of the state of Washington. While practicing law, he also served as adjunct professor at the University of Puget Sound from 1981 until 1984.

Miller was elected to Congress in 1984 and served four terms in office. A Republican with strong anticommunist views, he also had a commitment to the environment tempered by a dedication to the shipping and fishing industries, on which the Seattle area is dependent. Miller did not seek reelection in 1992. (MW)

MORGENTHAU, HENRY JR.
Secretary of the Treasury, 1934–1945

Henry Morgenthau Jr. was born May 11, 1891, in New York City. His father was a wealthy businessman, and both of his parents were Democratic Party activists. The younger Morgenthau frequently felt pressure to follow in his father's footsteps.

In 1909, Morgenthau Jr. was admitted to Cornell, but he left before finishing his second year. He worked odd jobs until a trip to Texas sparked his interest in farming. In 1913, Morgenthau Sr. helped his son purchase farmland in Dutchess County, New York. Morgenthau Jr. became a successful apple and dairy farmer. He developed a close relationship with Franklin D. Roosevelt, who lived in nearby Hyde Park. When Roosevelt was elected governor of New York in 1928, he appointed Morgenthau to chair the Agricultural Advisory Committee. When Roosevelt was elected president, Morgenthau was disappointed when his friend did not choose him to head the Agriculture Department. However, FDR did appoint him as head of the Federal Farm Board. He served only briefly, however, because Roosevelt's Treasury secretary, William Wooden, became terminally ill and his deputy, Dean Acheson, disagreed with the administration's views on key issues. FDR named Morgenthau as acting secretary in 1933. His appointment was eventually made permanent, and he remained in the post for eleven years. Only the second Jewish cabinet member, he was the longest-serving Jewish cabinet member and the longest-serving secretary of the Treasury in American history.

During World War II, Morgenthau helped develop the War Refugee Board to aid European Jewish refugees. At the Bretton Woods Conference, his work laid the foundation for the International Monetary Fund and the World Bank. After Roosevelt's death in 1945, Morgenthau served briefly under President Harry S. Truman, but he resigned when he was denied the opportunity to attend the Potsdam Conference. He returned to New York. Between 1947 and 1950, Morgenthau chaired the United Jewish Appeal. From 1951 to 1954, he was chairman of the board of the American Financial and Development Corporation for Israel.

Henry Morgenthau Jr. died in Poughkeepsie, New York, on February 6, 1967. (TW)

MORGENTHAU, HENRY SR.
Ambassador to Turkey, 1913–1916

Henry Morgenthau was born April 26, 1856, in Mannheim, Germany. He emigrated to the United States with his family in 1866. Morgenthau worked his way through school, graduating from Columbia Law School in 1877.

In 1879, Morgenthau formed the law firm Lachman, Morgenthau, and Goldsmith. He left the firm in 1899 and formed and served as president of the Central Realty Bond and Trust Company. In 1905, he formed his own real estate corporation, the Henry Morgenthau Company. In these endeavors, he amassed a sizable fortune.

Morgenthau chaired the finance committee of the Democratic National Committee during Woodrow Wilson's presidential campaigns in 1912 and 1916. In 1913, he retired from business and was appointed ambassador to Turkey. In that capacity, he represented the interests of Britain, France, Russia, and six other countries, when the Allied ambassadors pulled out of Turkey after its alignment with the Central Powers. Morgenthau resigned in 1916 and returned to the United States after the Turkish massacre of the Armenians. More than eighty years later, Morgenthau is still revered by Armenians for alerting the world to the Turkish genocide of their people.

In 1919, he was sent by President Wilson to investigate the persecution of Jews in Poland. As chair of the League of Nations Refugee Resettlement Commission, he went to Athens in October 1923 and successfully resettled the 1,250,000 Greeks deported from Turkey following the Greco-Turkish war, the pinnacle of his diplomatic career. Morgenthau later campaigned for President Franklin D. Roosevelt's New Deal and warned Americans of the dangers of Hitler. His son Henry Jr. subsequently served as FDR's secretary of treasury (1934–1945).

Henry Morgenthau Sr. died in New York City on November 25, 1946. (BF)

MORRIS, HANK
Political Consultant

Hank Morris has been a political consultant for Democrats throughout the nation for more than two decades. Born in New York on May 16, 1953, Morris graduated from Columbia College and Columbia Law School. He was a partner of New York political consultant David Garth, handling Tom Bradley's campaigns for mayor of Los Angeles in 1981 and for governor of California in 1982.

Morris formed his own firm in the early 1980s and in 1989 joined with Bill Carrick to form the firm now known as Morris, Carrick & Guma. Their first client was Dianne Feinstein in her 1990 campaign for governor of California. They have since handled media and strategy for her successful senatorial campaigns as well as for New York senator Chuck Schumer, Boston mayor Tom Menino, Mississippi governor Robbie Musgrove, and the Democratic Congressional Campaign Committee. (LSM)

MORRIS, RICHARD
Political Strategist

Dick Morris was born in New York in 1948. He earned a place at Stuyvesant, Manhattan's top high school, and then graduated from Columbia University in only three years.

After Columbia, Morris worked for Eugene McCarthy's presidential campaign in New Hampshire. He returned to Manhattan in 1969 and formed a group known as the "West Side Kids." The group promoted successful candidates for district leader seats; they gained control of a thirty-block area in Manhattan. Morris spent the next six years with a city budget watchdog organization and then served as issues director for an unsuccessful New York City gubernatorial candidate.

Morris met Bill Clinton in 1977 and obtained polling data that convinced Clinton to run for governor of Arkansas. Morris was called on in 1980 to save Clinton's reelection effort, but any help he offered came too late. He stayed close to the Clintons, while building up a business consulting with candidates of both parties, including the Republican senate majority leader at the time, Trent Lott.

When the Clinton presidency seemed to be floundering, following the Republican capture of the Congress in 1994, and the president's reelection was very much in doubt, Clinton turned once again to his old friend, bringing Morris into the White House to help devise a new strategy. Morris's strategy of triangulating, positioning Clinton between the Republicans and more liberal Democrats, drew criticism from some ideologues but was praised by pragmatists for its success in resurrecting a failing presidency.

Morris's stock in Washington was at its height during the summer of 1996. However, as Clinton prepared to accept his party's nomination for a second term, a tabloid newspaper revealed Morris's relationship with prostitute Sherry Rowlands. The details of the affair were graphic, and Morris was forced to separate himself from the White House.

Morris stayed out of the limelight for some time after his affair was revealed. But he has returned to public view in recent years, serving as a political commentator and columnist working for Fox News. In 1999, he launched Vote.com, a Web site asking visitors to vote on particular issues. (TW)

MORSE, LEOPOLD
Member of Congress, 1887–1889, 1877–1885

Leopold Morse was born in Wachenheim, Bavaria, on August 15, 1831. He emigrated to the United States in 1849. Settling in Boston, he worked in a clothing store, which he later purchased and owned until his death.

A Democrat, Morse ran unsuccessfully for Congress in 1870 and 1872. He ran a third time and was elected to Congress in 1876. He served four terms in office but declined renomination in 1884, the same year he was elected president of Post Publishing Company. After a brief absence from political life, Morse ran for Congress again in 1886, serving one more term before retiring to his business activities in Boston.

Leopold Morse died in Boston on December 15, 1892. (MW)

MOSES, ROBERT
New York Planner, 1918–1970s

Robert Moses was born in New Haven, Connecticut, on December 18, 1888, to a financially successful family. Moses and his family moved to New York City when Moses was a child. He graduated Phi Beta Kappa from Yale in 1909. He then went to Oxford, where he received an M.A. in political science in 1911, before returning to New York and to Columbia to earn his Ph.D. in 1914.

From 1915 until 1917, Moses served as technical expert for the New York City Civil Service Commission. When Al Smith became governor of New York in 1918, Moses became staff director of the commission to rewrite the state constitution. During Smith's second term, Moses was appointed president of the Long Island State Park Commission, which he led for the next thirty-nine years.

Throughout his very active participation in New York state and city planning, Moses was instrumental in engineering many major projects, including creating the Northern and Southern State Parkways in the 1920s. He served on the Triborough Bridge Authority from 1934 until 1968 and was an appointed city commissioner on the New York City Parks Department from 1934 until 1960. In 1934, he ran unsuccessfully for governor against incumbent Herbert Lehman, in the nation's first gubernatorial race between two Jews.

Moses's Triborough Bridge project employed more workers than any other Depression-era project. Using his authority as parks commissioner, Moses employed thousands to rebuild city facilities. Through these efforts he gained much public admiration. He also became known as a very powerful figure in New York, primarily through questionable managing of proceeds from major projects.

During the 1960s, with Moses serving on nearly all planning agencies, many felt that he wielded far too much power. Then-governor Nelson Rockefeller systematically removed him from many projects and committees. By then, Moses had gained a reputation for arrogant disregard for urban city dwellers, as most of his efforts favored car-driving suburbanites.

After 1974, Moses became more isolated, giving occasional speeches and writing several articles on parks, housing, and recreation, before his death on July 29, 1981. (MW)

MOSKOWITZ, BELLE LINDNER ISRAELS
Political Reformer and Welfare Worker

Born October 5, 1877, on the Upper East Side of New York City to immigrant parents, Isidor and Esther (Freyer) Lindner, Belle studied at the Horace Mann High School for Girls and at Teachers College, Columbia University. On completion of her formal education in 1900, she pursued her interests in social welfare reform by working at the Educational Alliance, a Jewish settlement house on New York's Lower East Side.

Moskowitz left the Alliance in 1903, when she married Charles Henry Israels but remained active in social service and worked part-time outside the home as she raised her children, volunteering for agencies including the United Hebrew Charities, the New York State Conference of Charities and Corrections, and the National Council of Jewish Women, New York Section.

After her husband's untimely death, she first worked as a grievance clerk for the Dress and Waist Manufacturers' Association and subsequently headed the labor department, adjusting thousands of industrial disputes. She married Henry Moskowitz, a former settlement work associate, on November 22, 1914.

Moskowitz became active in New York's political scene in 1918, when Alfred E. Smith, a man she believed had the same objectives that were held by herself, campaigned for the governorship. Becoming chair of the women's division of Smith's campaign committee, she helped attract the votes of newly enfranchised women. Moskowitz also laid out plans for an unofficial reconstruction commission to make over the state government. Governor Smith served eight years in Albany, and in each of his campaigns (including that for the presidency in 1928), Moskowitz was an efficient, ceaseless, but never conspicuous worker. She never held any public office but became the governor's fully trusted adviser on social and economic problems and his publicity director in all five campaigns.

Belle Moskowitz died of a heart attack on January 2, 1933. Four thousand New Yorkers crowded Temple Emanu-El to attend her funeral service. (JW)

Source: Elisabeth Israels Perry, *Belle Moskowitz: Feminine Politics and the Exercises of Power in the Age of Alfred E. Smith* (New York: Oxford University Press, 1987).

MULTER, ABRAHAM JACOB
Member of Congress, 1947–1967

Born on December 24, 1900, in New York City, Abe Multer attended public schools in Coney Island before graduating from Boys' High School in Brooklyn. While working during the day, Multer went to classes at night at the City College of New York. In 1923, he was admitted to the bar in New York following receiving his law degree from Brooklyn Law School. Multer earned his LL.D. from Yeshiva University in 1963.

While practicing law in New York City, Multer served as the special assistant attorney general of New York State. During World War II, from 1943 through 1945, he served in the United States Coast Guard. Multer served as special counsel to New York mayor William O'Dwyer in 1947.

Following the resignation of Leo Rayfiel, Multer was elected to Congress in a special election as a Democrat in November 1947. He was elected to a full term in 1948 and went on to represent New York in the Congress for the next two decades. Multer was elected to the New York Supreme Court on November 7, 1967, and resigned his seat in Congress to join that bench, on which he sat until January 1, 1977. Continuing his judicial service, Multer served as a special referee for the Brooklyn Appellate Division from 1979 until he retired in 1984.

Abraham Multer died on November 4, 1986. (DS)

N

NADLER, JERROLD
Member of Congress, 1992–present

Born in Brooklyn on June 13, 1947, Jerry Nadler has been involved in politics most of his adult life. He served as a member of the New York State Assembly from 1977 until 1992. In that year, Congressman Ted Weiss, who had represented the Upper West Side of Manhattan for many years, died the day before the primary election. Nadler was nominated to succeed Weiss and won easily in the general election. After surviving a difficult primary in 1994, Nadler has held his seat without difficulty and is considered among the safest of Democratic incumbents.

Nadler, whose district now includes not only Manhattan's Upper West Side but also parts of lower Manhattan and Brooklyn, is one of the most prominent liberals in the increasingly centrist House Democratic caucus. He gained prominence for his vociferous defense of President Bill Clinton as a member of the House Judiciary Committee during the impeachment inquiry. He has also championed other core liberal causes such as gay rights (including condemnation of Clinton's "don't ask, don't tell" policy), opposition to the death penalty, and progressive taxation.

Nadler is also legislative leader in transportation policy. He has used his position on the Transportation Committee to promote rail transport and is well known as an advocate for improvement of New York harbor to accommodate ever-larger cargo vessels. (JK)

NATHAN, MAUD
Suffragist and Community Leader

Maud Nathan, born October 20, 1862, in New York City, grew up in an orthodox Sephardic Jewish family. She attended private schools in New York until her family relocated to Green Bay, Wisconsin, where she completed public high school.

In 1880, Nathan returned to New York City, where she became involved in a variety of Jewish organizations. She was director of Mount Sinai Hospital's Nursing School and a volunteer English teacher for young Jewish immigrants at the Hebrew Free School Association in the 1880s. Nathan became an active member of her local chapter of the National Council of Jewish Women after it was formed in 1893. She was a member of the Congregation Shearith Israel Synagogue; she became president of their sisterhood in New York City.

Her community involvement, however, was not limited to Jewish organizations. In 1891, Nathan became one of the New York City Consumer League's first members. In 1897, she became chapter president, an office she held for twenty-one years. She was elected to the National Consumer League executive board in 1898. She also was a leading suffragist. She led New York City's Fifteenth Assembly

District's woman suffrage campaign and served as a delegate to the International Women's Suffrage Alliance convention in Budapest, 1913.

Nathan was the sister of Annie Nathan Meyer, who was opposed to the women's suffrage movement. After retiring from social work in the 1920s, Nathan lived in New York until her death on December 15, 1946. (TW)

NEUBERGER, RICHARD LEWIS
United States Senator, 1955–1960

Richard Lewis Neuberger was born near Portland, Oregon, on December 26, 1912. He received his education in the Portland public school system and attended the University of Oregon at Eugene in 1935. During this time, Neuberger worked as an author and reporter on issues of concern to the Pacific Northwest. He served as a correspondent for the *New York Times* from 1939 to 1954. In 1940, Neuberger was elected to the Oregon State House of Representatives. He held this position until July 15, 1942, when he resigned to accept a commission as an army second lieutenant; during the war, Neuberger rose to the rank of captain; he was a military aide at the founding conference of the United Nations in 1945.

Neuberger resumed his political life in 1949, when he was elected to the Oregon State Senate. He held this position until 1954, when he was elected to represent Oregon in the United States Senate.

Richard Neuberger died in office on March 9, 1960. He was succeeded by his wife, Maureen, who won a full term in her own right in the November 1960 election. (KJ)

NEWHOUSE, SAMUEL IRVING
Newspaper Publisher, 1920–1979

Born on May 24, 1895, in New York's Lower East Side, Solomon Neuhaus was the eldest of eight children born to Meier Neuhaus and Rose Arenfeldt, Jewish immigrants from Russia. The family moved to Bayonne, New Jersey, and in 1902 changed its name to *Newhouse;* Solomon also became *Samuel.* At age thirteen, Samuel left public school to become the primary breadwinner for the family, working first as an office boy for the Bayonne magistrate Hyman Lazarus, who became his mentor. Impressed by his ambitious nature, Lazarus soon involved Newhouse in overseeing the failing *Bayonne Times* until it could be sold. Under the care of this teenager, the newspaper was transformed into a profitable operation. In June 1916, after four years of night classes at the New Jersey College of Law, Newhouse passed the state bar examinations. He lost his first case due to a rigged jury and never practiced law again.

Instead, Newhouse began a career as a purchaser of newspapers, his first being the *News* of Fitchburg, Massachusetts. Throughout his career, he bought and revived declining papers whose location in potentially prosperous areas made them good risks. His profits were put right back into his family-owned enterprises in order to buy more papers without large bank loans. Unlike William Randolph Hearst and other media owners, Newhouse focused on raising profits, not on news content or editorials, with which he rarely interfered. He did so in part to counter fears of the people and papers being bought out by this now New York–based Jewish outsider.

Newhouse kept a low public profile and did not "go national" until 1955, when he paid a record-setting $5.6 million for the prestigious Portland *Oregonian.* In that year he also bought the *St. Louis Globe-Democrat* for $6.5 million and two Alabama newspapers—the *Birmingham News* and the *Huntsville Times*—plus a television station and three radio stations for $18.7 million. In 1959, he diversified into women's magazines by acquiring the famous Condé Nast publications *Vogue, Glamour, Young Brides,* and *House and Garden.* His empire grew from there.

Newhouse's life is a true Horatio Alger story: poor immigrant boy builds media empire and makes a fortune. At his death on August 29, 1979, that empire controlled thirty-one newspapers in twenty-two American cities, a string of magazines, radio and television stations, and cable television systems in a score of areas. (JW)

Source: Thomas Maier, *Newhouse: All the Glitter, Power, and Glory of America's Richest Media Empire and the Secretive Man behind It* (New York: St. Martin's, 1994).

NEWMAN, EDWIN
Journalist

Edwin Newman was born on January 25, 1919. After graduating from the University of Wisconsin, he became a dictation boy with the Washington bureau of the International News Service. His career in journalism was postponed in early 1942 when he entered the navy. He returned in 1945, however, to work for several news organizations. He freelanced in London for several years and began his long career at NBC in 1952.

In 1956, Newman was named the NBC bureau chief in London; the following year he was sent to Rome and finally to Paris, starting in 1958. He returned to New York in 1961 to make numerous contributions to NBC broadcasts as critic, correspondent, interviewer, anchorman, and commentator during the next twenty years. Newman reported on the coronation of Queen Elizabeth, anchored live coverage of the Kennedy and King assassinations, and moderated the presidential debates between Ford and Carter in 1976 and Reagan and Mondale in 1984. The longtime newsman left NBC later in 1984 after more than thirty years of reporting on events all over the world.

Newman wrote a novel, *Sunday Punch* (1979), as well as two authoritative works on the English language, *Strictly Speaking* (1975) and *A Civil Tongue* (1976). In 1996, at the age of seventy-six, Newman surprised many when he went to the USA Cable Network to host *Weekly World News.* (BMcN)

NOAH, MORDECAI MANUEL
Nineteenth-Century Political Activist;
U.S. Consul to Tunis, 1813–1815

Mordecai Noah was born in Philadelphia in July 1785. He was orphaned at a young age and was raised by his grandparents, first in Philadelphia and later in Charleston, South Carolina.

In 1811, Noah was appointed as the first American consul to Riga but was unable to assume the post due to outbreak of war. In 1813, Noah became the United States consul to Tunis. While serving in this post, Noah was entrusted to secure the safe release of eleven American seamen who were being held captive in Algiers. Noah succeeded in having only two of the seamen released. In 1815, Noah was recalled from his post on religious grounds by Secretary of State James Monroe.

Noah continued his career in political journalism in New York City, where he edited several newspapers, including the *New York Enquirer* and the *Evening Star.* He was appointed sheriff of New York City in 1821 and held the post until the following year. In 1824, he was the grand sachem of Tammany Hall. He also served as New York port inspector from 1829 until 1832 and judge on the New York Court of Sessions from 1841 until 1842.

Noah was very influential in the small American Jewish community, proclaiming America to be the Jewish people's "chosen country." In January 1820, he petitioned the New York legislature to sell him Grand Island, which lies in the Niagara River in western New York. Noah intended it to be the homeland for Jews from all over the world. Though he received no positive response from the state, an investor purchased a portion of the island and gave it to Noah. In September 1825, Noah dedicated "Ararat" as a haven for Jews from around the world. Though Ararat was a failure, Noah remained an outspoken advocate for Jews in America, pushing for all Jews to eventually relocate to Palestine.

Mordecai Noah died as a result of stroke on March 22, 1851. (MW)

OCHS, ADOLPH S.
Publisher, New York Times

For more than a century, the Ochs–Sulzberger family has owned and published the *New York Times.* Adolph S. Ochs was the son of Julius Ochs, a German Jewish immigrant with liberal political views, and his wife Bertha, a southerner who favored slavery as much as her husband opposed it. Adolph Ochs was born on the eve of the Civil War, on March 12, 1858, into a household that was divided, as were so many over loyalties during that great encounter.

Adolph grew up in the South and in the border states and worked from early on to help his family's finances. From the start he was involved in the newspaper business, literally working his way up from carrier, through journey printer, to reporter, editor, and eventually owner. His success was far from immediate. In fact, when he bought the *Times* in the summer of 1896, he was heavily in debt, and he was purchasing a paper proud in tradition but nearly bankrupt. The tradition was to continue, the reputation of the paper to be enhanced, and financial success and national and international power to follow.

Ochs brought to the paper a commitment to journalistic integrity. His credo—"to give the news impartially, without fear or favor, regardless of any party, sect, or interest involved"—appeared in the first editorial written under his ownership. Ochs tended to the paper's financial health as he watched over its editorial product. He built the famous Times Tower in the square in New York that bears his paper's name. He became a powerful figure, sought after by the leaders of the political world as well as those of industry. But he was not a man who sought the spotlight. While his fellow journalistic magnates, Hearst and Pulitzer, sought fame and fortune, Ochs sought admiration for his paper and the way he ran it. He achieved those goals.

Ochs made the paper a family business, not just his immediate family but his extended family; under his leadership they ran the *Chattanooga Times* as well as the *New York Times*. In a sense, the Tennessee paper was used as a farm system, developing talent to run the flagship enterprise.

Ochs and his wife, Effie, had only one child, their daughter Iphigene, born September 19, 1892. Ochs worshipped his daughter in every way, but in early twentieth-century America it was inconceivable that she could replace him at the paper. Iphigene, educated at Barnard, married Arthur Hays Sulzberger, the son of Cyrus Sulzberger, who had achieved prominence in business and was well known for his work on Jewish and civic causes, and his wife, Rachel, who was most proud that her Sephardic ancestors had emigrated to this country in the early years of the eighteenth century. Iphigene and Arthur Hays Sulzberger were married in 1917; after World War I he went to work for his bride's father's business, first in Chattanooga and then in New York.

When Adolph Ochs died, on April 8, 1935, it was not clear who would succeed him. The decision, to be made by the board of the Times Corporation, was between Sulzberger and Iphigene's cousin, Julius Ochs Adler. According to the terms of Adolph's will, the Ochs Trust controlled more than half of the voting stock of the corporation—and Iphigene had the deciding vote among the trustees. She chose her husband.

Arthur Hays Sulzberger ran the *Times* for nearly three decades with nearly despotic power, though Iphigene's influence and her control of the family fortune were always factors. Sulzberger, a strong internationalist, expanded the paper's influence around the world and hobnobbed with foreign leaders as much as with the American elite. He was a staunch anticommunist and an early supporter of Dwight D. Eisenhower's bid for the presidency, in an unprecedented move endorsing the general more than seven months before the election.

Sulzberger began to turn over the reins of the *Times* empire in the mid-1950s, first relinquishing his day-to-day control of the *Chattanooga Times* to his son-in-law Ben Golden, and the title of president of the *New York Times* to another son-in-law, Orvil E. Dryfoos, in 1957. Later that year, Sulzberger suffered the first of a series of strokes, and his control of the paper was never again so complete. In 1961, just after the paper had suppressed the prior knowledge it had of the Bay of Pigs invasion, Sulzberger named Dryfoos as the publisher of the *Times*.

Dryfoos's reign would be short but tumultuous. He was the paper's leader during the 114-day strike in 1962 and 1963. The burden of that strike took a toll on Dryfoos's already frail health. While on vacation in Puerto Rico with his wife, Marian, he collapsed. He returned to New York, still insisting on working from his hospital bed. He died from heart failure, without ever recovering full health, on May 25, 1963.

Dryfoos was succeeded as publisher by Arthur Ochs (Punch) Sulzberger. Punch Sulzberger's parents had not thought him ready to assume leadership of the family business some years earlier, but he had clearly learned a great deal during his brother-in-law's illness. Tutored by James (Scotty) Reston, the longtime Washington bureau chief for the *Times*, an intimate of the Sulzberger family, Punch assumed leadership as the paper was dominating American journalism. He saw the paper through another series of difficult times. Punch Sulzberger's finest hour as publisher might well have been when the United States Supreme Court ruled in favor of the *Times* in the Pentagon Papers case. The First Amendment had one of its finest hours.

Punch Sulzberger turned over the family business to his son, Arthur Ochs Sulzberger Jr., on January 16, 1962, after just under three decades of leading the paper. In his time and that of his son, the Times Corporation has expanded, contracted, and expanded again. The *Times* and the newspaper industry has had to adjust to the domination of instant news by television and more recently the Internet. The business side of the Times Corporation has demanded a significant amount of executive leadership. But through it all the *New York Times* has remained "the paper of record."

The Ochs–Sulzberger family has remained true to the credo of Arthur Ochs Sulzberger's great-grandfather. They have directed a paper that has been a voice of reason and a beacon of integrity in reporting on the business of the government, the politics of the nation, and the personalities who lead us. The family has viewed the *New York Times* as a trust. As such they have upheld the principles on which the First Amendment is based—and been worthy of the trust they have inherited. (LSM)

Source: Susan E. Tifft and Alex S. Jones, *The Trust: The Private and Powerful Family behind* The New York Times (Boston: Little, Brown, 1999).

OTTINGER, RICHARD LAWRENCE
Member of Congress, 1975–1985, 1965–1971

Richard Lawrence Ottinger was born on January 27, 1929. He grew up in the wealthy community of

Scarsdale, New York, where he attended public school before attending the Loomis School in Windsor, Connecticut. Ottinger earned his bachelor's degree from Cornell University and attained his law degree at Harvard University. After graduating from Harvard, Ottinger served in the United States Air Force for three years and was discharged in 1955 as a captain. That same year Ottinger was admitted to the New York Bar; for the next five years he practiced international and corporate law.

After graduate study in international law at Georgetown, Ottinger worked on the original plans for the Peace Corps and served as the director of programs for the West Coast of South America from 1961 to 1964. In 1964, Ottinger successfully ran for election to the Eighty-ninth Congress as a Democrat, winning in the Johnson landslide. He was re-elected twice but gave up his seat to run, unsuccessfully, for the United States Senate in 1970.

For the next few years, Ottinger organized the consumer group Grassroots Action, Inc., to oppose governmental regulation of communications. In 1974, Ottinger regained his seat in the House. He held this seat for the next ten years until he retired in 1984. Throughout his career as a congressman, Ottinger was known as a champion of the environment and as a consumer advocate. (KJ)

P

PALEY, WILLIAM
Chairman and CEO of CBS, 1929–1990

William Paley was born in Chicago on September 28, 1901, and grew up as the son of a wealthy cigar producer in Philadelphia. After graduating from a Philadelphia high school, Paley attended the Wharton School of Finance and Commerce at the University of Pennsylvania. Working for his father, Paley experimented with radio for advertising; to support his son's interest, Sam Paley bought the new radio network CBS in 1928.

Paley worked doggedly to build the failing network, building CBS into a broadcasting giant. He displayed a genius for merchandising that allowed the network to grow rapidly. In his first few years at the head of the network, he made his primary goal to reach the largest audience possible by allowing affiliates to use CBS programs for free. The strategy proved extremely fruitful. Paley insisted on controlling the smallest details of programming, which benefited the network greatly because he was an excellent judge of talent. He was personally responsible for bringing reporters Walter Cronkite and Edward

R. Murrow to the network and launching the careers of singers Bing Crosby and Frank Sinatra. Paley was responsible not only for developing CBS but also for establishing much of the structure of modern broadcasting.

After heading CBS for more than sixty years, William Paley died of a heart attack in 1990. (OS)

PEIXOTTO, BENJAMIN F.
Honorary U.S. Consul to Romania, 1870–1876

Born on November 13, 1834, in New York, Benjamin Franklin Peixotto was raised by his sister, Judith Salzedo Peixotto, after his father's untimely death in 1843. Judith was one of the first Jewish educators, and she became the first Jewish principal in New York. After moving to Cleveland, Ohio, Benjamin wrote for the *Cleveland Plain Dealer* and became an attorney, studying under Stephen Douglas. He moved to San Francisco and practiced law there. Peixotto served as national president of the B'nai B'rith from 1863 to 1864, advocating against human rights abuses of Jews.

During the Civil War, B'nai B'rith members played leadership roles in opposing General Ulysses S. Grant's attempt to expel Jews from several states under military rule. In 1870, with violence against Jews sweeping Romania, B'nai B'rith protested, and a chastened Grant, now president, chose Peixotto as honorary U.S. consul to Romania, where he served for five years without a salary. Peixotto focused on alleviating the civil and economic conditions of Romanian Jews. His original strategy was to encourage the masses to emigrate to America, which was very unpopular, and he eventually limited himself to education of Romanian Jewish youth. While in Romania, his expenses were sponsored by American Jews. Peixotto later served in the U.S. Consulate Office in Lyons, France.

Benjamin Peixotto died on September 18, 1890. (JM)

PENN, MARK
Democratic Pollster

Mark Penn was born in New York City on January 15, 1954. He graduated from Harvard College and also attended the Kennedy School of Government and Columbia Law School.

After completing his schooling, Penn worked in the Corporate Planning Division of NBC. He founded Penn & Schoen Associates in 1975 (now Penn, Schoen, and Berland Associates). This well-respected firm provides public opinion analysis and suggests public relations strategies for public and private clients, in the United States and abroad.

President Bill Clinton relied on Penn's media and message strategies during his 1996 reelection campaign, and Penn remained the Clintons' pollster during the second term. Numerous U.S. senators, members of the House of Representatives, and governors, including Daniel Patrick Moynihan, Joe Lieberman, and Evan Bayh, have depended on the firm's strategies. Penn's international clients have included President Belisario Bentacur of Colombia and Prime Minister Menachem Begin of Israel.

In addition to his consulting, Penn has done extensive foundation work. He studied the emergence of democratic values and antisemitism in post–Cold War Hungary, the Czech Republic, and Poland for the American Jewish Congress and Freedom House. (SB)

PERLE, RICHARD N.
Assistant Secretary of Defense for International Security Policy, 1981–1987

Richard N. Perle, son of Jack and Martha Perle, was born on September 16, 1941. He received his B.A. from the University of Southern California in 1964, did postgraduate work in economics at the University of London, and received his M.A. in political science from Princeton University in 1967.

He has served as a director of the *Jerusalem Post*, chairman and chief executive officer for Hollinger Digital, and an aide to Senator "Scoop" Jackson (D-Wash.). Perle drafted the Jackson–Vanik amendment linking Soviet trade concessions to freer emigration of Jews from the USSR. His staff service in the Senate covered more than a decade, from 1969 to 1980. Through most of the Reagan administration, Perle served as assistant secretary of defense for international security, a position in which he accrued a good deal of influence.

Perle, a resident fellow at the American Enterprise Institute since 1987, has used his expertise in the areas of defense, intelligence, Europe, the Middle East, Russia, and NATO as a basis for frequent contributions to contemporary policy debate. His articles have appeared in the *New York Times,* the *Washington Post, U.S. News & World Report,* the *Wall Street Journal,* as well as in British and Israeli newspapers. He authored *Hard Line* (1992) and edited *Reshaping Western Security* in 1991. (MP)

PERLMAN, NATHAN DAVID
Member of Congress, 1920–1927

Nathan David Perlman was born in Poland on August 2, 1887, and emigrated to New York City with his mother in 1891. He attended public school,

studied at the City College of New York, and graduated from New York University Law School in 1907. After beginning his legal practice in New York, Perlman was appointed special deputy attorney general of the state of New York in 1912, serving two years in that capacity. In 1914, he was elected as a Republican to the state legislature; he did not seek reelection.

Perlman won a special election to fill the vacant congressional seat caused by the resignation of Fiorello LaGuardia in 1920. He was reelected to three full terms but lost the 1926 election. Perlman returned to private practice for a few years; but in 1935, he became magistrate of the City of New York and was appointed justice of the court of special sessions in the city in 1936. He sat on that bench until his death on June 29, 1952. (LSM)

PEYSER, THEODORE ALBERT
Member of Congress, 1933–1937

Theodore Albert Peyser was born on February 18, 1873, in Charleston, West Virginia. After attending public school, Peyser went immediately to work. He switched occupations frequently until he finally settled down in Cincinnati, Ohio, when he was twenty years old. For the next seven years Peyser supported himself by working as a traveling salesman. In 1900, Peyser decided to change careers again and moved to New York City to work in the life insurance business. He became enamored with politics and tied his career to that of Franklin D. Roosevelt. In 1932, he was swept into office as a New Deal Democrat. He remained in the House as a Roosevelt supporter until his death on August 8, 1937. (KJ)

PHILLIPS, HENRY MYER
Member of Congress, 1857–1859

Henry Myer Phillips was born in Philadelphia on June 30, 1811, and was educated in that city. In 1832, Phillips was admitted to the bar and commenced practice in Philadelphia.

In 1856, Phillips was elected as a Democrat to the Thirty-fifth Congress; he was unsuccessful in his bid for reelection in 1858.

After his one term in Congress, Phillips resumed the practice of law in Philadelphia and was involved in various civic activities including terms on the boards of the Jefferson Medical College, the Fairmount Park Commission, the Board of City Trusts, and the Academy of Music.

Henry Phillips died in Philadelphia, August 28, 1884. (BB)

PHILLIPS, PHILIP
Member of Congress, 1853–1855

Philip Phillips was born in Charleston on December 13, 1807. His father was a German immigrant; his mother, the daughter of a Revolutionary War veteran. He was educated briefly in Charleston by a radical Reform rabbi, and then attended a military academy in Connecticut. Phillips returned to Charleston and was admitted to the bar when he was twenty-one.

Phillips began his political career amid the South Carolina nullification crisis. He was elected to the state's constitutional convention in 1832 as an opponent of nullification; he would maintain unionist proclivities throughout his career. In 1833 and 1834, he served in the South Carolina House of Representatives.

In 1835, Phillips moved to Mobile, Alabama, to practice law. He chaired the Alabama Democratic Party, was elected to that state's house of representatives in 1844 and 1850, and from 1853 to 1855 represented Alabama in Congress. He declined renomination, choosing to establish a law practice in Washington.

Phillips's wife Eugenia was a vocal secessionist. Eugenia's politics forced her family to leave Washington in 1861, after she was placed under house arrest. They resettled in New Orleans, but Union forces soon captured the city. She was arrested and incarcerated for three months in 1862.

After the war, the couple returned to Washington, where Phillips practiced law until his death on January 14, 1884. (MD)

PODELL, BERTRAM L.
Member of Congress, 1968–1975

Bertram L. Podell was born in Brooklyn on December 27, 1925. He attended primary school at Yeshiva of Flatbush and afterward entered Abraham Lincoln High School. Staying in Brooklyn, he received his undergraduate degree from St. John's University. Podell served in the United States Navy during World War II and then returned home to earn his law degree from Brooklyn Law School. In 1950, Podell was admitted to the New York Bar and began to practice law.

Within a short time, Podell became actively involved in New York state politics. After his first election in 1954, Podell served in the New York State Assembly for fourteen years. When the incumbent congressman from Podell's district resigned in 1968, Podell aggressively sought to fill the vacancy. Winning a special election on February 20, 1968,

Podell entered the Ninetieth Congress as a Democrat. Podell was reelected three more times, but he was accused in 1974 of improper use of his office, accepting $41,000 for influencing the Civic Aeronautics Board to award a Bahama route to a Florida airline. As this scandal brewed, Podell lost the 1974 Democratic primary. After losing the primary, Podell pled guilty to a charge that allowed him to resume his law career in New York City. (KJ)

PODHORETZ, NORMAN
Writer and Editor

Norman Podhoretz's career as a writer and editor has spanned the post–World War II era, and he has had a profound impact on intellectual currents on both the right and the left. Under his influence, *Commentary*, a liberal-left publication from its founding in 1945 and through the 1960s, has become a bastion of neoconservatism and an unwavering supporter of Israel. He has also written three memoirs, which chronicle not only his own intellectual journey but American intellectual life more generally.

Podhoretz was born to immigrant parents in Brooklyn on January 16, 1930. He attended New York City public school and then Columbia University, where he was awarded a B.A.; he later attended the Jewish Theological Seminary and Cambridge University, England.

After Podhoretz finished his schooling, Lionel Trilling, his professor at Columbia, recruited him to write for *Commentary*. He quickly became the youngest member of the New York Intellectuals, and by 1960, he had taken the helm of the publication.

A leftist himself in the early 1960s, though of stronger anticommunist tendencies than most of his colleagues, he became disenchanted with radical politics. By the early 1970s, he was convinced that the antiwar and antinuclear movements were undermining the American fight against the Soviet Union and totalitarianism. He also became, and remains, a critic of the gay rights movement.

Podhoretz is married to writer Midge Decter, whose political shift from left to right has paralleled his own. (MD)

Source: Norman Podhoretz, *Making It* (New York: Random House, 1967).

POLLACK, JACK
Political Leader

Jack Pollack was born in Baltimore in 1898 to Russian Jewish immigrant parents. Growing up in a working-class section of Baltimore, Pollack dropped out of school at age eleven to work full-time as a garment worker. The young Pollack became involved in the street life of Baltimore and began selling newspapers. When he became eighteen, Pollack decided that he would build a career in boxing. This venture lasted two years.

Pollack returned to Baltimore and became involved in the bail-bonding business. During Prohibition, Pollack rose to become a successful bootlegger of rum and whiskey, which made him very wealthy. In the 1930s, Pollack opened the James Pollack Insurance Agency and became active in real estate. He went on to become assistant to William Curran, powerful Baltimore political boss. From Curran, Pollack learned the details of city government and the importance of being influential. He became the leader of the Fourth District Trenton Democratic Club. Pollack became an influential figure in Baltimore city politics, promising jobs and food in exchange for political favors. Due to his knowledge and familiarity with the neighborhood and the residents, he was very influential in securing the Jewish vote for the Baltimore Democrats.

Like the stereotypical political leader Frank Skeffington in *The Last Hurrah*, Pollack was known for caring for his people and helping the needy, despite common knowledge of his questionable tactics. He died in Baltimore in 1977. (MW)

POLLITZER, ANITA
Chair, National Woman's Party, 1945–1949

Anita Pollitzer was born on October 31, 1894, in Charleston, South Carolina. She graduated from Columbia University, where she received her bachelor's degree in 1916 and later received her master's in international law.

After becoming involved in the suffrage movement at Columbia, Pollitzer continued her efforts as a leader of the National Woman's Party and an organizer of the movement to pass the Equal Rights Amendment. She served the National Woman's Party as its national secretary from 1921 to 1926, vice chair from 1927 to 1938, chair from 1945 to 1949, and honorary chair from 1949 to 1975. Pollitzer had considerable influence with several politicians, including President John F. Kennedy and her home-state senator, Strom Thurmond, who was an aspiring young Democrat during much of her career.

Pollitzer also fought for both female and male nationals to have the right to pass their nationality on to their children born abroad. She also backed the Copeland–Dickstein Bill, legislation that removed sex discrimination when women marry foreign nationals.

Anita Pollitzer died on July 3, 1975, in Queens, New York. (SB)

POSNER, RICHARD A.
U.S. Court of Appeals, 1981–present

One of the leading intellectuals on the federal bench, Richard Allen Posner was born January 11, 1939, in New York City. In 1959, he graduated from Yale University with an A.B.; he received an LL.B. in 1962 from Harvard Law School, where he served as president of the law review. After finishing at Harvard, Posner clerked for Supreme Court Justice William J. Brennan Jr.

Posner remained in Washington, practicing law for the Federal Trade Commission and in the office of the Solicitor General until he joined the Stanford Law faculty as an associate professor in 1968. A year later, he became a professor of law at the University of Chicago. Posner remained primarily in academia until 1981, when President Ronald Reagan appointed him to the U.S. Court of Appeals for the Seventh Circuit. He became chief judge of the court in 1993.

He is the author of more than twenty-five books and three hundred articles on legal issues, including economic perspectives and issues in law, law and literature, and antitrust law. Among his books are *An Affair of State: The Investigation, Impeachment, and Trial of President Clinton* (1999); *Economic Analysis of Law* (1972); and *Antitrust Law: An Economic Perspective* (1976). Posner is considered to be a pioneer in economic analysis of law and a conservative free-market advocate. In November 1999, he was appointed to serve as mediator in the Microsoft antitrust dispute, which he was unable to resolve. During his tenure on the court of appeals, Posner has continued to serve as a senior lecturer at the University of Chicago Law School. (JM)

PULITZER, JOSEPH
Member of Congress, 1885–1886;
Newspaper Publisher

Born on April 10, 1847, in Mako, Hungary, Joseph Pulitzer grew up in Budapest and emigrated to the

United States in 1864. He immediately enlisted in the Union Army, fighting for a year in the Civil War.

After demobilizing, Pulitzer embarked on an influential journalistic career that arguably has had no equal. After a brief stint on the staff of a German-language newspaper in St. Louis, he purchased a share of the paper and then resold it at a profit. It was a pattern that would repeat itself over the course of a lifetime, as Pulitzer soon acquired three more St. Louis newspapers and resold or reorganized them, taking control of the *St. Louis Post-Dispatch* by 1878.

Meanwhile, Pulitzer also pursued political interests. He was elected to the Missouri legislature in 1869, backed the Liberal Party presidential candidate Horace Greeley, and then became a Democrat. His paper reflected his political leanings; in 1882, his chief editorial writer was gunned down by a political opponent.

Within six months, Pulitzer had purchased the *New York World* from financier Jay Gould and turned the morning daily into a leading voice for the Democratic Party. He introduced illustrations, comics, and sports coverage to the paper, tempering a volatile mix of political coverage, exposés, and muckraking journalism. Circulation climbed to six hundred thousand, making the *World* the most widely read daily in America. Frustrated rivals attacked him viciously, calling him the "Jew who had denied his race and religion."

In 1885, Pulitzer was elected to the United States House of Representatives, where he served for a short time before resigning. He realized, he said later, that he had greater impact as a newspaperman, an observation that was born out with the start of the Spanish-American War—sparked in no small part by the circulation war between Pulitzer and William Randolph Hearst.

Poor health and eyesight led him to give up management of the paper, but Pulitzer's hand could clearly be seen in the paper's editorial policy until he died on October 29, 1911, in Charleston, South Carolina. His will endowed the Columbia University School of Journalism and the Pulitzer Prizes, awarded annually since 1917. (JB)

R

RABB, MAXWELL M.
Ambassador to Italy, 1981–1989;
Presidential Adviser, 1952–1957

"I never considered myself a symbol of America," Maxwell M. Rabb said in his ninetieth year. But he was.

Born on September 28, 1910, to Solomon and Rose Rabb of Boston, Rabb graduated from both Harvard College and Harvard Law School. After two years at the family law firm, he went to Washington in 1937 to serve as Senator Henry Cabot Lodge's chief administrative assistant, a post he held for six years.

From 1943 to 1951, Rabb's responsibilities alternated between his Boston law practice and a number of posts in Washington. In 1951, he served as an assistant campaign manager to General Dwight D. Eisenhower; he worked in the White House as cabinet secretary for the first five years of the Eisenhower administration. During that time, he quietly managed Eisenhower's desegregation efforts. In 1958, he returned to private life, joining the New York law firm of Stoock, Strook, and Lavan.

Rabb held a variety of appointments over the next two decades, including the chair of the U.S. delegation to UNESCO. After Ronald Reagan's election in 1980, the new president called on Rabb to serve his country once more—this time, as ambassador to Italy. Not long after his appointment, Rabb was targeted by a Libyan hit squad for assassination or kidnapping, but Italian police broke up the plot just hours before the attack was to take place.

Rabb served as ambassador for eight years. He continues to live and work in New York City. (JB)

RABIN, BENJAMIN J.
Member of Congress, 1945–1947

One of four children, Benjamin J. Rabin was born on June 3, 1896, in Rochester, New York, where he attended public schools. He entered New York University but left school to join the navy when the United States entered World War I. On discharge in 1919, he returned to New York University, graduated from the law department, and was admitted to the bar.

Rabin maintained a private practice and in the 1930s was counsel to the New York State joint legislative committee investigating guaranteed mortgages and to the State Mortgage Commission, which he chaired from 1937 to 1939. A Democrat, he was elected to the United States House of Representatives in 1944, representing the Bronx. After winning reelection in 1946, he served the first year of his second term before resigning on December 31, 1947, to assume the seat he had just won on the New York State Supreme Court.

In January 1955, Governor Averell Harriman designated Rabin associate justice of the appellate division of the state supreme court. In 1961, Rabin easily won a second fourteen-year stint on the bench. He died at his winter home in Palm Beach, Florida, on February 22, 1969, just eight years into the term. (JB)

RAFSHOON, GERALD MONROE
White House Media Adviser, 1978–1980

Gerald Monroe Rafshoon was born on January 11, 1934, to Jack and Helen Rafshoon in New York City. He attended the University of Texas, graduating in 1955.

Rafshoon began his rise to prominence in Atlanta with Century Fox Films, as a regional advertising and publicity manager. Within three years, he had become national advertising manager, a job that took him to New York from 1962 to 1963.

He left the film industry and returned to Atlanta to launch Gerald Rafshoon Advertising. Among his clients was an aspiring Georgia politician named Jimmy Carter. Rafshoon directed advertising for the 1976 presidential campaign and served as an informal adviser to Carter from the start of his administration. He became an official member of the Carter team in 1978, recruited to improve the president's standing with voters. Prior to Rafshoon's arrival, no one oversaw simple but crucial details such as the daily distribution of talking points to key White House personnel. More broadly, Rafshoon explained that his job was "developing the themes of the presidency, and getting them out." Rafshoon also advised Carter to hold televised town meetings, a radio call-in show, and dinners with news executives to enhance the president's image. In many ways, Rafshoon introduced the modern concept of message and image management as a crucial element in presidential politics.

Following Carter's 1980 election loss, Rafshoon became more involved in the movie industry, serving as executive producer for many television and big-screen movie projects. (JB)

RAPOPORT, BERNARD (B)
Democratic Party Fund-raiser

Bernard (B) Rapoport was born in San Antonio, Texas, on July 17, 1917, and educated in San Antonio public schools. He graduated from the University of Texas in Austin in 1939. Rapoport's career has been that of a successful businessman, a generous philanthropist, and an ardent, loyal Democrat.

Rapoport made his fortune as chairman and chief executive officer of the American Income Life Insurance Company, headquartered in Waco, Texas. He has used his money to benefit liberal causes that reflect his values and those of his wife, Audre. Thus, among many organizations he has supported, he has endowed a series of chairs at his alma mater and established the Bernard and Audre Rapoport Fund in support of the Freedom of Information Foundation of Texas.

Rapoport has also been most generous in his support of Democratic candidates for office, first in Texas and increasingly around the nation. He was an early and close supporter of both Lyndon Johnson (and he sits on the advisory board of the Lyndon Baines Johnson School at the University of Texas and is a member of the board of the Lyndon Baines Johnson Foundation) and former Speaker of the House, Jim Wright. He has been a major contributor to and fund-raiser for the Democratic National Committee and the Hill committees, as well as various individual campaigns.

Rapoport has also been active in many Jewish causes. As but one example, he is chairman of the board of the American Friends of Tel Aviv University and sits on the university's board of governors. (LSM)

RAUH, JOSEPH L. JR.
Founder, Americans for Democratic Action

Joseph L. Rauh Jr. was born in Cincinnati on January 3, 1911. His father was a Jewish immigrant from Batavia, Germany, and his mother, Sarah Weiler, was an American of German Jewish descent. The youngest of three children in the family, he attended Harvard, earning a bachelor's degree in 1932 and a law degree in 1935. He married Olie Westheimer the same year.

On graduating from law school, Rauh accepted a clerkship with Supreme Court Justice Benjamin Cardozo, on the recommendation of his professor, Felix Frankfurter. He later clerked for Frankfurter before joining the Roosevelt administration in the Lend-Lease Administration and the Office for Emergency Management.

Rauh entered World War II with a lieutenant's commission and served in the Pacific theater for the war's duration, attached to General Douglas MacArthur's headquarters. After his return, he tried private practice but within months found himself running the Veterans Emergency Housing Program under President Truman. Between 1946 and 1947, Rauh helped found the Americans for Democratic Action (ADA) with other prominent liberals such as Eleanor Roosevelt and Hubert Humphrey. As a leading voice for the ADA, he opposed Truman's loyalty program and the Smith Act, which made it criminal to advocate the violent overthrow of the government. He served as chair of the ADA from 1955 to 1957.

Much of Rauh's political influence came as general counsel to the United Auto Workers, the Leadership Conference on Civil Rights, and Miners for Democracy during the 1950s and 1960s. Rauh remained active in fighting for civil rights causes until his death in Washington in 1992. (JB)

RAYFIEL, LEO FREDERICK
Member of Congress, 1945–1947

Leo Frederick Rayfiel was born in New York City, March 22, 1888; attended city schools; and earned a law degree from New York University in 1908. Although he was not admitted to the state bar until 1918, he quickly established a flourishing private practice in Brooklyn that he would maintain until 1945.

His first experience with public office came in 1938, when he was elected to the New York State Assembly as a Democrat. He held the seat for six years before running and winning election to the United States House of Representatives. He served a term as the representative from the Fourteenth District, won reelection, but left the seat after president Harry Truman appointed him to a judgeship of the U.S. District Court for the Eastern District of New York.

In 1966, he assumed senior status on the court. He remained on the bench until his death in November 18, 1978, at the age of ninety. (JB)

RAYNER, ISIDOR
United States Senator, 1905–1912;
Member of Congress, 1891–1895, 1887–1889

Isador Rayner was born on April 11, 1850, in Baltimore. His father, a Bavarian immigrant, sent him to private schools and the University of Maryland. He later studied law at the University of Virginia and was admitted to the bar in 1871.

Rayner was elected to the Maryland House of Delegates in 1878, reelected twice, and elected to the state senate in 1884. In 1886, he was elected as a Democrat to the United States House of Representatives. He lost a reelection bid in 1888 but won the next two. From 1899 to 1903, he served as Maryland's attorney general. Rayner's political career ended with service in the United States Senate from 1905 until his death on November 25, 1912.

Rayner won his party's senatorial nomination by breaking with the state's Democratic machine. The break came over a proposed amendment to the state constitution that would have disenfranchised black voters. Rayner opposed the amendment, under pressure from Jewish leaders—and in an evident reversal of his earlier position, which had questioned the intellectual fitness of the black electorate. Apparently reversing his stand once more, Rayner supported a bill in 1907 that disenfranchised blacks and protected the rights of European immigrants.

Rayner was a nonobservant Jew but referred to his own Jewishness when campaigning for aid to Russian Jews. He married a Christian woman, and they raised their son in that faith. (MD)

REICH, ROBERT BERNARD
Secretary of Labor, 1993–1997

Born June 24, 1946, in Scranton, Pennsylvania, Robert Reich received a B.A. degree from Dartmouth College in 1968. He won a Rhodes Scholarship and met Bill Clinton while both men were studying at Oxford University. After returning to the United States, Reich went on to Yale, again with Clinton; he received his J.D. from Yale in 1973.

Reich is a true liberal, an advocate for a large government role in the economy. Between 1974 and 1976, he served as the assistant solicitor general in the Department of Justice. During the Carter administration, he was the director of policy planning for the Federal Trade Commission. With the election of Ronald Reagan, Reich left government for academia, accepting a position as a lecturer in political economy at the John F. Kennedy School of Government of Harvard University; he remained at Harvard until 1992.

During the 1992 campaign, Reich was one of the top policy advisers to candidate Bill Clinton. He had hoped for one of the top positions in the new administration; however, he was somewhat disappointed when his friend, the president-elect, asked him to join his cabinet as secretary of labor, not in a more prominent position. During his service as secretary, Reich was very concerned with narrowing the gap between rich and poor Americans and opposing antiworker developments in corporate America. Although his friendship with Clinton was still strong, he resigned the position in 1997, citing his desire to devote more time to his family.

Reich returned to Boston and accepted a position as the Maurice B. Hexter Professor of Economics and Social Policy at Brandeis University. Among Reich's several books is *Locked in the Cabinet* (1997), a memoir of his time as secretary of labor. His op-ed pieces frequently appear in the *New York Times* and the *Boston Globe*; he is the cofounder of the liberal publication *The American Prospect*.

Reich and his wife, Clare Dalton, the associate dean at the Northeastern University Law School, have two sons. (TW)

RENDELL, EDWARD
General Chair, Democratic
National Committee, 1999–2001;
Mayor of Philadelphia, 1992–2000

Edward Rendell was born in New York City on January 5, 1944. He attended the University of Pennsylvania, where he received a degree in political science in 1965. He then continued on to Villanova University, attaining his law degree in 1968. Rendell served in the Army Reserves during the Vietnam War.

Beginning in 1968, Rendell built his legal career as a prosecutor in Philadelphia, assistant district attorney, deputy special prosecutor, and, in 1977, the youngest district attorney in the city's history, a position he held until 1986.

In 1991, Rendell ran successfully for mayor of Philadelphia; his term was marked by the renaissance of the city. He balanced the city's budget within a year and succeeded in gaining privatization for many of Philadelphia's public works services. He gained a generally favorable rating among Philadelphians.

Rendell was chosen to serve as the general chairman of the Democratic National Committee in 1999, as his second term as mayor of Philadelphia was drawing to a close. He headed this group through the 2000 convention and presidential campaign. In 2001, he announced his candidacy for governor of Pennsylvania. (MW)

RESNICK, JOSEPH Y.
Member of Congress, 1965–1969

Joseph Resnick was born in Ellenville, New York, on July 13, 1924. He was interested in electronics and entered the United States Merchant Marine as a radio officer during World War II. Resnick returned from the war to found and run Channel Master Corporation, which was engaged in electronics research and development. The enterprise was extremely successful in a time of burgeoning electronics technology.

Active in local Democratic politics, Resnick sought the party nomination for Congress from his normally Republican upstate New York district in 1964. Resnick won the election, carried into office along with many other Democrats on the coattails of Lyndon Johnson. He was reelected once but chose to leave the House to seek a Senate nomination in 1968. He was unsuccessful in that race and returned to his business pursuits.

Joseph Resnick died at the age of forty-five, on October 6, 1969, while en route to California for a business trip. (LSM)

RIBICOFF, ABRAHAM A.
United States Senator, 1963–1981;
Secretary of Health, Education, and Welfare,
1961–1962; Governor of Connecticut, 1955–1961;
Member of Congress, 1949–1953

Abraham A. Ribicoff was born in New Britain, Connecticut, on April 9, 1910, to Rose and Samuel Ribicoff, the latter a Polish Jewish immigrant who earned a living as a peddler and a factory worker. As a boy, Ribicoff held a number of odd jobs and, after high school, worked in a zipper and buckle factory for a year to earn money for college. This background would later earn him the reputation of being a self-made man.

Ribicoff was admitted to New York University but earned his law degree at the University of Chicago without ever earning a bachelor's degree. He joined the Connecticut Bar and began practicing law in 1933.

He quickly became involved in Connecticut state politics, serving as a police court judge and state assemblyman before winning a seat to the United States House of Representatives in 1948. After two terms, he challenged Republican Prescott S. Bush (the father and grandfather of two American presidents) in a race to fill a Senate vacancy, losing by just three thousand votes. In 1954, Ribicoff ran for the Connecticut governor's office and beat John Davis Lodge by just 3,200 votes. In a state then dominated by Republicans, this was no small feat.

An early supporter of John F. Kennedy, Ribicoff became the secretary of health, education, and welfare in 1961. During his tenure, he worked on civil rights and school desegregation. In 1962, he ran for the United States Senate once more and won a seat that he would hold until 1981. Although he staked out a reputation for both his principles and his willingness to compromise, Ribicoff won the attention of the nation for his confrontation with Chicago mayor Richard J. Daley at the 1968 Democratic Convention, accusing Daley of Gestapo-like tactics for his heavy-handed treatment of Vietnam War protestors.

As a leading voice for Jews during the 1960s and 1970s, Ribicoff was part of an American effort to force open Soviet emigration policies. He also sponsored or supported major initiatives in auto safety standards, Medicare, and environmental law.

Ribicoff retired from the Senate in 1981. He kept a law practice in New York and Washington almost up until his death on February 22, 1998. (JB)

RICHMOND, FREDERICK WILLIAM
Member of Congress, 1975–1982

Frederick William Richmond was born to George and Frances Richmond on November 15, 1923, in Boston. After attending public schools, he entered Harvard College. His studies were interrupted by World War II, and after serving in the United States Navy from 1943 to 1945, Richmond graduated from Boston University. He entered the import-export business but soon assumed top positions with industrial companies in Pennsylvania, Connecticut, Ohio, and Michigan.

Richmond was a delegate to the 1964 Democratic National Convention and began to take an active role in politics. Having moved to New York City, he served as a city human rights commissioner before winning election to the City Council in 1973.

In 1974, he was elected to Congress from the Fourteenth District. He won election for three more terms but was forced to resign in 1982 after being indicted (and later convicted) on charges of income tax evasion and marijuana possession. He is the author of a book, *The Need for Businessmen to Become Active in Politics*. (JB)

RIVLIN, ALICE MITCHELL
Vice Chair, Federal Reserve System, 1996–1999; Director, Office of Management and Budget, 1994–1996; Director, Congressional Budget Office, 1975–1983

Born in Philadelphia on March 4, 1931, Alice Rivlin graduated from Bryn Mawr College in 1952 and re-

ceived a Ph.D. from Radcliffe College in 1958. She has been a staff member at the Brookings Institution off and on since the 1950s: from 1957 to 1966, 1969 to 1975, and 1983 to 1993. Between 1983 and 1987, she was the director of economic studies at Brookings.

From 1975 to 1983, Rivlin served as director of the Congressional Budget Office. After teaching public policy at George Mason University during 1992, she became deputy director of the Office of Management and Budget (OMB) in 1993. Rivlin was promoted to OMB director in 1994; she held the position until 1996. In 1996, she became vice chair of the Federal Reserve System. She stepped down from this post on June 3, 1999.

The author of several books, including *Reviving the American Dream: The Economy, the States, and the Federal Government* (1992) and *Caring for the Disabled Elderly: Who Will Pay?* (1988), she currently serves as a senior fellow of economic studies at Brookings. (TW)

ROHATYN, FELIX G.
Ambassador to France, 1997–2000

Born in Vienna in 1928, Felix G. Rohatyn moved to the United States in 1942 after receiving part of his secondary school education in France. He received his bachelor's degree in physics from Middlebury College in 1949.

Rohatyn joined the Lazard Frères & Company investment bank in New York in 1949. A partner as of 1961, Rohatyn became a top investment banker and the mergers and acquisitions specialist at Lazard Frères. Rohatyn was also the chair of the Municipal Assistance Corporation (MAC) of the City of New York from 1975 to 1993 and a member of the board of governors of the New York Stock Exchange from 1968 to 1972.

Rohatyn is a member of the Council on Foreign Relations and the American Academy of Arts and Sciences, and he served as vice chair of Carnegie Hall. After his reelection to a second term, President Bill Clinton appointed Rohatyn as the United States ambassador to France, a position he held until the end of the Clinton presidency. (BMcN)

ROSE, ALEX
Labor Leader and Founder of Liberal Party of New York

Alex Rose, son of a wealthy tanner, was born in Warsaw, Poland, on October 15, 1898. After completing high school, he emigrated to the United States, having been denied a university education in his native country because of discrimination against Jews. Although he planned to pursue a career in medicine, the outbreak of World War I forced him to abandon his studies and to take a job as a millinery worker.

In 1914, he made the fateful decision to join the Cloth Hat, Cap and Millinery Workers' International Union (CHCMW). Although Rose joined the British Army's "Jewish Legion" in 1918, he returned to the United States in 1920 and resumed his union-organizing activities. In his first campaign for a union office, he engaged in a bitter battle with a communist opponent, a fight that would set the tone for the rest of his career. He slowly worked his way through the union leadership until he was elected president of the Hatters' union in 1950. Three years later, he led a successful strike against the Connecticut-based Hat Corporation of America.

As a labor leader, Rose sought to root out the influence of communists and gangsters and to foster labor–management cooperation when others preferred confrontation. He also worked within the political system, helping found the American Labor Party in 1936 and the Liberal Party of New York, becoming its vice chair in 1944. The Liberal Party was extremely important under Rose's leadership, as Democrats with Liberal endorsement could add up the votes they received under each party to reach their total; often the Liberal line meant the difference between victory and defeat.

Rose was aware of the political power he wielded, but he never forgot his roots. An aide to Senator Edmund Muskie recalls visiting New York in the run-up to the 1972 presidential election, seeking Rose's endorsement. Rose's first question: "Do you wear a hat?"

Alex Rose died on December 28, 1976. (JB)

ROSE, ERNESTINE
Suffragist

Ernestine Louise Sismondi Potowski was born to an orthodox rabbi and his wealthy wife in Piotrkow, Poland, on January 13, 1810. Educated at an early age, she was sixteen when her mother died, leaving her a large inheritance. Rather than use the money as a dowry to marry an older man her father favored, young Ernestine used her inheritance to travel around Europe, settling in England in 1831 at the age of twenty-one. She immediately associated with social reformers and philanthropists and married William Ella Rose five years later.

The couple moved to New York, where Rose met Elizabeth Cady Stanton and became involved in the women's suffrage movement. She also took a prominent place in the freethinkers' movement and helped found a utopian community in 1843 near Syracuse, New York. As a suffragist, she was a widely acclaimed speaker and worked closely with Stanton and Susan B. Anthony on the executive committee of the Women's Suffrage Association.

Rose grew more radical, claiming that the Bible enslaved women and that religious institutions restricted women's freedoms. During the Civil War, Rose refused to abandon the cause, arguing that both women and blacks needed freedom. This, of course, only won her the enmity of the press.

In 1869, Rose and her husband toured Europe and ultimately returned to England. William Rose died in 1882. Ernestine Rose died a decade later, at age eighty-two, in Brighton, England. (JB)

ROSENBERG, ANNA M.
Undersecretary of Defense, 1950–1953

Anna M. Rosenberg's appointment, in 1950, as undersecretary of defense to George Marshall was then the highest office ever held by a woman in the military. Born in Budapest, Hungary, on June 19, 1902, to Charlotte and Albert Lederer, her family emigrated to the Bronx, New York. She was noted for selling Liberty Bonds and Thrift Stamps to promote America's effort in World War I, worked part-time in a military hospital in Manhattan, married Julius Rosenberg, a serviceman in 1919, and became a naturalized citizen.

As Rosenberg was known as a keen political observer, Governor Franklin Delano Roosevelt sought her advice. During the New Deal, she served in the federal government and in 1937 was named chair of the New York State Constitutional Committee.

During and after World War II, Rosenberg was active on boards and commissions. She directed the Office of Defense and regional Health and Welfare Services and was secretary of the President's Combined War Labor Board. In 1944 President Roosevelt, and in 1945 President Harry S. Truman, sent her to observe the European Theater of Operation. For her patriotism, she was awarded the Medal of Freedom in 1945 and the Medal of Merit in 1947. And in 1950, Truman appointed her undersecretary of defense. During the Korean War, she advised Air Secretary Stuart Symington on mobilization policy.

In 1962, Anna, who was divorced from Julius Rosenberg, married Paul G. Hoffman, the first administrator of the Marshall Plan. From 1968 to 1969, she served on President Lyndon B. Johnson's Commission on Income Maintenance.

Anna M. Rosenberg Hoffman died on May 9, 1983. (MP)

ROSENBLOOM, BENJAMIN
Member of Congress, 1921–1925

Benjamin Rosenbloom was not a native of West Virginia, though he committed his life to public service in that state. He was born in Braddock, Pennsylvania, on June 3, 1880. He was schooled in the public education system there and then attended the University of West Virginia in Wheeling, earning a law degree. He began practicing law in Wheeling after being admitted to the bar in 1904.

Rosenbloom campaigned successfully for election to the West Virginia State Senate in 1914 and served as a member until 1918. He was elected as a Republican to the United States House of Representatives in 1920, serving for two terms. He did not seek reelection in 1924 but rather unsuccessfully campaigned for his party's nomination for the United States Senate. After his loss, Rosenbloom resumed the practice of law in Wheeling. He published a weekly newspaper for two years beginning in 1933 and served as city councilman and vice mayor to Wheeling from 1935 to 1939. Rosenbloom retired from his law practice in 1951 and died on March 22, 1965. (CF)

ROSENMAN, SAMUEL I.
Presidential Adviser, 1933–1946

Though born in San Antonio, Texas, on February 13, 1896, Samuel Rosenman said he always considered himself a New Yorker, his home from the age of eight. Rosenman graduated summa cum laude from Columbia University in 1915. He went on to receive a law degree from Columbia University in 1919 after military service in World War I. On graduation, Rosenman entered New York politics, serving five terms in the state assembly.

Rosenman's seventeen-year association with Franklin Roosevelt began in 1928, when he worked on FDR's gubernatorial campaign. On his election, Roosevelt appointed Rosenman counsel to the governor. In 1933, after his initial nomination was blocked by Tammany Hall, Rosenman was appointed to the New York State Supreme Court, a position he held until 1943, when he resigned to become counsel to President Roosevelt.

Even while serving on the court, Rosenman was one of Roosevelt's most trusted and respected advisers throughout his career. He wrote most of the speeches Roosevelt made, including Roosevelt's 1932 acceptance speech at the convention in Chicago where the phrase "New Deal" was coined. Rosenman accompanied FDR to countless conferences during World War II, including the 1945 Yalta conference. He was also sent on a special mission to study the supply needs of Western Europe and on an important voyage to lay the groundwork for the war criminal trials.

After Roosevelt's death, Rosenman worked for President Harry S. Truman until 1946, when he resumed practice of private law. On his resignation, Truman awarded him the Medal of Merit for "outstanding services to the president of the United States and his country." Later in life Rosenman edited President Roosevelt's public papers and also wrote *Working with Roosevelt* (1952).

Samuel Rosenman died on June 24, 1973. (AE)

ROSENTHAL, ABRAHAM MICHAEL
New York Times *Foreign Correspondent and Associate Managing Editor*

A. M. Rosenthal was born on May 2, 1922, in Sault Sainte Marie, Ontario. Growing up in poverty in the Bronx, he was crippled as a teenager by osteomyelitis. While attending City College, he worked as a student correspondent for the *New York Times*; eventually, in 1943, he was made a full member of the *Times* staff, his disability preventing him from military service.

In 1946, Rosenthal was appointed to the new *Times* bureau at the United Nations, where he would stay for eight years, making a name for himself as a bright young journalist. Rosenthal's first overseas post was in India in 1954, and he soon moved to Poland and finally Japan. He received a Pulitzer Prize in 1959 for his outstanding reporting from Poland. Rosenthal's writing from abroad was extremely popular, and thus the *Times* management was reluctant to move him into a position as editor, but that decision was eventually made. Returning to New York in 1963, Rosenthal accepted the position of city editor and began to modernize the paper, making it more adventurous, concise, and readable. Starting in 1968, Rosenthal was promoted to associate managing editor, then to managing editor, and finally to executive editor, receiving nearly full authority over the daily paper. He left that position as he approached the *Times's* mandatory retirement age and began writing twice-weekly columns until his gradual full retirement some years later. (OS)

ROSENTHAL, BENJAMIN
Member of Congress, 1962–1983

Throughout his life, Benjamin Rosenthal frequently acknowledged that he had "chutzpah" and that some people found him abrasive; yet those qualities added to his effectiveness as a public servant.

Born in New York City on June 8, 1923, he attended public schools, Long Island University, and the City College of New York. He served in the United States Army from 1943 to 1946 and, on his discharge, earned law degrees from Brooklyn Law School and New York University. He was admitted to the New York Bar in 1949 and the Supreme Court Bar in 1954.

Rosenthal was first elected to Congress in a special election in 1962, following the resignation of the sitting member; he was reelected to the eleven succeeding congresses, serving until his death from cancer on January 4, 1983.

While in Congress, Rosenthal served on the Government Operations and Foreign Affairs Committees. He vigorously supported Israel and sought generous aid for that country. Along the same line, he was also an outspoken opponent of efforts to sell sophisticated weapons to Arab states that were at war with Israel, including President Carter's 1979 plan to sell advanced F-15 fighter aircraft to Saudi Arabia and President Ronald Reagan's 1981 sale of early-warning planes to the same government. He was never afraid to speak his mind, as was apparent in a 1969 speech in the House that angered President Lyndon Johnson. In this speech, he vigorously opposed the Vietnam War, declaring that the United States had become "virtually the puppet" of the Saigon government. He refused to abandon his position despite the president's reaction. (CF)

ROSS, DENNIS B.
Middle East Peace Envoy, 1992–2001

Dennis B. Ross was born in San Francisco in 1948. He received his bachelor's and graduate degrees from the University of California–Los Angeles.

Ross's political experience started in high school when he volunteered in the 1968 campaign for Robert F. Kennedy. In 1972, he was the director of field operations in California for George McGovern. He became a Defense Department analyst in the Carter administration. Moving through the establishment during the Reagan years, Ross held important policymaking jobs at the State Department, Defense Department, and National Security Council. A specialist in Soviet and Middle East affairs, Ross played a major role in much of the Bush administration's foreign policy, serving as deputy to Secretary of State James A. Baker. Most interestingly, Ross continued to work at the State Department when President Clinton came into office. His adaptability and nonpartisanship allowed him to transition smoothly from one administration to the next.

Ross is highly regarded among domestic and international leaders for his diligent, moderate, and nonpartisan style. Among his many accomplishments, he was instrumental in persuading Israel and its Arab neighbors to start peace talks in 1993. He played a major role in forwarding those peace efforts throughout the Clinton administration. Disheartened by the violence in the Middle East in 2000, Ross stepped down from his position to join the Washington Institute for Near East Policy in January 2001. (BMcN)

ROSSDALE, ALBERT BERGER
Member of Congress, 1921–1923

An unmarried postal clerk who started his own wholesale jewelry business, Albert Berger Rossdale was elected to the Sixty-seventh Congress in 1920.

Born on October 23, 1878, in New York City, Rossdale was educated in the public schools. On completing his education, he worked in the post office and worked his way up to a leadership role in the postal workers' union until 1910, when he left the postal service and entered the wholesale jewelry business.

A successful businessman, Rossdale was an active member of the state Republican Party during the early 1920s, attending the state convention as a delegate in 1922 and 1924 and attending the Republican National Convention in 1924. In 1920, he successfully ran for the House of Representatives. As the former president of the National Federation of Postal Clerks, Rossdale implemented various reforms to the postal system and advocated the present pension system for United States government employees during his tenure in Congress.

Rossdale was unsuccessful in his attempts at gaining reelection in 1922 and 1924. He returned to work in the wholesale jewelry business until his death on April 17, 1968. (KJ)

ROSTOW, EUGENE VICTOR
Undersecretary of State for Political Affairs, 1966–1969

A renowned scholar, Eugene Victor Rostow was born on August 25, 1913. He received three degrees from Yale University (A.B., 1933; LL.B., 1937; A.M., 1944). He also studied at King's College in Cambridge, England. He returned to the United States to practice law in New York City from 1937 to 1938, when he became a member of the law faculty at Yale. Rostow's career at Yale, interrupted by government service, lasted until 1984; for a ten-year period, from 1955 to 1965, he served as the law school dean.

Rostow's government service has been as distinguished as his career in legal education. He served as an adviser to the United States Department of State from 1942 to 1944 and served as the assistant executive secretary of the Economic Commission for Europe from 1949 to 1950. In 1953, he served for a year on the Attorney General's Committee to Study Anti-Trust Laws. In 1966, President Lyndon B. Johnson asked him to leave Yale to serve as the undersecretary of state for political affairs, a position he held until the end of the Johnson administration. In 1981, President Ronald Reagan recalled him to Washington for service as the director of the Arms Control and Disarmament Agency. Rostow left that job in 1983, just before he took emeritus status at Yale.

Rostow is the author of seven books, many of them on foreign policy, including *Toward a Managed Peace* (1993). (KJ)

ROSTOW, WALT WHITMAN
Special Assistant for National Security Affairs, 1966–1969

Walt Whitman Rostow has an impressive collection of awards for service, including the Order of the British Empire, the U.S. Legion of Merit, and the Presidential Medal of Freedom.

The son of a chemist, Rostow was born in New York City on October 7, 1916. He attended Yale University, where he earned his B.A. in 1936 and his Ph.D. in 1940. From 1936 until 1938, Rostow was a Rhodes Scholar at Oxford. He taught economics at Columbia until the outbreak of World War II.

From 1942 until 1945, Rostow was assigned to the army's Office of Strategic Services, where he was involved in recommending critical Nazi targets to the United States Air Force. In 1945, Rostow left the military with the rank of major and became the assistant chief of the German-Austrian Economic Division of the Department of State. In 1947, he served as the assistant to the executive secretary of the Economic Commission of Europe. Two years later, on completing his work with the commission, Rostow returned to teaching, first at Cambridge University for a year and then returning to the United States to accept a professorship at MIT in 1950.

When John F. Kennedy became president in 1961, he asked Rostow to join the White House Staff as deputy to the national security adviser to the president, McGeorge Bundy. After serving in this position for several months, Rostow was appointed counselor of the Department of State and chairman of the department's Policy Planning Council. In 1964, he also assumed membership on the Inter-American Committee on the Alliance for Progress (with the rank of ambassador). In 1966, Bundy left the White House, and President Lyndon B. Johnson appointed Rostow as his successor, a position in which he served until the end of the administration Throughout this tenure, Rostow was instrumental in providing advice on the critical issues of the day, including the Cuban missile crisis during the Kennedy administration and the Vietnam War during Johnson's tenure.

After this prolific career in public life, Rostow returned to teaching at the University of Texas at Austin. He is the author of more than thirty books, including the renowned *Stages of Economic Growth: A Non-Communist Manifesto* (1960), which is now in its third edition. (KJ)

ROTHMAN, STEVEN R.
Member of Congress, 1997–present

Born October 14, 1952, in Englewood, New Jersey, Steve Rothman received his B.A. from Syracuse University and his law degree from Washington University. Returning to his hometown to practice law, he was elected mayor at the age of thirty, holding that office from 1983 to 1989. Rothman subsequently served as judge of the Bergen County Surrogate's Court from 1993 to 1996. In 1996, he resigned his judgeship to run for New Jersey's open Ninth District. Receiving the Democratic Party endorsement, he won the primary easily and bested a better-known Republican in the general election. He was assigned to the House International Relations and Judiciary Committees.

During the 1998 impeachment proceedings, Rothman was initially critical of President Bill Clinton but soon became a vocal opponent of the divisive process. His seat on the Judiciary Committee has also positioned him to advocate reform of the juvenile justice system. (JS)

RUBIN, JAMES PHILLIP
Assistant Secretary of State for Public Affairs, 1997–2000

Born in New York City in 1960, James P. (Jamie) Rubin earned a bachelor's degree in political science in 1982 and a master's of international affairs in 1984, both from Columbia University.

Between 1985 and 1989, Rubin served as research director for the Arms Control Association in Washington. He later served as a senior foreign policy adviser to Senator Joseph R. Biden Jr., and a senior adviser to Madeleine K. Albright, when she was the U.S. representative to the United Nations. Rubin was the director of foreign policy and spokesman for the Clinton and Gore campaign in 1996. From 1997 until 2000, he was assistant secretary of state for public affairs and chief spokesman for Secretary of State Albright. He and Albright have developed a close professional relationship, which began with their mutual desire for United States intervention in Bosnia.

In 1997, while traveling to Bosnia with Secretary Albright, Rubin met Christiane Amanpour, a CNN foreign correspondent based in London. The two were married on August 8, 1998. Amanpour and Rubin had their first child, Darius John Rubin, in March 2000. Rubin left his position as assistant secretary of state to follow his wife to London and care for the baby while Amanpour continues to report for CNN. Rubin is currently an author, public speaker, and commentator based in London. (TW)

RUBIN, JERRY
Political Activist

Jerry Rubin burst into the limelight as one the most prominent and colorful leaders of the antiwar movement, protesting at the 1968 Democratic National Convention and the subsequent "Chicago Seven" trial.

Born in Cincinnati, Ohio, on July 14, 1938, the son of a union organizer, Rubin attended the University of Cincinnati before going on to study at Hebrew University in Jerusalem.

After returning from a trip to Cuba, Rubin came to prominence as one of the leaders of the 1967 Antiwar March on the Pentagon. He was a founding member of the Youth International Party, better known as the "Yippies." Following the 1968 Democratic National Convention, Rubin was arrested and charged with conspiracy to incite violence and with crossing state lines with the intent to riot. Rubin, famous for his flamboyance and flare for the dramatic, was able to turn his trial into simply another stage, wearing judicial robes to court and passing out jelly beans to spectators. The trial was highlighted by many outbursts, which resulted in one defendant being removed from the trial; nearly two hundred citations were issued for contempt. Each of the defendants was acquitted of conspiracy, but five of the Chicago Seven were convicted of incitement. The convictions were later overturned.

In the 1970s, Rubin became involved in the human potential movement, focusing on yoga, mediation, bioenergetics, and Rolfing. In 1991, he moved to Los Angeles, where he entered the nutrition business, marketing a nutritional drink that contained ginseng and bee pollen.

Jerry Rubin died from a heart attack on November 28, 1994, two weeks after being struck by a car while jaywalking, his last nonconformist act. (DS)

RUBIN, ROBERT
Secretary of the Treasury, 1995–1999

The grandson of a Democratic political machine leader from Brooklyn, Robert Rubin is widely credited with helping sustain the tremendous economic growth that occurred during his tenure as treasury secretary.

Born on August 29, 1938, in New York City, Rubin graduated summa cum laude from Harvard College in 1960, with a degree in economics. He went on to study at the London School of Economics and Yale Law School, receiving an LL.B. from Yale in 1964.

Rubin began practicing law at the firm of Cleary, Gottlieb, Steen, & Hamilton in New York City. In 1966, he left the firm to become an associate at Goldman, Sachs, and Co. Rubin worked for the firm for twenty-six years, becoming a general partner in 1971 and a member of the management committee in 1980. From 1987 to 1990, he served as vice chairman and co-chief operating officer for the company.

Rubin, an early supporter of Bill Clinton, came to the White House as the assistant to the president for economic policy when Clinton assumed office in 1993. In January 1995, Rubin succeeded Lloyd Bentsen as the secretary of the treasury. Leaders of the business community largely credit Rubin, along with Fed chairman Alan Greenspan, for leading the United States to the highest levels of economic growth in its history. He was able to do so while creating budget surpluses and maintaining extremely low levels of unemployment. A self-described centrist in relation to economic issues, Rubin strongly encouraged private investment in poor urban neighborhoods. Rubin left the administration in 1999 to be replaced by his deputy, Lawrence Summers. (DS)

RUDMAN, WARREN BRUCE
United States Senator, 1980–1993

Born in Boston on May 18, 1930, Rudman moved to Nashua, New Hampshire, where he attended public schools. In 1948, he graduated from Valley Forge Military School in Pennsylvania. Rudman went on to pursue his undergraduate studies at Syracuse University before attending Boston College Law School. After graduating in 1960, he was admitted to the New Hampshire Bar.

Rudman practiced law in New Hampshire before being appointed to serve as legal counsel to Governor Walter Peterson. From 1970 to 1976, he served as attorney general for New Hampshire. In 1975, Rudman was named president of the National Association of Attorneys General, a post in which he served for one year.

In 1980, Rudman emerged from a primary field of eleven candidates as the Republican nominee for the United States Senate. A moderate, he went on to defeat the Democratic incumbent, John Durkin. While in the Senate, Rudman was a member of Appropriations and Governmental Affairs Committees. Reelected in 1986, Rudman did not seek reelection in 1992, deciding to return to New Hampshire to resume his law practice. He stayed active in politics, however, as chair of the Concord Coalition, a bipartisan group interested in budget reform. (DS)

RUEF, ABRAHAM
Political Leader

Abraham Ruef was born on September 2, 1864, to French-born Jews living in San Francisco. His father was a successful merchant and real estate developer. He graduated from the University of California in 1883 with honors and went on to receive a law degree from Hastings College three years later.

Ruef began to practice law and became a leading Republican figure in San Francisco's Latin Quarter, a largely working-class section of the city. In 1901, he formed the Republican Primary League in an effort the challenge the established Republican presence in San Francisco. After failed labor strikes, Ruef encouraged his friend Eugene Schmitz to run for mayor on the Union Labor Party ticket. Schmitz won and named Ruef attorney for the mayor's office.

Ruef's practice soared as he received large retainers from the city's businesses. He was widely believed to be the true force behind the Schmitz administration but just as quickly gained a corrupt reputation. Fremont Older, editor of *The Bulletin,* began the call for investigations, slowly amassing support for his "graft prosecutions." Though offered immunity to testify against corporate officials, Ruef refused and was indicted four times between 1906 and 1907 and was convicted in 1908 on more than eighty-five charges. After many unsuccessful appeals, Ruef was sentenced to a fourteen-year term in San Quentin Prison, to begin in 1911. He was paroled in 1915 and eventually pardoned in 1920 due, ironically, to the work of Fremont Older, who believed that Ruef had been mistreated.

Ruef went on to become successful in real estate, though many of his businesses failed in the 1930s. (AE)

S

SABATH, ADOLPH JOACHIM
Member of Congress, 1907–1952

Born in Zabori, Czechoslovakia, on April 4, 1866, Adolph Sabath attended private schools in his native country before emigrating to the United States in 1881. He settled in Chicago, where he graduated from the Chicago College of Law in 1891. A year later he was admitted to the bar and began to practice law.

Sabath was the quintessential party politician in a city with a dominant political organization. He served the Democratic Party as ward committeeman and district leader from 1892 to 1944 and as a delegate to each Democratic National Convention from 1892 to 1944 and to all Democratic state conventions from 1890 through 1952. He was appointed justice of the peace in 1895, a position useful in registering new voters.

In 1906, the Democratic organization sent Sabath to Congress; he remained there, a loyal follower of party leaders, until his death. Earlier in his congressional career, he served as the chair of the Committee on Alcohol Liquor Traffic. Rising through the House seniority system, he eventually became chair of the powerful Rules Committee, well placed to obtain favors for his city and to do the party leaders' bidding. During his entire tenure in the House, he was a forceful advocate for increased immigration and, as early as the 1930s, an avid supporter of a Jewish state in Palestine.

Adolph Sabath died in office on November 6, 1952, before the Republicans could claim his chairman's seat. (DS)

SACKS, LEON
Member of Congress, 1937–1943

Leon Sacks was born October 7, 1902, in Philadelphia. He graduated from the Wharton School of the University of Pennsylvania in 1923 and that university's law school in 1926. He then commenced the practice of law in Philadelphia.

Sacks was appointed as the deputy attorney general of Pennsylvania in 1935 and served until 1937. In 1936, he was elected as a member of the Pennsylvania State Democratic Committee, on which he served for six years. Sacks was elected to the Seventy-fifth Congress from the Pennsylvania First District in 1936 and was successfully reelected twice. Defeated in 1942, Sacks served as a lieutenant colonel in the Army Air Forces Eastern Flying Training Command from 1943 until 1946. After leaving the military, he resumed his private law practice and chaired the registration commission of Philadelphia from 1952 until 1965.

Leon Sacks died in Philadelphia on March 11, 1972. (OS)

SAFIRE, WILLIAM
Columnist, 1973–present;
Presidential Adviser, 1969–1973

William Safire was born December 17, 1929. He enrolled at Syracuse University but left after two years. Safire began his career in journalism writing a profiles column for the *New York Herald Tribune*. He was also a correspondent and later producer for radio and television in New York.

From 1955 to 1960, Safire acted as the vice president of a major public relations firm, before becoming president of his own firm, Safire Public Relations, Inc. One of his greatest accomplishments as a public relations executive was bringing Richard Nixon and Nikita Khrushchev together for a debate in 1959.

Safire left his firm to join Nixon's presidential campaign in 1968 and served as a senior speechwriter through Nixon's first term. In 1973, he joined the *New York Times* editorial staff and won a Pulitzer Prize for his political column in 1978, he continues to write his acclaimed column and to comment on politics on television to this day.

Safire is also an accomplished novelist whose many works include the best-selling *Full Disclosure* (1977) and *Sleeper Spy* (1995). He also wrote *Safire's New Political Dictionary* (1993), which includes more than 1,800 important political terms. (OS)

SALOMAN, EDWARD SELIG
Governor, Washington Territory, 1870–1872

Edward S. Saloman was born December 25, 1836, in Schleswig-Holstein, Prussia. At the age of twenty, Saloman emigrated to the United States and settled in Chicago.

Saloman studied law, opened a practice, and was elected alderman on the Chicago City Council in 1860. He served in the Civil War, fighting in predominately German regiments. Entering as a second lieutenant in the First Illinois Infantry, he was a brevetted brigadier general by the end of his service.

On his return to Chicago following the war, Saloman was elected clerk of Cook County. On May 4, 1870, President Ulysses S. Grant appointed him governor of the Washington Territory, on the basis of his military service and pressure from the German American leadership. As governor, Saloman was the youngest and only Jewish chief executive of the territory. However, in 1872, Elisha P. Perry replaced him. The Treasury Department had conducted an unannounced audit, which found that a loan of approximately $30,000 given to the governor and his associates without secure collateral in 1870 by the receiver of public monies at Olympia was overdue. Although Saloman easily raised the necessary money, he was asked by federal officials to resign.

Following his resignation, Saloman moved to San Francisco and continued his political career. He served as district attorney and spent two terms in the California legislature.

Edward Saloman died July 18, 1913. (BF)

SANDERS, BERNARD
Member of Congress, 1991–present

Bernie Sanders was born September 8, 1941, in Brooklyn. Before embarking on a political career, he was the director of the American People's History Society. Sanders drew national attention when he was elected mayor of Burlington, Vermont, in 1981, as a socialist. Sanders pursued a progressive agenda over four two-year terms. Running without party label for Congress in 1988, Sanders lost the open seat contest to Republican Peter Smith, but in a 1990 rematch, Sanders prevailed in the state's single at-large district.

His congressional victory made Bernie Sanders the first independent elected to the House in forty years and only the third avowed socialist ever to serve in that body. He caucuses with the Democrats, who have even granted him party seniority.

In Congress, Sanders founded the Progressive Caucus, which now boasts fifty-eight members. His agenda has been an interesting mix of the pragmatic and the impractical. While the Progressive Caucus pursues the unlikely goals of progressive tax reform, single-payer health insurance, and radically reduced defense spending, he has had some success in the areas of corporate welfare and environmental health and safety. Looking out for Vermont's dairy farmers, Sanders led efforts to pass the Northeast Dairy Compact. (JS)

SCHAFFER, GLORIA
Secretary of State of Connecticut, 1971–1978

Born on October 3, 1930, Gloria Schaffer embarked on what has been a lifelong commitment to public service. In 1958, at the age of twenty-eight, Gloria

Schaffer successfully sought a seat in the Connecticut State Senate. She remained in the state senate for twelve years. In 1970, she gave up her safe senate seat to run statewide, winning election as Connecticut's secretary of state. In that post, Schaffer was among the state's most popular elected leaders. When she ran for reelection in 1974, she received a higher percentage of the statewide vote than any previous candidate had ever received.

With this strong support, Schaffer decided to challenge incumbent United States senator Lowell Weicker in the 1976 general election. This attempt was ultimately unsuccessful. Some reporters at the time attributed Schaffer's defeat to the fact that Connecticut currently had a female governor, Ella Grasso, and a Jewish senator, Abraham Ribicoff, and that the people of Connecticut were hesitant to elect an additional member of either of these groups to another prominent office. Regardless of the reasons surrounding her defeat, Schaffer resumed her duties as secretary of state until 1978, when she was appointed by President Jimmy Carter to the Civil Aeronautics Board (CAB); she was only the second woman to serve on that board. She remained on the CAB until it was dissolved in December 1984.

In 1985, Schaffer entered the private sector as a member of the board of directors for Emery Air Freight Corporation. In 1991, she reentered public life as Connecticut's state commissioner for consumer protection. She served in this capacity until 1995. Since leaving this position, she has worked as a consultant and spokesperson for Southern New England Telephone. (KJ)

SCHAKOWSKY, JANICE
Member of Congress, 1999–present

Jan Schakowsky was born May 26, 1944, in Chicago. She attended public schools in Chicago and earned a B.S. degree from the University of Illinois in 1965.

For two years after graduating from college, Schakowsky was an elementary school teacher in Chicago. She then worked as an organizer for the Illinois Public Action Council in Chicago until 1985. In 1985, she became executive director of the

Illinois State Council of Senior Citizens, a post in which she served for five years, until her election to the Illinois State House of Representatives; she served four terms in the state legislature.

Schakowsky was elected to the United States House of Representatives in 1998 and was reelected in 2000. A Democrat, she represents the Ninth District of Illinois, encompassing the Lakeshore district and the northern and northwestern suburbs of Chicago, including Evanston and Skokie.

Since 1990, Schakowsky has served on the governing council for the American Jewish Congress. She is also a member of the National Council of Jewish Women. (TW)

SCHECHTER, ARTHUR LOUIS
U.S. Ambassador to the Bahamas, 1998–2001; Democratic Activist

Arthur Schechter was born in Rosenberg, Texas, on December 6, 1939. He received his bachelor's and law degrees from the University of Texas at Austin. He practiced law in Houston and became a member of the boards of several local Jewish organizations, including the Anti-Defamation League's Southwest Region and the Texas Historical Society. He also served as president of the American Jewish Committee from 1992 to 1993 and as president of the Jewish Federation of Houston from 1994 to 1996.

Schechter has been very active in Democratic politics. He served as the Texas finance chair of President Bill Clinton's 1996 campaign and vice chair of the National Jewish Democratic Council. In 1994, Schechter was appointed by Clinton to the United States Holocaust Memorial Council. From 1998 to 2001, he served as U.S. ambassador to the Bahamas. After the end of the Clinton administration, Schechter returned to Houston, where he is currently of counsel to the law firm of Schechter, McElwee, and Shaffer. (IF)

SCHENK, LYNN
Member of Congress, 1993–1995

Lynn Schenk was born to Hungarian immigrants October 15, 1945, in New York City. Her family moved to California in her youth; there she attended high school and later earned her B.A. from the University of California–Los Angeles. She immediately went to earn a law degree at the University of San Diego. She then studied international law at the London School of Economics for a year, before returning to work first as California's deputy attorney general and then as an attorney for San Diego Gas and Electric Co.

From 1976 to 1977, Schenk was a White House fellow, working as a special assistant in the office of the vice president, during the transition from the Ford to the Carter administration. She was then appointed as California's first woman secretary of business, transportation, and housing, holding that position from 1978 to 1983. While practicing private law from 1983 to 1993, she was active in California, founding the Urban Corps of San Diego and serving as vice chair of the San Diego Port Commission.

Schenk was elected in 1992 as a Democrat to the 103d Congress, riding the tide of the Clinton victory in California. In 1994, however, like many other freshman Democrats, she was swept from office in the Republican landslide. She sought to reenter politics in 1998, running for attorney general of California, but was again unsuccessful. In 1999, she joined the staff of California governor Gray Davis as a top aide. (OS)

SCHEUER, JAMES HAAS
Member of Congress, 1975–1993, 1965–1973

James Scheuer was born February 6, 1920, in New York City. He graduated from Swarthmore College, Harvard Business School, and Columbia Law School, passing the bar in 1948 and beginning a legal practice.

Scheuer served as a member of the legal staff for the Office of Price Stabilization from 1951 to 1957. He ran unsuccessfully for Congress in 1962; in 1964, he was carried into office as part of the Johnson landslide. After redistricting prior to the 1972 election, he lost a reelection bid to Jonathan Bingham, a fellow Democratic incumbent whose district had been combined with Scheuer's. However, he returned to the House in 1974 and successfully won reelections until he retired in 1993. Extremely successful in real estate ventures, Scheuer served as president of the National Housing Conference from 1972 to 1974 and of the National Alliance for Safer Cities in 1972–1973, during his hiatus from Congress.

In the House, Scheuer chaired the Select Committee on Population. As a representative, he was known as a liberal Democrat and a champion of environmental issues. (OS)

SCHIFF, ADAM
Member of Congress, 2001–present

On June 22, 1960, Adam Schiff was born in Framingham, Massachusetts. He completed his undergraduate work at Stanford University in 1982 and in 1985 graduated from Harvard Law School.

For six years Schiff was a criminal prosecutor within the office of the U.S. attorney general. He had a 100 percent conviction record and is well known for his prosecution of the Miller/FBI case. He aided the government of the Czech Republic in reforming its criminal justice system in 1992.

Schiff was elected as a Democrat to the California State Senate in 1996 and chaired the Judiciary Committee, the Juvenile Select Committee, and the Joint Committee on the Arts. Many pieces of legislation that Schiff authored have been signed into law, including bills that reform the juvenile justice system, improve campaign ethics laws, and provide all California students with up-to-date textbooks.

In 2000, Schiff left the state senate to run for the United States House of Representative, winning over incumbent James Rogan, one of the Republicans who brought the House's case for impeachment of President Bill Clinton before the Senate, in the most expensive House race in history. (SB)

SCHIFF, DOROTHY
Publisher of the New York Post, *1939–1976*

Dorothy Schiff was born March 11, 1903, in New York City. She attended Bryn Mawr College in Pennsylvania from 1920 to 1921. Her life as a wealthy debutante and socialite changed in the 1930s when she became interested in social service and reform. At this point, she also shed her inherited affiliation with the Republican Party and became an active Democrat and New Dealer.

Schiff bought majority control of the *New York Post* in 1939. Over the years she held the titles of director, vice president, and treasurer of the *Post*, but she became president and publisher after her second husband, George Backer, resigned due to illness. Schiff was the first woman newspaper publisher in New York, assuming the titles of owner and

publisher in 1943 after she divorced Backer. Schiff also wrote a regular *Post* column, "Publishers Notebook," in 1958 and became the editor in chief of the news department in 1961.

During Schiff's long tenure directing the *Post*, it was a crusading paper devoted to liberal causes. She sold the *New York Post* in 1976 but remained a consultant to the paper until 1981.

Gloria Schiff died on August 30, 1989, in New York City. (BMcN)

SCHIFF, STEVEN HARVEY
Member of Congress, 1989–1997

Steve Schiff was born March 18, 1947, in Chicago. He graduated with a B.A. from the University of Illinois–Chicago in 1968 and a J.D. from the University of New Mexico Law School in 1972. After passing the bar in 1972, he began a private practice in Albuquerque. Schiff joined the Air National Guard during the Vietnam War; he stayed in the guard, rising in rank to become a lieutenant colonel and serving briefly in Bosnia and the Persian Gulf.

Schiff was appointed as the assistant district attorney of Bernaillo County, New Mexico, in 1972 and held that position until 1977; he was district attorney of Bernaillo County from 1980 to 1988. In 1988, Schiff was elected as a Republican to the United States House of Representatives and was reelected to the four succeeding congresses. While in Washington, he was best known for his participation in the ethics case against House Speaker Newt Gingrich.

Seriously ill with cancer that kept him out of Washington during his last term, he opted not to run for reelection in 1998. Steven Schiff died at age fifty-one in his Albuquerque home on March 25, 1998. (OS)

SCHNEIDERMAN, ROSE
Labor Leader

Born on April 6, 1882, in Saven, Poland, to Orthodox Jewish parents, Rose Schneiderman and her family emigrated to the United States in 1890, settling on New York City's Lower East Side.

Despite family efforts to keep her in school, by her teenage years Schneiderman went to work in a factory, manufacturing caps, and there was introduced her to socialism and trade unionism. In 1903, she organized her shop for the United Cloth Hat and Cap Maker's Union; in 1904, she was elected to the general executive board of the national union, becoming the first woman elected to a national office in an American labor union.

Schneiderman joined the National Women's Trade Union League (WTUL), an organization founded to help working women unionize and promote legislation protecting women in the workplace in 1905. By 1906, her talents at organizing won her the vice presidency of the New York league. Schneiderman helped pave the way for the great uprising of twenty thousand of New York's shirtwaist makers in 1909–1910, the largest strike by American women workers to that time. After brief interludes organizing for other unions and for women's suffrage, Schneiderman spent the remainder of her career in the WTUL, serving as president of the New York branch from 1917 to 1949 and as national president from 1926 to 1950.

Schneiderman looked to government to solve labor problems. She ran unsuccessfully for the United States Senate in 1920. Her growing friendship with Eleanor and Franklin D. Roosevelt eventually led to her increased interest in the Democratic Party and her appointment, in 1933, to the National Recovery Administration's (NRA) Labor Advisory Board. She was the only woman appointed to the NRA and was considered a trusted adviser to FDR. From 1937 to 1944, Schneiderman served as secretary of the New York State Department of Labor.

Rose Schneiderman died on August 11, 1972. (JW)

Source: Rose Schneiderman with Lucy Goldthwaite, *All for One* (New York: Eriksson, 1967).

SCHOEN, DOUGLAS
Democratic Pollster

Douglas Schoen was born on June 27, 1953, in New York City. In 1974, he graduated magna cum laude from Harvard College and later received his law degree from Harvard Law School. Schoen also holds a doctorate in philosophy from Oxford University in England.

During President Clinton's reelection campaign, Schoen was his chief research and strategic consultant. He has also guided campaigns for many United States political figures, including governors Cecil Andrus of Idaho and Paul Patton of Kentucky and senators John D. Rockefeller of West Virginia, John Breaux of Louisiana, and Daniel Patrick Moynihan of New York. Besides providing sound strategies for political candidates and officials, he also provides strategic research to many corporations, including Proctor & Gamble, Major League Baseball, AT&T, Frito Lay, and Citibank. Outside the United States, Schoen has designed successful messages for the heads of state in countries such as Turkey, Israel, Bermuda, Yugoslavia, and Greece. (SB)

SCHORENSTEIN, HYMAN
Democratic Party Leader

Hymie Schorenstein emigrated with his parents to the United States from Galiola, Poland, when he was an infant in 1870. He received little formal education and often bragged that he was making his own living from the age of ten.

Schorenstein began his career as an ice delivery man and rose to become one of Brooklyn's most vibrant and powerful leaders. He served as a deputy U.S. marshal in the Eastern District of New York from 1915 to 1922. Active in Brooklyn politics, he was the unanimous choice to succeed James Power in 1919 as the Democratic leader of the Twenty-third Assembly District, the Brownsville section of Brooklyn, a position he held until 1944. He was also named Kings County commissioner of deeds in 1923 and held the post until it was abolished in 1937.

In addition to his political posts, Schorenstein was a director of Beth-el Hospital from 1930 to 1934 and was instrumental in establishing the maternity pavilion there. Schorenstein's prominence in Brooklyn led to friendships with leading Democrats such as President Franklin D. Roosevelt and Governor Alfred Smith, both of whom stopped at his Brownsville home when campaigning in Brooklyn.

Hyman Schorenstein died on February 3, 1953, at the age of eighty-two. (AE)

SCHORR, DANIEL L.
Radio and Television News Analyst

Daniel L. Schorr was born on August 31, 1916, in New York City. He received his B.S.S. from the City College of New York in 1939.

Schorr, serving in United States Army intelligence during World War II, began writing from Western Europe for the *Christian Science Monitor,* the *New York Times,* and the *London Daily Mail* from 1948 to 1953. CBS News installed Schorr as its diplomatic correspondent in Washington, while also sending him on assignment to Latin America, Europe, and Asia. In 1955, he opened a CBS bureau in Moscow and conducted the first-ever exclusive television interview with Nikita Khrushchev. In 1960, Schorr was assigned to Bonn as CBS bureau chief and covered the Berlin crisis and the building of the Berlin Wall.

He returned to Washington in 1966 to work as a Washington correspondent for CBS. In 1972, Schorr was CBS's chief Watergate correspondent. His exclusive reports and coverage earned him three Emmys. The FBI, by order of President Richard Nixon, did a thorough investigation of Schorr because of Nixon's claim of "abuse of a Federal agency." Also in February 1976, he was suspended from CBS and investigated by the House Ethics Committee for his refusal to disclose his source from which he received an advanced copy of the final report of the Watergate investigations, which he intended to publish, despite government wishes that it be suppressed. The committee ultimately decided against such a contempt citation.

Despite CBS offers to return, Schorr decided to write a book about his tumultuous experience, *Clearing the Air* (1977). He was appointed Regents Professor of Journalism at University of California–Berkeley for two years. Schorr was also instrumental in Ted Turner's creation of CNN, serving as its senior correspondent in Washington.

Since leaving CNN in 1985, Schorr has worked primarily for National Public Radio as senior news analyst. (BMcN)

SCHUMER, CHARLES E.
United States Senator, 1999–present;
Member of Congress, 1981–1999

Elected to the United States Senate following a raucous campaign against incumbent Republican Alfonse D'Amato, Chuck Schumer has climbed steadily since first being elected to the New York state legislature at twenty-three in 1974. Schumer had served three terms in the New York State Assembly and nine terms in the House before moving to the Senate.

Born November 23, 1950, Chuck Schumer is a native of Brooklyn, where he still lives with his wife, Iris Weinshall, and their two daughters. He attended Harvard College and Harvard Law School. Immediately on graduation, Schumer successfully ran for an open seat in the state assembly. In 1980, he was elected to the House seat vacated by Elizabeth Holtzman when she ran for United States Senate. In the House, Schumer was an active member of both the Judiciary and Banking Committees. He was perhaps best known as one of the most vocal opponents of Speaker Newt Gingrich and the Contract with America.

In his quest to unseat three-term incumbent Al D'Amato, Schumer was a prolific fund-raiser. Draw-

ing on Wall Street connections and his House campaign account, which had been growing for several years in anticipation of the race, Schumer spent almost $17 million. At the time, the race was the most expensive in state history and one of the most costly races in the history of the United States.

In his congressional career, Schumer has been active in a number of policy areas, including the savings and loan bailout, immigration, gun control, and housing. (JK)

SCHWARTZ, TONY
Political Media Consultant

Tony Schwartz was born in Manhattan on August 19, 1923. After graduating from the Pratt Institute in 1944, he began his media career in 1945 by recording life around him in sound and pictures with his first Webster wire recorder.

This documentary turned into a weekly radio program called *Around New York* that Schwartz produced from 1946 to 1976. Widely regarded as a "media genius," he first started making commercials for companies such as Coke, Ivory, and Post Cereal and then ventured into general advertising. Schwartz was the first to produce antismoking radio ads and to use actual children's voices in ads, instead of adult voiceovers.

Perhaps Schwartz is most famous for one controversial political ad—namely, the "daisy ad" that showed a girl pulling petals from a daisy while a countdown is heard and an atomic bomb erupts into a mushroom cloud on the screen. Lyndon Johnson used the ad in his 1964 presidential campaign to illustrate the dangers of nuclear weapons and to express his stance on the issue. Aired only once, the ad was withdrawn amid controversy; yet it remains among the most well-known television spots in political history.

Almost two hundred political candidates have enlisted the expertise of Schwartz when planning their media campaigns. He created ads for successful presidential campaigns for Johnson in 1964 and Jimmy Carter in 1976, and for senatorial campaigns of Daniel Patrick Moynihan in New York and Edward Kennedy in Massachusetts, among others. (SB)

SEIDMAN, LEWIS WILLIAM
Presidential Adviser, 1974–1977

L. William Seidman was born April 29, 1921, to Frank E. and Ester (Lubetsky) Seidman. He graduated from Dartmouth College in 1943, served in

World War II, receiving a Bronze Star, and returned to school to earn his LL.B. from Harvard University in 1948 and his M.B.A. from the University of Michigan in 1949.

Seidman began his government service as the special assistant of financial affairs to the governor of Michigan, for three years from 1963 to 1966. He was managing partner of Seidman and Seidman Accounting Firm from 1969 until 1974, when his friend Gerald Ford asked him to join his White House staff. Seidman served as the chief adviser of economic affairs for President Ford from 1974 until the end of the administration in 1977.

Following his work with Ford, Seidman returned to the private sector, first as chief financial officer and vice chair of the Phelps Dodge Corporation (1977–1982) and then as dean of the Arizona State University College of Business (1982–1985). In 1985, President Ronald Reagan appointed Seidman chair of the Federal Deposit Insurance Corporation, a post that he held until 1991. Since 1991, Seidman has been the chief economic commentator for CNBC. (BF)

SELIGMAN, ARTHUR
Governor of New Mexico, 1931–1933

By developing a plan to process cotton cheaply, Arthur Seligman saved cotton growers in New Mexico $15 a bale. As a two-term governor of New Mexico from 1931 until his death in office on September 25, 1933, he efficiently and creatively utilized scarce resources to improve his state during a period of great economic depression. Seligman's life was perfect preparation for the difficult job of governing in these tough times.

Born in Santa Fe on June 14, 1871, he was educated at Swarthmore preparatory school, Pierce's College of Business, and Swarthmore College. In 1888, Seligman entered his father's merchant company and was named president of the corporation on his father's death in 1903. With his keen business mind, Seligman bought stock in the First National Bank of Santa Fe and was shortly thereafter named a director of the bank. Under his direction, this bank quickly became the most important bank between Denver and El Paso and in 1924 he was made its president.

Arthur Seligman was already involved in politics at the age of twelve, when he published his own small newspaper. From these humble beginnings, Seligman went on to become active in the Democratic Party. During the course of his life, he served as chair of the Santa Fe County Democratic Committee, chair of the state party, member of the Dem-ocratic National Committee, and delegate to Democratic national conventions. The only position that Seligman was elected to before governor was in 1910 when he was elected mayor of Santa Fe. (KJ)

SEMBLER, MELVIN
Finance Chair, Republican National Committee, 2000–2001; Ambassador to Australia and Nauru, 1989–1993

Antidrug activist, shopping-center developer, and Republican Party official, Melvin Sembler was born in 1930. He received a B.S. from Northwestern University in 1952 and served in the army from 1953 to 1955. In 1962, Sembler began developing shopping centers on the outskirts of small Tennessee towns. He went on to found The Sembler Company, a shopping-center development firm known for its creative designs and environmental integrity. He served as president of the International Council of Shopping Centers (ICSC) from 1986 to 1987 and is currently serving on the ICSC's board of trustees.

Sembler has been very active within the Republican Party, donating large sums and organizing fundraising. In 1989, President George H. W. Bush named Sembler as the ambassador to Australia and Nauru, a position he held until 1993. He also served as the finance chair for the Republican National Committee for the 2000 campaign and as Florida's national committeeman.

Sembler and his wife, Betty, have also been very active in the fight against drugs. In 1976, they founded STRAIGHT, an adolescent rehabilitation program that has been somewhat controversial. STRAIGHT has received praise from many clients, but several centers have shut down amid allegations of abuse and mismanagement. President Ronald Reagan appointed Sembler to the White House Conference for a Drug Free America in 1987. He is currently serving as the honorary chair for the Drug Free America Coalition.

Sembler has been very active within the Jewish community as well; he is currently serving as the honorary chair of the Republican Jewish Coalition. (AE)

SHAMANSKY, ROBERT
Member of Congress, 1981–1983

Robert Shamansky was born April 18, 1927, in Columbus, Ohio. He earned his B.A. from Ohio State University in 1947 as a member of Phi Beta Kappa and then an LL.B. from the Harvard University Law School in 1950. He served as a special agent for the United States Army Counter-Intelligence Corps from 1950 until 1952. Discharged due to injuries suffered in a car accident, he began a private law practice in his home state, which he continued for most of his life.

Shamansky originally ran for Congress as a Democrat against Republican Samuel L. Devine in 1966, but he was defeated by a considerable margin. Following his defeat, Shamansky engaged in little political activity until he ran against Devine again in 1980. Shamansky's victory was a major upset as Devine was an eleven-term incumbent and polls showed him leading by over 20 percent. As a member of Congress, Shamansky served on the Foreign Affairs Committee and its Europe and the Middle East subcommittee and on the Science, Space, and Technology Committee. Shamansky was defeated for reelection in 1982 and returned to the practice of law and local service in Columbus. (OS)

SHANKER, ALBERT
President of the American Federation of Teachers, 1974–1997

Born on September 14, 1928, Albert Shanker, son of a trade unionist, would rise to become a renowned force in education, for both his creative approaches and pioneering work in collective bargaining for teachers. Shanker was raised in New York City by his parents—Yiddish-speaking Russian immigrants. He received a B.A. with honors in philosophy from the University of Illinois and completed the coursework required for a Ph.D. in philosophy from Columbia University.

Shanker began his career as a teacher in the 1950s during the era of McCarthyism and quickly attempted to organize his colleagues. He served as president of New York City's United Federation of Teachers from 1964 to 1986. Shanker played a controversial role during the 1968 decentralization experiments in New York City. Amid racial and religious tensions, Shanker stood firm against decentralization and for teachers' rights, organizing a strike that closed the schools for fifty-three days. In 1974, he was elected president of the American Federation of Teachers; during his twenty-three-year tenure in this position, the union membership more than doubled to a size of 940,000. He also wrote a weekly column in the *New York Times*, "Where We Stand," as a means of promoting public education and teachers' issues during this time.

A staunch supporter of civil rights, Shanker marched with Dr. Martin Luther King Jr. in Selma and Montgomery, Alabama. He was the first teacher to become a member of the AFL-CIO Executive Council and served as its senior vice president and chair of its Education Committee. Shanker also founded Education International, a federation of more than twenty million teachers in democratic countries worldwide.

Shanker advised several presidents on education policy. He sought business's support for public education and was a staunch supporter of public education but acknowledged the need for reforms such as tougher discipline, teacher certification, and rigorous educational standards.

Al Shanker lost a three-year battle with bladder cancer on February 22, 1997. In 1998, he was awarded the nation's highest civilian honor, the Medal of Freedom, posthumously by President Bill Clinton. (AE)

SHAPIRO, SAMUEL HARVEY
Governor of Illinois, 1968–1969

Samuel Harvey Shapiro was named the 1968 Jewish National Fund Man of the Year, sixty-one years after his birth on April 25, 1907.

He displayed an interest in the political process at an early age, serving as the treasurer of the Young Democratic Club of Illinois. After pursuing an education from St. Viator College and receiving a law degree from the University of Illinois, Shapiro entered public life at the age of twenty-six. The first position that he held was the job of city attorney for Kankakee, Illinois. After holding this position for several years, Shapiro assumed the position of state's attorney for Kankakee County in 1936 and remained in this position until the outbreak of World War II, when he left to serve with the United States Navy.

Shapiro returned to public life as a member of the Illinois General Assembly, in which he served seven terms. During his legislative career, Shapiro served as chair for the state's public aid, health, welfare, and safety commission. In 1960, he was elected lieutenant governor and was reelected in 1964; he succeeded to the governorship in 1968 when Otto Kerner resigned to accept a federal judgeship. Shapiro's tenure in office was short-lived, however, as he lost his bid for election in his own right in the 1968 election.

Shapiro was an active member of a number of organizations including the American Legion and B'nai B'rith until his death on March 16, 1987. (KJ)

SHAPP, MILTON JERROLD
Governor of Pennsylvania, 1971–1979

The first major-party Jewish candidate for the presidency of the United States, Milton Jerrold Shapiro assumed the name Shapp to overcome discrimination. He was born on June 25, 1912, in Cleveland, Ohio, and attended school at the Case Institute of Technology. On graduating, Shapp found work as a truck driver and salesman during the Great Depression. When World War II began, Shapp was placed in charge of the army's Blue Danube radio network in Austria. After the war, he founded his own company, Jerrold Electronics, which brought cable television to mountain-locked communities. In 1966, he sold this company for more than $50 million.

Shapp first became involved in politics through his involvement with John F. Kennedy's campaign for the presidency in 1960. After the election, Shapp became an important consultant to the Kennedy administration on business and on the creation of the Peace Corps. In 1966, he decided to strike out a political life of his own and ran unsuccessfully for governor of Pennsylvania. Despite this loss, he ran again in 1970 and won the gubernatorial race in a landslide. Both of those campaigns were largely self-financed; they were among the first heavily financed media campaigns by a political neophyte seeking to begin a career in elective office with a high-level position. Shapp was reelected to a second term in 1974. In 1976, he declared himself a candidate for the presidency and attempted to secure the Democratic nomination. However, this campaign ended quickly when Shapp withdrew from the race after running behind "No Preference" in the Florida primary.

Despite his failure as a presidential candidate, Shapp was an enormous success as governor. During his tenure, Pennsylvania went from near bankruptcy to running large surpluses. He established a statewide lottery to provide funds for the elderly and introduced a local income tax to improve health care. Under his administration the public gained in-credible access to the political system through "sunshine laws" and citizen hotlines to various state agencies. Shapp created financial-disclosure laws for top state officials and enforced a strict ethics code for state employees. He left office in 1979 after serving the two terms he was limited to under state law.

Milton Jerrold Shapp died at the age of eighty-two on November 26, 1994. (KJ)

SHERMAN, BRAD
Member of Congress, 1997–present

Born October 24, 1954, in Los Angeles, Brad Sherman is a lifelong political junkie. He grew up in the San Gabriel Valley and as a child campaigned for Congressman George Brown. An accountant, Sherman's first elective office was the California Board of Equalization, the agency that collects state taxes. In 1996, he moved to the San Fernando Valley to run for the congressional seat vacated by retiring Representative Tony Beilenson. He won by five points, and two years later increased his margin to nearly 20 percent.

Sherman sits on the Banking and Financial Services Committee and the International Relations Committee. (JS)

SHEVIN, ROBERT LEWIS
Attorney General of Florida, 1971–1979

Robert L. Shevin was born January 19, 1934, to Aaron and Pauline (Bott) Shevin. He received his B.A. from the University of Florida in 1955 and his J.D. from the University of Miami in 1957.

Following law school, Shevin entered private practice in firms he formed. He began his political career in 1962, serving first as a member of the Florida House of Representatives (1963–1965) and then as a member of the Florida State Senate (1967–1971). In 1970, Shevin was elected attorney general of Florida; he served two terms, from 1971 until 1979. After serving as attorney general for eight years, Shevin returned to private practice. In 1996, he left private practice to become a judge of the Third District Court of Appeals in Miami. (BF)

SHORENSTEIN, WALTER
Democratic Party Fund-raiser

After his discharge from the army as a major in 1946, Walter Shorenstein joined the San Francisco real estate brokerage firm of Milton Meyer and Co. By 1951, he had become a partner in the firm; within ten years, he was the president and sole owner of the now-renamed Shorenstein Company. Under his leadership, the company has become the largest owner and operator of office buildings in San Francisco.

Shorenstein has used his wealth to support many causes. The family is among the nation's leading supporters of the United Way; he sponsors important programs for research into East Asia and the Pacific at the University of California–Berkeley and at Stanford University. With his late wife, Phyllis, he established the Joan Shorenstein Center on Press, Politics, and Public Policy at the John F. Kennedy School of Government at Harvard.

Shorenstein has also been a steadfast financial supporter of the Democratic Party, nationally and in California. In 1997, the party gave him the Lifetime Achievement Award in recognition of his efforts to raise money for the national committee and Democratic candidates. (LSM)

SHRIBMAN, DAVID MARKS
Washington Bureau Chief, Boston Globe

David M. Shribman was born March 2, 1954, in Salem, Massachusetts. He graduated summa cum laude from Dartmouth College in 1976 and did graduate study in England.

In 1992, when Shribman was named Washington bureau chief and an assistant managing editor of the *Boston Globe*, the *Globe* had hired an experienced and well-respected political reporter to succeed veteran Michael Putzel.

Shribman began his career in journalism reporting for the *Buffalo Evening News.* He moved to Washington with the Buffalo paper but soon joined the staff of the *Washington Star.* In 1981, he covered the Hill for the Washington Bureau of the *New York Times.* After three years at the *Times,* Shribman became a congressional reporter and national political correspondent at the *Wall Street Journal.*

After nine years at the *Journal,* Shribman assumed his present position at the *Boston Globe,* the same newspaper he used to deliver as a young boy. In addition to his duties as Washington bureau chief and assistant managing editor, he also writes a weekly syndicated political column. Shribman received a Pulitzer Prize for beat reporting in 1995. (BMcN)

SHULL, LEON
National Executive Director, Americans for Democratic Action, 1963–1981

Leon Shull's parents emigrated from Poland in the beginning of the twentieth century and settled their family in Philadelphia, where Shull was born on November 8, 1913. Shull entered Temple University but left after a year to focus on what he thought would be his future career—socialism.

From 1947 to 1949, Shull was the Philadelphia director of the Jewish Labor Committee, where his principal activity was working for civil rights in the labor movement. In 1950, he became the executive director of Americans for Democratic Action for Philadelphia and Southeast Pennsylvania. Between 1951 and 1962 he served as the regional campaign director for thirteen candidates, including Adlai Stevenson and John F. Kennedy, as well as Democratic candidates for governor and senator in Pennsylvania.

In 1963, Shull moved on to become the national director of Americans for Democratic Action (ADA), a position he held until 1981. Since his retirement, Shull has remained active within the ADA, serving on the governing boards and the executive committees at the local and national levels. He spends the majority of his time analyzing national legislation for the Washington ADA office. (AE)

SIEGEL, ISAAC
Member of Congress, 1915–1923

Isaac Siegel was born in New York City on April 12, 1880. He graduated from New York University Law School in 1901 and was admitted to the bar in 1902.

Siegel was first elected to Congress as a Republican in 1914. He served as the chair of the Committee on the Census from 1919 to 1923. He also visited war-torn France and Italy as a member of the Overseas Commission in 1918. Choosing not to run for reelection in 1923, Siegel returned to New York City to practice law. He served as the magistrate of New York City from 1939 to 1940. In 1940, he was appointed justice of the Domestic Relations Court of New York City, where he served until his death on June 29, 1947. (AE)

SILBERMAN, LAURENCE HIRSCH
Judge, U.S. Court of Appeals, 1985–present; Ambassador to Yugoslavia, 1975–1977

Born October 12, 1935, in York, Pennsylvania, Laurence Silberman earned an A.B. from Dartmouth

College in 1957 and an LL.B. in 1961 from Harvard Law School. After completing law school, Silberman practiced privately in Honolulu, Hawaii, until moving to Washington, D.C., in 1967, to serve as an attorney at the appellate division for the National Labor Relations Board.

Silberman became solicitor for the U.S. Department of Labor in 1969 and was named undersecretary of labor a year later. In 1974, he moved to the Justice Department as deputy attorney general. President Gerald Ford named Silberman ambassador to Yugoslavia in 1975; he served in Belgrade for two years.

Leaving government, Silberman accepted a position at the American Enterprise Institute (AEI). From 1979 until 1983, he also served as an officer of the Crocker National Bank of San Francisco, while remaining as a visiting fellow for the AEI.

During the 1980 campaign, Silberman served as a campaign aide for the Reagan–Bush ticket. Immediately following Ronald Reagan's election, he helped negotiate the release of American hostages from Iran's Khomeini regime. In 1985, President Reagan nominated Silberman for the U.S. Court of Appeals for the District of Columbia Circuit. One of Silberman's most famous decisions was overturning the convictions of Lieutenant Colonel Oliver North and Admiral John Poindexter in 1990, harming the case of the Iran-*contra* special prosecutor.

While serving on the federal bench, Silberman has also been an adjunct professor at Georgetown Law Center. (JM)

SIMON, JOSEPH
Mayor of Portland, Oregon, 1909–1911;
United States Senator, 1898–1903

Joseph Simon was born on February 7, 1851, in Bechtheim, Germany. At the age of six, the Simon family emigrated to Portland, Oregon. In Portland, Simon attended public school and studied law. In 1872, he entered the bar and began to practice law. In 1877, Simon was elected to the city council, and he served in this capacity until 1880, when he successfully sought election as a Republican to the Oregon State Senate. Simon served in the state senate for eight years.

In 1898, one of Oregon's seats in the United States Senate became vacant. Simon aggressively sought and won the election by the state legislature to fill that vacancy. However, Simon chose not to seek election to a full term when his seat came up for reelection in 1902. As a senator, Simon chaired the Committee on Irrigation and Reclamation of Arid Lands.

From 1909 to 1911, he returned to public life as mayor of Portland. After leaving office in 1911, Joseph Simon resumed his law practice, in which he remained active until his death in Portland on February 14, 1935. (KJ)

SIROVICH, WILLIAM IRVING
Member of Congress, 1927–1939

William Sirovich was born in York, Pennsylvania, on March 18, 1882. Sirovich moved with his parents to New York City in 1888 and attended public school. In 1902, he graduated from the College of the City of New York and went on to graduate from Columbia University's College of Physicians and Surgeons in 1906.

On graduation Sirovich began practicing medicine but also established himself as a lecturer and editor. He also wrote several plays that were produced on Broadway. Sirovich spent the next twenty years serving in several philanthropic positions, beginning with his appointment onto the commission to inquire into the subject of widows' pensions and of the state pension of New York in 1913. The following year he was appointed a member of the State Charities Convention. Sirovich also served as the superintendent of the Peoples' Hospital in New York City from 1910 through 1927 and on the Commission on Child Welfare from 1919 through 1931.

Sirovich was defeated in his first run for Congress in 1924 but succeeded in the following election, winning a House seat as Democrat. While serving, Sirovich was a delegate to the Congress held at Bucharest, Romania, in 1931 and served as the chair of the Committee on Patents from 1931 to 1937.

William Sirovich remained in Congress until his death in New York City on December 17, 1939. (AE)

SISISKY, NORMAN
Member of Congress, 1983–2001

Norman Sisisky was born June 9, 1927, in Baltimore, a child of Lithuanian immigrants. He grew up in Richmond and on graduating from high school enlisted in the navy during World War II.

In 1973, Sisisky was elected to the Virginia General Assembly as an independent. He subsequently became a Democrat and was reelected four times. He defeated an incumbent Republican in Virginia's Tidewater district in 1982.

Representing an area whose economy is dominated by defense installations, Sisisky sits on the National Security Committee and the Select Committee on Intelligence. He has been an outspoken advocate of the military, supporting projects in his district and even suggesting that the draft might be reinstated. He is a member of the "Blue Dogs" group of moderate Democrats.

Before he came to Congress, Sisisky was a successful soft-drink distributor, and he donated his congressional salary to charity.

Norman Sisisky died while still serving in the House on March 29, 2001. (JS)

SMITH, LAWRENCE J.
Member of Congress, 1983–1993

Lawrence Jack Smith was born in Brooklyn, New York, on April 25, 1941, and attended New York University. He graduated with an LL.B. and a J.D. from the Brooklyn Law School in 1964 and practiced law in New York City.

After moving to Hollywood, Florida, in 1972, Smith became active in Democratic politics. He was elected to the Florida House of Representatives in 1978. He ran successfully for United States House of Representatives in 1982 and remained in office until 1993. In the House, Smith was known as one of the most outspoken advocates of a strong U.S.-Israel relationship. He supported high foreign-aid levels for Israel and opposed arms sales to Arab nations at war with the Jewish state.

In 1992, Smith bought two minutes of time on south Florida television stations to make the surprise announcement that he did not intend to seek reelection, requiring that the stations not give the ad to the news divisions. At that time, the Florida media had been aggressively pursuing questions about Smith's finances. Smith wrote 161 overdrafts on his House bank account, and Common Cause had asked the House Ethics Committee to investigate whether Smith, in cashing an unexplained $10,000

check, was converting campaign funds to his personal use.

Smith remains active in community and political affairs in Hollywood, Florida. (JM)

SOFAER, ABRAHAM DAVID
Legal Adviser, U.S. Department of State, 1985–1990; Judge, U.S. District Court, 1979–1985

Abraham Sofaer was born on May 6, 1938, in Bombay, India. He came to the United States in 1948 and was naturalized in 1959. Sofaer served in the United States Air Force from 1956 to 1959. He received a B.A. from Yeshiva College in 1962 and an LL.B. from New York University in 1965.

Between 1965 and 1967 Sofaer clerked, first for Judge J. Skelly Wright on the U.S. Court of Appeals for the District of Columbia and then for Supreme Court Justice William C. Brennan Jr. From 1967 to 1969, he was the assistant U.S. attorney for the U.S. District Court (southern district) in New York. He became a professor of law at Columbia in 1969, where he remained until 1979. Between 1979 and 1985, Sofaer was a judge for the U.S. District Court in New York. From 1985 to 1990, he served as legal adviser to the U.S. Department of State. In early 1985, he changed his party affiliation from Democrat to Republican. His reinterpretation of the 1972 Anti-Ballistic Missile Treaty enraged many on Capitol Hill; it essentially gave the Reagan administration the legal underpinning for its "Star Wars" plans. After five years, he left the State Department to work for Hughes, Hubbard, & Reed in Washington. In 1993, Sofaer agreed to represent the Libyan government on issues related to Pan Am flight 103 but had to drop the case amid strong protest. Sofaer left the firm in 1994 to become a senior fellow at the Hoover Institution of Stanford University, where he remains today. (TW)

SOLARZ, STEPHEN JOSHUA
Member of Congress, 1975–1993

Stephen Solarz was born in New York City on September 12, 1940. He received a B.A. from Brandeis

University in 1962 and an M.A. from the Department of Public Law and Government at Columbia University in 1967.

Solarz taught political science at Brooklyn College for the academic year 1967–1968, while he was preparing to run for the state assembly. He served in the New York State Assembly from 1969 until 1974. In 1974, he was elected to the U.S. House of Representatives from the Thirteenth District of New York, one of the nation's most heavily Jewish districts. While in the House, Solarz served as the chair of two subcommittees of the House Foreign Affairs Committee, Asian and Pacific Affairs, and Africa. His leadership of the Subcommittee on Africa was particularly important as it coincided with a period of unusual turmoil in many parts of the continent.

Throughout his career, Solarz was a strong advocate of aid to Israel. He was defeated in 1992, after redistricting, partially due to his involvement in the House bank scandal. He was eventually cleared of all charges, and in 1992, President Bill Clinton nominated him as the U.S. ambassador to India, but the nomination was withdrawn without explanation. In 1993, President Clinton appointed Solarz chair of the Central Asian-American Enterprise Fund. He also serves as president of Solarz Associates, an international consulting firm. (AE)

SOLOMONT, ALAN D.
National Finance Chair,
Democratic National Committee, 1997–2000

Alan Solomont is an expert in and provider of eldercare in New England. Born on February 16, 1949, he was educated in Boston schools and is a 1970 graduate of Tufts University; after graduation he traveled for a year on a prestigious Thomas J. Watson Fellowship. He later returned to school, to earn a B.S. in nursing from the University of Lowell.

Solomont was the founder and CEO of the A•D•S Group, which built a broad and innovative network of postacute, elder care services in nursing homes, hospitals, assisted-living facilities, senior housing facilities, and at home. He sold that company in 1996 and recently launched Solomont Bailis Ventures, the goal of which is to launch new, innovative health services for the elderly.

Long active in the Democratic Party, Solomont was national chair of the Democratic Business Council and treasurer of the Massachusetts Democratic Party. In 1997, President Bill Clinton asked him to serve as national finance chair for the Democratic National Committee. He has also played leadership roles in the Gore 2000 campaign on the Leadership 2000 board. Solomont was recently named by President Clinton to serve on the board of the Corporation for National and Community Service, which oversees AmeriCorps, the National Senior Service Corps, and Learn & Serve.

Solomont has also been active in Jewish and community matters. As examples, he is a member of the boards of the Jewish Fund for Justice, the New Israel Fund, Jewish Community Housing for the Elderly, and Tufts University, and he chairs the advisory committee of the Institute of Health Policy at Brandeis's Heller School. He was chairman of the boards of the University of Lowell, guiding its merger with the University of Massachusetts, and of the Boston University Medical Center Hospital, which merged with Boston City Hospital to form the Boston Medical Center, on whose board he continues to serve. (LSM)

SONNENFELDT, HELMUT
Presidential Adviser, 1969–1977

Born on September 13, 1926, in Berlin, Germany, Helmut Sonnenfeldt and his family fled Nazi Germany, coming to the United States in 1944. He studied at Johns Hopkins University, receiving his B.A. in 1950 and his M.A. in 1951.

Joining the State Department, Sonnenfeldt earned a reputation as an expert political analyst and hard-line anticommunist. From 1965 to 1969, he directed the Soviet and East European Research Section of the Office of Research and Analysis. In 1969, his close friend Henry Kissinger, President Richard Nixon's newly appointed national security adviser, asked Sonnenfeldt to become his deputy on the National Security Council. Kissinger and Sonnenfeldt not only were close friends but also held strikingly similar views on almost every major foreign policy issue. Consequently, Sonnenfeldt was included in all of Kissinger's activities, including the Strategic Arms Limitation Talks, the reopening of China to the United States, and the Paris Peace Talks. Sonnenfeldt returned to the State Department when Kissinger became secretary of state, serving as counselor from 1974 to 1977.

Sonnenfeldt left the State Department after a politically damaging controversy regarding misconstrued comments about the Soviet Union and Eastern Europe. He joined the faculty of Johns Hopkins University's School for Advanced International Studies and in 1978 became a guest scholar at the Brookings Institution, a position he still holds. (JW)

SPECTER, ARLEN
United States Senator, 1981–present

Arlen Specter was born in Wichita, Kansas, on February 12, 1930. He received a B.A. from the University of Pennsylvania (1951) and his LL.B. from Yale University Law School (1956). Between 1951 and 1953, Specter served in the United States Air Force.

In 1956, Specter began practicing law in Pennsylvania, serving as assistant district attorney, as a Democrat, from 1959 to 1964. He left that post to work on the staff of the Warren Commission, investigating the assassination of President John F. Kennedy; in that role he helped devise the theory that a single bullet hit both the president and Texas governor John Connolly. Specter returned to the practice of law in Philadelphia and switched to the Republican Party. In 1965 and again in 1969, he was elected Philadelphia's district attorney, despite the city's Democratic leanings. Specter's rising political star was dimmed by a series of electoral losses: a reelection campaign for district attorney in 1973, a bid for the United States Senate in 1976, and a gubernatorial campaign in 1978. In 1980, however, as part of the Reagan landslide, Specter won election to the Senate; he was reelected in 1986, 1992, and 1998.

Specter was severely criticized by feminists in response to his questioning of Anita Hill during the confirmation hearings for Supreme Court Justice Clarence Thomas. In 1996, he unsuccessfully sought the Republican presidential nomination, withdrawing from the race before the first primary. He was, however, the first Jewish Republican candidate for the presidency.

In 1998, Arlen Specter introduced the Freedom from Religious Persecution Act, a law that allows the president to punish a country that violates religious rights. He is consistently one of the strongest supporters of Israel and is at odds with the conservative Christian right element in his own party. (TW)

SPELLMAN, GLADYS NOON
Member of Congress, 1975–1981

Gladys Noon Spellman was born in New York City on March 1, 1918. She attended George Washington University in Washington, D.C., and went to graduate school at the U.S. Department of Agriculture.

Spellman taught in the Prince George's County school system in Maryland and served on its board of commissioners from 1962 to 1970. In 1967, Lyndon Johnson appointed her to the Advisory Commission on Intergovernmental Relations. She also served as a councilwoman at large from 1971 to 1974 and as the president of the National Counties Association in 1972.

Spellman was elected as a Democrat from the Fifth District of Maryland to the Ninety-fourth Congress in 1974. Her popularity within the district grew each year, and she won all three of her reelection campaigns by large margins. Spellman focused much of her attention on health care and education reforms and worked tirelessly for her district. While in the House, she chaired the subcommittee on Compensation and Employee Benefits (of the Post Office and Civil Service Committee). Spellman suffered heart arrest while campaigning for reelection in 1980 but won reelection despite her comatose state. She was later removed by House Resolution 80 due to incapacitating illness in 1981. Her husband, Reuben, ran in the special election to fill her seat but was defeated.

Gladys Spellman died on June 19, 1988. (AE)

SPINGARN, JOEL E.
President of the National Association for the Advancement of Colored People, 1930–1939

Joel E. Spingarn was born May 17, 1875, in New York City. He graduated from Columbia with an A.B. degree in 1895, following which he spent a postgraduate year at Harvard before returning to Columbia to complete his Ph.D. (1899). He remained at Columbia for an additional twelve years, teaching from 1899 to 1911 (as the assistant to the comparative literature department from 1899 to 1904, as an adjunct professor from 1904 to 1909, and as a full professor from 1909 to 1911). His career at Columbia, and as a professor, ended after an acrid dispute with Columbia's president Nicholas Murray Butler over the university's academic administration in 1911.

Independently wealthy, an author, publisher, politician, lecturer, and soldier, Spingarn rebounded from his dismissal from Columbia by excelling at numerous pursuits. His crowning achievement was his service in the area of African American civil rights. While serving as an infantry major in the American Expeditionary Force in France during World War I, he led a successful movement to set up a training program for African American officers. In 1913, he established the Spingarn Medal, which is awarded each year to the African American who has best served his race. He was among the leaders who formed the National Association for the Advancement of Colored People (NAACP) in 1909. Spingarn served as an officer of the NAACP for many years and as the president from 1930 until his death on July 26, 1939, in New York City. (BF)

SPITZER, ELIOT
Attorney General of New York, 1999–present

Born on June 20, 1959, in New York City, Eliot Spitzer, who was elected as New York's attorney general in 1998, is a graduate of Princeton University and Harvard Law School, where he was editor of the law review. Following law school, he clerked for U.S. District Court Judge Robert W. Sweet.

Spitzer has split his professional time between private law practice and public service. From 1986 to 1992, he was assistant district attorney in Manhattan, eventually serving as chief of the labor racketeering division. A successful prosecutor, his efforts to confront organized crime, as in the Gambino case, have been credited with breaking its hold on New York City's garment district. In addition, his prosecutorial record included notable victories in cases involving political corruption, white-collar crime, and antitrust violations.

As a private lawyer and former prosecutor, Spitzer became known in New York through media appearances on show's such as CNN's *Burden of Proof* as well as on Court TV and CNBC before becoming state attorney general in 1999. (BF)

SPORKIN, STANLEY
U.S. District Court Judge, Washington, D.C., 1985–2000

Stanley Sporkin was born in Philadelphia in 1932. He received a B.A. from Penn State in 1953 and an LL.B. from Yale in 1957.

After clerking for the U.S. District Court in Delaware from 1957 to 1960, Sporkin spent one year in private law practice before becoming a staff attorney for a special study at the U.S. Securities and Exchange Commission (SEC). Throughout the next two decades, he worked with the SEC in several different capacities. Sporkin continued as a staff attorney and was promoted to chief enforcement attorney in 1966, assistant director in 1967, associate director in 1968, and deputy director of the division of trading and markets in 1972. Sporkin became director of the division of enforcement in 1973. As such, he broke the tradition of his predecessors and actively went after companies for making illegal payoffs and bribing foreign governments.

Sporkin left the SEC in 1981 to become general counsel to the Central Intelligence Agency, a position he held until 1985. In that capacity, he issued the legal finding that facilitated the Reagan administration's secret deal to trade arms for hostages with Iran. Sporkin was named a judge for U.S. District Court in Washington, D.C., and served from 1985 until 2000.

Since 2000, Sporkin has been a partner at the firm of Wiel Gotshal and Menges in Washington. (TW)

STEIGER, SAM
Member of Congress, 1967–1977

Sam Steiger was born in New York City on March 10, 1929. He attended Cornell University and received his B.S. from Colorado A & M in 1950. He was commissioned as an officer in the United States Army and served as a tank platoon leader from 1951 to 1953; during the course of his service, he was awarded a Silver Heart and a Purple Star. After his service, Steiger moved to Arizona, where he became interested in local politics. He served as a state senator from 1961 to 1965. In 1965, he became the Vietnam War correspondent for two local papers.

Steiger was elected as a Republican to the United States House of Representatives in 1966 and served there until 1977. In 1976, Steiger chose not to run for reelection, deciding instead to wage what would be a losing battle for the United States Senate. Six year late, running as a Libertarian, Steiger was defeated in a bid to become governor of Arizona. He went on to serve as special assistant to Governor Evan Mecham from 1987 until 1988 and also host a talk show. Steiger ran for governor again in 1990, on the Republican ticket, but was defeated once again. In 2000, Steiger was serving the mayor of Prescott, Arizona. (AE)

STEIN, HERBERT
President's Council of Economic Advisers, 1969–1974

Herbert Stein was born in Detroit, Michigan, on August 27, 1916, to David (an immigrant from Eastern Europe) and Jessie Stein. A scholarship made it possible for him to attend Williams College during the Depression. He received his B.A. from Williams in 1935, followed by a Ph.D. in economics from University of Chicago.

In 1938, Stein and his family moved to Washington, D.C. He worked for a number of federal agencies, including the Federal Deposit Insurance Corporation, National Defense Advisory Commission, War Production Board, and the Office of War Mobilization and Re-conversion, before he left to serve as a junior naval officer in World War II (1944–1945).

Following the war, Stein served as an economist for the Committee for Economic Development for twenty years, from 1945 until 1966. In 1969, President Richard Nixon named him to his Council of Economic Advisers and in 1972 promoted him to chair. When Gerald Ford replaced Nixon as president, he asked Stein to remain as chair, which he did briefly. On leaving he suggested to President Ford that he should appoint Alan Greenspan in his place. Stein spent the next ten years of his career as the Willis Robertson Professor of Economics at the University of Virginia.

At the age of eighty-three, Herbert Stein died September 8, 1999, of a heart attack in Washington.

STEINEM, GLORIA
Feminist Leader

Born on March 25, 1934, in Toledo, Ohio, to Leo Steinem, a Jewish antiques dealer, and Ruth Nuneviller Steinem, a rebellious Scotch Presbyterian newspaperwoman, Gloria Steinem is not considered a Jew by religious standards because her mother was not Jewish and she was baptized in the Congregationalist church. However, she has claimed that she has never identified herself as a Christian and, wherever there is antisemitism, identifies herself as a Jew.

Steinem's career has been far-ranging, from modeling to editing and writing to speaking out on behalf of women's rights. She began working as a writer in New York in 1960, frustrated at first because women were relegated to writing about light topics (e.g., fashion and celebrities), but eventually turning to serious political issues with the magazine *New York,* which she cofounded.

Steinem's feminist consciousness was raised and her second career born in 1969, as the result of a meeting she covered concerning abortion. Ensuing discussions with other women who, like herself, had experienced abortion made her realize women needed to fight for their own rights. Her writing on issues of gender equality and feminist concerns led to her launching of *Ms.* magazine. From 1971 to 1987, Steinem was the editor of *Ms.,* the first mass-market women's magazine with a revolutionary agenda and the first national magazine run and controlled entirely by women.

In addition to her new editorial responsibilities, in 1975 Steinem helped plan the women's agenda for the Democratic National Convention and continued to exert pressure on liberal politicians on behalf of women's concerns.

In September 2000, the woman who coined the phrase "a woman without a man is like a fish without a bicycle" got married for the first time, at age sixty-six, to David Bale. She currently maintains an office in New York City. (JW)

Source: Gloria Steinem, *Outrageous Acts and Everyday Rebellions* (New York: Holt, Rinehart & Winston, 1983).

STEINER, DAVID
Democratic Party Fund-raiser and Community Leader

Born on September 29, 1929, in Newark, New Jersey, David Steiner graduated from the Carnegie Institute of Technology in Pittsburgh in 1951 with a B.S. in civil engineering. Steiner went on to an extremely successful career as a real estate developer, building office and industrial parks and shopping centers in fifteen states.

Throughout his career, Steiner has been active in the various communities of which he has been a part. He has served as the president of his professional association, the National Association of Office and Industrial Parks; he has served his state as chair of the New Jersey Economic Development Council. He served as chair of the Political Education Project for the American Israel Public Affairs Committee (AIPAC) and later as AIPAC's national president. He is currently vice chair of the National Jewish Democratic Council.

Steiner has been one of the most prominent national Jewish fund-raisers in the past decade. He has served on the finance committees for many candidates for statewide office and was on the Gore 2000 Finance Committee. He is a member of the Jefferson Trust of the Democratic National Committee and sits on the board of trustees of the Democratic Senatorial Campaign Committee. He has also played a leading finance role for the Democratic Congressional Campaign Committee. (LSM)

STEINHARDT, LAURENCE ADOLPH
Ambassador to Six Nations, 1936–1950

Born October 6, 1892, in New York City to wealthy, influential parents of German Jewish ancestry, Laurence Steinhardt attended Columbia University, earning his B.A. in 1913 and his M.A. and LL.B. in 1915. After serving with the army during World War I, he returned to work with the law firm of his famous uncle, Samuel Untermeyer, a crusader for Jewish rights.

During the 1920s, Steinhardt became actively involved in New York's Democratic Party and the campaigns of Franklin D. Roosevelt. A major contributor to Roosevelt's presidential campaign, Steinhardt was named minister to Sweden after FDR's election in 1932. He successfully negotiated Sweden's first reciprocal trade agreement and also became enamored of the diplomatic life. He received his first of five ambassadorships in 1936. Posted to Peru, he concentrated on cultural and trade issues and played an important role in the successful Lima Pan-American Conference. More influential posts followed. In 1939, Roosevelt sent Steinhardt to Moscow; he provided our government with crucial evaluations of the ever-changing situation in the USSR. After the United States entered World War II, Roosevelt appointed Steinhardt to neutral Turkey; there he conducted a successful preemptive buying program to keep strategic items from the Germans. By 1944, he was using his influence to aid the passage of Jews from the Balkans to Palestine, atoning for his controversial role in limiting the flow of Jewish refugees to the United States during his service in Moscow.

In late 1944, Roosevelt appointed Steinhardt to Czechoslovakia; he tried, unsuccessfully, to convince the U.S. government of the pivotal nature of that country, which fell under Soviet control in the coup d'état of February 1948. After the coup, President Harry S. Truman appointed Steinhardt to be ambassador to Canada—his final position.

Laurence Steinhardt died in a plane crash near Ottawa on March 28, 1950, on his way to a political dinner in New York. (JW)

STONE, I. F.
Journalist

Born December 24, 1907, in Philadelphia, Isidor Feinstein was the eldest of four children of Bernard Feinstein, a retailer, and Katy Novack, both Russian Jewish immigrants. The family moved to Haddonfield, New Jersey, in 1914, where at the age of fourteen Isidor single-handedly published a few issues of his journal *The Progress*, which supported the League of Nations and opposed racism and intolerant religious fundamentalism. Stone always regarded himself as a proud, if agnostic, Jew. In 1937, however, he legally changed his name from *Feinstein* to *Stone*, arguing that he would influence readers better if seen as "less Jewish." While still in high school, he was hired as the Haddonfield correspondent for the liberal publisher J. David Stern's *Camden Evening Courier*. It ruined his academic standing but confirmed his future profession.

Stone entered the University of Pennsylvania in 1924, studying philosophy and working part-time for Philadelphia-area papers; he dropped out in his junior year, bored with classroom formality. Stern's *Philadelphia Record* hired Stone as an editorial writer in 1931. Subsequently working for the *New York Post*, *The Nation*, and other left-wing publications, including New York's newspaper *PM*, Stone maintained his liberal leanings while supporting intervention in the European war.

In 1946, Stone wrote a series of articles for *PM* on his experiences traveling with a group of Jewish "displaced persons," survivors of the Holocaust,

aboard a vessel that evaded the British blockade and brought them to Palestine. His articles expanded into a book, *Underground to Palestine*. In 1948, he wrote another pro-Zionist book, *This Is Israel*. Stone was a strong supporter of Israel but by 1967 also believed in the need for a separate Arab Palestine, a stance that alienated other Zionists.

In the 1950s, due to the decline of liberal newspapers and FBI surveillance of his activities, Stone found himself professionally isolated and jobless. As a result he started his own four-page newsletter, *I.F. Stone's Weekly*. Signing up 5,300 advance subscribers (including Albert Einstein and Eleanor Roosevelt), at five dollars a year, he published the first issue, with the help of his wife Esther, on January 17, 1953, from their Washington home. The *Weekly* reached conclusions on issues of the day based on close readings of ten newspapers and countless official documents read daily by Stone. Due to Stone's health problems, the publication went biweekly in 1968 and had to shut down in 1971, by which time the *Weekly* claimed a circulation of sixty-six thousand.

Until his death on June 18, 1989, I. F. Stone continued writing for the *New York Review of Books* and some of the same mainstream newspapers he once denounced. (JW)

STONE, RICHARD B.
Ambassador to Denmark, 1991–1993;
United States Senator, 1975–1980;
Secretary of State of Florida, 1970–1974

Richard Bernard Stone was born in New York City on September 22, 1928, but his family moved to Florida shortly thereafter. He graduated cum laude in 1944 from Harvard University and in 1954 from Columbia University Law School.

Stone practiced law in Miami, Florida, until he became the city attorney in 1966. He served as the secretary of state of Florida from 1970 until 1974, when he was elected to the United States Senate. Although a Democrat, Stone voted conservatively on many issues; thus, he opposed pardons for Vietnam draft resisters and the federal funding of abortions. Stone's vote for passage of the Panama Canal treaties, despite strong constituent opposition, likely led to his failure to be reelected in 1980.

In the 1980s, Stone practiced law in Washington, D.C., and was a registered foreign agent for the Government of Guatemala and the Government of Taiwan. He took a position as the vice chair of Capital Bank in Washington in 1982 and served as a consultant to the U.S. State Department for public diplomacy. President Ronald Reagan appointed him to be the president's special envoy to Central America from 1983 to 1984.

Stone returned to private law practice in 1984, but was named by President George H. W. Bush as the U.S. ambassador to Denmark from 1991 to 1993. He came out of retirement in the late 1990s to assist with the Dart Group Corp.'s legal difficulties and was eventually named acting chief executive during the turmoil. (JM)

STRAUS, ISIDOR
Member of Congress, 1894–1895

Born in Otterberg, Rhenish Bavaria, Germany, on February 6, 1845, Isidor Straus emigrated to the United States with his parents in 1854. Straus and his family settled in Talbotton, Georgia, where he pursued his education at Collinsworth Institute.

In 1865, he moved to New York City to enter the mercantile field. Straus and his brother later became the owners of famous R. H. Macy and Company department store. In 1894, he was elected to the Fifty-third Congress as a Democrat, following the resignation of Ashbel P. Fitch. Straus served in Congress from January 30, 1894, to March 3, 1895, not seeking reelection.

Following his service in Congress, Straus returned to New York to resume his business interests. He went on to become a member of the New York and New Jersey Bridge Commission.

Isidor Straus died on April 15, 1912, along with 1,500 others, while a passenger on the maiden voyage of the Royal Mail Steamer *Titanic*. (DS)

STRAUS, OSCAR SOLOMON
Ambassador to Turkey, 1909–1910; Secretary of Commerce and Labor, 1906–1909; Minister to Turkey, 1898–1899, 1887–1889

Oscar Straus, the younger brother of Isador, was the first Jew to serve in a president's cabinet. He was born December 23, 1850, in Otterberg, Bavaria, Germany. His family emigrated to the United States in 1854;

they lived in Georgia before moving to New York City. He graduated from Columbia College in 1871 and earned a law degree from Columbia in 1873.

Straus practiced law for several years before becoming a partner in L. Straus and Sons, merchants of glassware and china. Between 1887 and 1889, Straus served as minister to Turkey under President Grover Cleveland. As such, he was the first Jewish envoy appointed to the country that subsequently has hosted the largest number of Jewish ambassadors. In 1898, he was reappointed to the position by President William McKinley; he resigned in 1900. Originally a Cleveland Democrat, Straus increasingly identified with the Republican Party after the Democrats succumbed to silver mania and nominated William Jennings Bryan in 1896. Straus was frequently called on for advice during Theodore Roosevelt's administration and was appointed by Roosevelt to the International Court of Arbitration at The Hague in 1902. In 1906, President Roosevelt asked Straus to serve in his cabinet, as secretary of commerce and labor. He thus became the first Jew to serve in a president's cabinet. He held the post for three years.

In 1909, Straus returned to Turkey as an ambassador. He resigned from the post in 1910; two years later, he helped Roosevelt form the Progressive Party. In the fall of 1912, he ran unsuccessfully as the "Bull Moose" Party candidate in New York's gubernatorial race. He later helped President Woodrow Wilson raise support for inclusion of a League of Nations in the Versailles Treaty. He was also reappointed to the International Court of Arbitration in 1912 and 1920.

Straus was very active in the Jewish movement. While in Turkey, he met with Dr. Theodore Herzl, the founder of the Zionist movement. He was also active in several Jewish organizations, including the American Jewish Committee and the Jewish Welfare Board. He was founder and first president of the American Jewish Historical Society.

Oscar Straus died in New York City on May 3, 1926. (TW)

STRAUSS, LEO
Political Philosopher

Leo Strauss is often viewed as the primary philosophical influence on American neoconservatism, which began as a reaction against the New Left and the cultural revolutions of the 1960s. Among the popular political writers influenced by Strauss were Irving Kristol, William Kristol, Alan Bloom, and the more liberal William Galston.

Born on September 20, 1899, in Kirchhain, Hesse, Germany, by age seventeen Strauss had abandoned his Orthodox upbringing for Zionism. After receiving his doctorate in philosophy in 1925, he was granted a fellowship by the Academy for the Science of Judaism in Berlin. He wrote there until 1932, when he left for France and then England.

Strauss reached the United States in 1938 and spent eleven years teaching at the New School for Social Research in New York. In 1949, he went to the University of Chicago and taught there until 1968. He ended his teaching career at St. John's College in Maryland and died in Annapolis on October 18, 1973.

At the heart of Strauss's philosophy is a critique of cultural liberalism, which he deemed relativist, "historicist," and therefore nihilist and bankrupt. He suggested that "truth" could be found not in modern social thought but in the writings of medieval and ancient philosophers who favored natural law. He was also skeptical, if not critical, of political pluralism—thus his lifelong commitment to Zionism as a Jewish alternative.

Strauss's most famous works are *Natural Right and History* (1950) and *Persecution and the Art of Writing* (1952). His many students went on to become teachers and scholars throughout the country. Most "Straussians" stress the importance of close readings of historical texts as the most important element in the study of politics. Strauss had a parallel career as a scholar of Jewish philosophical texts and was considered one of the greatest interpreters of Maimonides.

Strauss married Miriam Petri in Europe, and they had a son and a daughter. The rest of his family died during World War II. (MD)

STRAUSS, LEWIS LICHTENSTEIN
Secretary of Commerce Designate, 1958–1959; Chair, Atomic Energy Commission, 1953–1958

Born January 31, 1896, in Charleston, West Virginia, Lewis Strauss was raised in Richmond, Virginia. He postponed and later abandoned a college education because of financial hardship and worked for his father's shoe company for three years.

During World War I, Strauss persuaded Herbert Hoover to grant him a position in the Food Administration. After the war, he was involved with the humanitarian work of the Jewish Joint Distribution Committee in Eastern Europe. In 1919, Strauss began working for the investment banking firm of Kuhn, Loeb, and Company. He was named partner by 1929. Strauss, a Republican, raised funds for Hoover, his former boss, during the 1928 presidential election. After the election, however, he chose to remain at Kuhn, Loeb. Strauss remained active in

the Naval Reserve throughout his career, rising to the rank of commander. He also worked directly for Secretary Forrestal during World War II.

Strauss divested his interest in Kuhn, Loeb to become a commissioner on the Atomic Energy Commission (AEC) in 1946. As a commissioner, he supported the development of the hydrogen bomb. In 1950, Strauss left the AEC to become a part-time financial consultant to the Rockefellers. In 1953, however, President Dwight D. Eisenhower recalled Strauss to government service, as chair of the AEC. Under his leadership, the commission ruled that J. Robert Oppenheimer was a security risk and should have his clearance revoked. This ruling later haunted Strauss. Eisenhower nominated Strauss to become the secretary of commerce in 1958, but his appointment was denied Senate confirmation in 1959. The Senate objected to the way Strauss had responded to criticism of his handling of the Oppenheimer matter.

Lewis Strauss died at his home in Virginia, January 21, 1974. To this day, Strauss is the only Jewish cabinet member to be denied Senate confirmation. (TW)

STRAUSS, ROBERT SCHWARTZ
Ambassador to Russia, 1991–1993; Chair, Democratic National Committee, 1972–1977

Born October 19, 1918, in Lockhart and raised in Stamford, Texas, Robert Strauss was the son of a Jewish German immigrant who owned a small-town dry-goods store and a strong-willed mother who encouraged his study of law and eventual entry into politics. Despite the Depression and his family's modest means, Strauss had earned both his undergraduate and law degrees from the University of Texas by 1941. His college experience introduced him to the world of politics and to John B. Connally—a connection that would affect his future career.

After service in the FBI during World War II, Strauss helped found the successful Dallas law firm Alin, Gump, Strauss, Hauer, & Feld. In 1962, he was the chief fund-raiser for the successful gubernatorial campaign of his friend John Connally. In 1968, appointed to the Democratic National Committee (DNC) by Connally, Strauss managed the Humphrey–Muskie campaign in Texas and established his political trademarks of financial savvy and the ability to find middle ground between disparate political elements. He was elected treasurer of the DNC in 1970 and given the daunting proposition of reducing the 1968 party debt of $9.3 million to manageable proportions. His success in working with all party elements to reduce that debt led to his election as chair of the DNC in 1972.

Following various appointments under the Carter administration, a return to his law practice, and participation in several bipartisan commissions in the 1980s, Strauss was called on by his fellow Texan, President George H. W. Bush, to be U.S. ambassador to Moscow in 1991. In the face of a rapidly changing situation in Russia, Strauss may not have seemed a likely candidate but was quickly approved based on his financial prowess and ability to bridge differences between factions. He spent most of his two years in Moscow dealing with economic issues, such as helping local businessmen run their enterprises according to free-market principles. (JW)

STROUSE, MYER
Member of Congress, 1863–1867

Born in Oberstrau, Bavaria, Germany, on December 16, 1825, Myer Strouse emigrated along with his father in 1832. He grew up in Pottsville, Schuylkill County, Pennsylvania, where he attended private schools.

From 1848 to 1852, Strouse worked as the editor of the *North American Farmer* in Philadelphia. Following his work in journalism, he went on to study law. In 1855, Strouse was admitted to the bar and commenced his practice in Pottsville.

Strouse was elected to Congress as a Democrat in 1862. He served in both the Thirty-eighth and Thirty-ninth Congresses, not seeking reelection 1866. Strouse returned to Pottsville to practice law. From 1876 to 1877, he served as an attorney and a solicitor for the "Molly Maguires," a secret mining organization in Pennsylvania.

Myer Strouse died on February 11, 1878. (DS)

SULZBERGER, ARTHUR HAYS
(see Adolph Ochs)

SULZBERGER, ARTHUR OCHS JR.
(see Adolph Ochs)

SULZBERGER, ARTHUR OCHS "PUNCH"
(see Adolph Ochs)

SUMMERS, LAWRENCE
Secretary, U.S. Department of Treasury, 1999–2001; Deputy Secretary, U.S. Department of Treasury, 1992–1999

Larry Summers was born in 1954 in New Haven, Connecticut. In 1975, he received a bachelor's degree from the Massachusetts Institute of Technology, followed by a Ph.D. from Harvard University in 1982.

Between 1979 and 1982, Summers was on the faculty at MIT. In 1982, he left to accept a public-sector position as a domestic policy economist for the President's Council of Economic Advisers. In 1983, he returned to the private sector as a professor at Harvard, where he remained until 1993. As the Nathaniel Ropes Professor, Summers was the youngest tenured professor at the university. Between 1991 and 1993, he served as the vice president of development economics and a chief economist at the World Bank.

In 1993, Summers became the undersecretary for international affairs at the U.S. Department of the Treasury. In 1995, he moved up within the organization to accept the position of deputy secretary, where he remained until 1999. In 1999, Summers succeeded his boss, Robert Rubin, as the secretary of the treasury. In the spring of 2001, Summers was chosen as the president of Harvard University. (TW)

SUTRO, ADOLPH
Mayor of San Francisco, 1894–1896

Adolph Sutro was born in Aachen, Prussia, on April 29, 1830. During his youth in Prussia, he was educated as a mining engineer. At the age of twenty, Sutro emigrated from Prussia to San Francisco, where he engaged in trade. This occupation supported Sutro until the Comstock Lode was discovered in Nevada and drew his attention. He moved to Nevada and utilized his mining education to create an ore-reducing mill that efficiently processed the silver that was mined at the lode. In addition to the mill, Sutro also created the Sutro Tunnel, which allowed miners to extract silver ore from the lode safely. In 1879, he sold his share of the mill and tunnel and returned to San Francisco. In San Francisco, Sutro invested heavily and successfully in real estate. Some estimates claim that at one point he held one-twelfth of the acreage in San Francisco; he amassed a considerable fortune.

In 1894, Sutro ran for mayor of San Francisco as a Populist. His campaign literature declared that he was the "Anti-Octopus" candidate, opposed to the policies of the Southern Pacific Railroad. He was elected on this platform and served one term as mayor.

Adolph Sutro died in San Francisco on August 8, 1898. (KJ)

SWOPE, HERBERT BAYARD
Journalist

Born on January 5, 1882, in St. Louis, Missouri, the son of Isaac Swope (formerly Schwab), a German immigrant who had set up a watchmaking business in St. Louis, and Ida Cohn, Swope graduated from Central High School in St. Louis in 1898 and briefly attended lectures at the University of Berlin the following year. His father's death in 1899 made it necessary for Swope to work.

Drawn to journalism, he worked as a reporter for the *St. Louis Post-Dispatch*, the *Chicago Inter-Ocean*, and then for several years on the *New York Herald*. In 1909, Swope joined the *New York World*, where he was recognized for his accounts of the Triangle Shirtwaist Company fire in 1911 and the sinking of the *Titanic* in 1912. During World War I, Swope made two trips to Europe to get an objective view of Germany. He summarized his observations in fourteen nationally syndicated installments (reprinted in 1917 as *Inside the German Empire*), for which he received the first Pulitzer Prize for reporting in 1917.

When the United States entered the war, Swope left his duties at the *World*, accepting a position as assistant to Bernard Baruch on the War Industries Board. At the war's end, Swope was sent to cover the Versailles Peace Conference. Elected head of the U.S. Press Delegation to the Peace Conference, he used his considerable political connections to obtain an advanced copy of the League of Nations covenant, which the *World* was the first to print.

From 1920 to 1928, Swope was executive editor of the *World*, and the paper reflected the flamboyance of its chief, engaging in crusades and investigations and creating the "Op Ed" (opposite editorial) page. He eventually resigned from the *World*, dissatisfied with Pulitzer's expanding role in managing the paper, and left journalism altogether.

Herbert Swope died in New York City on June 20, 1958. (JW)

SZOLD, HENRIETTA
Founder and President of Hadassah, 1912–1926; Zionist Leader

Henrietta Szold was born December 21, 1860, in Baltimore, Maryland. She graduated from Western Female High School with a liberal education that was supplemented by instruction from her father—a rabbi, Hebraist, and Talmudist.

Following graduation, Szold taught at both Adams' School in Baltimore and her father's congregational school. Inspired by the influx of Jewish immigrants to the United States in the 1880s, Szold helped found an evening school to teach immigrants in 1889. Working with the immigrants exposed Szold to Zionism. In 1910, she became secretary of the American-sponsored Jewish agricultural experiment station established in Palestine. To publicize and finance the cause, she organized women's study groups, called Hadassah. In 1912, she founded the national Hadassah and became its president. In 1918, Hadassah sent two public health nurses to Jerusalem and in 1922 dispatched, to Palestine, the American Zionist Medical Unit, forty-four doctors, nurses, and health care specialists. Beginning as a small organization with only forty members, Hadassah evolved into a large and efficient organization, unmatched in its attendance to the medical needs of Palestine and the State of Israel after 1948. In 1920, Szold went to Palestine to help in the administration of the unit and stayed for the remainder of her life. There she helped create a modern system of social service for Palestine Jewry and, working with the Jewish Agency's Aliya Bureau during World War II, helped rescue thirteen thousand children from Germany and Poland.

Henrietta Szold died in Jerusalem on February 3, 1945. (BF)

T

TELLER, LUDWIG
Member of Congress, 1957–1961

Except while in the military, Ludwig Teller was a resident of New York City his entire life. He was born in Manhattan in 1911 and educated in the New York City public schools. He completed both his undergraduate and law degrees at New York University, was admitted to the bar in 1936, and began to practice law. He served the War Department as an expert consultant to the Labor Relations Board in 1942.

Following the war, Teller served on the faculty at New York University and as a professor of law at New York Law School. In 1950, he won the first of three terms in the New York State Assembly; in 1956, he was elected as a Democrat to the United States House of Representatives. He served two terms but lost his party nomination in 1960. He stayed on the ballot as the Liberal Party nominee but was not reelected.

Ludwig Teller died in New York City on October 4, 1965. (CF)

TENZER, HERBERT
Member of Congress, 1965–1969

Herbert Tenzer was, in a sense, a jack-of all-trades, making his service to the public as a member of the United States Congress just one of many accomplishments in his lifetime.

Tenzer was born in New York City on November 1, 1905. He earned a law degree from New York City Law School in 1927 and began to practice in 1929. Eight years later, he formed the law firm Tenzer, Greenblatt, Fallon, and Kaplan. He was also the chairman of Barton's Candy Corporation from 1940 to 1960.

In 1964, Tenzer was the first Democrat-Liberal elected to represent New York's Fifth Congressional District, which he represented for two terms. While in Congress, he sponsored bills to create federal wetlands on Long Island and to curb jet aircraft noise. He did not seek reelection in 1968.

In 1965, he became a trustee of Yeshiva University and served as board chairman from 1977 until 1989. The university credits Tenzer as being especially influential in the creation of the Albert Einstein College of Medicine in 1955, the Benjamin N. Cardozo School of Law in 1976, and the Sy Sims School of Business in 1987. In addition to his service to Yeshiva University, Tenzer both founded and served as president of the United Jewish Appeal of Greater New York and devoted himself to service in many other Jewish and civic organizations, including Rescue Children, Inc., which cared for European war orphans following World War II.

After a very full and active life, Herbert Tenzer died of heart failure on March 24, 1993, one year after the death of his wife of more than sixty years. (CF)

TOLL, HERMAN
Member of Congress, 1959–1967

Though not a native of the United States, Herman Toll spent much of his adult life in public service to the people of Pennsylvania.

Born in Kiev, Russia, on March 15, 1907, Toll emigrated to the United States in 1910. Earning a law degree from Temple University, he was admitted to the bar and began to practice law in Philadelphia in 1930. In the twenty years that followed, Toll was a member of the Pennsylvania Prison Society, an organization that aids prisoners and their families during times of confinement and reintegration. He also was a member of the Philadelphia Housing Association and on the board of directors of the Crusader Savings and Loan Association.

In 1950, Toll ran for his first term in the Pennsylvania state legislature. He was elected for the two-year term and then reelected for three subsequent terms. In 1958, Toll was elected as a Democrat to the United States House of Representatives; he was reelected in 1960, 1962, and 1964. He did not seek reelection in 1966 and died on July 26, 1967, at the age of sixty. (CF)

V

VOLK, LESTER DAVID
Member of Congress, 1920–1923

Lester Volk's path to Congress through the medical profession was unusual, especially for someone in the early twentieth century, even if it was not unique.

Born on September 17, 1884, in Brooklyn, Volk was educated in the public schools, earned a degree from the Long Island School of Medicine in 1906, and began to practice medicine and serve as editor of the *Medical Economist*. While engaged in his practice, Volk felt called to the study of law and in 1911 earned a degree from St. Lawrence University Law School.

Volk served one term in the New York State Assembly, beginning in 1912, as a member of the Progressive Party, but he declined to seek reelection. During World War I, he served in the Medical Corps of the American Expeditionary Forces and, after the war, played a significant role in securing the Soldiers' Bonus offered by the state of New York. Following that, Volk was elected as a Republican in a special election in 1920 to fill the seat of Reuben Haskell, who resigned from the United States House of Representatives. He finished Haskell's term and earned a seat in Congress for the next term in his own right, though he was not reelected in 1922. For the next twenty years, Volk virtually vanished from the public eye, reemerging in 1943 to serve as assistant attorney general in New York until 1958.

Lester Volk died in New York City on April 30, 1962. (CF)

W

WALLACE, MIKE
Television Journalist

Born on May 9, 1918, in Brookline, Massachusetts, Myron Leon Wallace was educated in public schools and at the University of Michigan, from which he received his B.A. in 1939. He had intended to become an English teacher, but after working as an announcer for the university radio station, Wallace became enamored with the medium. After graduation, he worked at local radio stations in Grand Rapids, Detroit, and Chicago, before enlisting in the navy as a radio officer during World War II.

Returning to civilian life, Wallace spent most of the 1940s and 1950s as a game-show emcee, actor, announcer, and host of small talk shows. National prominence came with his 1957–1958 confrontational program, *The Mike Wallace Interview*, for ABC. But his major successes came with CBS.

After several years as anchor of the *CBS Morning News* and as a correspondent for the evening news, Wallace was chosen, along with Harry Reasoner, as coeditor and regular reporter for a new program called *60 Minutes*, conceived as the "*Life* magazine of the air." The show premiered in September 1968 and is now in its fourth decade. Wallace has prepared reports on issues ranging from heroin addiction and biological warfare to draft evasion and the plight of Syrian Jews. But his most notable contribution to *60 Minutes* has been as a skillful interviewer of important political figures, such as President Ronald Reagan, the Shah of Iran, and Spiro T. Agnew. (JW)

Source: Mike Wallace and Gary Paul Gates, *Close Encounters* (New York: Morrow, 1984).

WALTERS, BARBARA JILL
Television Journalist

Born on September 25, 1931, in Boston, Barbara Walters was the younger of two daughters of Louis Edward Walters, a vaudeville booking agent, and Dena Seletsky Walters. Although only minimally observant, the Walters lived in a succession of upper-middle-class Jewish neighborhoods. Barbara attended Sarah Lawrence College, intending to study acting, but turned instead to writing on graduation in 1951.

Shortly after graduation, Walters landed a position with NBC's New York affiliate. Her abilities in research, writing, editing, and filming led to a steady rise as a television journalist. In 1961, she went to work for the *Today* show. Occasional on-air appearances led to a chance to be the "Today girl," a role as a pretty small-talker. Walters turned that role into an essential part of the program and was taken more and more seriously. In 1974, she was finally named cohost of the *Today* show. She accepted a million-dollar-a-year contract for five years to move in 1976 to ABC, where she became television's first network

anchorwoman and the highest-paid newscaster at that time. At the anchor desk for only a year and a half, she fulfilled her ABC contract by producing her own TV specials.

The Barbara Walters Specials became legendary as Walters's probing but nonthreatening interview techniques earned the respect of leading political figures. She has interviewed every president since Richard Nixon. She arranged the first joint interviews with Egyptian president Anwar Sadat and Israeli prime minister Menachem Begin. In 1984, she helped develop one of the first investigative news programs, *20/20,* with friend and colleague Hugh Downs, an enterprise with which she continues today. (JW)

Source: Barbara Walters, *How to Talk with Practically Anybody about Practically Anything* (Garden City, N.Y.: Doubleday, 1970).

WANGER, IRVING PRICE
Member of Congress, 1893–1911

Born March 5, 1852, in North Coventry, Pennsylvania, Irving Wanger attended the Hill School in Pottstown, Pennsylvania.

Wanger was admitted to the bar in 1875 and began practicing law in Norristown and Media, Pennsylvania. In 1878, he became the Pennsylvania burgess from Norristown; he served as a delegate to the 1880 Republican National Convention. Wanger was the district attorney for Montgomery County, Pennsylvania, from 1881 to 1883 and again from 1887 to 1889. His 1890 bid for Congress was unsuccessful, but he was elected as a Republican to the Fifty-third Congress two years later. Wanger represented Pennsylvania's Seventh District between 1883 and 1903 and the Eighth District from 1903 to 1911, chairing the committee on post office expenditures. After losing his 1910 bid for reelection, Wanger resumed the practice of law.

Irving Wanger died on January 14, 1940, in Norristown, Pennsylvania. (TW)

WASSERMAN, LEW
Chair, Music Corporation of America, 1973–1995

Born March 15, 1913, in Cleveland, Ohio, to Jewish immigrant parents, Lew Wasserman attended Glenville High School in Cleveland, graduating in 1930.

Wasserman's show-business career began as an usher in Cleveland. His "break" came in 1936 when he was hired by Jules Stein to work for the fledgling talent agency, Music Corporation of America (MCA). In 1938, Wasserman was sent to Los Angeles to run the office, looking for motion picture talent. Within ten years, he built the agency into a powerhouse, ascended to its presidency, and was in charge of the day-to-day business. Among the stars on his roster were Bette Davis, Billy Wilder, Gene Kelly, Alfred Hitchcock, Joan Crawford, Jimmy Stewart, and Ronald Reagan.

But Wasserman knew the agency needed tangible assets beyond talent. Consequently, he obtained Paramount Pictures's pre-1948 film library for the then-exorbitant price of $10 million. This acquisition earned MCA more than $30 million from TV stations for broadcast rights to the films within the first month. In 1962, MCA purchased Universal Studios and its parent company, Decca Records, transforming this new company into Hollywood's first integrated entertainment corporation—though the Justice Department required the company to divest itself from the talent business.

Jules Stein named Wasserman his successor as MCA chair and CEO in 1973, and for much of his tenure the studio thrived. But despite Wasserman being tough, cost-conscious, and powerful, MCA's pockets were not as deep as the emerging competition's in the 1990s, and Wasserman sold MCA to the giant Japanese electronics firm Matsushita. "The Last Mogul" remained as chairman, but the company faltered under the conservative Japanese ownership and in 1995 it was sold to Seagram's Edgar Bronfman Jr., which effectively ended Wasserman's involvement in the day-to-day operations of the company. (JW)

WAXMAN, HENRY A.
Member of Congress, 1975–present

Henry Waxman, a member of Congress's 1974 class of "Watergate babies," has been a leading voice for liberal causes throughout his career in the House of Representatives. Chair of the Health and Environment Subcommittee from 1978 until the Republican takeover of the House in 1995, he is particularly noted for expanding the Medicaid program, crusading against the tobacco industry, and enacting a strong Clean Air Act.

Born September 12, 1939, in Los Angeles, Waxman's grandparents were Russian Jewish immigrants, and his parents operated a grocery store in Watts. As a student at the University of California–Los Angeles, he was a leader of the Young Democrats, where he met his longtime ally and future colleague Howard Berman. Waxman's first campaign, for the California State Assembly, launched the "Berman–Waxman machine," an alliance that would dominate southern California politics for two decades. In Waxman's 1968 campaign, Michael Berman, brother of Howard, pioneered the use of narrowly targeted direct mail and helped Waxman defeat incumbent Lester McMillan in the Democratic primary. Six years later, Waxman moved up to the United States House of Representatives.

After just two terms in the House, Waxman assumed the chair of the Energy and Commerce Committee's Subcommittee on Health. He was one of the first subcommittee chairmen elevated over more senior colleagues, and his success in a caucus vote was partly attributed to favor curried with campaign contributions to colleagues. For years Waxman was one of the largest redistributors of campaign funds, raising money from his affluent, liberal Jewish constituency on the West Side of Los Angeles and doling out contributions to fellow Democrats. As the Health Subcommittee chair, Waxman acquired a reputation as a skilled legislator and negotiator. Observers marveled that he was able to expand Medicaid coverage to poor women and children during the Reagan–Bush years, an era in which many domestic social programs were radically cut back. (JS)

WEINER, ANTHONY D.
Member of Congress, 1999–present

Born September 4, 1964, in Brooklyn, Anthony Weiner follows in the footsteps of his one-time boss, New York senator Chuck Schumer. Weiner's first job was as an aide to then-congressman Schumer. After six years in Washington and the district office, Weiner ran for and won a seat on the New York City Council in 1991. At age twenty-seven, he was the youngest person ever elected to that body.

When Schumer announced his 1998 United States Senate bid, Weiner entered the race to succeed him. In a four-way primary, Weiner defeated three other Jewish candidates—two members of the

New York Assembly and another City Council member—and went on to easily win the general election in the heavily Democratic Brooklyn district. In the House, he was appointed to the Judiciary and Science Committees. (JS)

WEISS, SAMUEL ARTHUR
Member of Congress, 1941–1946

Samuel Weiss was born in Poland on April 15, 1902, but spent only the first year of his life in his native land. Emigrating to the United States in 1903, Weiss and his family settled in Glassport, Pennsylvania, a suburb of Pittsburgh. Weiss earned both his undergraduate and his law degrees from Duquesne University and settled in Pittsburgh to begin his practice in 1927; he concurrently served as the director of the Roselia Maternity Hospital.

Weiss was first elected to the Pennsylvania state legislature in November 1934 and served two terms. After a two-year hiatus from politics, he sought and won election as a Democrat to the United States Congress in 1940. He was elected to two subsequent terms but resigned in 1946, when he was elected to serve as a judge to the Common Pleas Court in Allegheny County, Pennsylvania. Weiss's election to the court was for a ten-year term; he was reelected to two additional terms in 1956 and 1966. He retired from the bench in 1967, with nine years remaining in his final term, to become president of the Pennsylvania State Judicial Association.

Samuel Weiss died on February 1, 1977, in Pittsburgh, the city that had been his home nearly his entire life. (CF)

WEISS, THEODORE
Member of Congress, 1977–1992

Theodore Weiss, though he spent the last fifteen years of his life as a member of the United States Congress, did not even become a naturalized citizen of the United States until age twenty-six.

Born in Gava, Hungary, on September 17, 1927, Weiss and his family emigrated to the United States in 1938 to escape rising Nazi power in Europe. His family settled in New Jersey, where Weiss finished his public education; he then enlisted in the army and served until the end of World War II. After the war, Weiss enrolled at Syracuse University and earned both his undergraduate and law degrees. He was admitted to the bar in the state of New York in 1953, the same year he became a U.S. citizen. He had a private law practice from 1962 until 1977; during this period, he also began his political career,

attending state and national political conventions and winning a seat on the New York City Council.

Weiss was elected to the United States House of Representatives as a Democrat in 1976 after being defeated in the three previous primary elections. He filled the seat vacated by Bella Abzug, who had given it up to run for the United States Senate. Weiss proved to be just as determined as his predecessor to use his congressional seat to champion liberal causes. While in Congress, he fought for AIDS education and other human rights programs and vigorously opposed increased military spending. He led a small band of liberal congressmen in a quest to impeach Ronald Reagan after the invasion of Grenada. He also repeatedly voted against the stockpiling of nuclear weapons and cosponsored a joint resolution that denounced the first use of nuclear weapons in future conflicts. His liberal voting record made him exceedingly popular in New York's heavily Democratic Eighth Congressional District, and he won reelection handily every two years. He repeatedly received ratings of 100 percent from the Americans for Democratic Action, a group that assesses the representatives' commitment to liberal causes.

Theodore Weiss died of a heart attack on September 14, 1992, the night before the Democratic primary. Party leaders pleaded with voters to nominate a dead man for Congress, rather than support the fringe candidate who opposed Weiss. Weiss won the primary posthumously, allowing the Democratic Party to appoint State Assemblyman Jerry Nadler to fill Weiss's place on the ballot in the general election, virtually guaranteeing his election in the heavily Democratic district. (CF)

WELLSTONE, PAUL DAVID
United States Senator, 1991–present

Paul Wellstone, the son of Russian immigrants, was born July 21, 1944, in Washington, D.C. He received both his B.A. (in 1965) and his Ph.D. in political science (in 1969) from the University of North Carolina.

Wellstone moved to Minnesota to join the Political Science Department at Carleton College in Northfield; he taught there for over a decade. Hardly a traditional professor, he instructed his students in the politics of protest. Active in local politics, Wellstone was arrested for protesting at a bank that had foreclosed on farmers. He also organized Jesse Jackson's 1988 presidential campaign in Minnesota.

In 1990, Wellstone challenged incumbent Republican Rudy Boschwitz, who is also Jewish, for his seat in the United States Senate. This was the first Senate race between two Jewish candidates, a fact that is particularly ironic in that Minnesota has a relatively small Jewish community. To attract attention for the general election, Wellstone toured Minnesota on a green bus and ran ads stating, "I'm better looking." His victory was considered one of the most surprising upsets of the year.

Wellstone's voting record has been among the most liberal in Congress. In 1996, Boschwitz challenged Wellstone, seeking to regain his old seat; Wellstone prevailed again. In 1998, he began a tour across the country with the aim of convincing Americans to confront poverty; the tour was a trial balloon for a presidential run in 2000, but Wellstone bowed out before the race really began. In early 2001, Wellstone announced his intention to seek a third term in the Senate, despite an earlier pledge to limit himself to two terms. (TW)

WEXLER, ROBERT
Member of Congress, 1997–present

Born in Queens, New York, on January 2, 1961, Robert Wexler moved to Florida at the age of ten, attending the University of Florida before moving to Washington, D.C., to attend George Washington Law School. Returning to Florida, he practiced law in Boca Raton, until he ran for and won a seat in the state senate in 1990, at the age of twenty-nine. Wexler's six years in the senate were not without controversy as he sponsored bills, among others, calling for the chemical castration of sex offenders and a cap on the amount of money taxpayers should pay for the cleanup of the Everglades.

When Democrat Henry Johnston retired from the Nineteenth District seat prior to the 1996 election, Wexler and two other Democratic state legislators sought to succeed him. Wexler won a bitter primary; his opponent in the run-off primary filed a

$10-million defamation suit against him as a result of negative advertising, a suit that was dropped in 1997. Wexler won easily in this heavily Democratic district and continued to do so in 1998 and 2000. In Congress, he is a member of the House Judiciary Committee, a position from which he was a vocal critic of the 1998 impeachment proceedings against President Bill Clinton. (JS)

WHITE, THEODORE
Journalist and Author

Theodore White was born May 6, 1915, in Boston. He graduated from Boston Latin School in 1932 and Harvard University in 1938. From 1939 to 1945, he served as one of *Time* magazine's first foreign correspondents in East Asia. He moved on to work as a European correspondent for Overseas News Agency from 1948 to 1950 and the *Reporter* from 1950 to 1953.

Returning to the United States, he covered presidential elections in his renowned series of books that began with the Pulitzer Prize-winning *The Making of the President, 1960*. His accounts not only chronicled the presidential elections but also examined the personalities of all of those involved in the campaigns; they are considered standard histories of presidential campaigns. Later in his life, White drew on his years of experience covering presidents to write two more evaluative works, *Breach of Faith: The Fall of Richard Nixon* (1975) and *America in Search of Itself: The Making of the President, 1956–1980* (1982).

Theodore White died in New York City on May 15, 1986. (OS)

WIESNER, JEROME BERT
Chair, President's Science Advisory Committee, 1961–1964

Born on May 30, 1915, in Detroit to Joseph Wiesner, a shopkeeper, and Ida Freedman, Jerome grew up in Dearborn, Michigan, where he attended public schools and took an early interest in electrical equipment. He entered the University of Michigan, receiving a B.S. in both electrical engineering and mathematics in 1937 and an M.S. in electrical engineering in 1938. From 1942 to 1945, Wiesner was a part of MIT's radiation laboratory, leaving briefly at the end of World Ware II to work on atomic bomb testing at Los Alamos. In 1950, he received his Ph.D. in electrical engineering from the University of Michigan and returned to become a full professor at MIT.

Wiesner became a part of President Dwight D. Eisenhower's Presidential Science Advisory Committee (PSAC) in 1957. At the time, he strongly advocated the development of ballistic missiles. In the late 1950s, though, he became concerned with the environmental hazards associated with the production and testing of nuclear weapons and consequently became active in efforts to control and limit nuclear arms. He presented his views in his book *Where Science and Politics Meet* (1961). That same year he became special assistant to President John F. Kennedy for science and technology and chair of the PSAC. In 1962, he became head of the White House Office of Science and Technology. Among his accomplishments in these positions was preliminary work to ban all above-ground nuclear tests, aiding in the establishment of the Arms Control and Disarmament Agency, and leading efforts to restrict deployment of antiballistic missile systems.

Soon after Kennedy's assassination, Wiesner returned to MIT to assume its highest faculty post, institute professor. He became dean of the School of Science that year and MIT provost in 1966. In 1971, Wiesner was appointed president of MIT, retiring from the position in 1980.

Jerome Wiesner died at his home in Watertown, Massachusetts, on October 21, 1994. (JW)

WOLF, HARRY BENJAMIN
Member of Congress, 1907–1909

Harry Wolf was born on June 16, 1880, in Baltimore. He attended the public schools there and graduated from the law school of the University of Maryland; he was admitted to the bar in 1901. After several years of practicing real estate law and engaging in hotel property investments, he was elected in 1906, at the age of twenty-six, as a Democrat to the House of Representatives.

Wolf served a single term and then was defeated in the 1908 election. His defeat was blamed on the fact that he rarely attended sessions of the Congress or even showed up for roll call votes. Wolf then returned to Baltimore, resumed his law practice, and established a reputation as an outstanding criminal lawyer.

Harry Wolf died there on February 17, 1944. (MD)

WOLFF, LESTER LIONEL
Member of Congress, 1965–1981

A lifetime resident of New York, Lester Wolff had already spent a good bit of time in the public eye before beginning his political career. Born in New York City on January 4, 1919, Wolff received a degree from New York University and made a career in public relations. During World War II, he was a public relations officer and squadron commander in the Civil Air Patrol. At the end of the war, he began working as a television moderator and producer.

After leaving television in the early 1960s, Wolff was a member of the United States Trade Mission to the Philippines and to Malaysia and Hong Kong. He ran for Congress in 1964 and won in the Democratic landslide election. While in Congress, he worked to limit drug sales and abuse on both the domestic and international levels, serving on the Select Committee for Narcotics Abuse and Control and the Foreign Affairs Subcommittee on International Narcotics Control.

Wolff lost his seat in the House in the 1980 election in an extremely negative campaign. After leaving Congress, Wolff returned to television commentating and also became the chair of the Pacific Community Institute of Touro College, a Jewish independent institution of higher education. (CF)

WOLFOWITZ, PAUL DUNDES
Deputy Secretary of Defense, 2001–present;
Undersecretary of Defense, 1989–1993;
U.S. Ambassador to Indonesia, 1986–1989;
Assistant Secretary of State for East Asian
and Pacific Affairs, 1982–1986

Born December 22, 1943, in Brooklyn, Paul Wolfowitz grew up in Ithaca, New York. He received a B.A. from Cornell and an M.A. and Ph.D. from the University of Chicago.

From 1970 to 1973, Wolfowitz was an assistant professor at Yale. He left that position to work for the Arms Control and Disarmament Agency between 1973 and 1977. In 1980, Wolfowitz became the deputy assistant secretary of defense for regional programs. He was named director of the State Department's policy planning staff in 1981 and assistant secretary of state for East Asian and Pacific affairs in 1982. He served the Reagan administration in that post for four years. In 1986, President Ronald Reagan named Wolfowitz ambassador to Indonesia.

During the administration of George H. W. Bush, Wolfowitz worked with Dick Cheney as undersecretary of defense. With Bush's defeat in 1992, Wolfowitz returned to academia, first as George F. Kennan Professor of National Security Strategy at the National War College and beginning in 1994 as the dean of the Paul H. Nitze School of Advanced International Studies at the Johns Hopkins University. In 2001, President George W. Bush asked Wolfowitz to return to government service, as deputy secretary of defense.

Often known for his conservative nature, Wolfowitz has sometimes bought used cars rather than new ones. His favorite purchase was a 1953 Chrysler Imperial with 140,000 miles, bought for $350 in 1965. (TW)

WOLPE, HOWARD ELLIOT
Member of Congress, 1979–1993

Unlike many public servants, Howard Wolpe did not move to the state in which he served until well into his adult life.

Wolpe was born in Los Angeles on November 2, 1939, and received his public education there. He moved north to attend Reed College in Oregon and received his B.A. in 1960. He earned a Ph.D. in history from MIT in 1967.

Wolpe moved to Michigan to accept a position teaching African history at Western Michigan University in Kalamazoo. He quickly became interested in local politics. In 1972, Wolpe won the first of three elections to the Michigan state legislature as a Democrat. In 1976, Wolpe also accepted a position as regional representative for Senator Donald Riegle. In 1978, Wolpe ran for and won a seat in the United States House; he was reelected six times. While in Congress, Wolpe chaired the House Foreign Relations Subcommittee on Africa, drawing on his academic expertise.

Wolpe did not seek an eighth term in Congress in 1992. In 1994, he ran unsuccessfully for governor, running on a liberal platform in the year of a rising conservative tide. Following that defeat, President Bill Clinton named Wolpe special envoy to Africa. (CF)

WYDEN, RON
United States Senator, 1996–present;
Member of Congress, 1981–1996

Ron Wyden was born May 3, 1949, in Wichita, Kansas. He attended the University of California–Santa Barbara on a basketball scholarship and graduated from Stanford University. Wyden moved up the Pacific Coast in 1971 to enroll at the University of Oregon School of Law.

While still in law school Wyden became active in senior citizens' issues. In the 1970s, he was the director of the Oregon Gray Panthers and Oregon Legal Services for the Elderly. In 1980, at the age of thirty-one, Wyden ran for Congress from Portland, defeating the incumbent Democrat in a primary. Reelected seven times, Wyden compiled a liberal record in the House of Representatives and became the chair of the Subcommittee on Regulation, Business Opportunities, and Energy of the Small Business Committee. Wyden used his post to promote a consumer protection agenda, presiding over hearings on the cosmetics industry, plastic surgeons, diet companies, medical waste, child care, and computer crime.

Running in the first statewide mail ballot in the nation's history, Wyden was elected to the Senate in January 1996, narrowly defeating Republican Gordon Smith to fill the unexpired term of Bob Packwood. (Smith was elected to Oregon's other Senate seat, vacated by Mark Hatfield, in November of the same year.) As a United States Senator, Wyden has continued his interest in health care issues, sponsoring legislation to regulate HMO "gag rules." A member of the Senate Committee on Commerce, Science, and Transportation, Wyden cosponsored the airline passenger bill of rights and pressured the Federal Aviation Administration to disclose airline safety records. (JS)

WYMAN, ROSALIND (WEINER)
Democratic Party Activist

Rosalind Wyman was born on October 4, 1930, to Oscar Wiener and Sarah (Selten). She attended the University of Southern California, and in 1954, married Eugene Wyman. Together they played major roles in California Democratic politics.

Wyman has a long history of political work and activity. At age twenty-two, she was elected to the Los Angeles City Council, becoming the first Jew elected to public office in L.A. in the twentieth century. Wyman served three terms on the City Council and in the last was elected president pro tempore. As a member of the City Council in 1958, Wyman played a key role in bringing the Dodgers from Brooklyn to Los Angeles.

A member of the Democratic National Committee (DNC), Wyman has been a delegate to every Democratic National Convention since 1952, with the exception of the infamous 1968 convention in Chicago. In 1984, she was the chair and chief executive officer of the Democratic National Convention in San Francisco, becoming the first woman to be in charge of such an event. Wyman has also chaired each of Dianne Feinstein's campaigns since 1990. (BF)

Y

YATES, SIDNEY RICHARD
Member of Congress, 1965–1999, 1949–1963

Sidney Yates spent nearly two-thirds of his life as a member of the United States Congress in a career that spanned more than sixty years.

Yates was born in Chicago on August 27, 1909, the child of Lithuanian immigrants. He attended elementary school and high school there and earned his undergraduate and law degrees at the University of Chicago. Yates was admitted to the bar in 1933 and began to practice law in Chicago. After three years of wartime service in the navy, he returned to Chicago to run for Congress, winning in 1948 on the same ticket that included Democrats Adlai Stevenson for governor and Paul Douglas for the United States Senate.

Yates had a strong liberal voice and while in Congress worked to protect civil rights and free speech and to promote the arts. He gave up his seat in 1962 to challenge Republican Everett Dirksen in a hard-fought but losing campaign. For the next two years, Yates served as the American representative to the United Nations Trusteeship Council with the rank of ambassador. He won back his old seat in 1964, though he lost the seniority he had accrued. On his return, he was ranked twenty-seventh on the House Appropriations Committee; had he not dropped out, he would have been chair.

During his "second" congressional career, Yates was often called "the last of the New Deal liberals" for his commitment to helping the less fortunate in society that stayed with him until he retired. He supported measures for environmental protection and was an ardent supporter of Israel.

Nearing the age of ninety, Yates decided not to run for reelection in 1998. He died in October 2000 from complications from kidney failure and pneumonia. (CF)

YULEE, DAVID LEVY
United States Senator, 1855–1861, 1845–1851

Born David Levy on June 12, 1810, on St. Thomas, David Levy Yulee was the first Jewish United States Senator. His father, Moses Elias Levy, came to the United States from Morocco in 1800 and was part of an attempt to establish a Jewish colony in the Florida territory. Moses Levy spent more of his time in the Virgin Islands, however, as his business interests there flourished more than those in Florida.

David was schooled in Norfolk, Virginia, and studied law in St. Augustine. On admittance to the bar in 1836, he was quickly elected to the Florida territorial legislature. For eight years he served as a representative and led the effort to gain statehood. When Florida was admitted to the Union in 1845, he became one of the new state's senators.

It was at this point that he took the name Yulee, an ancestral patronymic. In 1846, he married the daughter of Kentucky's ex-governor and renounced Judaism. Despite his fervent Christianity, Yulee was an object of antisemitic derision throughout his senatorial career.

Yulee was a champion of Manifest Destiny, an antimonopolist in the Jacksonian tradition, and was known as the "Florida Fire-Eater" because of his passionate proslavery views. He also promoted the construction of a Florida railway and organized a corporation to build it, aided by land subsidies he encouraged the Senate to provide for railroad builders.

Yulee was a passionate secessionist. After the Civil War, he was imprisoned for nine months and, on release, devoted his energies to the Florida railroad. He spent the next decades trying to keep the corporation solvent.

David Yulee died on October 10, 1886. (MD)

Z

ZELENKO, HERBERT
Member of Congress, 1955–1963

Herbert Zelenko was born in New York City on March 16, 1906. He was educated in the city, at public schools, Columbia College, and Columbia University, earning his law degree in 1928 at the age of twenty-two. He practiced law in New York and became involved in Democratic politics; he was appointed to serve as the assistant U.S. attorney for the southern district of New York.

Zelenko won his first bid for elective office, gaining a seat in Congress in the 1954 election. He was reelected three times. In his 1956 reelection bid, he criticized the Eisenhower administration's failure to support Israel during the Sinai crisis. In 1962, however, he lost a primary election and never returned to public life. He resumed the private practice of law in New York.

Herbert Zelenko died on February 23, 1979. (LSM)

ZIMMER, RICHARD
Member of Congress, 1991–1997

Richard Zimmer, originally from what he calls "the New Jersey equivalent of a log cabin" in Newark, was born on August 16, 1944. He received his bachelor's degree from Yale in 1966 and his law degree from Yale School of Law in 1968. He practiced law in New York City until 1975 and for the New Jersey–based firm of Johnson and Johnson until 1990.

Zimmer began his political career as counsel to the campaigns of New Jersey governor Thomas Kean in 1981 and 1985. He also successfully sought election to the New Jersey State Assembly in 1981, where he served until 1990. In 1990, Zimmer ran for and was elected to the United States House of Representatives as a Republican to fill the seat of the retiring Jim Courter. In Congress, Zimmer's conservatism led him to favor tax cuts and oppose government spending on a number of projects, including the International Space Station and the creation of a new nuclear submarine. Caring for the needs of his constituents, Zimmer sponsored a bill to reduce aircraft noise in residential areas and another to halt gas and oil drilling up to one hundred miles off the Jersey shore.

Zimmer left his seat in the House in 1996 to run unsuccessfully for an open seat in the Senate. After a brief period in the private sector, he reentered the political arena in 2000, unsuccessfully seeking to recapture his old House seat. (CF)

ZORINSKY, EDWARD
United States Senator, 1977–1987;
Mayor of Omaha, 1973–1977

Edward Zorinsky, the man who eventually became the first Jew elected to statewide office in Nebraska, was born in Omaha on November 11, 1928. He attended public schools in Nebraska and then enrolled at the University of Minnesota in 1945. After transferring to Creighton University for two years, he changed universities once more, receiving his B.S. from the University of Nebraska in 1949.

Beginning in 1950, Zorinsky worked in the wholesale tobacco and candy business; he was also a member of the United States Army Reserves from 1949 until 1962. In 1966, Zorinsky began graduate work at Harvard University. On completion, he returned to Nebraska, serving as a member of the Nebraska Judicial Qualifications Commission and on the board of directors of the Nebraska Public Power Commission.

Zorinsky left the candy and tobacco business in 1973, when Omaha citizens elected him to serve as their mayor, a position he held for four years. In the fall of 1976, the longtime Republican switched parties and was elected as a Democrat to the United States Senate. Zorinsky's party switch was tactical, as it became apparent he would not win the Republican nomination to the Senate.

In the Senate, he served as a member of both the Foreign Relations Committee and the Agriculture, Nutrition, and Forestry Committee. He was reelected handily in 1982. Zorinsky believed strongly in the concept of "open government" and demonstrated this point by removing the door from his Senate office, thereby inviting members of the press and public to enter at any time.

On March 6, 1987, Zorinsky performed at the annual Omaha Press Club Gridiron Show, doing a soft-shoe dance and singing a humorous song poking fun at himself for switching parties. Shortly after the end of his skit, he suffered a massive heart attack and died en route to Methodist Hospital in Omaha, ending nearly two decades of service to the people of Nebraska. (CF)

ZUCKERMAN, MORTIMER BENJAMIN
Editor in Chief, U.S. News & World Report, *1984–present*

Born on June 4, 1937, in Montreal, Mort Zuckerman was educated at McGill University, graduating in 1957 with a B.A. in economics and political theory with first-in-class honors. He came to the United States in 1961 to attend the Wharton School of Business at the University of Pennsylvania from which he received an M.B.A. in 1962. He was naturalized in 1977.

He began his career as a real estate developer in Boston in the 1970s; despite being a major real estate mogul to this day, he has made his name as a publisher. His first major media purchase was *The Atlantic Monthly* in 1980. In 1984, he bought and became editor in chief of *U.S. News & World Report,* the nation's third-largest weekly publication. In 1992, he bought the *New York Daily News.* Zuckerman is not a man without controversy and not shy about promoting his own political beliefs in his publications. According to a *New York Times* article of February 14, 1992, after buying *The Atlantic Monthly,* Zuckerman issued a ban on articles that, in his own estimation, "challenged Israel's right to exist." (JW)

PART III

ROSTERS OF JEWISH LEADERSHIP AND VOTING

ROSTER A

Cabinet Secretary	Position (years in office)	Appointed by
Judah Philip Benjamin	Confederacy's attorney general, secretary of war, and secretary of state (1861–1865)	Jefferson Davis
Oscar S. Straus	Secretary of commerce and labor (1906–1909)	Theodore Roosevelt
Henry Morgenthau Jr.	Secretary of the treasury (1934–1945)	Franklin D. Roosevelt
Lewis L. Strauss	Secretary of commerce (unconfirmed) (1958–1959)	Dwight D. Eisenhower
Arthur J. Goldberg	Secretary of labor (1961–1962)	John F. Kennedy
Abraham A. Ribicoff	Secretary of health, education, and welfare (1961–1962)	John F. Kennedy
Wilbur J. Cohen	Secretary of health, education, and welfare (1968–1969)	Lyndon B. Johnson
Henry A. Kissinger	Secretary of state (1973–1977)	Richard M. Nixon
Edward H. Levi	Attorney general (1975–1977)	Gerald R. Ford
W. Michael Blumenthal	Secretary of the treasury (1977–1979)	Jimmy Carter
Harold Brown	Secretary of defense (1977–1981)	Jimmy Carter
Neil Goldschmidt	Secretary of transportation (1979–1981)	Jimmy Carter
Phillip M. Klutznick	Secretary of commerce (1979–1981)	Jimmy Carter
Robert Reich	Secretary of labor (1993–1997)	Bill Clinton
Robert Rubin	Secretary of the treasury (1995–1999)	Bill Clinton
Daniel R. Glickman	Secretary of agriculture (1995–2001)	Bill Clinton
Mickey Kantor	Secretary of commerce (1997–1997)	Bill Clinton
Lawrence Summers	Secretary of the treasury (1999–2001)	Bill Clinton

Officers listed by year of appointment.

ROSTER B

Senator	Party and State	Years of Service
Yulee, David Levy	D-Fla.	1845–1851, 1855–1861
Benjamin, Judah Philip	Whig-La.	1853–1861
Jonas, Benjamin Franklin	D-La.	1879–1885
Simon, Joseph	R-Oreg.	1898–1903
Rayner, Isidor	D-Md.	1905–1912
Guggenheim, Simon	R-Colo.	1907–1913
Lehman, Herbert Henry	D-N.Y.	1949–1957
Neuberger, Richard Lewis	D-Oreg.	1955–1960
Javits, Jacob Koppel	R-N.Y.	1957–1981
Gruening, Ernest Henry	D-Alaska	1959–1969
Ribicoff, Abraham A.	D-Conn.	1963–1981
Metzenbaum, Howard M.	D-Ohio	1974; 1976–1995
Stone, Richard Bernard	D-Fla.	1975–1980
Zorinsky, Edward F.	D-Neb.	1976–1987
Boschwitz, Rudolph Eli	R-Minn.	1978–1991
Levin, Carl Milton	D-Mich.	1979–
Rudman, Warren Bruce	R-N.H.	1980–1993
Specter, Arlen	R-Pa.	1981–
Lautenberg, Frank Raleigh	D-N.J.	1982–2001
Hecht, Jacob (Chic)	R-Nev.	1983–1989
Kohl, Herbert	D-Wis.	1989–
Lieberman, Joseph I.	D-Conn.	1989–
Wellstone, Paul David	D-Minn.	1991–
Feinstein, Dianne	D-Calif.	1992–
Boxer, Barbara	D-Calif.	1993–
Feingold, Russell Dana	D-Wis.	1993–
Wyden, Ronald Lee	D-Oreg.	1996–
Schumer, Charles Ellis	D-N.Y.	1999–

Senators listed by year of first election.

ROSTER C

Represenative	Party and State	Years of Service
Levin, Lewis Charles	Amer.-Pa.	1845–1851
Kaufman, David Spangler	D-Tex.	1846–1851
Hart, Emanuel Bernard	D-N.Y.	1851–1853
Phillips, Philip	D-Ala.	1853–1855
Phillips, Henry Myer	D-Pa.	1857–1859
Hahn, Michael	Unionist; R-La.	1862–1863; 1885–1886
Strouse, Myer	D-Pa.	1863–1867
Levy, William Mallory	D-La.	1875–1877
Morse, Leopold	D-Mass.	1877–1885; 1887–1889
Einstein, Edwin	R-N.Y.	1879–1881
Houseman, Julius	D-Mich.	1883–1885
Pulitzer, Joseph	D-N.Y.	1885–1886
Rayner, Isidor	D-Md.	1887–1889; 1891–1895
Frank, Nathan	R-Mo.	1889–1891
Meyer, Adolph	D-La.	1891–1908
Goldzier, Julius	D-Ill.	1893–1895
Wanger, Irving P.	R-Pa.	1893–1911
Straus, Isidor	D-N.Y.	1894–1895
Fischer, Israel Frederick	R-N.Y.	1895–1899
Littauer, Lucius Nathan	R-N.Y.	1897–1907
May, Mitchell	D-N.Y.	1899–1901
Levy, Jefferson	D-N.Y.	1899–1901; 1911–1915
Kahn, Julius	R-Calif.	1899–1903; 1905–1924
Goldfogle, Henry Mayer	D-N.Y.	1901–1915; 1919–1921
Lessler, Montague	R-N.Y.	1902–1903
Emerich, Martin	D-Ill.	1903–1905
Wolf, Harry Benjamin	D-Md.	1907–1909
Sabath, Adolph Joachim	D-Ill.	1907–1952
Berger, Victor Luitpold	Soc.-Wis.	1911–1913; 1919; 1923–1929
Cantor, Jacob Aaron	D-N.Y.	1913–1915
Bacharach, Isaac	R-N.J.	1915–1937

Represenative	Party and State	Years of Service
London, Meyer	Soc.-N.Y.	1915–1919; 1921–1923
Siegel, Isaac	R-N.Y.	1915–1923
Kraus, Milton	R-Ind.	1917–1923
Volk, Lester David	R-N.Y.	1920–1923
Perlman, Nathan David	R-N.Y.	1920–1927
Ansorge, Martin Charles	R-N.Y.	1921–1923
Rossdale, Albert Berger	R-N.Y.	1921–1923
Rosenbloom, Benjamin	R-W.V.	1921–1925
Marx, Samuel	D-N.Y.	Elected 1922; died before assuming office
Jacobstein, Meyer	D-N.Y.	1923–1929
Dickstein, Samuel	D-N.Y.	1923–1945
Bloom, Sol	D-N.Y.	1923–1949
Celler, Emanuel	D-N.Y.	1923–1973
Golder, Benjamin Martin	R-Pa.	1925–1933
Kahn, Florence Prag	R-Calif.	1925–1937
Cohen, William Wolfe	D-N.Y.	1927–1929
Sirovich, William Irving	D-N.Y.	1927–1939
Peyser, Theodore Albert	D-N.Y.	1933–1937
Ellenbogen, Henry	D-Pa.	1933–1938
Kopplemann, Herman Paul	D-Conn.	1933–1939; 1941–1943; 1945–1947
Citron, William Paul	D-Conn.	1935–1939
Sacks, Leon	D-Pa.	1937–1943
Edelstein, Morris Michael	D-N.Y.	1940–1941
Klein, Arthur George	D-N.Y.	1941–1945; 1946–1956
Weiss, Samuel Arthur	D-Pa.	1941–1946
Ellison, Daniel	R-Md.	1943–1945
Rabin, Benjamin J.	D-N.Y.	1945–1947
Rayfiel, Leo Frederick	D-N.Y.	1945–1947
Javits, Jacob Koppel	R-N.Y.	1947–1954
Multer, Abraham Jacob	D-N.Y.	1947–1967
Isacson, Leo	Am. Lab.-N.Y.	1948–1949
Irving, Theodore	D-N.Y.	1949–1953
Ribicoff, Abraham A.	D-Conn.	1949–1953
Heller, Louis Benjamin	D-N.Y.	1949–1954
Chudoff, Earl	D-Pa.	1949–1958
Dollinger, Isidore	D-N.Y.	1949–1959
Yates, Sidney Richard	D-Ill.	1949–1963; 1965–1999
Fine, Sidney Asher	D-N.Y.	1951–1956
Holtzman, Lester	D-N.Y.	1953–1961
Friedel, Samuel Nathaniel	D-Md.	1953–1971
Davidson, Irwin Delmore	D-N.Y.	1955–1956
Zelenko, Herbert	D-N.Y.	1955–1963
Teller, Ludwig	D-N.Y.	1957–1961
Farbstein, Leonard	D-N.Y.	1957–1971
Toll, Herman	D-Pa.	1959–1967
Halpern, Seymour	R-N.Y.	1959–1973
Gilbert, Jacob H.	D-N.Y.	1960–1971
Joelson, Charles Samuel	D-N.J.	1961–1969
Rosenthal, Benjamin S.	D-N.Y.	1962–1983
Resnick, Joseph Yale	D-N.Y.	1965–1969

Represenative	Party and State	Years of Service
Tenzer, Herbert	D-N.Y.	1965–1969
Ottinger, Richard L.	D-N.Y.	1965–1971; 1975–1985
Scheuer, James	D-N.Y.	1965–1973; 1975–1993
Wolff, Lester Lionel	D-N.Y.	1965–1981
Steiger, Sam	R-Ariz.	1967–1977
Eilberg, Joshua	D-Pa.	1967–1979
Podell, Bertram L.	D-N.Y.	1968–1975
Lowenstein, Allard K.	D-N.Y.	1969–1971
Mikva, Abner Joseph	D-Ill.	1969–1973; 1975–1979
Koch, Edward Irving	D-N.Y.	1969–1977
Abzug, Bella Savitsky	D-N.Y.	1971–1977
Gilman, Benjamin Arthur	R-N.Y.	1973–
Mezvinsky, Edward M.	D-IA	1973–1977
Holtzman, Elizabeth	D-N.Y.	1973–1981
Lehman, William	D-Fla.	1973–1993
Waxman, Henry Arnold	D-Calif.	1975–
Krebs, John Hans	D-Calif.	1975–1979
Spellman, Gladys Noon	D-Md.	1975–1981
Richmond, Frederick W.	D-N.Y.	1975–1982
Levitas, Elliott Harris	D-Ga.	1975–1985
Gradison, Willis David	R-Ohio	1975–1993
Solarz, Stephen	D-N.Y.	1975–1993
Marks, Marc Lincoln	R-Pa.	1977–1983
Weiss, Theodore S.	D-N.Y.	1977–1992
Glickman, Daniel Robert	D-Kans.	1977–1995
Beilenson, Anthony C.	D-Calif.	1977–1997
Green, Sedgwick William	R-N.Y.	1978–1993
Frost, (Jonas) Martin	D-Tex.	1979–
Kramer, Kenneth Bentley	R-Colo.	1979–1987
Wolpe, Howard Elliot III	D Mich.	1979–1993
Frank, Barney	D-Mass.	1981–
Lantos, Thomas Peter	D-Calif.	1981–
Shamanksy, Robert Norton	D-Ohio	1981–1983
Fiedler, Roberta Francis (Bobbi)	D-Calif.	1981–1987
Wyden, Ronald Lee	D-Oreg.	1981–1996
Schumer, Charles Ellis	D-N.Y.	1981–1999
Gejdenson, Samuel	D-Conn.	1981–2001
Ackerman, Gary Leonard	D-N.Y.	1983–
Berman, Howard L.	D-Calif.	1983–
Levin, Sander Martin	D-Mich.	1983–
Sisisky, Norman	D-Va.	1983–
Burton, Sala Galant	D-Calif.	1983–1987
Boxer, Barbara	D-Calif.	1983–1992
Erdreich, Benjamin Leader	D-Ala.	1983–1993
Levine, Meldon Edises	D-Calif.	1983–1993
Smith, Lawrence Jack	D-Fla.	1983–1993
Miller, John	R-Wash.	1985–1993
Cardin, Benjamin	D-Md.	1987–
Engel, Eliot Lanze	D-N.Y.	1989–
Lowey, Nita Melnikoff	D-N.Y.	1989–
Schiff, Steve	R-N.M.	1989–1997

Representative	Party and State	Years of Service
Sanders, Bernard	Ind.-Vt.	1991–
Zimmer, Richard	R-N.J.	1991–1997
Nadler, Jerrold Lewis	D-N.Y.	1992–
Deutsch, Peter R.	D-Fla.	1993–
Filner, Robert	D-Calif.	1993–
Coppersmith, Sam	D-Ariz.	1993–1995
Fingerhut, Eric	D-Ohio	1993–1995
Hamburg, Daniel	D-Calif.	1993–1995
Klein, Herbert Charles	D-N.J.	1993–1995
Levy, David A.	R-N.Y.	1993–1995
Mezvinsky, Margolis M.	D-Pa.	1993–1995
Schenk, Lynn	D-Calif.	1993–1995
Harman, Jane F.	D-Calif.	1993–1997; 2001–
Fox, Jon	R-Pa.	1995–1999
Rothman, Steven R.	D-N.J.	1997–
Sherman, Brad	D-Calif.	1997–
Wexler, Robert	D-Fla.	1997–
Berkeley, Shelley	D-Nev.	1999–
Schakowsky, Jan	D-Ill.	1999–
Weiner, Anthony	D-N.Y.	1999–
Cantor, Eric	R-Va.	2001–
Davis, Susan	D-Calif.	2001–
Israel, Steve	D-N.Y.	2001–
Schiff, Adam	D-Calif.	2001–

Representatives listed by year of first election.

ROSTER D

Jews on the United States Supreme Court

Justice	Years on the Court	Appointed by
Louis Dembitz Brandeis	1916–1939	Woodrow Wilson
Benjamin Nathan Cardozo	1932–1938	Herbert Hoover
Felix Frankfurter	1939–1962	Franklin D. Roosevelt
Arthur Joseph Goldberg	1962–1965	John F. Kennedy
Abe Fortas	1965–1969	Lyndon B. Johnson
Ruth Bader Ginsburg	1993–	Bill Clinton
Stephen Gerald Breyer	1994–	Bill Clinton

Justices listed by year of appointment.

ROSTER E

JEWS ON THE UNITED STATES CIRCUIT COURTS OF APPEALS

President	Judge	Circuit
Franklin Delano Roosevelt		
	Frank, Jerome N.	2d Circuit
Harry S. Truman		
	Kalodner, Harry Ellis	3d Circuit
	Bazelon, David L.	District of Columbia
Dwight D. Eisenhower		
	Sobeloff, Simon E.	4th Circuit
	Forman, Phillip	3d Circuit
	Friendly, Henry J.	2d Circuit
John F. Kennedy		
	Kaufman, Irving R.	2d Circuit
Lyndon B. Johnson		
	Freedman, Abraham L.	3d Circuit
	Leventhal, Harold	District of Columbia
	Feinberg, Wilfred	2d Circuit
	Goldberg, Irving L.	5th Circuit
	Bright, Myron H.	8th Circuit
	Stahl, David	3d Circuit
Richard M. Nixon		
	Adams, Arlin M.	3d Circuit
	Rosenn, Max	3d Circuit
	Rosen, James	3d Circuit
	Garth, Leonard I.	3d Circuit
Gerald R. Ford		
	Gurfein, Murray I.	2d Circuit
Jimmy Carter		
	Rubin, Alvin B.	5th Circuit
	Kravitch, Phyllis A.	5th Circuit
	Mikva, Abner J.	District of Columbia
	Newman, Jon O.	2d Circuit
	Pregerson, Harry	9th Circuit
	Reinhardt, Stephen R.	9th Circuit

President	Judge	Circuit
Jimmy Carter *(continued)*		
	Sloviter, Delores K.	3d Circuit
	Boochever, Robert	9th Circuit
	Breyer, Stephen G.	1st Circuit
	Ginsburg, Ruth Bader	District of Columbia
Ronald Reagan		
	Becker, Edward Roy	3d Circuit
	Posner, Richard A.	7th Circuit
	Flaum, Joel M.	7th Circuit
	Boggs, Danny Julian	6th Circuit
	Kozinski, Alex	9th Circuit
	Miner, Roger J.	2d Circuit
	Silberman, Laurence H.	District of Columbia
	Ginsburg, Douglas H.	District of Columbia
	Selya, Bruce M.	1st Circuit
	Cowen, Robert E.	3d Circuit
	Greenberg, Morton Ira	3d Circuit
George H. W. Bush		
	Jacobs, Dennis G.	2d Circuit
	Kleinfeld, Andrew J.	9th Circuit
	Wiener, Jacques Loeb Jr.	5th Circuit
	Stahl, Norman Harold	1st Circuit
	Rovner, Ilana Diamond	7th Circuit
	Boudin, Michael	1st Circuit
Bill Clinton		
	Sarokin, H. Lee	3d Circuit
	Tatel, David S.	District of Columbia
	Berzon, Marsha Siegel	9th Circuit
	Gilman, Ronald Lee	6th Circuit
	Gould, Ronald M.	9th Circuit
	Graber, Susan Pia	9th Circuit
	Katzmann, Robert A.	2d Circuit
	Lipez, Kermit V.	1st Circuit
	Marcus, Stanley	11th Circuit
	Pooler, Rosemary S.	2d Circuit
	Sack, Robert D.	2d Circuit
	Silverman, Barry G.	9th Circuit

Judges listed in order of nomination.

ROSTER F

President	Judge	District
Franklin Delano Roosevelt		
	Freed, Emerich B.	Ohio, N.D.
	Goodman, Louis Earl	California, N.D.
	Kalodner, Harry E.	Pennsylvania, E.D.
	Mandelbaum, Samuel	New York, S.D.
	Rifkind, Simon Hirsch	New York, S.D.
	Wyzanski, Charles E. Jr.	Massachusetts
Harry S. Truman		
	Edelstein, David Northon	New York, S.D.
	Holtzoff, Alexander	District of Columbia
	Kaufman, Irving Robert	New York, S.D.
	Kaufman, Samuel Hamilton	New York, S.D.
	Levin, Theodore	Michigan, E.D.
	Platt, Casper	Illinois, E.D.
	Rayfiel, Leo Frederick	New York, E.D.
	Solomon, Gus Jerome	Oregon
	Sugarman, Sidney	New York, S.D.
	Weinberger, Jacob	California, S.D.
	Weinfeld, Edward	New York, S.D.
Dwight D. Eisenhower		
	Bicks, Alexander	New York, S.D.
	Herlands, William B.	New York, S.D.
	Hoffman, Julius J.	Illinois, N.D.
	Metzner, Charles M.	New York, S.D.
	Miner, Julius H.	Illinois, N.D.
	Mishler, Jacob	New York, E.D.
	Morrill, Mendon	New Jersey
	Wollenberg, Albert C.	California, N.D.
John F. Kennedy		
	Blumenfeld, M. Joseph	Connecticut
	Cohen, Mitchell H.	New Jersey
	Cooper, Irving B.	New York, S.D.

President	Judge	District
John F. Kennedy *(continued)*		
	Feinberg, Wilfred	New York, S.D.
	Freedman, Abraham L.	Pennsylvania, E.D.
	Green, Ben C.	Ohio, N.D.
	Marovitz, Abraham Lincoln	Illinois, N.D.
	Rosenberg, Louis	Pennsylvania, W.D.
	Rosling, George	New York, E.D.
	Weigel, Stanley A.	California, N.D.
Lyndon B. Johnson		
	Frankel, Marvin E.	New York, S.D.
	Gordon, Myron Lee	Wisconsin, E.D.
	Gubow, Lawrence	Michigan, E.D.
	Hill, Irving	California, S.D.
	Kaufman, Frank A.	Maryland
	Lasker, Morris E.	New York, S.D.
	Pollack, Milton	New York, S.D.
	Port, Edmund	New York, N.D.
	Pregerson, Harry	California, C.D.
	Rubin, Alvin B.	Louisiana, E.D.
	Schwartz, Edward J.	California, S.D.
	Weiner, Charles R.	Pennsylvania, E.D.
	Weinstein, Jack B.	New York, E.D.
Richard M. Nixon		
	Becker, Edward R.	Pennsylvania, E.D.
	Finesilver, Sherman G.	Colorado
	Fogel, Herbert A.	Pennsylvania, E.D.
	Freedman, Frank H.	Massachusetts
	Garth, Leonard I.	New Jersey
	Gurfein, Murray I.	New York, S.D.
	Levin, Gerald S.	California, N.D.
	Newman, Jon O.	Connecticut
	Rubin, Carl B.	Ohio, S.D.
	Schwartz, Murray M.	Delaware
	Stern, Herbert Jay	New Jersey
	Teitelbaum, Hubert I.	Pennsylvania, W.D.
	Ward, Robert Joseph	New York, S.D.
Gerald R. Ford		
	Aronovitz, Sidney M.	Florida, S.D.
	Brotman, Stanley S.	New Jersey
	Flaum, Joel M.	Illinois, N.D.
	Schwartz, Charles Jr.	Louisiana, E.D.
	Sear, Morey L.	Louisiana, E.D.
Jimmy Carter		
	Ackerman, Harold Arnold	New Jersey
	Aspen, Marvin E.	Illinois, N.D.
	Beer, Peter H.	Louisiana, E.D.
	Black, Norman W.	Texas, S.D.
	Bloch, Alan Neil	Pennsylvania, W.D.
	Cohn, Avern	Michigan, E.D.
	Greene, Harold H.	District of Columbia
	Karlton, Lawrence Katz	California, E.D.
	Newblatt, Stewart A.	Michigan, E.D.

Jimmy Carter *(continued)*

Pollak, Louis H.	Pennsylvania, E.D.
Rice, Walter H.	Ohio, S.D.
Rothstein, Barbara J.	Washington, W.D.
Sachs, Howard F.	Missouri, W.D.
Sand, Leonard B.	New York, S.D.
Sarokin, H. Lee	New Jersey
Schwartz, Milton Lewis	California, E.D.
Shadur, Milton Irving	Illinois, N.D.
Shapiro, Norma L.	Pennsylvania, E.D.
Shoob, Marvin H.	Georgia, N.D.
Sofaer, Abraham D.	New York, S.D.
Spiegel, S. Arthur	Ohio, S.D.
Weinshienk, Zita L.	Colorado
Zobel, Rya W.	Massachusetts

Ronald Reagan

Feldman, Martin L. C.	Louisiana, E.D.
Glasser, Israel Leo	New York, E.D.
Katz, Marvin	Pennsylvania, E.D.
Kram, Shirley Wohl	New York, S.D.
Krenzler, Alvin I.	Ohio, N.D.
Miner, Roger J.	New York, N.D.
Rovner, Ilana Diamond	Illinois, N.D.
Selya, Bruce Marshall	Rhode Island
Wexler, Leonard D.	New York, E.D.
Cedarbaum, Miriam Goldman	New York, S.C.
Cowen, Robert E.	New Jersey
DuBois, Jan Ely	Pennsylvania, E.D.
Friedman, Bernard A.	Michigan, E.D.
Hittner, David	Texas, S.D.
Kleinfeld, Andrew Jay	Alaska
Korman, Edward R.	New York, E.D.
Marcus, Stanley	Florida, S.C.
Mukasey, Michael B.	New York, S.D.
Nevas, Alan H.	Connecticut
Rosenbaum, James M.	Minnesota
Smith, Fern M.	California, N.D.
Sporkin, Stanley	District of Columbia
Waldman, Jay C.	Pennsylvania, E.D.
Wilson, Stephen V.	California, C.D.
Wolf, Mark L.	Massachusetts
Wolin, Alfred M.	New Jersey
Zagel, James B.	Illinois, N.D.

George H. W. Bush

Boudin, Michael	District of Columbia
Brody, Anita B.	Pennsylvania, E.D.
Brody, Morton A.	Maine
Edmunds, Nancy G.	Michigan, E.D.
Garbis, Marvin J.	Maryland
Irenas, Joseph Eron	New Jersey
Levi, David F.	California, E.D.
Rosen, Gerald Ellis	Michigan, E.D.
Rosenthal, Lee Hyman	Texas, S.D.

President	Judge	District
George H. W. Bush *(continued)*		
	Schlesinger, Harvey E.	Florida, M.D.
	Spatt, Arthur D.	New York, E.D.
	Stahl, Norman H.	New Hampshire
Bill Clinton		
	Adelman, Lynn S.	Wisconsin, E.D.
	Atlas, Nancy Friedman	Texas, S.D.
	Baer, Harold Jr.	New York, S.D.
	Berman, Richard Miles	New York, S.D.
	Block, Frederic	New York, E.D.
	Borman, Paul David	Michigan, E.D.
	Breyer, Charles R.	California, N.D.
	Buchwald, Naomi R.	New York, S.D.
	Chasanow, Deborah Koss	Maryland
	Chatigny, Robert N.	Connecticut
	Cooper, Florence-Marie	California, C.D.
	Dlott, Susan J.	Ohio, S.D.
	Fogel, Jeremy Don	California, N.D.
	Friedman, Jerome B.	Virginia, E.D.
	Friedman, Paul L.	District of Columbia
	Furgeson, William Royal Jr.	Texas, W.D.
	Gershon, Nina	New York, E.D.
	Gertner, Nancy	Massachusetts
	Gettleman, Robert W.	Illinois, N.D.
	Gold, Alan S.	Florida, S.D.
	Hellerstein, Alvin K.	New York, S.D.
	Hochberg, Faith S.	New Jersey
	Kaplan, Lewis A.	New York, S.D.
	Katz, David A.	Ohio, N.D.
	Kauffman, Bruce William	Pennsylvania, E.D.
	Kessler, Gladys	District of Columbia
	Lasnik, Robert Stephen	Washington, W.D.
	Lenard, Joan A.	Florida, S.D.
	Lynn, Barbara M.	Texas, N.D.
	Matz, A. Howard	California, C.D.
	Messitte, Peter J.	Maryland
	Moskowitz, Barry Ted	California, S.D.
	Polster, Dan Aaron	Ohio, N.D.
	Pooler, Rosemary S.	New York, N.D.
	Pregerson, Dean D.	California, C.D.
	Rakoff, Jed S.	New York, S.D.
	Ross, Allyne R.	New York, E.D.
	Saris, Patti B.	Massachusetts
	Scheindlin, Shira A.	New York, S.D.
	Schiller, Berle M.	Pennsylvania, E.D.
	Schwartz, Allen G.	New York, S.D.
	Singal, George Z.	Maine
	Stein, Sidney H.	New York, S.D.
	Trager, David G.	New York, E.D.

N.D. = northern district; E.D. = eastern district; S.D. = southern district; W.D. = western district; C.D. = central district.

ROSTER G

JEWISH AMBASSADORS

Ambassador	Most Recent Embassy	Years
Abramowitz, Morton	Ambassador to Thailand	1989–1991
Alexander, Leslie M.	Ambassador to Ecuador	1996–2000
Annenberg, Walter H.	Ambassador to the United Kingdom	1969–1974
Baruch, Herman B.	Ambassador to the Netherlands	1947–1949
Belmont, August	Minister to the Netherlands	1853–1857
Berger, Samuel D.	Ambassador to Korea	1961–1964
Bernbaum, Maurice	Ambassador to Venezuela	1965–1969
Bernstein, Herman	Ambassador to Albania	1930–1933
Blinken, Alan John	Ambassador to Belgium	1993
Blinken, Donald M.	Ambassador to Hungary	1994–1997
Burns, Arthur F.	Ambassador to Germany	1981–1985
Cheshes, Martin L.	Ambassador to Djibouti	1993–1996
Cohen, Herman J.	Ambassador to the Gambia and Senegal	1977–1980
Davidow, Jeffrey	Ambassador to Venezuela	1993–1996
Davis, Arthur H.	Ambassador to Panama	1986–1990
De Leon, Edwin	Consul General to Egypt; minister to Czechoslavakia	1853–1861
Dreyfus, Louis G. Jr.	Ambassador to Iran	1939–1943
Edelman, Eric	Ambassador to Finland	1998–2001
Edelman, Mark L.	Ambassador to Cameroon	1987–1989
Einstein, Lewis	Ambassador to Czechoslovakia	1921–1930
Eizenstat, Stuart E.	Ambassador to European Union	1997–
Elkus, Abram Isaac	Ambassador to Turkey	1916–1917
Farkas, Ruth Lewis	Ambassador to Luxembourg	1973–1976
Feldman, George J.	Ambassador to Luxembourg	1967–1969
Feldman, Harvey J.	Ambassador to Papua New Guinea and Solomon Islands	1979–1981
Florman, Irving	Ambassador to Bolivia	1949–1951
Frank, Milton	Ambassador to Nepal	1988–1989
Fried, Daniel	Ambassador to Poland	1997–
Geisel, Harold W.	Ambassador to Comoros, Mauritius, and Seychelles	1996–1999

Ambassador	Most Recent Embassy	Years
Gelb, Bruce S.	Ambassador to Belgium	1991–1993
Gelbard, Robert	Ambassador to Indonesia	1999–
Gelber, Herbert D.	Ambassador to Mali	1990–1993
Gevirtz, Don L.	Ambassador to Fiji, Nauru, Tuvalu, and Tonga	1995–1997
Ginsburg, Marc C.	Ambassador to Morocco	1993–1997
Glassman, Jon David	Ambassador to Paraguay	1991–1994
Green, Steven J.	Ambassador to Singapore	1997–1998
Grossman, Marc	Ambassador to Turkey	1995–1997
Grunwald, Harry	Ambassador to Austria	1988–1990
Guggenheim, Harry	Ambassador to Cuba	1889–1892
Guggenheim, Robert	Ambassador to Portugal	1953–1954
Hart, Samuel F.	Ambassador to Ecuador	1982–1985
Hecht, Chic	Ambassador to the Bahamas	1989–1993
Hermelin, David B.	Ambassador to Norway	1998–2000
Hirsch, John L.	Ambassador to Sierra Leone	1995–
Hirsch, Solomon	Ambassador to Turkey	1889–1892
Holbrooke, Richard	Ambassador to the UN	1999–2001
Holzman, John C.	Ambassador to Bangladesh	1997–2000
Horowitz, Herbert E.	Ambassador to the Gambia	1986–1989
Hurwitch, Robert A.	Ambassador to the Dominican Republic	1973–1978
Hurwitz, Edward	Ambassador to Kyrgystan	1992–1994
Indyk, Martin S.	Ambassador to Israel	1995–1997; 2000–
Kaufman, David E.	Minister to Bolivia	1921–1924
Klutznick, Phillip M.	Ambassador to the UN Economic and Social Council	
Korn, David A.	Ambassador to Togo	1986–1988
Kornfeld, Joseph S.	Ambassador to Iran	1921–1924
Krys, Sheldon J.	Ambassador to Trinidad and Tobago	1985–1988
Kunin, Madeleine	Ambassador to Switzerland	1996–1999
Kurtzer, Daniel C.	Ambassador to Egypt	1997–
Lauder, Ronald S.	Ambassador to Austria	1986–1987
Lawrence, M. Larry	Ambassador Switzerland	1994–1996
Levin, Burton	Ambassador to Burma	1987–1990
Levitsky, Melvyn	Ambassador to Brazil	1994–1998
Lowenstein, Allard	Ambassador for Political Affairs to UN	1977–1978
Lowenstein, James	Ambassador to Luxembourg	1977–1981
Lyman, Princeton	Ambassador to Nigeria	1989–1986
Mann, Frederick R.	First Ambassador to Barbados	1913–1916
Merrill, Daniel N.	Ambassador to Bangladesh	1994–1997
Morgenthau, Henry	Ambassador to Turkey	1914–1923
Morris, Ira Nelson	Minister to Sweden	1867
Noah, Mordecai Manuel	Consul to Tunis	1813–1815
Okun, Herbert S.	Ambassador to the German Democratic Republic	1980–1983
Otterbourg, Marcus	Minister to Mexico	1867
Peixotto, Benjamin	First U.S. Consul in Bucharest, Romania	1870–1876
Polansky, Sol	Ambassador to Bulgaria	1987–1990
Popper, David H.	Ambassador to Chile	1973–1976
Rabb, Maxwell M.	Ambassador to Italy	1981–1989
Raphel, Arnold Lewis	Ambassador to Pakistan	1987–1988
Ratshesky, Abraham	Ambassador to Czechoslovakia	1930–1932

Ambassador	Most Recent Embassy	Years
Reich, Otto J.	Ambassador to Venezuela	1986–1989
Rivkin, William R.	Ambassador to the Gambia	1966–1967
Rohatyn, Felix	Ambassador to France	1997–2000
Ross, Dennis	Ambassador to Middle East Peace Talks	1992–2001
Sack, Leo R.	Ambassador to Costa Rica	1933–1937
Schneider, David T.	Ambassador to Bangladesh	1978–1981
Schecter, Arthur	Ambassador to the Bahamas	1998–2001
Schwartz, William B.	Ambassador to the Bahamas	1977–1981
Sembler, Melvin	Ambassador to Australia	1989–1993
Silberman, Laurence H.	Ambassador to Yugoslavia	1975–1976
Skol, Michael Martin	Ambassador to Venezuela	1990–1993
Solomon, Richard H.	Ambassador to the Philippines	1992–1993
Spiro, Herbert	Ambassador to Cameroon	1975–1977
Steigman, Arthur L.	Ambassador to Gabon and Equatorial Guinea	1975–1977
Steinhardt, Laurence A.	Ambassador to Canada	1948–1950
Stephansky, Ben S.	Ambassador to Bolivia	1961–1963
Stone, Richard B.	Ambassador to Denmark	1991–1993
Straus, Jesse Isidor	Ambassador to France	1933–1936
Straus, Oscar S.	Ambassador to Turkey	1909–1910
Strauss, Robert S.	Ambassador to Russia	1991–1992
Unger, Leonard	Ambassador to China	1974–1979
Warner, Marvin	Ambassador to Switzerland	1977–1979
Weiss, Seymour	Ambassador to the Bahamas	1974–1986
Weissman, Marvin	Ambassador to Bolivia	1980
Wold, Milton A.	Ambassador to Austria	1977–1980
Wolf, John Stern	Ambassador to Malaysia	1992–1995
Wolfowitz, Paul Dundes	Ambassador to Indonesia	1986–1989
Yalowitz, Kenneth Spencer	Ambassador to Belarus	1994–1997

Partial listing with dates if known.

ROSTER H

Governor	State	Term of Office
Emanuel, David	Ga.	1801
Hahn, Michael	La	1864–1865
Alexander, Moses	Idaho	1915–1919
Bamberger, Simon	Utah	1917–1921
Seligman, Arthur	N.M.	1931–1933
Meier, Julius L.	Oreg.	1931–1935
Horner, Henry	Ill.	1933–1940
Lehman, Herbert Henry	N.Y.	1933–1942
Gruening, Ernest Henry	Alaska	1939–1953
Ribicoff, Abraham	Conn.	1955–1961
Shapiro, Samuel Harvey	Ill.	1968–1969
Licht, Frank	R.I.	1969–1973
Mandel, Marvin	Md.	1969–1979
Shapp, Milton Jerrold	Pa.	1971–1979
Kunin, Madeleine M.	Vt.	1985–1991
Goldschmidt, Neil	Oreg.	1987–1991
Sundlun, Bruce G.	R.I.	1991–1995

Governors listed by year of election.

ROSTER I

JEWS HOLDING STATEWIDE CONSTITUTIONAL OFFICES

Officer	State	Office	Years
Abrams, Robert	N.Y.	Attorney general	1979–1995
Bettman, Gil	Ohio	Attorney general	1928–1932
Breslow, John	Neb.	State auditor	
Blumenthal, Richard	Conn.	Attorney general	1991–
Diamond, M. Jerome	Vt.	Attorney general	1975–1981
Firestone, George	Fla.	Secretary of state	1979–1987
Fisher, Lee	Ohio	Attorney general	1991–1995
Goldstein, Louis	Md.	Comptroller	1959–1998
Goldstein, Nathaniel	N.Y.	Attorney general	1943–1954
Hymans, Henry	La.	Lieutenant governor	1860–1864
Israel, Richard	R.I.	Attorney general	1971–1975
Javits, Jacob	N.Y.	Attorney general	1954–1956
Koenig, Samuel S.	N.Y.	Secretary of state	1909–1911
Kunin, Madeleine	Vt.	Lieutenant governor	1979–1981
Lefkowitz, Louis J.	N.Y.	Attorney general	1957–1979
Lehman, Herbert H.	N.Y.	Lieutenant governor	1929–1933
Levitt, Arthur	N.Y.	Comptroller	1955–1979
Lewis, Gerald	Fla.	Comptroller	1975–1995
Licht, Richard	R.I.	Lieutenant governor	1985–1989
Lieberman, Joseph I.	Conn.	Attorney general	1983–1988
Markell, Jack	Del.	Treasurer	1999–
Markowitz, Deborah	Vt.	Secretary of state	1999–
May, Mitchell	N.Y.	Secretary of state	
Mayer, Nancy	R.I.	Treasurer	1993–1999
Michaelson, Julius C.	R.I.	Attorney general	1975–1979
Miller, Jonathan	Ky.	Treasurer	2000–
Moise, Edwin	La.	Attorney general	1856–1860
Mosk, Stanley	Calif.	Attorney general	1959–1963
Pine, Jeffrey	R.I.	Attorney general	1993–1999
Rudman, Warren	N.H.	Attorney general	1971–1977
Sachs, Stephen H.	Md.	Attorney general	1979–1987
Sales, Steven	N.Y.	Attorney general	

Officer	State	Office	Years
Schaffer, Gloria	Conn.	Secretary of state	1971–1978
Shapiro, Samuel D.	Maine	Treasurer	1991–1999
Shapiro, Samuel H.	Ill.	Lieutenant governor	1961–1968
Shevin, Robert L.	Fla.	Attorney general	1971–1979
Spitzer, Eliot	N.Y.	Attorney general	1999–
Steinberg, Melvin	Md.	Lieutenant governor	1987–1995
Stone, Richard B.	Fla.	Secretary of state	1970–1974
Straus, Isaac L.	Md.	Attorney general	1907–1911
Woods, Harriet	Mo.	Lieutenant governor	1985–1989

Partial listing with dates if known.

ROSTER J

Mayor	City	Term of Service
Kalmon, Edmond	Albany, Ga.	1920s
Mandell, Michael	Albuquerque	
Jaffe, Henry N.	Albuquerque	
Harris, Robert J.	Ann Arbor	1969–1973
Brater, Elizabeth S.	Ann Arbor	1991–1993
Massell, Sam Jr.	Atlanta	1971–1973
Bacharach, Harry	Atlantic City	
Goodman, Phillip	Baltimore	1962–1963 (acting mayor)
Alexander, Moses	Boise	1897–1899; 1901–1903
Klein, Jacob	Bridgeport, Conn.	
Edelstein, Ruben H.	Brownsville, Tex.	1975–1979
Sanders, Bernard	Burlington, Vt.	1981–1989
Lupin, Henry	Butte	
Fleishmann, Julius	Cincinnati	1901–1909
Spiegel, Frederick	Cincinnati	1914–1916
Seasongood, Murray	Cincinnati	1926–1930
Bachrach, Walton H.	Cincinnati	1960–1967
Gradison, Willis David	Cincinnati	1971–1975
Springer, Jerry	Cincinnati	1977–1978
Strauss, Annette	Dallas	1987–1991
Londoner, Wolfe	Denver	1889–1890
Davis, Arthur	Des Moines	1995–1997
Naar, David	Elizabeth	1850–1852
Lashkowitz, Hershel	Fargo	
Seligson, Henry	Galveston	1855
Kemper, Isaac H.	Galveston	
Levy, Adrian	Galveston	
Houseman, Julius	Grand Rapids	1872–1873
Goldsmith, Steve	Indianapolis	
Dzialynski, Morris A.	Jacksonville	
Taussig, Isaac	Jersey City	1881–1883
Goodman, Oscar	Las Vegas	

Mayor	City	Term of Service
Levy, Jonas	Little Rock	1861–1865
Cohen, Bernard	Los Angeles	1878 (acting mayor)
Abramson, Jerry	Louisville	1986–1998
Aronovitz, Abraham	Miami	1953–1955
Naftalin, Arthur	Minneapolis	
Beame, Abraham David	New York	1974–1977
Koch, Edward I.	New York	1978–1989
Ellenstein, Meyer C.	Newark	1930s
Zimman, Harry	Omaha	1900s
Zorinsky, Edward F.	Omaha	1973–1977
Rosenblatt, Johnny	Omaha	
Goldman, Gerald	Passaic	1971–
Barnert, Nathan	Paterson	1883–1885; 1889–1891
Rendel, Edward	Philadelphia	1992–2000
Maslof, Sophie	Pittsburgh	
Simon, Joseph	Portland, Oreg.	1909–1911
Goldschmidt, Neil	Portland, Oreg.	1974–1979
Solis-Cohen, David D.	Portland, Oreg.	1896–1898
Steiger, Sam	Prescott, Ariz.	2000–
Jaffa, Nathan	Roswell and Santa Fe	
Sutro, Adolph	San Francisco	1895–1899
Feinstein, Dianne	San Francisco	1978–1988
Seligman, Arthur	Santa Fe	1911–1913
Myers, Herman	Savannah	1895–1897; 1899–1907
Meyers, Mordecai	Schenectady	1851–1854
Coleman, Norm	St. Paul	1993–
Glogowski, Herman	Tampa	1886
Karus, William	Toledo	1869–1870
Marx, Guido	Toledo	1880s
Schreiber, Cornell	Toledo	1916–1918
Miller, George	Tucson	1991–1999

Partial listing with dates if known.

ROSTER K

CONCENTRATION OF JEWISH POPULATION, 1800–2000

Concentration of Jewish Population, 1800–2000

Year	Total U.S. Jewish Population	NYC	NE NJ	Philadelphia	Boston	Charleston	Cincinnati	Baltimore	Chicago	Detroit	Cleveland	Pittsburgh
1800	2,000	400				500						
1820	3,000	500				700						
1840	15,000	7,000		1,000		700	1,250	150				
1850	50,000	16,000		6,000	40	700	2,500	700	200	60	120	
1860	150,000	35,000		7,000	360	700	8,000	6,000	1,500	150	1,000	100
1870	200,000	65,000	4,000	10,000	2,300	700	10,000	8,000	4,000	500	2,000	1,000
1880	250,000	80,000	6,000	12,000	2,500	700	10,000	10,000	10,000	1,000	3,500	2,000
1890	475,000	195,000	10,000	40,000	5,000	700	12,000	15,000	50,000	1,200	7,000	5,000
1900	1,000,000	500,000	29,000	77,000	7,000	1,000	15,000	25,000	75,000	10,000	20,000	10,000
1910	2,050,000	1,100,000	73,000	140,000	40,000	2,000	17,000	27,000	135,000	10,000	28,000	21,000
1920	3,150,000	1,600,000	125,000	215,000	70,000	2,000	18,000	60,000	230,000	50,000	55,000	35,000
1930	3,900,000	1,900,000	175,000	235,000	100,000	2,000	20,000	68,000	265,000	80,000	70,000	45,000
1940	4,200,000	2,100,000	210,000	250,000	150,000	2,000	22,000	73,000	290,000	92,000	80,000	54,000
1950	4,700,000	2,200,000	225,000	271,000	160,000	2,000	22,000	75,000	300,000	91,000	80,000	54,000
1960	5,200,000	2,325,000	273,000	360,000	170,000	2,400	25,000	80,000	269,000	90,000	80,000	47,000
1970	5,500,000	2,100,000	340,000	380,000	180,000	2,900	25,000	93,000	253,000	90,000	75,000	45,000
1980	5,500,000	1,800,000	375,000	340,000	210,000	3,200	22,200	92,000	248,000	85,000	75,000	45,000
1990	5,600,000	1,530,000	380,000	295,500	225,000	3,500	22,500	94,500	255,000	94,000	75,000	45,000
2000	5,800,000	1,500,000	386,000	276,000	230,000	3,500	22,500	94,500	261,000	94,000	80,000	40,000

(continued)

Concentration of Jewish Population, 1800–2000 *(continued)*

Year	Milwaukee	St. Louis	New Orleans	Atlanta	Dallas/ Ft. Worth	Houston	San Francisco	Los Angeles	San Diego	SE Florida	DC Metro	Denver
1800												
1820			50									
1840			150									
1850		500	500									
1860	500	1,000	2,000	50			5,000	150				250
1870	1,800	5,000	3,000	350		400	8,000	300				250
1880	2,500	7,000	5,000	550	400	1,000	16,500	500			1,500	250
1890	3,500	14,000	5,000	1,300	1,000	3,000	16,500	1,000			2,000	1,000
1900	7,500	25,000	5,000	2,000	3,000	6,000	16,500	2,500			3,000	4,000
1910	15,000	35,000	6,000	5,000	7,000	6,000	25,000	10,000			5,000	7,000
1920	17,000	42,000	8,000	11,000	10,000	6,000	32,000	30,000			12,000	11,000
1930	22,000	45,000	8,000	12,000	10,100	12,500	38,000	70,000	2,500	3,000	16,000	17,000
1940	25,000	48,000	8,000	12,000	10,600	15,000	48,000	130,000	3,000	9,000	20,000	18,000
1950	27,000	50,000	9,000	12,000	14,000	15,000	63,000	315,000	6,000	49,000	45,000	18,000
1960	27,000	50,000	10,100	14,500	20,600	16,000	91,000	410,000	8,500	90,000	81,000	20,000
1970	24,000	55,000	10,500	16,500	23,000	20,000	99,000	520,000	13,000	200,000	110,000	25,000
1980	24,000	53,500	10,600	27,500	23,000	28,000	125,500	575,000	32,500	410,000	135,000	30,000
1990	24,000	53,500	11,000	65,000	39,000	42,000	196,000	600,000	70,000	490,000	165,000	45,000
2000	21,300	54,000	13,000	77,000	50,000	42,000	210,000	600,000	75,000	507,000	180,000	63,000

(continued)

Concentration of Jewish Population, 1800–2000 *(continued)*

Year	Las Vegas	Phoenix	Tampa/St. Petersburg	Minneapolis/St. Paul	Seattle	Totals of Columns	% of Total
1800						900	45
1820						1,390	46
1840						10,290	69
1850						27,640	55
1860						70,700	47
1870						126,800	63
1880						175,400	70
1890				2,000		393,200	83
1900			200	7,000		883,700	88
1910			400	14,000	2,400	1,760,800	86
1920			1,000	25,000	6,000	2,701,000	86
1930			1,300	36,000	8,000	3,311,400	85
1940		1,000	1,700	35,000	10,000	3,727,300	89
1950	400	4,500	3,600	33,000	10,500	4,165,000	89
1960	1,000	8,750	7,330	30,200	13,500	4,630,880	89
1970	3,000	14,000	9,900	31,600	16,000	4,804,400	87
1980	16,000	29,000	17,500	32,400	21,000	4,890,900	89
1990	19,000	50,000	22,000	33,000	35,000	4,979,500	89
2000	55,600	60,000	44,200	42,000	40,000	5,121,600	88

Unless otherwise noted the geographic area covered by each of the cities or regions is defined as that area designated by the *American Jewish Yearbook 2000* as the "Metropolitan Region." Where a Metropolitan Region is not defined in the *Yearbook 2000*, or when an alternative definition is used (see notes below), the smaller "Metropolitan Area" (as defined in the *Yearbook 2000*) is used. NYC is defined as the Metropolitan Area (the city plus Nassau, Westchester and Suffolk counties) plus the New York counties of Orange, Putnam and Rockland and the Connecticut county of Fairfield. Northeastern New Jersey is defined as Bergen, Essex, Hudson, Middlesex, Morris, Passaic, Somerset, Union, Hunterdon, Sussex, Monmouth and Ocean counties (as defined in *Yearbook 2000*). Cleveland includes all of Cuyahoga County and portions of Lake, Geauga, Portage and Summit counties. Does not include Elyria, Lorain and Akron. Los Angeles includes Los Angeles County (including Long Beach area), the eastern edge of Ventura County and Orange County. Tampa-St. Petersburg includes Pinellas County (St. Petersburg) and Tampa.

Because the size of metropolitan areas are defined the same for all years, the above chart masks a very significant demographic change in the American Jewish community. Between the 1840s and the middle of the twentieth century nearly all Jewish populations were located in the central cities. Since World War II this population has dispersed: first into inner suburbs and then later outer suburbs. For example in 1920 essentially all of New York's 1.6 million Jews were located in the city itself. By the early 1990s only 1.05 million Jews lived in the city and another 450,000 lived in the New York state/Connecticut suburbs and nearly 400,000 lived in northeast New Jersey.

All figures are based on population figures from the following two sources: 1930, 1940, 1950, 1960, 1970, 1980, 1990 and 2000 *Yearbooks*: Marcus Jacob Rader, *To Count a People: American Jewish Population Data, 1585–1984* (Lanham 1990).

Ira Rosenwaike helped come up with estimates when the above sources did not have data for a given period, where there were conflicting sets of numbers, or where numbers were suspect. However, all final judgements in this chart are Ira Forman's.

ROSTER L

JEWISH VOTING PATTERNS

Jewish Voting Patterns in Selected Gubernatorial Elections

State	Year	Democrat	Percentage of Jewish Vote	Republican	Percentage of Jewish Vote	Other Candidate	Percentage of Jewish Vote	Source (number of respondents if known)
California	1966	Brown	85	Reagan	15			Levy and Kramer
	1970	Unruh	82	Reagan	18			Levy and Kramer
	1982	Bradley	75	Deukmejian	25			CBS News exit poll
	1986	Bradley	63	Deukmejian	37			ABCNews exit poll
	1994	Brown	61	Wilson	33			Voter News Service (92)
	1998	Davis	83	Lungren	13			Voter News Service (113)
Connecticut	1962	Dempsey	70	Alsop	30			Levy and Kramer
	1994	Curry	71	Rowland	12			Voter News Service (88)
Florida	1966	High	87	Kirk	13			Levy and Kramer
	1986	Pajcic	75	Martinez	25			ABCNews exit poll
Illinois	1964	Kerner	71	Percy	29			Levy and Kramer
	1968	Shapiro	84	Ogilvie	16			Levy and Kramer
	1998	Poshard	34	Ryan	62			CNN.com (146)
Maryland	1966	Mahoney	21	Agnew	44	Pressman[2]	35	Levy and Kramer
	1994	Glendening	78	Sauerbrey	22			Voter News Service (103)

State	Year	Democrat		Republican		Other		Source
Massachusetts	1966	McCormack	42	Volpe	58			Levy and Kramer
	1970	White	46	Sargert	54			Levy and Kramer
	1998	Harshbarger	69	Cellucci	30			Voter News Service (144)
Michigan	1966	Ferency	51	Romney	49			Levy and Kramer
New Jersey	1997	McGreevey	60	Whitman	36	Sabrin[5]	3	CNN.com (178)
New York	1950	Lynch[1]	71	Dewey	16	Others	13	McNickle (NYC only)
	1966	O'Connor	49	Rockefeller	32	Roosevelt[1],	16	Levy and Kramer
						Adams[3]	3	
	1970	Goldberg[1]	75	Rockefeller	23	Adams[3]	2	Levy and Kramer
	1982	Cuomo[1]	64	Lehrman[3]	33			Featherman, AJC, 1984
	1986	Cuomo	84	O'Rourke	15			ABCNews exit poll
	1994	Cuomo[1]	77	Pataki[3]	19			Voter News Service (173)
	1998	Vallone	54	Pataki[3]	37			Voter News Service (255)
Ohio	1966	Reams Jr.	40	Rhodes	60			Levy and Kramer
	1970	Gilligan	87	Cloud	13			Levy and Kramer
Pennsylvania	1966	Shapp	83	Shafer	17			Levy and Kramer
	1970	Shapp	85	Broderick	15			Levy and Kramer

[1]Liberal Party backing.
[2]Running as an Independent.
[3]Conservative Party backing.
[4]American Independent Party backing.
[5]Libertarian Party backing.

Jewish Voting Patterns in Selected United States Senatorial Elections

State	Year	Democrat	Percentage of Jewish Vote	Republican	Percentage of Jewish Vote	Other Candidate	Percentage of Jewish Vote	Source (number of respondents if known)
California	1968	Cranston	86	Rafferty	14	Jacobs[4]	1	Levy and Kramer
	1970	Tunney	85	Murphy	15			Levy and Kramer
	1980	Cranston	71	Gann	18	Others	5	CBS News/New York Times exit poll (158)
	1986	Cranston	86	Zschau	14			ABCNews exit poll
	1988	McCarthy	64	Wilson	33			ABCNews exit poll
	1998	Boxer	81	Fong	19			Voter News Service (113)
	2000	Feinstein	84	Campbell	10			Voter News Service (186)
Florida	1968	Collins	91	Gurney	9			Levy and Kramer
	1986	Graham	77	Hawkins	23			ABCNews exit poll
	1988	Mackay	78	Mack	21			ABCNews exit poll
Illinois	1968	Clark	80	Dirksen	20			Levy and Kramer
	1970	Stevenson	87	Smith	14			Levy and Kramer
	1998	Moseley-Braun	66	Fitzgerald	34			CNN.com (147)
Massachusetts	1966	Peabody	45	Brooke	55			Levy and Kramer
	1970	Kennedy	72	Spaulding	28			Levy and Kramer
	1996	Kerry	69	Weld	30			Voter News Service (101)
Maryland	1968	Brewster	63	Mathias	32	Mahoney[2]	5	Levy and Kramer
	1970	Tydings	80	Beall	20	Wilder[4]	0	Levy and Kramer

State	Year		%		%		%	Source
Michigan	1966	Williams	78	Griffin	22			Levy and Kramer
New Jersey	1984	Bradley	93	Mochary	7			ABCNews exit poll
	1988	Lautenberg	80	Dawkins	20			ABCNews exit poll
	1996	Torricelli	71	Zimmer	25			Voter News Service (162)
	2000	Corzine	72	Franks	25			Voter News Service (200)
New York	1949	Lehman[1]	92	Dulles	7	Others	1	McNickle (NYC only)
	1950	Lehman[1]	82	Hanley	7	Others	11	McNickle (NYC only)
	1956	Wagner[1]	81	Javits	19			McNickle (NYC only)
	1968	O'Dwyer	35	Javits[1]	60	Buckley[3]	5	Levy and Kramer
	1970	Ottinger	67	Gcodell[1]	20	Buckley[3]	13	Levy and Kramer
	1980	Holtzman	73	D'Amato[3]	6	Javits[1]	18	CBS News/New York Times exit poll (365)
	1986	Green	64	D'Amato[3]	34			ABCNews exit poll
	1988	Moynihan[1]	84	McMillan[3]	15			ABCNews exit poll
	1998	Schumer[1]	77	D'Amato[3]	23			Voter News Service (255)
	2000	Clinton[1]	53	Lazio[3]	45			Voter News Service (317)
Ohio	1968	Gilligan	74	Saxbe	26			Levy and Kramer
	1970	Metzenbaum	85	Taft Jr.	15			Levy and Kramer
Pennsylvania	1968	Clark	73	Schweiker	26			Levy and Kramer
	1970	Sesler	68	Scott	32			Levy and Kramer
	2000	Kink	55	Santorum	40			Jewish Exponent/Zogby poll

[1] Liberal Party backing.
[2] Running as an Independent.
[3] Conservative Party backing.
[4] American Independent Party backing.
[5] Libertarian Party backing.

Jewish Voting Patterns in Selected City Elections

Year	City	Democratic Candidate	Percentage of Jewish Vote	Republican Candidate	Percentage of Jewish Vote	Other Candidate	Percentage of Jewish Vote	Source (number of respondents if known)
1931	Chicago	Cermak	58	Thompson	42			Mazur
1971	Chicago	Daley	62	Friedman	38			Rose*
1983	Chicago	Washington	20	Epton	80			Rose*
1987	Chicago	Washington	20	Vrdolyak	75	Hyns	5	Rose*
1933	New York City	O'Brien	32	LaGuardia[1]	36	McKee[2]	23	McNickle
1937	New York City	Mahoney	31	LaGuardia[3]	69			McNickle
1941	New York City	O'Dwyer	31	LaGuardia[3]	69			McNickle
1949	New York City	O'Dwyer	41	Morris[4]	37	Marcantonio[3]	20	McNickle†
1950	New York City	Pecora[4]	62	Corsi	6	Impellitteri[6]	21	McNickle†
1953	New York City	Wagner	52	Riegleman	8	Halley[4]	34	McNickle†
1957	New York City	Wagner[4]	87	Christenberry	11			McNickle†
1969	New York City	Procacino	44	Marchi[7]	12	Lindsay[4, 5]	44	McNickle
1989	New York City	Dinkins	40	Giuliani[4]	60			*Jerusalem Post*, 11/10/89
1993	New York City	Dinkins	34	Giuliani[4]	65			*Jerusalem Post*, 11/4/93
1997	New York City	Messinger	27	Giuliani[4]	72			CNN.com (447)
1987	Philadelphia	Goode	25	Rizzo	74	Greta[8]	1	Featherman, AJC, 1988
1991	Philadelphia	Rendell	75	Egan	22			Featherman, AJC, 1992
1999	Philadelphia	Street	18	Katz	82	McDermott[9]	0sw	Featherman, AJC, 2000

*Estimates of Jewish vote by Don Rose, independent political consultant, based on sample precincts, exit polls, preelection polls, and anecdotal evidence from precinct workers.

†To isolate the Jewish vote, McNickle identified census tracts in which two of the following nationalities made up more than 20 percent of the population: Russian, Romanian, Austrian, and Polish. Because 90 percent of Russian immigrants, close to all Romanian immigrants, 70 percent of Austrian immigrants, and 60 percent of Polish immigrants were Jewish, and because there were about three native-born Jews for every Jewish immigrant during this period, McNickle concluded that such census tracts were probably well over 50 percent Jewish. McNickle then found the corresponding election districts to these census tracks and examined the names of registered voters there to confirm that the district was primarily Jewish. Hethen recorded the election results from that district (pp. 330–31).

[1] City Fusion Party backing.
[2] Recovery Party backing.
[3] American Labor Party backing.
[4] Liberal Party backing.
[5] Independent Party backing.
[6] Experience Party backing.
[7] Conservative Party backing.
[8] Socialist Workers Party backing.
[9] Constitutional Party backing.

INDEX

Page numbers in **boldface** are biographies. Page numbers in *italic* refer to art.

LIST OF CONTRIBUTORS

L. SANDY MAISEL is the William R. Kenan, Jr., Professor of Government and chair of the Department of Government at Colby College. A thirty-year veteran of the Colby faculty, Maisel is the author, coauthor, or editor of more than a dozen books, including *Parties and Elections in America: The Electoral Process*, *The Parties Respond*, and *Two Parties—or More?: The American Party System*. His current research examines the decision-making processes of those who consider running for elective office.

IRA N. FORMAN is the research director of the Solomon Project and executive director of the National Jewish Democratic Council. He previously served as a lobbyist and political director for AIPAC. Earlier in his career he was a research fellow at the Center for National Policy and ran a lobbying and political consulting firm.

DONALD ALTSCHILLER is a librarian at Boston University and has worked at Harvard, MIT, and the American Jewish Historical Society. An editor of eight books, he has also contributed to several reference works with essays covering Jewish, African American, and other historical subjects. He loves locating Jewish trivia.

CHARLES W. BASSETT is the Lee Family Professor of English and American Studies emeritus at Colby College. An expert on the life and writings of John O'Hara, Bassett was the American Studies Association's first winner of the Mary Turpie Award for contributions to the discipline; he was associate editor of *Parties and Elections in the United States: An Encyclopedia*.

Joyce Antler is the Samuel Lane Professor of American Jewish History and Culture at Brandeis University. She is the author of *The Journey Home: How Jewish Women*

Shaped Modern America and the editor of *America and I: Short Stories by American Jewish Women Writers* and *Talking Back: Images of Jewish Women in American Popular Culture.* She is a founding member and chair of the Academic Advisory Council of the Jewish Women's Archive.

Robert A. Burt is Alexander M. Bickel Professor of Law at Yale University. He is author of *Two Jewish Justices: Outcasts in the Promised Land* and *The Constitution in Conflict.*

Jerome A. Chanes is associate executive director of the National Foundation for Jewish Culture and an adjunct professor at Barnard College of Columbia University. He is the editor of *A Portrait of the American Jewish Community* and the author *of A Dark Side of History: Antisemitism through the Ages.* Chanes is a senior research fellow at the Center for Jewish Studies of the City University of New York Graduate Center.

David G. Dalin, a widely published American Jewish historian, is currently visiting professor in Judaic studies at the George Washington University. He is the author or coauthor of five books in the fields of American Jewish history and Jewish political thought. His most recent book, coauthored with Alfred J. Kolatch, is *The Presidents of the United States and the Jews.*

Benjamin Ginsberg is the David Bernstein Professor of Political Science and director of the Center for the Study of American Government at the Johns Hopkins University. He is the author or coauthor of a number of books, including *Politics by Other Means, American Government: Freedom and Power, The Captive Public, The Fatal Embrace: Jews and the State, We the People, The Consequences of Consent,* and the forthcoming *From Citizen to Customer: How America Downsized Citizenship and Privatized Its Public.*

Anna Greenberg is vice president of Greenberg Quinlan Rosner Research in Washington, D.C.; she is on leave as assistant professor of public policy at the John F. Kennedy School of Government at Harvard. She specializes in public opinion, political participation, gender politics, and religion and politics. She is currently working on a book entitled *Divine Inspiration: Revealing Faith in Politics,* which examines the role of congregations in politics and local communities.

Matthew R. Kerbel is professor of political science at Villanova University. A former news writer for public broadcasting, he is the author of a number of books, including *If It Bleeds It Leads: An Anatomy of Television News; Edited for Television: CNN, ABC, and the 1992 Presidential Election;* and *Remote and Controlled: Media Politics in a Cynical Age.*

Connie L. McNeely is associate professor of public policy in the School of Public Policy at George Mason University. Her work is concerned with issues of public policy and governance and addresses various aspects of politics, race and ethnicity, organizations, and culture. She is the author of *Constructing the Nation-State: International Organization and Prescriptive Action* and coauthor and editor of *Public Rights, Public Rules*, which examines matters of citizenship and polity participation

Gerald M. Pomper is Board of Governors Professor of Political Science at the Eagleton Institute of Politics of Rutgers University. Author or editor of sixteen books, his publications include *Passions and Interests*, *Elections in America*, and *Voters' Choice*. His most recent book is *The Election of 2000*, the seventh volume in a twenty-four-year series on U.S. national elections.

Miles Pomper is the foreign policy reporter for *CQ Weekly Report*. Previously, he served as a reporter for Legi-Slate News Service and a foreign service officer with the U.S. Information Agency.

Edward Shapiro is professor of history emeritus at Seton Hall University. His books include *A Time for Healing: American Jewry since World War II* and *Letters of Sidney Hook: Democracy, Communism, and the Cold War*. He is currently writing a book on the Crown Heights (Brooklyn) riots of 1991.

David M. Shribman is assistant managing editor and Washington bureau chief of the *Boston Globe*. He is a trustee of Dartmouth College and has taught courses on American politics at Brandeis University, Gettysburg College, and Virginia Commonwealth University. In 1995, he was awarded the Pulitzer Prize for his articles on American political culture.

Steven L. Spiegel is professor of political science and associate director of the Burkle Center for International Relations at the University of California–Los Angeles. He is also director of the Mideast Arms Control Program at the Institute on Global Conflict and Cooperation, the statewide international relations institute of the University of California. Among his many books are *World Politics in a New Era*, *The Other Arab-Israeli Conflict: Making American Middle East Policy from Truman to Reagan*, and *The Arab-Israeli Search for Peace in the Middle East*.

Susan J. Tolchin is professor of public policy at the School of Public Policy at George Mason University. She is the author of *The Angry American: How Voter Rage Is Changing the Nation*. Together with Martin Tolchin she has written six books, including *To the Victor: Political Patronage from the Clubhouse to the White House, Clout: Womanpower* *and Politics*, and *Glass Houses: Congressional Ethics and the Politics of Venom*. She received the Marshall Dimock Award for the best lead article in the *Public Administration Review* in 1996.

Kenneth D. Wald is professor of political science and director of the Center for Jewish Studies at the University of Florida. He is the author of *Religion and Politics in the United States* and *Private Lives, Public Conflicts: Conflicts over Gay Rights in American Communities*. He recently coedited *The Politics of Gay Rights* and has just completed a new book, *The Politics of Cultural Difference in U.S. Elections*.

Stephen J. Whitfield is a specialist in twentieth-century American politics and culture at Brandeis University, where he has been teaching since 1972. His most recent book is *In Search of American Jewish Culture*. He has served as visiting professor at the Hebrew University of Jerusalem, the Catholic University of Louvain in Belgium, and the Sorbonne.